CONTEMPORARY ISSUES IN WILLS, TRUSTS & ESTATES

CONTEMPORARY ISSUES IN WILLS, TRUSTS & ESTATES

By

Lucy A. Marsh

Professor of Law
University of Denver Sturm College of Law

VANDEPLAS PUBLISHING, LLC
UNITED STATES OF AMERICA

Contemporary issues in wills, trusts and estates

Marsh, Lucy A.

Published by:

Vandeplas Publishing, LLC – July 2013

801 International Parkway, 5th Floor
Lake Mary, FL. 32746
USA

www.vandeplaspublishing.com

ISBN 978-1-60042-194-5

TABLE OF CONTENTS

INTRODUCTION

Happily, because of recent changes to federal estate tax laws[1] fewer than 1% of the people in the United States need to have any concern with the possibility of estate taxes. So this book will not include any complex attempts at tax avoidance. Instead, the emphasis will be on estate planning for real people – with their multitude of different concerns.

The book is a collection of cases with interesting stories, about real people, and their attempts to make sure that when they die, the property they care most about will go to the right people. Relevant statutes are interspersed with the cases, since in this field statutes frequently do answer the questions.

The cases have been edited, of course, to make them easier to read. No case should be used in practice without going back to the full, official version. However, the cases in this book are designed to illustrate real situations, that do come up in practice, and to include stories that are so interesting that the law can be easily remembered – and understood.

Throughout the ages individuals have sought to control disposition of their property at death. As Justice O'Connor has stated, "In one form or another, the right to pass on property to one's family in particular - has been part of the Anglo-American legal system since feudal times...Total abrogation of the right to pass property is unprecedented and likely unconstitutional." *Hodel v. Irving, 481 U.S. 704 (1987).*

In the United States this important right is usually exercised by executing a will or by creating some sort of trust. Trusts may be created as one component of a will, (testamentary trusts), or as independent entities, (inter vivos trusts). This book will cover the basics of creation of wills, testamentary trusts, and inter vivos trusts – as well as other methods of passing on property at death.

First some basics. In this area of the law, the dead person is usually referred to as the decedent. Disposition of the property of a decedent is primarily controlled by state law, so most of the cases will be from state courts, usually called probate courts. Each state, of course, has slightly different laws. But the fundamental pattern is quite standard for every state. Uniform Acts, such as the Uniform Probate Code (UPC), and the Uniform Trust Code (UTC), provide patterns for state legislatures. The Restatement also provides guidance, although it is not, by itself, binding law.

Even though the right to be able to determine who receives one's property at death is an important right, most people, for one reason or another, do not get around to establishing a trust or writing a will. Their property, nevertheless, still goes to their closest relatives, as determined by state law.

If a person dies without a will, the person is said to have died intestate. Each

[1]An individual incurs no federal estate tax until his or her estate exceeds $5 million – or $10 million for a married couple.

state has specific rules on how the property of an intestate decedent is to be distributed. The basic pattern is that the property will be distributed to the decedent's closest relatives – in accordance with the specific provisions of the state statute. The statute is usually referred to as either the Intestate Statute, or the Statute of Descent and Distribution. Only if no such relatives can be found will the property of the decedent escheat to the state. That rarely happens.

Wills and trusts are convenient ways to exercise more control over distribution of one's property – rather than just leaving it to the provisions of the Intestate Statute. Even when a will or trust is created, however, all too often, there is some friend or family member who is not happy with the provisions of the will or trust, and litigation follows – to try to set aside the will or trust – or to get a court interpretation of an ambiguous provision of a will or trust that may be more beneficial to the unhappy friend or family member.

Most such litigation takes place in state courts, usually called probate courts. Federal courts are rarely involved with probate litigation. In most cases, even though the federal courts might technically have jurisdiction, (under diversity jurisdiction, for example), they simply refrain from exercising federal jurisdiction, and leave probate matters to the state courts. This pattern of federal courts refraining from exercising jurisdiction in probate matters is called the probate exception to federal jurisdiction.

Yet sometimes the federal courts do get involved. The first case in this book, *Hodel v. Irving*, is an example of an important probate issue that was ultimately decided by the U.S. Supreme Court.

Although *Hodel v. Irving* involves tribal lands which had been allocated to individual tribal members, some of the basic concepts are of importance to any system of distribution of the property of a decedent. Note, for example, how quickly problems arose when the same property was divided into increasingly smaller shares over successive generations.

Because of recent authorization by some states of very long-term private trusts, called Dynasty Trusts, (covered in Chapter 12), these same problems may now be expected to arise with regard to property owned by people who have never been members of any tribe, but are simply attracted by the concept of being able to provide for their descendants for many successive generations - thereby attempting to create a dynasty. Thus the discussion in *Hodel v. Irving* is important for non-tribal members and tribal members alike. The issues involved are some of the basic issues with regard to distribution of the property of a decedent.

As you get into the details of *Hodel v. Irving* you should see why the "new" concept of Dynasty Trusts is such a bad idea.

The lesson, for anyone, should be that it is very unwise to try to retain control over property for more than one or two generations after death. Freedom of testation must be tempered with wisdom.

Supreme Court of the United States.
Donald P. HODEL, Secretary of the Interior, Appellant,
v.
Mary IRVING et al.
Decided May 18, 1987

Justice O'CONNOR delivered the opinion of the Court.

The question presented is whether the original version of the "escheat" provision of the Indian Land Consolidation Act of 1983, effected a "taking" of appellees' decedents' property without just compensation.

I

Towards the end of the 19th century, Congress enacted a series of land Acts which divided the communal reservations of Indian tribes into individual allotments for Indians and unallotted lands for non-Indian settlement. This legislation seems to have been in part animated by a desire to force Indians to abandon their nomadic ways in order to "speed the Indians' assimilation into American society," and in part a result of pressure to free new lands for further white settlement. Two years after the enactment of the General Allotment Act of 1887, Congress adopted a specific statute authorizing the division of the Great Reservation of the Sioux Nation into separate reservations and the allotment of specific tracts of reservation land to individual Indians, conditioned on the consent of three-fourths of the adult male Sioux. Under the Act, each male Sioux head of household took 320 acres of land and most other individuals 160 acres. In order to protect the allottees from the improvident disposition of their lands to white settlers, the Sioux allotment statute provided that the allotted lands were to be held in trust by the United States. Until 1910, the lands of deceased allottees passed to their heirs "according to the laws of the State or Territory" where the land was located, and after 1910, allottees were permitted to dispose of their interests by will in accordance with regulations promulgated by the Secretary of the Interior. Those regulations generally served to protect Indian ownership of the allotted lands.

The policy of allotment of Indian lands quickly proved disastrous for the Indians. Cash generated by land sales to whites was quickly dissipated, and the Indians, rather than farming the land themselves, evolved into petty landlords, leasing their allotted lands to white ranchers and farmers and living off the meager rentals. The failure of the allotment program became even clearer as successive generations came to hold the allotted lands. Thus 40-, 80-, and 160-acre parcels became splintered into multiple undivided interests in land, with some parcels having hundreds, and many parcels having dozens, of owners. Because the land was held in trust and often could not be alienated or partitioned, the fractionation problem grew and grew over time.

A 1928 report commissioned by the Congress found the situation administratively unworkable and economically wasteful. Good, potentially productive, land was allowed to lie fallow, amidst great poverty, because of the difficulties of managing property held in this manner. In discussing the Indian Reorganization Act of 1934, Representative Howard said:

"It is in the case of the inherited allotments, however, that the administrative costs become incredible... On allotted reservations, numerous cases exist where the shares of each individual heir from lease money may be 1 cent a month. Or one heir may own minute fractional shares in 30 or 40 different allotments. The cost of leasing, bookkeeping, and distributing the proceeds in many cases far exceeds the total income. The Indians and the Indian Service personnel are thus trapped in a meaningless system of minute partition in which all thought of the possible use of land to satisfy human needs is lost in a mathematical haze of bookkeeping." 78 Cong.Rec. 11728 (1934).

In 1934, in response to arguments such as these, the Congress acknowledged the failure of its policy and ended further allotment of Indian lands.

But the end of future allotment by itself could not prevent the further compounding of the existing problem caused by the passage of time. Ownership continued to fragment as succeeding generations came to hold the property, since, in the order of things, each property owner was apt to have more than one heir. In 1960, both the House and the Senate undertook comprehensive studies of the problem. These studies indicated that one-half of the approximately 12 million acres of allotted trust lands were held in fractionated ownership, with over 3 million acres held by more than six heirs to a parcel. Further hearings were held in 1966, but not until the Indian Land Consolidation Act of 1983 did the Congress take action to ameliorate the problem of fractionated ownership of Indian lands.

Section 207 of the Indian Land Consolidation Act-the escheat provision at issue in this case-provided:

> "No undivided fractional interest in any tract of trust or restricted land within a tribe's reservation or otherwise subjected to a tribe's jurisdiction shall descedent [sic] by intestacy or devise but shall escheat to that tribe if such interest represents 2 per centum or less of the total acreage in such tract and has earned to its owner less than $100 in the preceding year before it is due to escheat."

Congress made no provision for the payment of compensation to the owners of the interests covered by § 207. The statute was signed into law on January 12, 1983, and became effective immediately.

The three appellees - Mary Irving, Patrick Pumpkin Seed, and Eileen Bissonette - are enrolled members of the Oglala Sioux Tribe. They are, or represent, heirs or devisees of members of the Tribe who died in March, April, and June 1983. Eileen Bissonette's decedent, Mary Poor Bear-Little Hoop Cross, purported to will all her property, including property subject to § 207, to her five minor children in whose name Bissonette claims the property. Chester Irving, Charles Leroy Pumpkin Seed, and Edgar Pumpkin Seed all died intestate. At the time of their deaths, the four decedents owned 41 fractional interests subject to the provisions of § 207. The Irving estate lost two interests whose value together was approximately $100; the Bureau of Indian Affairs placed total values of approximately $2,700 on the 26 escheatable interests in the Cross estate and $1,816 on the 13 escheatable interests in the Pumpkin Seed estates. But for § 207, this property would have passed, in the ordinary course, to appellees or those they represent.

Appellees filed suit in the United States District Court for the District of South Dakota, claiming that § 207 resulted in a taking of property without just compensation in violation of the Fifth Amendment. The District Court concluded that the statute was constitutional. It held that appellees had no vested interest in the property of the decedents prior to their deaths and that Congress had plenary authority to abolish the power of testamentary disposition of Indian property and to alter the rules of intestate succession.

The Court of Appeals for the Eighth Circuit reversed. Although it agreed that appellees had no vested rights in the decedents' property, it concluded that their decedents had a right, derived from the original Sioux allotment statute, to control disposition of their property at death. The Court of Appeals held that appellees had standing to invoke that right and that the taking of that right without compensation to decedents' estates violated the Fifth Amendment.

II

The Court of Appeals concluded that appellees have standing to challenge § 207. The Government does not contest this ruling. For obvious reasons, it has long been recognized that the surviving claims of a decedent must be pursued by a third party. At common law, a decedent's surviving claims were prosecuted by the executor or administrator of the estate. Permitting appellees to raise their decedents' claims is merely an extension of the common law's provision for appointment of a decedent's representative.

III

The Congress, acting pursuant to its broad authority to regulate the descent and devise of Indian trust lands, enacted § 207 as a means of ameliorating, over time, the problem of extreme fractionation of certain Indian lands. By forbidding the passing on at death of small, undivided interests in Indian lands, Congress hoped that future generations of Indians would be able to make more productive use of the Indians' ancestral lands. We agree with the Government that encouraging the consolidation of Indian lands is a public purpose of high order. The fractionation problem on Indian reservations is extraordinary and may call for dramatic action to encourage consolidation. The Sisseton-Wahpeton Sioux Tribe, appearing as amicus curiae, is a quintessential victim of fractionation. Forty-acre tracts on the Sisseton-Wahpeton Lake Traverse Reservation, leasing for about $1,000 annually, are commonly subdivided into hundreds of undivided interests, many of which generate only pennies a year in rent. The average tract has 196 owners and the average owner has undivided interests in 14 tracts. The administrative headache this represents can be fathomed by examining Tract 1305, dubbed "one of the most fractionated parcels of land in the world." Tract

1305 is 40 acres and produces $1,080 in income annually. It is valued at $8,000. It has 439 owners, one-third of whom receive less than $.05 in annual rent and two-thirds of whom receive less than $1. The largest interest holder receives $82.85 annually. The common denominator used to compute fractional interests in the property is 3,394,923,840,000. The smallest heir receives $.01 every 177 years. If the tract were sold (assuming the 439 owners could agree) for its estimated $8,000 value, he would be entitled to $.000418. The administrative costs of handling this tract are estimated by the Bureau of Indian Affairs at $17,560 annually.

This Court has held that the Government has considerable latitude in regulating property rights in ways that may adversely affect the owners. See *Penn Central Transportation Co. v. New York City*. The framework for examining the question whether a regulation of property amounts to a taking requiring just compensation is firmly established and has been regularly and recently reaffirmed.

As THE CHIEF JUSTICE has written: "This Court has generally 'been unable to develop any "set formula" for determining when "justice and fairness" require that economic injuries caused by public action be compensated by the government, rather than remain disproportionately concentrated on a few persons.' [*Penn Central Transportation Co. v. New York City*]. Rather, it has examined the 'taking' question by engaging in essentially ad hoc, factual inquiries that have identified several factors-such as the economic impact of the regulation, its interference with reasonable investment backed expectations, and the character of the governmental action-that have particular significance.

There is no question that the relative economic impact of § 207 upon the owners of these property rights can be substantial. Section 207 provides for the escheat of small undivided property interests that are unproductive during the year preceding the owner's death. Even if we accept the Government's assertion that the income generated by such parcels may be properly thought of as de minimis, their value may not be. While the Irving estate lost two interests whose value together was only approximately $100, the Bureau of Indian Affairs placed total values of approximately $2,700 and $1,816 on the escheatable interests in the Cross and Pumpkin Seed estates. These are not trivial sums. There are suggestions in the legislative history regarding the 1984 amendments to § 207 that the failure to "look back" more than one year at the income generated by the property had caused the escheat of potentially valuable timber and mineral interests.

Of course, the whole of appellees' decedents' property interests were not taken by § 207. Appellees' decedents retained full beneficial use of the property during their lifetimes as well as the right to convey it inter vivos. There is no question, however, that the right to pass on valuable property to one's heirs is itself a valuable right. Depending on the age of the owner, much or most of the value of the parcel may inhere in this "remainder" interest. See 26 CFR § 20.2031-7(f) (Table A) (value of remainder interest when life tenant is age 65 is approximately 32% of the whole).

The extent to which any of appellees' decedents had "investment-backed expectations" in passing on the property is dubious. Though it is conceivable that some of these interests were purchased with the expectation that the owners might pass on the remainder to their heirs at death, the property has been held in trust for the Indians for 100 years and is overwhelmingly acquired by gift, descent, or devise. Because of the highly fractionated ownership, the property is generally held for lease rather than improved and used by the owners. None of the appellees here can point to any specific investment-backed expectations beyond the fact that their ancestors agreed to accept allotment only after ceding to the United States large parts of the original Great Sioux Reservation.

Also weighing weakly in favor of the statute is the fact that there is something of an "average reciprocity of advantage," to the extent that owners of escheatable interests maintain a nexus to the Tribe. Consolidation of Indian lands in the Tribe benefits the members of the Tribe. All members do not own escheatable interests, nor do all owners belong to the Tribe. Nevertheless, there is substantial overlap between the two groups. The owners of escheatable interests often benefit from the escheat of others' fractional interests. Moreover, the whole benefit gained is greater than the sum of the burdens imposed since consolidated lands are more productive than fractionated lands.

If we were to stop our analysis at this point, we might well find § 207 constitutional. But the character of the Government regulation here is extraordinary. In *Kaiser Aetna v. United States*, we emphasized that the regulation destroyed "one of the most essential sticks in the bundle of rights that are commonly characterized as property-the right to exclude others." Similarly, the regulation here amounts to virtually the abrogation of the right to pass on a certain type of property-the small undivided interest-to one's heirs. In one form or another, the right to pass on property-to one's family in particular-has been part of the Anglo-American legal system since feudal times. The fact that it may be possible for the owners of these interests to effectively control disposition upon death through complex inter vivos transactions such as revocable trusts is simply not an adequate substitute for the rights taken, given the nature of the property. Even the United States concedes that total abrogation of the right to pass property is unprecedented and likely unconstitutional. Moreover, this statute effectively abolishes both descent and devise of these property interests even when the passing of the property to the heir might result in consolidation of property-as for instance when the heir already owns another undivided interest in the property. Since the escheatable interests are not, as the United States argues, necessarily de minimis, nor, as it also argues, does the availability of inter vivos transfer obviate the need for descent and devise, a total abrogation of these rights cannot be upheld.

In holding that complete abolition of both the descent and devise of a particular class of property may be a taking, we reaffirm the continuing vitality of the long line of cases recognizing the States', and where appropriate, the United States', broad authority to adjust the rules governing the descent and devise of property without implicating the guarantees of the Just Compensation Clause. The difference in this case is the fact that both descent and devise are completely abolished; indeed they are abolished even in circumstances when the governmental purpose sought to be advanced, consolidation of ownership of Indian lands, does not conflict with the further descent of the property.

It may be appropriate to minimize further compounding of the problem by abolishing the descent of such interests by rules of intestacy, thereby forcing the owners to formally designate an heir to prevent escheat to the Tribe. What is certainly not appropriate is to take the extraordinary step of abolishing both descent and devise of these property interests even when the passing of the property to the heir might result in consolidation of property. Accordingly, we find that this regulation, in the words of Justice Holmes, "goes too far."

The judgment of the Court of Appeals is Affirmed.

After this case was decided, Congress eventually passed the American Indian Probate Reform Act, (AIPRA), 25 U.S.C. 2201 et seq. which went into effect in 2006. The new act is remarkably complex, and limits the people to whom trust lands may be devised by will, with different rules for interests in trust lands depending on whether the interest is 5% or less of the total ownership in the specific tract. A tribal member is allowed to devise his or her share in trust land, of any size, to any descendant. Devises to other people are strictly limited. Without a will, in some situations the trust land may go by intestate succession only to the one oldest child, or the one oldest grandchild, or the one oldest great-grandchild, with nothing to the surviving spouse unless he or she was actually living on the land at the death of the decedent. There are also provisions for forced sales. AIPRA is a very complex attempt by Congress to decrease the remarkably inefficient fractionation caused by prior acts of Congress. Needless to say, there is now a great need for wills among tribal members throughout the country if they want to try to control how their property is distributed among their family and friends.

The fractionation which has occurred with trust land is exactly what is to be expected with the "great" new Dynasty Trusts now authorized for non-tribal members in a number of states.

The rest of this book will discuss methods available for more thoughtful estate planning.

CHAPTER 1. WHAT HAPPENS WITHOUT A WILL

The first thing lawyers need to know for estate planning is what happens when a person dies without having executed a valid will.[1] Contrary to popular belief, the property does not go to the state. Instead, the property goes to the person's closest relatives, as determined by the applicable state Intestate Statute. Statutes vary considerably from state to state, and may be called by various names, including the statute of Descent and Distribution - but some form of intestate statute does exist in every state.

Which state's statute controls for a person who spends time in several different states? The state statute that controls the distribution of the property of the decedent, (the person who has died), is the statute of the state in which the person was *domiciled* at death - not the state in which the person happened to be physically at the time of death. Thus, if a woman who is domiciled in Maine dies while visiting relatives in California, or while vacationing in France, it will be the laws of her state of domicile, Maine, that control distribution of her property - not the laws of California, or the laws of France.

Not surprisingly, states change their laws of intestate distribution fairly frequently, as social customs change, (such as more frequent use of adoption, for example), or as problems or gaps in existing legislation become apparent. It is the statute that was in effect at the time of death of the decedent, in the state of decedent's domicile, that controls. So sometimes it is necessary to go back to a superseded statute if an issue of intestate distribution arises when some time has passed between the death of the decedent and the determination of the issue of distribution.

But remember, states have had statutes of intestate distribution since colonial times - or since the times when the states were first admitted to the union. So with appropriate research, you should always be able to determine how a person's property would have been distributed under the statutes in effect at the time of the decedent's death. One nice thing about intestate statutes is that they do, very specifically, tell you what the law actually is for a specific situation.

Intestate statutes are used for two primary purposes. One is to determine distribution of the property of someone who has died without a valid will. The other purpose is to determine distribution of property of someone who had a valid will which for some reason failed to distribute all of the decedent's property. Any of the decedent's property that is not successfully distributed under the terms of the will, (or trust), is then distributed in accordance with the provisions of the intestate statute.

You will notice that in the following brief sample of the basic components of an intestate statute in some cases the statute will include reference to sections that have

[1]Or a valid trust, or other will substitute, all of which will be covered later in the book. For this chapter, all of those other possible documents will simply be included in the term "will".

been repealed. When the legislature makes small changes to statutes it frequently leaves the older numbering system intact - to cause as little disruption as possible. That way the section numbers of the older parts of the statute stay the same – until the legislature makes a major change in the statute, and renumbers everything.

For example, in the statute below, when section 15-11-103(1) was repealed, to be replaced by different provisions elsewhere in the intestate statute, the legislature intentionally did not renumber the sections which followed the repealed section. Thus a document that had referred to section 15-11-103(2) prior to the most recent statutory change would still refer to that same part of the law. In other words, 15-11-103(2) kept the same number – even when the prior section was deleted. It is convenient when the legislature does this. But it doesn't always happen this way.

So, this should serve as a warning to all lawyers that it is NOT a good idea to refer to specific statutory sections by number – because the numbers *may* be changed by subsequent changes to the statute.

Also remember that although a client may be domiciled in Maine when her will is written, she may later move permanently to Colorado, and thus end up domiciled in Colorado at the date of her death. In that case, the intestate statue of Colorado, not Maine, will control distribution of her intestate property – because she was *domiciled* in Colorado at her death. So it is usually best to put all of the necessary provisions right in the will – and avoid specific reference to any particular statute as it exists when the will is written. Remember, statutes change, and people move permanently to different states.

In the brief statutory excerpt below, only the basics of the intestate statute are included. Other important parts of the intestate statute will be included in other parts of this chapter, and in other parts of this book.

If you are curious about specific situations which are not covered in this brief excerpt, feel free to look at the complete intestate statute in your state.

The Colorado statute which is used here is typical of most intestate statutes, and is based on the Uniform Probate Code. But remember that each state will be slightly different – and it is the particular state statute in effect at the time of the decedent's death – not any Uniform Act – or any subsequent statute – that controls distribution of the intestate property of the decedent.

As you read through the following statute it may be helpful to think about how your property, or that of your parents or grandparents, would be distributed under the terms of this statute. Do not worry if you do not fully understand all of the concepts at this point.

Just notice that some property goes to the surviving spouse, (or perhaps a surviving partner), and the rest of the property goes first down to descendants of the decedent, and then up to various ancestors of the decedent – or their descendants. This statute actually answers a number of questions frequently asked by clients – or neighbors – as to the distribution of property of someone who dies.

A. SAMPLE INTESTACY STATUTE

C.R.S.15-11-101. Intestate estate

(1) Any part of a decedent's estate not effectively disposed of by will or otherwise passes by intestate succession to the decedent's heirs as prescribed in this code, except as modified by the decedent's will.

(2) A decedent by will may expressly exclude or limit the right of an individual or class to succeed to property of the decedent passing by intestate succession. If that individual or a member of that class survives the decedent, the share of the decedent's intestate estate to which that individual or class would have succeeded passes as if that individual or each member of that class had disclaimed his or her intestate share.

15-11-102. Share of <u>spouse</u>

The various possible circumstances describing the decedent, his or her surviving spouse, and their surviving descendants, if any, are set forth in this section to be utilized in determining the intestate share of the decedent's surviving spouse. The intestate share of a decedent's surviving spouse is:

(1) The entire intestate estate if:

(a) No descendant or parent of the decedent survives the decedent; or

(b) All of the decedent's surviving descendants are also descendants of the surviving spouse and there is no other descendant of the surviving spouse who survives the decedent;

(2) The first three hundred thousand dollars, plus three-fourths of any balance of the intestate estate, if no descendant of the decedent survives the decedent, but a parent of the decedent survives the decedent;

(3) The first two hundred twenty-five thousand dollars, plus one-half of any balance of the intestate estate, if all of the decedent's surviving descendants are also descendants of the surviving spouse and the surviving spouse has one or more surviving descendants who are not descendants of the decedent;

(4) The first one hundred fifty thousand dollars, plus one-half of any balance of the intestate estate, if one or more of the decedent's surviving descendants are not descendants of the surviving spouse.

15-11-102.5. Share of designated beneficiary

[This may be a same sex partner, or any other person designated in a Designated Beneficiary Agreement, covered later in the book.]

(1) If the decedent is survived by a person with the right to inherit real or personal property from the decedent in a designated beneficiary agreement

executed pursuant to article 22 of this title, the intestate share of the decedent's designated beneficiary is:

(a) The entire estate if no descendent of the decedent survives the decedent; or

(b) One half of the intestate estate if one or more descendants of the decedent survive the decedent.

15-11-103. Share of heirs other than surviving spouse and designated beneficiary

Any part of the intestate estate not passing to the decedent's surviving spouse under section 15-11-102, or to the decedent's surviving designated beneficiary under section 15-11-102.5, or the entire intestate estate if there is no surviving spouse and no surviving designated beneficiary, passes in the following order to the individuals who survive the decedent:

(1) Deleted by Laws 2010, Ch. 374, § 5, eff. July 1, 2010.

(2) To the decedent's descendants per capita at each generation;

(3) If there is no surviving descendant, to the decedent's parents equally if both survive, or to the surviving parent if only one survives;

(4) If there is no surviving descendant or parent, to the descendants of the decedent's parents or either of them per capita at each generation;

(5) If there is no surviving descendant, parent, or descendant of a parent, but the decedent is survived on both the paternal and maternal sides by one or more grandparents or descendants of grandparents:

(a) Half to the decedent's paternal grandparents equally if both survive, to the surviving paternal grandparent if only one survives, or to the descendants of the decedent's paternal grandparents or either of them if both are deceased, the descendants taking per capita at each generation; and

(b) Half to the decedent's maternal grandparents equally if both survive, to the surviving maternal grandparent if only one survives, or to the descendants of the decedent's maternal grandparents or either of them if both are deceased, the descendants taking per capita at each generation;

(6) If there is no surviving descendant, parent, or descendant of a parent, but the decedent is survived by one or more grandparents or descendants of grandparents on the paternal but not the maternal side, or on the maternal but not the paternal side, to the decedent's relatives on the side with one or more surviving members in the manner as described in subsection (5) of this section;

15-11-104. Requirement of <u>survival</u> by one hundred twenty hours--individual in gestation

(1) For purposes of intestate succession the following rules apply:

(a) An individual born before a decedent's death who fails to survive the decedent by one hundred twenty hours is deemed to have predeceased the decedent. If it is not established by clear and convincing evidence that an individual born before the decedent's death survived the decedent by one hundred twenty hours, it is deemed that the individual failed to survive for the required period.

(b) An individual in gestation at a decedent's death is deemed to be living at the decedent's death if the individual lives one hundred twenty hours after birth. If it is not established by clear and convincing evidence that an individual in gestation at the decedent's death lived one hundred twenty hours after birth, it is deemed that the individual failed to survive for the required period.

(2) This section is not to be applied if its application would result in a taking of intestate estate by the state under section 15-11-105.

15-11-105. No taker

If there is no taker under the provisions of this article, the intestate estate passes to the state of Colorado, subject to the provisions of section 15-12-914. *[That section deals with how much time relatives have to reclaim the assets.]*

15-11-111. Alienage

No individual is disqualified to take as an heir, devisee, grantee, lessee, mortgagee, assignee, or other transferee because the individual or an individual through whom he or she claims is or has been an alien.

15-11-114. <u>Parent barred from inheriting</u> in certain circumstances

(1) A parent is barred from inheriting from or through a child of the parent if:

(a) The parent's parental rights were terminated and the parent-child relationship was not judicially reestablished; or

(b) The child died before reaching eighteen years of age and there is clear and convincing evidence that immediately before the child's death the parental rights of the parent could have been terminated under the laws of this state other than this code on the basis of nonsupport, abandonment, abuse, neglect, or other actions or inactions of the parent toward the child.

(2) For the purpose of intestate succession from or through the deceased child, a parent who is barred from inheriting under this section is treated as if the

parent predeceased the child.

15-11-117. No distinction based on marital status
Except as otherwise provided in section 15-11-114, 15-11-119, 15-11-120, or 15-11-121, a parent-child relationship exists between a child and the child's genetic parents, regardless of the parents' marital status.

B. ADOPTION

Under the intestate statute, who counts as a child? With increasing frequency there are issues involving the inheritance rights of people who have been adopted. Of course, specific provisions for adopted people can always be made by will. But when that has not been done, what happens? The following cases provide some answers, and some warnings about important issues of adoption.

(1) REMOVAL FROM ORIGINAL FAMILY TREE

Court of Special Appeals of Maryland.
Eva C. HALL et al.
v.
Joseph VALLANDINGHAM,
for the Estate of William Vallandingham, Jr.
May 9, 1988

OPINION BY: GILBERT

Adoption did not exist under the common law of England,[2] although it was in use among the ancient peoples of Greece, Rome, Egypt and Babylonia. The primary purpose for adoption was, and still is, inheritance rights, particularly in France, Greece, Spain and most of Latin America. Since adoption was not a part of the common law, it owes its existence in this State, and indeed in this nation, to statutory enactments.

The first two general adoption statutes were passed in Texas and Vermont in 1850. Maryland first enacted an Adoption Statute in 1892, and that law has continued in existence, in various forms, until the present time. The current statute provides in pertinent part:

> "(b) After a decree of adoption is entered:
> (1) the individual adopted:

---

2 According to J.W. Madden, *Handbook of the Law of Persons and Domestic Relations* (Wash.1931) § 106, adoption in the sense of the term as used in this country was not a part of the English law until 1926.

(i) is the child of the petitioner for all intents and purposes; and

(ii) is entitled to all the rights and privileges of and is subject to all the obligations of a child born to the petitioner in wedlock;

(2) each living natural parent of the individual adopted is:

(i) relieved of all parental duties and obligations to the individual adopted; and

(ii) divested of all parental rights as to the individual adopted; and

(3) *all rights of inheritance between the individual adopted and the natural relations shall be governed by the Estates and Trusts Article*."

Notwithstanding Maryland law, a child who is eligible for social security survivor's benefits through a deceased natural parent under Federal law does not lose eligibility for the continuation of those benefits because of a subsequent adoption.

The applicable section of the Md. Estates and Trusts Code Ann., *§ 1-207(a)*, provides:

"An adopted child shall be treated as a natural child of his adopted parent or parents. On adoption, a child no longer shall be considered a child of either natural parent, except that upon adoption by the spouse of a natural parent, the child shall be considered the child of that natural parent."

With that "thumbnail" history of adoption and the current statutes firmly in mind, we turn our attention to the matter *sub judice*.

Earl J. Vallandingham died in 1956, survived by his widow, Elizabeth, and their four children. Two years later, Elizabeth married Jim Walter Killgore, who adopted the children.

In 1983, twenty-five years after the adoption of Earl's children by Killgore, Earl's brother, William Jr., died childless, unmarried, and intestate. His sole heirs were his surviving brothers and sisters and the children of brothers and sisters who predeceased him.

Joseph W. Vallandingham, the decedent's twin brother, was appointed Personal

Representative of the estate. After the Inventory and First Accounting were filed, the four natural children of Earl J. Vallandingham noted exceptions, alleging that they were entitled to the distributive share of their natural uncle's estate that their natural father would have received had he survived William.

The Orphan's Court transmitted the issue to the Circuit Court for St. Mary's County. That tribunal determined that the four natural children of Earl, because of their adoption by their adoptive father, Jim Walter Killgore, were not entitled to inherit from William M. Vallandingham Jr.

Patently unwilling to accept that judgment which effectively disinherited them, the children have journeyed here.

When the four natural children of Earl J. Vallandingham were adopted in 1958 by Jim Killgore, then Md. Ann. Code art. 16, § 78(b) clearly provided that adopted children retained the right to inherit from their natural parents and relatives. That right of inheritance was removed by the Legislature in 1963.

The right to receive property by devise or descent is not a natural right but a privilege granted by the State. Every State possesses the power to regulate the manner or term by which property within its dominion may be transmitted by will or inheritance and to prescribe who shall or shall not be capable of receiving that property.

Family Law Art. § 5-308(b)(1)(ii) entitles an adopted person to all the rights and privileges of a natural child insofar as the adoptive parents are concerned, but adoption does not confer upon the adopted child *more* rights and privileges than those possessed by a natural child. To construe *Est. & Trusts Art. § 1-207(a)* so as to allow dual inheritance would bestow upon an adopted child a superior status. That status was removed in 1963.

Family Law Art. § 5-308 plainly mandates that adoption be considered a "rebirth" into a completely different relationship. Once a child is adopted, the rights of both the natural parents and relatives are terminated. Because an adopted child has no right to inherit *from* the estate of a natural parent who dies intestate, it follows that the same child may not inherit *through* the natural parent by way of representation. What may not be done directly most assuredly may not be done indirectly. The elimination of dual inheritance in 1963 clearly established that policy, and the current language of *§ 1-207(a)* simply reflects the continuation of that policy.

We hold that because *§ 1-207(a)* eliminates the adopted child's right to inherit from the natural parent it concomitantly abrogated the right to inherit through the natural parent by way of representation.

"The Legislature giveth, and the Legislature taketh away."

JUDGMENT AFFIRMED.

The result in the preceding case seems very unfortunate - particularly in light of the fact that the law was *changed* after the adoption took place! This emphasizes how dangerous it is to rely on the provisions of any existing statute.

In some states, although there has not been a legal adoption, the state may recognize an old aspect of the common law, called equitable adoption. Basically, when a child has been raised within a family and treated as if adopted, though a legal adoption has not actually taken place, under some circumstances, the courts, by means of equity, will treat the matter as if the child had been legally adopted, thus treating the child as equitably adopted.

(2) ADULT ADOPTION

In the next case, the issue is adult adoption. It is because of cases like this that any estate planning attorney should specifically ask the client what the client wishes to do about people who are adopted after the client's documents have been signed. Most clients usually want to include adopted grandchildren, as long as the children were adopted when they were fairly young. But the client usually feels quite differently about the possibility that the client's son, for example, might adopt all six of his college roommates, or all eleven of the other people with whom he plays touch football. Adult adoptions are frequently legal.

Colorado Court of Appeals.
In the Matter of the Petition of P.A.L. von R., Plaintiff-Appellant,
For the Adoption of an Adult, K.M.F.
June 8, 2000.

Opinion by Judge Kapelke.

P.A.L. von R. appeals from the judgment of the trial court dismissing the petition to adopt his adult sister, K.M.F. We reverse and remand for entry of an adoption decree.

Petitioner filed his petition pursuant to § 14-1-101, C.R.S.1999, together with a consent to the adoption and a waiver and acceptance of service signed by his sister. Following an evidentiary hearing, the trial court denied the petition. No party opposed the requested adoption.

The court found that petitioner, age 60, was seeking the adoption to allow his sister, a German citizen, age 55, to change her name to the original family name. Petitioner stated that his sister had been unable to effect the name change by any court proceeding in Germany, but that an adoption decree would be recognized.

The court also found that there was nothing in the statute that expressly prevented an adult from adopting another adult of any age. However, the court indicated that it would exercise its discretion and decline to decree the adoption because it appeared to the court to violate public policy. The transcript shows that the court was concerned with the lack of age differential between petitioner and his sister and with the fact that they were siblings.

Petitioner contends that § 14-1-101 contains no exception based upon age differential or blood relationship. Therefore, he argues that the trial court erred in denying the petition for adoption. We agree.

Section 14-1-101, the adult adoption statute, provides in pertinent part:

> (1) "Any person desiring to adopt an adult as heir at law shall file his petition in the juvenile court of the county and thereupon summons shall issue ... and be served on the person sought to be adopted. Said person shall file in the court a written answer to the petition ... and shall either consent to such adoption or deny or disclaim all desire to be adopted by such person.
> (2) Upon the filing, by the person sought to be adopted, of a disclaimer of all desire to become the heir at law of the petitioner, the petition shall be dismissed by the court, but *upon the filing of a consent to such adoption, ... the prayer of the petition shall be granted, and a decree of adoption shall be rendered and entered by the court declaring such person the heir at law of the petitioner* and entitled to inherit from the petitioner any property in all respects as if such adopted person had been the petitioner's child born in lawful wedlock, and such decree may or may not change the name of such adopted person, as the court rendering the decree may deem advisable." (Emphasis added.)

The statute authorizes the adoption of adults for the purpose of giving the adoptee the status of an heir at law. An adult adoption has been described as "merely a means of giving effect to a personal transaction mutually agreeable between two adults.

If we can give effect to the ordinary words used by the General Assembly, we must apply the statute as written. Use of the word "shall" implies a mandatory meaning.

The plain language of § 14-1-101 requires the trial court to grant an adult adoption when there is valid service and the adoptee consents to such adoption. Both requirements were met here. There is no additional requirement that there be a minimum age differential between the adoptor and the adoptee. Nor is adoption precluded based upon the prior relationship of the parties. *See* Berston v. Minnesota Department of Public Welfare, 296 Minn. (1973) (under statute allowing adoption of an adult by "any person," son's petition to adopt mother granted even though admitted motive was to bring her within terms of trust established by father who had divorced mother).

Finally, we are not aware of any public policy in Colorado that would be violated by permitting a person to adopt his or her own adult sibling.

Accordingly, we conclude that pursuant to the mandatory language of § 14-1-101, the court was required to grant the petition and enter a decree of adoption.

The judgment is therefore reversed, and the cause is remanded for entry of a decree of adoption.

C. SPECIAL FAMILY SITUATIONS

There are numerous special family situations that are best addressed by specific drafting. What happens, for example, if while H and W are married to each other, H adopts all of W's children from her prior marriage. Then, five years later, H and W are involved in a bitter divorce. If W leaves, taking the children with her, and neither W nor the children ever have any contact with H again, would H's mother (Mom), want the children H had adopted to be beneficiaries under Mom's will? The children, once adopted by H, will always remain H's legal children. Their status does not change because of a divorce between H and W. And it may be that the adopted children will still remain close to H. Or, it may be that they may entirely forget about H, and move on. With careful drafting, Mom could provide for such contingencies in her will.

A similar situation may arise when a same sex couple adopts a child, and then the couple splits up, and the child may or may not continue to have contact with both adoptive parents.

The parent/child relationship, unlike marriage, is very seldom terminated by any court. So appropriate drafting of estate planning documents is important.

D. CHILDREN BY ASSISTED REPRODUCTION

In the statute included earlier in this chapter terms such as "child of assisted reproduction" and "gestational child" were used. Those terms, and many related terms, are defined by the statute. They refer to what are sometimes referred to, collectively, as sperm bank children. All of this comes about because of recent medical advances that allow a child to be created in a number of non-traditional ways.

Before attempting to plow through a very complex statute on the matter, it may be helpful, first, to read the May 2012 U.S. Supreme Court case, *Astrue v. Capato*, which shows one of the many reasons these complex statutory definitions matter.

(1) ASTRUE V. CAPATO

Supreme Court of the United States.
Michael J. ASTRUE, Commissioner of Social Security, Petitioner
v.
Karen K. CAPATO, on behalf of B.N.C., et al.
Decided May 21, 2012.

Ginsburg, J., delivered the opinion for a unanimous Court.

Karen and Robert Capato married in 1999. Robert died of cancer less than three years later. With the help of in vitro fertilization, Karen gave birth to twins 18 months after her husband's death. Karen's application for Social Security survivors benefits for the twins, which the Social Security Administration (SSA) denied, prompted this litigation. The technology that made the twins' conception and birth possible, it is safe to say, was not contemplated by Congress when the relevant provisions of the Social Security Act (Act) originated in 1939 or were amended in 1965 to read as they now do.

Karen Capato, respondent here, relies on the Act's initial definition of "child" in 42 U.S.C. § 416(e): "'Child' means the child or legally adopted child of an [insured] individual." Robert was an insured individual, and the twins, it is uncontested, are the biological children of Karen and Robert. That satisfies the Act's terms, and no further inquiry is in order, Karen maintains. The SSA, however, identifies subsequent provisions, § 416(h)(2) and (h)(3)(C), as critical, and reads them to entitle biological children to benefits only if they qualify for inheritance from the decedent under state intestacy law, or satisfy one of the statutory alternatives to that requirement.

I

Karen Capato married Robert Capato in May 1999. Shortly thereafter, Robert was diagnosed with esophageal cancer and was told that the chemotherapy he required might render him sterile. Because the couple wanted children, Robert, before undergoing chemotherapy, deposited his semen in a sperm bank, where it was frozen and stored. Despite Robert's aggressive treatment regime, Karen conceived naturally and gave birth to a son in August 2001. The Capatos, however, wanted their son to have a sibling.

Robert's health deteriorated in late 2001, and he died in Florida, where he and Karen then resided, in March 2002. His will, executed in Florida, named as beneficiaries the son born of his marriage to Karen and two children from a previous marriage. The will made no provision for children conceived after Robert's death, although the Capatos had told their lawyer they wanted future offspring to be placed on a par with existing children. Shortly after Robert's death, Karen began in vitro fertilization using her husband's frozen sperm. She conceived in January 2003 and gave birth to twins in September 2003, 18 months after Robert's death.

Karen Capato claimed survivors insurance benefits on behalf of the twins. The SSA denied her application, and the U.S. District Court for the District of New Jersey affirmed the agency's decision. In accord with the SSA's construction of the statute, the District Court determined that the twins would qualify for benefits only if, as § 416(h)(2)(A) specifies, they could inherit from the deceased wage earner under state intestacy law. Robert Capato died domiciled in Florida, the court found. Under that State's law, the court noted, a child born posthumously may inherit through intestate succession only if conceived during the decedent's lifetime.

The Court of Appeals for the Third Circuit reversed. Under § 416(e), the appellate court concluded, "the undisputed biological children of a deceased wage earner and his widow" qualify for survivors benefits without regard to state intestacy law.

II

Congress amended the Social Security Act in 1939 to provide a monthly benefit for designated surviving family members of a deceased insured wage earner. "Child's insurance benefits" are among the Act's family-protective measures. An applicant qualifies for such benefits if she meets the Act's definition of "child," is unmarried, is below specified age limits (18 or 19) or is under a disability which began prior to age 22, and was dependent on the insured at the time of the insured's death. § 402(d)(1).[3]

To resolve this case, we must decide whether the Capato twins rank as "children" under the Act's definitional provisions. Section 402(d) provides that "every child (as defined in section 416(e) of this title)" of a deceased insured individual "shall be entitled to a child's insurance benefit." Section 416(e), in turn, states: "The term 'child' means (1) the child or legally adopted child of an individual, (2) a stepchild [under certain circumstances], and (3) the grandchild or step grandchild of an individual or his spouse [who meets certain conditions]."

A subsequent definitional provision further addresses the term "child." Under the heading "Determination of family status," § 416(h)(2)(A) provides: "In determining whether an applicant is the child or parent of an insured individual for purposes of this subchapter, the Commissioner of Social Security shall apply the intestacy law of the insured individual's domiciliary State." [4]

An applicant for child benefits who does not meet § 416(h) (2) (A)'s intestacy-law criterion may nonetheless qualify for benefits under one of several other criteria the Act prescribes, not applicable here.

A

Nothing in § 416(e)'s definition suggests that Congress understood the word "child" to refer only to the children of married parents.

Nor does § 416(e) indicate that Congress intended "biological" parentage to be prerequisite to "child" status under that provision. As the SSA points out, "in 1939, there was no such thing as a scientifically proven biological relationship between a child and a father, which is ... part of the reason that the word 'biological' appears nowhere in the Act." Notably, a biological parent is not necessarily a child's parent under law. Ordinarily, a parent-child relationship does not exist between an adoptee and the adoptee's genetic parents. Moreover, laws directly addressing use of today's assisted reproduction technology do not make biological parentage a universally determinative criterion. See, *e.g.*, Mass. Gen. Laws, ch. 46, § 4B (West 2010) ("Any child born to a married woman as a result of artificial insemination with the consent of her husband, shall be considered the legitimate child of the mother and such husband.").

---

[3] A "legitimate" child, even if she is not living with or receiving support from her parent, is ordinarily "deemed dependent" on that parent.

[4] An equitably adopted child may be eligible for benefits if the agreement to adopt the child would be recognized under state law as enabling the child to inherit upon the intestate death of the adopting parent.

We note, in addition, that marriage does not ever and always make the parentage of a child certain, nor does the absence of marriage necessarily mean that a child's parentage is uncertain. An unmarried couple can agree that a child is theirs, while the parentage of a child born during a marriage may be uncertain.

Finally, it is far from obvious that Karen Capato's proposed definition—"biological child of married parents," —would cover the posthumously conceived Capato twins. Under Florida law, a marriage ends upon the death of a spouse.

B

The SSA finds a key textual cue in § 416(h) (2) (A)'s opening instruction: "In determining whether an applicant is the child ... of an insured individual *for purposes of this subchapter,*" the Commissioner shall apply state intestacy law.

The original version of today's § 416(h) was similarly drafted. It provided that, "in determining whether an applicant is the child of an insured individual *for purposes of sections 401–409* of this title, the Board shall apply state intestacy law."

Reference to state law to determine an applicant's status as a "child" is anything but anomalous. Quite the opposite. Section § 416(h)(1)(A) directs that, "*for purposes of this subchapter,*" the law of the insured's domicile determines whether "the applicant and the insured individual were validly married," and if they were not, whether the applicant would nevertheless have "the same status" as a wife under the State's intestacy law.

Indeed, as originally enacted, a single provision mandated the use of state intestacy law for "determining whether an applicant is the wife, widow, child, or parent of an insured individual."

Just as the Act generally refers to state law to determine whether an applicant qualifies as a wife, widow, husband, widower, child or parent, so in several sections the Act sets duration-of-relationship limitations. See Weinberger v. Salfi, 422 U.S. 749,(1975) (discussing § 416(e)(2)'s requirement that, as a check against deathbed marriages, a parent-stepchild relationship must exist "not less than nine months immediately preceding insured's death"). Time limits also qualify the statutes of several States that accord inheritance rights to posthumously conceived children. See Cal. Prob.Code (allowing inheritance if child is in utero within two years of parent's death); Colo.Rev.Stat. (child in utero within three years or born within 45 months); Iowa Code Ann. (child born within two years); La.Rev.Stat. (child born within three years); N.D. Cent.Code (child in utero within three years or born within 45 months).

The paths to receipt of benefits laid out in the Act and regulations, we must not forget, proceed from Congress' perception of the core purpose of the legislation. The aim was not to create a program "generally benefiting needy persons"; it was, more particularly, to "provide ... dependent members of a wage earner's family with protection against the hardship occasioned by the loss of the insured's earnings." It is Congress' prerogative to legislate for the generality of cases. It did so here by employing eligibility to inherit under state intestacy law as a workable substitute for burdensome case-by-case determinations whether the child was, in fact, dependent on her father's earnings.

The SSA's construction of the Act, respondent charges, raises serious constitutional concerns under the equal protection component of the Due Process Clause. We have applied an intermediate level of scrutiny to laws "burdening illegitimate children for the sake of punishing the illicit relations of their parents, because 'visiting this condemnation on the head of an infant is illogical and unjust.' No showing has been made that posthumously conceived children share the characteristics that prompted our skepticism of classifications disadvantaging children of unwed parents. We therefore need not decide whether heightened scrutiny would be appropriate were that the case. Under rational-basis review, the regime Congress adopted easily passes inspection. That regime is "reasonably related to the government's twin interests in reserving benefits for those children who have lost a parent's support, and in using reasonable presumptions to minimize the administrative burden of proving dependency on a case-by-case basis."

IV

As we have explained, § 416(e)(1)'s statement, "the term 'child' means the child of an individual," is a definition of scant utility without aid from neighboring provisions. Under the completed definition, §416(h)(2)(A) refers to state law to determine the status of a posthumously conceived child. Under Florida law a child born posthumously may inherit through intestate succession only if conceived during decedent's lifetime.

V

Tragic circumstances—Robert Capato's death before he and his wife could raise a family—gave rise to this case. But the law Congress enacted calls for resolution of Karen Capato's application for child's insurance benefits by reference to state intestacy law. We cannot replace that reference by creating a uniform federal rule the statute's text scarcely supports.

For the reasons stated, the judgment of the Court of Appeals for the Third Circuit is reversed, and the case is remanded for further proceedings consistent with this opinion.

It is so ordered.

(2) STATUTES ON ASSISTED REPRODUCTION

As the preceding case has illustrated, different states have different statutes in the area of assisted reproduction. The following statute is based on the Uniform Act, but in nearly all such "adoptions" of Uniform Acts, there are individual state variations.

Before attempting to plow through the following statute, please realize that it would be nearly impossible to understand this statute except in specific, limited situations. It is just important to know that the act exists, and that it does cover many different situations. Undoubtedly, there will be additional medical procedures developed in the future, which are not presently covered by this statute.

However, it *is* worthwhile to skim through the statute, just to get an idea of how many different circumstances are covered by the statute – and to realize that when a particular situation arises, it may very well be covered by the statute, and then the statute will control – including on issues of eligibility for Social Security benefits.

Note that under this version of the statute, because of section 15-11-120(11), it may not be possible to ascertain the existence, and identity, of the children of a decedent for up to forty-five months after the death of the decedent. Clearly, that could significantly delay distribution of the decedent's estate.

Sample Statute on Assisted Reproduction

C.R.S. 15-11-115. Definitions

In this subpart 2:

(1) "Adoptee" means an individual who is adopted.

(2) "Assisted reproduction" means a method of causing pregnancy other than sexual intercourse.

(3) "Divorce" includes an annulment, dissolution of marriage, and declaration of invalidity of a marriage.

(4) "Functioned as a parent of the child" means behaving toward a child in a manner consistent with being the child's parent and performing functions that are customarily performed by a parent, including fulfilling parental responsibilities toward the child, recognizing or holding out the child as the individual's child, materially participating in the child's upbringing, and residing with the child in the same household as a regular member of that household.

(5) "Genetic father" means the man whose sperm fertilized the egg of a child's genetic mother. If the father-child relationship is established under the presumption of paternity under section 19-4-105, C.R.S., the term means only the man for whom that relationship is established.

(6) "Genetic mother" means the woman whose egg was fertilized by the sperm of a child's genetic father.

(7) "Genetic parent" means a child's genetic father or genetic mother.

(8) "Incapacity" means the inability of an individual to function as a parent of a child because of the individual's physical or mental condition.

(9) "Relative" means a grandparent or a descendant of a grandparent.

115-11-116. Effect of parent-child relationship

Except as otherwise provided in section 15-11-119, if a parent-child relationship exists or is established under this subpart 2, the parent is a parent of the child and the child is a child of the parent for the purpose of intestate succession.

15-11-119. Adoptee and adoptee's genetic parents

(1) Parent-child relationship between adoptee and genetic parents. Except as otherwise provided in this section, a parent-child relationship does not exist between an adoptee and the adoptee's genetic parents.

(2) Stepchild adopted by stepparent. A parent-child relationship exists between an individual who is adopted by the spouse of either genetic parent and:

(a) The genetic parent whose spouse adopted the individual; and

(b) The other genetic parent, but only for the purpose of the right of the adoptee or a descendant of the adoptee to inherit from or through the other genetic parent.

(2.5) Child of a second-parent adoption. A parent-child relationship exists between an individual who is adopted by a second parent and:

(a) A genetic parent who consented to a second-parent adoption; and

(b) Another genetic parent who is not a third-party donor, but only for the purpose of the right of the adoptee or a descendant of the adoptee to inherit from or through the other genetic parent.

(3) Individual adopted by relative of genetic parent. A parent-child relationship exists between both genetic parents and an individual who is adopted by a relative of a genetic parent, or by the spouse or surviving spouse of a relative of a genetic parent, but only for the purpose of the right of the adoptee or a descendant of the adoptee to inherit from or through either genetic parent.

(4) Individual adopted after death of both genetic parents. A parent-child relationship exists between both genetic parents and an individual who is adopted after the death of both genetic parents, but only for the purpose of the right of the adoptee or a descendant of the adoptee to inherit through either genetic parent.

(5) Child of assisted reproduction or gestational child who is subsequently adopted. If, after a parent-child relationship is established between a child of assisted reproduction and a parent or parents under section 15-11-120 or between a gestational child and a parent or parents under section 15-11-121, the child is adopted by another or others, the child's parent or parents under section 15-11-120 or 15-11-121 are treated as the child's genetic parent or parents for the purpose of this section.

15-11-120. Child conceived by assisted reproduction other than child born to gestational carrier

(1) Definitions. In this section:

(a) "Birth mother" means a woman, other than a gestational carrier under section 15-11-121, who gives birth to a child of assisted reproduction. The term is not limited to a woman who is the child's genetic mother.

(b) "Child of assisted reproduction" means a child conceived by means of assisted reproduction by a woman other than a gestational carrier under section 15-11-121.

(c) "Third-party donor" means an individual who produces eggs or sperm used for assisted reproduction, whether or not for consideration. The term does not include:

(I) A husband who provides sperm, or a wife who provides eggs, that are used for assisted reproduction by the wife;

(II) The birth mother of a child of assisted reproduction; or

(III) An individual who has been determined under subsection (5) or (6) of this section to have a parent-child relationship with a child of assisted reproduction.

(2) Third-party donor. A parent-child relationship does not exist between a child of assisted reproduction and a third-party donor.

(3) Parent-child relationship with birth mother. A parent-child relationship exists between a child of assisted reproduction and the child's birth mother.

(4) Parent-child relationship with husband whose sperm were used during his lifetime by his wife for assisted reproduction. Except as otherwise provided in subsections (9) and (10) of this section, a parent-child relationship exists between a child of assisted reproduction and the husband of the child's birth mother if the husband provided the sperm that the birth mother used during his lifetime for assisted reproduction.

(5) Birth certificate--presumptive effect. A birth certificate identifying an individual other than the birth mother as the other parent of a child of assisted reproduction presumptively establishes a parent-child relationship between the child and that individual.

(6) Parent-child relationship with another. Except as otherwise provided in subsections (7), (9), and (10) of this section, and unless a parent-child relationship is established under subsection (4) or (5) of this section, a parent-child relationship exists between a child of assisted reproduction and an individual other than the birth mother who consented to assisted reproduction by the birth mother with intent to be treated as the other parent of the child. Consent to assisted reproduction by the birth mother with intent to be treated as the other parent of the child is established if the individual:

(a) Before or after the child's birth, signed a record that, considering all the facts and circumstances, evidences the individual's consent; or

(b) In the absence of a signed record under paragraph (a) of this subsection (6):

(I) Functioned as a parent of the child no later than two years after the child's birth;

(II) Intended to function as a parent of the child no later than two years after the child's birth but was prevented from carrying out that intent by death, incapacity, or other circumstances; or

(III) Intended to be treated as a parent of a posthumously conceived child, if that intent is established by clear and convincing evidence.

(7) Record signed more than two years after the birth of the child--effect. For the purpose of paragraph (a) of subsection (6) of this section, neither an individual who signed a record more than two years after the birth of the child, nor a relative of that individual who is not also a relative of the birth mother, inherits from or through the child unless the individual functioned as a parent of the child before the child reached eighteen years of age.

(8) Presumption--birth mother is married or surviving spouse. For the purpose of paragraph (b) of subsection (6) of this section, the following rules apply:

(a) If the birth mother is married at the time of conception and no divorce proceeding is then pending, her spouse is presumed to satisfy the requirements of subparagraph (I) or (II) of paragraph (b) of subsection (6) of this section.

(b) If the birth mother is a surviving spouse and at her deceased spouse's death no divorce proceeding was pending, her deceased spouse is presumed to satisfy the requirements of subparagraph (II) or (III) of paragraph (b) of subsection (6) of this section.

(9) Divorce before placement of eggs, sperm, or embryos. If a married couple is divorced before placement of eggs, sperm, or embryos, a child resulting from the assisted reproduction is not a child of the birth mother's former spouse, unless the former spouse consented in a record that if assisted reproduction were to occur after divorce, the child would be treated as the former spouse's child.

(10) Withdrawal of consent before placement of eggs, sperm, or embryos. If, in a record, an individual withdraws consent to assisted reproduction before placement of eggs, sperm, or embryos, a child resulting from the assisted reproduction is not a child of that individual, unless the individual subsequently satisfies subsection (6) of this section.

(11) When posthumously conceived child treated as in gestation. If, under this section, an individual is a parent of a child of assisted reproduction who is conceived after the individual's death, the child is treated as in gestation at the time of the individual's death for purposes of section 15-11-104(1)(b) if the child is:

(a) In utero not later than thirty-six months after the individual's death; or

(b) Born not later than forty-five months after the individual's death.

§ 15-11-121. Child born to gestational carrier

(1) In this section:

(a) "Gestational agreement" means an enforceable or unenforceable agreement for assisted reproduction in which a woman agrees to carry a child to birth for an intended parent, intended parents, or an individual described in subsection (5) of this section.

(b) "Gestational carrier" means a woman who is not an intended parent who gives birth to a child under a gestational agreement. The term is not limited to a woman who is the child's genetic mother.

(c) "Gestational child" means a child born to a gestational carrier under a gestational agreement.

(d) "Intended parent" means an individual who entered into a validated gestational agreement providing that the individual will be the parent of a child born to a gestational carrier by means of assisted reproduction. The term is not limited to an individual who has a genetic relationship with the child.

(2) Court order adjudicating parentage--effect. A parent-child relationship is conclusively established by a court order designating the parent or parents of a gestational child.

(3) Gestational carrier. A parent-child relationship between a gestational child and the child's gestational carrier does not exist unless the gestational carrier is:

(a) Designated as a parent of the child in a court order described in subsection (2) of this section; or

(b) The child's genetic mother and a parent-child relationship does not exist under this section with an individual other than the gestational carrier.

CHAPTER 2 - WILL SUBSTITUTES

A. INTER VIVOS GIFTS

One way to avoid having to make a will is to give the property away while alive. An outright inter vivos gift is complete when made, is irrevocable, and will not be part of the probate estate. Sometimes, however, it may not be clear whether or not a gift has actually been made.

Supreme Court of Errors of Connecticut.
HEBREW UNIVERSITY ASSOCIATION
v.
George O. NYE et al., Executors
(ESTATE OF Ethel S. YAHUDA).
March 28, 1961.

KING, Associate Justice.

The plaintiff obtained a judgment declaring that it is the rightful owner of the library of Abraham S. Yahuda, a distinguished Hebrew scholar who died in 1951. The library included rare books and manuscripts, mostly relating to the Bible, which Professor Yahuda, with the assistance of his wife, Ethel S. Yahuda, had collected during his lifetime. There is no dispute that all of the library had become the property of Ethel before 1953 and was her property when she died on March 6, 1955, unless by her dealings with the plaintiff between January, 1953, and the time of her death she transferred ownership to the plaintiff. While the defendants in this action are the executors under the will of Ethel, the controversy as to ownership of the library is, in effect, a contest between two Hebrew charitable institutions, the plaintiff and a charitable trust or foundation to which, as hereinafter appears, Ethel bequeathed the bulk of her estate.

The pertinent facts recited in the finding may be summarized as follows:

Professor Yahuda and his wife had indicated to their friends their interest in creating a scholarship research center in Israel which would serve as a memorial to them. In January, 1953, Ethel went to Israel and had several talks with officers of the plaintiff, a university in Jerusalem. On January 28, 1953, a large luncheon was given by the plaintiff in Ethel's honor and was attended by many notables, including officials of the plaintiff and the president of Israel. At this luncheon, Ethel described the library and announced its gift to the plaintiff. The next day, the plaintiff submitted to Ethel a proposed newspaper release which indicated that she had made a gift of the library to the plaintiff. Ethel signed the release as approved by her. From time to time thereafter she stated orally, and in letters to the plaintiff and friends, that she 'had given' the library to the plaintiff. She refused offers of purchase and explained to others that she could not sell the library because it did not belong to her but to the plaintiff. On one occasion, when it was suggested that she give a certain item in the library to a friend, she stated that she could not, since it did not belong to her but to the plaintiff.

Early in 1954, Ethel began the task of arranging and cataloguing the material in the library for crating and shipment to Israel. These activities continued until about the time of her death. She sent some items, which she had finished cataloguing, to a warehouse for crating for overseas shipment. No consignee was named, and they remained in her name until her death.

Until almost the time of her death, she corresponded with the plaintiff about making delivery to it of the library. In September, 1954, she wrote the president of the plaintiff that she had decided to ship the library and collection, but that it was not to be unpacked unless she was present, so that her husband's ex libris could be affixed to the books.

The complaint alleged that the plaintiff was the rightful owner of the library and was entitled to possession ... The judgment found the 'issues' for the plaintiff, and further recited that 'a trust in relation to the library was created by a declaration of trust made by Ethel S. Yahuda, indicating her intention to create such a trust, made publicly by her.' We construe this language, in the light of the finding that, at the luncheon in Jerusalem, Ethel orally constituted herself a trustee of the library for future delivery to the plaintiff.

The difficulty with the trust theory adopted in the judgment is that the finding contains no facts even intimating that Ethel ever regarded herself as trustee of any trust whatsoever, or as having assumed any enforceable duties with respect to the property. The facts in the finding, in so far as they tend to support the judgment for the plaintiff at all, indicate that Ethel intended to make, and perhaps attempted to make, not a mere promise to give, but an executed, present, legal gift inter vivos of the library to the plaintiff without any delivery whatsoever.

A gift which is imperfect for lack of a delivery will not be turned into a declaration of trust for no better reason than that it is imperfect for lack of a delivery. Courts do not supply conveyances where there are none. This is true, even though the intended donee is a charity. The rule is approved in 1 Scott, Trusts § 31.

> "It is true that one can orally constitute himself a trustee of personal property for the benefit of another and thereby create a trust enforceable in equity, even though without consideration and without delivery. But he must in effect constitute himself a trustee. There must be an express trust, even though oral. It is not sufficient that he declare himself a donor. While he need not use the term 'trustee,' nor even manifest an understanding of its technical meaning or the technical meaning of the term 'trust,' he must manifest an intention to impose upon himself enforceable duties of a trust nature."

There are no subordinate facts in the finding to indicate that Ethel ever intended to, or did, impose upon herself any enforceable duties of a trust nature with respect to this library. The most that could be said is that the subordinate facts in the finding might perhaps have supported a conclusion that at the luncheon she had the requisite donative intent so that, had she subsequently made a delivery of the property while that intent persisted, there would have been a valid, legal gift inter vivos. The judgment, however, is not based on the theory of a legal gift inter vivos but on that of a declaration of trust. Since the subordinate facts give no support for a judgment on that basis, it cannot stand.

To support a factual conclusion of an executed inter-vivos gift, there would have to be a donative intention and at least a constructive delivery. It is true that the donative intention need not be expressed, nor the delivery made, in any particular form or mode. Here, there was no actual delivery of the library; nor was there any constructive delivery. No manual delivery of the library could have been made at the time of the expression of the donative intention in Jerusalem, since the library was then in the United States. But there is nothing in the finding to show that constructive delivery was attempted in Jerusalem or that any delivery of any kind was attempted after Ethel's return to the United States. Ethel did not, for instance, make any delivery either of the library or of a document of title purporting to represent the ownership of the library. For a constructive delivery, the donor must do that which, under the circumstances, will in reason be equivalent to an actual delivery. It must be as nearly perfect and complete as the nature of the property and the circumstances will permit. Just what, if any, form of constructive delivery would have been adequate, under the circumstances of this case, when Ethel was in Jerusalem, or what form of actual or constructive delivery would have been adequate after her return to the United States, we have no occasion to determine, since the finding discloses no delivery whatsoever.

The judgment declaring that the plaintiff is the owner of the library is without support in the finding and cannot stand.

The case must therefore be remanded for a new trial.

Then five years later the same case came before the court, and the court reached a different result – finding that there had been sufficient delivery. Hmm. Some of the techniques used in the second case might be of use in other situations.

Superior Court of Connecticut, New Haven County, at New Haven.
The HEBREW UNIVERSITY ASSOCIATION
v.
George O. NYE et al., Executors (ESTATE of Ethel S. YAHUDA).
Sept. 12, 1966.

PARSKEY, Judge.

Most of the facts in this case are recited in Hebrew University Assn. v. Nye, 148 Conn. 223. Additionally, it should be noted that at the time of the announcement of the gift of the 'Yahuda Library' the decedent gave to the plaintiff a memorandum containing a list of most of the contents of the library and of all of the important books, documents and incunabula. At some time prior to the summer of 1954 and during the lifetime of Mrs. Yahuda, the Hebrew University began the project of erecting its library. As a part of its effort to finance the construction of the library, the Hebrew University adopted a plan whereby various portions or rooms in the library were assigned certain respective money values, thereby permitting a person desiring to contribute toward the construction of such building, by making a contribution of the amount so assigned for such portion of the building or room, to have it dedicated to himself or some person designated by him. In setting up this plan for the library building, the Hebrew University designated a room in the building as the Yahuda room and indicated upon its plan that such room was not open for subscription or contribution because it had already been assigned for the Yahuda collection. The assigned value of this room was $21,600. By thus removing such room from possible subscription or contribution, the Hebrew University deprived itself of a possible source of substantial revenue.

The plaintiff claims a gift inter vivos based on a constructive or symbolic delivery, and alternatively that because of the decedent's conduct and the plaintiff's action in reliance thereon the defendants are estopped to deny the gift. In addition there are two other theories upon which the plaintiff may prevail. These are constructive trust based on action in reliance on a promise to make a gift and constructive trust arising out of an ineffective conveyance of an intended gift made by one who has died believing that he has made an effective gift.

I

Constructive Delivery

A gift inter vivos is complete when there is an intention to give, accompanied by a delivery of the thing given and an acceptance by the donee. It is not necessary that there should be a manual delivery of the thing given; nor is there any particular form or mode in which the transfer must be made or by which the intention of the donor must be expressed. While the change of possession may be either actual or constructive, it must be such as is consistent with the nature of the property and the situation of the parties. For a constructive delivery, the donor must do that which, under the circumstances, will in reason be equivalent to an actual delivery. It must be as nearly perfect and complete as the nature of the property and the circumstances will permit. The gift may be perfected when the donor places in the hands of the donee the means of obtaining possession of the contemplated gift, accompanied with acts and declarations clearly showing an intention to give and to divest himself of all dominion over the property. It is not necessary that the method adopted be the only possible one. It is sufficient if manual delivery is impractical or inconvenient.

Constructive delivery has been found to exist in a variety of factual situations: delivery of keys to safe deposit box; pointing out hiding places where money is hidden; informal memorandum.

Examining the present case in the light of the foregoing, the court finds that the delivery of the memorandum coupled with the decedent's acts and declarations, which clearly show an intention to give, and to divest herself of any ownership of the library, was sufficient to complete the gift. If the itemized memorandum which the decedent transmitted had been incorporated in a formal document, no one would question the validity of the gift. But formalism is not an end in itself. Where the purpose of formalities is being served, an excessive regard for formalism should not be allowed to defeat the ends of justice. The circumstances under which this gift was made - a public announcement at a luncheon attended by a head of state, accompanied by a document which identified in itemized form what was being given - are a sufficient substitute for a formal instrument purporting to pass title.

II

Constructive Trust-Action In Reliance

If it be assumed that there was an insufficient constructive delivery to consummate the gift, the question arises whether the facts justify the imposition of a constructive trust. It is undisputed that the decedent intended to give the Yahuda Library to the Hebrew University. She had reason to expect that the plaintiff would act in reliance on the eventual delivery of the library. In fact it did so act. It removed from the fund-raising market a room which was set aside to house the Yahuda collection. "A promise which the promisor should reasonably expect to induce action or forbearance of a definite and substantial character on the part of the promisee and which does induce such action or forbearance is binding if injustice can be avoided only by enforcement of the promise." Restatement, 1 Contracts s 90.

Courts cannot be oblivious to the techniques of fund raising for charitable purposes. It is no small task to build a university library. Plans must be made, architects employed, cost estimates arrived at, fund-raising committees named, solicitations made. The key to any such fund raising is the knowledge of the insatiable human desire to perpetuate one's name in brick and marble. Substantial sums of money are pledged and paid for suitable plaques on doors, rooms, wings and buildings. The setting aside of a room in a university library is no small matter. The withdrawal of such a room from the fundraising market for a considerable period of time in reliance on a promise that it will house a valuable collection of rare books is a matter of substance. The conditions justifying the application of s 90 of the Restatement of the Law of Contracts are present.

III

Constructive Trust - Ineffective Conveyance by Decedent

There is authority for the proposition that where an owner of property makes an ineffective conveyance of it as an intended gift he will not ordinarily be compelled to complete the gift, but if he dies believing that he has made an effective gift and if the donee was a natural object of his bounty, such as a wife or child, the donee can obtain the aid of the court of equity to complete the gift as against the heirs or next of kin. The question here presented is whether the rule should be extended to cover gifts to charities. "It is now fully recognized as a rule of our jurisprudence that gifts to charitable uses are to be highly favored, and will be most liberally construed in order to accomplish the intent of the donor, and trusts for such purposes may be established and carried into effect where, if not of a charitable nature, they could not be supported."

Although it is true that even in the case of a charity an imperfect gift will not be turned into a declaration of trust for no better reason than that it is imperfect; there is ample reason on the facts of this case for equity to impose a constructive trust. It is abundantly clear from the evidence that Ethel Yahuda wanted to house her husband's collection of rare books and manuscripts in a single repository so that they might be easily accessible to scholars. Yet if this collection remains part of the estate the trustees, who are directed under the second clause of Ethel's will to sell, call in and convert into money such parts of the trust as shall not consist of money, may have no alternative but to sell these books and documents piecemeal, in which event the library may be scattered over universities and colleges throughout the world. The net effect would be to frustrate the foundation which Ethel Yahuda established in the fifth clause of her will, for of what value would be a foundation in Israel, one of the purposes of such foundation being to complete the publication of the work of decedent's husband, if the source material was scattered?

Rules of law must, in the last analysis, serve the ends of justice or they are worthless. For a court of equity to permit the decedent's wishes to be doubly frustrated for no better reason than that the rules so provide makes no sense whatsoever. Who is helped by completing the gift to the plaintiff? The plaintiff, obviously; scholars, of course; the Ethel Yahuda foundation, to be sure. Who is hurt? No one. According to Ethel's will, after the specific bequests the remainder of the estate is to be converted into money and this money is to be used to establish Ethel Yahuda's foundation. The Yahuda library, however, is essential if the foundation is to serve the purpose for which it is founded. By the housing of library at the Hebrew University, the decedent's wishes will be carried out in full.

The court recognizes, in arriving at this result, that it is abrogating in some respects the requirement of delivery in a case involving an intended gift inter vivos. Obviously, it would be neither desirable nor wise to abrogate the requirement of delivery in any and all cases of intended inter vivos gifts, for to do so, even under the guise of enforcing equitable rights, might open the door to fraudulent claims. But neither does it mean that the present delivery requirement must remain inviolate. The facts of this case are so peculiarly suited for an extension to charities of the rule applicable to family settlements; that the court can find no good reason for not so extending it.

Accordingly, judgment may enter declaring that the plaintiff is the legal and equitable owner of the 'Yahuda Library' and has a right to the immediate possession of its contents.

B. JOINT TENANCY

Another standard will substitute is to put property into joint tenancy. Any property held by two or more people as joint tenants automatically becomes the property of the surviving joint tenants when one joint tenant dies. For example, if A, B, and C own Blackacre as joint tenants, when B dies, A and C automatically become the owners of all of Blackacre. B's interest in Blackacre ceases at the moment of B's death, and there is no interest in B's estate which B might convey by will.

There is also no need for any probate involving Blackacre at B's death. To clarify in the land records that A and C are now the sole owners of Blackacre, it is only necessary to record a copy of B's death certificate in the land records – and sometimes an affidavit that B, the person who has died, was one of the joint tenants of Blackacre.

So joint tenancy is a very simple, effective way of making sure that property owned by husband and wife, for example, as joint tenants, automatically goes to the surviving spouse upon the death of the first spouse to die, without any necessity for probate for the property held in joint tenancy.

If joint tenancy is used as an estate planning tool, however, it should be kept in mind, that a joint tenancy may be severed at any time by any joint tenant, without the consent of, or prior notice to, any other joint tenant. After severance, the land goes not to the surviving joint tenant(s), but into the *estate* of the person who was previously a joint tenant.

(1) UNILATERAL SEVERANCE OF JOINT TENANCY

Supreme Court of Colorado.
En Banc.
Noah TAYLOR, as personal representative of the Estate of Terrell Taylor, Petitioner
v.
Lucy I. CANTERBURY, Respondent.
June 28, 2004.

Justice KOURLIS delivered the Opinion of the Court.

I. Introduction

The question we address in this case is whether one joint tenant may extinguish a joint tenancy by conveying his interest in real property back to himself as a tenant in common. In the past, courts did not honor such transactions because of two premises: one, that someone could not be both a grantor and a grantee in the same real property transaction; and two, that in order to extinguish a joint tenancy, a joint tenant had to destroy one of the "four unities" of time, title, interest, or possession.

What is not at issue in this opinion is whether a joint tenant may destroy a joint tenancy without the consent of the other joint tenant or tenants. It is indisputable under Colorado law that one joint tenant may unilaterally dissolve the survivorship interest by creating a tenancy in common in lieu of a joint tenancy. However, for a joint tenant to sever the joint tenancy yet remain an owner of the property, courts required the use of a "strawman" transaction whereby the joint tenant executed a deed to a third person, and then a deed back from that third person to the joint tenant—this time as a tenant in common. By transferring legal title to the property held in joint tenancy to a third party, the transferor destroyed the unities of time and title and severed the joint tenancy.

We conclude that this circuitous process is no longer required under Colorado law because the two premises undergirding it are no longer valid. In Colorado and other jurisdictions around the country, joint tenancy law has evolved. The four unities are no longer the compass; rather, the polestar by which joint tenancies are now measured is the intent of the parties. For this reason, we have recognized in recent cases that acts inconsistent with the right of survivorship operate to sever the joint tenancy. Similarly, by operation of statute, the notion that a property owner may not be both the grantor and grantee in the same transaction has evaporated. Currently, the owner of real property may create a joint tenancy by conveying real property back to himself and one or more persons as joint tenants. Hence, the common law notions that once drove the jurisprudence of joint tenancy are gone. In their place are principles that focus on the intent of the property owners.

Therefore, we find no common law or legislative support for preventing a landowner from doing directly what he can do indirectly. We hold that a joint tenant who unilaterally conveys his interest in real property back to himself, with the intent of creating a tenancy in common, effectively severs the joint tenancy as to that joint tenant and the remaining joint tenant or tenants. We reverse the court of appeals and remand the case for further proceedings consistent with this opinion.

II. Facts and Procedural History

Terrell Taylor (Taylor) was the owner in fee simple of a 666–acre ranch in Fremont County, Colorado. The Petitioner, Noah Taylor, is the personal representative for Taylor, now deceased. On March 4, 1991, Taylor executed a warranty deed that conveyed that property from Taylor as sole owner to Taylor and Lucy I. Canterbury as joint tenants. The validity of that deed is not in dispute.

In 1997, Taylor executed a second deed: this time a quitclaim deed purporting to transfer the property back to himself and Canterbury as tenants in common. Taylor's manifest intent to sever the joint tenancy between himself and Canterbury, and to create a tenancy in common, could not have been clearer. The second deed stated: "It is my intention by this deed to sever the joint tenancy created by the 1991 deed, and to create a tenancy in common." The deed was duly recorded on June 16, 1997—the same day it was executed. Taylor died on August 20, 1999.

Canterbury filed an action to quiet title to the property to herself as surviving joint tenant. In that complaint, she also asked the trial court to set aside the 1997 conveyance and award her damages arising out of Taylor's attempted conveyance. Following a bench trial, the trial court found that "as a matter of law, the right of survivorship interest of a joint tenant is an estate in land which vests on the creation of the joint tenancy. The court concluded "that the rights of a joint tenant or joint tenants are vested and fixed at the time of the creation of the joint tenancy" and therefore the 1997 deed failed to effectively sever the joint tenancy between Canterbury and Taylor. On that basis, the court determined that "all interests which Taylor owned at the time of his death passed to Canterbury pursuant to the 1991 deed."

The court of appeals affirmed the trial court's judgment, holding that a joint tenant cannot effectively sever a joint tenancy by executing a deed which purports to convey title back to the two individuals as tenants in common.

We granted certiorari to address the issue of whether it is "permissible for a joint owner of real estate to sever the joint tenancy by unilaterally conveying his interest in the property back to himself to create a tenancy in common with the other joint tenant." We answer that question in the affirmative. Therefore, we reverse the court of appeals and remand this case for further proceedings consistent with this opinion.

III. Analysis

This case presents an issue of first impression in Colorado: whether the holder of an interest in joint tenancy may unilaterally sever that joint tenancy by conveying property back to himself as a tenant in common. We begin our analysis by discussing the basic characteristics of the two forms of concurrent ownership implicated in this case: tenancies in common and joint tenancies. Next, we analyze the law regarding the termination of joint tenancies in Colorado. Finally, we examine the specific subject of the validity of the transaction at issue in this case and conclude that, in light of the evolution of joint tenancy law in Colorado and other jurisdictions throughout the country, the common law principles that once supported the prohibition against a unilateral self-conveyance no longer have vitality.

A. Tenancy in Common and Joint Tenancy

A tenancy in common is a form of ownership in which each co-tenant owns a separate fractional share of undivided property. All co-tenants share a single right to possession of the entire interest. Each co-tenant also possesses the right to: unilaterally alienate his or her interest through sale, gift or encumbrance; to exclude third parties from the property; and to receive a portion of any income derived from the property.

just good to know def

Conversely, joint tenancy is a form of ownership in which each joint tenant possesses the entire estate, rather than a fractional share. Upon the death of one joint tenant, the remaining joint tenant or tenants automatically inherit that tenant's share in the property. ("Upon the death of one joint tenant, that tenant's share in the property does not pass through will or the rules of intestate succession; rather, the remaining tenant or tenants automatically inherit it."). This feature, called the "right of survivorship," is the principal distinction between a joint tenancy and a tenancy in common. ("Upon the death of one of the co-tenants in joint tenancy, the entire undivided interest of the deceased passes, by operation of law, to the surviving joint tenant.").

At common law, joint tenancies were the favored form of concurrent ownership of real property. If property was conveyed to two or more persons, the law presumed that a joint tenancy was intended. For purposes of establishing a joint tenancy, the "four unities" of time, title, interest, and possession were essential components. This requirement meant that to create a joint tenancy, "a conveyance had to convey to two or more persons at the same time the same title to the same interest with the same right of possession." If one of the four unities ceased to exist, a tenancy in common remained.

Today, in Colorado, joint tenancies are no longer the presumptive form of concurrent ownership of real property. Rather, tenancies in common are favored and the very existence of the joint tenancy is circumscribed by statute. Courts strictly construe instruments purporting to create a joint tenancy and do not recognize joint tenancies created by instruments that lack statutorily prescribed language.

B. Termination of Joint Tenancies

We turn to the question of how a joint tenancy may be terminated. In that inquiry, we pause to address the notion that the interests associated with the ownership of real property held in joint tenancy are fixed and vested. That principle comes most recently from our decision in *Lee's Estate v. Graber* where we held that "in the case of real property, rights under a joint tenancy are fixed and vested in the joint tenants at the time of the creation of the joint tenancy." As a result, once a donor creates a joint tenancy, he or she may not convey or otherwise interfere with the property interests vested in the other joint tenant by virtue of the conveyance. ("A joint tenant cannot alienate, encumber, or transfer the interest of other joint tenants without their consent."). What *Graber* restates is the axiom that once a joint tenancy is created, each joint tenant owns a vested interest in the property, which cannot be extinguished or alienated without that particular tenant's consent.

Graber does *not* hold that the right of survivorship itself is irrevocable or "fixed and vested" and cannot be eliminated without the consent of the other joint tenant or tenants. Indeed, such a holding would fly in the face of years of precedent to the contrary. Even characterizing survivorship as a "right" is somewhat misleading. Rather, survivorship is an expectancy that is not irrevocably fixed upon the creation of the estate; it arises only upon success in the ultimate gamble—survival—and then only if the unity of the estate has not theretofore been destroyed by voluntary conveyance, by partition proceedings, by involuntary alienation under an execution, or by any other action which operates to sever the joint tenancy.

Thus, in order for an *expectancy* of a survivorship interest to become a vested right, one joint tenant must survive the death of another joint tenant during the period of time that the joint tenancy remains intact.

Hence, the right of survivorship is not fixed in such a way as to constrain a joint tenant from changing his mind and abrogating it. Rather, a joint tenant may unilaterally eliminate the survivorship element of the ownership rights, and by doing so, eliminate his own survivorship rights as well. Stated otherwise, a joint tenant has the absolute right to terminate a joint tenancy unilaterally.

In this case, therefore, we are not dealing with whether a joint tenant may sever the tenancy and create a tenancy in common; we are dealing with the question of how that can be accomplished. Historically, whether the severance of a joint tenancy was effective turned on the question of whether the act was sufficient to destroy any of the four unities. Thus, conveying the property to a third party, transferring legal title into a trust, executing a lien, or foreclosing on a mortgage, were all considered to be effective means of severing a joint tenancy. We also specifically recognized the antiquated convention whereby the joint tenant wishing to terminate a joint tenancy would convey the property to a strawman who would in turn reconvey the property back to the former joint tenant as a tenant in common. The rationale underlying all of these transactions was that because legal title was transferred, the unities of time and title were destroyed, and therefore the joint tenancy, and the survivorship interest associated with it, were destroyed as well.

Along these same lines, mortgages, leases, and other encumbrances that did not involve the transfer of legal title were considered insufficient to sever a joint tenancy. Again, the underlying rationale was that because the grantor had not transferred title to the real property, the unities remained intact and the transaction did not sever the joint tenancy.

In stark contrast to traditional common law, "the modern tendency is to not require that the act of the co-tenant be destructive of one of the essential four unities of time, title, possession or interest before a joint tenancy is terminated." In *Mann*, we recognized that a joint tenancy may be terminated by mere agreement between the joint tenants, despite the fact that no property is conveyed or interests alienated. Thus, in determining whether a joint tenancy has been created or severed, we look not to the four unities, but rather to the intent of the parties. Actions that are inconsistent with the right of survivorship may terminate a joint tenancy.

C. Unilateral Self–Conveyance

As we have noted, historically, a joint tenant wishing to sever the joint tenancy used a strawman transaction. That method satisfied the common law proscription that "a conveyance to oneself has no legal consequence and therefore does not destroy any unities." This "two-to-transfer" artifice stemmed from the English common law feoffment ceremony with livery of seisin. Under the livery of seisin, the grantor of property had to transfer a physical remnant of the land (such as a lump of dirt or a twig) to the grantee. Therefore, the grantor could not be both grantor and grantee simultaneously.

In light of the changes to joint tenancy law in Colorado, the justifications for prohibiting unilateral self-conveyances no longer exist. For example, section 38–31–

101 expressly allows the owner of property to become both the grantor and the grantee for purposes of establishing a joint tenancy. This concept directly conflicts with the four unities doctrine and the notion that one could not be a grantor and a grantee. Further, the livery of seisin requirement has been explicitly abolished in Colorado. In short, none of the underpinnings that led to the artifice of a third-party transfer to sever a joint tenancy have continuing vitality.

Other jurisdictions have similarly concluded that it no longer makes sense to prohibit joint tenants from doing directly what they are already able to do indirectly through a strawman transaction. For instance, in Hendrickson v. Minneapolis Fed. Sav. & Loan Ass'n, the Supreme Court of Minnesota rejected the strawman requirement. The court in that case recognized the validity of a "Declaration of Election to Sever Survivorship of Joint Tenancy" by one joint tenant for purposes of severing the joint tenancy.

We conclude, in light of Colorado's statutory and precedential approach to joint tenancy, that a joint tenant may sever a joint tenancy by conveying the property to himself or herself as a tenant in common, without the need for an intermediary strawman. The statute, which permits the grantor and grantee to be one and the same, and which bypasses the four unities, does not preclude such a termination of the joint tenancy. The underlying premises that gave rise to the fiction of the strawman transaction in the first place have disappeared in the law of real property; and the law does not require a futile act. The strawman transaction does not protect the other joint tenant to any greater degree than the direct transfer, and, we repeat, the overriding consideration is that the survivorship interest is *not* vested.

IV. Conclusion

We reverse the court of appeals and thus the trial court's conclusion that the deed from Taylor to Taylor as a tenant in common was not valid for purposes of severing the joint tenancy. Rather, we conclude that Taylor had the right to sever the joint tenancy by means of a conveyance to himself. Taylor retained an undivided one-half interest in the property as a tenant in common at the time of his death in 1999. We return this case to the court of appeals for remand to the trial court for proceedings consistent with this opinion.

(2) EFFECT OF MURDER ON JOINT TENANCY

Even if there is no severance of a joint tenancy during the lives of the joint tenants, the law may impose a severance. For example, the act of one joint tenant murdering another joint tenant is likely to cause a severance of the joint tenancy – so that the murderer does not become the sole owner of the land – by "prematurely" terminating the life of the other joint tenant. The following statutes are illustrative.

Florida, for example, provides that:

732.802. Killer not entitled to receive property or other benefits by reason of victim's death

(1) A surviving person who unlawfully and intentionally kills or participates in procuring the death of the decedent is not entitled to any benefits under the will or under the Florida Probate Code, and the estate of the decedent passes as if the killer had predeceased the decedent. Property appointed by the will of the decedent to or for the benefit of the killer passes as if the killer had predeceased the decedent.

(2) Any joint tenant who unlawfully and intentionally kills another joint tenant thereby effects a severance of the interest of the decedent so that the share of the decedent passes as the decedent's property and the killer has no rights by survivorship. This provision applies to joint tenancies with right of survivorship and tenancies by the entirety in real and personal property; joint and multiple-party accounts in banks, savings and loan associations, credit unions, and other institutions; and any other form of co-ownership with survivorship incidents.

(3) A named beneficiary of a bond, life insurance policy, or other contractual arrangement who unlawfully and intentionally kills the principal obligee or the person upon whose life the policy is issued is not entitled to any benefit under the bond, policy, or other contractual arrangement; and it becomes payable as though the killer had predeceased the decedent.

(4) Any other acquisition of property or interest by the killer, including a life estate in homestead property, shall be treated in accordance with the principles of this section.

(5) A final judgment of conviction of murder in any degree is conclusive for purposes of this section. In the absence of a conviction of murder in any degree, the court may determine by the greater weight of the evidence whether the killing was unlawful and intentional for purposes of this section.

The California provision is more concise:

§ 251. Joint tenants; rights by survivorship
A joint tenant who feloniously and intentionally kills another joint tenant thereby effects a severance of the interest of the decedent so that the share

of the decedent passes as the decedent's property and the killer has no rights by survivorship. This section applies to joint tenancies in real and personal property, joint and multiple-party accounts in financial institutions, and any other form of co-ownership with survivorship incidents.

C. POD, TOD, Totten Trusts

All three of these WILL SUBSTITUTES are just forms in which bank accounts or other financial assets may be held. POD stands for Pay on Death. TOD stands for Transfer on Death. Totten Trust is just an early form of bank account trust, in which the pay on death provision was recognized. It was known as the "poor man's trust." With all of these forms of ownership, the original depositor is allowed to take out all of the funds, or change the form of the account at any time prior to death. But if money does remain in the account at the death of the original depositor, the remaining funds will go directly to the named beneficiary on the account – though subject, in most cases, to the ability of the Personal Representative to use the funds, if necessary, to pay the debts and final expenses of the decedent.

D. DESIGNATED BENEFICIARY AGREEMENT

As an alternative to a Civil Union or a same-sex marriage provision, a state may have authorized a document called a Designated Beneficiary Agreement, which may serve as a will substitute. In Colorado, for example, C.R.S. 15-15-401*et seq.* provides that any two unmarried people, (which might include, for example, a grandmother and granddaughter; same sex partners; elderly person and her caregiver, etc.) may execute a Designated Beneficiary Agreement, using the form provided in the statute. Unless the parties specify otherwise, execution of a Designated Beneficiary Agreement will give each partner the right to hospital visitation and the like, *plus* a right to an intestate share of the other partner's estate. The Designated Beneficiary Agreement must be recorded in the county in which one of the partners is domiciled at the time of the agreement. The whole agreement may be revoked at any time by *one* partner recording a revocation of the agreement in the county in which the agreement was originally recorded – *without* giving any prior notice to the other partner to the agreement. The county clerk and recorder is just directed to send notice of the revocation to the last known address of the other partner.

A will, executed *before or after* execution of the Designated Beneficiary Agreement, will prevail over the Designated Beneficiary Agreement. But when the Designated Beneficiary Agreement is in effect, it will serve as a will substitute to give one person a right to an intestate share of the other person's estate.

E. BENEFICIARY DEED

A number of states have recently authorized another will substitute, a ***revocable*** deed, usually called a Beneficiary Deed. A Beneficiary Deed is a ***revocable*** deed, which must be recorded prior to the death of the grantor, and is *unilaterally revocable* by the grantor at any time – even after it is recorded. The grantor of the Beneficiary Deed never needs to give any notice to the grantee of the existence of the deed, or of the revocation of the deed. As long as the grantor is alive, the grantor may treat the property just as if it still belonged to the grantor – including taking out a mortgage on the land, selling the land, or giving the land to another person. In fact, if the grantor gives ten acres of land to A by Beneficiary Deed, and then gives one acre of the *same* land to B by Beneficiary Deed, B will then become the grantee of the one acre of land, and the *entire* Beneficiary Deed to A will be thereby revoked. (C.R.S. 15-15-405(2)) A Beneficiary Deed may *not* be revoked by will.

Although it was intended, at least in Colorado, to serve as a "poor man's will," in some cases a Beneficiary Deed may actually be a trap for the unwary, because of a provision at C.R.S. 15-15-403 that provides:

> "No person who is an applicant for or recipient of medical assistance for which it would be permissible for the department of health care policy and financing to assert a claim pursuant to [various sections] shall be entitled to such medical assistance if the person has in effect a beneficiary deed. Notwithstanding the provisions of [another section] the execution of a beneficiary deed by an applicant for or recipient of medical assistance as described in this section shall cause the property to be considered a countable resource in accordance with [various sections]."

So under this statute a low income person who has executed a Beneficiary Deed is automatically disqualified for Medicaid, and in addition, a house, which would otherwise not have been a countable asset in determining a person's eligibility for Medicaid, is now a countable asset – thus almost certainly preventing the person from qualifying for Medicaid.

So the first step in estate planning for a relatively low income person may be to make sure to revoke any outstanding Beneficiary Deed.

CHAPTER 3. WILL BASICS

A. SAMPLE OF A COMPLETE WILL

When studying the details of a great car, or a great painting, it is best, first, to get an overview of the car or painting, and then to zero in on the details. Similarly, as we study the details of wills and trusts, it should be helpful first to look at a complete will, which includes a testamentary trust. Do not expect to understand all of the details of the document at this point. That will come later. For now, just read through the complete, real will of Elvis Presley, included in the appendix, to see an example of a real will.

B. INTEGRATION OF THE COMPONENTS OF A WILL

There is a basic rule that all components of a will must be integrated. That means that it must be clear that all the parts of a will are included as a single document. This rule is intended to insure that a disappointed friend or relative does not simply substitute a new page, within an existing will, after the death of the testator. The following case illustrates the importance of this rule of integration.

It is because of situations like the one that occurred in the following case that careful attorneys staple all pages of a will together *before* the will is signed, and then do *not* remove the staples when the Xerox copies of the will are made after the signing. Just fold the pages of the will back, when making the Xerox copy. Because any computer may now be set to print out a page with exactly the same font as the font used on some other page, it may be tempting for someone to substitute a page 2 that is significantly different from the original page 2 of the will. But it is almost impossible to hit the same staple holes twice! So a careful attorney today will integrate the will, and staple all of the pages of the will together *before* the client signs the will. Then just fold back the pages, *without removing the staples,* to make the copies. The following case illustrates why that is good practice for an attorney.

Court of Appeals of Colorado.
In the Matter of the Estate of SKY DANCER, Deceased. Laura J. Fisher, Appellee, v. Lawrence Barnes, Appellant.
Decided October 12, 2000

Opinion by JUDGE ROY

In this probate proceeding, Lawrence Barnes, (the legatee, who would have taken under the provisions of the will), appeals the trial court's order finding that Sky Dancer (the decedent) died intestate, and appointing the decedent's mother, Laura J. Fisher (the heir, who would take if the decedent died intestate), as personal representative of the decedent's estate. We affirm.

The decedent died in December 1997 of gunshot wounds. The circumstances of her death prompted an investigation during which the investigating officers allegedly took into possession the original copy of a document which purported to be her last will and testament (the "Will").

Thereafter, an attorney retained to represent the estate commenced summary administration pursuant to *§ 15-12-1201, et seq., C.R.S. 2000*, which provides simplified procedures for the administration of small estates. At that time, the interested parties agreed that the decedent's testamentary intent was expressed in the "Will" which was considered to be a photocopy of the original document retained by the police. Based upon that agreement, partial distribution of the decedent's personal property was made in accordance with the terms of the "Will." However, after becoming aware of certain information developed by the police investigation suggesting that the legatee might have been involved in the decedent's death, the heir objected to any further distributions under the "Will," and none was made.

In October 1998, the heir filed a petition for adjudication of intestacy, determination of heirs, and formal appointment as personal representative of the decedent's estate. The legatee, who was living with the decedent at the time of her death and was a beneficiary under the "Will," filed an objection to the petition.

The "Will" consisted of four typewritten pages entitled "Last Will and Testament of Sky Dancer," dated September 10, 1997, to which were stapled two additional typewritten pages entitled "AFFIDAVIT," which takes the form of a notarized will attestation signed by the decedent and two witnesses and dated April 8, 1996.

The document which purported to be the testamentary instrument, contained incomplete portions, the end of the testamentary text was followed by a large segment of blank page, and the signatures and attestation clauses were on a page separate from any testamentary text.

The legatee argued in the trial court that the decedent died testate, conceding, however, that the "Will" was not executed pursuant to statute. The legatee maintained that the documents making up the "Will" constituted a holographic will and, in any event, when considered with certain supporting documents, were sufficient to make a determination of intestacy improper. The legatee further argued that he and the decedent had contracted a common law marriage and he was, therefore, an heir.

Following an evidentiary hearing, the trial court found or concluded that the legatee had failed to prove: (1) that he and the decedent had contracted a common law marriage; (2) that the "Will" was a holographic will; or (3) that the decedent intended the "Will" to be her last will and testament. The trial court concluded that the decedent had died intestate and appointed the heir as personal representative of the estate.

The formalities associated with the execution of a will have historically served as proof of the testator's intent to dispose of property as set forth in the document, and the absence of undue influence, duress, or deceit.

In this instance, we are not dealing with a minor deviation from the formal requisites of the preparation or execution of a will. Here, the "Will," or at least the dispositive portion of it, cannot be attributed to the decedent. It was not written by her in her own hand, it was not signed by her, and there is no evidence that she represented it to anyone, either orally or in writing, as her will. And, while there is no affirmative evidence to support the proposition here, the "Will" does not foreclose the possibility that some other person prepared or assembled the dispositive provisions of it.

The order declaring that the decedent died intestate is affirmed.

To be blunt, the pages which had been submitted as decedent's will were not *integrated* into a single document. There was no proof that all of the pages had been together when the decedent and the witnesses had signed the affidavit, which was dated _April 8, 1996._ The dispositive parts of the "will" had been signed on _September 10, 1997_, roughly *a year and five months* _after_ the date on the attestation clause. Yet despite this serious difference in dates, partial distribution had been made, under the terms of the will, before anyone noticed the problem.

C. STATUTORY REQUIREMENTS FOR FORMAL WILL

There are certain statutory requirements for a formal will. These vary a bit from state to state, but the current Uniform Probate Code demonstrates a basic pattern of one of the most liberal types of the traditional statutory provisions for a formal will.

U.P.C. 2-502(a) provides:

"2-502(a) **Witnessed or Notarized Wills.** Except as provided in subsection (b) and in Sections 2-503, 2-506, and 2-513, a will must be:

(1) in writing;

(2) signed by the testator or in the testator's name by some other individual in the testator's conscious presence and by the testator's direction; and

(3) either:

(A) signed by at least two individuals, each of whom signed within a reasonable time after the individual witnessed either the signing of the will as described in paragraph (2) or the testator's acknowledgment of that signature or acknowledgment of the will; or

(B) acknowledged by the testator before a notary public or other individual authorized by law to take acknowledgments."

D. SIGNED BY THE TESTATOR

The following case provides a number of dramatic illustrations of the very unfortunate consequences that may follow if the statutory provisions are not complied with exactly as specified in the applicable statue. The dissent in this case is a classic.

The Supreme Court of Pennsylvania
Estate of PAVLINKO
January 15, 1959

OPINION BY MR. JUSTICE BELL.

Vasil Pavlinko died February 8, 1957; his wife, Hellen, died October 15, 1951. A testamentary writing dated March 9, 1949, which purported to be the will of Hellen Pavlinko, was signed by Vasil Pavlinko, her husband. The residuary legatee named therein, a brother of Hellen, offered the writing for probate as the will of Vasil Pavlinko, but probate was refused. The orphans' court, after hearing and argument, affirmed the decision of the register of wills.

The facts are unusual and the result very unfortunate. Vasil Pavlinko and Hellen, his wife, retained a lawyer to draw their wills and wished to leave their property to each other. By mistake Hellen signed the will which was prepared for her husband, and Vasil signed the will which was prepared for his wife, each instrument being signed at the end thereof. The lawyer who drew the will and his secretary, Dorothy Zinkham, both signed as witnesses. Miss Zinkham admitted that she was unable to speak the language of Vasil and Hellen, and that no conversation took place between them. The wills were kept by Vasil and Hellen. For some undisclosed reason, Hellen's will was never offered for probate at her death; in this case it was offered merely as an exhibit.

The instrument which was offered for probate was short. It stated, with emphasis added:

> "I, *Hellen* Pavlinko, of... do hereby make, publish and declare this to be *my* Last Will and Testament..."
>
> In the first paragraph she directed her executor to pay her debts and funeral expenses. In the second paragraph she gave her entire residuary estate to "my husband, Vasil Pavlinko... absolutely".
>
> She then provided: "Third: If my aforesaid husband, Vasil Pavlinko, should predecease me, then and in that event, I give and bequeath: (a) To my brother-in-law, Mike Pavlinko, of McKees Rocks, Pennsylvania, the sum of Two hundred ($200.00) Dollars. (b) To my sister-in-law, Maria Gerber, (nee Pavlinko), of Pittsburgh, Pennsylvania, the sum of Two hundred ($200.00) Dollars. (c) The rest, residue and remainder of *my* estate, of whatsoever kind

and nature and wheresoever situate, I give, devise and bequeath, absolutely, to *my brother,* Elias Martin, now residing at 520 Aidyl Avenue, Pittsburgh, Pennsylvania.

"I do hereby nominate, constitute and appoint my husband, Vasil Pavlinko, as Executor of this my Last Will and Testament." It was then mistakenly signed: "Vasil Pavlinko".

While no attempt was made to probate, as Vasil's will, the writing which purported to be his will but was signed by Hellen, it could not have been probated as Vasil's will, because it was not signed by him at the end thereof.

The Wills Act of 1947 provides in clear, plain and unmistakable language in § 2: "Every will shall be in writing and shall be signed *by the testator* at the end thereof" with certain exceptions not here relevant. The court below correctly held that the paper which *recited* that it was the will of Hellen Pavlinko and intended and purported to give Hellen's estate to her husband, could not be probated as the will of Vasil and was a nullity.

In order to decide in favor of the residuary legatee, almost the entire will would have to be rewritten. The court would have to substitute the words "Vasil Pavlinko" for "Hellen Pavlinko" and the words "my wife" wherever the words "my husband" appear in the will, and the relationship of the contingent residuary legatees would likewise have to be changed. To consider this paper - as written - as Vasil's will, it would give his entire residuary estate to "my husband, Vasil Pavlinko, absolutely" and "Third: If my husband, Vasil Pavlinko, should predecease me, then... I give and bequeath my residuary estate to my brother, Elias Martin." The language of this writing, which is signed at the end thereof by *Vasil* Pavlinko, is unambiguous, clear and unmistakable, and it is obvious that it is a meaningless nullity.

While no authority is needed to demonstrate what is so obvious, there is a case which is directly in point and holds that such a writing cannot be probated as the will of Vasil Pavlinko. This exact situation arose in *Alter's Appeal, 67 Pa. 341.* The facts are recited in the unanimous opinion of the Court, speaking through Mr. Justice AGNEW:

> "This is a hard case, but it seems to be without a remedy. An aged couple, husband and wife, having no lineal descendants, and each owning property, determined to make their wills in favor of each other, so that the survivor should have all they possessed. Their wills were drawn precisely alike, mutatis mutandis, and laid down on a table for execution. Each signed a paper, which was duly witnessed by three subscribing witnesses, and the papers were enclosed in separate envelopes, endorsed and sealed up. After the death of George A. Alter, the envelopes were opened and it was found that each had by mistake signed the will of the other. To remedy this error the legislature conferred authority upon the Register's Court of this county to take proof of the mistake, and proceed as a court of chancery, to reform

> the will of George A. Alter and decree accordingly.... Was the paper signed by George A. Alter his will? Was it capable of being reformed by the Register's Court? The paper drawn up for his will was not a will in law, for it was not 'signed by him at the end thereof,' as the Wills Act requires. *The paper he signed was not his will, for it was drawn up for the will of his wife and gave the property to himself. It was insensible and absurd.* It is clear, therefore, that he had executed no will, and there was nothing to be reformed. There was a mistake, it is true, but that mistake was the same as if he had signed a blank sheet of paper. He had written his name, but not to his will. He had never signed his will, and the signature where it was, was the same as if he had not written it at all. He therefore died intestate, and his property descended as at law."

The Court further decided that the Legislative Act was void because it had no power to divest estates which were already vested at law on the death of George A. Alter without a will.

In *Bryen's Estate,* a testator received from his lawyer a three page will. He wished to add an additional clause providing for a grandchild. The lawyer thereupon rewrote the last page "backed and bound together with brass eyelets the first, second and new third page, unnumbered, and inserted the original third page loosely between the last of the fastened pages and the backer." Bryen executed the loose sheet at the end thereof in the presence of two subscribing witnesses. He then placed the enclosure in his safe deposit box where it was found after his death. The Court held that the instrument could not be probated as Bryen's last will because it was not signed at the end thereof in conformity with the statute, nor could any part or pages thereof be probated as his last will. This Court, speaking through Mr. Justice, later Chief Justice, STERN, said: "The obvious truth of the matter is that the loose sheet was signed by mistake... While decedent's mistake is regrettable, it cannot be judicially corrected; the situation thus created must be accepted as it exists. The question is not what a testator mistakenly thinks he is doing, but what he actually does... It is of paramount importance to uphold the legal requirements as to the execution of wills, so that the possibility of fraud may be reduced to a minimum."

In *Churchill's Estate,* the Court refused to probate Churchill's will, which was written by him. He failed to sign his name "at what was so clearly the end of the paper as a will. What he did do was to write his name in three blank spaces in the paper - first at the top and then in the testimonium and attestation clauses.... he said to one of the two attesting witnesses, 'This is my will, I have signed it,' and to the other, 'I wish you to witness my name to a paper,' and subsequently handed it to a physician, saying, 'This is my will, and I want you to keep it for me,'...

> "The decedent may have thought he had made a will, but the statute says he had not. The question is not one of his intention, but of what he actually

> did, or rather what he failed to do. He failed to sign the paper at the end thereof, and this essential requirement of the statute is not met by the insertion of his name in his own handwriting in three blank spaces in the printed form of the paper which he may have intended to use in executing his will. 'It may happen, even frequently, that genuine wills, namely, wills truly expressing the intentions of the testators, are made without observations of the required forms; and whenever that happens, the genuine intention is frustrated by the act of the legislature, of which the general object is to give effect to the intention. The courts must consider that the legislature, having regard to all probable circumstances, has thought it best, and has therefore determined, to run the risk of frustrating the intention sometimes, in preference to the risk of giving effect to or facilitating the formation of spurious wills, by the absence of forms."

Once a court starts to ignore or alter or rewrite or make exceptions to clear, plain and unmistakable provisions of the Wills Act in order to accomplish equity and justice in that particular case, the Wills Act will become a meaningless, although well intentioned, scrap of paper, and the door will be opened wide to countless fraudulent claims which the Act successfully bars.

DISSENTING OPINION BY MR. JUSTICE MUSMANNO:

Vasil Pavlinko and his wife, Hellen Pavlinko, being unlettered in English and unlearned in the ways of the law, wisely decided to have an attorney draw up their wills, since they were both approaching the age when reflecting persons must give thought to that voyage from which there is no return. They explained to the attorney, whose services they sought, that he should draw two wills which would state that when either of the partners had sailed away, the one remaining ashore would become the owner of the property of the departing voyager. Vasil Pavlinko knew but little English. However, his lawyer, fortunately, was well versed in his clients' native language, known as Little Russian or Carpathian. The attorney thus discussed the whole matter with his two visitors in their language. He then dictated appropriate wills to his stenographer in English and then, after they had been transcribed, he translated the documents, paragraph by paragraph, to Mr. and Mrs. Pavlinko, who approved of all that he had written. The wills were laid before them and each signed the document purporting to be his or her will. The attorney gave Mrs. Pavlinko the paper she had signed and handed to her husband the paper he had signed. In accordance with customs they had brought with them from the old country, Mrs. Pavlinko turned her paper over to her husband. It did not matter, however, who held the papers since they were complementary of each other. Mrs. Pavlinko left her property to Mr. Pavlinko and Mr. Pavlinko left his property to Mrs. Pavlinko. They also agreed on a common residuary legatee, Elias Martin, the brother of Mrs. Pavlinko.

Mrs. Pavlinko died first, but for some reason her will was not probated. Then Mr. Pavlinko died and Elias Martin came forth to claim his inheritance. The Register of Wills of Allegheny County refused to accept the Vasil Pavlinko will for probate. It now developed for the first time that, despite every care used by her attorney, a strange thing had happened. Mr. Pavlinko had signed his wife's will and Mrs. Pavlinko had signed her husband's will.

Everyone in this case admits that a mistake was made: an honest, innocent, unambiguous, simple mistake, the innocent, drowsy mistake of a man who sleeps all day and, on awakening, accepts the sunset for the dawn.

No one disputes this brute fact, no one can dispute this granitic, unbudgeable truth. Cannot the law, therefore, dedicated as it is to the truth, and with all its wisdom and majestic power, correct this mistake which cries out for correction? May the law not untie the loose knot of error which begs to be freed? I know that the law is founded on precedent and in many ways we are bound by the dead hand of the past. But even, with obeisance to precedent, I still do not believe that the medicine of the law is incapable of curing the simple ailment here which has not, because of any passage of time, become aggravated by complications.

We have said more times than there are tombstones in the cemetery where the Pavlinkos lie buried, that the primary rule to be followed in the interpretations of a will is to ascertain the intention of the testator. Can anyone go to the graves of the Pavlinkos and say that we do not know what they meant? They said in English and in Carpathian that they wanted their property to go to Elias Martin.

We have also said time without number that the intent of the testator must be gathered from the four corners of his will. Whether it be from the four corners of the will signed by Vasil Pavlinko or whether from the eight corners of the wills signed by Vasil and Hellen Pavlinko, all set out before the court below, the net result is always the same, namely that the residue of the property of the last surviving member of the Pavlinko couple was to go to Elias Martin. In the face of all the pronouncements of the law as to the fidelity with which the intention of the testator must be followed, on what possible basis can we now ignore the intention expressed by the Pavlinkos so clearly, so conclusively, and so all-encompassingly?

The results do not need to be unfortunate. "What offends against an innate sense of justice, decency and fair play offends against good law." Certainly the results being affirmed by this Court offend against an innate sense of justice. Elias Martin is being turned out of court when there is no need for such a peremptory eviction.

The Wills Act itself specifically provides: "A devise or bequest not being part of the residuary estate which shall fail or be void because the beneficiary fails to survive the testator or because it is contrary to law *or otherwise incapable of taking effect,* shall be included in the residuary devise or bequest if any contained in the will."

I see no insuperable obstacle to probating the will signed by Vasil Pavlinko. Even though it was originally prepared as the will of his wife, Hellen, he did adopt its testamentary provisions as his own. Some of its provisions are not effective but their ineffectuality in no way bars the legality and validity of the residuary clause which is complete in itself. I would, therefore, probate the paper signed by Vasil Pavlinko. Here, indeed, is a situation where we could, if we wished, consistent with authority and precedent, and without endangering the integrity of the Wills Act, put into effect the time-honored proverb that "where there's a will, there's a way."

In fact, we have here two wills, with proper signposts unerringly pointing to the just and proper destination, but the Court still cannot find the way.

E. HARMLESS ERROR

Because of the unfortunate results in the Pavlinko case, and others like it, a number of states have recently adopted some version of UPC 2- 503, the "Harmless Error" provision.

UPC 2-503 provides:

> "Although a document or writing added upon a document was not executed in compliance with Section 2-502, the document or writing is treated as if it had been executed in compliance with that section if the proponent of the document or writing establishes by clear and convincing evidence that the decedent intended the document or writing to constitute:

(1) the decedent's will,

(2) a partial or complete revocation of the will,

(3) an addition to or an alteration of the will, or

(4) a partial or complete revival of his or her formerly revoked will or of a formerly revoked portion of the will."

Although this provision might have helped in the *Pavlinko* case, it also creates some dangers, which will be covered later in the book.

A recent case, decided soon after the adoption of the Harmless Error rule, demonstrates how the provision on harmless error might be applied to carry out the intent of a testator.

Colorado Court of Appeals.
In the Matter of the ESTATE of Ronald WILTFONG, Deceased.
Randall Rex, Claimant-Appellant,
v.
Margaret L. Tovrea, Respondent-Appellee.
Oct. 19, 2006.

Opinion by Judge BERNARD.

In this formal testacy probate proceeding, Randall Rex (proponent), the proponent of a document alleged to be a will, appeals the trial court's order finding decedent, Ronald Wiltfong, died intestate. We reverse and remand for further proceedings.

I. Background

The following facts are undisputed. Proponent and decedent were domestic partners for twenty years until decedent's death. They lived together and intermingled most of their finances.

On proponent's birthday in 2003, proponent and decedent celebrated with two friends. In the presence of the friends, decedent gave proponent a birthday card containing a typed letter decedent had signed. The letter expressed decedent's wish that if anything should ever happen to him, everything he owned should go to proponent. The letter also stated that proponent, their pets, and an aunt were his only family, and "everyone else is dead to me." Decedent told proponent and the friends the letter represented his wishes.

Decedent died from a heart attack the following year. Proponent filed a petition to have the letter admitted to probate as decedent's will. Margaret Tovrea (contestant), the mother of decedent's three nephews who would be decedent's heirs if he died intestate, objected to the petition.

The trial court ruled the letter was not a will because it did not meet the requirements of § 15-11-503(2), C.R.S., and therefore the nephews would take decedent's estate by intestate succession. This appeal followed.

While scrupulous adherence to the formalities associated with executing wills serves the important purpose of preventing fraud, it can also "defeat intention ... or work unjust enrichment." Restatement (Third) of Property: Wills & Other Donative Transfers § 3.3 To address this concern, among others, the Code was amended to align Colorado's law with extensive changes suggested by the Uniform Probate Code.

One of these changes was effected by § 15-11-503(1), C.R.S. This statute governs how potential donative documents are treated when they have not been executed pursuant to the usual statutory requirements. Section 15-11-503(1) states:

> "Although a document, or writing added upon a document, was not executed in compliance with section 15-11-502, the document or writing is treated as if it

had been executed in compliance with that section if the proponent of the document or writing establishes by clear and convincing evidence that the decedent intended the document or writing to constitute:

(a) The decedent's will..."

The purpose of adding § 15-11-503(1) was to provide a mechanism for the application of harmless error analysis when a probate court considers whether the formal requirements of executing a will have been met.

Thus, the question is whether a defect is harmless in light of the statutory purposes, not in light of the satisfaction of each statutory formality, viewed in isolation. To achieve those purposes, the issue is whether the evidence of the conduct proves the decedent intended the document to be a will.

Certain errors cannot be excused as harmless, like the failure of a proponent to produce a document. Other errors are difficult, although not impossible, to excuse as harmless, like the absence of a signature on a document. In this regard, § 15-11-503(2) reads: "Subsection (1) of this section shall apply only if the document is signed or acknowledged by the decedent as his or her will...."

§ 15-11-503(2) was designed to limit the harmless error concept to minor flaws in the execution of wills. Thus, § 15-11-503(2) establishes the condition precedent that a document be "signed or acknowledged by the decedent as his or her will" before a court may move to the next step and decide whether there is clear and convincing evidence the decedent intended the document to be a will.

Under § 15-11-503, a proponent of a document must show, by clear and convincing evidence, the decedent intended the document to be a will. The greater the deviation from the requirements of due execution established by § 15-11-502, the heavier the burden on the document's proponent to prove, by clear and convincing evidence, that the instrument establishes the decedent's intent.

Proponent contends the trial court erred in interpreting § 15-11-503(2) to require a document to be both signed *and* acknowledged by a decedent as his or her will. We agree.

The trial court found decedent signed the letter, but did not acknowledge the letter as his will. The court ruled the phrase "signed or acknowledged" must be read in the conjunctive and therefore, the letter could not be admitted to probate. We conclude the court's interpretation was erroneous.

The term "or" in a statute is presumed to be used in the disjunctive sense unless the legislative intent is clearly contrary. Here, there is no indication the General Assembly intended a document to be both signed and acknowledged to satisfy § 15-11-503(2).

Hence, the trial court erred in interpreting § 15-11-503(2) to require a document to be both signed and acknowledged by a decedent.

Conclusion

look at whole picture

In this case, the court found decedent's letter did not satisfy the formal requirements of a will pursuant to § 15-11-502(1) and that it was not a holographic will pursuant to § 15-11-502(2). We agree.

Two of the formal requirements of § 15-11-502 were met in this case because the letter was in writing and signed by decedent. However, the letter was not signed by at least two witnesses who had witnessed either decedent's signing of the letter or decedent's acknowledgment of the signature or of the document as a will. Thus, the letter was not a formal will.

The letter was also not a holographic will. Although it was signed by decedent, the material portions of the letter were typed, and, therefore, they were not in decedent's handwriting.

Thus, it was appropriate to determine whether the letter was a writing intended as a will under § 15-11-503.

On remand, once a court determines that a decedent has signed or acknowledged a document as a will, as the trial court did here, the issue becomes whether the proponent can establish by clear and convincing evidence that the decedent intended the document to be a will.

This proof may take the form of extrinsic evidence, such as decedent's statements to others about the letter.

The language of the letter is also relevant evidence, including, for example, whether the letter disposes of all decedent's property and whether the letter identifies a beneficiary.

The trial court's order is reversed, and the case is remanded for further proceedings consistent with the views expressed in this opinion.

F. REQUIREMENTS FOR A HOLOGRAPHIC WILL

About half of the states of the United States give recognition to a will, even though it does not comply with the usual statutory formalities requiring witnesses, *if* the will complies with the requirements for a holographic will. Basically, the requirements for a holographic will are that the will, or at least all of the dispositive parts of the will, are in the *handwriting* of the testator; that there are words, in the handwriting of the testator, demonstrating the testator's intent that the document serve as his or her will; and that the document is signed by the testator. In a holographic will this rather large sample of the testator's own handwriting is considered to be sufficient proof of the validity of the document – and thus the will is valid, without any witnesses.

Over the years, these requirements for holographic wills have caused many problems – most frequently when someone fills in a standard pre-printed will form, signs the document, but does not have anyone sign as a witness. There have been many cases in which a document, which the testator considered to be his or her will, was held to be invalid either because there was nothing in the testator's handwriting demonstrating testamentary intent, or because important dispositive provisions were on the printed form – not in the handwriting of the testator.

Today, in states which have adopted the "Harmless Error" provision of the UPC, such documents might be held to be valid. But in states which have not adopted a harmless error provision, the document which someone downloads on his or her computer, prints, and signs, is likely to be held to be void, because of the absence of witnesses, (thus not a formal will), and the absence of sufficient provisions in the testator's own handwriting (thus not a holographic will).

On the other hand, over the years, many documents, including letters, have been held to constitute valid wills, as illustrated by the well-known case below.

Supreme Court of Pennsylvania.
In re KIMMEL'S ESTATE.
Jan. 7, 1924.

SIMPSON, J.

One of decedent's heirs at law appeals from a decree of the orphans' court, directing the register of wills to probate the following letter:

'Johnstown, Dec. 12.

'The Kimmel Bro. and Famly We are all well as you can espec fore the time of the Year. I received you kind & welcome letter from Geo & Irvin all OK glad you poot your Pork down in Pickle it is the true way to keep meet every piece gets the same, now always poot it down that way & you will not miss it & you will have good pork fore smoking you can keep it from butchern to butchern the hole year round. Boys, I wont agree with you about the open winter I think we are gone to have one of the hardest. Plenty of snow & Verry cold verry cold! I dont want to see it this way but it will will come see to the old sow & take her away when the time comes well I cant say if I will come over yet. I will wright in my next letter it may be to ruff we will see in the next letter if I come I have some very valuable papers I want you to keep fore me so if enny thing hapens all the scock money in the 3 Bank liberty lones Post office stamps and my home on Horner St goes to George Darl & Irvin Kepp this letter lock it up it may help you out. Earl sent after his Christmas Tree & Trimmings I sent them he is in the Post office in Phila working.

'Will clost your Truly,

Father.'

This letter was mailed by decedent at Johnstown, Pa., on the morning of its date-Monday, December 12, 1921-to two of his children, George and Irvin, who were named in it as beneficiaries; the envelope being addressed to them at their residence in Glencoe, Pa. He died suddenly on the afternoon of the same day.

Two questions are raised: First. Is the paper testamentary in character? Second. Is the signature to it a sufficient compliance with our Wills Act? Before answering them directly, there are a few principles, now well settled, which, perhaps, should be preliminarily stated.

While the informal character of a paper is an element in determining whether or not it was intended to be testamentary this becomes a matter of no moment when it appears thereby that the decedent's purpose was to make a posthumous gift. On this point the court below well said:

'Deeds, mortgages, letters, powers of attorney, agreements, checks, notes, etc., have all been held to be, in legal effect, wills. Hence, an assignment, a deed, a letter of instructions, a power of attorney, and an informal letter of requests were all held as wills.'

It is equally clear that where, as here, the words 'if enny thing hapens,' condition the gift, they strongly support the idea of a testamentary intent; indeed they exactly state what is expressed in or must be implied from every will. True, if the particular contingency stated in a paper, as the condition upon which it shall become effective, has never in fact occurred, it will not be admitted to probate. In the present case, however, it is clear the contingency, 'if enny thing hapens,' was still existing when testator died suddenly on the same day he wrote and mailed the letter; hence, the facts not being disputed, the question of testamentary intent was one of law for the court.

As is often the case in holographic wills of an informal character, much of that which is written is not dispositive; and the difficulty, in ascertaining the writer's intent, arises largely from the fact that he had little, if any, knowledge of either law, punctuation, or grammar. In the present case this is apparent from the paper itself; and in this light the language now quoted must be construed:

> 'I think we are gone to have one of the hardest [winters]. Plenty of snow & Verry cold Verry cold! I dont want to see it this way but it will come * * * well I cant say if I will come over yet. I will wright in my next letter it may be to ruff we will see in the next letter if I come I have some very valuable papers I want you to keep fore me so if enny thing hapens all * * * [the real and personal property specified] goes to George Darl and Irvin Kepp this letter lock it up it may help you out.'

When resolved into plainer English, it is clear to us that all of the quotation, preceding the words 'I have some very valuable papers,' relate to the predicted bad weather, a doubt as to whether decedent will be able to go to Glencoe because of it, and a possible resolution of it in his next letter; the present one stating 'we will see in the next letter if I come.' This being so, the clause relating to the valuable papers begins a new subject of thought, and since the clearly dispositive gifts which follow are made dependent on no other contingency than 'if enny thing happens,' and death did happen suddenly on the same day, the paper, so far as respects those gifts, must be treated as testamentary.

It is difficult to understand how the decedent, probably expecting an early demise - as appears by the letter itself, and the fact of his sickness and inability to work, during the last three days of the first or second week preceding - could have possibly meant anything else than a testamentary gift, when he said 'so if enny thing hapens [the property specified] goes to George Darl and Irvin'; and why, if this was not intended to be effective in and of itself, he should have sent it to two of the distributees named in it, telling them to 'Kepp this letter lock it up it may help you out.'

The second question to be determined depends on the proper construction of section 2 of the Wills Act of June 7, 1917, which is a re-enactment of section 6 of the Wills Act of April 8, 1833, reading as follows:

> 'Every will shall be in writing, and, unless the person making the same shall be prevented by the extremity of his last sickness, shall be signed by him at the end thereof, or by some person in his presence and by his express direction.'

The letter now being considered was all in the handwriting of decedent, including the word 'Father,' at the end of it; and hence the point to be decided would appear to resolve itself into this: Does the word 'Father,' when taken in connection with the contents of the paper, show that it was 'signed by him?' When stated thus bluntly - in the very language of the statute - the answer seems free from doubt; but we must go further and determine whether or not the word 'Father' was 'meant as a signature.'

Under the statute it has been held that the signing may be by a mark, or by initials only, or by a fictitious or assumed name, or by a name different from that by which the testator is designated in the body of the will.

If, then, the word 'Father,' was intended as a completed signature to this particular character of paper, it answers all the purposes of the Wills Act. That it was so intended we have no doubt. It was the method employed by decedent in signing all such letters, and was mailed by him as a finished document. In these respects it varies from Brennan's Estate, supra, so much relied on by appellant, where the writing of 'your misserable father,' was construed to be not a signature, but part of an unfinished paper, which decedent retained, and to which his signature was not subsequently attached.

In the present case, as already pointed out, testator used the word 'Father,' as a complete signature, and mailed the paper as a finished document. True, a formal will would not be so executed; but this is not a formal will. It is a letter, signed by him in the way he executed all such letters, and, from this circumstance, his 'intent to execute is apparent' beyond all question.

Decree affirmed and appeal dismissed.

G. TESTAMENTARY CAPACITY

For any will to be held to be valid, and thus accepted for probate, there must be proof that the testator had sufficient testamentary capacity to write a will. The next case includes an excellent discussion of what is required for testamentary capacity.

SUPREME COURT OF COLORADO.
In The Matter of the Estate of Spicer H. Breeden, Deceased
HOLLY BREEDEN CONNELL, and VIC E. BREEDEN, III, Petitioners,
v.
SYDNEY STONE, Respondent.
January 18, 2000

JUSTICE RICE delivered the Opinion of the Court.

I. FACTS AND PROCEDURAL HISTORY

This case involves a contested probate of a handwritten (holographic) will executed by Spicer Breeden, the decedent. Mr. Breeden died in his home on March 19, 1996, from a self-inflicted gunshot wound two days after he was involved in a highly publicized hit-and-run accident that killed the driver of the other vehicle.

Upon entering the decedent's home following his suicide, the Denver police discovered on his desk a handwritten document that read:

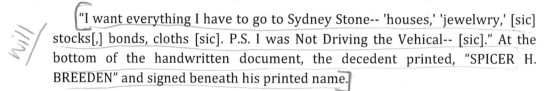

> "I want everything I have to go to Sydney Stone-- 'houses,' 'jewelwry,' [sic] stocks[,] bonds, cloths [sic]. P.S. I was Not Driving the Vehical-- [sic]." At the bottom of the handwritten document, the decedent printed, "SPICER H. BREEDEN" and signed beneath his printed name.

Sydney Stone (Respondent) offered the handwritten document for probate as the holographic will of the decedent. The decedent had previously executed a formal will in 1991 and a holographic codicil leaving his estate to persons other than Respondent. Several individuals filed objections to the holographic will, including Petitioners, who alleged lack of testamentary capacity.

On September 3-6, 1996, a hearing was held on the petition for formal probate. On September 26, 1996, the court made several findings based on the evidence presented. First, the court found that the decedent used cocaine and alcohol for several years prior to his death, based on the testimony of his friends Jennifer Chelwick and Michael Crow. Relying on the autopsy report and testimony from the decedent's sister, the court found that the decedent used alcohol and cocaine on the evening of March 17 and between March 17 and 19, and that substantial alcohol was consumed proximate to the time of death. Based on the testimony of a number of the decedent's friends, the court found that the decedent's moods were alternately euphoric, fearful, and depressed, and that he was excessively worried about threats against himself and his dog from government agents, friends, and others.

In addition, the probate court considered the testimony of a number of expert witnesses, including two forensic toxicologists, two forensic psychiatrists, a forensic document examiner, and two handwriting experts. After considering conflicting evidence from the various expert witnesses, the court concluded that the decedent possessed the motor skills necessary to write his will and that his handwriting on the holographic will was unremarkable when compared to other writing exemplars. The court also considered the testimony of the decedent's friends Ken McSpadden and Rick Eagan, who testified that in the two weeks prior to his death, the decedent had indicated to each of them in separate conversations that he did not intend to leave his estate to his family.[1]

After considering the evidence, the probate court found that Petitioners did not prove by a preponderance of the evidence that, because of the decedent's chronic use of alcohol and drugs or their use between March 17 and 19, he was not of sound mind when he executed the holographic will. In addition, the probate court held that the stress and anxiety that compelled the decedent to commit suicide did not deprive him of testamentary capacity. The court also found that the decedent's insane delusions regarding his friends, government agencies, and others, did not affect or influence the disposition of his property. In reaching the conclusion that the decedent was of sound mind at the time he executed the will, the probate court relied on the will itself, which evidenced a sufficient understanding of the general nature of his property and the disposition under the will, the testimony of two doctors regarding the decedent's motor skills at the time he wrote the will, evidence that the decedent had omitted his father and sister from his will in the past, and testimony from two friends that indicated the decedent had been considering revising his will in the future.

Petitioners appealed. The court of appeals affirmed the decision of the probate court. We granted certiorari.

II. TESTAMENTARY CAPACITY

Underlying Colorado's law of wills is the fundamental concept of freedom of testation; namely that a testator "may dispose of his property as he pleases, and that he may indulge his prejudice against his relations and in favor of strangers, and that, if he does so, it is no objection to his will." This principle, however, is subject to the

[1] In particular, McSpadden testified that at a March 14, 1996 lunch meeting, the decedent told him that he intended to leave his estate to McSpadden and Respondent.

requirement that the maker of the will possess testamentary capacity at the time he executes the will. A person has testamentary capacity if he is an "individual eighteen or more years of age who is of sound mind." *§ 15-11-501, 5 C.R.S.*

Until 1973, the proponents of a will assumed the burden of proving that the testator had testamentary capacity at the time he executed a will. However, in 1973, the legislature shifted this burden to the contestants of a will. Under *section 15-12-407*, once a proponent of a will has offered prima facie proof that the will was duly executed, any contestant then assumes the burden of proving a lack of testamentary capacity, including a lack of sound mind, by a preponderance of the evidence. The issue of what constitutes sound mind has developed along two separate lines of inquiry, summarized below.

A. The Cunningham Test

We initially defined sound mind as having sufficient understanding regarding "the extent and value of one's property, the number and names of the persons who are the natural objects of one's bounty, their deserts with reference to their conduct and treatment toward oneself, their capacity and necessity, and that one shall have sufficient active memory to retain all of these facts in one's mind long enough to have one's will prepared and executed."

Later this court further refined the test for sound mind in the landmark case *Cunningham v. Stender*, when we held that mental capacity to make a will requires that: (1) the testator understands the nature of her act; (2) she knows the extent of her property; (3) she understands the proposed testamentary disposition; (4) she knows the natural objects of her bounty; and (5) the will represents her wishes.

B. The Insane Delusion Test

This court has also held that a person who was suffering from an insane delusion at the time he executed the will may lack testamentary capacity. We first defined an insane delusion in 1924 as "a persistent belief in that which has no existence in fact, and which is adhered to against all evidence." We held that a party asserting that a testator was suffering from an insane delusion must meet the burden of showing that the testator suffered from such delusion.

We also have addressed the issue of the causal relationship necessary between an individual's insane delusion and his capacity to contract. See *Hanks v. McNeil Coal Corp.* In Hanks, we noted that contractual capacity and testamentary capacity are the same. In that case, a prosperous farmer suffered mental and physical deterioration after being diagnosed with diabetes. He became irritable and critical of his son's work, and in 1934 he developed a "secret formula" for a medicine to cure fistula [2] in horses that was

[2] Fistula is "an abnormal passage leading from an abscess or hollow organ to the body surface . . . and permitting the passage of fluids or secretions." Webster's Ninth New Collegiate Dictionary

comprised of ground china, brick dust, burnt shoe leather and amber-colored glass.

This mixture was to be poured into the ear of the horse opposite the shoulder suffering from the fistula infection. In 1937, the farmer began to devote most of his time and money to peddling his medicine. In 1940, he was adjudicated insane and his son was appointed conservator of his estate. His son subsequently brought suit against a coal manufacturer to put aside a contract, alleging that his father was insane at the time he entered the contract. The lower court held that, although the farmer was suffering from insane delusions related to his fistula cure, there was no evidence of delusions in connection with his other businesses at that time. We affirmed, holding that one may have insane delusions regarding some matters and be insane on some subjects, yet [be] capable of transacting business concerning matters wherein such subjects are not concerned, and such insanity does not make one incompetent to contract unless the subject matter of the contract is so connected with an insane delusion as to render the afflicted party incapable of understanding the nature and effect of the agreement or of acting rationally in the transaction.

The Hanks case sets out a standard for the requisite causal connection between insane delusions and contractual capacity that is equally applicable to testamentary capacity. A number of other courts have applied a similar standard in the context of testamentary capacity by phrasing the inquiry as whether the delusion materially affects the contested disposition in the will.

Based on Colorado precedent and the persuasive authority from other jurisdictions discussed above, we hold that before a will can be invalidated because of a lack of testamentary capacity due to an insane delusion, the insane delusion must materially affect the disposition in the will.

C. Cunningham and Insane Delusion Tests Are Not Mutually Exclusive

As the preceding case law indicates, the Cunningham and the insane delusion tests for sound mind have developed independently of each other.

The Cunningham test is most commonly applied in cases in which the objectors argue that the testator lacked general testamentary capacity due to a number of possible causes such as mental illness, physical infirmity, senile dementia, and general insanity. See, e.g., *White v. White,* (holding that physical illness was insufficient to render a testator incapacitated to make a will where there was no evidence that she did not understand the nature of the transaction); *Calloway v. Miller,* (effects of advanced age do not establish lack of testamentary capacity where the testator had knowledge of meaning of making a will, of character and extent of the estate, and of the natural objects of his bounty).

The insane delusion test ordinarily involves situations in which the testator,

---

467 (1988).

although in possession of his general faculties, suffers from delusions that often take the form of monomania or paranoia. See, e.g., *Davis v. Davis,* (father who believes his son is not his son suffers from an insane delusion); *In re Haywood's Estate,*(fact that a testator dislikes the natural objects of his bounty is *not* an insane delusion); *McReynolds v. Smith,* (belief that property worth several million dollars is only worth ten thousand dollars *is* an insane delusion); *Power v. Overholt,,* (a testator's belief, not based on any evidence, that his niece stole from him *is* an insane delusion); *In re Hanson's Estate,* (holding that a testator did *not* suffer from insane delusions though she was afraid of men, was afraid to go out at night, was self-conscious about a deformed back, was untidy and disheveled, was sensitive, believed that others were plotting against her, and disliked talking to more than one person at a time).

As such, the Cunningham and insane delusion tests, although discrete, are not mutually exclusive. In order to have testamentary capacity, a testator must have a sound mind. In Colorado, a sound mind includes the presence of the Cunningham factors and the absence of insane delusions that materially affect the will. As noted above, insane delusions are often material to the making of the will, and thus will defeat testamentary capacity. However, just as in the Hanks case, not all insane delusions materially affect the making of a will. Nonetheless, a testator suffering from an immaterial insane delusion must still meet the Cunningham sound mind test.

Accordingly, we hold that an objector may challenge a testator's soundness of mind based on both or either of the Cunningham and insane delusion tests.

Upon reviewing the decision of the probate court, we hold that the court correctly applied these two tests for testamentary capacity to find that the decedent was of sound mind at the time he executed his holographic will. The court found that the decedent had used alcohol and cocaine for several years prior to his death, had used alcohol and cocaine between March 17 and 19, suffered from mood swings, and worried excessively about threats against his and his dog's life. Despite these adverse findings, the court found that the decedent was of sound mind.

First, the court applied the Cunningham test and found that the decedent: (1) could index the major categories of the property comprising his estate; (2) knew his home and rental addresses; and (3) identified the devisee by name and provided her current address. The court noted that the will was "legible, logical in content, and reasonably set out the decedent's intent." In addition, the probate court considered the testimony of handwriting experts that indicated that at the time the decedent wrote the will, he was in command of his motor skills and his handwriting was unremarkable when compared to other exemplars. Based upon these factors, the trial court found that the decedent met the Cunningham test for sound mind.

Then, the probate court applied the insane delusion test to hold that although the decedent was suffering from insane delusions at the time he executed his will, "his insane delusions did not affect or influence the disposition of property made in the will." In so finding, the probate court considered the decedent's delusions regarding listening devices in his home and car and assassination plots against himself and his dog. In addition, the court weighed the testimony of numerous expert witnesses regarding the decedent's handwriting, his mental state near the time he executed the will, and the impact of his drug and alcohol use on his mental faculties. Further, the court considered testimony from several persons who stated that the decedent was not close to Petitioners, had infrequent contact with them, indicated to friends that he believed his father was irresponsible with money, disliked his sister's husband, and that his relationship with his brother was distant. In fact, the decedent had not made provisions for either Breeden Sr. or Connell in his earlier 1991 will. As such, the probate court concluded that the insane delusions from which the decedent suffered did not materially affect or influence the disposition made in the holographic will.

In sum, the probate court order reflects that the court thoroughly considered all of the evidence presented by the parties and concluded that (1) the testator met the Cunningham test for sound mind and (2) the insane delusions from which the decedent was suffering did not materially affect or influence his testamentary disposition.

CONCLUSION

We therefore hold that the probate court correctly applied the two tests for testamentary capacity to find that the testator, Spicer Breeden, was of sound mind at the time he executed the holographic will. Accordingly, we affirm the decision of the court of appeals upholding the probate court's ruling that the decedent was of sound mind.

H. DUTY OF ATTORNEY TO VERIFY CAPACITY

As you have noticed by now, it is frequently the case that people who are omitted from a will, or do not like the specific provisions of a will, try to contest the validity of the will in the probate court, as part of the probate process.

But sometimes that is not the end of it for a disappointed friend or relative who feels that he or she should have received a larger share of the decedent's estate. With increasing frequency, the disappointed person turns around and sues the lawyer who drafted the will, or the beneficiaries who took under the will – in separate suits which are not limited to the short time limits which must be met for initiating a contest in probate.

Suits against an attorney may be particularly attractive, because in that way one part of the family will receive assets from the probate estate, and another part of the family may receive money, as damages, from the pocket of the attorney. The next case includes descriptions of a variety of situations in which disappointed family members have been allowed to sue the attorneys involved with wills or estate plans.

In the case itself, the quite novel claim was made that the attorney had a duty – to family members not included in the will – to ascertain the testamentary capacity of the decedent. The case raises a number of ethical and practical problems.

Court of Appeal, First District, Division 2, California.

CHERYL T. MOORE et al., Plaintiffs and Appellants,

v.

ANDERSON ZEIGLER DISHAROON GALLAGHER & GRAY, P.C., et al., Defendants and Respondents.

June 20, 2003.

KLINE, P. J.

In an issue of first impression in this state, we consider whether an attorney has a duty to beneficiaries under a will to evaluate and ascertain the testamentary capacity of a client seeking to amend the will or to make a new will and whether the attorney also has a duty to beneficiaries to preserve evidence of that evaluation. We shall conclude the attorney owes the beneficiaries no such duties.

Facts and Procedural History

Appellants Jeffrey K. Smith (and others) appeal from the judgment dismissing their action for legal malpractice against respondents Attorney Rob Disharoon and the law firm of Anderson Zeigler. Appellants sued respondents for malpractice in connection with respondents' preparation of amendments to the estate plan of appellants' father, Clyde P. Smith (Clyde).

The complaint alleged as follows:

> "Appellants are five of the nine adult children of decedent Clyde. Respondent law firm represented Clyde. Attorney Disharoon, one of the partners of the firm, prepared an estate plan for Clyde in 1985, and helped him amend the estate plan in 1999. Under both the 1985 plan and the 1999 plan the remainder of Clyde's estate was to be distributed to eight of Clyde's nine adult children (including appellants). Both plans provided that the ninth child, Michael D. Smith, was not a beneficiary.
>
> Michael had already received substantial benefits and advantages from Clyde in that Clyde's company, Argonaut had employed and promoted Michael and Michael had received substantial financial compensation and benefit from his employment. Attorney Disharoon had prepared the September 1999 plan and knew that Clyde intended that Michael not receive anything and that Clyde intended to benefit his eight other children with equal shares in the remainder.
>
> Clyde became terminally ill. By June 2000, Clyde was "extremely sick,

debilitated, and confused. Clyde had undergone chemotherapy and was under the influence of powerful medications, including pain medication. Clyde had to be hospitalized. By June 2000, Clyde lacked the capacity to know or understand his estate plan. He did not recollect nor understand the nature of his property or trust dispositions, nor recall his relation to his family members and children."

Disharoon was aware that Clyde was terminally ill and extremely weak. Nevertheless, in June 2000, Disharoon prepared new estate planning documents, including a new will, whereby the estate plan was fundamentally changed.

The new documents provided that all of Clyde's common shares of Argonaut would be distributed to Michael D. Smith outright for no payment or consideration. Clyde executed these documents on *June 21, 2000.*

When Clyde did so, he lacked testamentary capacity, was not competent and did not truly know or understand his appointments and property disposition. Clyde died on *June 23, 2000.*

A dispute arose among the children as to which documents should govern the disposition of Clyde's property. Appellants retained counsel. Expenses of the litigation were substantial and continuing and assets were being diminished by attorney fees. After extensive discovery, the parties to the litigation reached a settlement. No determination was made of Clyde's capacity. The terms of the settlement allocated to appellants a portion of what they would have received under the 1999 plan, before the June 23, 2000 amendments."

Following settlement of the trust litigation, on June 20, 2001, appellants sued respondents Disharoon and Anderson Zeigler for malpractice. They filed a complaint on January 25, 2002. In addition to the foregoing, the complaint alleged that:

"A competent estate planning attorney in the circumstances should have recognized that Clyde's testamentary capacity was "questionable because of Clyde's weakened and confused condition and medical treatment. A competent attorney in such circumstances should exercise reasonable care to confirm his client's capacity, competence, and intentions regarding the client's property dispositions, and should document such confirmation. Attorney Disharoon negligently failed to do so in June 2000, and thereby breached the duty of care to effectuate his client's intent to benefit his eight children. The complaint also alleged that "a competent attorney would have recognized that litigation between the children was likely, unless the attorney took reasonable steps to investigate, confirm and document the client's capacity, competence, and testamentary intent."

Respondents demurred to the complaint on the grounds that, as a matter of law, an attorney owes no duty of care to nonclients to determine whether the testator client possesses testamentary capacity. As a separate ground for demurrer, respondents asserted that the settlement of the will contest in the probate proceeding barred appellants from asserting the malpractice action under principles of estoppel and waiver.

On June 12, 2002, judgment was entered dismissing the action. This timely appeal followed.

Discussion

A key element of any action for professional malpractice is the establishment of a duty by the professional to the claimant. Absent duty there can be no breach and no negligence. As a general rule, an attorney has no professional obligation to nonclients and thus cannot be held liable to nonclients for the consequences of the attorney's professional negligence.

As an exception to this general rule, it has been settled in California that an attorney may be liable to nonclients in limited circumstances where the nonclient was the *intended beneficiary* of the attorney's services. The lack of privity will not necessarily preclude an intended beneficiary under a will from maintaining an action against the testator's attorney on either a contractual theory of third party beneficiary or a tort theory of negligence. Such liability is not, however, automatic.

All of the authorities indicate that a determination whether liability exists in a specific case is a matter of policy and involves the balancing of various factors, including: 1) the extent to which the transaction was intended to affect the plaintiff; 2) the foreseeability of harm to him; 3) the degree of certainty that the plaintiff suffered injury; 4) the closeness of the connection between the defendant's conduct and the injury suffered; 5) the moral blame attached to the defendant's conduct; and 6) the policy of preventing future harm. These factors were identified by the Supreme Court in Biakanja v. Irving, in which a notary public was held liable in tort to the intended beneficiary of a will which was ineffective because of the notary's negligent supervision of its attestation.

* there are situations where you can be sued

Later cases have considered two additional factors to be critical to the duty determination. One is the likelihood that imposition of liability might interfere with the attorney's ethical duties to the client. The Supreme Court has also considered the related question of whether the imposition of liability would impose an undue burden on the profession.

Heyer v. Flaig similarly involved negligence in the drafting of a document which did not carry out the testator's intent. In that case, the testator had retained the attorney to prepare her will, telling him she wished her estate to pass to her two daughters and that she intended to remarry. The attorney drafted the will providing for the two daughters, but failed to include any mention of the intent of the testator to remarry and to not make any provision for her new spouse. The testator remarried 10 days after the will was executed. Upon her death, the new spouse claimed a portion of the estate as a post testamentary spouse. The attorney was sued by the testator's daughters.

In Radovich v. Locke-Paddon, the court held that the defendant attorney and his firm owed no duty of care to the client's husband, as a potential beneficiary named in an *unsigned* will. In *Radovich*, the attorney had prepared a new will for a client naming the husband as a beneficiary. The client had died without executing the will. The husband sued the attorney and the firm for malpractice, alleging that they owed a duty to the husband to carry out the decedent's testamentary wishes in a reasonably prompt and diligent fashion and had breached that duty in failing to remind the decedent to execute the will or even to find out whether she had done so.

The *Radovich* court recognized that the will was not defective by reason of its draftsmanship. It was not clear that the decedent had not changed her mind. Moreover, the *Radovich* court saw "both practical and policy reasons for requiring more evidence of commitment than is furnished by a direction to prepare a will containing specified provisions. From a policy standpoint, we must be sensitive to the potential for misunderstanding and the difficulties of proof inherent in the fact that disputes such as these will not arise until the decedent - the only person who can say what he or she intended - has died.

Most importantly, the *Radovich* court recognized strong countervailing policy considerations that in the circumstances cut against imposition of a duty. Imposition of liability in a case such as this could improperly compromise an attorney's primary duty of undivided loyalty to his or her client, the decedent. Imposition of liability would create an incentive for an attorney to exert pressure on a client to complete and execute estate planning documents summarily, without the additional consideration the decedent intended to give them, and fear of liability to potential third party beneficiaries would contravene the attorney's primary responsibility to ensure that the proposed estate plan effectuates the client's wishes and that the client understands the available options and the legal and practical implications of whatever course of action is ultimately chosen. On weighing the relevant policy considerations, the court concluded the attorney owed no duty to the beneficiary to inquire whether the decedent had any question or wished further assistance in completing the change in testamentary disposition she had discussed with him.

Conclusion

The considerations identified in *Radovich*, as well as in the negligent drafting and execution cases, lead to the conclusion that an attorney preparing a will for a testator *owes no duty to the beneficiary of the will or to the beneficiary under a previous will* to ascertain and document the testamentary capacity of the client.

First and foremost, we believe the duty of loyalty of the attorney to the client may be compromised by imposing a duty to beneficiaries in these circumstances. Our own Supreme Court has recently reaffirmed the fundamental importance of an attorney's duty of undivided loyalty to his or her client. Regarding the duty of loyalty, the court has stated, "'This obligation is a very high and stringent one. It is also an attorney's duty

If you botch up drafting, then bens can sue you!

to protect his client in every possible way, and it is a violation of that duty for him to assume a position adverse or antagonistic to his client without the latter's free and intelligent consent given after full knowledge of all the facts and circumstances. *By virtue of this rule an attorney is precluded from assuming any relation which would prevent him from devoting his entire energies to his client's interests.*

In the negligent drafting line of cases, there is clearly no potential for conflict between the duty the attorney owes to the client and the duty the attorney owes to intended beneficiaries. The testator and the beneficiaries want the will allowed. The intention of the testator is certain in the circumstance presented in those cases. Only the negligence of the attorney, resulting in the invalidity of the document or bequest, frustrates the intention of the testator.

In contrast, where the testamentary capacity of the testator is the basis for a will challenge, the true intent of the testator *is* the central question. That intent cannot be ascertained from the will or other challenged estate plan document itself. The attorney who is persuaded of the client's testamentary capacity by his or her own observations and experience, and who drafts the will accordingly, fulfills that duty of loyalty *to the testator.* In so determining, the attorney should not be required to consider the effect of the new will on beneficiaries under a former will or beneficiaries of the new will.

The extension of the duty to intended beneficiaries recognized in negligent drafting cases to this context would place an intolerable burden upon attorneys. Not only would the attorney be subject to potentially conflicting duties to the client and to potential beneficiaries, but counsel also could be subject to conflicting duties to different sets of beneficiaries. The testator's attorney would be placed in the position of potential liability to either the beneficiaries disinherited if the attorney prepares the will or to the potential beneficiaries of the new will if the attorney refuses to prepare it in accordance with the testator's wishes. The instant case, where some children benefited under the previous will and others benefited under the later, challenged will is a perfect illustration of that burden.

Ascertaining testamentary capacity is often difficult and the potential for liability to beneficiaries who might deem any investigation inadequate would unjustifiably deny many persons the opportunity to make or amend their wills.

Factors which might suggest lack of testamentary capacity to some attorneys do not necessarily denote a lack of capacity. It has been held over and over in this state that old age, feebleness, forgetfulness, filthy personal habits, personal eccentricities, failure to recognize old friends or relatives, physical disability, absent-mindedness and mental confusion do not furnish grounds for holding that a testator lacked testamentary capacity. Even hallucinations and delusions do not demonstrate lack of capacity if not related to the testamentary act.

Any doubts as to capacity might be resolved by counsel by refusing to draft the will as desired by the testator, turning the presumption of testamentary capacity on its head and requiring the testator represented by a cautious attorney to prove his competency.

In the situation presented in the negligent drafting cases the intended beneficiaries of the invalid will or trust documents were left with no remedy and no way to secure the undisputed intention of the testator. Their only avenue for redress was via a malpractice action against the negligent attorney. In contrast, beneficiaries disinherited by a will executed by an incompetent testator have a remedy in the probate court. They may contest the probate and challenge the will on the ground that the testator lacked testamentary capacity at the time of executing the will. That is precisely what appellants did in this case.

As drafted, the will here is effective to carry out the presumed intention of the testator. It does exactly what it purports to do. The question of Clyde's capacity or lack thereof is one that cannot be determined from the will itself, unlike those cases involving invalidly drafted or executed wills in which the document itself demonstrates the intention of the testator to benefit the beneficiary.

No California case directly addresses the duty question in the alleged incapacity context presented here. However, our conclusion is reinforced by the Restatement and by out-of-state cases.

Finally, appellants rely upon several secondary sources, including Model Rules of Professional Conduct

> Rule 1.14 of the Model Rules provides; "(a) When a client's ability to make adequately considered decisions in connection with the representation is impaired, whether because of minority, mental disability or for some other reason, the lawyer shall, as far as reasonably possible, maintain a normal client-lawyer relationship with the client. (b) A lawyer may seek the appointment of a guardian or take other protective action with respect to a client only when the lawyer reasonably believes that the client cannot adequately act in the client's own interest."

> The ACTEC Commentaries on the Model Rules have advised, "*Testamentary Capacity.* If the testamentary capacity of a client is uncertain, the lawyer should exercise particular caution in assisting the client to modify his or her estate plan. The lawyer generally should not prepare a will or other dispositive instrument for a client who the lawyer reasonably believes lacks the requisite capacity. *On the other hand, because of the importance of testamentary freedom, the lawyer may properly assist clients whose testamentary capacity appears to be borderline.* In any such case the lawyer should take steps to preserve evidence regarding the client's testamentary capacity." (ACTEC Commentaries (3d ed. 1999, italics added.)

It may be that prudent counsel should refrain from drafting a will for a client the attorney reasonably believes lacks testamentary capacity or should take steps to preserve evidence regarding the client's capacity in a borderline case. However, that is a far cry from imposing malpractice liability to nonclient potential beneficiaries for the attorney's alleged inadequate investigation or evaluation of capacity or the failure to sufficiently document that investigation. We conclude that the policy considerations present in these circumstances and discussed above strongly militate against imposition on the testator's lawyer of a duty to nonclient beneficiaries to investigate, evaluate and ascertain the testator's capacity or to document the same.

The judgment is affirmed.

I. CONTESTING THE WILL - TIME LIMITS

As indicated by the preceding case, the time limits for a will contest in the probate court are quite short. These rules will be discussed later. For now, a sample statute is sufficient.

> C.R.S.15-12-803 provides:
> "All claims against a decedent's estate ... including claims of the state of Colorado... absolute or contingent, liquidated or unliquidated, founded on contract, tort, or other legal basis, if not barred earlier by other statutes of limitations, are barred against the estate, the personal representative, any transferee or other person incurring liability ... and the heirs and devisees of the decedent unless presented ... within one year of the decedent's death."

CHAPTER 4 - NUNCUPATIVE WILLS

A nuncupative will is technically defined as "A will declared orally by a testator during his last illness, before witnesses, and later reduced to writing by a person who was present during the declaration." *Ballentine's Legal Dictionary.*

A nuncupative will was designed as a testamentary tool available for someone such as a soldier in combat, who might express his last wishes to his comrades while in a fox hole, for example. The first case in this chapter is an illustration of such a use.

Nuncupative wills are rarely used, for many good reasons. But there are still occasionally instances of the use of such wills. Approximately twenty-three jurisdictions currently have statutes permitting some sort of nuncupative will.[1]

A. TRADITIONAL USE

New York Surrogate's Court, Kings County.
In the Matter of Proving the Last Will and Testament of ERNEST CHARLTON MASON, Deceased,
as a Nuncupative Will of Personal Property.
June, 1923.

WINGATE, S.

This is a proceeding to probate the oral will of a soldier, last seen or heard of in a German prison camp.

The first question to be determined is whether or not the soldier is dead. The contestant admits that the inherent probabilities are that the soldier is dead, but questions whether there is proof enough before the court to establish the fact.

The soldier involved was a member of the One Hundred and Sixth Infantry of the army of the United States, and was captured on September 27, 1918, by troops of the German army, during the attack of the Twenty-seventh American Division upon the enemy position known as the Hindenburg line. He was taken by his captors, with other prisoners, to the German rear. On October first he was stricken with influenza.

Quartered at that time in a schoolhouse or barn, he was there attended by Loomis, one of his regimental comrades, who was his fellow prisoner, and his only medication was some aspirin given him by a British hospital orderly, also a fellow prisoner. He was so sick as to be unable to rise, and on October fourteenth and fifteenth was delirious. On the latter date he was, during the absence of his comrade, removed

[1] Alaska, District of Columbia, Georgia, Indiana, Kansas, Louisiana, Massachusetts, Mississippi, Missouri, Nevada, New Hampshire, New York, North Carolina, Ohio, Oklahoma, Rhode Island, South Dakota, Tennessee, Texas, Vermont, Virginia, Washington, West Virginia. 1 Restatement (Third) of Prop: Wills, 3.2.

from the schoolhouse or barn in a German ambulance.

Since then, he has never been heard from. All the Americans captured by the German army have been repatriated, but he is not among them. The United States army authorities have classified him as dead. His comrades have never heard from him. The members of his family have never heard from him. The young lady to whom he told his comrades he was engaged, and who was the object of his affectionate solicitude, designated by him as the beneficiary of his alleged will, has never heard from him. His uncle, who holds his funds, has never heard from him. No reason is known to exist why he should not, if alive, communicate with some or all of them.

The well-known character of the malady from which he was suffering, so fatal even under the best of care and medical attention, taken in conjunction with the other facts disclosed in the record, lead to the inevitable conclusion that, under the conditions confronting him during his illness, aggravated by the lack of proper medicines, he died.

It is true that his grave has not been located, but the graves of prisoners dying in prison camps of a defeated and retreating army are not always accurately recorded, and many graves have been found of dead whom it is impossible to identify.

The law only requires that the proof should remove the reasonable probability of Ernest Charlton Mason's being alive. There is no probability at all that he is alive. Indeed, the proof does not admit of conflicting inferences, but points clearly to his death; and it is found, as matter of law and of fact, that the evidence is sufficient to show that he is dead and does establish the fact of his death.

The second question to be determined is as to whether decedent made a valid will.

The decedent, Mason, on the night before the attack of September 27, 1918, was on duty as a signalman at the telephone in a dugout, with other members of his company, awaiting the hour of attack. He was on duty forty-eight hours, and in the intervals between messages talked to his comrade, Westgate, who at times relieved him at the telephone. Westgate testified that during the night Mason said: 'In the event that I get killed, I want everything that I have to go to Miss Knapp, including my insurance.' When he made the statement, no one was present within hearing but Mason and Westgate. They talked about the matter considerably and Mason referred to it more than once.

After Mason was captured, as recited above, and about two days before he was taken away in the German ambulance, about October thirteenth, according to the testimony of Loomis, the latter expressed to Mason some wishes in regard to messages to his folks and asked Mason what he wanted him to do. Mason replied, 'Ted, I haven't much in this world, but what I do have I want to go to Miss Knapp.' When he made this statement no one was present within hearing but Mason and Loomis.

The statutory provision as to nuncupative or unwritten wills is found in section 16 of the Decedent Estate Law, which provides that they shall not be valid 'unless made by a soldier while in actual military service, or by a mariner, while at sea;' and in section 141 of the Surrogate Court Act, which requires that 'before a nuncupative will is admitted to probate, its execution and the tenor thereof must be proved by at least two witnesses.'

Except for these limitations, the common-law rules as to nuncupative wills are still in force. As we have previously stated, 'in addition to the general rules regarding testamentary capacity and freedom from restraint, the only essentials are that the act shall be performed with testamentary intent and shall be sufficiently explicit and intelligible to permit a finding of its purport and scope, and that its execution must be proved by at least two witnesses.'

It has been urged in this case that apprehension of death must also be shown. It is not the law that, to be valid, the oral will of a soldier must be made in immediate apprehension of death, arising from circumstances equivalent to his being *in extremis.* It cannot, however, seriously be contended that this young soldier, either upon the occasion of his first declaration, when in the dugout awaiting the order to assault the enemy's strongly intrenched position, which up to that time had successfully resisted many attacks, or upon the occasion when he lay prostrate upon the floor of his prison suffering from a dread sickness, was not in apprehension of death. He undoubtedly was subject to that apprehension upon both occasions.

The deceased was a soldier and was in actual military service. His testamentary intent was very clearly expressed upon the first occasion mentioned, and was quite apparent upon the second. The words used were sufficiently explicit and intelligible to permit a finding of the scope and purpose of his testamentary desires. 'Everything to Miss Knapp' is unequivocal and precise as to *quantum* and beneficiary.

We come to the question as to whether a statement of testamentary purpose made in substantially identical terms upon two occasions, each time to a single witness, is a sufficient compliance with the statute.

The execution of a written will is required by statute to be observed with certain prescribed formalities, but even these formal requirements permit the testator to acknowledge his signature and declare the instrument to the witnesses upon separate occasions. There seems to be no stronger restriction in regard to the execution of a soldier's nuncupative will.

The latitude permitted in regard to nuncupative wills of soldiers and the origin and history of so called 'soldiers' wills' is interestingly discussed in the opinion of Surrogate Bradford in *Ex parte Thompson,* which closes with the statement: 'Nor has any particular mode been prescribed in respect to the manner of making the testament. The very essence of the privilege consists in the absence of all ceremonies as legal requisites; or, as Merlin states the proposition -'Their form was properly to have no form.' It is true, the Roman law required two witnesses; this, however, did not relate to the essence of the act, but only to the proof. In respect to evidence, we do not follow the civil or the canon law; no particular number of witnesses is required to verify an act judicially, and all the court demands, is to be satisfied by sufficient evidence, as to the substance of the last testamentary request or declaration of the deceased. This ascertained, the law holds it sacred, and carries it into effect, with as much favor and regard as would be paid to the most formal instrument, executed with every legal solemnity.

The very preservation of the right of soldiers to make nuncupative wills while in service indicates the appreciation by the legislature of the peculiar circumstance of their existence and the uncertainty of its tenure and the desire to relax in their favor the restrictions placed upon others in regard to the effectuation of their testamentary purposes.

There is no express requirement of statute that there must be a declaration of testamentary purpose by a soldier in actual service to two persons present at the same time, in order that the declaration may be proved as a nuncupative will. There was no such requirement at common law. Though not express, does the statute plainly imply such a requirement?

'Statutes in derogation of the common law are to be construed strictly. Where the statute not only affects a change in the common law, but is also in derogation of common rights, it must be construed with especial strictness.'

In the light of this rule of construction, the surrogate is of the view that section 141 of the Surrogate Court Act does not require the execution of a soldier's oral will to be proved by the testimony of two witnesses who were present together at the time of the testamentary declaration, but that two single declarations, of like tenor, each to a separate witness, upon a separate occasion, will suffice, there being no evidence of testamentary declarations by the decedent at variance with those propounded as his will.

A like ruling has recently been made by Surrogate Foley of New York county in Matter of Hickey, in which case he admitted as the oral will of a soldier portions of two letters, relating to the disposition of his estate. One of the letters had been addressed to the beneficiary of the will, and the second to another person.

Cases, from other jurisdictions, as to nuncupative wills of nonsoldiers and non-sailors, are not controlling upon the question under discussion; for, except as to the privileged classes (soldiers and seamen), oral wills are not favored, and the courts require strict compliance with statutory formalities before decreeing probate. A far more liberal rule obtains with respect to the oral wills of soldiers.

A recent example of the generosity of the law in their behalf is to be found in the case of *Rice v. Freeland,* in which the Supreme Court of Appeals of Virginia says: 'We are frankly, and we believe properly, relaxing in some measure the ordinary rules of construction in this case, and we are doing so in recognition of the general tendency of the Legislatures and the courts to treat soldiers in actual service as belonging to a class of persons entitled to public gratitude and to special consideration in respect to their private and property interests.'

The execution of the will is deemed sufficient. The statements of the witnesses and their earnest demeanor on the stand gave every indication of truthfulness. The reticence of one witness in regard to expressing to decedent's *fiancée* the facts indicating his death is easily understandable.

The testamentary declarations of the decedent referred to in this opinion are admitted to probate as his last will and testament, valid in law to pass his personal property.

Settle decision and decree on notice.

Decreed accordingly.

B. MORE MODERN USE

As you will see from the following case, by 2008 some states had very specific statutory requirements for nuncupative wills. However, it was still possible that an oral will might be effective to devise property at death.

Court of Appeals of Texas, Waco.
In the Matter of the ESTATE of Stephen Ellis ALEXANDER, Deceased.
Jan. 30, 2008.

FELIPE REYNA, Justice.

This appeal involves the question of whether the decedent Stephen Ellis Alexander (Stephen), made a nuncupative will before his death or died intestate. The trial court determined that Stephen died intestate. Appellant Ben C. Lambeth (Ben), who claims to be the beneficiary under Stephen's nuncupative will, appeals the judgment of the trial court.

Background

In April 2001, Stephen, and his sisters, Cheryl, and Deborah each received a substantial inheritance when their paternal grandmother died. According to the terms of a testamentary trust established by their paternal grandfather in his will, they were each to receive: (1) monthly payments of the net income from their portion of the corpus; (2) partial distributions at the ages of twenty-five and thirty; and (3) a final distribution at the age of thirty-five.[2] Stephen consulted with an attorney regarding the need to prepare a will. They discussed the matter on several occasions, but no will was ever executed.

Stephen suffered from several chronic conditions and was hospitalized at the Veterans Administration Medical Center in Temple from June 18 to July 8, 2002 for complications associated with these conditions, exacerbated by alcohol abuse. He allegedly made the nuncupative will on July 4, 2002, while hospitalized in Temple.

After being released from the VA hospital in Temple, according to the affidavits of several friends, Stephen was taken to the VA hospital in Waco for "a few days" because he was retaining fluids. "The staff drained some fluids, but finally sent him home

---

[2] Stphen, Cheryl, and Deborah were each older then thirty-five when their grandmother died.

because they could do nothing else for his condition."

Stephen was taken by ambulance to another Waco hospital on July 24, 2002, due to extreme intoxication. He died two days later.

Cheryl filed an application to determine heirship and for an independent administration of Stephen's estate. Ben filed an application to probate Stephen's alleged nuncupative will.

Cheryl and Deborah filed a motion for summary judgment, which was granted by the trial court.

Nuncupative Will

Section 65 of the Probate Code states the requisites of a nuncupative will.

> No nuncupative will shall be established unless it be made in the time of the last sickness of the deceased, at his home or where he has resided for ten days or more next preceding the date of such will, except when the deceased is taken sick away from home and dies before he returns to such home; nor when the value exceeds Thirty Dollars, unless it be proved by three credible witnesses that the testator called on a person to take notice or bear testimony that such is his will, or words of like import.

Cheryl's and Deborah's summary-judgment motion challenged virtually every element of Ben's claim that Stephen had made a nuncupative will. The first challenged element concerns whether Stephen was "in the time of the last sickness" when he made the alleged nuncupative will. The rule in Texas has long been that the testator must be "in extremis" to make a valid nuncupative will. "A nuncupative will is not good, unless it be made by a testator when he is in extremis, or overtaken by sudden and violent sickness, and has not time or opportunity to make a written will."

In McClain v. Adams the decedent had called a tenant to her bedside on a Thursday afternoon and told him that she knew she was about to die. She then told him that she wanted her friend Adams to inherit her estate. The decedent's activities were unclear between Thursday afternoon and Saturday, but on Saturday the decedent went to a neighbor's house and a nearby grocery store before returning home, where she died that night.

The court concluded:

> Applying the approved rule to the facts of this case, it is obvious that the decedent was not in extremis when she uttered the words claimed to constitute her will. Thereafter she had the time, ability and opportunity to prepare or have prepared a written will. About that there is no dispute in the record. Certain it is that she could have attended to that matter on Saturday morning when she was able to transact business and go in person to a store to purchase groceries.

The language of the statute has not changed in any significant way since McClain was decided and our research has disclosed no subsequent decision altering the holding in McClain.

The summary judgment record shows that Stephen suffered from several chronic conditions which ultimately contributed significantly to his death. He allegedly made the nuncupative will while hospitalized in Temple for complications associated with these conditions. He died eighteen days after his release from the Temple hospital, with one brief intervening hospitalization of "a few days."

Ben presented the affidavit of a nurse who reviewed Stephen's medical records and reached the following conclusions regarding the cause of his death:

> "*Cause of* Death The patient, Steven [sic] Ellis Alexander, died of an exacerbation of these chronic illnesses. From the date of his admittance to the VA Hospital in Temple, the patient had the same chronic condition that he died from at the Providence Health Center in Waco, Texas. This was a continuing and ongoing ir-reversible [sic] physical condition which could not be reversed and from which the patient subsequently died. Thus, Steven [sic] Ellis Alexander was under the same continuing chronic illness from the date he entered VA Temple to the time of his demise at Providence in Waco. There was no intervening recovery in his medical condition but instead there was a temporary abatement of gastrointestinal hemorrhage. Once the patient was released by the hospital in Temple he was not actively bleeding, but his medical condition remained the same. This condition at VA Temple was the same medical aliment [sic] that caused his hemorrhaging, resulting in respiratory and cardiac arrest, and his death at Providence Waco."

However, the fact that the chronic conditions which afflicted Stephen when he was admitted to the VA hospital in Temple (and apparently many months before) were the very same chronic conditions which substantially contributed to his death thirty-eight days later is no evidence that Stephen was "in extremis" during his hospitalization in Temple.

As stated in McClain,

> If nuncupative wills can be permitted at all, in the cases of chronic disorders, which make silent and slow, but sure and fatal approaches, it is only in the very last stage and extremity of them. In no other period can such a disorder be deemed, within any reasonable construction of the Statute, a man's last sickness. Such diseases continue for months, and sometimes for years. In one of Captain Cook's voyages he states that he lost his first lieutenant, Mr. Hicks, near the conclusion of the voyage of three years, and almost within sight of the English coast. But he adds that as his disease was the consumption, and as it existed when he left England, it might be truly said that he was dying during the

> whole voyage. What would the law call that man's last sickness? Not the whole voyage surely, and probably it would be narrowed down to the last day, and to the last hour of his existence. We must give a reasonable interpretation to the Statute, in reference to the mischief, and to the remedy. We cannot safely apply a man's last sickness to the whole continuance of a protracted disease, without giving to the Statute an absurd construction.

Although the Supreme Court did not directly address the issue of chronic illness in McClain, it appears from the lower court's opinion that the decedent in that case died as a result of complications from a chronic illness.

> "Annie became sick in 1930. She gradually grew worse, and in 1934 was practically helpless—she was then having some sort of "spells." This continued until she died on September 8, 1934."

We believe that the correct rule is that, "in the cases of chronic disorders, which make silent and slow, but sure and fatal approaches, it is only in the very last stage and extremity of them" that a nuncupative will can be made.

Viewed in the light most favorable to Ben, the summary judgment evidence conclusively establishes that Stephen was not "in extremis" during his hospitalization in Temple. Thus, the court properly granted Cheryl's and Deborah's summary judgment motion on this element of Ben's claim. Because summary judgment was proper on this element, we need not address the other elements challenged in the motion.

We affirm the judgment.

C. AS A SUBSTITUTE FOR A HOLOGRAPHIC WILL

In a state such as Vermont, which does not recognize holographic wills, the concept of a nuncupative will may sometimes be available when an attempted formal will does not meet all of the necessary statutory requirements. Note how the statutory requirements in Vermont differ from the statutory requirements in Texas. As with other parts of probate law, the specific statute of the state of testator's domicile will control.

Supreme Court of Vermont.
In re ESTATE OF Gerald Thomas COTE
(Teresa Cooper, Appellant).
Feb. 13, 2004.

AMESTOY, C.J.

Appellant Teresa Cooper seeks reversal of the Franklin Superior Court's order affirming the Franklin Probate Court's disallowance of her deceased fiancée's nuncupative will. We affirm.

The relevant undisputed facts are as follows.

In July 1998, the decedent Gerald Thomas Cote executed a will disposing of his property that conforms to statutory requirements. See 14 V.S.A. § 5 (will must have signature of three witnesses who sign in presence of each other and testator). After Cote's wife died, he reestablished a relationship he had with appellant many years earlier. Eventually, Cote gave appellant a diamond ring, and they planned to marry.

In December 2000, Cote wrote and signed a handwritten will while he sat alone at appellant's kitchen table. He brought the document to Edna Sauvigney, appellant's mother, and declared to her that it was his will and that he wanted appellant "to be taken care of" after he died. Sauvigney then signed the will as a witness. During his life, Cote gave the will to Edna Sauvigney, along with the key to his safety deposit box. He asked Ms. Sauvigney to keep the will safe and to deliver it to appellant if anything happened to him. In September 2001, without having married appellant, Cote died. At the time of his death, Cote's personal property was worth well over $200.

The present dispute arose when appellant filed the December 2000 will with the probate court following Cote's death. The probate court disallowed the December 2000 document, and concluded that Cote's 1998 will was valid as his last will and testament. Appellant appealed to the superior court, and now to this Court, claiming the December 2000 will is a valid nuncupative will, or in the alternative, it is a valid holographic will. She argues that because the December 2000 will is valid and supersedes Cote's original 1998 will, the probate court should have allowed it and not the earlier will. We disagree.

Whether the December 2000 document is a valid will depends on its conformance to Vermont's nuncupative will statute. The statute provides:

> "A nuncupative will shall not pass personal estate when the estate thereby bequeathed exceeds the value of $200.00, nor shall such will be proved and allowed, unless a memorandum thereof is made in writing by a person present at the time of making such will, within six days from the making of it, nor unless it is presented for probate within six months from the death of the testator." 14 V.S.A. § 6.

Appellant claims that 14 V.S.A. § 6 unambiguously allows a nuncupative will to pass an estate in excess of $200 as long as it is put in writing within six days and presented to probate within six months. Appellant argues that, according to an exception to the "last antecedent rule," the presence of the comma before the word "unless" requires that the clause "unless a memorandum thereof is made in writing" modify not just the immediately preceding phrase, but also the first clause. Appellant thus suggests that the statute provides: "A nuncupative will shall not pass personal estate when the estate thereby bequeathed exceeds the value of $200.00 unless a memorandum thereof is made ... nor unless it is presented for probate within six months." To construe the statute otherwise, appellant argues, renders the clause beginning with "unless" superfluous.

Under appellant's reading of the statute, Cote's nuncupative will is valid even though his personal estate is worth more than $200 because it substantially conforms to the statute's requirements for proof and admission. The will was written and affirmed in the presence of a witness, Sauvigney, and appellant filed it within six months of Cote's death.

The superior court found, however, that the statute was not ambiguous "when its words are given their plain and ordinary meaning, particularly in light of the readily evident intent of the Legislature." The court interpreted § 6 as allowing a nuncupative will to be effective only when all the conditions are met: (1) the will must relate to personal property; (2) the personal property must be worth no more than $200; (3) someone present when the testator made the will must prepare a memorandum of it within six days; and (4) the probate court must receive the memorandum within six months of the testator's death. Under the superior court's interpretation, the statute does not apply to Cote's will, since Cote's estate does not meet the $200 limitation requirement.

When interpreting a statute, our principal objective is to implement legislative intent. Here, however, both parties' interpretations are plausible, and therefore we must ascertain legislative intent through consideration of the entire statute, including its subject matter, effects and consequences, as well as the reason and spirit of the law. All relevant parts of the applicable statutory scheme are to be construed together to create, if possible, a harmonious whole.

Vermont's nuncupative will statute is one of three statutes dealing with the creation of testamentary instruments. Those provisions can and should be construed in harmony with each other. When 14 V.S.A. § 6 is read in context with the other two statutes, its purpose becomes apparent. Section 5 establishes the general requisites for a valid will: in order to pass any real or personal estate, a will must be in writing, signed by the testator, and witnessed by three individuals. The obvious purpose of such provisions is to supply ample evidence of the decedent's testamentary intent and capacity and to prevent fraud.

Sections 6 and 7, as exceptions to the general requisites for proper execution, must be of more limited application than the general rule. Section 7 allows individuals in the military to create soldier's wills in order to bequeath wages and personal property when they are engaged in "actual military service," i.e., when the circumstances may make compliance with formal execution and probate requirements difficult, if not impossible. Significantly, this provision, unlike § 6, does not limit the size of the personal estate that can be passed. As the superior court noted, "the additional restrictions and limitations included in § 6, as to nuncupative wills generally, must be accorded their evident purpose, as the Legislature was (and remains) obviously capable of providing for more liberal allowance of oral wills if that is the lawmakers' choice." That "evident purpose" is to provide an alternative, less formal testamentary instrument for small bequests only.

If we interpreted § 6, as appellant urges, to permit an oral will to pass estates of any size, the safeguards against fraud provided by § 5 would be easily defeated, rendering the section superfluous. Because we presume that legislative language is inserted advisedly and not intended to create surplusage, we decline to construe 14 V.S.A. § 6 in this manner.

Under appellant's interpretation of the statute the possibilities of fraudulent claims against wealthy estates would be great. Since § 6 does not even require the testator's signature for the will to be proved, alleged beneficiaries of estates with significant assets would be able to contest a duly executed will by presenting a purported nuncupative will, delaying the probate process and forcing the courts to engage in extensive fact-finding to determine the validity of the claim. It is difficult to believe that the Legislature intended to impose detailed evidentiary requisites under 14 V.S.A. § 5, only to defeat them by allowing such lax standards for the execution of nuncupative wills, which can be proved only through prolonged hearings. We presume that "the Legislature does not intend an interpretation that would lead to absurd or irrational consequences."

We note that although no real property was at issue in this dispute, the probate court construed § 6 to limit the use of nuncupative wills solely to the bequest of personal property. The provision is ambiguous, because it makes no reference to the disposition of real property. From this silence it is possible to infer that the statute does not impose any limits on the use of nuncupative wills to pass real estate, or that the statute does not apply to real property at all. To resolve the ambiguity, we must ascertain legislative intent through consideration of the whole statutory scheme. Any implication of allowance of nuncupative wills for real property leads to a construction of the exception that conflicts with the general rule established in § 5, which specifically provides the requirements for passing real estate. Such interpretation is contrary to our preference to construe all relevant parts of the statutory scheme to create a harmonious whole. Further, it is irrational to conclude that the Legislature intended to strictly limit the size of personal estate that can pass by nuncupative wills, but permit such wills to pass real estate property of any size, thereby undermining the evidentiary safeguards against fraud erected in § 5. We presume that the Legislature did not intend an interpretation of the nuncupative will provision that would lead to such an irrational result. Therefore, we agree with the probate court's interpretation of § 6 as applicable to personal property only.

Our construction thus continues the long accepted interpretation of the Vermont statute as limiting the right to dispose of property by a nuncupative will to personal property with a value of $200, or less. Vermont is among the States which treat nuncupative wills of property beyond a specified amount as invalid.

This interpretation is also consistent with statutory schemes in other jurisdictions. Twenty-one jurisdictions provide for nuncupative wills, and all impose significant restrictions on such wills. The overwhelming majority limit its use to personal property and most impose a low cap on the monetary value of the estate that can pass. In sum, no jurisdiction has a statute comparable to appellant's construction of the Vermont statute, that would permit an estate of virtually any size to pass through a nuncupative will. The superior court correctly limited the application of 14 V.S.A. § 6 to personal estates not exceeding the value of $200.

In the alternative, appellant claims that Cote's December 2000 will is a valid holographic will. The validity of a holographic will, that is, one that is written in the testator's handwriting, is ascertained by reference to statutory authority.

Although handwriting provides superior evidence of genuineness, handwriting does not serve the protective and cautionary policies, nor does it serve the evidentiary values associated with having attesting witnesses observe and participate in executing the will. Accordingly, the legislature's decision to recognize holographic testation represents a determination to accept a lower level of formality.

Vermont does not have a statutory provision for holographic wills, and from this silence it is logical to infer that the Legislature does not intend to exempt such handwritten wills from formal execution requirements.

There was no error below.

Affirmed.

CHAPTER 5 - LAPSED GIFTS

A. LAPSED GIFTS IN FIRST PART OF WILL

Normally there are a number of specific gifts at the beginning of the will. For each of these specific gifts, to a specific person, there is the chance that the specified beneficiary may die before the testator. For example, in Article Three of his will the testator might say, "I leave the home which I own at the time of my death to my daughter, Sally, if she survives me." If, at the time the testator dies, it turns out that Sally has predeceased the testator, then the intended gift to Sally will lapse - in other words, the gift will fail.

Better drafting should have provided what was to happen in that contingency. For example, the will might have been written to state, that "I leave the home which I own at the time of my death to my daughter, Sally, if she survives me, but if Sally does not survive me, then to my friend, Fred, if he survives me." Yet this drafting still leaves a gap. What if both Sally and Fred predecease the testator?

The basic rule is that if a specific gift in a will fails, then that item will become part of the residuary estate. In the above example, the testator probably would have expected either Sally or Fred to have survived the testator. But if neither one survived, then the home simply would not have been successfully given away by the specific gift provisions of the will. So the home would then become part of the residuary estate, which might be discussed very near the end of the will. Somewhere near the end of the will every will should have what is usually referred to as a *residuary clause* - a provision which states what should happen to all of the testator's property which has not been successfully given away by any other provision of the will. Normally the residuary clause will start out with words such as, "All the rest, residue, and remainder of my estate I give to ..."

Sometimes a residuary clause will blindly try to exercise any power of appointment that the testator might have. As demonstrated in Chapter 13, it is usually *not* a good idea to attempt to exercise a power of appointment without knowing the details of the power - whether it is general or special, whether specific words are required for the exercise, and the like.

But basically the residuary clause should take care of the disposition of any remaining property of the testator.

B. LAPSE IN RESIDUARY CLAUSE

So what happens if the attempted gifts in the residuary clause fail because of some sort of lapse? Then that property will simply be distributed as the intestate property of the decedent.

The basic pattern is quite simple. Gifts which lapse in the first parts of the will fall down into the residuary estate. Gifts which lapse in the residuary estate pass as intestate property.

Frequently, however, there will be some sort of legislation designed to prevent gifts – at least gifts to close relatives - from lapsing. Different states have enacted different kinds of Antilapse statutes.

Examples from two states are given below.

C. SAMPLE ANTILAPSE STATUTES

Notice the differences between the relatively clear statute from California, and the painfully complex statute from Colorado. And remember that any state may change its antilapse statute at any time.

So even if you drafted a document to comply with a particular antilapse statute, that statute might be changed prior to the death of the testator – or the testator might die domiciled in a different state, with a different antilapse statute. Emphasis has been added to the following statutes, to try to point out the most important parts of each statute.

(1) CALIFORNIA ANTILAPSE STATUTE

§ 21110. Transferee's death; taking by representation; contrary intent in instrument

(a) Subject to subdivision (b), if a transferee is dead when the instrument is executed, or fails or is treated as failing to survive the transferor or until a future time required by the instrument, the issue of the deceased transferee take in the transferee's place in the manner provided in Section 240. [By representation.] A transferee under a class gift shall be a transferee for the purpose of this subdivision unless the transferee's death occurred before the execution of the instrument and that fact was known to the transferor when the instrument was executed.

(b) The issue of a deceased transferee do not take in the transferee's place if the instrument expresses a contrary intention or a substitute disposition. A requirement that the initial transferee survive the transferor or survive for a specified period of time after the death of the transferor constitutes a contrary intention. A requirement that the initial transferee survive until a future time that is related to the probate of the transferor's will or administration of the estate of the transferor constitutes a contrary intention.

(c) As used in this section, "transferee" means a person who is **kindred of the transferor or kindred of a surviving, deceased, or former spouse of the transferor.**

§ 21111. Failed transfers

(a) Except as provided in subdivision (b) and subject to Section 21110, if a transfer fails for any reason, the property is transferred as follows:

(1) If the transferring instrument provides for an alternative disposition in the event the transfer fails, the property is transferred according to the terms of the instrument.

(2) If the transferring instrument does not provide for an alternative disposition but does provide for the transfer of a residue, the property becomes a part of the residue transferred under the instrument.

(3) If the transferring instrument does not provide for an alternative disposition and does not provide for the transfer of a residue, or if the transfer is itself a residuary gift, the property is transferred to the decedent's estate.

(b) Subject to Section 21110, if a residuary gift or a future interest is transferred to two or more persons and the share of a transferee fails for any reason, and no alternative disposition is provided, the share passes to the other transferees in proportion to their other interest in the residuary gift or the future interest.

(c) A transfer of "all my estate" or words of similar import is a residuary gift for purposes of this section.

(d) If failure of a future interest results in an intestacy, the property passes to the heirs of the transferor determined pursuant to Section 21114.

(2) COLORADO ANTILAPSE STATUTE

– this is default statute –

By comparison to California, the Colorado antilapse statute, below, which is patterned after the Uniform Probate Code, is a remarkably convoluted statute, that may, or may not, comport with the wishes of the average testator.

§ 15-11-603. Antilapse; deceased devisee; class gifts

Only applies to grandparents

(1) **Definitions.** As used in this section, unless the context otherwise requires:

(a) "Alternative devise" means a devise that is expressly created by the will and, under the terms of the will, can take effect instead of another devise on the happening of one or more events, including survival of the testator or failure to survive the testator, whether an event is expressed in condition-precedent, condition-subsequent, or any other form. A residuary clause constitutes an alternative devise with respect to a nonresiduary devise only if the will specifically provides that, upon lapse or failure, the nonresiduary devise, or nonresiduary devises in general, pass under the residuary clause.

(b) "Class member" includes an individual who fails to survive the testator but who would have taken under a devise in the form of a class gift had he or she survived the testator.
(c) "Devise" includes an alternative devise, a devise in the form of a class gift, and an exercise of a power of appointment.
(d) "Devisee" includes (i) a class member if the devise is in the form of a class gift, (ii) the beneficiary of a trust but not the trustee, **(iii) an individual or class member who was deceased at the time the testator executed his or her will** as well as an individual or class member who was then living but who failed to survive the testator, and (iv) an appointee under a power of appointment exercised by the testator's will.
(e) (Reserved)
(f) "Surviving devisee" or "surviving descendant" means a devisee or a descendant who neither predeceased the testator nor is deemed to have predeceased the testator under section 15-11-702.
(g) "Testator" includes the donee of a power of appointment if the power is exercised in the testator's will.

(2) **Substitute gift.** If a devisee fails to survive the testator **and is a grandparent or a descendant of a grandparent of either the testator or the donor of a power of appointment exercised by the testator's will**, the following apply:
(a) Except as provided in paragraph (d) of this subsection (2), if the devise is not in the form of a class gift and the deceased devisee leaves surviving descendants, a substitute gift is created in the devisee's surviving descendants. They take per capita at each generation the property to which the devisee would have been entitled had the devisee survived the testator.
(b) Except as provided in paragraph (d) of this subsection (2), **if the devise is in the form of a class gift, other than a devise to "issue", "descendants", "heirs of the body", "heirs", "next of kin", "relatives", or "family", or a class described by language of similar import**, a substitute gift is created in the deceased devisee's or devisees' surviving descendants. The property to which the devisees would have been entitled had all of them survived the testator passes to the surviving devisees and the surviving descendants of the deceased devisees. Each surviving devisee takes the share to which he or she would have been entitled had the deceased devisees survived the testator. Each deceased devisee's surviving descendants who are substituted for the deceased devisee takes per capita at each generation the share to which the deceased devisee would have been entitled had the deceased devisee survived the testator. For the purposes of this paragraph (b), "deceased devisee" means a class member who failed to survive the testator and left one or more surviving descendants.
(c) For purposes of this part 6, words of survivorship, such as in a devise

to an individual "if he survives me" or in a devise to "my surviving children", are not, in the absence of additional evidence, a sufficient indication of an intent contrary to the application of this section. The use of language such as "and if he does not survive me the gift shall lapse" or "to A and not to A's descendants" shall be sufficient indication of an intent contrary to the application of this section.

(d) If the will creates an alternative devise with respect to a devise for which a substitute gift is created by paragraph (a) or (b) of this subsection (2), the substitute gift is superseded by the alternative devise only if an expressly designated devisee of the alternative devise is entitled to take under the will.

(e) Unless the language creating a power of appointment expressly excludes the substitution of the descendants of an appointee for the appointee, a surviving descendant of a deceased appointee of a power of appointment can be substituted for the appointee under this section, whether or not the descendant is an object of the power.

(3) **Dispositions under separate writing.** The provisions of this section shall not apply to dispositions of tangible personal property made under section 15-11-513. **[In other words, the Colorado antilapse statute does NOT apply to gifts made by the Memorandum Disposition of Tangible Personal Property, discussed in Chapter 10.]**

(4) **More than one substitute gift; which one takes.** If, under subsection (2) of this section, substitute gifts are created and not superseded with respect to more than one devise and the devises are alternative devises, one to the other, the determination of which of the substitute gifts takes effect is resolved as follows:

(a) Except as provided in paragraph (b) of this subsection (4), the devised property passes under the primary substitute gift.

(b) If there is a younger-generation devise, the devised property passes under the younger-generation substitute gift and not under the primary substitute gift.

(c) In this subsection (4):

(I) "Primary devise" means the devise that would have taken effect had all the deceased devisees of the alternative devises who left surviving descendants survived the testator.

(II) "Primary substitute gift" means the substitute gift created with respect to the primary devise.

(III) "Younger-generation devise" means a devise that:

(A) Is to a descendant of a devisee of the primary devise;

(B) Is an alternative devise with respect to the primary devise;

(C) Is a devise for which a substitute gift is created; and

(D) Would have taken effect had all the deceased devisees who left surviving descendants survived the testator except the deceased devisee or devisees of the primary devise.

(IV) "Younger-generation substitute gift" means the substitute gift created with respect to the younger-generation devise.

§ 15-11-604. Failure of testamentary provision

(1) Except as provided in section 15-11-603, a devise, other than a residuary devise, that fails for any reason becomes a part of the residue.

(2) Except as provided in section 15-11-603, if the residue is devised to two or more persons, the share of a residuary devisee that fails for any reason passes to the other residuary devisee, or to other residuary devisees in proportion to the interest of each in the remaining part of the residue.

Fortunately, this convoluted and complex Colorado antilapse statute is just a default provision. A testator may opt out of having any of these complex provisions applied to his or her will.

Because of the complexity of the antilapse statutes in some states, and because of the fact that any statute may be changed at any time by any state legislature, it may be best just to provide in the will that no antilapse statue, in any jurisdiction, is to apply to the terms of the will.

Then you must be certain, of course, to provide for all possible contingencies in the will itself. There are two easy ways to do this. One way is to provide a final gift that might state, for example, "Then to all of my descendants living at my death, by representation."

Another way, which might be included even after the gift to descendants, would be to provide a final gift to a charity, if everyone the testator actually cares about turns out to have predeceased the testator. Then be sure to add a provision that the testator has a general charitable intent, and requests that the court apply the doctrine of cy pres, to shift the gift to another charity, if the named charity is no longer in existence at the time of the death of the testator.

For example, there might be a final provision stating, "then to the Sierra Club, and if it is no longer in existence, then to the Nature Conservancy, and if they are no longer in existence then I direct the court to apply the doctrine of cy pres to implement my general charitable intent by directing that this gift shall go to some other charitable institution which is concerned with the protection of the environment."

In that way, there should be no need for any antilapse statute to be applied to the terms of the will – if the will has been appropriately drafted.

CHAPTER 6 - BASIC OUTLINE OF TRUSTS

You have already seen several cases involving trusts. This chapter will just be a basic outline of the components of a trust – and a description of the three major types of trusts which are used most frequently today. Subsequent chapters will go into more details on trusts.

It may be easiest to think of a trust just as a box – into which assets are put. Then a trustee is appointed to administer the assets in the trust. And one or more beneficiaries are named, or otherwise identified, as those who are to benefit from the trust. The person who sets up the trust is called the settlor, the person who manages the assets is called the trustee, and those who are to benefit from the assets are called the beneficiaries.

The three major types of trusts in use today are: Living Trusts, (also called Inter Vivos trusts); Testamentary Trusts; and Pour- Over Trusts. The fundamental mechanism of all three kinds of trusts is basically the same – they differ in when and how they are established.

Living Trusts, as the name suggests, are trusts established while the settlor is still alive. Testamentary trusts are established in the will of a testator, and come into effect at the death of the testator. Pour- Over Trusts are funded when assets are "poured over" from one legal entity to another. The assets in a living trust may be poured over into a testamentary trust at the death of the settlor. Or the assets owned by a person at death may be poured over into a living trust, which was established by that person, or by some other person, prior to the death of the testator. So the term "pour over trust" really just means that assets from one legal entity are poured over into another legal entity at a specified time, or upon the happening of a specified event.

So the distinction in names is primarily just an indication of how the trust came into existence, or was funded.

Now to the fundamentals of a trust – which will be applicable to all three types of trusts. Every trust must have a settlor, a trust *res*, a trustee, and one or more beneficiaries.

Legal title to the trust assets is in the trustee. So unless otherwise limited, the trustee has full authority to sell, manage, and invest all of the assets in the trust. That is the primary job of the trustee.

The beneficiaries of a trust are said to have equitable title to the assets. The beneficiaries have no authority to sell, manage, or invest the particular trust assets. Yet all such actions are to be taken only for the benefit of the beneficiaries – *not* in any way for the benefit of the trustee.

There are several major reasons for establishing a trust – to secure expert management of trust assets; to keep the assets out of the hands of minor children, or others who are thought to need special financial protection; to facilitate management of assets as one unit; and, for Living Trusts, to help to provide a smooth transition to a new set of beneficiaries at the death of the settlor.

In a number of situations a skillful trustee may manage trust assets more effectively than the beneficiaries would have been able to manage the assets on their own. But remember that any trustee is entitled to payment for his or her services, out of the assets of the trust. And very often disputes arise between the trustee and the beneficiaries as to management of the trust assets.

A. LIVING TRUSTS

Living trusts, (also called Inter Vivos trusts), are trusts which go into effect during the life of the settlor. Normally, the settlor will be both the trustee and the sole beneficiary of the trust, as long as the settlor is alive. However, at the death – or incapacity – of the settlor, a named successor trustee will take over administration of the trust, and there normally will be no need for probate for the assets included in the living trust. The assets are already in a legal entity called a trust, and the assets will stay in that same legal entity. Only the beneficiaries, and possibly the trustee, will change when the settlor dies.

So living trusts have become popular as a way of avoiding probate – and possibly avoiding some estate tax. Note that in many states, however, both of these reasons are no longer valid.

First, as to estate tax. As of January 2013 there is no federal estate tax until the estate exceeds $5 million for a single person, or $10 million for a married couple. Fewer than 1% of the people in the United States actually have estates that large. So, for more than 99% of the people in the country, federal estate taxes are irrelevant.

Second, if a living trust may be amended during life by the settlor, to change the beneficiaries, for example, or if the settlor retains various other types of control over the assets of the living trust, the assets in the living trust *are* subject to federal estate tax, even though they would not be part of the settlor's probate estate. So even though the assets in the living trust would not go through probate, they would be subject to federal estate tax - if the settlor turned out to be in the top 1%.

So a living trust will not save anything on federal estate taxes if the settlor retains control of the assets of the living trust. If the settlor gives up all control over the trust, and makes the trust irrevocable, then the assets *might* escape federal estate tax – which applies to less than 1% of the population, anyway.

So living trusts are not appropriate for saving estates taxes.

What about the goal of avoiding probate? In many states, that is no longer a valid goal, either. In states which have adopted the Uniform Probate Code, probate is now a simple, relatively smooth process. The major expense of probate is attorneys fees. In most states today, the fees attorneys may charge for probate must be based on the hours actually worked. The time required to set up a good living trust, and to transfer all of the assets into the trust, is usually about the same amount of time as the time required for basic probate. So the cost of attorneys fees is about the same. With a

The trust agreement, however, does not contain a "paragraph 1. (d)."

The parties stipulated:

> The Oyloes intended for the Trustee to sell the home if neither Ruth nor Clifford resided in the home. The Oyloes further intended that, after the sale of the home, the Trustee shall distribute the sales proceeds to the residuary beneficiaries of the trust. The Oyloes' attorney who assisted them with the drafting and establishment of the Trust inadvertently failed to change the dispositive provision of section 2(b) of the Trust. Specifically, the attorney failed to change the reference in section 2(b) to "paragraph 1. (d)" to read, "paragraph 2. (c)."

Paragraph "2. (c)" of the trust agreement provides for distribution of trust assets to residuary beneficiaries upon the Oyloes' deaths and states:

> "Upon the death of the survivor of the Grantors, the Trustee shall divide the trust estate into as many equal shares as shall equal in number those of the children of the Grantors who shall be then living, and those of the children of the Grantors who shall have predeceased the surviving Grantor leaving issue then living. The Trustee shall pay over and distribute outright one such equal share to the issue of each such deceased child, by representation, and one such equal share to each such child who shall be living at the death of the surviving Grantor. If there be no such children or issue of the Grantors then living, to the persons who would be entitled to inherit the same in accordance with the laws of the State of North Dakota, then in force, as if the Grantors had then died intestate, a resident of the State of North Dakota, and owning such property."

On September 28, 2006, the trustee sold the Oyloes' home and the net sale proceeds of $122,498.90 were deposited into the trust account. The Oyloes applied for Medicaid, but their applications were denied because their home and its sale proceeds were considered countable assets which exceeded Medicaid eligibility limits. The Department did not take the position that the other trust assets were countable assets for Medicaid purposes. The Administrative Law Judge ("ALJ") concluded the trust agreement was a Medicaid-qualifying trust because it failed to specify how the proceeds of the sale of the home were to be distributed before the Oyloes' deaths, and consequently, the home sale proceeds reverted to the Oyloes and remained available assets to pay for their care. The Department adopted the ALJ's recommendations, and the district court affirmed the Department's decision.

II

On appeal, the Oyloes argue the Department erred in determining the home sale proceeds are countable assets in determining Medicaid eligibility because the terms of the trust provide for the sale proceeds to be distributed under the provisions of paragraph 2(c), which relate to distributions to residuary beneficiaries. In the alternative, they argue the Department erred in refusing to consider extrinsic evidence of their intentions for distribution of the home sale proceeds.

A

Medicaid is a cooperative federal-state program designed to furnish financial assistance to needy persons for their medically necessary care. A person must lack sufficient assets to meet the cost of necessary medical care and services to be eligible for Medicaid benefits. North Dakota participates in the Medicaid program and the Department has adopted rules to implement the program and to determine the conditions of eligibility for Medicaid benefits. The Medicaid program is intended to be the payor of last resort, and an individual's resources must be virtually exhausted before Medicaid will pay for care. An applicant for Medicaid benefits has the burden of proving eligibility.

Under the Department's rules for determining Medicaid eligibility, a one-person unit is eligible for Medicaid benefits if the total value of that person's assets does not exceed $3,000. An "asset" is defined as "any kind of property or property interest, whether real, personal, or mixed, whether liquid or illiquid, and whether or not presently vested with possessory rights. Although certain assets are exempt or excluded from consideration, other assets that are "actually available" must be considered in determining the applicant's eligibility for Medicaid. Assets are "actually available" when the assets are at the disposal of the applicant, recipient, or responsible relative who has a legal interest in a liquidated sum and that person has the legal ability to make the sum available for support, maintenance, or medical care.

don't label it MQT

A Medicaid-qualifying trust is considered an available asset for Medicaid eligibility purposes. The federal law in effect at the time the Oyloes established the trust defined a Medicaid-qualifying trust as "a trust, or similar legal device, established (other than by will) by an individual (or an individual's spouse) under which the individual may be the beneficiary of all or part of the payments from the trust and the distribution of such payments is determined by one or more trustees who are permitted to exercise any discretion with respect to the distribution to the individual." A trust that meets this definition is a Medicaid-qualifying trust "whether or not the medicaid qualifying trust is irrevocable or is established for purposes other than to enable a grantor to qualify for medical assistance," or "whether or not the discretion described in paragraph (2) is actually exercised." This Court has noted "the statutory definition of a Medicaid qualifying trust in 42 U.S.C. § 1396a (k) (1992) 'does not require that a trustee have unbridled discretion, but indicates that *any* discretion to distribute assets is sufficient.'

The Oyloes contend the trust is not a Medicaid-qualifying trust because under the terms of the trust agreement, the trustee has the option to either distribute the home sale proceeds in accordance with nonexistent paragraph 1(d) or hold them for distribution under the residuary beneficiary provision of paragraph 2(c), and because paragraph 1(d) does not exist, the trustee is obligated to hold the proceeds for the residuary beneficiaries of the trust until the Oyloes' deaths. We reject the Oyloes' argument because it does not comport with the actual language of the trust and conflicts with this Court's precedent.

Paragraph 2(b) of the trust agreement gives the trustee the option to sell the Oyloes' personal residence and "*immediately* distribute the proceeds from the sale in accordance with the terms of paragraph 1. (d)." (Emphasis added.) The trustee is given only an option to sell or not to sell the residence. If the trustee exercises the option to sell, the trust agreement does not grant the trustee another option to hold the sale proceeds until the Oyloes deaths and then distribute the proceeds to the residuary beneficiaries. The trustee's retention of the sale proceeds for distribution to residuary beneficiaries under paragraph 2(c) would violate the requirement in paragraph 2(b) that the proceeds be "immediately" distributed.

> If a trust fails and the settlor made no provision for distribution, the trustee must restore the trust property to the settlor. The cases are so numerous and the rule so well settled that it is unnecessary to cite them. If a trust is terminated by exercise of a trustee's discretion, and the settlor has not specified "who shall receive the trust property on the termination of the trust, the trustee will ordinarily hold the trust property upon a resulting trust for the settlor or his successors in interest." *Scott on Trusts* § 345.3

"A resulting trust in favor of the settlor arises not only where an intended trust fails altogether but also where it fails in part. Where the intended trust fails in part, there is a resulting trust of so much of the property as is not appropriated to the part of the trust that does not fail." *Scott on Trusts* § 411.2 (1989). *See also* Ronald Chester and George G. Bogert, The Law of Trusts and Trustees § 451,(2005) (resulting trust arises when express trust "fail[s] in whole or in part"); 76 Am.Jur.2d Trusts § 135, (2005) (resulting trust may arise "where an express trust fails in whole or in part").

The trustee in this case was given the discretionary power to sell the Oyloes' personal residence and immediately distribute the proceeds from the sale. Because the distribution provision related to the sale of the personal residence failed, a resulting trust arose in favor of the Oyloes, and all proceeds from the sale reverted to the Oyloes. The result would not differ if the trustee had not exercised his discretion to sell the home. Under federal and state Medicaid law, those proceeds must be considered an asset available to the Oyloes for purposes of determining their eligibility for Medicaid benefits.

B

The Oyloes contend the reference to a nonexistent paragraph renders the trust ambiguous and, therefore, the Department erred in failing to consider the undisputed extrinsic evidence of the Oyloes' intentions in resolving the ambiguity.

In Allen this Court rejected an identical contention:

> "Allen contends that the hearing officer and Department were required to consider extrinsic evidence about his intent and were bound by the county court's findings interpreting the Trust. Allen urges that his intent to preserve

> the Trust assets for family members is not against public policy. On the other hand, the Department takes the position that extrinsic evidence and the county court decision are irrelevant and contrary to federal law for the Medicaid program."

The Department ruled that both Allen's intent to preserve his assets for relatives and the county court's construction of the Trust were irrelevant to Allen's eligibility for Medicaid benefits. These rulings by the Department correctly applied the federal law. As Bleazard v. Utah Dep't of Health, explained, "State Medicaid plans must comply with federal requirements, including those regarding eligibility."

> "If Allen's indicated intent is actually carried out, Allen will have transferred his considerable wealth to two cousins and two nephews, and will have largely shifted the cost of his medical care to the public and taxpayers. This intent is against public policy."

Public policy will not allow the social safety net for persons who are old, poor, and unfortunate to be exploited by those who are affluent.

As in Allen, the Oyloes' stated intention to have the sale proceeds distributed to their children conflicts with public policy, and we conclude the Department did not err in refusing to consider this extrinsic evidence.

We conclude the Oyloes' trust is a Medicaid-qualifying trust and the Department did not err in refusing their applications for benefits.

The judgment upholding the Department's decision is affirmed.

B. TESTAMENTARY TRUSTS

You have already seen several examples of testamentary trusts – and will see many more. The main thing to remember is just that a testamentary trust is a trust created by the will of the settlor, and therefore does not come into existence until the death of the settlor. Because a will, (except a contract will), is always revocable and amendable until the moment of the testator's death, all documents creating testamentary trusts are revocable until the moment of the settlor's death, and may be amended or revoked by any subsequent will of the testator.

All testamentary trusts automatically become irrevocable when the settlor dies.

C. POUR- OVER TRUSTS

Pour- Over Trusts are merely a means of pouring assets from one legal entity to another. Assets covered by the provisions of a will may be poured over into a pre-existing inter vivos trust. Or assets in an inter vivos trust may be poured over into the estate of a decedent, to be made subject to the provisions of a will. So assets may be poured from a trust into a will, or may be poured from a will into a pre-existing inter vivos trust.

The following case is included as an example of a pour-over trust. It should also be a reminder that simply putting assets into a trust does not ensure that the assets will be managed appropriately.

Office of the Presiding Disciplinary Judge of the Supreme Court of Colorado.
The PEOPLE of the State of Colorado, Complainant
v.
Alex Frank GALLEGOS, Respondent.
Feb. 3, 2010.

DECISION AND ORDER IMPOSING SANCTIONS

I. *ISSUE*

Disbarment is generally appropriate when a lawyer knowingly converts property belonging to a client or third-party and causes injury or potential injury. Respondent converted trust funds while serving as Trustee and caused injury to the sole beneficiary of the Trust. He also failed to answer the complaint or otherwise participate in these proceedings. What is the appropriate sanction for his misconduct?

II. *ESTABLISHED FACTS AND RULE VIOLATIONS*

Respondent took and subscribed the Oath of Admission and gained admission to the Bar of the Colorado Supreme Court on June 8, 1994.[1]

A. Background

In October of 1999, Respondent prepared a will and revocable trust for William H. Sherman. The Will had a pour-over provision to the revocable trust, which provided in relevant part:

> "Section 1. Pour-Over to Trust. All of the rest and remainder of the property which I shall own at my death, excluding any property over which I might have a power of appointment, and after payment of expenses and taxes which are paid pursuant to this Will, shall be distributed to the Trustee or Trustees of the WILLIAM SHERMAN REVOCABLE TRUST dated October 24, 1999 ... to be added to the property of that trust and disposed of in accordance with its terms and any amendments thereto prior to my death."

[1] The Court takes judicial notice of the fact that the Colorado Supreme Court immediately suspended Respondent from the practice of law pursuant to C.R.C.P. 251.8 on April 13, 2009.

The revocable trust for Mr. Sherman provided the following:

> "On the death of William H. Sherman, the Trustee shall establish the Hanna-Sherman Charitable Trust for the benefit of the Rio Grande Hospital, located in Del Norte, Colorado. From the Hanna-Sherman Charitable Trust, the Trustee shall make an annual contribution to the hospital of Fifteen Thousand Dollars ($15,000.00) for the purchase of medical equipment which, in the exercise of the Trustee's sound discretion, is in the best interest and benefit to the community as a whole, until such time the trust fund is exhausted."

The Trust does not identify any specific beneficiaries upon Mr. Sherman's death other than the Rio Grande Hospital. Valley Citizens' Foundation for Health Care, Inc. is the owner and operator of the Rio Grande Hospital.

The Trust notes that upon Mr. Sherman's death, Respondent shall serve as the Trustee, with the power to appoint a successor Trustee. Prior to Mr. Sherman's death, the Trust had bank accounts with at least three different banking institutions-San Luis Valley Federal Bank, Rio Grande Savings & Loan and Del Norte Federal Bank.

On January 20, 2008, Mr. Sherman died in an automobile accident. Respondent went to Mr. Sherman's house the next day and contacted San Luis Valley Moving Company to move Mr. Sherman's things into storage. Respondent did not inventory the assets of Mr. Sherman's house before he moved them into storage. Instead, Respondent specifically requested that the company refrain from completing an inventory and told them he would complete it at a future time.

B. Respondent Begins Taking Money from the Trust Bank Accounts

Following Mr. Sherman's death, Respondent opened at least two bank accounts for the Trust-another account at Del Norte Federal Bank and one at Sunflower Bank.[2] The following transactions occurred:

- On or about February 6, 2008, a check was drawn on Del Norte Federal Bank in the amount of $10,000.00, made payable to Gallegos Law Office.

- On or about February 8, 2008, a check was drawn on Del Norte Federal Bank in the amount of $10,000.00, made payable to A. Frank Gallegos.

- On or about February 13, 2008, a check was drawn on Del Norte Federal Bank in the amount of $50,000.00, made payable to Gallegos Law Office, with a memo for "home improve expense."

---

[2] The People attempted to determine "date of death" balances for the Trust bank accounts. The approximate total was $1,238,737.68.

- On or about February 25, 2008, a check was drawn on San Luis Valley Federal Bank in the amount of $20,000.00, made payable to Frank Gallegos.

This pattern continued, so that in the approximately five months following Mr. Sherman's death, Respondent received a total of $260,812.26 through checks payable to him personally, to his law firm or to "cash," through cash-out transactions on deposits and through payment of personal expenses.

C. The Estate Proceedings

Respondent was appointed Personal Representative of the William H. Sherman estate on or about April 21, 2008. Beginning in March 2008, William Dunn, counsel for the Foundation, had requested information from Daniel Powell, counsel for Respondent, regarding the Foundation's interest in the estate. Mr. Powell told Mr. Dunn that he did not have authorization to give him Mr. Sherman's Will or Trust information. On April 17, 2008, Mr. Powell told Mr. Dunn it would be six months before he knew what assets the hospital might receive from the estate and not to call his office in the meantime.

On or about June 26, 2008, the Foundation filed a claim to the assets of the estate of William H. Sherman. On June 30, 2008, they filed a: a) Motion for Interim Accounting, requesting that the court require the Personal Representative to file an interim accounting of the income and expenses of the estate as of July 1, 2008; b) Request for Copy or Filing of Inventory, requesting that the Personal Representative prepare and provide the Foundation, or file with the court, a complete and detailed inventory of assets of the estate of William H. Sherman; and c) Petition for Supervised Administration and Request for Performance Bond.

On July 8, 2008, the court set a hearing date on the Foundation's claim. Mr. Powell, as attorney for the Personal Representative, objected to the claim and all other requests made by the Foundation. He asserted that the Foundation was not an "interested party" and therefore had no standing in the estate of William H. Sherman. Mr. Powell requested that the court hold an evidentiary hearing that was subsequently held on August 12, 2008. The court thereafter granted the Foundation's motion for supervised administration of Mr. Sherman's probate estate.

On September 18, 2008, the court found the Foundation to be an "interested person" to the estate and ordered it to be provided access to all of the pleadings of the estate. The court directed Respondent to communicate with the Foundation as "befits his fiduciary obligations to this sole beneficiary of the estate."

On October 15, 2008, Respondent filed an inventory of the real and personal property of Mr. Sherman's estate. The only item listed in the inventory was proceeds from an insurance company in the amount of $15,587.74. The inventory did not identify any personal assets, vehicles, bank accounts, personal property or real property.

D. Removal of Respondent as Trustee and Personal Representative

On December 15, 2008, the Foundation filed a Petition for Supervised Trust Administration and Replacement of Trustee. On December 30, 2008, the court held a hearing on the Foundation's petition. Notwithstanding the bank account records showing Respondent withdrew significant amounts of funds from the Trust bank accounts, he testified at the hearing that he only withdrew funds from the Trust assets to maintain Mr. Sherman's property and home, including mowing the lawn and trimming the shrubs. Respondent testified that he had not paid any bill or disposed of property other than to pay for Mr. Sherman's funeral expenses. Respondent testified that he has not paid personal bills out of the Trust assets.

On January 2, 2009, *nunc pro tunc* to December 30, 2008, the court issued an Order for Supervised Administration and Removal of Trustee. The court found that Respondent had failed to fulfill his fiduciary obligation to take inventory of the assets of Mr. Sherman's estate or the Trust; failed to keep accurate records of his withdrawals from Mr. Sherman's trust accounts and that his sworn testimony was in conflict with the bank records admitted into evidence; and failed to manage the Trust for the benefit of the Rio Grande Hospital, as sole beneficiary of the Trust.

In the order, the court temporarily "removed" Respondent as the Personal Representative of the estate of William H. Sherman and as Trustee of the William H. Sherman Revocable Trust and suspended Respondent from his duties as the Personal Representative of the estate of William H. Sherman and as Trustee of the William H. Sherman Revocable Trust. The court further ordered Mr. Dunn to inform the court of the name and address of a certified public accountant with a background in forensic accounting so that a complete inventory and accounting of the amount and whereabouts of Mr. Sherman's assets could be prepared for the court.

On February 13, 2009, the court issued an Order for Turnover of Financial Records and Appointment of Replacement Personal Representative and Trustee. In the order, the court noted that it had previously removed Respondent as the Personal Representative of the estate and as Trustee of the Trust and appointed Matthew K. Hobbs to serve as the replacement Personal Representative of the estate of William H. Sherman and as successor Trustee of the William H. Sherman Revocable Trust. As of April 30, 2009, Mr. Hobbs noted that the amount definitively known that Respondent and others converted is approximately $500,000.00.

E. Violations of Rule of Professional Conduct

Respondent did not give the Foundation, as the sole beneficiary of the Trust, any of the funds from the Trust. He instead knowingly exercised unauthorized dominion and/or ownership over the Trust's funds. As a result of such conduct, Respondent knowingly converted or misappropriated funds belonging to the Trust and violated Colo. RPC 8.4(c).

In addition, by removing the Trust's funds from the Trust's bank accounts, Respondent failed to keep third party funds separate from his own property. As a result

** a trust never fails for lack of a trustee!! **

of such conduct, Respondent technically converted or misappropriated funds belonging to the Trust and violated Colo. RPC 1.15(a).

Finally, Respondent engaged in dishonest conduct when he testified under oath at the hearing held on December 28, 2008. He testified that he only took out funds from the Trust's assets to maintain Mr. Sherman's property and home, including mowing the law and trimming the shrubs; that he had not paid any bill or disposed of property other than to pay for Mr. Sherman's funeral expenses; and that he has not paid personal bills out of the trust assets. As a result of such conduct, Respondent falsely testified and violated Colo. RPC 8.4(c).

III. SANCTIONS

The Court finds that several aggravating factors exist in this case including a dishonest or selfish motive, a pattern of misconduct, multiple offenses, substantial experience in the practice of law, and illegal conduct.[3] The People conceded that Respondent has no prior disciplinary record. They also acknowledged that Respondent went through a divorce and received a diagnosis of Multiple Sclerosis, and that he has been sentenced to a lengthy prison term as a result of a criminal conviction.

The ABA *Standards* suggest that disbarment is the presumptive sanction for the most serious misconduct demonstrated by the admitted facts and rule violations in this case.

Colorado Supreme Court case law applying the ABA *Standards* also holds that disbarment is the presumptive sanction for conversion of client or third-party funds. Knowing conversion or misappropriation of client money "consists simply of a lawyer taking a client's money entrusted to him, knowing that it is the client's money and knowing that the client has not authorized the taking." Neither the lawyer's motive in taking the money, nor the lawyer's intent regarding whether the deprivation is temporary or permanent, are relevant for disciplinary purposes. *

IV. CONCLUSION

One of the primary goals of our disciplinary system is to protect the public from lawyers who pose a danger to them. The facts established in the complaint, without explanation or mitigation, reveal the harm Respondent has caused his client and the public. He knowingly converted or misappropriated funds belonging to the Trust and engaged in dishonest conduct when he falsely testified under oath at the hearing. Upon consideration of the nature of Respondent's misconduct, his mental state, the actual and potential harm he caused, and the absence of mitigating factors, the Court concludes that the ABA *Standards* and Colorado Supreme Court case law both support

---

[3] On August 17, 2009, Respondent entered a plea of guilty to a violation of C.R.S. § 18-4-401(1), (2) (c) (theft), a class 4 felony. He was sentenced to two years in the Department of Corrections with three years of parole on October 19, 2009.

revocable trusts have strings attached — would be in pe box

disbarment in this case.

V. ORDER

The Court therefore ORDERS:

Alex Frank Gallegos, Attorney Registration No. 24144, is hereby DISBARRED from the practice of law and his name shall be stricken from the list of attorneys licensed to practice law in the State of Colorado.

CHAPTER 7 - PRIVATE TRUSTS

A. BASIC TRUST REQUIREMENTS

Many of the same basic rules apply for either private trusts or charitable trusts. For both kinds of trusts the settlor must have the intent to establish a trust, there must be some assets in the trust (corpus), there must be one or more beneficiaries, and there must be a trustee.

However, the rule is that no trust will ever fail for lack of a trustee. If the settlor has not appointed a trustee who is available, and willing to serve, then the court will appoint a trustee. For the other three requirements, intent, corpus, and beneficiaries, the settlor must have taken the necessary steps to meet these three requirements.

B. BENEFICIARIES OF A PRIVATE TRUST

When the beneficiaries of a private trust are ascertainable people, such as the children of the settlor, there will be no difficulty with the requirement that there must be a beneficiary of a private trust. However, there are two special situations involving trust beneficiaries of a private trust. The first is when a pet is intended to be the beneficiary of a trust. The second special situation is when the beneficiary, for some reason, is considered to be especially unable to handle financial matters, so that a "spendthrift" trust may be advisable.

(1) PETS AS TRUST BENEFICIARIES

It may turn out that an elderly client's best friend, toward the end of life, is actually the client's pet. And clients are increasingly likely to want to establish some protection for surviving pets. Probably the best known case is that of Leona Helmsley, who left nearly all of her estate for the benefit of her dog, appropriately named Trouble. In the Leona Helmsley case, after a great deal of litigation, the courts finally cut down the amount of money that had been left for the benefit of Trouble, and specified that a portion of the money was to be spent for the benefit of humans, instead.

It is not just millionaires who care about their pets. Many clients, regardless of the size of their estates, want to provide for the care of their pets after death. Then the question arises: May a pet be the designated beneficiary of a private trust? The following two cases illustrate some of the orthodox responses to that question.

In the first case, there is also a good discussion of the rules regarding use of extrinsic evidence in will contests, comparing the rules for use of such evidence in the case of a latent ambiguity compared to a patent ambiguity in the will. In this case the whole outcome of the case may have turned on whether or not certain extrinsic evidence - the notes on the address book - were admissible in evidence. Finding a way to persuade a judge to admit or exclude certain evidence frequently determines the outcome.

Does the dog win? Does the court uphold the intent of the testatrix? Should an attorney have been able to do a better job of drafting?

(a) PET AS A DIRECT BENEFICIARY

Supreme Court of California.
In re ESTATE of Thelma L. RUSSELL, Deceased.
Georgia Nan Russell HEMBREE, Plaintiff and Appellant,
v.
Chester H. QUINN, Defendant and Respondent.
Aug. 19, 1968.

SULLIVAN, Associate Justice.

Georgia Nan Russell Hembree appeals from a judgment entered in proceedings for the determination of heirship decreeing inter alia that under the terms of the will of Thelma L. Russell, deceased, all of the residue of Thelma's estate should be distributed to Chester H. Quinn.

Thelma L. Russell died testate on September 8, 1965, leaving a validly executed holographic will written on a small card. The front of the card reads:

'Turn the card
March 18—1957
I leave everything
I own Real &
Personal to Chester
H. Quinn & Roxy Russell

Thelma L. Russell'

The reverse side reads:
'My ($10.) Ten dollar gold
Piece & diamonds I leave to Georgia Nan Russell.
Alverata, Geogia (sic).'

Chester H. Quinn was a close friend and companion of testatrix, who for over 25 years prior to her death had resided in one of the living units on her property and had stood in a relation of personal trust and confidence toward her. Roxy Russell was testatrix' pet dog which was alive on the date of the execution of testatrix' will but predeceased her.[1] Plaintiff is testatrix' niece and her only heir-at-law.

In her petition for determination of heirship plaintiff alleges, inter alia, that 'Roxy Russell is an Airedale dog';[2] that section 27 enumerates those entitled to take by will; that 'Dogs are not included among those listed in Section 27. Not even Airedale dogs'; that the gift of one-half of the residue of testatrix' estate to Roxy Russell is invalid and void; and that plaintiff was entitled to such one-half as testatrix' sole heir-at-law.

At the hearing on the petition, plaintiff introduced without objection extrinsic evidence establishing that Roxy Russell was testatrix' Airedale dog which died on June 9, 1958. To this end plaintiff, in addition to an independent witness, called defendant. Upon redirect examination, counsel for Quinn then sought to introduce evidence of the latter's relationship with testatrix 'in the event that your Honor feels that there is any necessity for further ascertainment of the intent above and beyond the document.' Plaintiff's objections on the ground that it was inadmissible under the statute of wills and the parole evidence rule 'because there is no ambiguity' and that it was inadmissible under section 105, were overruled.

Over plaintiff's objection, counsel for Quinn also introduced certain documentary evidence consisting of testatrix' address book and a certain quitclaim deed 'for the purpose of demonstrating the intention on the part of the deceased that she not die intestate.' Of all this extrinsic evidence only the following infinitesimal portion of Quinn's testimony relates to care of the dog:

> 'Q (Counsel for Quinn) Prior to the first Roxy's death did you ever discuss with Miss Russell taking care of Roxy if anything should ever happen to her? A Yes.'

Plaintiff carefully preserved an objection running to all of the above line of testimony and at the conclusion of the hearing moved to strike such evidence. Her motion was denied.

The trial court found, so far as is here material, that it was the intention of testatrix that CHESTER H. QUINN was to receive her entire estate, excepting the gold coin and diamonds bequeathed to plaintiff and that Quinn was to care for the dog, ROXY RUSSELL, in the event of Testatrix's death. The language contained in the Will

---

1 Actually the record indicates the existence of two Roxy Russells. The original Roxy was an Airedale dog which testatrix owned at the time she made her will, but which, according to Quinn, died after having had a fox tail removed from its nose, and which, according to the testimony of one Arthur Turner, owner of a pet cemetery, was buried on June 9, 1958. Roxy was replaced with another dog (breed not indicated in the record before us) which, although it answered to the name Roxy, was, according to the record, in fact registered with the American Kennel Club as ' Russel's (sic) Royal Kick Roxy.'

2 In his 'Petition for Probate of Holographic Will and for Letters of Administration with the Will Annexed,' Quinn included under the names, ages and residences of the devisees and legatees of testatrix the following: 'Roxy Russell, A 9 year old Airedale dog, (residing at) 4422 Palm Avenue, La Mesa, Calif.'

concerning the dog, ROXY RUSSELL, was precatory in nature only, and merely indicative of the wish, desire and concern of Testatrix that CHESTER H. QUINN was to care for the dog, ROXY RUSSELL, subsequent to Testatrix's death.'[3] The court concluded that testatrix intended to and did make an absolute and outright gift to Mr. Quinn of all the residue of her estate, adding: 'There occurred no lapse as to any portion of the residuary gift to CHESTER H. QUINN by reason of the language contained in the Will concerning the dog, ROXY RUSSELL, such language not having the effect of being an attempted outright gift or gift in trust to the dog. The effect of such language is merely to indicate the intention of Testatrix that CHESTER H. QUINN was to take the entire residuary estate and to use whatever portion thereof as might be necessary to care for and maintain the dog, ROXY RUSSELL.' Judgment was entered accordingly. This appeal followed.

The trial court found further: 'Testatrix intended that GEORGIA NAN RUSSELL HEMBREE was not to have any other real or personal property belonging to Testatrix, other than the gold coin and diamonds.' This finding also was elaborated on in the memorandum decision: 'In making the will it is apparent she had Georgia on her mind. While there is other evidence in the case about Thelma Russell's frame of mind concerning her real property and her niece, which was admitted by the Court, over counsel's vigorous objection, because it concerned testatrix' frame of mind, a condition relevant to the material issue of intent, nevertheless this additional evidence was not necessary to this Court in reaching its conclusion.' The additional evidence referred to included an address book of testatrix upon which she had written: 'Chester, Don't let Augusta and Georgia have one penny of my place if it takes it all to fight it in Court. Thelma.'

Not allowed - extrinsic evidence

Plaintiff's position before us may be summarized thusly: That the gift of one-half of the residue of the estate to testatrix' dog was clear and unambiguous; that such gift was void and the property subject thereof passed to plaintiff under the laws of intestate succession; and that the court erred in admitting the extrinsic evidence offered by Quinn but that in any event the uncontradicted evidence in the record did not cure the invalidity of the gift.

We proceed to set forth the rules here applicable which govern the interpretation of wills.

First, as we have said many times: 'The paramount rule in the construction of wills, to which all other rules must yield, is that a will is to be construed according to the intention of the testator as expressed therein, and this intention must be given effect as far as possible.

---

[3] The memorandum decision elaborates on this point, stating in part: 'The obvious concern of the human who loves her pet is to see that it is properly cared for by someone who may be trusted to honor that concern and through resources the person may make available in the will to carry out this entreaty, desire, wish, recommendation or prayer. This, in other words, is a most logical example of a precatory provision. It is the only logical conclusion one can come to which would not do violence to the apparent intent of Mrs. Russell.'

When the language of a will is ambiguous or uncertain resort may be had to extrinsic evidence in order to ascertain the intention of the testator. We have said that extrinsic evidence is admissible to explain any ambiguity arising on the face of a will, or to resolve a latent ambiguity which does not so appear. A latent ambiguity is one which is not apparent on the face of the will but is disclosed by some fact collateral to it.

As to latent ambiguities, this court has said: 'Broadly speaking, there are two classes of wills presenting latent ambiguities, for the removal of which ambiguities resort to extrinsic evidence is permissible. The one class is where there are two or more persons or things exactly measuring up to the description and conditions of the will. The other class is where no person or thing exactly answers the declarations and descriptions of the will, but where two or more persons or things in part, though imperfectly, do so answer.

Extrinsic evidence always may be introduced initially in order to show that under the circumstances of a particular case the seemingly clear language of a will describing either the subject of or the object of the gift actually embodies a latent ambiguity for it is only by the introduction of extrinsic evidence that the existence of such an ambiguity can be shown. Once shown, such ambiguity may be resolved by extrinsic evidence.

A patent ambiguity is an uncertainty which appears on the face of the will. When an uncertainty arises upon the face of a will as to the meaning of any of its provisions, the testator's intent is to be ascertained from the words of the will, but the circumstances of the execution thereof may be taken into consideration, excluding the oral declarations of the testator as to his intentions. The rule is well established that where the meaning of the will, on its face, taking the words in the ordinary sense, is entirely clear, and where no latent ambiguity is made to appear by extrinsic evidence, there can be no evidence of extrinsic circumstances to show that the testatrix intended or desired to do something not expressed in the will. However, this ancient touchstone has not necessarily uncovered judicial material of unquestioned purity.

In order to determine initially whether the terms of any written instrument are clear, definite and free from ambiguity the court must examine the instrument in the light of the circumstances surrounding its execution so as to ascertain what the parties meant by the words used. Only then can it be determined whether the seemingly clear language of the instrument is in fact ambiguous.

Words are used in an endless variety of contexts. Their meaning is not subsequently attached to them by the reader but is formulated by the writer and can only be found by interpretation in the light of all the circumstances that reveal the sense in which the writer used the words.

When a judge refuses to consider relevant extrinsic evidence on the ground that the meaning of written words is to him plain and clear, his decision is formed by and wholly based upon the completely extrinsic evidence of his own personal education and experience.

The foregoing reflects the modern development of rules governing interpretation. Accordingly, we think it is self-evident that in the interpretation of a will, a court cannot determine whether the terms of the will are clear and definite in the first place until it considers the circumstances under which the will was made so that the judge may be placed in the position of the testator whose language he is interpreting. Failure to enter upon such an inquiry is failure to recognize that the 'ordinary standard or 'plain meaning,' is simply the meaning of the people who did *not* write the document.'

If the evidence offered would not persuade a reasonable man that the instrument meant anything other than the ordinary meaning of its words, it is useless. On the other hand an ambiguity is said to exist when, in the light of the circumstances surrounding the execution of an instrument, the written language is fairly susceptible of two or more constructions.

Under the application of this general principle in the field of wills, extrinsic evidence of the circumstances under which a will is made may be considered by the court in ascertaining what the testator meant by the words used in the will. If in the light of such extrinsic evidence, the provisions of the will are reasonably susceptible of two or more meanings claimed to have been intended by the testator, 'an uncertainty arises upon the face of a will' and extrinsic evidence relevant to prove any of such meanings is admissible,

If, on the other hand, in the light of such extrinsic evidence, the provisions of the will are not reasonably susceptible of two or more meanings, there is no uncertainty arising upon the face of the will and any proffered evidence attempting to show an intention different from that expressed by the words therein, giving them the only meaning to which they are reasonably susceptible, is inadmissible.

The making of a will raises a presumption that the testator intended to dispose of all his property. Residuary clauses are generally inserted for the purpose of making that disposition complete and these clauses are always to receive a broad and liberal interpretation, with a view of preventing intestacy as to any portion of the estate of the testator. But there is no room for application of the rule if the testator's language, taken in the light of surrounding circumstances, will not reasonably admit of more than one construction. If testator used language which results in intestacy, and there can be no doubt about the meaning of the language which was used, the court must hold that intestacy was intended. Therefore, if having ascertained in the instant case that the provisions of the will are not reasonably susceptible of two or more meanings, we conclude that the only meaning to which the words expressed by testatrix are reasonably susceptible results in intestacy, we must give effect to her will accordingly.

Examining the will in the light of the foregoing rules, we arrive at the following conclusions: Extrinsic evidence offered by plaintiff was admitted without objection and indeed would have been properly admitted over objection to raise and resolve the latent ambiguity as to Roxy Russell and ultimately to establish that Roxy Russell was a dog. Extrinsic evidence of the surrounding circumstances was properly considered in order to ascertain what testatrix meant by the words of the will, including the words: 'I leave everything I own Real & Personal to Chester H. Quinn & Roxy Russell' or as those words can now be read 'to Chester H. Quinn and my dog Roxy Russell.'

However, viewing the will in the light of the surrounding circumstances as are disclosed by the record, we conclude that the will cannot reasonably be construed as urged by Quinn and determined by the trial court as providing that testatrix intended to make an absolute and outright gift of the entire residue of her estate to Quinn who was to use whatever portion thereof as might be necessary to care for and maintain the dog. No words of the will give the entire residuum to Quinn, much less indicate that the provisions for the dog is merely precatory in nature. Such an interpretation is not consistent with a disposition which by its language leaves the residuum in equal shares to Quinn and the dog. A disposition in equal shares to two beneficiaries cannot be equated with a disposition of the whole to one of them who may use 'whatever portion thereof as might be necessary' on behalf of the other. Neither can the bare language of a gift of one-half of the residue to the dog be so expanded as to mean a gift to Quinn in trust for the care of the dog, there being no words indicating an enforceable duty upon Quinn to do so or indicating to whom the trust property is to go upon termination of the trust. While no particular form of expression is necessary for the creation of a trust, nevertheless some expression of intent to that end is requisite.

Accordingly, since in the light of the extrinsic evidence introduced below, the terms of the will are not reasonably susceptible of the meaning claimed by Quinn to have been intended by testatrix, the extrinsic evidence offered to show such an intention should have been excluded by the trial court. Upon an independent examination of the will we conclude that the trial court's interpretation of the terms thereof was erroneous. Interpreting the provisions relating to testatrix' residuary estate in accordance with the only meaning to which they are reasonably susceptible, we conclude that testatrix intended to make a disposition of all of the residue of the estate to Quinn and the dog in equal shares; therefore, as tenants in common. As a dog cannot be the beneficiary under a will the attempted gift to Roxy Russell is void.[4]

There remains only the necessity of determining the effect of the void gift to the dog upon the disposition of the residuary estate. That portion of any residuary estate that is the subject of a lapsed gift to one of the residuary beneficiaries remains undisposed of by the will and passes to the heirs-at-law. The rule is equally applicable with respect to a void gift to one of the residuary beneficiaries. Therefore, notwithstanding testatrix' expressed intention to limit the extent of her gift by will to plaintiff one-half of the residuary estate passes to plaintiff as testatrix' only heir-at-law. We conclude that the residue of testatrix' estate should be distributed in equal shares

---

[4] As a consequence, the fact that Roxy Russell predeceased the testatrix is of no legal import. As appears, we have disposed of the issue raised by plaintiff's frontal attack on the eligibility of the dog to take a testamentary gift and therefore need not concern ourselves with the novel question as to whether the death of the dog during the lifetime of the testatrix resulted in a lapsed gift.

to Chester H. Quinn and Georgia Nan Russell Hembree, testatrix' niece.

The judgment is reversed and the cause is remanded.

Perhaps it would have been better if the testatrix had been willing to use just a little more paper to express her full testamentary intent.

In the following case, there is the same problem about having a dog as a beneficiary, but the court reaches a different resolution of the problem. What is the important difference in wording between the two wills?

(b) HONORARY TRUSTS

Court of Appeals of Ohio, Ninth District, Wayne County.
In re SEARIGHT'S ESTATE.
DEPARTMENT OF TAXATION OF OHIO
v.
MILLER.
June 7, 1950.

HUNSICKER, Judge.

George P. Searight, a resident of Wayne County, Ohio, died testate on November 27, 1948. Item 'third' of his will provided:

> 'I give and bequeath my dog, Trixie, to Florence Hand of Wooster, Ohio, and I direct my executor to deposit in the Peoples Federal Savings and Loan Association, Wooster, Ohio, the sum of $1000.00 to be used by him to pay Florence Hand at the rate of 75 cents per day for the keep and care of my dog as long as it shall live. If my dog shall die before the said $1000.00 and the interest accruing therefrom shall have been used up, I give and bequeath whatever remains of said $1000.00 to be divided equally among those of the following persons who are living at that time, to wit: Bessie Immler, Florence Hand, Reed Searight, Fern Olson and Willis Horn.'

At the time of his death, all of the persons, and his dog, Trixie, named in such item third, were living.

Florence Hand accepted the bequest of Trixie, and the executor paid to her from the $1000 fund, 75 cents a day for the keep and care of the dog. The value of Trixie was agreed to be $5.

The Probate Court made a determination of inheritance tax due from the estate of George P. Searight, deceased.

The Department of Taxation of Ohio appeals to this court from such judgment.

The questions presented by this appeal on questions of law are:

1. Is the testamentary bequest for the care of Trixie (a dog) valid in Ohio--
(a) as a proper subject of a so-called 'honorary trust'?
(b) as not being in violation of the rule against perpetuities?

2. Is the bequest set forth in item third of testator's will subject to the inheritance tax laws of Ohio?

The creation of a trust for the benefit of specific animals has not been the subject of much litigation in the courts, and our research, and that of able counsel in this case, have failed to disclose any reported case on the subject in Ohio. The few reported cases in this country, in England and in Ireland have been the subject of considerable comment by the writers of text books and by the law reviews of leading law schools.[5]

We do not have, in the instant case, the question of a trust established for the care of dogs in general or of an indefinite number of dogs, but we are here considering the validity of a testamentary bequest for the benefit of a specific dog. This is not a charitable trust, nor is it a gift of money to the Ohio Humane Society or a county humane society, which societies are vested with broad statutory authority for the care of animals.

Text writers on the subject of trusts and many law professors designate a bequest for the care of a specific animal as an 'honorary trust'; that is, one binding the conscience of the trustee, since there is no beneficiary capable of enforcing the trust.

In 1 Scott on the Law of Trusts, the author says:

> "In certain classes of cases, as for example, bequests for the erection or maintenance of tombstones or monuments or for the care of graves, and bequests for the support of specific animals, even though the legatee cannot be compelled to apply the property to the designated purpose, the courts have very generally held that he can properly do so, and that no resulting trust arises so long as he is ready and willing to carry it out. The legatee will not, however, be permitted to retain the property for his own benefit; and if he refuses or neglects to carry out the purpose, a resulting trust will arise in favor of the testator's residuary legatee or next of kin."

---

[5] See: Mitford v. Reynolds, (trust for horses); Pettingall v. Pettingall, (trust for horses and hounds); In re Dean, Cooper-Dean v. Stevens, (trust for horses and hounds); Willett v. Willett, (trust for dog allowed on the basis of a statute exempting both trusts for humane purposes and those for charitable purposes from the definite beneficiary requirement); In re Howells' Estate, (trust for 5 household pets and one human being declared invalid as violating the New York statute forbidding the suspension of the absolute ownership of personal property for a period longer than two lives in being); In re Renner Estate, (a gift of residue in trust to maintain a dog and parrot held valid).

The object and purpose sought to be accomplished by the testator in the instant case is not capricious or illegal. He sought to effect a worthy purpose - the care of his pet dog.

Whether we designate the gift in this case as an 'honorary trust' or a gift with a power which is valid when exercised is not important, for we do know that the one to whom the dog was given accepted the gift and indicated her willingness to care for such dog, and the executor proceeded to carry out the wishes of the testator.

To call this bequest for the care of the dog, Trixie, a trust in the accepted sense in which that term is defined is, we know, an unjustified conclusion. The modern authorities, as shown by the cases cited earlier in this discussion, however, uphold the validity of a gift for the purpose designated in the instant case, where the person to whom the power is given is willing to carry out the testator's wishes. Whether called an 'honorary trust' or whatever terminology is used, we conclude that the bequest for the care of the dog, Trixie, is not in and of itself unlawful.

In Ohio, by statute, Section 10512-8, General Code, the rule against perpetuities is specifically defined, and such statute further says:

> 'It is the intention by the adoption of this section to make effective in Ohio what is generally known as the common law rule against perpetuities.'

It is to be noted, in every situation where the so-called 'honorary trust' is established for specific animals, that, unless the instrument creating such trust limits the duration of the trust - that is, the time during which the power is to be exercised - to human lives, we will have 'honorary trusts' established for animals of great longevity, such as crocodiles, elephants and sea turtles.

The lives, in being, which are the measure of the period set out in the rule against perpetuities, must be determined from the creating instrument.

If we then examine item third of testator's will, we discover that, although the bequest for his dog is for 'as long as it shall live,' the money given for this purpose is $1000 payable at the rate of 75c a day. By simple mathematical computation, this sum of money, expended at the rate determined by the testator, will be fully exhausted in three years and 238-1/3 days. If we assume that this $1000 is deposited in a bank so that interest at the high rate of 6% per annum were earned thereon, the time needed to consume both principal and interest thereon (based on semi-annual computation of such interest on the average unused balance during such six month period) would be four years, 57 1/2 days.

It is thus very apparent that the testator provided a time limit for the exercise of the power given his executor, and that such time limit is much less than the maximum period allowed under the rule against perpetuities.

We must indulge the presumption that the testator was cognizant of the rule against perpetuities and the construction placed upon it by the courts, and that he prepared his will possessed of such knowledge.

We therefore conclude that the bequest in the instant case for the care of the dog, Trixie, does not, by the terms of the creating instrument, violate the rule against perpetuities.

We next consider the problem of the inheritance tax, if any, to be levied on the bequest contained in item third of testator's will.

We have hereinabove indicated that the bequest for the dog, Trixie, comes within the designation of an 'honorary trust,' and, as such, is proper in the instant case. A tax based on the amount expended for the care of the dog cannot lawfully be levied against the monies so expended, since it is not property passing for the use of a 'person, institution or corporation.' silly

We therefore conclude that no succession tax may be levied against such funds as are expended by the executor in carrying out the power granted to him by item third of testator's will.

The judgment of the Probate Court is affirmed.

(c) SAMPLE PET TRUST STATUTE

Occasionally, you may find that a state has enacted a statutory solution for the problems illustrated in the preceding cases. The statute below is an outstanding example of such a statute.

C.R.S.§ 15-11-901 Honorary trusts; trusts for pets

(1) **Honorary trust.** Subject to subsection (3) of this section, and except as provided under sections 38-30-110, 38-30-111, and 38-30-112, C.R.S., if (i) a trust is for a specific, lawful, noncharitable purpose or for lawful, noncharitable purposes to be selected by the trustee and (ii) there is no definite or definitely ascertainable beneficiary designated, the trust may be performed by the trustee for twenty-one years but no longer, whether or not the terms of the trust contemplate a longer duration.

(2) **Trust for pets.** Subject to this subsection (2) and subsection (3) of this section, a trust for the care of designated domestic or pet animals and the animals' offspring in gestation is valid. For purposes of this subsection (2), the determination of the "animals' offspring in gestation" is made at the time the designated domestic or pet animals become present beneficiaries of the trust. Unless the trust instrument provides for an earlier termination, the trust terminates when no living animal is covered by the trust. A governing instrument shall be liberally construed to bring the transfer within this subsection (2), to presume against the merely precatory or honorary nature of the disposition, and to carry out the general intent of the transferor. Extrinsic evidence is admissible in determining the transferor's intent. Any trust under

this subsection (2) shall be an exception to any statutory or common law rule against perpetuities.

(3) **Additional provisions applicable to honorary trusts and trusts for pets.** In addition to the provisions of subsection (1) or (2) of this section, a trust covered by either of those subsections is subject to the following provisions:

(a) Except as expressly provided otherwise in the trust instrument, no portion of the principal or income may be converted to the use of the trustee, other than reasonable trustee fees and expenses of administration, or to any use other than for the trust's purposes or for the benefit of a covered animal or animals.

(b) Upon termination, the trustee shall transfer the unexpended trust property in the following order:

(I) As directed in the trust instrument;
(II) If the trust was created in a nonresiduary clause in the transferor's will or in a codicil to the transferor's will, under the residuary clause in the transferor's will; and
(III) If no taker is produced by the application of subparagraph (I) or (II) of this paragraph (b), to the transferor's heirs under part 5 of this article.

(c) (Reserved)
(d) The intended use of the principal or income can be enforced by an individual designated for that purpose in the trust instrument, by the person having custody of an animal for which care is provided by the trust instrument, by a remainder beneficiary, or, if none, by an individual appointed by a court upon application to it by an individual.
(e) All trusts created under this section shall be registered and all trustees shall be subject to the laws of this state applying to trusts and trustees.
(f) (Reserved)
(g) If no trustee is designated or no designated trustee is willing or able to serve, a court shall name a trustee. A court may order the transfer of the property to another trustee, if required to assure that the intended use is carried out and if no successor trustee is designated in the trust instrument or if no designated successor trustee agrees to serve or is able to serve. A court may also make such other orders and determinations as shall be advisable to carry out the intent of the transferor and the purpose of this section.

This statute certainly gives some good protections to the pet, but as a practical matter there may be a number of difficulties. First, does anyone really want to have his or her pet cared for by someone who is doing it, at least partially, for the money? Wouldn't it be better, in most cases, just to use a will to name a person to take care of the pet, with provisions for back-up caretakers if the first person named can no longer take care of the pet? Then, you might structure some sort of cash gift to anyone who takes on care of the pet – and leave it at that.

There is also the potential issue of a pet being kept alive, in pain, attached to all kinds of equipment, just so that the trustee of the pet trust continues to have a job – and an ability to charge fees. Such issues should be covered by careful drafting.

C. SPENDTHRIFT TRUSTS FOR PEOPLE

Pets, of course, need special protections. Frequently settlors also seek to establish special protections for human beneficiaries of a trust. Thus the settlor may attempt to make the trust a spendthrift trust, to try to prevent any creditors of the beneficiary from having access to the trust assets – and to try to prevent the beneficiary from taking out a loan from someone, to try to get the benefit of trust assets before the assets have actually been distributed to the beneficiary by the trustee.

The efficacy of the extra protections intended to be provided by a spendthrift trust vary from state to state. In some states, the children of a beneficiary of a spendthrift trust can reach the assets in the trust, for child support, no matter what words the settlor has used in putting up the protective wall of a spendthrift trust. In some states a former spouse can also reach the assets of the trust – for court ordered maintenance or alimony. It all depends on state law.

The following case illustrates some of the issues involved.

United States Bankruptcy Court.
In re Barbara T. BLAKELY a/k/a Barbara Ann Blakely, Debtor.
Sept. 23, 2011.

MICHAEL E. ROMERO, Bankruptcy Judge.

BACKGROUND

On February 27, 2011, the Debtor, Barbara T. Blakely, (the "Debtor"), filed her voluntary petition under Chapter 13 of Title 11, of the United States Bankruptcy Code. The Debtor's father, Gerald A. Tokle, passed away on February 24, 2011 — three days before the Debtor filed her petition. The Debtor's father left a will, titled "Will of Gerald A. Tokle" executed on April 18, 2007.

On April 7, 2011, the Chapter 13 Trustee filed her Objection to Confirmation of Chapter 13 Plan based in part on the Debtor's omission of proceeds she received as a beneficiary of her father's estate under the Will.

Debtor seeks a determination that the Debtor's interest in the Will is protected by the alleged spendthrift clause in the Will and is of no consequential value to her bankruptcy estate.

DISCUSSION

"The scope of §541(a)(1) is broad, and includes property of all types, tangible and intangible, as well as causes of actions." However, §541(c)(2), carves out an exception to the general rule: "a restriction on the transfer of a beneficial interest of the debtor in a trust that is enforceable under applicable nonbankruptcy law is enforceable in a case under this title.[6]

Article 8.2 of the Will provides its validity and construction "shall be determined by the laws of Colorado." In Colorado, only trusts which are enforceable under state law as spendthrift trusts fall within the exception and are excluded from the assets of a bankruptcy estate. The characteristics of a valid spendthrift trust are as follows: (1) the terms of the trust restrain the voluntary or involuntary transfer of the beneficiary's interest; (2) a spendthrift trust which names the settlor as beneficiary is invalid; and (3) the operative issue is the extent of dominion and control a beneficiary possesses over the trust corpus.

As noted by Judge Sidney B. Brooks of this Court:

> To qualify as a spendthrift trust it is appropriate and necessary that the trust instrument contain articulated spendthrift provisions and the trust be administered in a correct and legally sufficient manner. If the provisions, administration and integrity of a spendthrift trust are disregarded, so too will be its status as a special, protected asset of the Debtor.

Here, for the proposition that a spendthrift trust is created the Debtor relies solely upon Article 6.4 of the Will, which provides:

> 6.4 INALIENABILITY: No beneficiary shall have any right to anticipate, sell, assign, mortgage, pledge, or otherwise dispose of or encumber all or any part of any trust estate established for his or her benefit under this instrument. No part of such trust estate, including income, shall be liable for the debts or obligations of any beneficiary or be subject to attachment, garnishment, execution, creditor's bill, or other legal or equitable process.

Under the above-cited Colorado law, Article 6.4 does provide an argument in favor of a spendthrift trust inasmuch as it restrains the transfer of a beneficiary's interest. However, Article 6.4 itself does not provide for the creation of such a trust. Specifically, the only provision in the Will which provides for a trust to be created is found in the opening paragraph of Article 6.5:

> 6.5. If any beneficiary to whom my personal representative is directed to

[6]The natural reading of the provision entitles a debtor to exclude from property of the estate any interest in a plan or trust that contains a transfer restriction enforceable under any relevant nonbankruptcy law.

> distribute any share of my probate estate is under the age of 21 or is, in the opinion of the fiduciary, under any disability which renders such beneficiary unable to administer distributions properly when the distribution is to be made, such fiduciary, in its discretion, acting as trustee, may continue to hold such beneficiary's share as a separate trust until he or she reaches the age of 21 or overcomes the disability, when my trustee shall distribute such beneficiary's trust to him or her.

Thus, Article 6.5 clearly states the creation of a trust under the Will only occurs if the testator dies before any beneficiary reaches the age of 21 or the beneficiary is under a disability which renders such beneficiary unable to administer distributions properly when the distribution is to be made. In paragraph 15 of her Motion for Summary Judgment, the Debtor expressly states she is "over the age of twenty-one and is not disabled nor incompetent" Therefore, any provision pertaining to the creation of a spendthrift trust is moot under the facts of this case.

CONCLUSION

Accordingly, absent a spendthrift trust created under the narrow circumstances set forth in Article 6.5, circumstances which are not present in this case, the Debtor's interest under the Will is property of the estate under § 541(a).

IT IS THEREFORE ORDERED the *Motion for Summary Judgment* filed by the Debtor, Barbara T. Blakely, is DENIED.

CHAPTER 8 – CHARITABLE TRUSTS

Charitable trusts are trusts that are established for some charitable purpose, and may last forever, because they are not subject to the Rule Against Perpetuities. In many ways, as to day to day operations, charitable trusts are just like private trusts. But there are a few rules which are applicable only to charitable trusts. This chapter will cover three of the major rules applicable only to charitable trusts.

The first rule is that a charitable trust must have an authorized charitable purpose. If the purpose of the trust does not meet the legal requirements for a charitable purpose, it will be deemed to be merely a private trust, and must comply with the applicable Rule Against Perpetuities.

The second rule is that the state Attorney General usually is the only entity with authority to enforce the terms of a charitable trust. There are several reasons that the Attorney General is charged with enforcement of charitable trusts. First, since charitable trusts may last forever, no individual person will be able to provide the necessary enforcement. Second, since charitable trusts have the benefit of being tax exempt, it is necessary that some governmental entity have authority to check to insure that the activities of the trust really are worth the tax exemption granted.

The final rule to be studied is that if the original purpose of the charitable trust becomes impossible or highly impractical, (such as providing scholarships for students at a college that has gone out of existence), and the court finds that the settlor of the charitable trust had a general charitable purpose, then the court is authorized to apply the doctrine of *cy pres* to modify the trust, so that the funds may be used for a similar purpose, at some other college, for example.

The following two cases illustrate the importance of finding that the purpose of the trust is an authorized charitable purpose.

A. CHARITABLE PURPOSE

Supreme Court of Appeals of Virginia.
SHENANDOAH VALLEY NATIONAL BANK, EXECUTOR
v.
HARRIET H. TAYLOR, AND OTHERS.
March 12, 1951.

MILLER, J., delivered the opinion of the court.

Charles B. Henry, a resident of Winchester, Virginia, died testate on the 23rd day of April, 1949. His will dated April 21, 1949, was duly admitted to probate and the Shenandoah Valley National Bank of Winchester, the designated executor and trustee, qualified thereunder.

Subject to two inconsequential provisions not material to this litigation, the testator's entire estate valued at $86,000, was left as follows:

> 'SECOND: All the rest, residue and remainder of my estate, real, personal, intangible and mixed, of whatsoever kind and wherever situate, * * *, I give, bequeath and devise to the Shenandoah Valley National Bank of Winchester, Virginia, in trust, to be known as the 'Charles B. Henry and Fannie Belle Henry Fund', for the following uses and purposes:
>
> '(a) My Trustee shall invest and reinvest my trust estate, shall collect the income therefrom and shall pay the net income as follows:
>
> '(1) On the last school day of each calendar year before Easter my Trustee shall divide the net income into as many equal parts as there are children in the first, second and third grades of the John Kerr School of the City of Winchester, and shall pay one of such equal parts to each child in such grades, to be used by such child in the furtherance of his or her obtainment of an education.
>
> '(2) On the last school day of each calendar year before Christmas my trustee shall divide the net income into as many equal parts as there are children in the first, second and third grades of the John Kerr School of the City of Winchester, and shall pay one of such equal parts to each child in such grades, to be used by such child in the furtherance of his or her obtainment of an education. '

By paragraphs (3) and (4) it is provided that the names of the children in the three grades shall be determined each year from the school records, and payment of the income to them 'shall be as nearly equal in amounts as it is practicable ' to arrange.

Paragraph (5) provides that if the John Kerr School is ever discontinued for any reason the payments shall be made to the children of the same grades of the school or schools that take its place, and the School Board of Winchester is to determine what school or schools are substituted for it.

The John Kerr School is a public school used by the local school board for primary grades and had an enrollment of 458 boys and girls so there will be that number of pupils or thereabouts who would share in the distribution of the income.

The testator left no children or near relatives. Those who would be his heirs and distributees in case of intestacy were first cousins and others more remotely related. One of these next of kin filed a suit against the executor and trustee, and others challenging the validity of the provisions of the will which undertook to create a charitable trust.

Paragraph No. 10 of the bill alleges:

> 'That the aforesaid trust does not constitute a charitable trust and hence is

invalid in that it violates the rule against the creation of perpetuities. '

Other heirs and distributees appeared and joined in the cause and asked that the trust be declared void and the estate distributed among testator's next of kin.

The contention of the heirs and distributees was sustained. From decrees that adjudicated the principles of the cause and held that the trust was not charitable but a private trust and thus violative of the rule against perpetuities and void, this appeal was awarded.

The sole question presented is: does the will create a valid charitable trust?

Construction of the challenged provisions is required and in this undertaking the testator's intent as disclosed by the words used in the will must be ascertained. If his dominant intent as expressed was charitable, the trust should be accorded efficacy and sustained.

But on the other hand, if the testator's intent as expressed is merely benevolent, though the disposition of his property be meritorious and evince traits of generosity, the trust must nevertheless be declared invalid because it violates the rule against perpetuities.

The Restatement of the Law of Trusts gives a comprehensive classification definition of charitable purposes, which include:

'(a) the relief of poverty;
'(b) the advancement of education;
'(c) the advancement of religion;
'(d) the promotion of health;
'(e) governmental or municipal purposes; and
'(f) other purposes the accomplishment of which is beneficial to the community.'

In a recent decision we approved and adopted the following definition. It reads:

A charity, in a legal sense, may be described as a gift to be applied, consistently with existing laws, for the benefit of an indefinite number of persons. It is essential that a charity be for the benefit of an indefinite number of persons; for if all the beneficiaries are personally designated, the trust lacks the essential element of indefiniteness, which is onc characteristic of a legal charity.

In the law of trusts there is a real and fundamental distinction between a charitable trust and one that is devoted to mere benevolence. The former is public in nature and valid; the latter is private and if it offends the rule against perpetuities, it is void.

It is quite clear that trusts which are devoted to mere benevolence or liberality, or generosity, cannot be upheld as charities. Benevolent objects include acts dictated by mere kindness, good will, or a disposition to do good. Charity in a legal sense must be distinguished from acts of liberality or benevolence. To constitute a charity the use must be public in its nature.

We are, however, reminded that charitable trusts are favored creatures of the law enjoying the especial solicitude of courts of equity and a liberal interpretation is employed to uphold them.

Charitable gifts are viewed with peculiar favor by the courts, and every presumption consistent with the language contained in the instruments of gift will be employed in order to sustain them. All doubts will be resolved in their favor.

Appellant contends that the gift qualifies as a charitable trust. It not only meets the requirements of a charitable trust as defined above, but specifically fits two of those classifications, *viz.:*

'(b) trusts for the advancement of education;
'(f) other purposes the accomplishment of which is beneficial to the community.'

Our first duty is to construe the will; and this we must do, exactly in the same way as if the rule against perpetuities had never been established, or were repealed when the will was made; not varying the construction in order to avoid the effect of that rule, but interpreting the words of the testator wholly without reference to it.

> "The Rule against Perpetuities is not a rule of construction, but a peremptory command of law. It is not, like a rule of construction, a test, more or less artificial, to determine intention. Its object is to defeat intention. Therefore every provision in a will or settlement is to be construed as if the Rule did not exist, and then to the provision so construed the Rule is to be remorselessly applied." Gray's Rule Against Perpetuities, sec. 629.

The will provides that yearly on the last school day before Easter and Christmas each youthful beneficiary of the testator's generosity is to be paid an equal share of the income

Without more, that language and the occasions specified for payment of the funds to the children being when their minds and interests would be far removed from studies or other school activities definitely indicate that no educational purpose was in the testator's mind. It is manifest that there was no intent or belief that the funds would be put to any use other than such as youthful impulse and desire might dictate. But in each instance immediately following the above-quoted language the sentence concludes with the words or phrase 'to be used by such child in the furtherance of his or her obtainment of an education. ' It is significant that by this latter phrase the trustee is given no power, control or discretion over the funds so received by the child. Full and complete execution of the mandate and trust imposed upon the trustee accomplishes no educational purpose. Nothing toward the advancement of education is attained by the ultimate performance by the trustee of its full duty. It merely places the income irretrievably and forever beyond the range of the trust.

Appellant says that the latter phrase, 'to be used by such child in furtherance of his or her obtainment of an education', evinces the testator's dominant purpose and intent. In construing wills, we may not forget or disregard the experiences of life and the realities of the occasion. Nor may we assume or indulge in the belief that the testator by his injunction to the donees intended or thought that he could change childhood nature and set at naught childhood impulses and desires.

Appellant asserts that the funds could be administered by a guardian or a court could direct payment to be made to the recipient's parents.

With these statements, we agree. But because the funds could be administered under applicable statutes has no bearing upon nor may that device be resorted to as an aid to prove or establish the testator's intent. We are of opinion that the testator's dominant intent appears from and is expressed in his unequivocal direction to the trustee to divide the income into as many equal parts as there are children beneficiaries and pay one share to each. This expressed purpose and intent is inconsistent with the appended direction to each child as to the use of his respective share and the latter phrase is thus ineffectual to create an educational trust. The testator's purpose and intent were, we think, to bestow upon the children gifts that would bring to them happiness on the two holidays, but that falls short of an educational trust.

If it be determined that the will fails to create a charitable trust for *educational purposes* (and our conclusion is that it is inoperative to create such a trust), it is earnestly claimed that the two yearly payments to be made to the children just before Christmas and Easter produce 'a desirable social effect' and are 'promotive of public convenience and needs, and happiness and contentment' and thus the fund set up in the will constitutes a charitable trust.

It is argued that the word 'charity', as used in law, has a broader meaning and includes substantially any scheme or effort to better the condition of society or any considerable portion thereof. It has been well said that any gift not inconsistent with existing laws, which is promotive of science or tends to the education, enlightenment, benefit, or amelioration of the condition of mankind or the diffusion of useful knowledge, or is for the public convenience, is a charity.

However, upon examination it will be found that where a gift results in mere financial enrichment, a trust was sustained only when the court found and concluded from the entire context of the will that the ultimate intended recipients were poor or in necessitous circumstances.

A trust from which the income is to be paid at stated intervals to each member of a designated segment of the public, without regard to whether or not the recipients are poor or in need, is not for the relief of poverty, nor is it a social benefit to the community. It is a mere benevolence - a private trust - and may not be upheld as a charitable trust.

> 'If a large sum of money is given in trust to apply the income each year in paying a certain sum to every inhabitant of a city, whether rich or poor, the trust is not charitable, since although each inhabitant may receive a benefit, the social interest of the community as such is not thereby promoted.'

In the *Mellody Case* income from the trust fund was to be used by the trustee "to provide an annual treat or field day for the schoolchildren of Turton or as many of such children as the same will provide for." 'It will thus be seen that the trustee had control of and administered the income from the fund and it was devoted to a supervised annual outing for school children as such. Its intended use bore a direct relationship to their schooling and education. The court held that it was a charitable trust because it (1) tended to the advancement of education, and (2) was "for purposes beneficial to a particular section of the community." Speaking of the annual treat or field day provided for, it said:

> "It may well be made, and, I doubt not, often is made, the occasion for pointing out to the children those objects of the countryside and nature about which during their school hours they have read in their books, or which they have seen in the pictures displayed upon the walls of their schoolroom."

In the *Nilson Case,* the testator, a then resident of Nebraska, recited in his will that -

> "Sixth. Being a native of the Tjosvold, Harmoen, Kingdom of Norway, where fishing and sailing are the chief industries, and being acquainted with the social and industrial conditions of the poorer classes of Norway, my sympathies go out to industrious and deserving servant girls, and to widows and orphans of deceased fishermen and sailors. Desiring to relieve such servant girls and widows and orphans, I give and bequeath to Akre church congregation (Akre Kirksogn) six thousand dollars, to be invested and the interest to be distributed on each Christmas to worthy and needy servant girls and the widows and orphans of deceased sailors and fishermen who are not a public charge."

The pastor of the congregation or parish, the president of the county commissioners, and the county treasurer of Akre Kirksogn, Norway, and their successors in office were designated trustees. They were peculiarly well situated to know and select who were in need of and deserving of the testator's assistance. Though the language used excludes from the class of beneficiaries those who are public charges, the context of the entire will when the trustees selected and their implied powers and discretion are taken into account sufficiently authorizes selection by them of beneficiaries from the designated class who are in need, deserving and worthy of help. The court said:

> 'We are also of the opinion that the designation of the respective officers whose duty it shall be 'to carry out the provisions of this bequest' impliedly confers upon these officials the power to select from within the class the individuals who shall receive the bounty. It was, no doubt, with reference to the peculiar opportunities for knowledge as to the condition of the poor servant girls and widows and orphans afforded to these officers by virtue of their church relations that the testator selected them to execute the trust. It was impossible for him to select the individuals. He could only designate a class, and leave it to his trustees to select the individual beneficiaries of the charity, and no one seemed to him to be better fitted or to possess better qualities than those who resided among the poor people whom he wishes to help.'

In *Goodell v. Union Association of Children* a bequest of $1,000 was left to Trinity Church Sunday School with directions that it be safely invested and the interest used to secure Christmas presents for the scholars of that school. There was no indication that the recipients were to be those found to be in necessitous circumstances nor is any implied power or discretion given to limit or apply the income to such individuals. In the following language, the court declared that no charitable trust was created:

> 'What the gifts are to be does not appear. It does not appear that they are even to be rewards of merit, or to be used as means of inducing attendance on the part of the scholars at the school, or of promoting their good conduct there, or of inciting them to attention to religious instruction given to them there; nor whether they are to be given to all the scholars or part only. The gift is in trust, and it is not a charity in the legal sense. It is void.'

Of similar import is *Pleasants v. Attorney General.* There property was left in trust with the direction that the trustee, among other things, buy at a certain time each year a pennyworth of sweets for each boy and girl below fourteen years of age residing within a certain parish. It was decided that the trust was non-charitable and void.

Nor do we find any language in this will that permits the trustee to limit the recipients of the donations to the school children in the designated grades who are in necessitous circumstances.

Payment to the children of their cash bequests on the two occasions specified would bring to them pleasure and happiness and no doubt cause them to remember or think of their benefactor with gratitude and thanksgiving. That was, we think, Charles B. Henry's intent. Laudable, generous and praiseworthy though it may be, it is not for the relief of the poor or needy, nor does it otherwise so benefit or advance the social interest of the community as to justify its continuance in perpetuity as a charitable trust.

In 1946 the General Assembly enacted what is now commonly called the *cy pres* statute. If the trust set up is in other respects valid as a charitable trust - that is, if the instrument creating the trust discloses a general charitable intent. This legislation empowers the court, to determine to what purpose the trust estate shall be applied. If the necessary charitable intent be found, defects in the trust may be cured, beneficiaries selected and determined upon, purposes for the trust supplied, and suitable plans and details of execution and administration adopted. But the court is not given carte blanche to change a mere benevolent intent and generous bequest (private trust) into a charitable trust.

Here the ultimate beneficiaries of the class are not uncertain or indefinite. They are the pupils in the three designated grades of John Kerr School. Testator's true intent is that the school children receive their two payments on the designated times and occasions and that, as we have said, evinces no general charitable intent. No intent to apply the income to educational, charitable or eleemosynary purposes as required by the statute is disclosed.

The statute does not permit or allow the fundamental and dominant intent of a testator or grantor to be altered. It may not be used to transform a private trust into a charitable trust and thus employed to evade, impair or set at naught the rule against perpetuities.

No error is found in the decrees appealed from and they are affirmed. The attempted trust fails because it is not a charitable trust, and might last longer than the time allowed by the Rule Against Perpetuities.

Affirmed.

Where will the assets of the trust go, now that the trust has been held not to meet the requirements for a charitable trust? Back to the estate of the testator, and then, by intestacy, to the closest relatives of the testator, who were obviously NOT the people to whom the testator wanted to give his money.

If you had been the attorney representing the school children, what might you have argued, leaving the facts and law the same, in order to convince the court to uphold the trust as a charitable trust? If a child takes his $5 bill from school and buys three apples for 50 cents each, (or three candy bars), and counts his change, is that the sort of transaction a second-grader would have been reading about in math class? A form of "experiential learning?"

Is it likely, in a case like this, that any high-powered lawyer will actually be representing the school children?

What might you do, in drafting a trust like this, to make it far less likely that the trust would be challenged by any relative, and far more likely that the assets would be used to benefit the school children, exactly as the testator intended, for as many years in the future as possible? Remember, the testator really did not seem to want to buy math books for the children – he wanted them to have gifts of money at certain times of year that they could spend for anything they liked. So what could you do, in drafting, to try to make sure that would happen for as long a time as possible?

Hint: Under the Rule Against Perpetuities a *private* trust would be allowed to last for the life of some person (or readily ascertainable group of persons, such as current second grade students at Kerr school), plus 21 years. Would the testator's first cousins have much motivation to fight for money which might come to them after about 100 years?

With regard to the following case, from 2004, probably all of us - or our descendants - would have enjoyed having the trust succeed. For an illustration of a charitable trust that did succeed, for the 200 years for which it was established, see Benjamin Franklin's charitable trust for the City of Boston.

The testator in the following case was actually someone who had worked as a carpenter, and was unlikely to have had sufficient assets to fund the trust with the original amount specified, anyway. But it was a nice idea.

Unfortunately, this carpenter did not have quite as good drafting skills as Benjamin Franklin.

Court of Appeals of Texas.
Anna Spohn Welch MARSH, Noel Marsh, and Holly McKee, Appellants,
v.
THE FROST NATIONAL BANK, as Independent Executor of the estate of Charles Vartan Walker and Greg Abbott, Texas Attorney General, Appellees.

Jan. 29, 2004.

Opinion by Justice RODRIGUEZ.

This is a declaratory judgment action. Appellants, Anna Spohn Welch Marsh, Noel Marsh, and Holly McKee, appeal from a probate order that modified a provision in the will of Charles Vartan Walker, deceased, and question whether the trial court properly applied the *cy pres* doctrine[1] to reform a will provision.

I. Factual Background

Charles Walker died on March 13, 2000, leaving a holographic will. The will named appellee, Frost National Bank (Frost Bank), as independent executor. On July 11, 2000, Frost Bank filed an original petition for declaratory judgment for clarification of several probate matters including the construction of Article V of the Charles Walker will, the provision at issue in this appeal. Article V reads in relevant part:

> "I hereby direct my Executor to sell tract 3 of the V.M. Donigan 456.80 Partition for cash and to invest the proceeds in safe and secure tax-free U.S.

[1] The doctrine of *cy pres* gives the court equitable power to effectuate the general charitable intent of a testator when his particular purpose becomes impossible, impractical, or illegal to carry out. The court directs the trust funds or property to be utilized in a charitable manner as near (*cy pres*) to the donor's intent as possible.

> government bonds or insured tax-free municipal bonds. This trust is to be called the James Madison Fund to honor our fourth President, the Father of the Constitution. The ultimate purpose of this fund is to provide a million dollar trust fund for every American 18 years or older. At 6% compound interest and a starting figure of $1,000,000.00, it would take approximately 346 years to provide enough money to do this. My executor will head the Board of Trustees... When the Fund reaches $15,000,000 my Executor's function will cease, and the money will be turned over to the Sec. of the Treasury for management by the federal government. The President of the U.S., the Vice President of the U.S., and the Speaker of the U.S. House of Representatives shall be permanent Trustees of the Fund. The Congress of the United States shall make the final rules and regulations as to how the money will be distributed. No one shall be denied their share because of race, religion, marital status, sexual preference, or the amount of their wealth or lack thereof."

Appellants filed an answer alleging that Article V of the will is void under the rule against perpetuities. Appellee, John Cornyn, Texas Attorney General, intervened, alleging that a general charitable intent could be found and that Article V of the will created a charitable trust. The Attorney General then moved for the application of the *cy pres* doctrine to Article V. After a hearing on this issue, the trial court found in relevant part that: (1) the will evidenced a general charitable intent; (2) Article V of the will established a valid charitable trust not subject to the rule against perpetuities; and (3) the Attorney General's request to have the court exercise its *cy pres* powers should be granted.

II. Interpretation of Article V

In Texas, under the rule against perpetuities, an interest is not good unless it must vest, if at all, not later than twenty-one years after some life in being at the time of the creation of the interest, plus a period of gestation. Both perpetual trusts and trusts for an indefinite duration violate the rule against perpetuities and are void. The rule against perpetuities does not, however, apply to charitable trusts. Therefore, we must first address whether Article V of the will establishes a trust for a charitable purpose.

Where the question of whether a given purpose is or is not charitable arises, the words "charitable purpose" have a definite ascertainable meaning in law, and a judicial determination may be made with satisfactory certainty in every case. Legal concepts of what are "charitable purposes" are categorized in section 368 of the Restatement Second of Trusts. Section 368 provides as follows:

> Charitable purposes include
> (a) the relief of poverty;
> (b) the advancement of education;
> (c) the advancement of religion;
> (d) the promotion of health;

(e) governmental or municipal purposes;
(f) other purposes the accomplishment of which is beneficial to the community.

Article V of the will clearly states that the purpose of the fund is to provide a million dollar trust fund for every American eighteen years or older with no one being denied his share due to race, religion, marital status, sexual preference, or the amount of his wealth. Thus, it is clear from the language of Article V that if the purpose is to be found charitable, it must fall under the broad category (f) of section 368 of the Restatement; other purposes the accomplishment of which is beneficial to the community. To be included in category (f), the purpose set out in Article V must go beyond merely providing financial enrichment to the individual members of the community; the purpose must promote the social interest of the community as a whole. The Restatement provides this Court with the following illustration applicable to the facts of this case:

> "If a large sum of money is given in trust to apply the income each year in paying a certain sum to every inhabitant of a city, whether rich or poor, the trust is not charitable, since although each inhabitant may receive a benefit, the social interest of the community as such is not thereby promoted. Furthermore, trusts created to distribute money out of liberality or generosity, without regard to the need of the donees and the effect of the gifts, do not have the requisite public benefit necessary to a charity."

Charles Walker expressly states in Article V that "The ultimate purpose of this fund is to provide a million dollar trust fund for every American 18 years or older." From this language, it is obvious Walker intended nothing more than to financially enrich the American public. While this act is generous and benevolent, it is not necessarily beneficial to the community. There is no evidence referenced or argument made by appellees to persuade us that the effect of the trust contemplated by Walker would promote the social interest of the community. Article V does not place restrictions or limitations on the beneficiaries of the trust, thus allowing them to use the funds for any purpose, whether it be one that benefits the community or one that burdens it. The trust would provide a personal, individual benefit to each beneficiary but would fail to promote the social interest of the community as a whole. Furthermore, the trust is established without regard to the need of the beneficiaries or the effect of the trust and as a result lacks the requisite public benefit necessary to a charity. The trust created by Walker is nothing more than a generous distribution of money with no contemplation or recognition of public benefit. We conclude the trust established by Walker is devoid of any charitable intent or purpose and is therefore not charitable as defined by law.

Appellees argue that Texas courts have a long history of favoring charitable bequests and that where a bequest is open to two constructions, the interpretation that gives the charity effect should be adopted, and that which will defeat the charity should be rejected.

In this case, however, we find no charitable intent or purpose. Therefore, these rules of law do not apply. Appellees would have us use these rules to create a charitable intent where none exists. We decline to do so.

Having concluded Article V of the will does not establish a charitable trust, the rule against perpetuities is applicable. In this case, the trust is of indefinite duration and therefore violates the rule against perpetuities. Accordingly, appellants' first issue is sustained.

III. Reformation of Noncharitable Trusts

When a noncharitable trust is in violation of the rule against perpetuities, a trial court is authorized to reform the trust pursuant to section 5.043 of the Texas Property Code. A court has the power to reform or construe the trust according to the doctrine of *cy pres* by giving effect to the general intent of the testator within the limits of the rule. It is clear from the language in Article V that Walker's general intent in creating the trust was to financially enrich the American public. Therefore, application of section 5.043 requires the court to reform or construe Article V within the limits of the rule against perpetuities and consistent with this intent. If reformation is not possible however, the trust is void as being in violation of the rule.

IV. Conclusion

Accordingly, we reverse the trial court's judgment to the extent it established a charitable trust and remand this case for further proceedings consistent with this opinion.

B. STANDING TO ENFORCE CHARITABLE TRUST

In both of the two preceding cases, the settlor of the attempted trust was dead by the time the trust was to go into effect, so there was no live person available to try to enforce the terms of the trusts. However, when an institution, such as a foundation, sets up the trust, or if the trust is established while the settlor is alive, then there may well be an institution, or an individual, who is readily available to try to enforce the terms of the trust.

The following case illustrates the problems which a settlor may have in trying to enforce the terms of a trust which has been established by the settlor.

(1) ENFORCEMENT BY DONOR

Supreme Court of Connecticut.
CARL J. HERZOG FOUNDATION, INC.
v.
UNIVERSITY OF BRIDGEPORT.
Decided Aug. 26, 1997.

NORCOTT, Associate Justice.

The sole issue in this certified appeal is whether the Connecticut Uniform Management of Institutional Funds Act (CUMIFA), establishes statutory standing for a donor to bring an action to enforce the terms of a completed charitable gift. Because we conclude that the legislature did not intend to establish donor standing under the circumstances of this case, we reverse the judgment of the Appellate Court.

The plaintiff Carl J. Herzog Foundation, Inc. commenced an action against the defendant, the University of Bridgeport, seeking injunctive and other relief in connection with a gift made by it to the defendant. The plaintiff alleged that prior to August 12, 1986, it made various grants to the defendant 'to provide need-based merit scholarship aid to disadvantaged students for medical related education.' On August 12, 1986, the plaintiff agreed, by letter, to participate in a matching grant program that would provide need-based merit scholarships to disadvantaged students for medical related education on a continuing basis. On September 9, 1986, the defendant wrote a letter accepting the offer of a matching grant of up to $250,000. Over a period of time, the defendant raised the necessary $250,000, which the plaintiff matched in accordance with the agreement. The grants were used to provide scholarships to students in the defendant's nursing program. On November 21, 1991, however, the plaintiff was informed that the defendant had closed its nursing school on June 20, 1991.

The plaintiff's alleged injury is that the funds are no longer being used for their specified purpose - that the said institutional funds have been co-mingled with the general funds of the defendant, that said institutional funds are not being used in accordance with the "Gift Instrument" under which said institutional funds were transferred to the defendant, and that said institutional funds have in fact been spent for general purposes of the defendant.

The plaintiff requested a temporary and permanent injunction, ordering the defendant 'to segregate from its general funds matching grants totaling $250,000,' an accounting for the use of the fund from the date of receipt until present, and a reestablishment of the fund in accordance with the purposes outlined in the gift instrument, and, in the event that those purposes could not be fulfilled, to revert the funds and direct them to the Bridgeport Area Foundation, which is prepared to administer the funds in accordance with the original agreement.

The defendant moved to dismiss the action for lack of subject matter jurisdiction on the ground that the plaintiff lacked standing. The trial court agreed, and dismissed the complaint.

The Appellate Court reversed the judgment of the trial court. The Appellate Court concluded that the statute, although silent on the matter, *implicitly* confers donor standing on the plaintiff. We disagree.

At common law, a donor who has made a completed charitable contribution, whether as an absolute gift or in trust, had no standing to bring an action to enforce the terms of his or her gift or trust unless he or she had expressly reserved the right to do so. Where property is given to a charitable corporation and it is directed by the terms of the gift to devote the property to a particular one of its purposes, it is under a duty, *enforceable at the suit of the attorney general,* to devote the property to that purpose.

The theory underlying the power of the attorney general to enforce gifts for a stated purpose is that a donor who attaches conditions to his gift has a right to have his intention enforced. The donor's right, however, is enforceable only at the instance of the attorney general. The donor himself has no standing to enforce the terms of his gift when he has not retained a specific right to control the property, such as a right of reverter, after relinquishing physical possession of it. The fact that the charity is bound to use contributions for the purposes for which they were given does not confer to the *donor* standing to bring an action to enforce the terms of the gift.

Having concluded that the plaintiff would have had no standing at common law, we now turn to its contention that the common law has been altered by the legislature's adoption of CUMIFA, specifically that portion codified at § 45a-533. Subsection (a) of § 45a-533 empowers the governing board of an institution to seek a release of an onerous or obsolete restriction without resort to the courts by obtaining the donor's consent. Subsection (b) of § 45a-533 empowers the board to apply to the courts for such release in the event of the donor's death, disability or other unavailability.

The plaintiff bases its statutory standing claim primarily on the language of subsection (a) of § 45a-533, which provides that "with the written consent of the donor, the governing board may release, in whole or in part, a restriction imposed by the applicable gift instrument on the use or investment of an institutional fund." The plaintiff maintains, that "it would be anomalous for a statute to provide for written consent by a donor to change a restriction and then deny that donor access to the courts to complain of a change without such consent." We disagree.

The plaintiff concedes, as it must, that nothing in the plain language of § 45a-533 (a) or any other portion of CUMIFA expressly provides statutory standing for donors to charitable institutions who have not somehow reserved a property interest in the gift such as a right of reverter.

We agree with the defendant that the drafters of UMIFA did not intend to confer donor standing in the matter of the release of gift restrictions, and that our legislature provided no indication when it enacted CUMIFA that it intended any other result.

First, it is unmistakable that the drafters of UMIFA regarded charitable institutions, particularly colleges and universities, as the principal beneficiaries of their efforts. The drafters set forth the explanation of their purpose in the prefatory note to UMIFA. "Over the past several years the governing boards of eleemosynary institutions, particularly colleges and universities, have sought to make more effective use of endowment and other investment funds. They and their counsel have wrestled with questions as to permissible investments, delegation of investment authority, and use of the total return concept in investing endowment funds. Some gifts and grants contained restrictions on use of funds or selection of investments which imperiled the effective management of the fund. An expeditious means to modify obsolete restrictions seemed necessary."

UMIFA, drafted in the early 1970s, was set against the backdrop of a state of flux for colleges and universities. In a time of dramatic social change that cast new light on many older charitable gift restrictions, these institutions saw their operating costs rise significantly without a similar increase in endowment funds. It is evident that the drafters of UMIFA attempted to offer as much relief as possible *to charitable institutions,* without any mention of concern regarding a donor's ability to bring legal action to enforce a condition on a gift.

The specific area of relief to institutions focused upon § 7, of UMIFA, entitled "Release of Restrictions on Use or Investment." The prefatory note to that section provides: "It is established law that the donor may place restrictions on his largesse which the donee institution must honor. Too often, the restrictions on use or investment become outmoded or wasteful or unworkable. There is a need for review of obsolete restrictions and a way of modifying or adjusting them. The Act authorizes the governing board to obtain the acquiescence of the donor to a release of restrictions and, in the absence of the donor, to petition the appropriate court for relief in appropriate cases." In the comment to § 7, the drafters of UMIFA expressly provided that the donor of a completed gift would not have standing to enforce the terms of the gift. "*The donor has no right to enforce the restriction,* no interest in the fund and no power to change the eleemosynary beneficiary of the fund. He may only acquiesce in a lessening of a restriction already in effect." (Emphasis added.) .

These clear comments regarding the power of a donor to enforce restrictions on a charitable gift arose in the context of debate concerning the creation of potential adverse tax consequences for donors, if UMIFA was interpreted to provide donors with control over their gift property after the completion of the gift. Pursuant to § 170(a) of the Internal Revenue Code and § 1.170A-1 (c) of the Treasury Regulations, an income tax deduction for a charitable contribution is disallowed unless the taxpayer has permanently surrendered "dominion and control" over the property or funds in question. Where there is a possibility not "so remote as to be negligible" that the charitable gift subject to a condition might fail, the tax deduction is disallowed.

The drafters of UMIFA worked closely with an impressive group of professionals, including tax advisers, who were concerned with the federal tax implications of the proposed act. The drafters' principal concern in this regard was that the matter of donor restrictions not affect the donor's charitable contribution deduction for the purposes of federal income taxation. In other words, the concern was that the donor not be so tethered to the charitable gift through the control of restrictions in the gift that the donor would not be entitled to claim a federal charitable contribution exemption for the gift.

Although the comments and the prefatory note to UMIFA do recognize that a donor has an interest in a restriction, as analyzed herein we find no support in any source for the proposition that the drafters of either UMIFA or CUMIFA intended that a donor or his heirs would supplant the attorney general as the designated enforcer of the terms of completed and absolute charitable gifts.[2]

On the basis of our careful review of the statute itself, its legislative history, the circumstances surrounding its enactment, the policy it was intended to implement, and similar common law principles governing the same subject matter, we conclude that CUMIFA does not establish a new class of litigants, namely donors, who can enforce an unreserved restriction in a completed charitable gift. Nothing in our review supports the conclusion that the legislature, in enacting CUMIFA, implicitly intended to confer standing on donors.

The judgment of the Appellate Court is reversed and the case is remanded to that court with direction to affirm the judgment of the trial court.

McDONALD, Associate Justice, with whom BERDON, J., joins, dissenting.

I would affirm the thoughtful and well reasoned opinion of the Appellate Court.

The majority here holds that the donor itself may not enforce a restriction in a gift to an educational institution when the institution had specifically agreed to that restriction. This decision is simply an approval of a donee, in the words of the donor, "double crossing the donor," and doing it with impunity unless an elected attorney general does something about it.

This decision will not encourage donations to Connecticut colleges and universities. I fail to see why Connecticut, the home of so many respected schools that would honor their promises, should endorse such sharp practices and create a climate in this state that will have a chilling effect on gifts to its educational institutions.

Accordingly, I respectfully dissent.

(2) STANDING UNDER THE UNIFORM TRUST CODE

Although the preceding case definitely represents the common law rule, there have been statutory modifications in some states. The current provisions of the Uniform Trust Code illustrate a possible modification with regard to enforcement by the settlor of the provisions of a charitable trust.

Uniform Trust Code

§ 405. Charitable Purposes; Enforcement.

[2] The brief of the amici curiae in this appeal, the Connecticut Conference of Independent Colleges, Inc., the Connecticut Association of Independent Schools, Inc., and the National Association of Independent Colleges and Universities persuasively posits that, should the establishment of donor standing become the law, the infinite variety of charitable gift restrictions that affect educational institutions would create the potential for a flood of "time-consuming, fact-sensitive litigation." This "mischief," they argue, would harm the very institutions that the CUMIFA intended to protect. We agree.

(a) A charitable trust may be created for the relief of poverty, the advancement of education or religion, the promotion of health, governmental or municipal purposes, or other purposes the achievement of which is beneficial to the community.

(b) If the terms of a charitable trust do not indicate a particular charitable purpose or beneficiary, the court may select one or more charitable purposes or beneficiaries. The selection must be consistent with the settlor's intention to the extent it can be ascertained.

(c) The settlor of a charitable trust, among others, may maintain a proceeding to enforce the trust. (Emphasis added)

(different than a donation)

C. MODIFICATIONS TO CHARITABLE TRUSTS – CY PRES

Both the preceding case and the Uniform Trust Code refer to the doctrine of cy pres – a doctrine which allows a court to vary the terms of a charitable trust when the provisions of the trust become illegal or seriously impractical. The following two cases are illustrations of possible applications of the doctrine of cy pres.

Court of Appeals of New York.
In re NEHER'S WILL.
VILLAGE OF RED HOOK
v.
BENNETT et al.
Jan. 10, 1939.

LOUGHRAN, Judge.

The will of Ella Neher was admitted to probate by the Surrogate's Court of Dutchess County December 22, 1930. Paragraph 7 thereof made these provisions:

> 'I give, devise and bequeath my home in Red Hook Village, on the east side of South Broadway, consisting of house, barn and lot of ground to the incorporated Village of Red Hook, as a memorial to the memory of my beloved husband, Herbert Neher, with the direction to said Village that said property be used as a hospital to be known as 'Herbert Neher Memorial Hospital.' The trustees of the Village of Red Hook, consisting of the President and the Trustees, shall constitute the managing board with full power to manage and operate said hospital as they deem wise for the benefit of the people of Red Hook, and each succeeding Board of Trustees shall constitute the Board of Trustees for said hospital, so that any person duly elected and qualified or duly appointed and qualified as a President or Trustee of the said Village of Red Hook shall be a trustee of said hospital during such person's lawful term of office, and shall be succeeded as a trustee on the hospital board by his successor on the Village

Board.'

All her other estate Mrs. Neher gave to relatives and friends.

On September 1, 1931, the trustees of Red Hook (hereinafter called the village) resolved to 'accept the real property devised and bequeathed by the Will of Ella Neher, deceased, according to the terms of the Will of said Ella Neher.'

In March, 1937, the village presented to the Surrogate's Court its petition asserting that it was without the resources necessary to establish and maintain a hospital on the property devised to it by the testatrix and that a modern hospital theretofore recently established in the neighboring village of Rhinebeck adequately served the needs of both communities. The prayer of this petition was for a decree 'construing and reforming paragraph Seven of the last Will and Testament of said decedent directing and permitting your petitioner to receive said property and to erect and maintain thereon a building for the administration purposes of said Village to be known and designated as the Herbert Neher Memorial Hall, with a suitable tablet placed thereon expressing such memorial.'

This petition the Surrogate denied on the single ground 'that to read into the will a general intention to devote the property to charitable purposes instead of an intention to limit the use of the property to the operation of a hospital, would do violence to the expressed testamentary design of Mrs. Neher.' The Appellate Division has affirmed the Surrogate. The village brings the case here by our leave.

This gift was not a gift to a particular institution. There was to be no singular object of the bounty. This gift was one to a whole community-'to the incorporated Village of Red Hook.' The idea initially expressed by the testatrix was that her home should be dedicated to the village in the name of her husband. The only question is whether this first stated design of beneficence at large is necessarily to be denied prime import, because of the words that immediately follow-'with the direction to said Village that said property be used as a hospital to be known as 'Herbert Neher Memorial Hospital.' This last phrase, it is to be noticed, gave no hint in respect of a predilection for any certain type of the manifold varieties of medical or surgical care. Nor did the will make any suggestion as to management or control, save that the village trustees (as such) were designated as a governing board. So great an absence of particularity is a strong circumstance against the view that the instruction of the testatrix was of the substance of the gift.

When paragraph 7 of the will is taken as a whole, the true construction, we think, is that the paramount intention was to give the property in the first instance for a general charitable purpose rather than a particular charitable purpose, and to graft on to the general gift a direction as to the desires or intentions of the testator as to the manner in which the general gift is to be carried into effect. Such a grafted direction may be ignored when compliance is altogether impracticable and the gift may be executed cy pres through a scheme to be framed by the court for carrying out the general charitable purpose.

The order of the Appellate Division and the decree of the Surrogate's Court should be reversed and the matter remitted to the Surrogate's Court for further proceedings in accordance with this opinion, without costs.

Another case, from 2008, in which the court refused to apply the doctrine of cy pres, follows. Notice how active the Attorney General was in this case, for some reason.

Court of Appeals of Ohio.
In re TRUST OF LOWRY
The State of Ohio ex rel. Dann, Atty. Gen., Appellant.
Decided Feb. 11, 2008.

SHAW, Presiding Judge.

Appellant, the State of Ohio ex rel. Marc Dann, Attorney General of Ohio ("the state") appeals the July 27, 2007 judgment of the probate court of Henry County, Ohio, partially terminating the trust of Earl Lowry.

This matter began with a trust created by Earl Lowry, upon his death, in his last will and testament. The trust was created expressly for the purpose of beautification and upkeep of three cemeteries located in Damascus Township, Henry County. Prior to this action, the trust has been in force for over 35 years.

On April 23, 2007, the trustees, who are also the township trustees, filed an application to terminate or modify the trust so that the trust could be modified to "distribute a portion of the funds accumulated in the Trust by the consent of the beneficiary for the reason that the Trust property is more than sufficient to satisfy the Trust's current purposes and maintaining all the funds in the Trust has become impracticable."

A hearing was held on July 3, 2007, with the parties stipulating to the following facts as articulated in the July 24, 2007 judgment of the court:

1. The trust balance as of September 30, 2005 was $74,521.11.
2. The entire trust balance is invested in a bank certificate of deposit drawing five percent interest per annum.
3. The trust expenses over the first thirty-five years of the trust's existence totaled $19,058.00 for the beautification and upkeep of the three Damascus Township Cemeteries. Said sum does not include real estate taxes, fiduciary bond premiums, attorney fees and court costs.
4. The Trustees of the Trust of Earl Lowry, deceased, believe that Twenty-five Thousand Dollars ($25,000.00) would be more than sufficient to satisfy the Trust's stated purpose.

Based on these stipulations, the court made the following findings:

> 1. The charitable purpose of the Trust of Earl Lowry, deceased has become impracticable to the extent that income from the Trust property exceeds the funds necessary to satisfy the Trust's stated purpose.
> 2. Twenty-five Thousand Dollars ($25,000.00) is more than sufficient to satisfy the current purpose of the Trust.

The court entered its judgment and ordered the following:

> 1. The Court orders a partial termination of the Trust for funds in the Trust in excess of Twenty-five Thousand Dollars ($25,000.00).
> 2. The Trust funds in excess of the Twenty-five Thousand Dollars ($25,000.00) shall be used for other charitable purposes of Damascus Township, Henry County, Ohio expended by the Trustees in the manner consistent with a general charitable purpose.
> 3. The Trustees shall first consider capital improvements for the three cemeteries in Damascus Township, Henry County, Ohio and shall hold at least one public hearing advertised at least once in the Northwest Signal with thirty (30) days prior notice to the hearing. At the hearing, the Trustees shall hear and receive any suggestions from Damascus Township residents as to capital improvements to the three cemeteries in Damascus Township, Henry County, Ohio.
> 4. Thereafter, at their sole and exclusive discretion, the Trustees may expend the funds in excess of Twenty-five Thousand Dollars ($25,000.00) for capital improvements to the cemeteries as determined by a resolution of a majority of the Trustees and, thereafter, may expend said funds for other capital improvements in Damascus Township, Henry County, Ohio. "Capital Improvements" as used herein shall be defined as real estate or equipment with a useful life estimated at ten years or more.

Snow plows

The state now appeals. The state argues that partial termination was inappropriate under cy pres because the capital improvements allowed by the termination are too dissimilar to Lowry's original charitable purpose and because the court misapplied the phrase "general charitable intent."

The rule of construction by which charitable gifts are preserved for the public benefit is known as the Cy Pres doctrine. In the law of trusts it refers to a rule of construction used by courts of equity to effectuate the intention of a charitable donor "as near as may be" when it has become impossible or impractical by reason of changing conditions or circumstances to give literal effect to the donor's intention.

At common law, Ohio courts have followed the traditional view that before the cy pres doctrine will be applied by a court, the following three essentials must be present:

> (1) there must be a valid charitable trust and one that is invalid will not be cured by an application of the doctrine;
> (2) it must be established that it is impossible or impractical to carry out the specific purposes of the trust;
> (3) it must be established that the donor evinced a general charitable intent.

The common-law doctrine of cy pres has recently been codified at R.C. 5804.13, which provides:

> (A) Except as otherwise provided in division (B) of this section, if a particular charitable purpose becomes unlawful, impracticable, or impossible to achieve, all of the following apply:
> (1) The trust does not fail in whole or in part.
> (2) The trust property does not revert to the settlor or the settlor's successors in interest.
> (3) The court may apply cy pres to modify or terminate the trust by directing that the trust property be applied or distributed, in whole or in part, in a manner consistent with the settlor's charitable purposes. In accordance with section 109.25 of the Revised Code, the attorney general is a necessary party to a judicial proceeding brought under this section.
>
> (B) A provision in the terms of a charitable trust for the distribution of the trust property to a noncharitable beneficiary prevails over the power of the court under division (A) of this section to apply cy pres to modify or terminate the trust.

The official comment to R.C. 5804.13 indicates that this codification "modifies the doctrine of cy pres by presuming that the settler had a general charitable intent when a particular charitable purpose becomes impossible or impracticable to achieve."

At the outset, we question whether the administration of the trust has become impossible or impracticable, as found by the probate court. The judgment of the probate court states that the trust has become "impracticable to the extent that income from the Trust property exceeds the funds necessary to satisfy the Trust' stated purpose."

Impracticability occurs when:

> Even though it is possible to carry out the particular purpose of the settlor, if to do so would not accomplish the settlor's charitable objective, or would not do so in a reasonable way. In such a case, it is "impracticable" to carry out the particular purpose in the sense in which that word is used in this Section.

We are mindful that "the direction of the testator should prevail, although the carrying out of the trust is inconvenient or even undesirable."

We are not convinced that this notion of impracticability is present in this case. For over 35 years, the trust has carried out Lowry's original purpose, accomplishing his objective through reasonable means of upkeep and beautification of the cemeteries. Moreover, the trust provides a resource of funds should the mausoleum be condemned or abandoned, necessitating the removal of the remains of Lowry and others.

However, even if impracticability were to be established or conceded in this case, R.C. 5804.13 still requires that if a trust is modified or terminated, it must be "in a manner consistent with the settlor's charitable purposes." Lowry's charitable intent is specifically expressed in his last will and testament. Lowry provided in Item 28 of his last will and testament for the creation of a trust for the following purpose:

> "The employment of a recognized Horticulturist or Landscaping Firm or individual to oversee and direct the beautification by planting, trimming and cultivation of trees, shrubbery and flowers and landscaping the same in the three (3) Cemeteries now in Damascus Township, Henry county, Ohio, and also to be used for the upkeep, care and maintenance and beautification of the Mausoleum in the United Brethren Cemetery, the income shall be used for all three (3) cemeteries and for the Mausoleum, and not to be expended on any one particular Cemetery or Mausoleum, to the detriment of any one of the Cemeteries.
>
> "In the event, that the mausoleum be condemned or abandoned, I direct said Trustees to expend said income for the purchase of suitable burial lot or lots in Hockman Cemetery and to transfer the remains of Calvin S. Lowry, Addie Lowry, Clyde Wilcox, Alma Wilcox, and Marguerite Wilcox to said Hockman Cemetery, and to purchase and cause to be erected monuments and grave markers for the above named."

On reading Item 28, it is clear that Lowry intended to provide for upkeep and beautification of three cemeteries and for the indefinite care of his remains and the remains of other specified individuals. Although R.C. 5804.13 may now permit the court to presume a general charitable intent, we have a serious question as to whether general capital expenditures on behalf of local government for "real estate or equipment" purchases constitute a "charitable purpose" under the statute as a matter of law.

More important, however, even if R.C. 5804.13 allows for modification based upon a general charitable intent, the purpose of the court-ordered modification must still be consistent with the settlor's specific charitable intent. There is nothing in the language of Lowry's last will and testament providing for the beautification and upkeep of three cemeteries as well as a family mausoleum that evinces any intent to provide for other capital improvements to Damascus Township. As a result, in this instance, it is our conclusion that the modification of the trust ordered by the probate court allows for the use of the trust for a purpose too dissimilar to Lowry's original intent.

Finally, one might argue that the trust could still be modified if waste was occurring. When excess resources remain in a trust, waste can be a justification for modification of a trust. Waste occurs when "the amount of property held in the trust exceeds what is needed for the particular charitable purpose to such an extent that the continued expenditure of all of the funds for that purpose, although possible to do, would be wasteful." Restatement of the Law 3d, Trusts (2003).

> Faced with circumstances of the type required for cy pres intervention in a surplus-funds case, a court might broaden the purposes of the trust, direct application of the surplus funds to a like purpose in a different community, or otherwise direct the use of funds not reasonably needed for the original purpose to a different but reasonably similar charitable purpose.

Impt to know! i treat as black

The trust at issue contained $74,521.11 as of September 30, 2005. Although the record indicates that over 35 years of trust administration, only $19,058 have been expended for the beautification and upkeep of the three Damascus Township cemeteries, we cannot say with certainty that this spending pattern would continue. For example, Damascus Township could allocate less of its own funding to the cemeteries in the future, requiring additional funds from the trust to maintain the cemeteries in their current condition.

Moreover, this court is mindful of the provision in the last will and testament that provides as follows:

> In the event, that the mausoleum be condemned or abandoned, I direct said Trustees to expend said income for the purchase of suitable burial lot or lots in Hockman Cemetery and to transfer the remains of Calvin S. Lowry, Addie Lowry, Clyde Wilcox, Alma Wilcox, and Marguerite Wilcox to said Hockman Cemetery, and to purchase and cause to be erected monuments and grave markers for the above named.

If it were necessary to carry out the above provision, this could cause a significant increase in the expenditures from the trust. As a result, there is nothing in the record to support a finding of waste here, and we note that the probate court did not appear to make waste a basis of its ruling in any event. Accordingly, it is our conclusion that the funds contained in Lowry's trust are not so excessive, in this case, as to constitute waste.

In sum, we do not find sufficient evidence in the record to establish that the trust has become impracticable or has become wasteful. Moreover, it is our conclusion that even if modification were appropriate, the current modification is too dissimilar to Lowry's original charitable purpose.

Accordingly, the July 27, 2007 judgment of the probate court of Henry County, Ohio, partially terminating the trust of Earl Lowry is reversed.

Judgment reversed.

ROGERS, J., concurring separately.

I concur with the result reached in the majority's opinion. However, I write separately to further note that there is no evidence that the trustees have ever fully complied with the directives of the trust. The trust provides for "the employment of a recognized Horticulturist or Landscaping Firm or individual to oversee and direct the beautification by planting, trimming and cultivation of trees, shrubbery and flowers and landscaping and also the upkeep, care and maintenance and beautification of the mausoleum." See Item 28 of the will. The expenditure of less than $20,000 over a period of 35 years suggests that the trustees have not recognized the requirement that persons or firms be employed for landscaping and planting. The evidence suggests that any action by the trustees has been limited to maintenance. I would find the lack of evidence of the hiring of a landscaper or horticulturist sufficient cause, in and of itself, to reverse the decision of the trial court.

CHAPTER 9 - NECESSITY OF A TRUSTEE

A. NECESSITY OF HAVING A TRUSTEE

(1) RESIGNATION OR REPLACEMENT OF TRUSTEE

As you have seen in earlier cases, a trust will never fail for lack of a trustee. But what happens when one or more of the designated trustees wish to resign? And what happens if the beneficiaries become very dissatisfied with the performance of one or more of the trustees? The following case should illustrate why it is important to make specific provisions for such possibilities when drafting a trust.

Supreme Court of Pennsylvania.
In re C.A. WHITE and Flo B. White, Deed of Trust
Appeal of Raymond WHITE and J. Nevin White, Trustees.
Appeal of the JUNIATA VALLEY BANK.
Decided Nov. 20, 1984.

ZAPPALA, Justice.

Before this Court is a review of the Superior Court order reversing the order of the lower court granting the petition of Juniata Valley Bank to resign as a corporate trustee and denying a petition to remove Raymond White as an individual trustee.[1]

By an agreement dated December 13, 1965, C.A. White and Flo B. White, his wife, created an inter vivos trust naming their thirteen grandchildren as beneficiaries, and appointing C.A. White (co-settlor); his two sons, Raymond White and J. Nevin White; and the settlor's son-in-law, Roy A. Wingate; and Juniata Valley Bank (Bank) as Trustees. The purpose of the trust is to provide income to the minor beneficiaries until such time as each beneficiary reaches twenty-five years of age. At twenty-five, each beneficiary is entitled to receive one-half of his share of the trust corpus. The remaining one-half is to be distributed upon reaching the age of thirty.

The trust assets consist mostly of timber and coal properties situate in central Pennsylvania and valued by the Bank as of May 28, 1980 at $3,245,773.83. The agreement grants broad discretionary powers to the Trustees, including the power to: hold and continue to hold investment property; invest and reinvest without restriction in any securities or property deemed to be for the best interest of the trust or the beneficiaries; rent or lease property for such time and upon such terms as the Trustees

---

[1] Roy A. Wingate joined in on the bank's petition to resign as a trustee. However, there is no indication of record that the lower court ruled on this petition. In October, 1982, Mr. Wingate died, thereby making this omission moot.

in their discretion deem appropriate; sell and convey any trust property which they determine is in the best interest of the trust and its beneficiaries; and, finally, act as they shall see fit under the circumstances based upon their judgment as to the best course to pursue on behalf of the trust and its beneficiaries. In exercising their powers, the Trustees are not required to obtain the consent of any other person or any court.

C.A. White resigned as a Trustee on December 15, 1965. On June 25, 1980, the Bank and Wingate filed a Petition to Resign as Trustees. In their Petition, they indicated that a dispute arose between Raymond White (Raymond), and themselves regarding investment and management of certain timber and coal resources of the trust. As a result of the actions of the Bank and Wingate, one of the trust beneficiaries filed a Petition to Remove Raymond as a Trustee. Hearings on both Petitions were held on August 18 and 20, 1980. As the result of these hearings, the lower court entered an order granting the Bank's Petition to Resign and denying the beneficiaries' Petition to Remove Raymond. Five of the trust beneficiaries, Kenneth K. King, Sarah King, Thomas F.B. King, John King and Mary King, appealed to the Superior Court, which reversed. We now reverse.

Our review of the trial court's action in removing a trustee and permitting another trustee to resign is limited to determining whether that court abused its discretion or committed an error of law in so acting. If a trial court's adjudication is supported by the record, we cannot disturb its determination because we would have arrived at a different result.

This appeal raises two issues, the propriety of removing one trustee and the propriety of permitting another trustee to resign. The removal of a trustee is controlled by statute. The Fiduciary Code sets forth the grounds for removing a trustee. The applicable section of the Code sets forth that a trustee may be removed:

> (1) for wasting or mismanaging the estate, or when the estate is likely to become insolvent, ... or
> (5) when, for any other reason, the interests of the estate are likely to be jeopardized by his continuation in office.

The beneficiaries contend that Raymond's action had the potential of mismanaging the trust, thereby jeopardizing it. Specifically, the beneficiaries claim that Raymond's proposals of investing in canned foods, wheat, corn, oats, livestock, Swiss francs and German marks were so speculative as to cause harm to the trust. The Superior Court agreed with this allegation and used these proposals as a basis for removing Raymond. However, in addition to the fact that these proposals were not and could not be implemented by Raymond alone, Raymond testified that he did not consider these investments as poor or risky.

In *Croessant Estate,* we refused to remove a trustee who had neglected the administration of a trust but promised to actively participate in the future. There we held that the removal of a trustee is a drastic remedy, and the need for such action must be clear. We also indicated that such action must be viewed in conjunction with the settlor's expressed confidence in the trustee, evinced by the trustee's appointment. In a case where a settlor appoints a particular trustee, removal should only occur when required to protect the trust property. (*See also, In Re Crawford's Estate,* in which we refused to remove a trustee appointed by the settlor but accused of being hostile to the corporate trustee and of being prone to speculative investments.)

The present record is devoid of any *actual* wrongdoings by Raymond. Although the Bank was of the opinion that Raymond's proposals were speculative, Raymond, as a successful businessman, disagreed. In any event, no such proposal could be implemented without the approval of the majority of the Trustees. Apparently, the settlors had sufficient confidence in Raymond to appoint him as a Trustee. Until such time as Raymond violates some fiduciary duty, he cannot be removed. Furthermore, the fact that some of the trust beneficiaries are unhappy with Raymond as a Trustee is of no importance. Obviously, the settlor intended that an independent party have control of the trust corpus, not the beneficiaries. Without a demonstration that the trust corpus is in danger of dissipation, mere displeasure of a beneficiary is an insufficient reason for removing a testamentary trustee.

The second issue presented for review is the Superior Court's reversal of the lower court's approval of the Bank's resignation as a Trustee. Both the trial court and the Superior Court relied upon § 106 of the Restatement (Second) of Trusts which provides:

> A trustee who has accepted the trust cannot resign except
> (a) with the permission of a proper court; or
> (b) in accordance with the terms of the trust; or
> (c) with the consent of all the beneficiaries, if they have capacity to give such consent.

Although our statutes do not speak directly of a trustee's right to resign, § 3184 of the Code sets forth the procedure to be followed when the court permits the discharge of a trustee. Implicitly, a trustee has the power to resign subject to court approval.

The general rule is that a trustee may relieve himself from the liabilities arising from a trust relation by submitting the administration of the trust to the jurisdiction of the court. In our State the right of a trustee to be discharged is recognized by statutes which provide the method of procedure. Appellant has complied with the statutory requirements and has done everything that the law requires to be done antecedently to the asking of a discharge. There may be, and no doubt there are, cases in which a court would be justified in refusing a discharge.

There is nothing in this record to indicate that the remaining trustees are not fully competent to manage the trust estate, or that they are unwilling to do so. The trust estate will be as safe in their hands as it was in the hands of those who preceded them in its management. The argument that the cestuis que trustent will lose some advantage if the trustee be discharged is without merit.

Furthermore, Comment (c) to § 106 of the Restatement (Second) of Trusts suggests that a trustee may resign so long as his resignation will not be unduly detrimental to the administration of the trust. This determination is at the discretion of the trial court, subject to a review of whether an abuse has occurred in the exercise of that discretion.

In the lower court, the Bank indicated that it wished to resign as a Trustee. No evidence was presented to demonstrate that the trust would be harmed by permitting this resignation. While some of the trust beneficiaries contended that Raymond's investment proposals were harmful, and thus the Bank's position as a Trustee was necessary, such contentions were unfounded. Even if Raymond's proposals were harmful, he could not act unilaterally. There appearing no evidence of *actual* harm to the trust, the lower court did not abuse its discretion in permitting the Bank's resignation as a Trustee. [2]

The order of the Superior Court is reversed, and the order of the Court of Common Pleas of Juniata County is reinstated.

McDERMOTT, Justice, dissenting.

The record is replete with examples of risky and sometimes bizarre investment ideas proffered by Raymond. Perhaps such ideas were magic for him in his private affairs, and doubtless he wishes to enhance the trust; but his duties to the trust differ materially from his own fortunes. Again, without impugning integrity, the trustee, Raymond, would have made a considerable personal profit had the bank not refused the purchase of lumber from Raymond.

The majority insists that until there is evidence of actual wrongdoing a trustee should not be removed. Fair enough. Certainly, however, all the trustees should be kept in place. Permitting the bank to resign under the circumstances is to dilute the intention of the testator by at least a third, perhaps, indeed, excusing the very persons most relied upon to guard the trust. The majority insists upon a salutary principle of law, that a testator should have who he will be his trustee. If more than one trustee is named however, the intention of the settlor in diversifying their backgrounds should be honored: particularly so where one is a bank, lawyer or other professional trustee appointed for their expertise. To allow one to resign, unreplaced by a similar person or institution, is to dilute the full intention of the settlor. Indeed, trustees may be driven from their post by actions they were designated to prevent or warn against. A good reason for a trustee to resign is a good reason to replace his kind. To allow a trustee to remain and another to resign, under the circumstances here, is to dissolve the full intention of the testator and leave the trust in hands not intended. As the Superior

---

In its opinion, the Superior Court suggests that a corporate fiduciary must show greater cause for resignation than an individual. This principle has never been adopted by this Court and is explicitly rejected.

Court noted, "the bank's presence as a trustee is clearly more beneficial to the trust than Raymond's continuing as a trustee."

I would affirm the decision of the Superior Court.

(2) WHEN ALL TRUSTEES ARE BENEFICIARIES – MERGER?

The doctrine of merger basically holds that when any one person holds all of the interests in a piece of property, that ownership merges into a fee simple absolute. For example, if the owner of a life estate becomes the owner of the reversion, and no one else owns any rights in the property, then the life estate and the reversion will merge into a fee simple absolute.

Similarly, if one person is the sole trustee of a trust, and that same person is the sole beneficiary of the same trust, then usually the doctrine of merger will apply, and the person will own the assets free and clear of any trust provisions. The following case provides an analysis of whether or not the doctrine of merger should be applied to terminate a trust when all of the trustees are also all of the beneficiaries of a trust.

Supreme Court of Alabama.
FIRST ALABAMA BANK OF TUSCALOOSA, N.A., a National Banking Association, as Executor and Trustee of the Last Will and Testament of Mary Webb Cleveland, Deceased
v.
C. A. WEBB, Jr., et al.
July 27, 1979.

EMBRY, Justice.

Plaintiffs/appellees, four of the five children of the late Mrs. M. E. Webb: namely, C. A. Webb, Jr., J. C. Webb, Katherine, and Elizabeth, filed this action seeking a declaratory judgment. Appellees sued both in their individual capacities as well as in their fiduciary capacities under the Webb Trust.

The basic relief sought was a judgment declaring: (1) the trust was valid; (2) the doctrine of merger did not apply to the Webb Trust; and (3) the death of Mary (a daughter of Mrs. M. E. Webb), without children surviving her, terminated all her interest in and to the income and corpus of the Webb Trust.

The trial court found the Webb Trust was valid and the doctrine of merger did not apply to it, and that the death of Mary terminated all her interest in the Trust. After entry of that judgment the Bank's appeal ensued.

Appellant/defendant First Alabama Bank of Tuscaloosa brings this appeal as executor and trustee of the Last Will and Testament of Mary. We affirm the trial court's determination that the Webb Trust is valid.

On 15 July 1940, Mrs. M. E. Webb executed a trust indenture granting to her five children, as trustees, certain property. These same children, and the surviving children of them in the event of their death prior to termination of the trust, were designated as the beneficiaries of the Webb Trust. The trust instrument provided that the trust would terminate at the death of the last surviving trustee, but could be terminated prematurely, at any time after the death of the first trustee to die, upon unanimous consent of all trustees and all beneficiaries who were at that time sui juris. The distributive share of income and principal of each beneficiary was to go to any surviving child or children of each beneficiary and, if there were no children, be distributed to the surviving beneficiaries in equal parts at the time of the termination of the trust.

Three grandchildren of the settlor are presently living. They constitute contingent alternative remaindermen of the Webb Trust.

The Webb Trust contains language typically employed in the creation of trusts in Alabama. In paragraph 6 is the following provision:

> "In case one or more of the above-named beneficiaries should die prior to the termination of this trust and should not leave surviving any child or children, then in that case the remaining beneficiaries hereinabove named shall take, share and share alike, the interests of said deceased beneficiary in and to disbursements from the trust property and in and to the final distribution of said trust property."

On 15 August 1975, Mary, a daughter of the settlor and one of the trustees under the Webb Trust, died without any surviving child or children. The Last Will and Testament of Mary designated the defendant/appellant Bank as executor.

In August 1977, the Bank sent a letter to the plaintiffs/appellees stating it was its position the doctrine of merger applied to the Webb Trust and that Mary owned in fee simple a twenty percent (20%) interest in the principal of the Trust at the time of her death.

The different position taken by the parties resulted in this litigation.

I

The doctrine of merger applies when one person becomes the simultaneous owner of identical legal and equitable interests in the same property. The equitable interest merges into the legal interest and absolute ownership ensues, without any division into legal and equitable interests. For example, a trustee, who holds fee simple title in trust in certain real estate which makes up the corpus of a trust may become the absolute owner of that realty if he becomes the beneficiary of the trust, or in other words, the owner of the equitable interest. The doctrine of merger would merge the legal interest into the equitable interest, since the same person now holds both interests, consequently destroying the trust. The doctrine of merger, however, is an equitable doctrine and would not apply if "serious injustice would result or if the settlor's intent would be frustrated." Bogert, Trusts and Trustees.

The key ingredient to the application of the doctrine of merger is that *one* person holds both the equitable and legal interests or estates. The great weight of authority supports the proposition that the doctrine of merger cannot apply to trusts where there are two or more trustees. This is demonstrated by the following excerpt:

> " For example, if there is a single trustee and he is also sole beneficiary, the legal interest may well be a legal fee simple owned in severalty and the equitable interest may be an equitable fee simple owned in severalty. Hence the stage may be set for merger. But if there are two or more trustees or two or more beneficiaries a diversity arises. The two or more trustees hold their interest (generally legal) as joint tenants, title vesting in them as a unit, while the beneficiaries hold their equitable interests as tenants in common in almost all cases. This slight difference in the character of legal and equitable interests may justify the refusal to apply merger. Even if A and B hold a legal fee as trustees for A and B who have the complete equitable interest, the difference between joint tenancy and tenancy in common may be sufficient grounds for not applying the doctrine of merger." Bogert, Trusts and Trustees.

In the case of Black v. Black this court refused to apply the doctrine of merger to a trust where three of the seven beneficiaries of the trust were also trustees. Again, this court described the merger doctrine in terms of *one* person acquiring or holding both legal and equitable interest. The Black court made the following statement:

> "The fact that the persons named as executor (trustees) are also beneficiaries does not affect the validity of the trust. It is true that the same person cannot be at the same time sole trustee and sole beneficiary of the same identical interest, but a Cestui que trust, a beneficiary, is not prohibited from occupying the position of trustee for his own benefit where he is a trustee for others as well as for himself."

Because we now expressly hold the doctrine of merger does not apply to trusts with multiple trustees, the Webb Trust is a valid trust. Consequently, all of Mary's interest in the trust terminated upon her death without surviving children as provided by the trust instrument.

II

There is also no merit in the Bank's argument that the trust instrument gave the trustees too much discretion in administering the trust and thus created a tenancy in common among the trustees. Because the discretion of the trustees was limited by ascertainable standards we need not further address that argument.

For the reasons assigned the judgment below is affirmed.

discretion

B. DUTY TO REGISTER – SAMPLE STATUTE

One reason some people may prefer to have an inter vivos trust, rather than a will, is that wills are nearly always a matter of public record. So any person, sufficiently motivated to search through the public records, might learn the contents of a will.

For that reason, some celebrities may prefer to have most of the dispositive provisions for their assets included in the provisions of an inter vivos trust. The contents of an inter vivos trust are not a matter of public record. But the existence of the trust itself should be a matter of record, under the provisions of a state statute such as the statute set forth below.

C.R.S.§ 15-16-101. Duty to register trusts

(1) The trustee of a trust having its principal place of administration in this state shall, within thirty days after his acceptance of the trust, register the trust in the court of this state at the principal place of administration. ...

(3) Registration of a fully and presently revocable inter vivos trust shall not be required until such time as the grantor's power to revoke such trust has terminated, nor shall registration be required if all the assets of such a trust become then distributable outright to the beneficiaries. ...

§ 15-16-102. Registration procedures and content of statement

(1) Registration shall be accomplished by filing a statement indicating the name and address of the trustee in which it acknowledges the trusteeship. The statement shall indicate whether the trust has been registered elsewhere.

(2) The statement shall identify the trust as follows:

(a) In the case of a testamentary trust, by the name of the testator and the date and place of domiciliary probate;

(b) In the case of a written inter vivos trust, by the name of each settlor and the original trustee and the date of the trust instrument;

(c) In the case of an oral trust, by information identifying the settlor or other source of funds and describing the time and manner of the trust's creation and the terms of the trust, including the subject matter, beneficiaries, and time of performance.

(3) If a trust has been registered elsewhere, registration in this state is ineffective until the earlier registration is released by order of the court where prior registration occurred, or an instrument executed by the trustee and all beneficiaries, filed with the registration in this state.

§ 15-16-103. Effect of registration

(1) By registering a trust, or accepting the trusteeship of a registered trust, the trustee submits personally to the jurisdiction of the court in any

proceeding relating to the trust that may be initiated by any interested person while the trust remains registered.

(2) To the extent of their interests in the trust, all beneficiaries of a trust properly registered in this state are subject to the jurisdiction of the court of registration for the purposes of proceedings [involving the trust].

§ 15-16-104. Effect of failure to register

Any trustee who, within thirty days after receipt of a written demand by a settlor or beneficiary of the trust, fails to register a trust as required is subject to removal and denial of compensation or to surcharge as the court may direct. **A provision in the terms of the trust purporting to excuse the trustee from the duty to register, or directing that the trust or trustee shall not be subject to the jurisdiction of the court, is ineffective.** If any trustee wrongfully and willfully fails to register within thirty days of his acceptance of a trust which is required to be registered, the court in which the trust should have been registered shall impose on the trustee a civil penalty of one hundred dollars per day for each day the trustee fails to register the trust, but not more than one thousand dollars. Such civil penalty shall not be paid from the corpus or income of the trust.

CHAPTER 10 - RULES OF CONSTRUCTION

Unfortunately, it frequently turns out that the words of a will are not clear enough to prevent controversy among various people who feel entitled to some of decedent's estate. Even though courts all agree that the intent of the testator should control, it is not always easy to ascertain that intent. The problem usually arises either because the testator actually did not anticipate the particular issue involved, or because the words used by the testator turn out to be ambiguous, and might legitimately be interpreted in several different ways.

To assist courts in the search for the intent of the testator, several "rules of construction" have been developed. These rules of construction are to be applied unless it is clear that the testator would not have wanted the particular rule of construction to be applied to the particular problem at hand.

Does this make rules of construction fairly weak? Definitely. But when in doubt, courts will frequently decide the issue by applying one of a large selection of rules of construction. Some of the major rules of construction are illustrated in this chapter.

A. IMPORTANCE OF SPECIFIC WORDS

The rule of construction illustrated by the following case is that "Every will should be construed to give effect to every word therein."

Court of Appeals of Tennessee.
Deborah Delaine PRESLEY, Plaintiff-Appellant,
v.
Joseph A. HANKS, Priscilla B. Presley and National Bank of Commerce, co-executors Estate of the Estate of Elvis A. Presley, Deceased, Defendants-Appellees.
July 20, 1989.

CRAWFORD, Judge.

This is a will construction case. On February 18, 1988, appellant, Deborah Delaine Presley, acting pro se, filed a petition in the probate court entitled "Petition To Determine Heirship And For Share of Estate Under Will Heretofore Admitted To Probate." In essence, the petition alleges that petitioner is the illegitimate daughter of the testator, Elvis A. Presley, and pursuant to the terms and provisions of his Last Will and Testament, she, as his daughter, is entitled to a share of the estate.

The Answer of the co-executors, Joseph A. Hanks, Priscilla B. Presley and National Bank of Commerce, filed September 23, 1988, denies the material allegations of the complaint and joins issue thereon. The Answer specifically avers that the decedent's will expressly excludes petitioner as a beneficiary. On the same date, the co-executors also filed a motion for summary judgment asserting that the express language of Elvis Presley's will manifests his intent "that only those children born in lawful wedlock to Mr. Presley are entitled to inherit from and through him, and that Lisa Marie Presley" is the only such child.

The motion for summary judgment was supported by the affidavit of Priscilla B. Presley and D. Beecher Smith, II. The Presley affidavit asserts that Elvis Presley was married only once in his lifetime and that was to the affiant. The affidavit further states that the daughter of the affiant and Elvis Presley, Lisa Marie Presley, is the only child born to Elvis Presley during a lawful marriage.

Smith's affidavit states that pursuant to Elvis Presley's instructions, he prepared the Last Will and Testament in question. Affiant further states that Mr. Presley had previously successfully defended a paternity suit in California and was cognizant of the need to specify in his will those he wanted to take thereunder.

Appellant filed affidavits from her mother, Barbara Jean Young, and from Gene Smith, purportedly Elvis Presley's first cousin. These affidavits, in general, establish the relationship between appellant's mother and Elvis Presley in support of appellant's claim that Mr. Presley was her father.

The probate judge found that appellant failed to establish that she was the daughter of Elvis Presley, and further construed the Presley will to exclude illegitimate children as beneficiaries. Appellant presents various issues for review.

The dispute in this case involves Item IV of Elvis Presley's will which is as follows:

ITEM IV

Residuary Trust

Item IV (b) directs the Trustee to pay for the support and maintenance of "(1) my daughter, Lisa Marie Presley, and *any other lawful issue* I might have." (Emphasis supplied). Paragraph (d) of Item IV provides for a division of the residuary trust by creating a separate and equal trust for "each of my *lawful children.*" (Emphasis supplied). Paragraph (c) of Item IV provides for distribution of the assets of the respective trusts "as each of my *respective children* attains the age of twenty-five (25) years." (Emphasis supplied). The trial court held that by the use of the foregoing language, the decedent intended only for "Lisa Marie Presley or other legitimate children to take under the will."

The cardinal rule in construction of all wills is that the court shall seek to discover the intention of the testator and give effect to it unless it contravenes some rule of law or public policy. The testator's intention is to be ascertained from the particular words used in the will itself, from the context in which those words are used, and from the general scope and purposes of the will, read in the light of the surrounding and attending circumstances.

Every will is *sui generis* and therefore reference to other cases involving the testator's intention is usually of little assistance.

In the case before us, it is uncontroverted that Elvis Presley had been involved in a paternity case and was cognizant of claims placed against him for children born out of wedlock. In Item IV, paragraph (b), the testator makes provision for the support and maintenance of his family, vesting the trustee with absolute discretion in the manner and amount to be used for that purpose. At the time the will was executed, the testator had one child of his only marriage. The provision for the child is coupled with the provision "and any *other* lawful issue I might have." (Emphasis supplied) There was no doubt in Mr. Presley's mind that Lisa Marie was his issue, nor was there any doubt on his part that she was born in lawful wedlock. With this knowledge of the status of his daughter, he explicitly describes the other objects of his bounty as "any other lawful issue."

Moreover, the clause provides for issue the testator "might have" indicating his intent to provide for those coming into existence after the execution of the will. The intent of the testator to provide for only legitimate children becomes even more clear when we consider his disposition of the corpus of the trust. Here again, he utilizes the descriptive word "lawful" when referring to his children who should receive his bounty. A will should be construed to give effect to every word and clause contained therein. Unless we disregard and give no meaning to the word "lawful," we are compelled to believe that the word was used to denote those born in lawful wedlock.

"Lawful" is the antithesis of "unlawful" or "illegitimate." In popular usage, the words "lawful issue" have an accepted meaning. All children are "issue" of their parents, for the operation of natural laws favorable to the procreation and birth of offspring is not affected by the existence or nonexistence of a marital contract. But when this word relating to children is qualified by the adjective "lawful," it is ordinarily understood to mean those begotten and born in lawful wedlock, and none others. At common law the words "child," "son," "issue," even when unqualified by the adjective "lawful," excluded all but the latter class.

We note also that even without the use of the qualifying word "lawful," the general rule recognized in Tennessee is that absent clear evidence of contrary intention, words such as "children" in a will are construed to mean legitimate children and not to include illegitimate children. This appears to be the majority rule in the United States.

Accordingly, we construe the will of Elvis Presley to exclude illegitimate children as beneficiaries.

B. SPECIFIC AND GENERAL BEQUESTS

Basically, a "specific bequest" is a gift of a specific, particular thing, such as "the quilt made by my mother." A "general bequest" is usually a gift of money, such as "$1,000 to each of my grandchildren." For a general bequest such as this, it is the general amount of money, not any specific dollar bills, which is the gift intended by the testator.

When there are not enough assets in the decedent's estate to fulfill all of the gifts stated in the will, or when there is an issue as to which assets in the estate should be used for payment of decedent's debts, taxes, and expenses of administration, then the difference between a specific bequest and a general bequest may become important, as illustrated by the following case.

Court of Appeals of Texas.
In the ESTATE OF Melvin J. ANDEREGG, Deceased.
Feb. 1, 2012.

CHRISTOPHER ANTCLIFF, Justice.

Melvin Anderegg's will bequeathed money and securities to his sister, Hazel Davitt, and the remainder of his property to his great-nephew, Bryan Cosper and Bryan's wife, Marie Cosper. The Cospers were named as executors of the estate. Following Anderegg's death, Davitt filed a motion to remove the Cospers as executors, accusing them of embezzlement. The Cospers contested the removal and sought a declaratory judgment regarding the correct interpretation of the will.

The trial court found for Davitt on all issues. The Cospers appeal, raising three issues. We affirm.

Will Interpretation

The Cospers' first two issues require interpretation of the will. When interpreting a will, our focus is on the testator's intent, which, absent an ambiguity, must be ascertained solely from the will's language. In this case, neither party relies on extrinsic evidence.[1] Accordingly, whether Anderegg's will is ambiguous or unambiguous; we must determine its meaning from the words used.

After an introductory paragraph, Anderegg's will has three sections, each serving a separate purpose. The first section provides for the payment of debts and expenses. The second disposes of Anderegg's property. The third governs administration of the estate, by appointing executors, describing the executors' powers, and providing for probate of the will. The sections are worded as follows:

> FIRST: I do hereby direct that all of my just debts and all expenses of my last illness, funeral, and the administration of my estate shall be paid out of my estate by my executrix hereinafter appointed as soon after my death as may be

---

[1] The attorney who drafted the will testified regarding its meaning, but his testimony indicated that he did not know the answers to the questions of intent and interpretation raised by the parties. Neither side refers to his testimony on appeal.

Should have made a memo to the file

practicable.

SECOND: Subject to the provisions of the foregoing paragraph hereof, I do hereby give and bequeath, all monies I may have at the time of my death, be they in the form of cash, checking accounts or savings accounts, all stocks, bonds, annuities, etc., and any accounts I may have with A.G. Edwards & Sons, Inc., Farm Bureau or others to my beloved sister, HAZEL DAVITT.

In the event that my said sister, HAZEL DAVITT should predecease me, the property that would have otherwise been distributed to her shall instead pass to her children in equal shares, or their children should a child of Hazel Davitt also predecease me.

All the rest and residue of my estate being primarily the 115.20 acres of land, more or less, I own in Kimble County, Texas, all personal property located on such real estate to included [sic], but not limited to all my guns, livestock, vehicles, buck horns, four wheeler, etc. I give, devise, and bequeath to BRYAN and MARIE COSPER.

THIRD: I do hereby appoint the said BRYAN and MARIE COSPER, Independent Executors...

In their first issue, the Cospers argue that the trial court erred in requiring that all debts and expenses of the estate be paid *pro rata* from all of the estate's assets. Debts and expenses are generally paid from the residuary estate. The Probate Code provides that a decedent's property is liable for debts and expenses of administration other than estate taxes, and that **bequests abate in the following order: property passing by intestacy; personal property of the residuary estate; real property of the residuary estate; general bequests of personal property; general devises of real property; specific bequests of personal property; and specific devises of real property.** (Emphasis added) The statute further provides that the decedent's intent, as expressed in a will, controls over the statutory order of abatement.

The question presented here is whether Anderegg's will expresses an intent to deviate from the statutory order of abatement. The first section of Anderegg's will states that debts and expenses "shall be paid out of my estate." The Probate Code defines "estate" as "the real and personal property of a decedent." Thus, the word encompasses all of Anderegg's property. The first section, standing alone, supports the trial court's decision.

In arguing that the trial court erred in charging their devise with a *pro rata* portion of the debts and expenses, the Cospers rely principally on the words "subject to the provisions of the foregoing paragraph...." These words appear in the second section, immediately before the bequest to Davitt. The Cospers believe that this wording demonstrates Anderegg's intent that debts and expenses be deducted from Davitt's bequest. Furthermore, because the wording only appears before the bequest to Davitt, and not before the devise and bequest to them, they argue that all of the debts and expenses should be deducted solely from Davitt's bequest.

Considering the overall structure of the will, we believe the trial court's interpretation is better than the one offered by the Cospers. The words appear at the beginning of the second section, which contains all of the devises and bequests. Accordingly, they apply to the entire section, not merely to Davitt's bequest.

In their second issue, the Cospers argue that the trial court erred in determining that Anderegg's lump sum death benefit and income tax refund should be paid to Davitt. The will gives Davitt "all monies I may have at the time of my death, be they in the form of cash, checking accounts or savings accounts, all stocks, bonds, annuities, etc., and any accounts I may have with A.G. Edwards & Sons, Inc., Farm Bureau or others." The Cospers contend that the death benefit and tax refund do not fit within the literal meaning of "monies I may have at the time of my death," "cash," "stocks," "bonds," "annuities," or "accounts" of any type.

"Courts have generally construed the testamentary terms 'money' and 'cash' to mean only coins, paper money and demand deposits." (See cases holding that "all cash money that may be on hand at the time of my decease" did not include certificate of deposit because it was not payable on demand and the money was not available to the testator at the time of his death). However, the Texas Supreme Court has noted that "money" is a word "of flexible meaning that ordinarily refers to cash or coin, but it has often been construed in will cases to mean wealth or property."

The Cospers assert that Anderegg defined what he meant by "monies" when he provided the description "be they in the form of cash, checking accounts or savings accounts." But the will also gives Davitt brokerage accounts and "all stocks, bonds, annuities, etc." Although the death benefit and tax refund are not literally securities or annuities, the abbreviation "etc." suggests that Anderegg contemplated that Davitt would receive other items that were neither securities nor annuities. This abbreviation means "and other things" and usually "indicates additional, unspecified items in a series." Black's Law Dictionary. All of the specific items given to Davitt are relatively liquid financial assets. The death benefit and tax refund fall into this category. Given that "money" can have a flexible meaning, that the bequest uses the abbreviation "etc.," that the will gives Davitt financial assets of various kinds, and that the death benefit and tax refund are of a similar nature, we believe that the death benefit and tax refund were properly awarded to Davitt.

This interpretation is reinforced by the remainder of the will. The will describes the residuary estate, which was given to the Cospers, as consisting of illiquid non-financial assets, such as land, livestock, and vehicles. This contrasts with the relatively liquid financial assets that were given to Davitt. This distinction suggests that Anderegg contemplated that Davitt would receive his "monies" in the broad sense of the word.

The Cospers argue that the maxim *expressio unius est exclusio alterius,* "meaning

exclusio unius

that the naming of one thing excludes another," applies here. More precisely, this maxim refers to the supposition that "the expression in a contract of one or more things of a class implies the exclusion of all not expressed, even though all would have been implied had none been expressed." Even when applicable, the maxim is merely an aid to interpretation, and is not conclusive. Here, Anderegg's use of the term "etc." negates the idea that he intended the listed items to be exclusive.

The trial court was correct in apportioning all debts and expenses among all assets of the estate.

Petition for Removal

Bryan Cosper testified that Anderegg had given Marie Cosper a key to his safe. After Anderegg died, they found a credit card in the safe and "figured he left that in the safe to be used." The Cospers proceeded to use the credit card for personal expenses. For example, they bought tires, made a truck payment, purchased college text books for their daughter, and charged various restaurant meals to the credit card. According to the Cospers, the attorney who drafted the will initially told them that they could use the credit card, but two days later, the attorney changed his mind and said not to use it. Marie testified that she believed this was good advice.

Nevertheless, the majority of the charges occurred after the attorney said not to use the credit card.

Bryan Cosper insisted that he was not a thief. He admitted that he signed the court's written instructions for executors, but he did not read the instructions. The instructions said not to borrow money from the estate. Marie Cosper stated that the judge went over the instructions with them and that she understood the instructions. Although she needed the money and she intended to pay it back, she knew she was "doing wrong" and she "didn't think it was right" when she charged personal expenses to the credit card.

The attorney testified that he did not remember whether he told the Cospers that they could use the credit card. He could not recall ever giving that advice to an executor. The attorney was present when the judge gave the Cospers their instructions and he thought they understood the instructions.

Executors may be removed if they misapply or embezzle property of the estate of if they commit some other type of gross misconduct. Davitt sought to remove the Cospers on the grounds of embezzlement and gross misconduct.

The evidence is both legally and factually sufficient to support a finding of objective bad faith. Considering the admissions they made in their testimony, their subjective belief in the viability of their defense to removal was not reasonable in light of the existing law.

Conclusion

All of the Cospers' issues are overruled, and the judgment of the trial court is affirmed.

UNIFORM PROBATE CODE PROVISIONS

The UPC sets forth rules of construction which may be applied in a variety of other situations which may arise with respect to specific bequests or devises. At common law a gift of personal property was termed a bequest, and a gift of real property was called a devise. The UPC uses the term devise for all testamentary gifts, including gifts of both personal and real property.

U.P.C. § 2-607. Change in Securities; Accessions; Nonademption.

(a) If the testator intended a specific devise of certain securities rather than the equivalent value thereof, the specific devisee is entitled only to:

(1) as much of the devised securities as is a part of the estate at time of the testator's death;

(2) any additional or other securities of the same entity owned by the testator by reason of action initiated by the entity excluding any acquired by exercise of purchase options;

(3) securities of another entity owned by the testator as a result of a merger, consolidation, reorganization or other similar action initiated by the entity; and

(4) any additional securities of the entity owned by the testator as a result of a plan of reinvestment.

(b) Distributions prior to death with respect to a specifically devised security not provided for in subsection (a) are not part of the specific devise.

And what happens if land which has been specifically devised is still subject to a mortgage at the death of the testator? According to the applicable rule of construction in the UPC, the devisee takes the land subject to the mortgage.

U.P.C. § 2-609. Non-Exoneration.

A specific devise passes subject to any mortgage interest existing at the date of death, without right of exoneration, regardless of a general directive in the will to pay debts.

It is a fundamental rule of drafting that a testator should virtually never bequeath specific securities, such as "my 100 shares of Ford," to a specific beneficiary. That is because it is highly likely that between the time the will is written, and the time the testator dies, there will have been changes to the Ford stock owned by the testator when the will was written. Ford may have issued some stock dividends, so that the original 100 shares have become 102.5 shares. Or Ford may have been purchased by

Apple. Or merged with General Motors. Or have gone out of business, like the maker of Hostess "Twinkies," perhaps.

It is not unusual for clients to come in with a list of investments, with the idea of leaving all of the Ford stock, for example, to grandchild A; all of the Apple stock to grandchild B; and all of the General Motors stock to grandchild C. At the time the client is making the will, the value of the three different investments may be about equal. But that is very unlikely to be true ten years in the future. It would be much wiser for the client just to leave each grandchild one-third of whatever stocks the client may happen to own at the time of death.

C. INCORPORATION BY REFERENCE

Very often clients write notes about who should get specific items of personal property. Or they put "stickies" on various items. For the most part, those notes and "stickies" have no binding legal effect whatsoever. The following case illustrates the problems created when a client attempts to make gifts of specific property without including those specific bequests in the formal will.

It *is* possible to incorporate a list of gifts in a will by reference, under the doctrine of *Incorporation by Reference.* But for any document to be incorporated by reference, it must be a pre-existing document in existence *prior* to execution of the will.

Supreme Judicial Court of Massachusetts.
Virginia Marston CLARK
v.
Frederic GREENHALGE, II, Executor of Estate of Helen Nesmith
Decided Dec. 16, 1991.

NOLAN, Justice.

We consider in this case whether a probate judge correctly concluded that specific, written bequests of personal property contained in a notebook maintained by a testatrix were incorporated by reference into the terms of the testatrix's will.

We set forth the relevant facts as found by the probate judge. The testatrix, Helen Nesmith, duly executed a will in 1977, which named her cousin, Frederic T. Greenhalge, II, as executor of her estate. The will further identified Greenhalge as the principal beneficiary of the estate, entitling him to receive all of Helen Nesmith's tangible personal property upon her death except those items which she "designated by a memorandum left by her and known to Greenhalge, or in accordance with her known wishes," to be given to others living at the time of her death. [2] Among Helen Nesmith's possessions was a large oil painting of a farm scene signed by T.H. Muckley and dated 1833. The value of the painting, as assessed for estate tax purposes, was $1,800.00.

[2] The value of Ms. Nesmith's estate at the time of her death exceeded $2,000,000.00, including both tangible and nontangible assets.

In 1972, Greenhalge assisted Helen Nesmith in drafting a document entitled "MEMORANDUM" and identified as "a list of items of personal property prepared with Miss Helen Nesmith upon September 5, 1972, for the guidance of myself in the distribution of personal tangible property." This list consisted of forty-nine specific bequests of Ms. Nesmith's tangible personal property. In 1976, Helen Nesmith modified the 1972 list by interlineations, additions and deletions. Neither edition of the list involved a bequest of the farm scene painting.

Ms. Nesmith kept a plastic-covered notebook in the drawer of a desk in her study. She periodically made entries in this notebook, which bore the title "List to be given Helen Nesmith 1979." One such entry read: "Ginny Clark farm picture hanging over fireplace. Ma's room." Imogene Conway and Joan Dragoumanos, Ms. Nesmith's private home care nurses, knew of the existence of the notebook and had observed Helen Nesmith write in it. On several occasions, Helen Nesmith orally expressed to these nurses her intentions regarding the disposition of particular pieces of her property upon her death, including the farm scene painting. Helen Nesmith told Conway and Dragoumanos that the farm scene painting was to be given to Virginia Clark, upon Helen Nesmith's death.

Virginia Clark and Helen Nesmith first became acquainted in or about 1940. The women lived next door to each other for approximately ten years (1945 through 1955), during which time they enjoyed a close friendship. The Nesmith-Clark friendship remained constant through the years. In more recent years, Ms. Clark frequently spent time at Ms. Nesmith's home, often visiting Helen Nesmith while she rested in the room which originally was her mother's bedroom. The farm scene painting hung in this room above the fireplace. Virginia Clark openly admired the picture.

According to Ms. Clark, sometime during either January or February of 1980, Helen Nesmith told Ms. Clark that the farm scene painting would belong to Ms. Clark after Helen Nesmith's death. Helen Nesmith then mentioned to Virginia Clark that she would record this gift in a book she kept for the purpose of memorializing her wishes with respect to the disposition of certain of her belongings. [3] After that conversation, Helen Nesmith often alluded to the fact that Ms. Clark someday would own the farm scene painting.

Ms. Nesmith executed two codicils to her 1977 will: one on May 30, 1980, and a second on October 23, 1980. The codicils amended certain bequests and deleted others, while ratifying the will in all other respects.

Greenhalge received Helen Nesmith's notebook on or shortly after January 28, 1986, the date of Ms. Nesmith's death. Thereafter, Greenhalge, as executor, distributed

[3]According to Margaret Young, another nurse employed by Ms. Nesmith, Ms. Nesmith asked Ms. Young to "print in the notebook, beneath her own handwriting, 'Ginny Clark painting over fireplace in mother's bedroom.' " Ms. Young complied with this request. Ms. Young stated that Ms. Nesmith's express purpose in having Ms. Young record this statement in the notebook was "to insure that Greenhalge would know that she wanted Ginny Clark to have that particular painting."

Ms. Nesmith's property in accordance with the will as amended, the 1972 memorandum as amended in 1976, and certain of the provisions contained in the notebook. [4] Greenhalge refused, however, to deliver the farm scene painting to Virginia Clark because the painting interested him and he wanted to keep it. Mr. Greenhalge claimed that he was not bound to give effect to the expressions of Helen Nesmith's wishes and intentions stated in the notebook, particularly as to the disposition of the farm scene painting. Notwithstanding this opinion, Greenhalge distributed to himself all of the property bequeathed to him in the notebook. Ms. Clark thereafter commenced an action against Mr. Greenhalge seeking to compel him to deliver the farm scene painting to her.

The probate judge found that Helen Nesmith wanted Ms. Clark to have the farm scene painting. The judge concluded that Helen Nesmith's notebook qualified as a "memorandum" of her known wishes with respect to the distribution of her tangible personal property, within the meaning of Article Fifth of Helen Nesmith's will. [5] The judge further found that the notebook was in existence at the time of the execution of the 1980 codicils, which ratified the language of Article Fifth in its entirety. Based on these findings, the judge ruled that the notebook was incorporated by reference into the terms of the will. The judge awarded the painting to Ms. Clark.

The Appeals Court affirmed. We allowed the appellee's petition for further appellate review and now hold that the probate judge correctly awarded the painting to Ms. Clark.

A properly executed will may incorporate by reference into its provisions any "document or paper not so executed and witnessed, whether the paper referred to be in the form of a mere list or memorandum, if it was in existence at the time of the execution of the will, and is identified by clear and satisfactory proof as the paper referred to therein." The parties agree that the document entitled "memorandum," dated 1972 and amended in 1976, was in existence as of the date of the execution of Helen Nesmith's will. The parties further agree that this document is a memorandum regarding the distribution of certain items of Helen Nesmith's tangible personal property upon her death, as identified in Article Fifth of her will. There is no dispute, therefore, that the 1972 memorandum was incorporated by reference into the terms of the will.

The parties do not agree, however, as to whether the documentation contained in the notebook, dated 1979, similarly was incorporated into the will through the

---

[4] Helen Nesmith's will provided that Virginia Clark and her husband, Peter Hayden Clark, receive $20,000.00 upon Helen Nesmith's death. Under the terms of the 1972 memorandum, as amended in 1976, Helen Nesmith also bequeathed to Virginia Clark a portrait of Isabel Nesmith, Helen Nesmith's sister with whom Virginia Clark had been acquainted. Greenhalge honored these bequests and delivered the money and painting to Virginia Clark.

[5] Article Fifth of Helen Nesmith's will reads, in pertinent part, as follows: "that Greenhalge distribute such of the tangible property to and among such persons *as I may designate by a memorandum left by me and known to him, or in accordance with my known wishes,* provided that said persons are living at the time of my decease" (Emphasis added).

language of Article Fifth. Greenhalge advances several arguments to support his contention that the purported bequest of the farm scene painting written in the notebook was not incorporated into the will and thus fails as a testamentary devise. The points raised by Greenhalge in this regard are not persuasive. First, Greenhalge contends that the judge wrongly concluded that the notebook could be considered a "memorandum" within the meaning of Article Fifth, because it is not specifically identified as a "memorandum." Such a literal interpretation of the language and meaning of Article Fifth is not appropriate.

"The 'cardinal rule in the interpretation of wills, to which all other rules must bend, is that the intention of the testator shall prevail, provided it is consistent with the rules of law.' " The intent of the testator is ascertained through consideration of "the language which the testatrix has used to express her testamentary designs," as well as the circumstances existing at the time of the execution of the will. The circumstances existing at the time of the execution of a codicil to a will are equally relevant, because the codicil serves to ratify the language in the will which has not been altered or affected by the terms of the codicil.

Applying these principles in the present case, it appears clear that Helen Nesmith intended by the language used in Article Fifth of her will to retain the right to alter and amend the bequests of tangible personal property in her will, without having to amend formally the will. The text of Article Fifth provides a mechanism by which Helen Nesmith could accomplish the result she desired; i.e., by expressing her wishes "in a memorandum." The statements in the notebook unquestionably reflect Helen Nesmith's exercise of her retained right to restructure the distribution of her tangible personal property upon her death. That the notebook is not entitled "memorandum" is of no consequence, since its apparent purpose is consistent with that of a memorandum under Article Fifth: It is a written instrument which is intended to guide Greenhalge in "distributing such of Helen Nesmith's tangible personal property to and among ... persons who are living at the time of her decease." In this connection, the distinction between the notebook and "a memorandum" is illusory.

The appellant acknowledges that the subject documentation in the notebook establishes that Helen Nesmith wanted Virginia Clark to receive the farm scene painting upon Ms. Nesmith's death. The appellant argues, however, that the notebook cannot take effect as a testamentary instrument under Article Fifth, because the language of Article Fifth limits its application to "a" memorandum, or the 1972 memorandum. We reject this strict construction of Article Fifth. The language of Article Fifth does not preclude the existence of more than one memorandum which serves the intended purpose of that article. As previously suggested, the phrase "a memorandum" in Article Fifth appears as an expression of the manner in which Helen Nesmith could exercise her right to alter her will after its execution, but it does not denote a requirement that she do so within a particular format. To construe narrowly Article Fifth and to exclude the possibility that Helen Nesmith drafted the notebook contents as "a memorandum" under that Article, would undermine our long-standing policy of interpreting wills in a manner which best carries out the known wishes of the testatrix. The evidence supports the conclusion that Helen Nesmith intended that the bequests in her notebook be accorded the same power and effect as those contained in the 1972 memorandum under Article Fifth. We conclude, therefore, that the judge properly accepted the notebook as a memorandum of Helen Nesmith's known wishes as referenced in Article Fifth of her will.

The appellant also contends that the judge erred in finding that Helen Nesmith intended to incorporate the notebook into her will, since the evidence established, at most, that she intended to bequeath the painting to Clark, and not that she intended to incorporate the notebook into her will. Our review of the judge's findings on this point proves the appellant's argument to be without merit. The judge found that Helen Nesmith drafted the notebook contents with the expectation that Greenhalge would distribute the property accordingly. The judge further found that the notebook was in existence on the dates Helen Nesmith executed the codicils to her will, which affirmed the language of Article Fifth, and that it thereby was incorporated into the will pursuant to the language and spirit of Article Fifth. It is clear that the judge fairly construed the evidence in reaching the determination that Helen Nesmith intended the notebook to serve as a memorandum of her wishes as contemplated under Article Fifth of her will.

Lastly, the appellant complains that the notebook fails to meet the specific requirements of a memorandum under Article Fifth of the will, because it was not "known to him" until after Helen Nesmith's death. For this reason, Greenhalge states that the judge improperly ruled that the notebook was incorporated into the will. One of Helen Nesmith's nurses testified, however, that Greenhalge was aware of the notebook and its contents, and that he at no time made an effort to determine the validity of the bequest of the farm scene painting to Virginia Clark as stated therein. There is ample support in the record, therefore, to support the judge's conclusion that the notebook met the criteria set forth in Article Fifth regarding memoranda.

We note, as did the Appeals Court, that "one who seeks equity must do equity and that a court will not permit its equitable powers to be employed to accomplish an injustice." To this point, we remark that Greenhalge's conduct in handling this controversy fell short of the standard imposed by common social norms, not to mention the standard of conduct attending his fiduciary responsibility as executor, particularly with respect to his selective distribution of Helen Nesmith's assets. We can discern no reason in the record as to why this matter had to proceed along the protracted and costly route that it did.

Judgment affirmed.

D. UNIFORM PROBATE CODE MEMO PROVISION

The drafters of the Uniform Probate Code have attempted to come up with a moderate solution for this problem, with authorization for a legally binding memo provision, executed and signed by the testator, which may give away various items of tangible personal property – not including land or money.

Remember that this memo provision in the UPC has been revised several times within the last twenty years, and that not all of the states which have adopted the UPC have adopted the memo provision of the UPC. So the version of the UPC which follows is not available in every state. But it could have been helpful if it had been adopted in Massachusetts at the time of the preceding case.

U.P.C. **§ 2-513. Separate Writing Identifying Bequest of Tangible Property.** Whether or not the provisions relating to holographic wills apply, a will may refer to a written statement or list to dispose of items of tangible personal property not otherwise specifically disposed of by the will, other than money, evidences of indebtedness, documents of title, and securities, and property used in trade or business. To be admissible under this section as evidence of the intended disposition, the writing must either be in the handwriting of the testator or be signed by him and must describe the items and the devisees with reasonable certainty. The writing may be referred to as one to be in existence at the time of the testator's death; it may be prepared before or after the execution of the will; it may be altered by the testator after its preparation; and it may be a writing which has no significance apart from its effect upon the dispositions made by the will.

On the following page you will find a sample memo pattern for use in a state which has adopted the UPC memo provision. Note that the pattern does not include reference to any specific will, or specific part of a will. This is an important safety precaution so that memos written by someone like Helen Nesmith, in the prior case, will continue to be valid whether or not Helen Nesbit executes a subsequent will.

Of course if Helen Nesmith, or any other testator decides to put some of the specific gifts into a new will, then the will controls over any attempted gift made of the same item in a prior or subsequent will. The UPC memo provision applies only to "items of tangible personal property not otherwise specifically disposed of by the will." And the UPC requires that the possibility of a memo must be mentioned in a valid will.

So the UPC memo provision is valuable for clients who have first written a formal will, and have mentioned the possibility of a memo in that will. The UPC does not validate the mere use of "stickies."

SAMPLE MEMO PATTERN

MEMORANDUM OF DISPOSITION OF TANGIBLE PERSONAL PROPERTY

Pursuant to the terms of my Will, I hereby make this Memorandum of Disposition of Tangible Personal Property.

Description of Items Tangible Personal Property	First Beneficiary	Second Beneficiary – if the first beneficiary is not alive when I die
____________________	________________	______________
____________________	________________	______________
____________________	________________	______________
____________________	________________	______________
____________________	________________	______________
____________________	________________	______________
____________________	________________	______________
____________________	________________	______________
____________________	________________	______________
____________________	________________	______________

If the first beneficiary and the second beneficiary listed for any item shall predecease me, then the attempted gift of that item shall lapse and that item shall be distributed in accordance with the terms of my Will.

__________________________ __________________________________

Date Signature

E. LIFE ESTATE & POWER TO CONSUME – THE RULE OF REPUGNANCY

What the testator attempted to do in the following case seems quite logical. But it turns out to be void, under the Rule of Repugnancy. How could you have drafted a valid provision which would have effectuated the testator's intent?

Supreme Court of Nebraska.
Gladys Pauline STERNER et al., Appellants,
v.
Leatha NELSON, Successor Personal Representative of the Estate of Mary Viola Rose, et al., Appellees.
Jan. 8, 1982.

KRIVOSHA, Chief Justice.

The instant case involves the construction of the last will and testament of Oscar Wurtele, deceased. The appellants appeal from a summary judgment entered by the District Court finding that the nature of the devise and bequest made by Oscar Wurtele to his wife, Mary Viola Wurtele, by his last will and testament was a fee simple absolute. We believe the trial court was correct and affirm the judgment.

The appeal herein arises out of the last will and testament of Oscar Wurtele, executed on August 4, 1939. While the will is simple and to the point, it is not a model for estate planners. It reads in total as follows:

> "I, the undersigned, Oscar Wurtele do hereby make, publish and declare the following as and for my Last Will and Testament:
>
> "I hereby give, devise and bequeath all of my property of every kind and nature to my wife Mary Viola Wurtele to be her property absolutely with full power in her to make such disposition of said property as she may desire; conditioned, however, that if any of said property is remaining upon the death of said Mary Viola Wurtele, or in the event that she predeceases me then and in such event such of said property as remains shall vest in my foster daughter Gladys Pauline Sterner and her children.
>
> "I hereby nominate and appoint my said wife, Mary Viola Wurtele, of Nebraska City, Nebraska, as executrix of this My Last Will and Testament.
>
> "Dated at Nebraska City, Nebraska, this 4th day of August, 1939. Oscar Wurtele."

this should have been in a trust

Following Oscar Wurtele's death in 1955 his will was admitted to probate. Certain of the property, including two commercial buildings, a farm, and a residence, were held in joint tenancy and passed to Mary Viola Wurtele by action of law and are not in any manner involved in this case. Two other commercial buildings, however, did pass to Mary Viola Wurtele by reason of the will of her husband, Oscar Wurtele, as well as certain personal property having an estimated value of $19,000. Mary Viola Wurtele thereafter married one Aaron Rose with whom she lived until her death on March 7, 1978. Mary Viola Rose died testate leaving her property to various individuals, including her husband, Aaron, and certain other nieces and nephews, but leaving no property to the appellants herein who are the foster daughter and her children referred to in the last will and testament of Oscar Wurtele. Aaron Rose died on June 24, 1979.

The evidence further discloses that in 1963 Mary Viola Rose sold the four commercial buildings for a total sale price of $70,000. No division of the sale price was made between the joint tenancy property and the property received under the will of her former husband. It is, however, clear from the evidence that none of the original property devised and bequeathed to Mary Viola Wurtele remained at the time of her death, though she did die owning property, some of which may have been purchased from the proceeds of either the personal property or the sale of the real estate. Following a hearing, the trial court found that the will of Oscar Wurtele devised and bequeathed all of his property to his wife, Mary Viola Wurtele, in fee simple absolute, and granted the personal representative's motion for summary judgment.

Appellants have raised a number of errors, but the principal issue which needs to be addressed is whether the devise and bequest by Oscar Wurtele to Mary Viola Wurtele was a fee simple absolute or merely a life estate with authority to dispose of so much of the property as she chose during her lifetime. For, obviously, if we conclude, as the trial court did, that the devise and bequest was a fee simple absolute, then Mary Viola Rose was entitled to do whatever she wished with her property, both during her lifetime and upon her death, and Gladys Pauline Sterner and her children would not be entitled to any portions of the property remaining at the death of Mary Viola Rose. While the issue as so stated is clear, the decisions of our court concerning this matter are not so clear.

The general and majority rule is as expressed in 28 Am.Jur.2d Estates (1966), wherein it provides in part: "It is a well-settled, general rule that where there is a grant, devise, or bequest to one in general terms only, expressing neither fee nor life estate, and there is a subsequent limitation over of what remains at the first taker's death, if there is also given to the first taker an unlimited and unrestricted power of absolute disposal, express or implied, the grant, devise, or bequest to the first taker is construed to pass a fee. The attempted limitation over, following a gift which is in fee with full power of disposition and alienation, is void. It is the well-settled rule that a general or indefinite grant or gift, coupled with an absolute or unlimited power of disposition, passes a fee even though the will purports to make a gift over of whatever may remain at the death of the grantee or devisee, the purported gift over merely being an invalid repugnancy."

In the case of Moffitt v. Williams we said: " 'It has been regarded by the courts that it is impossible to convey an absolute title to real estate in fee simple by deed or will, and at the same time in the same instrument convey to the same person a limited right or title in the same land. It therefore follows that when there was an attempt to do so, and no other disposition of the land was made in the will, the courts, on the theory that real estate must have an owner, rejected the attempt to convey the limited title, and treated the conveyance as of a fee simple title."

The settled rule of law is that, if a deed or will conveys an absolute title in fee simple, an inconsistent clause in the instrument attempting merely to limit that title or convey to the same person a limited title in the same land will be disregarded.

Cases may likewise be found in a majority of the jurisdictions which support the general rule. In the case of Moran v. Moran, the Michigan Supreme Court was presented a will which provided in part as follows: "I give and bequeath to my beloved wife ... all my property real and personal, of every name, nature and description to be hers absolutely, providing however, that if at her death any of the said property be still hers, then the residue still hers shall go to my, not her, nearest heir or heirs." The court held that such language created a fee simple absolute in the wife and the provision for the property remaining was void and unenforceable.

While this might at first blush seem to make the disposition of this matter relatively easy, unfortunately there are cases to be found in Nebraska which appear to hold to the contrary. The principal case is Merrill v. Pardun, (1933). In Merrill, the testator's will provided in part as follows: "I give and bequeath to my wife, Maggie Brown, all the rest, residue and remainder of my property of whatever kind and wherever situated to be hers absolutely. It is my request, however, that any of said property remaining on the death of my said wife, shall go to my daughter, Mildred I. Merrill, to be hers absolutely and in case of her prior death then to her children, share and share alike." This court held that the conveyance was simply a life estate with the power to dispose during one's lifetime. In so holding, we said in Merrill "The general rule under the common law is that, where an estate in fee simple is given in one clause of a will, subsequent clauses attempting to cut down said estate would be void; but in Nebraska, on account of the peculiar provisions of our statute regarding the intentions of the testator, in construing a will it is held that, where a will in one clause makes an apparently absolute bequest of property, but in a subsequent clause makes a further bequest of the remainder after the death of the legatee taking under the first clause, the two clauses are to be construed and considered together to ascertain the true character of the estate in fact granted by the first clause; and in such case, contrary to the ancient rule at common law, the second clause is effective and operative to define and limit the estate granted by the first to and as a life estate with power of disposition, and the second is effective and operative to grant an estate in remainder in the unused, unexpended or undisposed property granted for life by the first."

However, neither the rationale of the Merrill case nor the earlier decisions seems to justify abandoning the general common-law majority rule for what appears to have developed as the Nebraska rule.

Both the statute, s 76-205, and the common law provide that in attempting to ascertain the true intent of the testator you cannot ignore the rules of law applicable to a situation. A testator may intend to violate the rule against perpetuities in his will. The statute, nevertheless, cannot permit such action even if the testator's intent to that effect is absolute and clear.

It is the general rule that a grant or devise of real estate to a designated person in fee simple, with provisions therein that are inconsistent or repugnant thereto such as a restriction against the power to sell, mortgage, or otherwise encumber, conveys an absolute fee and such restrictions are void. One of the primary incidents of ownership of property in fee simple is the right to convey or encumber it. It is the general rule that a testator may not create a fee simple estate to vest at his death and at the same time restrict alienation thereof.

"We do not say that a testator may not create a vested fee simple estate subject to a condition subsequent, or a determinable or defeasible fee. What we do say is that a restriction against alienation of a vested fee simple estate is not any one of these, nor, since it is void, can it be used as the sole basis for the creation of any of these estates. A restraint on alienation in the form of a condition subsequent, forfeiting or terminating the fee simple estate, or providing for a limitation over upon breach of the condition, is void. The right of alienation is inherent in the vested fee simple estate and it arises by virtue of the fact that such an estate is created."

In the instant case it is not possible to reconcile the devise given by Oscar Wurtele to his wife, on the one hand, and the expression of desire concerning his foster daughter, on the other.

The grant to Mary Viola Wurtele was clear and unambiguous. She was to have the property to "be her property absolutely with full power in her to make such disposition of said property as she may desire." That intent is clear. By having the property as hers "absolutely" and with "full power" to "dispose" of the property as she may desire, she had not only the right to sell or give away the property during her lifetime but the right to will the property upon her death as well. Anything less would not have granted her the property "absolutely" with "full power in her to make such disposition" as she desired. The authority given was not limited to sale or disposition during her lifetime, but rather was to be absolute.

A life tenant cannot dispose of property by will, and the sale of the property often does not constitute a "disposition" but only a change in form.

No reason is given to us nor are we able to find any on our own as to why the majority rule following the common law should not be the rule in this jurisdiction. Certainly the reason suggested by the court in the Merrill decision, to wit, the particular nature of our statute, is not very persuasive. If the testator does not desire for the devisee to have a fee simple, it is easy enough to say so. But having once granted the devise or bequest in language which standing alone constitutes an absolute conveyance, the balance of the limitations should be disregarded, regardless of the intent of the testator, on the basis that the intent is in conflict with the first grant. Either a devisee has received the property absolutely or the devisee has not received the property absolutely. Like honesty, morality, and pregnancy, an absolute devise cannot be qualified.

To be sure, a testator can give less than an absolute grant, as was done in the case of Annable v. Ricedorff, where the testator provided his property to his wife " 'to her own use and benefit forever; and it is my desire and wish that after her death, that all the property remaining' " go to his children. In such a case it can be argued that only a life estate was granted to the wife for her use and benefit during her lifetime. But where, as here, the devise is "absolute," we can reach no other conclusion but that the grant was a fee simple. As such, it is without qualification regardless of what the testator may intend.

We, therefore, now adopt the majority rule to the effect that where there is a grant, devise, or bequest to one in general terms only, expressing neither fee nor life estate, and there is a subsequent limitation over of what remains at the first taker's death, if there is also given to the first taker an unlimited and unrestricted power of absolute disposal, express or implied, the grant, devise, or bequest to the first taker is construed to pass a fee. The attempted limitation over, following a gift which is in fee with full power of disposition and alienation, is void. To the extent that our previous decision in Merrill and cases of similar import are to the contrary, they are overruled.

Having thus concluded that the trial court was correct in ruling that the devise and bequest by Oscar Wurtele to his wife, Mary Viola Wurtele, was as a matter of law a fee simple absolute, there remained no question of fact to be resolved and the trial court was correct in granting summary judgment. The judgment of the trial court, therefore, is affirmed.

F. "SURVIVES"

The word "survives" would not seem to be a particularly troublesome word – and yet it frequently raises important questions. Survives whom? Survives until when? Is survival by five minutes sufficient?

All of these issues should be clearly spelled out in the particular testamentary documents. The choices are up to the client – with advice from the lawyer.

But if the client has not made any specific provisions as to the exact meaning of "survives," then most states have a default provision, similar to the UPC provision set forth below.

UPC § 2-601. Requirement That Devisee Survive Testator by 120 Hours.

A devisee who does not survive the testator by 120 hours is treated as if he predeceased the testator, unless the will of decedent contains some language dealing explicitly with simultaneous deaths or deaths in a common disaster, or requiring that the devisee survive the testator or survive the testator for a stated period in order to take under the will.

G. PER STIRPES, BY REPRESENTATION, OR PER CAPITA AT EACH GENERATION

(1) DESCRIPTION OF PER STIRPES, BY REPRESENTATION, AND PER CAPITA AT EACH GENERATION

When a testator gives property to his or her descendants, as a group, it is likely that the testator will choose one of three usual forms of distribution: per stirpes; by representation; or per capita at each generation.

Per stirpes just means "by the root," and the distribution of property will always be based on the number of people in the generation closest to the testator – (or a specifically designated person) - whether or not anyone in that generation is still alive at the death of the testator. Clients sometimes select this form of distribution as a way of treating the families of their children equally. The family of each child of the testator will get the same size share.

If all of the children of the testator survive the testator there will be no difference between distribution per stirpes and distributions using either of the other two methods. However, if at least one of the testator's children predeceases the testator, then it will matter which form of distribution is selected by the testator.

If ALL of the children of the testator predecease the testator, and the testator has selected "by representation" as the method of distribution, then the testator's property will be divided into equal shares for each of the *grandchildren who survive the testator, plus one share for each grandchild who predeceased the testator, but left issue who survived the testator.* This method of distribution is attractive to testators who want to treat the grandchildren equally. Each surviving grandchild will get the same share, no matter how many siblings the grandchild may have.

One easy way to remember the distinction between per stirpes and by representation is that the "arrow" indicating at which generation the shares will be cut *stays* at the closest level to the testator when the distribution is per stirpes.

When the distribution is made by *representation* the arrow roams to the closest generation in which there is someone alive.

The third method of distribution, per capita at each generation, is usually a refinement of the by representation method of distribution. Under per capita at each generation, the shares are cut at the closest level to the testator in which at least one person survived the testator. Then the shares of any people in that closest generation who died before the testator, but who left issue surviving, are combined and then sent down to the next generation, to be distributed in equal shares to all of the great-grandchildren, for example, whose parents were not alive to get a share. That way each of these great-grandchildren will get the same size share, per capita.

With all three methods of distribution no share is ever cut for anyone who predeceased the testator and did *not leave any issue who survived the testator.* In other words, *you never cut a share if there is no one to whom that share can be given.*

Also, with all three methods, no child ever takes a share if his or her parent is alive to take a share.

If you try to explain all of this to clients in words, they will generally not have any idea what you are saying. However, if you draw them pictures, and explain the differences, they seem to have no difficulty in making a choice.

The following case makes it clear that the attorney who is drafting a will should be certain about the intent of the testator, so that the will can make it clear which generation is to serve as the "root" for a distribution which is to be made per stirpes. Usually, plain English is the best solution.

(2) WHERE IS THE ROOT?

Court of Chancery of Delaware.
Re: In re Trust Under WILL Dated August 14, 1997 Created by Elizabeth Haskell FLEITAS.
Decided: Nov. 30, 2010.

WILLIAM B. CHANDLER III, Chancellor.

I. BACKGROUND

Before the Court are cross-motions for summary judgment.

Valerie and Elizabeth are sisters; their mother was Elizabeth Fleitas ("Fleitas"), whose will and trust are at the heart of this dispute.

On August 14, 1997, Fleitas executed her Will in which she created the Trust with Wilmington Trust Company ("Trustee"). The testamentary Trust language is at issue here. Fleitas died on July 12, 1999, bequeathing her estate by the distribution scheme prescribed in her Will. At the time of Fleitas's death, she had two living daughters, Elizabeth and Valerie, and four living adult grandchildren, all of whom were Valerie's children. Fleitas's other daughter, Elizabeth, had no children at the time of Fleitas's death. On May 5, 2009, almost ten years after Fleitas's death, Elizabeth adopted a seven-year-old daughter, Kaylee.

A. Procedural History

On August 14, 2009, the petitioner Wilmington Trust Company ("WTC") filed a verified petition for instructions asking this Court to interpret the Trust distribution language. WTC believes that the Will's language is ambiguous as to the generational level at which the per stirpital division of the beneficial Trust interest should first occur.

On June 9, 2010, Elizabeth and Kaylee filed a motion for summary judgment, seeking a judicial declaration that, as a matter of law, the initial per stirpes distribution of the Trust assets at issue begins with Elizabeth and Valerie, the testatrix's daughters. On the same day, Valerie's children also filed a motion for summary judgment, seeking judicial determination that, as a matter of law, the initial per stirpes distribution of the Trust assets at issue begins with the testatrix's five grandchildren.

B. The Will Language Regarding the Trust

A few articles of the Will are relevant to my discussion, some being the actual testamentary Trust text for which the parties have diverging interpretations, and some being other parts of the Will that may indicate Fleitas's intent. I will examine each separately.

I begin with Article 5.

Article 5, Paragraph C, states as follows with reference to Fleitas's Trust:

> For so long after my death as both of my daughters, VALERIE FLEITAS JOHNSON and ELIZABETH H. FLEITAS, are living, Trustee shall distribute forty percent (40%) of the net income to each daughter, and shall distribute the balance of the net income to such of my issue more remote than children as are living from time to time, *per stirpes.* On the death of the first of my daughters to die or, on my death, if only one daughter survives me, Trustee shall distribute fifty percent (50%) of the net income to such surviving daughter during the remainder of her life, and shall distribute the balance thereof to such of my issue more remote than children as are living from time to time, *per stirpes.* On the death of the survivor of my daughters and me, Trustee shall distribute the net income to such of my issue as are living from time to time, *per stirpes.*

Article 5, Paragraph D, states as follows with reference to Fleitas's Trust:

> Upon the termination of the trust period ... such property shall vest in interest in my then living issue more remote than children, *per stirpes* ... Trustee shall continue to hold and administer the trust property as follows: If both my daughter, VALERIE FLEITAS JOHNSON, and my daughter ELIZABETH H. FLEITAS, are then living, Trustee shall distribute forty percent (40%) of the net income to each daughter, and Trustee shall distribute the balance of the net income to such of my issue more remote than children as are living from time to time, *per stirpes.* On the death of the first of my daughters to die or, upon the termination of the trust period if only one daughter is then living, Trustee shall distribute fifty percent (50%) of the net income to such surviving daughter and the balance thereof to such of my issue more remote than children as are living from time to time, *per stirpes.*

The dispute regarding Paragraph D is like that regarding Paragraph C. One interpretation, which favors Kaylee, is that the initial division of the Trust property in the per stirpes scheme occurs at the generational level directly below the testatrix, namely with her daughters Elizabeth and Valerie. This would entitle Kaylee right now to one-half of the 20% balance of the Trust income reserved for Fleitas's "issue more remote than children" and Valerie's four children to the other one-half of the 20% balance. It would also entitle Kaylee's line of heirs to half of the vested interest in the Trust corpus after the Trust terminates.

The second interpretation, which favors Valerie's children, is that the initial division of the Trust property in the per stirpes scheme occurs at the generational level of Fleitas's grandchildren, including Kaylee and the other grandchildren. This interpretation provides each grandchild with one-fifth of the 20% beneficial Trust income while Elizabeth and Valerie are alive and one-fifth of the vested interest in the

Trust principal once the Trust terminates and Fleitas's daughters die.

C. The Will Language in the Personal Property, Residuary, and Definitions Sections

In Article 1 of the Will ("Personal Property Provision"), concerning tangible personal property, the testatrix directs her personal property to be divided between Valerie and Elizabeth "in such manner as they agree in as nearly equal shares as practicable." Article 1 also provides that if either daughter predeceases Fleitas "but is represented by children who survive me, such children shall take, equally, the share which such deceased daughter would otherwise have taken had she survived me." Fleitas directs her personal property to be divided per capita among her grandchildren if both her daughters predecease her.

Article 5, Paragraph B ("Pecuniary Gifts Provision"), which is part of the Trust provisions, provides $1 million to Valerie and $1 million to Elizabeth, assuming they survive Testatrix. Paragraph B also provides $100,000 to each living grandchild or to the living issue of a grandchild that predeceases testatrix, per stirpes.

Article 6 ("Residue Provision"), which concerns the residue of Fleitas's estate, divides the residue in equal shares between Elizabeth and Valerie "and to the issue, *per stirpes,* of either of them who predeceases me but is represented by issue who survive me." This Article divides the residue of testatrix's estate equally between Elizabeth's line of heirs and Valerie's line of heirs.

Importantly, Article 17, the definitions section of the Will, defines "per stirpes" thusly: "In applying any provision of this my Will which refers to a person's issue, 'per stirpes,' the children of that person are the heads of their respective stocks of issue, whether or not any child is then living." The Will's definition of "issue, per stirpes" is consistent with Delaware's statute, 12 Del. C. § 3301(g)(3) (2008), which states that "issue" shall denote a distribution per stirpes, such that the children of the person whose issue is referred to shall be taken to be the heads of the respective stock of issue and that adopted persons such as Kaylee are considered issue of the adopting person. This means that in Delaware, children of a testator or testatrix are the heads of the stirpes, absent a different intent explicitly conveyed by the testator or testatrix. Therefore, under the Will's definitions section, a distribution to Fleitas's "issue, per stirpes" makes Fleitas's *children* the heads of the respective stock of issue.

II. ANALYSIS

The issue here is straightforward: in the Will, do the phrases "my issue more remote than children as are living from time to time, *per stirpes,*" "my issue as are living from time to time, *per stirpes,*" and "my then living issue more remote than children, *per stirpes,*" make Elizabeth and Valerie the stirpital roots of the Trust distribution or alternatively make Fleitas's grandchildren the stirpital roots. Elizabeth and Kaylee argue that, under the clear language of the Will, Elizabeth and Valerie are the heads of the stirpes, regardless of their position as non-takers of the 20% Trust interest. Valerie's children argue that Fleitas's grandchildren are the heads of the stirpes because they are the first possible takers of the 20% Trust balance, and testatrix Fleitas intended to treat all her grandchildren equally as a class, as evidenced in other paragraphs of the Will.

When language in a written instrument is potentially ambiguous regarding a per stirpes distribution, this Court applies the following test:

> A testator's intent, unless unlawful, shall prevail; that intent shall be ascertained from a consideration of (a) all the language contained in his will, and (b) his scheme of distribution, and (c) the circumstances surrounding him at the time he made his will, and (d) the existing facts, and (e) canons of construction will be resorted to only if the language of the will is ambiguous or conflicting or the testator's intent is for any reason uncertain.

In deciding whether parol evidence should be considered, I must first determine if the language in the Will is ambiguous. "Ambiguity exists when the terms in question 'are reasonably or fairly susceptible of different interpretations or may have two or more different meanings.' " Ambiguity does not exist merely because parties disagree on proper construction of the words in a written instrument. Absent a double meaning in the Will language, I must take the Will to mean what it says, not what I suppose it was meant to say. Furthermore, "if a mistake was made in the writing of the will ... this court has no power to correct a mistake, and it cannot, by introduction of parol evidence, rewrite the will." "Extrinsic evidence can do no more than explain language and show intent, but cannot furnish an intent itself which the language does not do."

Both parties argue that the Will is clear and unambiguous, but both argue for different interpretations of the phrases containing the "per stirpes" language. The dispute between the parties is one over the interpretation of the words regarding which generation represents the heads of stock in the stirpital distribution of the Trust assets, not over any double meaning. In light of the Will's definitions section, which explicitly designates the heads of stock to be the testatrix's daughters, the only reasonable interpretation of the Will read in its entirety is that Elizabeth and Valerie are the stirpital roots. Furthermore, the meaning of the phrases at issue, considering Fleitas's equal distribution between Elizabeth's and Valerie's lines of heirs in various articles of the Will and canons of construction under 12 Del. C. § 3301, is clear and unambiguous. Since no ambiguity exists in the language, I need not resort to extrinsic evidence.

Having determined that no ambiguity exists in the Will, I now must interpret the Will's terms as written. It is undisputed that the first generation that qualifies as "issue more remote than children" or "then living issue more remote than children" are Fleitas's grandchildren. The Will's definitions section, Article 17, aids the Court in understanding Article 5's plain language. It states that when determining a person's issue per stirpes, "the children of that person are the heads of their respective stocks of issue."

The distinction between an equal distribution among heirs under a Will and a per stirpes distribution is clear. " 'Equal shares' denotes per capita distribution." On the other hand, "those who take per stirpes are substituted heirs who collectively take the share of the deceased ancestor." Therefore, a per stirpes distribution indicates that descendants take the share that their parent would have taken, had the parent been alive. Looking only within the four corners of the Will, I conclude that the testatrix, by her inclusion of the definitions section, understood that her daughters would be the heads of the stock. Had Fleitas clearly indicated that she wanted a per capita distribution of the Trust income and corpus, then I would conform my analysis to that intention.

As a preliminary matter, an equal division among the grandchildren is essentially a "per capita" distribution for the purposes of that generation. The Will mandates a per stirpes distribution in the definitions section, which states that in a per stirpes distribution, "the children [Elizabeth and Valerie] of that person [Fleitas] are the heads of their respective stocks of issue." The existence of this definitions section makes it unequivocally clear that Fleitas understood what "per stirpes" meant and that she did not intend for an equal distribution among the first generation qualifying as her "issue more remote than [her] children."

Four separate provisions in the Will indicate Fleitas's intent to treat her daughters and her daughters' lines of descendants equally: Article 1 (the Personal Property Provision), Article 6 (the Residue Provision), Article 5, Paragraph B (the Pecuniary Gifts Provision), and Article 5, Paragraph D (containing Fleitas's devise when one or both of her daughters die).

1. Personal Property Provision

In Article 1, the Will provides that the testatrix's personal property should be divided between Valerie and Elizabeth in "as nearly equal shares as practicable." That paragraph provides that if one daughter predeceases Fleitas but the deceased daughter has living children, those children (i.e., Fleitas's grandchildren) "shall take, equally, the share which such deceased daughter would otherwise have taken had she survived me [Fleitas]." This indicates that Fleitas understood the difference between equitable divisions of her personal property, for which she willed equally between her two daughters, versus taking by representation, for which she willed among her grandchildren.

It is also evident that Fleitas knew the difference between a per capita and per stirpes distribution based on her use of the term "issue" versus "children" or "grandchildren" in the different clauses of her Will. Article 1 states that if *both* Elizabeth and Valerie predecease her, Fleitas's personal property should be divided among "such of my grandchildren who survive me, *per capita.* " This statement indicates that Fleitas understood that "per capita" means equally, and she specifically wanted her personal belongings to be divided equally among her grandchildren who could bequeath those items as they pleased in their respective wills. Had Fleitas wanted the 20% Trust balance to be likewise distributed to her grandchildren equally, she would have provided that her grandchildren take equal shares and that the issue of any deceased grandchild take per stirpes the share that that deceased grandchild would have taken if he or she were alive. The Will does not state this, and I cannot now redraft the Will to implement something that was not Fleitas's intent. Therefore, the Personal Property Provision serves as additional evidence that the Will, taken as an entirety, was intended to divide Fleitas's assets equally between her two daughters' lines of heirs, unless otherwise stated. This provision also demonstrates Fleitas's understanding of the distinction between "per capita" and "per stirpes" and demonstrates that she did not intend to treat her grandchildren as a class concerning the Trust distribution.

2. Residue Provision

Article 6 of the will provides for "equal shares to such of my children [Fleitas's daughters] ... who survive me, and to the issue, *per stirpes,* of either of them who predeceases me but is represented by issue who survive me." I agree that Article 6 provides an equal distribution of Fleitas's residue assets to her two daughters. Under this language, Valerie and Elizabeth are clearly the heads of their respective stocks of issue and will each receive 50% of the residue. Upon the deaths of Elizabeth and Valerie, their children will then receive a fractional portion of their mothers' interest in the residue.

Assuming, for the sake of argument, that Valerie had predeceased the testatrix but Elizabeth had survived her, under the Residuary Provision, Elizabeth would receive 50% of the residue, and Valerie, having died, would pass her 50% interest in the residue to her issue, per stirpes, that is, to her four children. Kaylee would get none of the residue until Elizabeth died. Under the Respondents' argument that the heads of the stirpes should be the grandchildren, however, Elizabeth would get 50% of the interest in the residue and the five grandchildren, including Kaylee, would evenly divide up the other half of the residue. This scheme does not make sense, considering Kaylee is a "substituted heir" and should not take until Elizabeth can no longer take. Contrary to respondents' argument, the Residue Provision further supports the reading that "issue, per stirpes" throughout the Will means that the stirpital roots lie with Elizabeth and Valerie, *not* with Fleitas's grandchildren.

3. Pecuniary Gifts Provision of Article 5

Article 5, Paragraph B, provides $1 million to each of Fleitas's children and $100,000 to each of her grandchildren, "and if any one or more of my [Fleitas's] grandchildren is then deceased with issue then living, to the then living issue, *per stirpes,* of each such deceased grandchild of mine." This bequest again indicates Fleitas's understanding of the distinction between an equal distribution and a per stirpes distribution. For this particular provision only, Fleitas bequeaths $100,000 per capita to each of her grandchildren.

This provision also indicates Fleitas's intent to treat her two daughters equally, giving them both $1 million. The equal bequests to her grandchildren, which are substantially smaller than those to her daughters, only suggest that Fleitas intended to treat all of Valerie's children, the only grandchildren who existed at the time of Fleitas's death, equally; it has no bearing on what the testatrix might have bequeathed had she known Elizabeth would have a child. The Pecuniary Gifts Provision treats Fleitas's grandchildren equally and their issue, per stirpes, taking what their parents have by representation; the Trust language in Paragraphs C and D treat Elizabeth and Valerie equally and their issue, per stirpes, taking by representation of what their mothers would have *if they could take* (which they cannot). The Pecuniary Gifts Provision therefore reinforces the argument that Fleitas intended for the heads of the stirpital distribution of the Trust to be her daughters and that she understood the meaning of per stirpes.[6]

4. Article 5, Paragraph D

Finally, Article 5, Paragraph D itself provides an indication of how Fleitas intended to divide her Trust assets. Paragraph D provides that when one of Fleitas's daughters dies or at the termination of the Trust period, if only one of Fleitas's daughters is alive, the surviving daughter will get 50% of the Trust income, and the other 50% goes to Fleitas's "issue more remote than children as are living from time to time, *per stirpes.*" Paragraph D also says that, if no issue more remote than her children are alive at the termination of the Trust period, the Trust property goes equally to Elizabeth and Valerie if they are alive. Under Paragraph D, if Valerie had predeceased Fleitas, Elizabeth would take 50% of the Trust income, and Valerie's children would evenly divide the other 50%. This provision indicates that Fleitas intended to divide the Trust interest between her two daughters' lines of heirs equally, whether they were both alive or one died; the daughter that died first would pass her 50% share by dividing that share evenly among her children. Therefore, Article 5, the actual Trust provision, also indicates Fleitas's intent to treat both her daughters' lines of heirs equally.

Under the Will's clear terms, the initial division of the 20% net balance of the Trust income occurs with Elizabeth and Valerie, daughters of the testatrix.

III. CONCLUSION

Based on the definitions section in Fleitas's Will and Delaware statutory law, I conclude that Elizabeth and Valerie, as daughters of the testatrix, are the heads of the stirpital distribution of Fleitas's Trust. In applying a per stirpes distribution with Elizabeth and Valerie as the heads of the stirpes, I treat Elizabeth and Valerie as having predeceased the testatrix for purposes of the 20% balance of the Trust interest because they are not entitled to that 20%. Therefore, Kaylee will receive one-half of the 20% Trust income balance, or 10% of the total Trust income presently and her line of heirs will receive 50% of the Trust corpus once the Trust period terminates and Elizabeth

---

[6] Respondent Beneficiaries argue that this equal distribution of pecuniary gifts among grandchildren indicate Fleitas's intent to treat her grandchildren equally. There are many equally plausible reasons, however, why Fleitas would have wanted a per stirpes distribution to begin with her daughters, one being that the testatrix possibly thought that a grandchild without siblings would have less financial support. I will not delve into these possible reasons because I do not think it is necessary; the plain words of the Will speak for themselves.

and Valerie die. Valerie's four children will share the other one-half of the 20% Trust income balance, each receiving 2.5% of the total Trust income presently and each receiving 12.5% of the Trust corpus following the termination of the Trust period and both Elizabeth's and Valerie's deaths.

IT IS SO ORDERED.

H. "YOUNGEST" WHEN?

Normally, the phrase, "when my youngest grandchild reaches the age of 21," would seem to be fairly clear. However, the following case illustrates that there may be at least four different ways in which that simple phrase could be interpreted. So an attorney must always be careful to spell out youngest – when?

Supreme Court of Rhode Island.
Anthony J. Lux, Jr., as Executor u/w Philomena Lux v. Donna M. Lux et al.
March 21, 1972
OPINION BY: KELLEHER

The artless efforts of a draftsman have precipitated this suit which seeks the construction of and instructions relating to the will of Philomena Lux who died a resident of Cumberland on August 15, 1968. We hasten to add that the will was drawn by someone other than counsel of record.

Philomena Lux executed her will on May 9, 1966. She left her residuary estate to her husband, Anthony John Lux, and nominated him as the executor. Anthony predeceased his wife. His death triggered the following pertinent provisions of Philomena's will:

> "*Fourth*: In the event that my said husband, Anthony John Lux, shall predecease me, then I make the following disposition of my estate: ...
>
> "2. All the rest, residue and remainder of my estate, real and personal, of whatsoever kind and nature, and wherever situated, of which I shall die seized and possessed, or over which I may have power of appointment, or to which I may be in any manner entitled at my death, I give, devise and bequeath to my grandchildren, share and share alike.
>
> "3. Any real estate included in said residue shall be maintained for the benefit of said grandchildren and shall not be sold until the youngest of said grandchildren has reached twenty-one years of age.
>
> "4. Should it become necessary to sell any of said real estate to pay my debts, costs of administration, or to make distribution of my estate or for

any other lawful reason, then, in that event, it is my express desire that said real estate be sold to a member of my family."

Philomena was survived by one son, Anthony John Lux, Jr., and five grandchildren whose ages range from two to eight. All the grandchildren were children of Anthony. The youngest grandchild was born after the execution of the will but before Philomena's death. The son is named in the will as the alternate executor. He informed the trial court that he and his wife plan to have more children. At the time of the hearing, Anthony was 30. The Superior Court appointed a guardian ad litem to represent the interests of the grandchildren. It also designated an attorney to represent the rights of individuals who may have an interest under the will but who are at this time unknown, unascertained or not in being.

At the time of her death, the testatrix owned real estate valued at approximately $35,000 and tangible and intangible personal property, including bank accounts, that totaled some $7,400. The real estate consists of two large tenement houses located in Cumberland. The sole dispute is as to the nature of the devise of the real estate. Did Philomena make an absolute gift of it to the grandchildren or did she place it in trust for their benefit? The guardian takes the view that the grandchildren hold the real estate in fee simple. All the other parties take a contrary position.

Admittedly, the language before us is unclear. Accordingly, it is the duty of this court to ascertain the testator's intent as it is expressed in the will having in mind the circumstances surrounding its formulation and effectuate that intent so long as it is not contrary to law.

From the record before us, we believe that Philomena intended that her real estate be held in trust for the benefit of her grandchildren. In reaching this conclusion, we must emphasize that there is no fixed formula as to when a testamentary disposition should be classified as an outright gift or a trust. The result reached depends on the circumstances of each particular case.

looking @ circumstances

We are not unmindful of the formal requirements necessary for the creation of a testamentary trust. It is an elementary proposition of law that a trust is created when legal title to property is held by one person for the benefit of another. It is generally accepted that such a relationship cannot be created by will unless the beneficiaries of the trust are identifiable. However, no particular words are required to create a testamentary trust. The absence of such words as "trust" or "trustee" is immaterial where the requisite intent of the testator can be found. A trust never fails for lack of a trustee.

The guardian contends that the testatrix has vested in the grandchildren an absolute and unconditional title to her real and personal property and that any subsequent conditions which purport to limit such an estate are repugnant and void.

When the residuary clause in the instant case is viewed in its entirety, it is clear that Philomena did not give her grandchildren a fee simple title to the realty. It appears that she, realizing the nature of this bequest and the age of the beneficiaries, intended that someone would hold and manage the property until they were of sufficient age to do so themselves. The property is income-producing and apparently she felt that the ultimate interest of her grandchildren would be protected if the realty was left intact until the designated time for distribution. The use of the terms "shall be maintained" and "shall not be sold" is a strong indication of Philomena's intent that the property was to be retained and managed by some person for some considerable time in the future for the benefit of her son's children. This is a duty usually associated with a trustee. We therefore hold that Philomena's will does create a trust on her real estate.

Having found the trust, the question of who shall serve as trustee is easily answered. The general rule is that, unless a contrary intention appears in the will or such an appointment is deemed improper or undesirable, the executor would be named to the position of trustee.

Before determining the individuals who may benefit from Philomena's benevolence, it should be noted that the residuary devise to the grandchildren is a class gift [7] which in no way violates the rule against perpetuities. The rule, in seeking to insure the free administration of property, requires that interests must vest, if at all, within a life or lives in being at the time of the creation of the future interest plus twenty-one years thereafter including an allowance for the period of gestation in those instances where there is a posthumous birth. The person whose life serves as the measuring rod need not be mentioned in the will, nor need he take any interest in the property. He need not be connected in any way with the property or the persons designated to take it. The life in being is Philomena's son. No grandchild will be born to the testatrix once her son dies with a possible exception of an allowance being made for the gestation period.

The ascertainment of time within which a person who answers a class description such as "children" or "grandchildren" must be born in order to be entitled to share in a testator's bounty is not an easy matter. In seeking a solution, the court must seek to effectuate the testator's intent. We have said that where there is a testamentary gift to a class, persons who take are to be ascertained at the testator's death unless the will expressly or impliedly directs otherwise. Accordingly, depending upon the circumstances of each case, the class may be closed as of the date of the execution of the will, at the termination of an intervening life interest, or when there is no possibility of the birth of additional children or grandchildren.

The rationale for permitting a class to increase in size until the time for distribution

---

[7] A testamentary class gift is a gift to a group whose number at the time of the gift is uncertain but which will be ascertained at some future time when all who constitute the class will take an equal or other definite portion, the amount of the share of each being dependent upon the number that ultimately constitutes the class.

stems from a judicial recognition that generally, when a testator describes the beneficiaries of his bounty by some group designation, he has in mind all those persons whenever born who come within the definition of the term used to describe the group. Normally, if he had in mind the individual members of the designated group, he would have described them by name. This recognition is tempered by the presumption that testators usually would not intend to keep the class open at the expense of an indefinite delay in the distribution of the estate. Since there is no good reason to exclude any person who is born before the period of distribution, all such persons are, in the absence of a contrary testamentary intent, deemed to be members of the class.

Despite our invocation of the rule requiring the class to remain open until the corpus is distributed, we still must determine what Philomena intended when she said that the corpus has to be preserved until the "youngest grandchild" becomes twenty-one.

There are four possible distribution dates depending on the meaning of "youngest." Distribution might be made when the youngest member of the class in being when the will was executed attains twenty-one; or when the youngest in being when the will takes effect becomes twenty-one; or when the youngest of all living class members in being at any one time attains twenty-one even though it is physically possible for others to be born; or when the youngest whenever it is born attains twenty-one. This last alternative poses a question. Should we delay distribution here and keep the class open until the possibility that Philomena's son can become a father becomes extinct? We think not.

We are conscious of the presumption in the law that a man or a woman is capable of having children so long as life lasts. A construction suit, however, has for its ultimate goal the ascertainment of the average testator's probable intent if he was aware of the problems that lead to this type of litigation. It is our belief that the average testator, when faced with the problem presented by the record before us, would endorse the view expressed in 3 *Restatement, Property § 295, comment k* which states:

> "When all existent members of the class have attained the stated age, considerations of convenience * * * require that distribution shall then be made and that the property shall not be further kept from full utilization to await the uncertain and often highly improbable conception of further members of the group. The infrequency with which a parent has further children after all of his living children have attained maturity, makes this application of the rule of convenience justifiable and causes it to frustrate the unexpressed desires of a conveyor in few, if any, cases."

We hold, therefore, that distribution of the trust corpus shall be made at any time when the youngest of the then living grandchildren has attained the age of twenty-one. When this milestone is reached, there is no longer any necessity to maintain the trust to await the possible conception of additional members of the class.

Although Philomena declared that the real estate was not to be sold until the youngest grandchild became twenty-one, her later statements about the necessity of its sale amounted to her awareness that future circumstances might require the liquidation of her real estate sometime prior to the time her youngest grandchild becomes twenty-one. The Superior Court was informed and documentary evidence was introduced which showed such a precipitous drop in the rental income as would warrant a trustee to seek a better investment.

Section 18-4-2(b) provides that in the absence of any provision to the contrary, every trust shall be deemed to have conferred upon the trustee a discretionary power to sell the trust estate, be it real or personal property. Section 18-4-10 specifically authorizes a trustee, whenever he believes it desirable to sell trust property, to seek the Superior Court's approval for such a transaction.

When the real estate is sold, the proceeds from such sale shall, because of the doctrine of the substitute res, replace the realty as the trust corpus.

The impending sale brings into focus the testatrix's "express *desire* that said real estate be sold to a member of my family." (Emphasis added) The words "express desire" are purely precatory. We have said that precatory language will be construed as words of command only if it is clear that the testator intended to impose on the individual concerned a legal obligation to make the desired disposition. We think it clear that since Philomena's primary goal was to benefit her grandchildren, we see nothing in the record that would justify a conclusion that she intended that the potential purchasers of her real estate be limited to the members of her family.

Finally, we come to the allocation of income. The will is silent as to this item. Over a half-century ago, we said that if the will shows no intention on the part of the testator that income be accumulated, income is payable to the beneficiary as it accrues. This rule has been reaffirmed on many occasions. Should Philomena's son's hope for additional progeny become a reality, the quantum of each share of income received by a grandchild would be reduced as each new member of the class joins his brothers and sisters.

The parties may present to this court for approval a form of judgment in accordance with this opinion.

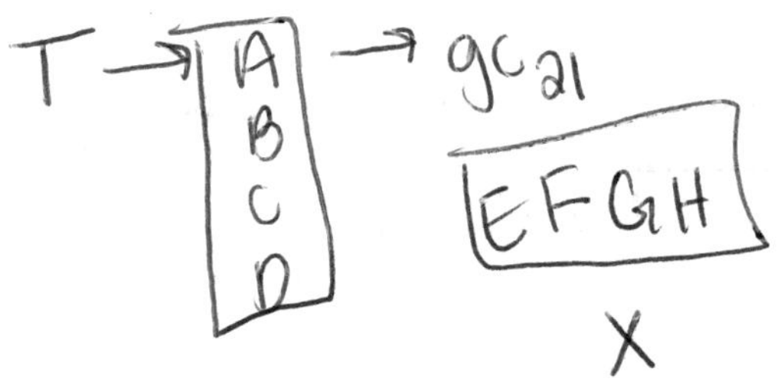

CHAPTER 11 – CONTINUING CONTROL OF PROPERTY AFTER DEATH - FUTURE INTERESTS

A. THE BASICS OF FUTURE INTERESTS

As you have noticed, nearly every will or trust includes some sort of future interest. So it should be helpful to review the fundamentals now.

There are only five kinds of future interests:

(1) Reversions
(2) Possibilities of Reverter
(3) Rights of Entry
(4) Remainders
(5) Executory Interests.

The first three of these (Reversions, Possibilities of Reverter, and Rights of Entry), are all created in the grantor, and are not subject to the Rule Against Perpetuities. Only the last two kinds of future interests, (Remainders and Executory Interests), are created in a third person – not the grantor. And only the last two, Remainders, and Executory Interests, are subject to the Rule Against Perpetuities.

Here is a brief definition of each of these interests.

(1) REVERSION

A reversion is simply what is left in the grantor, after he has given away less than he had – (as long as the interest left in the grantor does not meet the special requirements of a Possibility of Reverter, or a Right of Entry.) Here are some examples. In each example assume that G, the grantor, started off with full ownership of the land, a fee simple absolute.

EXAMPLE: G gives land "To A for life."

Under this example A will have a life estate, and G will have a reversion. When A dies, the land will go back to G. While A is still alive, G could sell his reversion to B. Then, when A died, B would have a right to the land. A reversion is an interest which remains in the grantor when the grantor creates some other interest in a third party. In the example above, a reversion is what is left in G when G creates a life estate in A, but then doesn't specify what is to happen when A dies. After A is granted a life estate, all the rest of the interest in the land remains in G, who thus has a reversion.

Once the reversion comes into existence in G, the reversion can be sold or given to another person – and it will still be called a reversion. The reversion just has to start off as the "leftovers" that remain in the grantor.

Any time the grantor gives away less than he has, he retains a reversion – *unless* the grantor specifically provided that the retained interest was a possibility or reverter or a right of entry.

(2) POSSIBILITY OF REVERTER

A Possibility of Reverter is an interest which remains in the grantor after he has given away a "fee simple determinable."

EXAMPLE: The grantor gives land, "To the University of Denver so long as the land is used for law school purposes, and when no longer used for law school purposes, then to revert to me."

This grant would create a "fee simple determinable" in DU, and would leave a Possibility of Reverter in the grantor. The interest created in DU is some sort of fee interest, because it might last forever. It is a fee simple determinable because it will automatically end, or "determine," whenever DU stops using the land for law school purposes. So the interest created in DU is a fee simple determinable. And what is left in the grantor – the possibility of getting the land back if DU stops using the land for law school purposes sometime in the future – is called a Possibility of Reverter. In most states, the grantor, after creating a Possibility of Reverter in himself, could convey the Possibility of Reverter to another person – and the interest would still be a Possibility of Reverter, (and not subject to the Rule Against Perpetuities), because it was originally *created* in the grantor.

A few states do not allow a Possibility of Reverter to be conveyed, but nothing serious happens if the grantor tries to convey a Possibility of Reverter in those states. The Possibility of Reverter just bounces back to the grantor.

When the grantor dies, if the grantor has not successfully conveyed the Possibility of Reverter, then the Possibility of Reverter will simply be part of the grantor's estate.

In any case, when the specified event happens, such as DU no longer using the land for a law school, the land will *automatically* revert back to whoever then owns the Possibility of Reverter.

(3) RIGHT OF ENTRY (also called a Power of Termination)

This looks a lot like a Possibility of Reverter, but the law treats it very differently.

EXAMPLE: The grantor gives land "to A, *but if* liquor is ever sold on the land, then I have a *right to re-enter* and take the land back."

not automatic

By this provision the grantor has created a "fee simple subject to condition subsequent" in A, and has retained a Right of Entry in himself.

The interest in A in this example might last forever, and that is why it is some sort of a fee interest. But since it may be ended, if anyone sells liquor on the land, the interest created in A is called a "fee simple subject to condition subsequent."

Notice that with a right of entry the grantor has to DO something to get the land back. It will NOT come back to the grantor automatically. This may be a good thing, for the grantor, if it turns out that the land is filled with toxic substances when A sells that bottle of liquor. At that time, after inspecting the land, the grantor might decide that he doesn't want the land back after all, with all the possible expenses of clean-up under the provisions of CERCLA. So the grantor might just decide NOT to assert his right of entry – and thus leave A with ownership of the land. Usually, under the applicable statute of limitations, the grantor has about two years to decide whether or not to assert the right of entry.

Another important thing to remember about a right of entry is that at common law, any attempt to convey a right of entry will DESTROY it! So if a grantor, after retaining a right of entry in himself, tries to sell the right of entry to B, the whole right of entry self-destructs – and A will then have full ownership of the land, a fee simple absolute, instead of just a fee simple subject to condition subsequent. \ FSA

Remember, no one of the three future interests described above is subject to the Rule Against Perpetuities – so, in the absence of some special statute, each of the interests might last forever.

Now for a discussion of the remaining two future interests, the ones which are created in a third person, and are subject to the Rule Against Perpetuities. These two interests are Remainders, and Executory Interests.

(4) REMAINDERS

A remainder is an interest created in a third person, (not the grantor). A remainder nearly always is the interest that follows a life estate, when the property goes on to a third person, (not the grantor), after the death of the life tenant.

EXAMPLE: If the grantor gives land, "To A for life, then to B," the grantor has created a life estate in A, and a remainder in B.

There are four different kinds of remainders, and it is important to know the difference between them, because different rules apply to each of them. The four types of remainders are: Contingent; Vested; Vested Subject to Open; and Vested Subject to Divestment. Here are some examples.

(a) CONTINGENT REMAINDER

EXAMPLE: "To A for life, then to A's children."

If A *doesn't yet have any children*, then the remainder in A's children will be contingent – contingent on the children being born. *Any remainder in unborn, or unascertained people, will always be a contingent remainder.*

You may also have a contingent remainder if there is some condition which has to be met before the remainderman is entitled to the remainder – some condition *other* than just the death of the person who has the life estate.

For example, if the grantor says, "To A for life, then *if* B graduates from law school, to B" that would create a life estate in A, and a contingent remainder in B *until* B graduates from law school. As soon as B graduates from law school, even though A is still alive, B's remainder becomes a *vested* remainder, because there is no longer anything that has to happen before B gets the land – except the death of A. If B happens to die before A dies, B's vested remainder will be part of B's estate.

In both of these examples, while the remainder is contingent, there is also a *reversion* in the grantor –
If it turns out that A never has any children, or if B never graduates from law school.

(b) VESTED REMAINDER

EXAMPLE: "To A for life, then to B."

This remainder in B is called a vested remainder. B doesn't have to do anything to get the remainder – except wait for A to die. And if B dies before A, the vested remainder will be part of B's estate. So B has a vested remainder – we know who he is, and he doesn't have to do anything except wait for A to die.

(c) REMAINDER WHICH IS VESTED SUBJECT TO OPEN

EXAMPLE: "To A for life, then to A's children" - IF A already has at least one child.

Since all that A's children have to do to be entitled to the remainder is to be A's children, then as soon as each child is born, that child has a vested remainder. But since more and more children may be born to A, the remainder in each of A's children is considered to be vested subject to open – subject to letting in more children, as each new child is born to A.

As long as this remainder stays *open*, as long as more people might enter the class, is has *not yet complied with the Rule Against Perpetuities.*

(d) REMAINDER WHICH IS VESTED SUBJECT TO DIVESTMENT

EXAMPLE: "To A for life, then to B, but if B ever goes skiing when she should be in Trusts & Estates class, then to C."

This creates a life estate in A; a remainder in B which is vested subject to divestment; and a shifting executory interest in C. B's interest is vested, because we know who B is, and she doesn't have to do anything before she gets the gift. But, if B goes skiing when she should be in class, then the remainder will be taken away from her – it will be divested. So B has a remainder which is vested, subject to divestment.

The interest C has is called a *shifting executory interest* – because it will *shift* from B to C if B cuts class to go skiing. An executory interest is the *only* interest, in a third party, that can follow a previously vested estate.

(5) EXECUTORY INTERESTS - SHIFTING & SPRINGING

There are two kinds of executory interests – shifting and springing. A *shifting* executory interest *shifts* from one grantee to another grantee. A *springing* executory interest *springs* from the grantor, over an interval of time, to a grantee. Needless to say, you will hardly ever find a *springing* executory interest that was created on purpose. It is usually found in cases in which a court is trying to save an attempted gift someone tried to make in a will, when the will is void because it doesn't have enough witnesses. In order to save the gift, the court may hold that the attempted gift was really just a springing executory interest – created in a document that was actually a deed, not a will. So springing executory interests are extremely rare.

But shifting executory interests are used frequently. In addition to the example given above, in which C has a shifting executory interest that will take effect if B cuts class to go skiing, there are two other kinds of shifting executory interests.

If the grantor creates a fee simple determinable, and then, instead of retaining a possibility of reverter in himself, he says that if the land is no longer used by DU for a law school, for example, it will go to CU, then the grantor will have created a shifting executory interest in CU. As soon as DU stops using the land for a law school, the ownership of the land will shift to CU.

Likewise, in theory, a shifting executory interest could follow a fee simple subject to condition subsequent, though there are some cases that say that would not be allowed, because the right to re-enter must only be created in the original grantor. In a jurisdiction which does allow a shifting executory interest to follow a fee simple subject to condition subsequent, the provision might be worded as follows: Grantor conveys land "To Denver, to be used for park purposes, *but if Denver* ever builds a two-story building on the land, then the Audubon Society has a right to enter, and become owner of the land." In this example, the Audubon Society would have a shifting executory interest, following a fee simple subject to condition subsequent which was created in Denver.

Notice that in both these examples of shifting executory interests a solid line of charities was used. (All schools, cities, hospitals, etc. are considered to be charities, whether or not they are profit-making institutions.) So the executory interest shifts, at some uncertain time, from one charity to another. That is permissible under the Rule Against Perpetuities – which does not apply to a solid line of charities.

But if any person or entity involved with a shifting executory interest is *not* a charity, then the Rule Against Perpetuities says that the shifting executory interest is *void* unless it is certain, from the time the shifting executory interest is created, that the shifting executory interest will either vest *in possession*, or fail, within the time allowed by the Rule Against Perpetuities. The time allowed by the Rule Against Perpetuities is a life in being at the creation of the interest, plus 21 years.

The Rule Against Perpetuties (RAP), will be covered in more detail later in Chapter 12. For now, just remember that Reversions, Possibilities of Reverter, and Rights of Entry are not subject to RAP. All of the other future interests must vest, if at all, within the time allowed by RAP. And executory interests must become vested *in possession* within the time allowed by RAP.

The following case illustrates why it is important to be able to distinguish a vested remainder from a contingent remainder.

B. CASE ON LIFE ESTATES AND REMAINDERS

Court of Appeal of California.
Estate of HAROLD EVANS WOODWORTH, Deceased. WELLS FARGO BANK, N.A., as Trustee, etc., Petitioner and Respondent, v. THE REGENTS OF THE UNIVERSITY OF CALIFORNIA, Claimant and Appellant; JAMES V. WOODWORTH et al., Claimants and Respondents.
September 10, 1993

OPINION BY: DIBIASO

The Regents of the University of California (Regents) appeal from an order of the probate court which rejected their claim to the remainder of a testamentary trust. We will reverse. We will apply the common law preference for early vesting and hold that, absent evidence of the testator's intent to the contrary, the identity of "heirs" entitled to trust assets must be determined at the date of death of the named ancestor who predeceased the life tenant, not at the date of death of the life tenant.

STATEMENT OF CASE AND FACTS

Harold Woodworth died testate in 1971. His will was thereafter admitted to probate; in 1974 a decree of distribution was entered. According to this decree, a portion of the estate was distributed outright to the testator's surviving spouse, Mamie Woodworth. The balance of the estate was distributed to Mamie Woodworth and the

Bank of America, to be held, administered and distributed in accord with the terms of a testamentary trust established by the will of Harold Woodworth. The life tenant of the trust was Mamie Woodworth. Among the trust provisions was the following:

> "This trust shall terminate upon the death of Mamie Woodworth. Upon the termination of this trust, my trustee shall pay, deliver and convey all of the trust estate then remaining, including all accrued and/or undistributed income thereunto appertaining, to Elizabeth Woodworth Plass, [Elizabeth Plass] whose present address is 90 Woodland Way, Piedmont, California, if she then survives, and if not then to her heirs at law."

Elizabeth Plass was the testator's sister; he also had two brothers who predeceased him. One died without issue. The other was survived by two children, Elizabeth Woodworth Holden, a natural daughter, and James V. Woodworth, an adopted son.

Elizabeth Plass died in 1980; she was survived by her husband, Raymond Plass. Raymond Plass died testate in 1988. In relevant part, he left the residue of his estate to the Regents for use on the university's Berkeley campus.

Mamie Woodworth, the life tenant, died in 1991. Thereafter, Wells Fargo Bank, as successor trustee of the Woodworth trust, petitioned the probate court pursuant to *Probate Code section 17200* to determine those persons entitled to distribution of the trust estate. The petition alleged that "The petitioner was uncertain as to whether Elizabeth Plass's 'heirs at law' should be determined as of February 14, 1980, the date of her death, or August 13, 1991, the date of Mamie Woodworth's death."

It is undisputed that (1) as of February 14, 1980, Elizabeth Plass's heirs at law were her husband, Raymond Plass; her niece, Elizabeth Woodworth Holden; and her nephew, James V. Woodworth; and (2) as of August 13, 1991, Elizabeth Plass's heirs at law were Elizabeth Woodworth Holden and James V. Woodworth (the Woodworth heirs).

The probate court concluded that the identity of the heirs entitled to the trust assets must be determined as of the date of death of the life tenant. The probate court therefore ordered the trustee to deliver the remaining trust assets in equal shares to the Woodworth heirs.

1. *ISSUES.*

The Regents contend the probate court erroneously failed to apply the general rule of construction which requires that the identity of "heirs" entitled to take a remainder interest be determined as of the date of death of the denominated ancestor, in the absence of any contrary intent expressed by the testator. Had the probate court construed the decree in accord with this principle, the Regents would have been entitled to share in the trust assets as a residuary legatee of Raymond Plass, an heir at law of Elizabeth Plass at the time of her death in 1980.

The Woodworth heirs respond by asserting the probate court's decision is consistent with an exception to the general rule which requires that the determination be made at the date of death of the life tenant. Under this principle, the Regents have no interest in the trust assets, because Raymond Plass predeceased Mamie Woodworth. [1]

2. *THE EARLY VESTING RULE.*

Estate of Liddle reflects the common law preference for vested rather than contingent remainders. Thus, unless a particular instrument disclosed a different intent on the part of the testator, a remainder to a class of persons, such as children, became vested in the class when one or more of its members came into existence and could be ascertained, even though the class was subject to open for future additional members. Furthermore, the fact that takers of a postponed gift were described by a class designation did not, under the common law rule, give rise to any implied condition of survival.

The circumstances involved in *Liddle* are substantially indistinguishable from those of the present case. In *Liddle*, the remainder of a testamentary trust was to be distributed to the testatrix's attorney or, in the event of his death, the attorney's heirs at law. Although the attorney survived the testatrix, he predeceased the life tenant. The attorney's only heir, his wife, died intestate several years before the death of the life tenant. The wife's heirs and the administrator of her estate clashed with certain remote cousins of the attorney over the ownership of the trust assets.

The appellate court ruled in favor of the wife's estate. The court construed the phrase "heirs at law" according to its technical meaning, that is, the person or persons who are entitled to succeed to the property of an intestate decedent. The rule was summarized as follows: "Normally, when a gift has been made to the 'heirs' or 'next of kin' of a named individual, the donor has said in effect that he wants the property distributed as the law would distribute it if the named person died intestate. Accordingly, the normal time for applying the statute of descent or distribution is at the death of the named individual. This is, however, merely a rule of construction, and if the testator or grantor manifests an intention that the statute be applied either at an earlier or a later time, such intention will be given effect."

The designated ancestor in *Liddle* was the attorney. Because his wife was his intestate heir at the time he died, the court found she was the proper recipient of the trust estate.

---

[1]It is undisputed that had the testator in this case died on or after January 1, 1985, the Regents would have no claim to the trust assets. Under *Probate Code sections 6150* and *6151*, which have been in effect since 1985, a devise of a future interest to a class, such as heirs, includes only those who fit the class description at the time the legacy is to take effect in enjoyment.

3. *THE CONTINGENT SUBSTITUTIONAL GIFT EXCEPTION.*

On the other hand, *Wells Fargo Bank* reflects the application of an exception to the early vesting principle. In *Wells Fargo Bank*, a woman had conveyed, by a grant deed, a life estate in certain real property to her daughter, with remainders to the grantor's two other children. If the life tenant died without issue and the two other children died without issue before the grantor's death, the instrument provided that the remainder interest in the property would belong to the grantor's "heirs."

Because the remainder to the other children or their issue was contingent upon their surviving the life tenant, the court held the substitutional gift to the heirs was also contingent, thereby requiring the identification of the class members as of the death of the life tenant: "In this type of case . . . the class of heirs is determined upon termination of the trust because the question whether the testator's heirs would take at all having been postponed until the resolution of contingency, the question of the identity of the heirs has likewise been deemed to have been postponed by the testator."

4. *APPLICATION.*

The will of Harold Evans Woodworth created a contingent remainder in Elizabeth Plass, with a substitutional gift to her heirs at law. Although it appears we are therefore free to choose between *Liddle* and *Wells Fargo Bank*, in reality this is not so; the contingent, substitutional gift exception to the rule of early vesting applies only to grants of remainder interests which differ materially from the one now before us.

An authority relied upon is Simes & Smith, The Law of Future Interests. "Where a testator devises a life estate or defeasible fee to *a person who is one of his heirs*, followed by a remainder or executory interest to the testator's heirs in such circumstances, some courts have rejected the general rule that the members of the class are to be determined at the death of the ancestor (i.e., the testator), and instead have applied an exception which identifies the heirs who will take the remainder as those in being upon the death of the holder of the life estate or defeasible fee. The rationale for these decisions is an assumption the testator did not intend to give both a present and a future interest to the same person."

Thus, we believe the exception to the general rule of early vesting, as implemented in *Wells Fargo Bank*, should not be applied to the remainder interest contained in the decree of distribution here.

5. *OTHER CONSIDERATIONS.*

First, the fact that the university, an entity, is not a relative of Elizabeth Plass or one of her heirs at law is not material. We are unwilling to say that application of the general rule "would result in thwarting the expressed intention of the Grantor by distributing the corpus of the trust to persons or entities other than Elizabeth Plass's heirs."

It would be pure speculation for us to conclude that Harold Woodworth would not have wanted Raymond Plass to inherit a portion of the trust assets. It appears from the record that Raymond Plass and Elizabeth Plass were married at the time the testator executed his will. It has long been the law in California that a husband is an heir of his deceased wife. Nothing in the record forecloses the possibility the testator took into account the fact that Elizabeth Plass might predecease, and Raymond Plass might outlive, Mamie Woodworth, resulting in Raymond Plass's succession to a portion of the trust remainder.

Second, the rule of construction which favors descent according to blood in cases of ambiguity in testamentary dispositions should not determine the result in this case. The general rule favoring early vesting was well established long before the testator died. We do not think it should be abandoned in order to carry out some purportedly perceived, but entirely speculative, notion about the intent of the testator based upon events which occurred well after the testator's death. As we noted earlier, it is perfectly conceivable that Harold Woodworth took into account in making his will the possibility that his property would pass to Raymond Plass and thereafter be transferred to strangers to the Woodworth line.

In the absence of any firm indication of testamentary intent, the rules of construction must be implemented in order to ensure uniformity and predictability in the law, rather than disregarded in order to carry out a court's ad hoc sense of what is, with perfect hindsight, acceptable in a particular set of circumstances.

The crucial question in this case is whether the language imposes a survivorship condition to membership in the class of Elizabeth Plass's heirs. We have determined it does not.

Last, none of the other exceptions identified in *Wells Fargo Bank* to the early vesting rule applies under the circumstances of this case. This is not a situation where the ". . . life tenant is the sole heir, but the will devises the remainder to the testator's 'heirs.' "

In addition, the language does not contain any "expression of futurity in the description of the ancestor's heirs" When, as here, "the gift is in terms 'then to the heirs' of a designated person, the word 'then' merely indicates the time of enjoyment and has no significance in relation to the rule of early vesting."

Finally, and contrary to the contention of the Woodworth heirs, we do not find the words "pay to" contained in the will to be equivalent to the word "vest" or otherwise constitute an "expression of futurity" for purposes of determining the identity of the relevant heirs. Rather, the instruction pertains to the time when the recipients of the assets are entitled to have them.

DISPOSITION

Accordingly, we must reverse the probate court's ruling that the Regents have no claim to the assets of the testamentary trust.

The judgment appealed from is reversed.

C. CASE ON POSSIBILITY OF REVERTER

The next case illustrates how a feisty grandmother, appearing pro se, used a possibility of reverter to defeat a major financial institution in 2008. Enjoy.

Court of Appeals of South Carolina.

GREEN TREE SERVICING, LLC, Plaintiff
v.
Reniata L. WILLIAMS a/k/a Reniata Garvin Williams, Defendant,
and
Green Tree Servicing, Respondents,
v.
Lueveania Garvin, Appellant.
Decided Feb. 20, 2008. Certiorari Denied July 23, 2009.

Lueveania Garvin, for Appellant.

Pearce Fleming, Randolph Whitt, and Martha Phillips, all of Columbia, for Respondents.

HUFF, J.:

Lueveania Garvin appeals the order of the special referee holding her interest in certain property was subject and junior to Green Tree's mortgages and that she was not entitled to damages for trespass. We reverse and remand.

FACTUAL/PROCEDURAL BACKGROUND

In September of 1995, Garvin deeded .23 acres of property to her granddaughter, Reniata Williams. The deed provided the property was to be used for residential purposes and further provided:

> In the event Reniata L. Garvin Williams shall fail to use said property for residential purposes for a consecutive period of sixty (60) days or more, the aforementioned property shall revert back to Grantor or Grantor's heirs and assigns, in fee simple.

Thus, the interest Garvin transferred to Williams was a fee simple determinable while she retained a possibility of reverter.

Williams subsequently obtained two notes secured by mortgages on the property. Garvin was not a party to these mortgages. Williams had a mobile home placed on the property. The mobile home encroached onto Garvin's property by six feet.

On June 1, 2004, Williams wrote to Garvin that she no longer resided on the property and in recognition of the condition in the deed, she wished to return the property to Garvin.

Green Tree then brought this action for foreclosure of the mortgages in August of 2004. In an order filed December 30, 2004, the special referee ordered foreclosure of the mortgages. Garvin was not named a party to the action at this time. In April of 2005 Garvin wrote to Green Tree stating she would charge it $25.00 a day storage fee effective June 1, 2004 for the mobile home on her property. She explained $10.00 a day was for the part of the mobile home on the far end of her yard previously deeded to Williams and $15.00 a day was for the part of the mobile home that extended into her front yard.

Green Tree subsequently filed a petition for a rule to show cause requesting the court to order Garvin to show cause why she should not be bound by the previous order and determine whether Garvin's interest was junior to Green Tree's mortgages. The court issued the rule as requested. Garvin answered asserting that Green Tree executed the mortgages with knowledge of the possibility of reverter. She also asserted a claim for trespass.

After a hearing on the matter, the special referee held Garvin had no estate in the property until the possibility of reverter was triggered, which was after Green Tree had perfected its mortgage. Thus, the referee held Garvin's interest in the property was subject and junior to Green Tree's mortgage that was already in place when she acquired an estate in the property. In addition, the referee held that as Garvin had submitted no evidence of any diminution in the market value of her property due to the mobile home's presence on her property, she was not entitled to damages for trespass. However, the referee did order Green Tree to remove the trailer from Garvin's property. This appeal followed.

LAW/ANALYSIS

1. Mortgages

Garvin argues the special referee erred in holding her interest in the property was subject to and junior to Green Tree's mortgages. We agree.

A fee simple determinable is a grant that can be cut short when a given term expires. "It is an estate in fee 'with a qualification annexed to it by which it is provided that it must determine whenever that qualification is at an end.'" The wording of the grant allows for defeasance of the grantee upon the terms, covenants and conditions of the grant. A possibility of reverter is the future interest that accompanies a fee simple determinable. In the case of a possibility of reverter, the possessory estate vests immediately and automatically upon the happening of the event whereby the determinable or conditional fee is terminated.

Although the grantee of a fee simple determinable may transfer or assign the estate, the determinable quality of the estate follows the transfer or assignment. The determinable fee may be mortgaged, subject to the qualification. The creator of the estate would have to join in the mortgage to subject the entire fee interest to the lien.

The deed granting Williams the fee simple determinable estate was duly recorded and was referred to in the mortgage. Green Tree was on notice of the nature of the estate. *See* S.C.Code Ann. § 30-9-30 (2007) (stating recording of instrument is notice to all persons, sufficient to put them upon inquiry of the purport of the filed instrument and the property affected by the instrument. Notice of a deed is notice of its whole contents. Garvin never joined in the mortgages and the mortgages were subject to the determinable quality of the estate. When the determinable fee was terminated, Green Tree's interest in the property terminated. Therefore, the special referee erred in holding Garvin's interest in the property was subject to Green Tree's mortgages.

2. Trespass

Garvin argues the special referee erred in holding her claim for trespass failed. We agree.

If a plaintiff establishes a willful trespass, the damages from invasion of the plaintiff's legal rights will be presumed sufficient to sustain the action even though such damages may be only nominal and not capable of measurement. Thus, Garvin did not need to establish a diminution in value to her property to maintain her claim for trespass. We reverse the order of the special referee and remand the trespass claim for further proceedings.

CONCLUSION

We reverse the special referee's holding that Garvin's interest in the property was subject and junior to Green Tree's mortgages. We further reverse the special referee's ruling on Garvin's trespass claim and remand for further proceedings consistent with this opinion.

REVERSED AND REMANDED

D. CASE ON SHIFTING EXECUTORY INTERESTS

The following case is a fairly dramatic illustration of the use of a shifting executory interest, to try to enforce the provisions of a charitable gift. The final resolution seems excellent, but it will not always be available in every state.

Court of Appeal, California.
CITY OF PALM SPRINGS, Plaintiff and Respondent,
v.
LIVING DESERT RESERVE, Defendant and Appellant.
March 3, 1999.

McKINSTER, J.

standard stuff

Not infrequently, wealthy individuals, intending both to promote the common weal and to memorialize themselves, give property to a city on the condition that it be used in perpetuity for some specified purpose. With disturbing regularity, however, the city soon tires of using the donated property for the purpose to which it agreed when it accepted the gift, and instead seeks to convert the property to some other use.

In this case, for instance, the City of Palm Springs (City) built a golf course on 30 acres of donated property which it had accepted in 1986 on the express condition that it be used in perpetuity as a desert wildlife preserve. The trial court reluctantly approved. We reverse.

Factual and Procedural Background

In June of 1986, the Bank of America, as trustee of the McCallum Desert Foundation (Foundation) under the will of Pearl M. McManus, deceased, executed a grant deed conveying 30 acres of land to the City. The Deed provides:

> "This Deed Is Made and Accepted on the Express Condition that the land hereby conveyed be used solely as the site of the McCallum Desert Preserve and Equestrian Center, and that grantee, its successors or assigns shall forever use the land and premises for the purpose of maintaining a public park for the exposition of desert fauna and flora, named as the McCallum Desert Preserve and Equestrian Center.
>
> "In the event that the property is not used solely and perpetually as the site of the McCallum Desert Preserve and Equestrian Center, then the interest in the land and premises herein conveyed shall pass to the Living Desert Reserve, Palm Desert, California, and grantee shall forfeit all rights thereto."

The City expressly accepted the grant in October of 1986. Less than three years later, however, the City decided that it would rather build a golf course on the Land. Believing that the golf course would be inconsistent with the condition in the Deed, the City asked the Living Desert for permission to buy other property for use as a preserve instead of the Land. Those negotiations continued periodically without success. The City's final offer was made in November of 1992, when it offered to buy the Living Desert's reversionary interest in the Land for $200,000 and threatened to take the interest by eminent domain if the Living Desert did not agree.

After the Living Desert declined that offer, the City adopted a resolution of necessity by which it found that the public health, safety and welfare required the acquisition of the Living Desert's reversionary interest in the Land for the purpose of expanding the City's municipal golf course. In March of 1993, the City filed a complaint in eminent domain by which it sought to do so. Simultaneously, the City applied for an order for immediate possession of the reversionary interest within 30 days, relying on an appraisal valuing that interest at $200,000 and on a deposit in an equal amount. The trial court granted the application and issued the order for immediate possession.

In October of 1993, the Living Desert recorded a notice of breach of condition subsequent. The notice alleges that the City breached the conditions of the Deed by (1) adopting the resolution by which it declared the necessity of acquiring the reversionary interest to permit the golf course expansion and (2) implementing that resolution by filing its eminent domain action and obtaining an order for immediate possession. In the same month, the Living Desert cross-complained against the City to quiet title to the Land. It alleged that, as a result of the City's breach of the conditions and the notice of that breach, the fee simple interest of the City in the Land had reverted to the Living Desert.

The parties stipulated that the issues of whether (1) the reversionary interest held by the Living Desert is a compensable interest and (2) the City had breached the conditions of the Deed would be bifurcated from and tried before the issue of the amount of any compensation due for the reversionary interest.

The trial court ruled that the reversionary interest was not a compensable interest and hence no payment was due to the Living Desert, and entered judgment in favor of the City.

The Living Desert appeals. The Attorney General of the State of California appears as an amicus curiae.

Contentions of the Parties

In its opening brief, the Living Desert contends that the trial court erred by relying on Code of Civil Procedure section 1265.410, to determine that the reversionary interest was not compensable. Specifically, it argues that the statute does not apply to efforts by a condemner to relieve itself of the obligation to comply with conditions accompanying a gift of property, and that if it does, the statute permits the taking of property without just compensation, in violation of the federal and state Constitutions.

The Attorney General contends that the Foundation gave the Land to the City in a charitable trust, not in fee simple subject to a condition subsequent, that the effect of the judgment was to terminate that trust, and that therefore the judgment must be reversed because the trial court lacked subject matter jurisdiction to terminate a charitable trust.

Discussion

A. *The Deed Granted a Fee Simple Subject to a Condition Subsequent.*

The Attorney General raises a fundamental issue: What is the nature of the interests created by the Deed? Was the Land given to the City in trust, or in fee simple subject to a condition subsequent?

"A charitable trust is a fiduciary relationship with respect to property arising as a result of a manifestation of an intention to create it, and subjecting the person by whom the property is held to equitable duties to deal with the property for a charitable purpose." The elements essential to its creation are a proper manifestation by the settlor of an intention to create a trust, a trust res, and a charitable purpose promoting the welfare of mankind or the public at large, of a community, or of some other class of persons which is indefinite as to numbers and individual identities

The legal title of the res or corpus of any trust is held by the trustee, but the beneficiaries own the equitable estate or beneficial interest. In the event of a breach of duty by the trustee of a private trust, the beneficiaries may sue the trustee for damages and for an equitable decree enforcing the trust. But because a charitable trust has an indefinite class of beneficiaries, standing to enforce the trust is generally limited to the Attorney General as the representative of the public.

"However, a gift may have a charitable purpose and yet not constitute a charitable trust." Rather than create a trust, the owner of property may transfer it to another on the condition that if the latter should fail to perform a specified act the transferee's interest shall be forfeited either to the transferor or to a designated third party. "In such a case the interest of the transferee is subject to a condition subsequent [2] and is not held in trust."

A gift of property in fee subject to a condition subsequent differs from a gift of that same property in trust in at least two ways. First, the transferee of a conditional gift receives both legal and equitable title to the property. Unless and until the transferee breaches the conditions imposed by the transferor, he or she is in the same position as an owner in fee simple absolute. Second, the transferee has no enforceable duties. The breach of condition may result in the termination of the transferee's interest, but it does not subject the transferee to actions for damages or to enforce the condition.

"Whether a trust or a condition is created depends upon the manifested intention of the transferor; the mere fact that the word 'condition' is used does not necessarily indicate that a condition and not a trust is intended." Trusts can be created by words of condition. Property given "upon condition" that it be applied to certain charitable purposes is especially likely to be construed as having been given in a charitable trust. The question in each case is whether (1) the donor intended to provide that if the property were not used for the designated charitable purposes it should revert either to the donor's estate or to a contingent donee, or (2) the donor intended to impose an enforceable obligation on the donees to devote it to those purposes.

Courts favor the construction of a gift as a trust over a conditional gift for several reasons. Because forfeiture is a harsh remedy, any ambiguity is resolved against it. Moreover, the transferor's objective is to use the transferee to confer a benefit upon the public. To ensure that the benefit is conferred as intended, the transferor ordinarily wants the intended beneficiary to be able to enforce that intent. Because the only remedy for the breach of a condition is a forfeiture, a condition is not a very effective method of accomplishing those goals. For both of those reasons, courts will generally

---

[2] Under the common law, there were two types of defeasible estates: a fee simple determinable, the reversionary interest of which was the possibility of reverter; and a fee simple subject to a condition subsequent, the reversionary interest of which was the right of reentry. The distinctions between these two defeasible estates were statutorily abolished by the adoption of Civil Code section 885.020 in 1982. All defeasible fees *in California* are now known as fees simple subject to a condition subsequent, and all executory interests reserved by the grantor after granting such fees are known *in California* as powers of termination.

construe a conveyance as one upon trust rather than upon condition.

However, if the donor clearly manifests an intention to make a conditional gift, that intention will be honored. The gift will be construed as one of a fee simple subject to a condition subsequent if " it is expressly provided in the instrument that the transferee shall forfeit it or that the transferor or his heir or a third person may enter for breach of the condition."

The Deed in this case expressly states the Foundation's intent that, in the event of a breach of the condition, the transferee (City) shall forfeit its interest in favor of a third party (the Living Desert). Accordingly, the Deed must be construed as granting to the City a fee simple subject to a condition subsequent, and assigning to the Living Desert a power of termination.

B. *Because the Deed Did Not Create a Charitable Trust, the Attorney General Is Not a Necessary Party to the Action.*

Under the Uniform Supervision of Trustees for Charitable Purposes Act, "the primary responsibility for supervising charitable trusts in California, for insuring compliance with trusts and articles of incorporation, and for protection of assets held by charitable trusts and public benefit corporations, resides in the Attorney General" Accordingly, "no court shall have jurisdiction to modify or terminate any trust of property for charitable purposes unless the Attorney General is a party to the proceedings." Noting that he has never been made a party to the City's action, the Attorney General asserts that the trial court lacked subject matter jurisdiction over that action.

As explained above, the Deed created a fee simple subject to a condition subsequent, not a charitable trust. Therefore, the Attorney General is not a necessary party to the action, and the trial court did not lack subject matter jurisdiction.

C. *The Living Desert's Future Interest Is Compensable.*

The general rule in California is that, when a condemner takes property the ownership of which is split into an estate in fee simple subject to a condition subsequent and a power of termination, the owner of the future interest is not entitled to any compensation unless the condition has been breached as of the date of valuation. If no such breach has yet occurred, then the possibility of a reversion is too remote and speculative to be valued, and the reversionary interest is deemed to be valueless for purposes of condemnation.

However, the general rule denying compensation to the holder of the reversionary interest applies only "in the absence of exceptional circumstances." One of the exceptions is that the reversionary interest is compensable if the reversion would have been likely to occur within a reasonably short time. That exception was codified in 1975 as section 1265.410(a)(1), which provides: "Where the acquisition of property for public use violates a use restriction coupled with a contingent future interest granting a right to possession of the property upon violation of the use restriction: (1) If violation of the use restriction was otherwise reasonably imminent, the owner of the contingent future interest is entitled to compensation for its value, if any."

The trial court found that this exception did not apply because a violation of the restriction by the City was not reasonably imminent. It reasoned (1) that the City did not intend to violate the condition until it was relieved from the obligation of complying with it, either by agreement with Living Desert or by eminent domain, and (2) that the City's preparation to exercise its power of eminent domain could not be considered in determining whether a violation was reasonably imminent. As will be explained below, both its reasoning and its conclusion are mistaken. To the contrary, the undisputed evidence demonstrates that the violation was imminent. Therefore, the exception to the general rule did apply, and the Living Desert's interest was compensable.

D. The Trial Court Applied the Wrong Standard When Deciding Whether a Violation Was Reasonably Imminent.

On the facts of this case, both parts of the trial court's analysis were incorrect.

(1) *That the City Did Not Intend to Violate the Condition Is Irrelevant.*

The reasonable imminence of a violation is to be determined objectively. It is not determined by the City's subjective understanding of the legal consequences of its actions.

(2). *When the Condemner Already Owns the Present Interest, Actions Taken by the Condemner to Condemn the Future Interest Must Be Considered to Determine Whether a Violation of the Condition Is Reasonably Imminent.*

If further use of the property by the grantee in conformance with the use restriction is prevented by the divestiture of the grantee's title through eminent domain, the failure to perform is excused as being involuntary on the part of the grantee, and the future interest is not compensated.

In short, section 1265.410(a)(1) contemplates a situation in which the grantee of the conditional deed intends to continue to comply with the condition indefinitely, but is prevented from doing so because a paramount authority seizes title to the property through the power of eminent domain. And because it is designed to apply in situations in which the intentions and desires of the grantee of the present interest are contrary to and frustrated by the condemner, it necessarily assumes that the grantee and the condemner are separate entities dealing at arm's length.

The circumstances before us are radically different from those assumed by the statutory rule, in two respects.

First, the grantee of the present interest and the condemner of the power of termination are one and the same entity: the City. Given that identity, we cannot ignore the actions of the City as condemner when considering whether a voluntary violation of the use restriction by the City as grantee was reasonably imminent. Instead, we must evaluate the conduct of the grantee regardless of what other hats it may be wearing. When one of those hats is that of a condemner, the actions of the condemner are, and must be recognized to be, those of the grantee.

Second, the condemnation of the future interest did not divest the City of its present interest in the Land, and thus did not prevent the City from continuing to use the Land in conformance with the use restriction. That it did not plan to do so was not a decision forced upon it by the condemnation, but rather was its own voluntary choice, for which it should be held accountable.

For both of these reasons, that portion of section 1265.410(a)(1) which precludes the consideration of the condemnation proceedings to determine whether a violation of the use restriction is reasonably imminent, does not apply here.

E. The Violation of the Conditions of the Gift Was Imminent.

When the condemnation proceedings are considered, the undisputed evidence proves that a violation of the use restriction was reasonably imminent.

In its resolution of necessity, the City expressly found that the public welfare required the construction of a golf course on the Land, and that the acquisition of the future interest was necessary to do so. Similarly, in its application for an order for immediate possession, the City stated that it "must acquire the reversionary interest in order to devote the property to the public recreational uses" specified in the resolution of necessity.

Moreover, the City believed that the use of the Land as a golf course would violate the conditions of the gift. In one of its letters to the Living Desert, it offered to exchange adjacent property for the Land, explaining that "a golf course does not appear to be consistent with the intent of this grant."

Even in the absence of that express statement, the City's actions demonstrate its belief that the golf course would violate the use restriction: If a golf course was consistent with the conditions, then there would have been no need to buy the future interest. It is beyond belief that the City would have offered to pay $200,000 to purchase the future interest, and thereafter incurred the attorney's fees necessary to initiate the condemnation action, unless it believed that the planned golf course would violate the conditions. The only reason to do so was to attempt to eliminate the conditions by merging the present and future interests.[3]

Those circumstances establish that the violation of the conditions was reasonably imminent. Although we have found no California case involving similar facts, the Supreme Court of Texas has addressed that precise issue on a substantially identical factual record. (*Leeco Gas & Oil Co.* v. *Nueces County* (Tex. 1987) The Supreme Court although noting that a future interest is generally not compensable unless the reversion is imminent, held that the evidence was undisputed that the county sought to

---

[3]Noting that the trial court expressly declined to decide whether use of the Land for a golf course would violate the conditions, the City argues that the issue must be remanded for trial. It is mistaken. Trials are reserved for disputed factual issues. No trial is necessary when a factual issue cannot be disputed. The Deed provides that the Land is to be used "solely" for the exhibition of desert flora and fauna. Even if we were to accept the City's questionable assertion that a golf course could be landscaped in such a fashion as to exhibit desert plants and animals, the fairways and greens would obviously not be devoted to such an exhibition, and thus such a course would not comply with the conditions of the Deed.

purchase the reversionary interest in order to permit uses of the property which were inconsistent with the restrictive condition. "Thus, this is not a case of condemning a 'remote' possibility of reverter, but rather an attempt by the County to remove the 'burden' of the reversionary interest by condemning the interest and paying nominal damages."

The Texas Supreme Court held that when the purpose of taking the future interest was to permit the holder of the present interest to use the property in a manner which violates the conditions under which the present interest was given to the condemner, the violation of those conditions is imminent and the taking is compensable. The court explained that any other result would be contrary to public policy. "To allow a governmental entity, as grantee in a gift deed, to condemn the grantor's reversionary interest by paying only nominal damages would have a negative impact on gifts of real property to charities and governmental entities. It would discourage these types of gifts in the future. This is not in the best interests of the citizens of this State."

That analysis is persuasive, for several reasons. First, it is consistent with the concerns, voiced by this court and others, that if a public entity which had accepted a gift of property subject to a condition limiting the use of that property were permitted to avoid the force of the donor's restriction, donors would be discouraged from making such gifts in the future.

Second, denying compensation under these facts would frustrate the public policy in favor of the enforcement of existing charitable gifts.

The Eminent Domain Law promotes that policy by specifically requiring a donor's charitable intent to be continued even when the actual gift has been taken for a different public use. If a condemner takes property subject to a use restriction which requires the property to "be devoted to a particular charitable or public use, the compensation for the property shall be devoted to the same or similar use coupled with the same contingent future interest." Thus, the happenstance that a public entity finds it necessary to take the physical property, thereby converting the gift into cash, does not relieve the donee of its obligation to continue to use the gift for charitable purposes. That policy of enforcing the donor's charitable intent, even when the original gift has been taken by eminent domain, is totally inconsistent with a rule which would permit a public entity receiving a conditional gift to destroy the condition through condemnation without compensation to the holder of the reversionary interest.[4]

Finally, this analysis ensures that the City does not profit from its unfair and unseemly tactics. When offered 30 acres of valuable property on the condition that it be used exclusively and perpetually as a public park devoted to the display of desert plants and animals, the City eagerly accepted, apparently without voicing any objection

---

[4] For the same reason, we question whether the City's condemnation solely of the reversionary interest relieves it of its duty under the Deed to comply with the use restriction. However, the parties have not raised that issue, and we do not decide it.

to the condition imposed by the donor. In reliance upon the City's agreement to that condition, the Foundation conveyed the Land. But only a few years later, the City unilaterally renounced its agreement to devote the Land to the charitable use specified by the Foundation and hatched a plan not only to terminate that restrictive condition but to do so in a manner which would deprive the Living Desert of the means of carrying on the Foundation's charitable intent. Whether the City's refusal to comply with the condition is the result of promissory fraud or a subsequent change of heart, the unfairness to the donor is palpable.

One of the maxims of equity is that "He who takes the benefit must bear the burden." In this context, that means that the donee of a conditional gift may not keep the gift unless the donee complies with the donor's conditions. That the donee in this case is a public entity, endowed with the power of eminent domain, does not exempt it from that rule. To the contrary, public entities should exemplify equitable conduct. "A public office is a public trust created in the interest and for the benefit of the people." As trustees for and representatives of the public, local public officials are required to discharge their responsibilities with the utmost fidelity and integrity. They should be "standard-bearers of public virtue."

The City, by contrast, has been unfaithful both to the Foundation's intent and to the spirit of the conditions under which it accepted the Foundation's gift. And whether the City's policymakers genuinely believed that the law might permit it to keep the Land without either complying with the Foundation's wishes or paying fair compensation-indeed, without paying *any* compensation whatsoever-the decision to assert that position did not display the high degree of fairness, justice, and virtue that should characterize public entities. Such inequitable behavior must not be rewarded.

In summary, we hold that if a public entity accepts a gift of property by the terms of which the public entity receives a fee simple subject to a condition subsequent restricting the use of the property to a particular charitable use, and if that same public entity thereafter uses its power of eminent domain to take the power of termination reserved by the donor or given by the donor to a third party, with the intention of eliminating the use restriction and thereby permitting a use of the property which would violate the condition, then a violation of that condition is reasonably imminent. Accordingly, the public entity must pay compensation to the holder of the power of termination.

E. The Requirement to Pay Compensation Is Not an Improper Limitation on the Power of Eminent Domain.

The City argues that because eminent domain is an inherent governmental power, the exercise of that power can never constitute a breach of contract, and thus its decision to take the future interest by eminent domain to build a golf course cannot constitute a breach of the conditions of the Deed.

The issue here is not whether the condemner had the power to take the condemnee's property interest. The Living Desert did not contest the City's right to take either below or on appeal. Instead, the only issue is whether the property interest taken by the City has compensable value. The requirement to pay compensation is not an improper limitation on the power of eminent domain.

Conclusion

Given the identity of the grantee and the condemner, the trial court prejudicially erred in refusing to consider the City's condemnation proceedings when deciding whether a violation of the use restriction by the City was reasonably imminent.

Had the condition been violated before the City commenced its condemnation action, the measure of compensation payable to the Living Desert would have been the fair market value of an estate in fee simple absolute. The violation here had not yet occurred when this action was filed but was reasonably imminent. Indeed, given that the City was requesting possession of the Land within 30 days, that violation was likely to occur within a matter of months. Under that circumstance, the trial court should apply the same measure of compensation to determine the value of Living Desert's power of termination, i.e., 100 percent of the value of the unrestricted fee in the Land. [5]

Disposition

The matter is remanded to the trial court to determine the compensation due, in accordance with the views expressed in this opinion. The Living Desert Reserve shall recover its costs on appeal.

---

[5] Code of Civil Procedure section 43 requires an appellate court to determine all questions of law involved in the case which are necessary to the final determination of the case upon retrial. Because we are remanding the matter for a new trial to determine the amount of compensation due for the taking of the future interest, it is proper for us to instruct the trial court concerning the measure of valuation to be used.

CHAPTER 12 - THE RULE AGAINST PERPETUITIES

Clearly, it is necessary for anyone drafting wills, deeds, or trusts to have a basic understanding of the Rule Against Perpetuities. It is not that hard.

> **"No interest is good, unless it must vest, if at all, not later than 21 years after some life in being at the creation of the interest."**

Gray, The Rule Against Perpetuities s 629 (4th Ed.1942).

As a practical matter, this means that a testator should not try to hold onto control of property for more than 21 years after the death of the last of his children to die. That is long enough. After that, as Thomas Jefferson said, "The earth belongs always to the living generation. They may manage it then, and what proceeds from it, as they please."[1]

A skilled lawyer, in fact, can make it possible for a client to hold onto control for a much longer time. For more details, and for a simple, sure way to ascertain whether or not a provision violates the common law Rule Against Perpetuities (RAP), see Chapter 8, "Rule Against Perpetuities", Drafting Wills and Trusts, Lucy A. Marsh, Vandeplas Publishing (2009).

In the meantime, here are some cases illustrating the basics of RAP. The first case includes some of the important rules regarding class gifts, the interesting concept of *infectious invalidity,* and a demonstration of some of the difficulties involved with drafting a good RAP savings clause.

A. CASES ON THE RULE AGAINST PERPETUITIES

Supreme Court of Virginia.
Anne Mutter Woodward HAGEMANN and Fletcher D. Woodward, Jr.
v.
NATIONAL BANK AND TRUST COMPANY, Administrator, C. T. A. of the Estate of Mildred Hart Woodward, Deceased, and Trustee U/W Mildred Hart Woodward, Malcolm P. Woodward, Katherine D. Woodward and infant beneficiaries, now born or as yet unborn, under Article Eight of the Will of Mildred Hart Woodward.
September 1, 1977
POFF, Justice.

In this appeal, we are asked to construe a will to determine whether the residuary clause violates the rule against perpetuities.

[1] Thomas Jefferson, Letter to James Madison, September 6, 1789.

The will of Mildred Hart Woodward, executed January 15, 1971, was admitted to probate on March 16, 1971. National Bank and Trust Company, the trustee named in the will, qualified as administrator, c. t. a. The testatrix was survived by her children, Anne, Fletcher, and Malcolm, her sole heirs at law, all of whom were named as beneficiaries in her will.

Article Eight, the residuary clause of the will, creates two equal trust funds, one for Fletcher and his descendants and the other for Malcolm and his descendants. The clause contains eight paragraphs. Paragraph 1 provides that the son will receive the income so long as he lives and has living children under the age of 25 years and that, upon the son's death, the income shall be paid to his surviving wife and children for their "support, comfort and education." Paragraph 2 authorizes the trustee to invade the corpus for such purposes. Paragraph 3 provides:

> "3. When the youngest living child of such son of mine has reached age twenty-five years, that trust shall end and the fund shall be divided one-third to such son of mine and two-thirds equally to his then living descendants, per stirpes. Should such son of mine not then be living, the whole of the fund shall go to his then living descendants, per stirpes."

Under paragraph 4, if the last surviving child of one of the testatrix's sons dies before attaining the age of 25 years, the corpus will be paid on that date to that son, if living, and if not, will be added to the corpus of the other trust fund. The provisions of paragraph 8, considered in context with those of paragraph 3, are of crucial relevance:

> "8. Notwithstanding the foregoing, if any portion of my estate is in any contingency capable of being held in trust for a longer period than is permitted by the law of the state of my domicile, or if in any such contingency the vesting of any interest hereunder may occur after the expiration of such permissive period, then upon the happening of any such contingency such portion of my estate shall not be held in further trust, but shall rather be paid over absolutely to the person or persons to whom, and in the proportions in which, such portion would ultimately go under the provisions hereof."

Anne and Fletcher, complainants, filed a bill of complaint seeking construction of the will. The administrator-trustee, Malcolm, and infant beneficiaries, now born or as yet unborn, were named respondents. The chancellor appointed a guardian ad litem to represent the infant respondents and later joined Katherine D. Woodward, one of Fletcher's children who had attained her majority, as a party-respondent. Complainants prayed that the residuary clause "be declared null and void and of no effect as violating the rule against perpetuities, and that as a consequence thereof it be declared that the testatrix died intestate as to her residuary estate".

On appeal, all parties agree that under the rule against perpetuities as applied in this Commonwealth, the remainder interests granted the children (or descendants) of the testatrix's sons by paragraph 3 are void unless "saved" by paragraph 8.

The rule against perpetuities in Virginia voids a contingent remainder or executory interest, created inter vivos or by will, which may, by some possibility, however unlikely that possibility may be, vest beyond a life or lives in being at the effective date of the instrument creating the interest, plus 21 years and 10 months.

The effective date of the Woodward will is the date of Mrs. Woodward's death. In paragraph 3, she disposes of two-thirds of each of the two funds there created to the descendants of her sons living when the youngest living child of a son attains 25 years. The words "then living" create an express condition that a descendant, as a member of the class of descendants, must survive to the time at which the youngest child of the son attains 25 years of age. A contingent remainder is created in the class of "descendants".

By the familiar rule in Leake v. Robinson, 35 Eng.Rep. 979 (1817), generally followed in the United States and discussed in detail in Simes and Smith, The Law of Future Interests, a class must stand or fall as a unit when the rule against perpetuities is applied. If the interest of one member of that class could vest beyond the time permitted by the rule, the interests of all members of that class fail for remoteness. Here, it is possible that the sons could die survived by a child in gestation or by a child under the age of three years and two months. In such case the interest of descendants of the testatrix would vest upon the 25th birthday of that child which is beyond the time permitted by the rule. It is not actuality or probability but possibility, viewed from the effective date of the will, that actuates the rule against perpetuities.

As respondents point out, these contingent remainders *could* vest before expiration of the term permitted by the rule upon the happening of any of several events. For example, the rule could be satisfied if the testatrix's son should die survived by children, none of whom are under the age of three years and two months and none of whom are in gestation at his death. There are other possibilities, even probabilities, of valid vesting. Respondents say, in effect, that we should so construe the will that the trustee will be allowed to "wait and see" whether any such future event occurs, and if not, then "upon the happening of any such contingency" which violates the rule, the trustee will be allowed to terminate the trust and distribute the corpus.

A statute embodying the "wait and see" doctrine has been adopted in England, and in some of the states. But a majority of the states, including Virginia, apply the common law rule in its orthodox form. As respondents tacitly acknowledge, the "wait and see" rule is actuated by the possibility of timeliness. The common law rule is actuated by the possibility of remoteness. Absent statutory mandate, we reject the "wait and see" rule and adhere to the common law rule.

Turning to respondents' first rationale, we examine the chancellor's ruling that paragraph 8 "saved" the residuary clause.

The rule against perpetuities "is a rule adopted in furtherance of public policy to prevent excessive restraints or limitations upon the alienation of an estate." The language of the Woodward will leaves nothing ambiguous about the possibility of remoteness or the thrust of testamentary intent. The testatrix intended to forbid alienation of her residuary estate until her youngest grandchild, living at the time of her death *or later born*, reached the age of 25 years. Nor can there be any doubt that she attempted to do so knowing that what she attempted posed the possibility of remoteness and constituted a violation of the rule as applied in the state of her domicile. She knew, too, that what she attempted would succeed so long as her will was not challenged in court.

Against the hazard of such a challenge, she added a "savings clause". That clause provides that

> "If the vesting of any interest hereunder may occur after the expiration of (the period permitted by the rule), then upon the happening of any such contingency such portion of my estate shall not be held in further trust but shall be paid over absolutely."

Manifestly, the testatrix's deliberate purpose was to violate but, if possible, evade the effect of the rule against perpetuities, and if the rule were ever invoked, to rewrite the rule so that it would be actuated only upon the "happening" of an event which made remoteness an inevitability. But, as we have said, the rule is actuated by the possibility of remoteness, and that possibility must be determined as of the date of the testatrix's death.

The savings clause was patterned after a model form found in Rabkin & Johnson, 3 Current Legal Forms, Form 8.24(30). Indeed, with one exception, the language was identical. The Woodward clause provided that, upon the happening of a contingency that violated the rule against perpetuities, the corpus would be paid "to the person or persons to whom, and in the proportions in which, such portion would ultimately go under the provisions hereof"; the model form provided that in such event the corpus would be paid to those to whom "the income therefrom was then payable." While we do not decide what impact the model form might have had if its exact language had been employed in the Woodward will, we do note that the effect of such language is to fix the date for determining the remaindermen at a time within the term permitted by the rule against perpetuities. The language of the Woodward will, on the other hand, fixes the date at a time which could fall beyond the end of that term, for it identifies the remaindermen as those to whom the corpus "would ultimately go under the provisions hereof."

Under the provisions of paragraph 3, the interests of the grandchild-remaindermen would be void for remoteness. A "savings clause" cannot save a void interest by adopting the very provisions which make it void.

Invoking the principle that testamentary intent "is the 'Pole star' and 'sovereign guide' in construction of a will", respondents say that, even if the original testamentary design violated the rule, the "overriding" testamentary intent was to avoid a violation and that we should give effect to such intent in obedience to the maxim that the law does not favor intestacy. As we have indicated, we believe that the testatrix's dominant intent was to violate the rule against perpetuities with the hope that the violation would never be challenged and that the savings clause would never have to be applied.

The whole function of the rule is to defeat testamentary intent to violate its mandate.

> "The Rule against Perpetuities is not a rule of construction, but a peremptory command of law. It is not, like a rule of construction, a test, more or less artificial, to determine intention. Its object is to defeat intention. Therefore every provision in a will or settlement is to be construed as if the Rule did not exist, and then to the provision so construed the Rule is to be remorselessly applied." Gray, The Rule Against Perpetuities s 629 (4th Ed.1942).

When the maxim that the law does not favor intestacy collides with the "public policy to prevent excessive restraints or limitations upon the alienation of an estate", the former must yield.

Nor do we intend to imply that all savings clauses are inherently ineffectual in Virginia. If the language of a will leaves it ambiguous whether there is a possibility of remoteness, then a savings clause may be effective. But where, as here, the language reasonably permits no construction but that remoteness is a possibility, the use of a savings clause only reinforces the conclusion that the paramount testamentary intent was to violate the very rule which condemns such intent.

Accordingly, we hold that paragraph 8 of the residuary clause in the Woodward will did not save the remainder interests granted by paragraph 3 to the children (or descendants) of the testatrix's sons.

Finally, we consider whether the failure of these interests caused the other interests created by the residuary clause to fail.

Neither party has cited a case we consider controlling. The cases discovered in our research are conflicting, but the conflicts result not so much from jurisprudential differences as from factual, syntactical, and statutory diversity. We have concluded that the most succinct exposition of the general rule is that found in 28 A.L.R. Prior Estate-Remainder Void for Remoteness:

> "The general rule is that a remainder which is void because in violation of the rule against perpetuities does not necessarily render invalid the prior estate, but that the latter will be sustained notwithstanding the invalidity of the ulterior estate, where the two are not inseparable and dependent parts of a general testamentary scheme, and to uphold the one without the other would not defeat the primary or dominant purpose of the testator.."

Unless infected by the invalidity of the ulterior estates, the anterior estates created by the residuary clause of the Woodward will are valid: the income interest of the son will vest, if at all, within his lifetime; the income interests of the "surviving wife" of the son and his children will vest, if at all, not later than the death of the son; and the son's interest in the corpus will vest, if at all, within his lifetime. Under the rule quoted above, these anterior estates are not infected by the invalidity of the ulterior estates when "the two are not inseparable and dependent parts of a general testamentary scheme, and to uphold the one without the other would not defeat the primary or dominant purpose" of the testatrix.

As reflected in the will as a whole, the testatrix's "general testamentary scheme" was to make roughly equivalent provision for her three children and their descendants. In Article Seven, she created a specific trust for the benefit of her daughter and her daughter's children, and in Article Eight she created residuary trusts for her two sons and their descendants. If the invalidity of the ulterior interests infects the anterior interests, the entire residuary estate will pass by intestacy. In such case, the daughter would receive a portion of the estate intended for the sons and their descendants. This would effectively thwart the general testamentary scheme and defeat what we perceive to be the primary or dominant purpose of the testatrix. Clearly, with respect to her residuary estate, the testatrix's dominant purpose was to make available, during the critical period her grandchildren were to be reared and educated, not only the income from the trust but also such portion of the corpus as might be necessary for "support, comfort and education." Only after the expiration of that critical period was the corpus to be distributed and, then, only what had not been consumed.

We are of opinion that the anterior and ulterior estates were not "inseparable and dependent parts" of the general testamentary scheme and that to uphold the former would not defeat but, rather, would substantially promote the "primary or dominant purpose" of the testatrix.

We hold, therefore, that the anterior estates which, as we have said, will vest, if at all, within the term permitted by the rule against perpetuities, are not infected by the invalidity of the ulterior estates. We will reverse the final decree insofar as it upholds the remote remainders and affirm the final decree insofar as it upholds the other estates created by the residuary clause. And this cause will be remanded with instructions to restore it to the docket and enter a new decree consistent with this opinion.

Reversed in part, affirmed in part, and remanded.

The next case is even more frightening than it is complex. It illustrates an important concept – that standard options to buy property may – or may not – be subject to the Rule Against Perpetuities. But the frightening part of the case is that the court requires that drafting be so clear that no lawyer could *mistakenly* believe that a provision violated the Rule Against Perpetuities. Not only must you get it right, but you must also make it clear to any other lawyer that it *is* right. The penalty, if some other lawyer *mistakenly* believes that you have violated the Rule Against Perpetuities, may be

$5 million!

Colorado Court of Appeals.
The TEMPLE HOYNE BUELL FOUNDATION, a Colorado nonprofit corporation, and Buell Development Corporation, a Colorado corporation, Plaintiffs-Appellees
v.
HOLLAND & HART, a partnership and Bruce T. Buell, Defendants-Appellants.
Aug. 27, 1992. Certiorari Denied May 10, 1993.

Opinion by Judge SMITH.

In this legal malpractice action, defendants, Holland & Hart and Bruce Buell, appeal the final judgment entered on a jury verdict awarding plaintiffs, Buell Development Corporation, $3,364,011 in damages and $2,125,195 in pre-judgment interest. We reverse the judgment and remand for a new trial.

The judgment at issue here arose from defendants' representation of plaintiffs in connection with the sale of stock in Kings County Development Corporation (KCDC), to John Rocovich. As part of the transaction, defendants drafted an option contract which provided that part of the consideration for the stock sale was an option in favor of plaintiffs to acquire from Rocovich a percentage of KCDC's minerals underlying its California farmland should KCDC ever distribute these interests to its shareholders.

In 1982, KCDC and Rocovich, were involved in another lawsuit. While that lawsuit was pending, as part of a settlement, Rocovich conveyed all of his KCDC stock to the corporation. KCDC, meanwhile, decided to distribute its mineral interest to the corporation's shareholders within the year 1982.

While the KCDC lawsuits were pending, plaintiffs attempted to exercise their option under the contract executed with Rocovich. KCDC refused to honor the agreement between plaintiffs and Rocovich and to transfer the mineral interests, asserting that the option violated the Rule Against Perpetuities and was therefore unenforceable.

In 1984, plaintiffs, who had discharged defendants as counsel in 1981, during the KCDC lawsuits, settled their dispute with the corporation. Under the terms of this settlement, plaintiffs received one-half of the mineral interests that they would have been entitled to under the option.

In 1989, plaintiffs initiated this lawsuit against defendants, asserting claims of negligence and breach of contract relating to the option contract with Rocovich. Soon after the litigation commenced, defendants sought a determination from the trial court that the option did not violate the Rule Against Perpetuities.

At the evidentiary hearing on this issue, defendants attempted to establish that the option was exclusively contractual in nature and, thus, outside the Rule. The trial court disagreed, concluding that the option was subject to, and in violation of, the Rule. Moreover, the court ruled that there were no public policy reasons to allow the enforcement of the option in spite of the violation. Finally, the trial court ruled that no testimony on this particular issue would be admissible at trial.

Numerous expert witnesses for both parties testified at trial concerning the effects of the Rule Against Perpetuities violation as it related to the rights of the parties under the option contract.

The jury returned a verdict that plaintiffs' losses were caused solely by defendants' negligence.

I.

Defendants contend that the jury verdict in favor of plaintiffs on their claim for legal malpractice is erroneous as a matter of law. The crux of defendants' argument is the trial court's pre-trial ruling that the option contract violated the Rule Against Perpetuities. Defendants argue that the trial court's ruling was erroneous, tainted the entire trial, and justifies entry of judgment in their favor. We agree that the trial court's ruling was in error and that such error did, indeed, pervade the trial proceedings. We disagree, however, that these conclusions dispose of plaintiffs' claim of legal malpractice.

As relevant here, the option provided:

> In further consideration of the mutual promises of the parties as herein provided, we agree as follows with respect to the mineral interests *owned by KCDC...*
>
> 2. I Rocovich will use my best efforts to have the mineral interests distributed or made available to shareholders of KCDC as soon as possible.
>
> 3. From and after the time of distribution, plaintiffs will have *six months to purchase, at its option,* 31.73576% of *the mineral interests now owned by KCDC,* and I Rocovich agree to sell to plaintiffs said interest for the sum of $305,500; if plaintiffs should not exercise its option, I Rocovich will, nevertheless, have the option, at any time during said six-month period, to offer plaintiffs the said 31.73576% of KCDC mineral interests which plaintiffs shall be required to purchase for the sum of $305,500.00.
>
> This agreement will bind and enure to the benefit of the heirs, successors and assigns of the respective parties.

A. The Rule Against Perpetuities Issue

The Rule Against Perpetuities is a rule of property law, the fundamental purpose of which is to keep property "unfettered," that is, free from inconvenient limitations. As such, the Rule operates to invalidate future interests in property, real or personal, legal or equitable, which [might] vest too remotely, specifically, "later than twenty-one years after some life in being at the creation of the interest."

An option to purchase, such as that at issue here, may or may not be subject to the Rule. If the option may continue for a period longer than 21 years and it creates an interest in a specific parcel of land or in any "specific identifiable thing," the option is required to comply with the Rule. In such instances, the option, because it is specifically enforceable, "fetters" the property which is the subject matter of the option by imposing upon it an unfulfilled condition precedent for too long a time.

If the option is determined *not* to create an enforceable interest in a specific parcel of land or in any "specific identifiable thing," then no specific property is "fettered" or chargeable with performance under the option. Nor is any particular property subject to a potentially objectionable unfulfilled condition precedent. Such option, therefore, while creating enforceable contract rights between the parties, "involves no fettering of any property and hence, presents no occasion for applying the Rule." Restatement of Law of Property § 401.

Defendants contend that the uncertainty created by the unknown date of the mineral distribution, if any, was an irrelevant circumstance because the Rule had no applicability to the option. The essence of defendants' argument is, thus, that the trial court erred in its initial conclusion that the option concerned specific property.

A cursory review of the terms of the option reveals that the parties clearly *identified* a specific property interest as the subject matter of the option. However, based on the following principles of property and corporate law, we conclude that the terms were insufficient to *create an interest* in the property described.

It is fundamental that a grantor can convey no more rights in property than he himself owns. Accordingly, for the option here to have created an interest in a specific property, to wit, the mineral property identified in the option, Rocovich, the "grantor," would have to have had, at the time the option was executed, an interest, legal or equitable, in this property.

The record discloses, however, that, at the pertinent time, Rocovich's status was only that of a shareholder in KCDC. As a shareholder, Rocovich was entitled to an interest in the minerals only *if and when* they were *distributed.* However, until such time, he held no interest in specific property of the corporation.

As succinctly stated by the United States Supreme Court in Rhode Island Hospital Trust Co. v. Doughton:

> "The owner of the shares of stock in a company is not the owner of the corporation's property. He has a right to his share in the earnings of the corporation, as they may be declared in dividends, arising from the use of all its property. In the dissolution of the corporation he may take his proportionate share in what is left, after all the debts of the corporation have been paid and the assets are divided in accordance with the law of its creation. *But he does not own the corporate property.*"

Thus, when the parties executed their contract, Rocovich's rights and interests, while, indeed, valuable and enforceable, were in KCDC's earnings and profits not in its *divisible assets,* such as the mineral interests.

At most, Rocovich held only a hope or chance of acquiring *specific* corporate property. Neither a hope or a chance, however, are sufficient to create an interest in property.

Hence, until the mineral interests were *distributed,* Rocovich had no rights in the mineral interests which he could convey or "fetter." The option contract could not, thus, subject this particular property to an unfulfilled condition precedent. Indeed, KCDC was equally free, both before and after the parties executed the option, to dispose of the mineral interests at issue in any particular manner it chose and to any particular person or entity.

The option contract, in sum, involved no fettering of a specific parcel of property or of any specific identifiable thing and, hence, presented no opportunity to invoke the Rule.

This is not to say that the option was unenforceable. Indeed, between plaintiffs and Rocovich, the contract created rights and obligations enforceable by one against the other, their heirs, successors, and assigns. Of critical significance, however, the contract, in the words of defendants' expert, did "nothing whatsoever to the subject matter of their contract - property owned by a stranger to that contract."
Under the terms of the contract here, no interest in the minerals could arise in Rocovich or in plaintiffs *unless and until* the mineral interests were distributed by KCDC to its shareholders. Once the interest was created by distribution, moreover, the option to purchase it was to be exercised promptly, specifically, six months "from and after the time of distribution" or it would lapse. Hence, there was no "mathematical possibility" that once created, the interest would vest beyond the period of perpetuities.

In conclusion, we hold that the trial court erred in ruling that the option contract violated the Rule Against Perpetuities.

B. Effect of the Erroneous Ruling

Defendants argue that the trial court's erroneous pre-trial ruling tainted the entire trial and thus constituted prejudicial error. Under the particular circumstances here, we agree.

At trial the jury was instructed that:

> "The court has ruled as a matter of law that the option violated the Rule Against Perpetuities and there is no public policy reason for not applying the rule."

This instruction states, unequivocally, that, in drafting the option contract, defendants committed an error.

Moreover, the transcript discloses that extensive reference was made to the option's "unenforceability" by both the trial court and plaintiffs' counsel. Indeed, as pointed out by defendants in their brief, mention of this matter was made "10 times by the court, 56 times by the plaintiffs' counsel and 7 times by witnesses."

The trial court's erroneous ruling pervaded the trial proceedings and, most critically, influenced the instructions given to the jury. Accordingly, we conclude that defendants are entitled to a new trial on plaintiffs' claim of legal malpractice.

Defendants argue, however, that if the option is valid and enforceable, there can be no malpractice claim as a matter of law, thus entitling them to entry of judgment in their favor. We disagree.

An attorney owes a duty to his client to employ that degree of knowledge, skill, and judgment ordinarily possessed by members of the legal profession in carrying out the services for his client. One of these obligations is anticipating *reasonably foreseeable risks.*

Thus, although we hold here that the option did not violate the Rule Against Perpetuities, the question remains whether defendants, as reasonably prudent attorneys, should have foreseen that the option, as drafted, was likely to result in litigation and whether other attorneys, in similar circumstances, would have taken steps to prevent such a result.

Plaintiffs argued at trial, and presented expert testimony in support of their assertion, that the principal negligence of defendants was their not protecting plaintiffs from loss by failing to research and analyze the Rule's applicability in the option, to recognize the likelihood that a good faith dispute could occur over the enforceability of the option because of the Rule, and to take the simple step of either adding a time limitation or "savings clause" or recommending the deletion of the provision that made the option binding on heirs, successors, and assigns.

Bruce Buell testified that he had given no specific consideration to the Rule in drafting the Agreement. Nor did he perform any legal research, consider the choice of law, consult with experts, or even consult with other members of his own firm on the question of whether the Rule could apply to the option. He concluded that he had no duty to do any of these things because he "was an experienced business transactions lawyer" who "knew the rule against perpetuities" and "knew when it applied," and could "spot issues like that." As a result, plaintiffs argue, Buell did not advise his clients of the real likelihood that a good faith dispute could arise over the enforceability of the option under the Rule.

On the issue of defendant's negligence, one expert attorney-witness testified that a reasonable attorney would have no reason to include a savings clause in the option and concluded that defendants met the standard of care in drafting it. However, conflicting testimony was offered by two other attorney-experts who testified that defendants had failed to meet the standard of care and should have considered the possibility that the Rule might apply to the option and should have protected it against a Rule challenge.

Perhaps the strongest testimony on this issue was that of defendant's own attorney-expert. On cross-examination, he unequivocally testified that, in his opinion, an attorney would be guilty of malpractice if he: (a) did not research the issue of the

Rule in the context of this transaction, (b) failed to consider the potential for a dispute over the applicability of the Rule to the option, and (c) failed to utilize a savings clause to protect against that potential dispute.

Thus, although there was a conflict in the expert testimony as to attorney negligence in drafting the option, no witness disagreed with the premise that the option would have been protected from any Rule dispute if defendants had considered the Rule, had recognized the clear potential for dispute, and had either included a savings clause or excluded the language making the option binding on heirs, successors, and assigns.

In short, resolution of the Rule of Perpetuities issue does not conclusively resolve the issue of whether defendants met the applicable standard of care in preparing the option contract. Hence, we reject defendant's argument that judgment be entered in their favor.

The judgment is reversed, and the cause is remanded for a new trial on plaintiffs' claims for legal malpractice.

Note: Rather than submitting to a new trial, defendants simply settled the case – for a very large sum of money.

B. DRAFTING A GOOD RAP SAVINGS CLAUSE

As you could see from the *Hagemann* case, it is not sufficient to say, in a savings clause, that the property which is part of a void gift should be distributed in the same way that has already turned out to be void.

Another frequent problem with RAP savings clauses is that the savings clause directs that if a gift in a trust fails, then the property of the trust is to be distributed to the people then "entitled" to the income from the trust assets. In a great many trust provisions, the trustee has some discretion as to distribution of income. So, technically, no one is "entitled" to distribution of income.

Recently, the Colorado Estate Planning Forms Committee promulgated an excellent pattern for a RAP savings clause, which should work in most situations involving trust income. But as always, do not blindly copy any existing form into a document you are drafting – be sure that the words will be appropriate for your specific document.

SAMPLE SAVINGS CLAUSE

"Every trust hereunder, and every trust created by the exercise of a power of appointment hereunder, shall terminate no later than the end of the period allowed by the applicable Rule Against Perpetuities and the trust property shall be distributed to the persons then entitled to the income from the trust in the proportions in which they are entitled to such income. For this purpose only, any person eligible to receive discretionary distributions of income from a particular trust shall be treated as being entitled to receive the income. If two or more persons are so treated, they shall be treated as being entitled to receive the income by representation if they have a common ancestor, or in equal shares if they do not."

C. STATUTORY MODIFICATIONS TO RAP – DYNASTY TRUSTS

Within the last decade or two various states have been working to bring more trust business into their states – to increase the income for banks, other corporate entities, and attorneys who may serve as trustees. In response to lobbying by such groups, various states have scrambled to make statutory modifications to RAP – to allow private trusts to last for up to 1,000 years! Really?! One thousand years?! Yes.

It is hard to picture just what was happening in the United States 1,000 years ago. But most of us do remember learning that in 1066 (*less* than 1,000 years ago), William the Conqueror came over from France and invaded England. So of course it makes a great deal of sense to try to establish a trust, today, that will last farther into the future than 1066 is in the past.

What establishing a Dynast Trust *will* do is allow beneficial ownership to become as fractionated as the trust lands in the first case in this book, *Hodel v. Irving.* As you remember, in that case, one $8,000 parcel of land, after only a few generations, had become so fractionated that one of the heirs was entitled to $.01 of income every 177 years. And the U.S. government was spending $17,500 per year just to tabulate and distribute the various shares of income.

Obviously, only corporate entities, such as banks, will be able to serve as trustees for such long-term trusts. Looks like nice, steady work for a bank, which will take management fees off the top – if some owner can be persuaded to set up a Dynasty Trust.[2]

Despite the possibility, in a number of states, of setting up a Dynasty Trust, it is probably best to stay close to the time allowed by the common law Rule Against Perpetuities.

[2] For one of the few articles pointing out the *flaws* in the concept of Dynasty Trusts, see Lucy A. Marsh, *The Demise of Dynasty Trusts: Returning the Wealth to the Family,* 5 Estate Planning & Community Property Law 23 (2012).

*donor is giving donee the power to appoint for donor's property

avoid a general power of appointment if worried about estate tax — general power of appointment is viewed by IRS as part of donee's estate

CHAPTER 13 - POWERS OF APPOINTMENT

A. DESCRIPTION OF POWERS OF APPOINTMENT

Powers of appointment are a very popular, useful tool to provide valuable flexibility to an estate plan. The most frequent use of a power of appointment is when the testator gives property to A for life, and then gives A the power to decide to whom the property should go at A's death. In other words, the testator gives A the power to fill in a blank in the testator's will. This delegated power given to A is acceptable in all states.

The person who creates the power, frequently a testator, is called the Donor of the power of appointment. He gives someone else the power to exercise the power of appointment. So the Donor (creator) of the power gives the Donee of the power the authority to fill in the blank in the donor's document. The donor may authorize the donee to exercise the power while the donee is still alive – in which case the power would be called an inter vivos power. Or the donor may authorize the donee to exercise the power only by the donee's will – in which case the power would be called a testamentary power.

In labeling a power of appointment it does not matter whether the donor *creates* the power in a deed or in a will. What matters is how the *donee may exercise the power.* If the donee may exercise the power while the donee is alive the power is called an inter vivos power. If the donee is only allowed to exercise the power by the donee's will, the power is called a testamentary power.

When creating the power, the donor may authorize the donee to appoint to anyone the donee chooses – including the donee, the creditors of the donee, the donee's own estate, or anyone else the donee likes. If the donee is allowed to appoint to anyone, including the donee, then the power is called a General Power. If the donee is allowed to appoint only to a special group, *not* including the donee – for example to a group such as the children of the donee – then the power is called a Special Power. -designated group of people

There are only four kinds of powers of appointment: General Inter Vivos, General Testamentary, Special Inter Vivos, and Special Testamentary. The distinctions are really quite easy. A General power may be exercised on behalf of anyone – including the donee, the donee's creditors, the donee's estate, the creditors of the donee's estate – or anyone else. A Special power may be exercised only for the group of people specially defined by the donor of the power. A Special Power may not be exercised for the benefit of the donee of the power, the donees's creditors, the donee's estate, or the creditors of the donee's estate

In defining the special group for whom a Special power of appointment may be exercised, the donor may require that the donee give at least something, (a non-illusory amount), to every member of the group. If every member of the group must get at least something, the power is called a *non-exclusive* power of appointment – no member of the group may be excluded.

On the other hand, if the donor of the power says that the power may be exercised for "one or more" of the members of a designated group, then the power is called an *exclusive* power of appointment – it is permissible for the donee to *exclude* one or more members of the group when the donee exercises the power.

The people for whom the power of appointment may be exercised – the people to whom the property may be appointed – are called the Objects of the power. The donee of a Special power is not allowed to appoint the property to anyone who is not within the group specified by the donor to be proper Objects of the power. If the donee attempts to appoint to a non-object of the power, that attempted appointment is called a "fraud on the power," and is void.

What happens if the donee of a power of appointment never gets around to appointing the property to anyone? Then the property just remains the property of the donor of the power. That might cause a difficulty, if, at the death of the donee, the property went back into the estate of the donor, who might have been dead for 30 years. So whenever anyone creates a power of appointment the donor should also provide for a "gift in default" - a gift which will take effect if the donee fails to exercise the power of appointment properly.

The gift in default for a Special power frequently says that if the donee fails to exercise the power, then the property goes, in default, to the Objects of the power, in equal shares. Or if the power of appointment was a General power of appointment, which could have been appointed to anyone in the world, then the donor will frequently provide that if the donee fails to exercise the power – that is, in default of appointment – the property shall go the descendants of the donor who are living at the death of the donee, by representation. That will keep the property in the family, even if the donee fails to exercise the power of appointment.

B. "JUST BEFORE GENEROUS"

There is one more interesting rule, which applies only to General powers of appointment. That rule is that the donee of a General power of appointment must be *"Just before generous."* In other words, if the donee of a General Power, who has the authority to appoint to himself, his creditors, or anyone else, decides to exercise the power, the donee must first make sure that his own creditors will be paid – either from the donee's own assets, or from the property subject to the power of appointment. In essence, the donee must be *just*, and pay his own debts, before he is *generous* in giving appointive property to others.

The donee is never *required* to exercise the power of appointment. But if the donee does exercise a *General* power of appointment, the donee must be "J*ust before generous."*

An example of a General testamentary power of appointment might be, "I give my vacation home in Malibu to my son, Sam, for life, and then to whomever my son may appoint by will, and in default of appointment in equal shares to my grandchildren who are living at the death of my son Sam." Under this provision, if Sam did not exercise the power of appointment, then the home in Malibu would go to the grandchildren living at Sam's death.

However, if Sam *exercised* this General power of appointment by his will, and appointed the home in Malibu "to my wife, W," then W would normally get the house at Sam's death, and the grandchildren would get nothing. Remember, since Sam had a General power of appointment, he was authorized to appoint the Malibu property to *anyone.* So the appointment to Sam's wife would certainly be appropriate.

But there is always some danger when a person exercises a General power of appointment. If it turned out that at Sam's death, he had more creditors than could be paid by using Sam's own property, then the rule of *"Just before Generous"* would be applied, and the home in Malibu could be taken by Sam's creditors - to the extent needed to pay Sam's debts to his own creditors. That is because of the rule that if a donee *exercises* a General power of appointment, under which he could have appointed the appointive property to his own creditors, then the creditors can come in and take the appointive property, to the extent necessary to provide for payment of Sam's own debts in full.

By contrast, if Sam had *not* exercised the General power, the home in Malibu would have ended up with the grandchildren of the donor - and would *not* have been subject to any claims by any of Sam's creditors.

So, when exercising a General power of appointment it would seem to be clear malpractice by the attorney involved to *exercise* a general power of appointment for the takers in default. In the example above, if Sam just declines to exercise the General power of appointment the home in Malibu will go directly to the grandchildren, free of any claims by Sam's creditors. But if Sam, (not being properly advised), *exercises* the General power of appointment, by appointing to the grandchildren in equal shares, then all that appointment has really accomplished is to open up the possibility that Sam's creditors will get some of the property.

So NEVER exercise a General power of appointment *on behalf of the takers in default.* If the donee really wants the appointive property to go to someone other than the takers in default, then the risks incurred by exercising a General power of appointment are probably worth it. But a General power should never be exercised for the takers in default. Just let them get the property in the safe way - by default.

C. EXAMPLE OF SPECIAL TESTAMENTARY POWER

An example of a Special testamentary power of appointment which might be included in a testator's will might say: "I give my ranch to my daughter, Debby, for life, and then to such one or more of Debby's children as she may appoint by her will, and if she fails to appoint, then to Debby's children who survive her, in equal shares."

In this situation the testator is the donor of the power. The daughter, Debby, is the donee of the power. Debby has a special, exclusive, testamentary power of appointment – because she has the power to exclude one or more of her children, if she wishes to do so. And there is a gift in default to Debby's children who survive her, in equal shares.

This sort of provision would allow testator to keep the ranch in the family for two more generations, and it would also give Debby the flexibility to decide which of her children should have the ranch – based on events which testator might not have been able to anticipate when testator wrote his or her will. Since this is a *Special* power, which could not be exercised for the donee or the donee's creditors anyway, there would be no application of the *Just before generous"* rule, and no creditors of Debby could take the ranch, whether or not Debby actually exercised the power.

D. LIMITS TO POWERS – RAP SECOND LOOK DOCTRINE

In a state which still has the common law Rule Against Perpetuities (RAP), there will be limits to how long this process of powers of appointment may be used to keep the ranch in the family.

The rule is that with any power of appointment other than a General Inter Vivos Power (which the donee could appoint to herself immediately), the time allowed by the Rule Against Perpetuities begins to run with the *creation of the power* – when the document that *creates the power* goes into effect.

So, in the example above, when testator *creates* the power in testator's will, the power is considered to have been created when testator dies, because testator's will goes into effect at testator's death. So testator is able to control who will own the ranch only for a time measured by "some life in being at the creation of the interest," plus 21 years. Usually the donee will be someone who was alive at testator's death, so the donee of the power will be a good "measuring life" - a good "life in being at the creation of the interest." But then the donee will have to be sure that the property actually gets to someone – outright – within 21 years after the donee's death.

There are lots more details on the application of the Rule Against Perpetuities elsewhere in the book. For now, just remember the important concept, for powers of appointment, that with all powers of appointment, (except General Inter Vivos powers), the time allowed by the Rule Against Perpetuities begins to run *at the creation of the power.*

It is, of course, impossible to know, at the time that the power is *created* exactly how the donee will exercise the power later on – how the donee will choose to fill in the blank in the donor's document. So in all jurisdictions, the court is allowed to take a *Second Look*, when the donee actually exercises the power, to ascertain how the power has been exercised, and to consider the facts as they actually exist when the donee finally exercises the power.

For example, if in his will *testator* made a direct gift, "To Debby for life, and then to such of Debby's children as reach the age of twenty-five," that attempted gift to

Debby's children would be void, under RAP, because it *might* turn out that at Debby's death she was survived by a one year old child, who would make it to age 25 - but could not do so within twenty-one years after A's death. So the attempted gift to Debby's children would be *void*, as soon as the *testator's* will went into effect.

On the other hand, if in testator's will he had instead provided that the gift should go "To Debby for life, then to such of Debby's children as *she may appoint by will*," it might turn out that the age restriction of twenty-five would be valid, because of the application of the Second Look doctrine.

Here's how that would work. If in her will Debby, the donee of the power of appointment said, "Then to those of my children who reach the age of twenty-five," AND *at Debby's death* her youngest child was already at least four years old, then by application of the Second Look doctrine - looking at the facts as they exist *when the power of appointment is exercised*, we would know that in fact, the gift to Debby's children would vest, if at all, within twenty-one years after Debby's life. Debby would not have any more children after Debby was dead, and any child of Debby's who ever made it to 25 would do so within twenty-one years after Debby's death, because at the time of Debby's death her *youngest* child was already four years old. So the gift to such of Debby's children as reach 25 would be good, when *Debby* exercised the power of appointment.

Note that we did not expand the time allowed by the common law Rule Against Perpetuities - 21 years after some life in being at the creation of the interest. RAP started running at the time testator's will went into effect. We merely waited until the blank left in testator's will was filled in by Debby, by her exercise of the power of appointment. Then, at the time the blank was filled in - when Debby exercised the power of appointment - it was clear under the facts at that time that all of Debby's children would reach twenty-five, if they ever did, within twenty-one years after the death of Debby.

So the use of a power of appointment, and application of the Second Look doctrine, allowed a gift to be made of testator's property which testator would not have been able to do, without use of a power of appointment.

Just remember that for the purposes of the Rule Against Perpetuities, the time begins to run at the *creation* of the power, and the court will take a *Second Look*, when the power is actually exercised, to be sure that the property *will* get to someone, (if at all), within the time allowed by the Rule Against Perpetuities. The court, of course, may take into account whatever has actually happened between the time the power was created and the time that the power was exercised. The is called *The Second Look Doctrine.*

The following cases should make all of this a bit easier to understand.

E. CASES INVOLVING POWERS OF APPOINTMENT

(1) EXERCISE OF A GENERAL TESTAMENTARY POWER

In the following case, what do you think of the donee of the power? Is there some argument that *you* could have made, leaving the facts just as they are, which would have allowed the children to win? Should anything special have happened in the following case when the donee exercised a General testamentary power of appointment? Just before Generous

Notice that the "blank" in the testator's will was not filled in until fifty-two years after his death, when his son finally exercised the General power of appointment.

Supreme Court, New York County, New York.
Samuel B. SEIDEL and Robert L. Werner as Trustees under a Trust Agreement made by Abraham L. Werner dated December 29, 1919, Plaintiffs,
v.
Edith Fisch WERNER, Individually and as Executrix of the Last Will and Testament of Steven L. Werner, deceased, et al., Defendants.
Feb. 24, 1975.

SAMUEL J. SILVERMAN, Justice:

Plaintiffs, trustees of a trust established in 1919 by Abraham L. Werner, sue for a declaratory judgment to determine who is entitled to one-half of the principal of the trust fund—the share in which Steven L. Werner, decedent (hereinafter 'Steven'), was the life beneficiary and over which he had a testamentary power of appointment. The dispute concerns the manner in which Steven exercised his power of appointment and is between Steven's second wife, Harriet G. Werner (hereinafter 'Harriet'), along with their children, Anna and Frank Werner (hereinafter 'Anna' and 'Frank') and Steven's third wife, Edith Fisch Werner (hereinafter 'Edith').

Anna and Frank claim Steven's entire share of the trust remainder on the basis of a Mexican consent judgment of divorce, obtained by Steven against Harriet on December 9, 1963, which incorporated by reference an approved a separation agreement, entered into between Steven and Harriet on December 1, 1963. That agreement included the following provision:

> '10. The Husband shall make, and hereby promises not to revoke, a will in which he shall exercise his testamentary power of appointment over his share in a trust known as 'Abraham L. Werner Trust No. 1' by establishing with respect to said share a trust for the benefit of the aforesaid Children.'

Paragraph 9 in relevant part provides for the wife to receive the income of the trust, upon the death of the husband, for the support and maintenance of the children, until they reach twenty-one years of age, at which time they are to receive the principal in equal shares.

On March 20, 1964, less than four months after entry of the divorce judgment, Steven executed a will in which instead of exercising his testamentary power of appointment in favor of Anna and Frank, he left everything to his third wife, Edith:

> 'First, I give, devise and bequeath all of my property * * * including * * * all property over which I have a power of testamentary disposition, to my wife, EDITH FISCH WERNER.'

Steven died in April 1971 and his Will was admitted to probate by the Surrogate's Court of New York County on July 11, 1973.

Paragraph 10 of the Separation Agreement is a contract to exercise a testamentary power of appointment not presently exercisable and as such is invalid under EPTL 10—5.3, which provides as follows:

> '(a) The donee of a power of appointment which is not presently exercisable or of a postponed power which has not become exercisable, cannot contract to make an appointment. Such a contract, if made, cannot be the basis of an action for specific performance or damages, but the promisee can obtain restitution of the value given by him for the promise unless the donee has exercised the power pursuant to the contract.'

This is a testamentary power of appointment. The original trust instrument provided in relevant part that:

> 'Upon the death of such child (Steven) the principal of such share shall be disposed of as such child shall by its last will direct, and in default of such testamentary disposition then the same shall go to the issue of such child then surviving per stirpes .'

It is not disputed that New York law is determinative of the validity of Paragraph 10 of the Separation Agreement; the Separation Agreement itself provides that New York law shall govern.

The reasoning underlying the refusal to enforce a contract to exercise a testamentary power was stated by Justice Cardozo in the case of Farmers' Loan & Trust Co. v. Mortimer, (1916):

> 'The exercise of the power was to represent the final judgment, the last will, of the donee. Up to the last moment of his life he was to have the power to deal with the share as he thought best. To permit him to bargain that right away would be to defeat the purpose of the donor. Her command was that her property should go to her son's issue unless at the end of his life it remained his will that it go elsewhere. It has not remained his will that it go elsewhere; and his earlier contract cannot nullify the expression of his final purpose. 'It is not, I apprehend, to be doubted,' says Rolt, L.J., in Cooper v. Martin, 'that equity will never uphold an act which will defeat what the person creating the power has declared, by expression or necessary implication, to be a material part of his intention.'

The question then is whether entry of the Mexican divorce decree, incorporating the Separation Agreement, alters this result; I do not think it does.

Whatever the judgment in this case, it would not impair the Mexican decree, which did not direct Steven to exercise his power of appointment, or to do anything at all with respect to the power, but merely 'approved' the separation agreement, as fair and reasonable.

Since this is a foreign divorce decree, and one entered into by consent, it is at most entitled to the respect which derives from principles of comity. I think comity does not require enforcing a Mexican consent judgment in a manner that the Mexican court did not pass upon or consider under rules of New York property law with which the Mexican court was presumably unfamiliar and which would seriously affect the rights of New York litigants.

However, under New York law, EPTL 10—5.3(b) permits a donee of a power to release the power, and that release, if in conformity with EPTL 10—9.2, prevents the donee from then exercising the power thereafter.

Under the terms of the trust instrument, if Steven fails to exercise his power of appointment, Anna and Frank (along with the children of Steven's first marriage) take the remainder, i.e., the property which is the subject of Steven's power of appointment. Therefore, Harriet, Anna and Frank argue that at a minimum Steven's agreement should be construed as a release of his power of appointment, and that Anna and Frank should be permitted to take as on default of appointment.

There is respectable authority—by no means unanimous authority, and none binding on this Court—to the effect that a promise to appoint a given sum to persons who would take in default of appointment should, to that extent, be deemed a release of the power of appointment. See Restatement of Property (1940); Simes and Smith, The Law of Future Interests (1956).

This argument has the appeal that it seems to be consistent with the exception that the release statute (EPTL 10—5.3(b)) carves out; and is also consistent with the intentions and reasonable expectations of the parties at the time they entered into the agreement to appoint, here in the separation agreement; and that therefore perhaps in these circumstances the difference between what the parties agreed to and a release of the power of appointment is merely one of form.

Whatever may be the possible validity or applicability of this argument to other circumstances and situations, I think it is inapplicable to this situation because:

It is clear that the parties did not intend a release of the power of appointment. Indeed, the agreement—unlike a release of a power of appointment—expressly contemplates that something will be done by the donee of the power in the future, and that that something will be an exercise of the power of appointment. Thus, the agreement, in the very language said to be a release of the power of appointment, says (Par. 10):

> 'The Husband *shall* make a will in which he *shall* exercise his testamentary power of appointment'. (Emphasis added)

Nor is the substantial effect of the promised exercise of the power the same as would follow from release of, or failure to exercise the power.

Under the separation agreement, the power is to be exercised so that the entire appointive property shall be for the benefit of Anna and Frank; under the trust instrument, on default of exercise of the power, the property goes to all of Steven's children (Anna, Frank and the two children of Steven's first marriage). Thus the agreement provides for appointment of a greater principal to Anna and Frank than they would get in default of appointment.

Under the trust instrument, on default of exercise of the power, the property goes to the four children absolutely and in fee. The separation agreement provides that Steven shall create a Trust, with Income payable to Harriet as trustee, for the support of Anna and Frank until they both reach the age of 21, at which time the principal shall be paid to them or the survivor; and if both fail to attain the age of 21, then the principal shall revert to Steven's estate. Thus, Anna and Frank's interest in the principal would be a defeasible interest if they did not live to be 21; and indeed at Steven's death they were both still under 21 so that their interest was defeasible.

Finally, under the separation agreement, as just noted, if Anna and Frank failed to qualify to take the principal, either because they both died before Steven or before reaching the age of twenty-one, then the principal would go to Steven's estate. Under the trust instrument, on the other hand, on default of appointment and an inability of Anna and Frank to take, Steven's share of the principal would not go to Steven's estate, but to his other children, if living, and if not, to the settlor's next of kin.

In these circumstances, I think it is too strained and tortuous to construe the separation agreement provision as the equivalent of a release of the power of appointment. If this is a release then the exception has swallowed and destroyed the principal rule.

Accordingly, I hold that the separation agreement is not the equivalent of a total or partial release of the power of appointment.

Anna and Frank also seek restitution out of the trust fund of the value given by them in exchange for Steven's unfulfilled promise. EPTL 10—5.3(a) provides that although the contract to make an appointment cannot be the basis for an action for specific performance or damages, 'the promisee can obtain restitution of the value given by him for the promise unless the donee has exercised the power pursuant to contract.'

Anna and Frank's remedy is limited, however, to the claim for restitution that they have (and apparently have asserted) against Steven's estate. They may not seek restitution out of the trust fund, even if their allegation that the estate lacks sufficient assets to meet this claim were factually supported, because the trust fund was not the property of Steven, except to the extent of his life estate, so as to be subject to the equitable remedy of restitution, but was the property of the donor of the power of appointment until it vested in someone else.

Finally, Edith moves for summary judgment that she is entitled to receive Steven's share of the trust fund on the ground that Steven exercised his testamentary power in her favor in his will of March 20, 1964, in the provision quoted at the beginning of this decision.

Since there are no factual questions raised as to Steven's exercise of his testamentary power of appointment in Edith's favor in that will provision, and since each of the other defendants' conflicting claims to the share of trust principal has been dismissed, Edith's motion for summary judgment is granted.

Accordingly, on the motions for summary judgment I direct judgment declaring that defendant Edith Fisch Werner is entitled to the one-half share of Steven C. Werner in the principal of the Abraham L. Werner trust.

Note: Could a better attorney have secured some of the trust money for the children? What about "Just Before Generous?"

(2) PARTIAL EXERCISE OF A SPECIAL POWER

This next case is more challenging to read, but you have to admire a woman who, in 1898, was trying to make sure that Harvard would admit women to the Medical School on the same footing as men. Almost ninety years after her death, the careful, specific wording of her power of appointment still controls.

Supreme Judicial Court of Massachusetts.
Augustus P. LORING et al. trustees,
v.
Colin Sam. MARSHALL et al.
Decided Nov. 7, 1985.

WILKINS, Justice.

This complaint seeks instructions as to the disposition of the remainder of a trust created under the will of Marian Hovey.[1] In Massachusetts Inst. of Technology v. Loring, (1951), this court held that the President and Fellows of Harvard College, the Boston Museum of Fine Arts, and Massachusetts Institute of Technology (the charities) would not be entitled to the remainder of the trust on its termination. The court, however, did not decide, as we now must, what ultimate disposition should be made of the trust principal.

Marian Hovey died in 1898, survived by a brother, Henry Hovey, a sister, Fanny H. Morse, and two nephews, John Torrey Morse, Third, and Cabot Jackson Morse. By her will, Marian Hovey left the residue of her estate in trust, the income payable in equal shares to her brother and sister during their lives. Upon her brother's death in 1900, his share of the income passed to her sister, and, upon her sister's death in 1922, the income was paid in equal shares to her two nephews.

John Torrey Morse, Third, died in 1928, unmarried and without issue. His share of the income then passed to his brother, Cabot Jackson Morse, who remained the sole income beneficiary until his death in 1946.

At that point, the death of the last surviving income beneficiary, Marian Hovey's will provided for the treatment of the trust assets in the following language:

> "At the death of the last survivor of my said brother and sister and my two said nephews, or at my death, if none of them be then living, the trustees shall divide the trust fund in their hands into two equal parts, and shall transfer and pay over one of such parts to the use of the wife and issue of each of my said nephews as he may by will have appointed; provided, that if his wife was living at my death he shall appoint to her no larger interest in the property possessed by me than a right to the income during her life, and if she was living at the death of my father, he shall appoint to her no larger interest in the property over which I have a power of disposition under the will of my father than a right to the income during her life; and the same limitations shall apply to the appointment of income as aforesaid. If either of my said nephews shall leave no such appointees then living, the whole of the trust fund shall be paid to the appointees of his said brother as aforesaid. If neither of my said nephews leave such appointees then living the whole trust fund shall be paid over and transferred in equal shares to the Boston Museum of Fine Arts, the Massachusetts Institute of Technology, and the President and Fellows of Harvard College for the benefit of the Medical School; provided, that if the said Medical School shall not then admit women to instruction on an equal footing with men, the said President and Fellows shall not receive any part of the trust property, but it shall be divided equally between the Boston Museum of Fine

[1] Questions involving the wills of Marian Hovey and her nephew, Cabot Jackson Morse, have been before this court on four prior occasions. (1948), (1951), (1953), and (1954).

Arts and the Massachusetts Institute of Technology."[2]

The will thus gave Cabot Jackson Morse, the surviving nephew, a special power to appoint the trust principal to his "wife and issue" with the limitation that only income could be appointed to a widow who was living at Marian Hovey's death. Cabot Jackson Morse was survived by his wife, Anna Braden Morse, who was living at Marian Hovey's death, and by his only child, Cabot Jackson Morse, Jr., a child of an earlier marriage, who died in 1948, two years after his father. Cabot Jackson Morse left a will which contained the following provisions:

> "*Second*: I give to my son, Cabot Jackson Morse, Jr., the sum of one dollar ($1.00), as he is otherwise amply provided for.
>
> "*Third*: The power of appointment which I have under the wills of my aunt, Marian Hovey, and my uncle, Henry Hovey, both late of Gloucester, Massachusetts, I exercise as follows: I appoint to my wife, Anna Braden Morse, the right to the income during her lifetime of all of the property to which my power of appointment applies under the will of Marian Hovey, and I appoint to my wife the right during her widowhood to the income to which I would be entitled under the will of Henry Hovey if I were living.
>
> "*Fourth*: All the rest, residue and remainder of my estate, wherever situated, real or personal, in trust or otherwise, I leave outright and in fee simple to my wife, Anna Braden Morse."

this is all he can give her

In 1948, we held that the appointment of a life interest to Anna Braden Morse was valid, notwithstanding Cabot Jackson Morse's failure fully to exercise the power by appointing the trust principal. Consequently, the trust income following Cabot Jackson Morse's death was paid to Anna Braden Morse until her death in 1983, when the principal became distributable. The trustees thereupon brought this complaint for instructions.

G

The complaint alleges that the trustees "are uncertain as to who is entitled to the remainder of the Marian Hovey Trust now that the trust is distributable and specifically whether the trust principal should be paid in any one of the following manners: (a) to the estate of Cabot Jackson Morse, Jr. as the only permissible appointee of the remainder of the trust living at the death of Cabot Jackson Morse; (b) in equal shares to the estates of Cabot Jackson Morse, Jr. and Anna Braden Morse as the only permissible appointees living at the death of Cabot Jackson Morse; (c) to the estate of Anna Braden Morse as the only actual appointee living at the death of Cabot Jackson Morse; (d) to the intestate takers of Marian Hovey's estate on the basis that Marian Hovey failed to

[2] The parties have stipulated that at the relevant time Harvard Medical School admitted women to instruction on an equal footing with men.

make a complete disposition of her property by her will; (e) to Massachusetts Institute of Technology, Museum of Fine Arts and the President and Fellows of Harvard College in equal shares as remaindermen of the trust; or (f) some other disposition." Before us each named potential taker claims to be entitled to trust principal.

In our 1951 opinion we explained why in the circumstances the charities had no interest in the trust: "The rights of the petitioning charities as remaindermen depend upon the proposition that Cabot J. Morse, Senior, did not leave an 'appointee' although he appointed his wife Anna Braden Morse to receive the income during her life. The time when, if at all, the 'whole trust fund' was to be paid over and transferred to the petitioning charities is the time of the death of Cabot J. Morse, Senior. At that time the whole trust fund could not be paid over and transferred to the petitioning charities, because Anna Braden Morse still retained the income for her life. We think that the phrase no 'such appointees then living' is not the equivalent of an express gift in default of appointment, a phrase used by the testatrix in the preceding paragraph." In 1953 the court reiterated that the charities had no interest in the trust fund.

It is apparent that Marian Hovey knew how to refer to a disposition in default of appointment from her use of the terms elsewhere in her will. She did not use those words in describing the potential gift to the charities. A fair reading of the will's crucial language may rightly be that the charities were not to take the principal unless no class member who could receive principal was then living (i.e., if no possible appointee of principal was living at the death of the surviving donee). Regardless of how the words "no such appointees then living" are construed, the express circumstances under which the charities were to take did not occur. The question is what disposition should be made of the principal in the absence of any explicit direction in the will.

Although in its 1951 opinion this court disavowed making a determination of the "ultimate destination of the trust fund," the opinion cited the Restatement of Property § 367(2) (1940), and 1 A. Scott, Trusts § 27.1 (1st ed.1939) [3] to the effect that when a special power of appointment is not exercised and absent specific language indicating an express gift in default of appointment, the property not appointed goes in equal shares to the members of the class to whom the property could have been appointed.

Applying this rule of law, we find no specific language in the will which indicates a gift in default of appointment in the event Cabot Jackson Morse should fail to appoint

[3] "In Restatement: Property, § 367(2), it is said, with certain immaterial exceptions, that 'where there is a special power and no gift in default of appointment in specific language, property not effectively appointed passes to those living objects to whom the donee could have appointed at the time of expiration of the power, unless the donor has manifested an intent that the objects shall receive the property only so far as the donee elects to appoint it to them.' In Scott, Trusts, § 27.1, the author says, 'Where there is no express gift over in default of appointment the inference is that the donor intended the members of the class to take even though the donee should fail to exercise the power. The inference is that he did not intend that they should take only if the donee should choose to exercise the power. The cases are numerous in which it has been held that the members of the class are entitled to the property in equal shares where the donee of a power to appoint among them fails to exercise the power.'

the principal. The charities argue that the will's reference to them suggests that in default of appointment Marian Hovey intended them to take. On the other hand, in one of the earlier cases we commented that Marian Hovey's "will discloses an intent to keep her property in the family." The interests Marian Hovey gave to her sister and brother were life interests, as were the interests given to her nephews. The share of any nephew who died unmarried and without issue, as did one, was added to the share of the other nephew. Each nephew was limited to exercising his power of appointment only in favor of his issue and his widow.[4] We think the apparent intent to keep the assets within the family is sufficiently strong to overcome any claim that Marian Hovey's will "expressly" or "in specific language" provides for a gift to the charities in default of appointment.[5]

If we were to depart from the view taken thirty-four years ago in the 1951 case, and now were to conclude that under the terms of Marian Hovey's will the charities were to receive the trust principal, we would face the problem that, under normal principles of res judicata, our earlier decision against the charities is binding on them. Any suggestion that our 1951 decision did not bind the charities because the Attorney General was not a party to that proceeding is not supported by authority. The charities themselves brought the earlier action and chose not to name the Attorney General as a party. To conclude now that the Attorney General's involvement was indispensable to a valid determination in the 1951 action would cast a shadow over hundreds of pre-1954 decisions concerning charitable interests under wills and trusts.

The same arguments made by the charities and the Attorney General in this case were considered and rejected in 1951.

What we have said also disposes of the claim that the trust principal should pass to Marian Hovey's heirs as intestate property, a result generally disfavored in the interpretation of testamentary dispositions.

The claim of the executors of the estate of Anna Braden Morse that her estate should take as the class, or at least as a member of the class, must fail because Marian Hovey's will specifically limits such a widow's potential stake to a life interest.

A judgment shall be entered instructing the trustees under the will of Marian Hovey to distribute the trust principal to the executors of the estate of Cabot Jackson Morse, Jr. The allowance of counsel fees, costs, and expenses from the principal of the trust is to be in the discretion of the single justice.

So ordered.

---

[4] The gift to any widow was to be a life interest if she were living at Marian Hovey's death.

[5] The nominal distribution made to his son in the donee's will provides no proper guide to the resolution of the issues in this case. We are concerned here with the intention of Marian Hovey, the donor of the special power of appointment. The intentions of the donee of the power of appointment are irrelevant in construing the donor's intent. Cabot Jackson Morse's intention with regard to his exercise of the power of appointment is irrelevant in determining his aunt's intention concerning the consequences of his partial failure to exercise that power.

Note: So much for Cabot, Sr.'s attempt to give Cabot, Jr. only $1.

(3) CREDITORS OF A DONEE

The following case deals with the issue of whether or not a judgment creditor can *force* the donee of a General power of appointment to exercise that power – so that the creditor can get paid. The trust provision at issue is one that is frequently included in trusts, so it might be expected that this issue will arise often. The following case represents an orthodox resolution of the issue.

Court of Appeals of Indiana
Irwin Union Bank and Trust Company
Philip W. Long v. Victoria B. Long
June 25, 1974

OPINION BY: LOWDERMILK

On February 3, 1957, Victoria Long, appellee herein, obtained a judgment in the amount of $15,000 against Philip W. Long, which judgment emanated from a divorce decree. In this action appellee sought satisfaction of that judgment by pursuing funds allegedly owed to Philip W. Long as a result of a trust set up by Laura Long, his mother.

Appellee alleged that the Irwin Union Bank and Trust Company (Union Bank) was indebted to Philip W. Long as the result of its position as trustee of the trust created by Laura Long. On April 24, 1969, the trial court ordered that any income, property, or profits, which were owed to Philip Long and not exempt from execution should be applied to the divorce judgment. Thereafter, on February 13, 1973, the trial court ordered that four percent (4%) of the trust corpus of the trust created by Laura Long which benefited Philip Long was not exempt from execution and could be levied upon by appellee and ordered a writ of execution. Union Bank, as trustee, appealed.

The pertinent portion of the trust created by Laura Long is as follows, to-wit:

> "ITEM VC
> "Withdrawal of Principal.
> When Philip W. Long, Jr. has attained the age of twenty-one (21) years and is not a full-time student at an educational institution as a candidate for a Bachelor of Arts or Bachelor of Sciences degree, Philip W. Long shall have the right to withdraw from principal once in any calendar year upon thirty (30) days written notice to the Trustee up to four percent (4%) of the market value of the entire trust principal on the date of such notice, which right shall not be cumulative."

The primary issue raised on this appeal is whether the trial court erred in allowing execution on the 4% of the trust corpus.

Appellant contends that Philip Long's right to withdraw 4% of the trust corpus is, in fact, a general power of appointment. Union Bank further contends that since Philip Long has never exercised his right of withdrawal, pursuant to the provisions of the trust instrument, no creditors of Philip Long can reach the trust corpus. Appellant points out that if the power of appointment is unexercised, the creditors cannot force the exercise of said power and cannot reach the trust corpus in this case.

Appellee posits that the condition precedent to Philip Long's right of withdrawal has been met and therefore Philip Long has an absolute right to the present enjoyment of 4% of the trust corpus simply by making a written request to the trustee. Appellee contends that this is a vested right and is consistent with the intentions of the donor, Laura Long. Appellee further contends in her brief that the right of withdrawal is not a power of appointment, but is, rather, a power of augmentation and relies upon the *Restatement of the Law of Property, § 318*, which reads as follows, to-wit:

> "Definition -- Power of Appointment.
> (1) Except as stated in Subsection (2), a power of appointment, as the term is used in this Restatement, is a power created or reserved by a person (the donor) having property subject to his disposition enabling the donee of the power to designate, within such limits as the donor may prescribe, the transferees of the property or the shares in which it shall be received.
> (2) The term power of appointment does not include a power of sale, a power of attorney, a power of revocation, a **power to cause a gift of income to be augmented out of principal,** a power to designate charities, a charitable trust, a discretionary trust, or an honorary trust." (Emphasis added.)

It is the position of appellee that if the right of withdrawal is not a power of appointment under *§ 318, supra*, then the cases and authorities relied upon by appellant which relate to powers of appointment will not be in point.

Appellee also argues that Philip has absolute control and use of the 4% of the corpus and that the bank does not have control over that portion of the corpus if Philip decides to exercise his right of withdrawal. Appellee argues that the intention of Laura Long was to give Philip not only an income interest in the trust but a fixed amount of corpus which he could use as he saw fit. Thus, Philip Long would have a right to the present enjoyment of 4% of the trust corpus. A summation of appellee's argument, as stated in her brief, is as follows: "So it is with Philip -- he can get it if he desires it, so why cannot Victoria get it even if Philip does not desire it?"

We have had no Indiana authority directly in point cited to us by either of the parties and a thorough research of this issue does not reveal any Indiana authority on point. Thus, this issue so far as we can determine is one of first impression in Indiana.

The distinction which appellee seeks to rely upon based on the Restatement of the Law of Property in regard to a power of augmentation is apparently such a distinction only in that authority. We have found no cases or treatises which follow the distinction made in the Restatement. We have found one treatise which expressly refutes the distinction between a power of appointment and a power of augmentation, as set out in the Restatement.

Further, appellee has failed to point out exactly how the distinction made in the Restatement would affect the case at bar. Appellee cites no authority which says that an unexercised power of augmentation can be reached by creditors.

Broadly speaking, a power is said to be general if it can be exercised in favor of anyone whom the donee may select. A power is defined in Thompson on Real Property as follows:

> "§ 2025. What a 'power' is. -- Broadly stated, a 'power' is an authority enabling one person to dispose of an interest which is vested in another. It is an authority reserved by or limited to one to do certain acts in relation to the subject matter of the gift for his own benefit or for the benefit of another.
> "Powers are either general or special. They are general when they are capable of being exercised by the donee in favor of any person, including himself, and are not restricted as to the estate or interest over which he may exercise the power, while the power is special if its exercise is restricted to particular persons, or a particular class of persons, or if it can be exercised only for certain named purposes or under certain conditions. "

The Supreme Court of Texas, in the case of *Republic National Bank of Dallas v. Fredericks* discussed and defined power of appointment and stated:

> "Subject to certain restrictions, the common law accords to the individual a right to delegate to another person the power of designating or selecting the takers of his property. The authority thus to control the disposition of the estate of the grantor or testator is referred to as a 'power of appointment.'

An examination of the pertinent parts of the trust created by Laura Long indicates that the power which was given to Philip Long in Item VC falls under the definition of power of appointment, as set out above. Philip Long may exercise the power which was delegated to him by Laura Long, that being to distribute property not his own.

A reading of Item VC, *supra*, does not disclose any direct reference to a power of appointment. However, it is not necessary that the actual words "power of appointment" be used in order to create such a power.

Thompson on Real Property, *supra*, § 2025, states:

> "No particular form or words is necessary for the creation of a power; any expression, however, informal, is sufficient if it clearly indicates an intention to give a power. Where the intention to create the power is plain, it should be given effect. All that is necessary is an indication of a clear intention to accomplish some proper purpose by the donor through the donee. It may be conferred by express words, or may be necessarily implied."

Appellee contends that the right of withdrawal of Philip Long is a vested property right rather than a power of appointment. However, it is our opinion that such is not the case. This problem was discussed in *62 Am. Jur. 2d, Powers, § 107,* as follows:

> ". . Creating a general power of appointment is virtually an offer to the donee of the estate or fund that he may receive or reject at will, and like any other offer to donate property to a person, no title can vest until he accepts the offer, nor can a court of equity compel him to accept the property or fund against his will, even for the benefit of creditors."

Blue

The leading case on this issue is *Gilman v. Bell (1881),* wherein the Illinois Supreme Court discussed powers of appointment and vesting as follows:

> "No title or interest in the thing vests in the donee of the power until he exercises the power. It is virtually an offer to him of the estate or fund, that he may receive or reject at will, and like any other offer to donate property to a person, no title can vest until he accepts the offer, nor can a court of equity compel him to accept the property or fund against his will, even for the benefit of creditors. Until accepted, the person to whom the offer is made has not, nor can he have, the slightest interest or title to the property. So the donee of the power only receives the naked power to make the property or fund his own. And when he exercises the power, he thereby consents to receive it, and the title thereby vests in him."

Contrary to the contention of appellee, it is our opinion that Philip Long has no control over the trust corpus until he exercises his power of appointment and gives notice to the trustee that he wishes to receive his 4% of the trust corpus. Until such an exercise is made, the trustee has the absolute control and benefit of the trust corpus within the terms of the trust instrument.

While not controlling as precedent, we find that the Federal Estate Tax laws are quite analogous to the case at bar. Under *§ 2041*, Powers of Appointment, of the Internal Revenue Code, it is clear that the interest given to Philip Long under Item VC would be considered a power of appointment for estate tax purposes. A general power of appointment is defined in *§ 2041(B) (1)* as follows:

"(1) General Power of Appointment. -- The term 'general power of appointment' means a power which is exercisable in favor of the decedent, his estate, his creditors, or the creditors of his estate"

The regulations pertinent to this issue discuss a power of appointment as it is used for estate tax purposes as follows:

"(b) Definition of 'power of appointment' (1) In general. The term 'power of appointment' includes all powers which are in substance and effect powers of appointment regardless of the nomenclature used in creating the power and regardless of local property law connotations. For example, if a trust instrument provides that the beneficiary may appropriate or consume the principal of the trust, the power to consume or appropriate is a power of appointment. "

For estate tax purposes even the failure to exercise a power of appointment may lead to tax consequences. Under *§ 2041(B) (2)* the lapse of a power of appointment will be considered a release of such power during the calendar year to the extent of the value of the power in question. However, the lapsed power will only be considered a release and includable in the gross estate of a decedent if the value of the lapsed power is greater than $ 5,000 or 5% of the aggregate value of the assets out of which the lapsed power could have been satisfied.

The trust instrument signed by Laura Long was obviously carefully drawn with the tax consequences bearing an important place in the overall intent of the testator. The trust as a whole is set up to give the grandchildren of Laura Long the substantial portion of the assets involved. We note with interest that the percentage of corpus which Philip Long may receive is carefully limited to a percentage less than that which would be includable in the gross estate of Philip Long should he die within a year in which he had allowed his power of appointment to lapse.

It is elementary that courts will seek to ascertain the intention of the testator by giving a full consideration to the entire will. The trust created in the will of Laura Long, in our opinion, has the legal effect of creating a power of appointment in Philip Long under Item VC of the trust.

Philip Long has never exercised his power of appointment under the trust. Such a situation is discussed in II Scott on Trusts, § 147.3 as follows:

"Where the power is a special power, a power to appoint only among a group of persons, the power is not beneficial to the donee and cannot, of course, be reached by his creditors. Where the power is a general power, that is, a power to appoint to anyone including the donee himself or his estate, the power is beneficial to the donee. If the donee exercises the power by appointing to a volunteer, the property appointed can be reached by his creditors if his other assets are insufficient for the payment of his debts. ***[Editor's Note: This rule is frequently referred to as the rule that the donee must be just before generous – in other words that the donee must pay his or her own debts, before making generous gifts to others.]*** But where the donee of a general power created by some person other than himself fails to exercise the power, his creditors cannot acquire the power or compel its exercise, nor can they reach the property covered by the power, unless it is otherwise provided by statute."

Indiana has no statute which would authorize a creditor to reach property covered by a power of appointment which is unexercised.

The doctrine has been long established in the English courts, that the courts of equity will not aid creditors in case there is a non-execution of the power.

Appellee concedes that if we find that Philip Long had merely an unexercised power of appointment then creditors are in no position to either force the exercise of the power or to reach the trust corpus. Thus, it is clear that the trial court erred when it granted the writ of execution.

Reversed and remanded.

CHAPTER 14 - DUTIES OF THE TRUSTEE

A. THE PRUDENT MAN RULE

In the early Massachusetts case of Harvard College v. Amory (1830), the rule was laid down that when a trustee invests the assets of the trust, the trustee must "observe how men of prudence, discretion, and intelligence manage their own affairs, not in regard to speculation, but in regard to the permanent disposition of their funds, considering the probable income, as well as the probable safety of the capital to be invested." This standard of investment became known as the "Prudent Man Rule," and was the basic standard for trustees until some states adopted a modified standard in recent years. Whether or not the particular trustee had any special expertise in handling financial matters, the trustee was expected to live up to the dictates of the prudent man rule.

The prudent man rule is the basic guideline for all actions by a trustee. In addition, there are many standard rules for specific situations.

B. DUTY NOT TO DELEGATE

One traditional rule which is still in effect in many states is the rule that the trustee is not allowed to delegate investment decisions to another. Whether or not the trustee has any particular expertise in investments, the trustee is expected to live up to the dictates of the Prudent Man Rule, and to make all significant decisions as to trust investments – without delegation of the investment authority.

The following case illustrates one way in which these two rules, the Prudent Man Rule and the Duty not to Delegate, were applied to the actions of a family member trustee, who clearly had no special expertise in investments. Is the result in this case what the settlor would have wanted for her daughter, Mary Jane?

Supreme Court of Arizona.
SHRINERS HOSPITALS FOR CRIPPLED CHILDREN, Petitioner-Appellant, v. Mary Jane GARDINER, Trustee; the Laurable Gardiner Trust, Respondents-Appellees
February 3, 1987

OPINION BY: HAYS

Laurabel Gardiner established a trust to provide income to her daughter, Mary Jane Gardiner; her two grandchildren, Charles Gardiner and Robert Gardiner; and a now deceased daughter-in-law, Jean Gardiner. The remainder of the estate passes to Shriners Hospitals for Crippled Children (Shriners) upon the death of the life income beneficiaries. Laurabel appointed Mary Jane as trustee, Charles as first alternate trustee, and Robert as second alternate trustee. Mary Jane was not an experienced investor, and she placed the trust assets with Dean Witter Reynolds, a brokerage house. Charles, an investment counselor and stockbroker, made all investment decisions concerning the trust assets. At some point in time, Charles embezzled $317,234.36 from the trust. Shriners brought a petition to surcharge Mary Jane for the full $317,234.36. The trial court denied the petition, but a divided court of appeals reversed. We granted review.

1. BREACH OF FIDUCIARY DUTY

In Arizona, a trustee has the duty to "observe the standard in dealing with the trust assets that would be observed by a prudent man dealing with the property of another." If the trustee breaches that responsibility, he is personally liable for any resulting loss to the trust assets. A trustee breaches the prudent man standard when he delegates responsibilities that he reasonably can be expected personally to perform.

We believe that Mary Jane breached the prudent man standard when she transferred investment power to Charles. Mary Jane argues, and we agree, that a trustee lacking investment experience must seek out expert advice. Although a trustee must seek out expert advice, "he is not ordinarily justified in relying on such advice, but must exercise his own judgment." (A trustee must not only obtain information concerning investment possibilities but also is "under a duty to use a reasonable degree of skill in selecting an investment"). Mary Jane, though, did not evaluate Charles' advice and then make her own decisions. Charles managed the trust fund, not Mary Jane. A prudent investor would certainly participate, to some degree, in investment decisions.

Mary Jane unquestionably transferred trustee discretion to Charles.

Mary Jane's second accounting of the Gardiner trust states:

> "From time to time the Trustee made investments ("investments") in the money market and also in the purchase and sale of shares of stock listed on the New York Stock Exchange, the American Stock Exchange and the Over-the-Counter Markets . . . . *All of said investments were made on behalf of the Trust Estate by a person qualified in that business,* [Charles] *who was selected by and in whom the Trustee justifiably had the utmost trust and confidence.*" (Emphasis added)

Most damning, however, are the admissions of Mary Jane's own attorney.

> "Now, we can show, if the Court pleases, by way of evidence if counsel will not accept my avowal, we can show that Charles Gardiner for the past many years, including several years prior to and since these assets were placed in his hands for investment, was in the business of a consultant and in the business of

> investing and selecting investments in the stock market, and this he did. And it was only natural that Mary Jane would turn to him to make that selection, to invest those funds and to account in an appropriate proceeding if, as and when required. So the prudent man rule has been adhered to here. She got a man who is capable and fortunately he was a man who was designated as an alternate trustee *and for all practical purposes really served as trustee*." (Emphasis added)

yikes

Together, the accounting and admissions establish that Charles was functioning as a surrogate trustee. Mary Jane was not exercising any control over the selection of investments. She clearly breached her duties to act prudently and to personally perform her duties as a trustee. A fiduciary may not delegate to another the performance of a duty involving discretion and judgment.

Even on appeal, Mary Jane does not argue that she, in fact, exercised any discretionary investment power. Instead, she argues that her lack of investment experience made it prudent for her to delegate her investment power. She relies on the *Restatement (Second) of Torts § 171*.

> "*§ 171*. Duty Not To Delegate
>
> "The trustee is under a duty to the beneficiary not to delegate to others the doing of acts which the trustee can reasonably be required personally to perform."

Mary Jane asserts that her lack of investment experience prevented her from personally exercising investment power and consequently permitted delegation of that power. The standard of care required, however, is measured objectively. The standard of care required of a trustee does not take into account the "differing degrees of education or intellect possessed by a fiduciary". The trustee must be *reasonable* in her delegation. A delegation of investment authority is unreasonable and therefore Mary Jane's delegation is a breach of trust. *See Estate of Baldwin* (Me.1982) (bank trustee liable for losses incurred when it failed to monitor management of grocery store despite bank's lack of expertise in grocery store management).

It is of no import that Charles was named as alternate trustee. A trustee is not permitted to delegate his responsibilities to a co-trustee. Certainly, then, a trustee is subject to liability when she improperly delegates her investment responsibility to an alternate trustee.

Mary Jane also argues that broad language in the trust document permitted her to delegate her investment authority to Charles. A trust document may allow a trustee to delegate powers ordinarily non-delegable. The Gardiner Trust permits the trustee "to employ and compensate attorneys, accountants, agents and brokers." This language does not bear on Mary Jane's delegation of investment authority. Mary Jane did not

spell it out

use for family member trustee

simply employ Charles; she allowed him to serve as surrogate trustee. We view this language as merely an express recognition of the trustee's obligation to obtain expert advice, not as a license to remove herself from her role as a trustee.

2. PROXIMATE CAUSE

Mary Jane next argues that there is no causal connection between her breach and the loss suffered by the trust. The court of appeals rejected this argument in a summary fashion, stating that "the trustee offers no evidence to meet this burden of showing that the loss would have occurred anyway." We disagree.

The very nature of the loss indicates that the breach was not causally connected to the loss. The accounting indicates that Charles embezzled the funds.

> "Without the knowledge or consent of the Trustee, said person received from said investments, and diverted to his own use, a total believed by the Trustee to aggregate $317,234.36 ($116,695.55 on January 16, 1981 and $200,537.81 on March 4, 1981). The trustee did not learn of said diversions until long after they occurred. No part of the amount so diverted had been returned or paid to the Trustee or the Trust Estate."

If the trust had suffered because poor investments were made, the delegation of investment authority would unquestionably be the cause of the loss. Otherwise, a causal connection between Charles' diversion of funds and Mary Jane's breach is absent unless the delegation of investment authority gave Charles control and dominion over the trust fund that permitted the defalcation.

A causal connection does not exist simply because "but for" Mary Jane's opening of the account at Dean Witter Reynolds, no loss would have occurred. A trustee is not personally liable for losses not resulting from a breach of trust. Mary Jane did not breach her duty by establishing an account at Dean Witter Reynolds, a major brokerage house. Charles was not only the type of person Mary Jane was obliged to seek out for investment advice, but he was a person whom Laurabel Gardiner indicated was trustworthy by naming him as second alternate trustee. Furthermore, the Dean Witter Reynolds account was apparently in Mary Jane's name. If Dean Witter Reynolds wrongfully allowed Charles access to the fund, Mary Jane is not personally liable. A trustee is not generally liable for wrongful acts of agents employed in administration of estate.

Unfortunately, the record does not reveal the nature of the diversion. The relative culpability of Charles, Mary Jane and Dean Witter Reynolds is unclear. The trial court found that Mary Jane was without fault and, therefore, did not consider the causal connection between Mary Jane's breach and Charles's defalcation. The inadequacy of the record demands a remand for a determination of the relationship between Mary Jane's delegation of investment authority and Charles' diversion of funds.

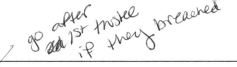

3. ROBERT GARDINER AS TRUSTEE

If, after remand, the trial court determines that Mary Jane is personally liable for the diversion of funds, Robert must be removed as trustee.[1]

A trustee is liable to a beneficiary if he fails to "redress a breach of trust committed by the predecessor trustee." *Restatement (Second) of Trusts § 223(2)*. Robert would, therefore, have a duty to enforce the surcharge against his aunt and ward, Mary Jane. The conflict between personal responsibilities and trust obligations is obvious and great. *Estate of Rothko, (1977)* (while a trustee is administering the trust he must refrain from placing himself in position where his personal interest does or may conflict with interest of beneficiaries). Another trustee, without such conflicts, would have to be appointed.

The decision of the court of appeals is vacated, and the case is remanded for further proceedings consistent with this opinion.

C. THE PRUDENT INVESTOR RULE

Cases such as the preceding case have caused many jurisdictions to adopt more liberal rules, such as The Uniform Prudent Investor Act, as set forth in the Colorado version below. These newer rules allow a trustee to diversify investments using a "portfolio" approach, so that the appropriateness of the investments will be evaluated based on the whole portfolio, rather than on each individual investment.

This list of rules is a good, basic statement of the duties of a trustee, including someone like Mary Jane, or any other person who agrees to serve as a trustee.

Would any part of these rules have changed the outcome in the prior case?

C.R.S. § 15-1.1-101. Prudent investor rule

(a) Except as otherwise provided in subsection (b) of this section, a trustee who invests and manages trust assets owes a duty to the beneficiaries of the trust to comply with the prudent investor rule set forth in this article.

(b) The prudent investor rule, a default rule, may be expanded, restricted, eliminated, or otherwise altered by the provisions of a trust. A trustee is not liable to a beneficiary to the extent that the trustee acted in reasonable reliance on the provisions of the trust.

---

[1] Robert Gardiner is currently serving as trustee because Mary Jane is an invalid and Charles is untrustworthy. Robert is also Mary Jane's guardian-conservator.

§ 15-1.1-102. Standard of care--portfolio strategy--risk and return objectives

(a) A trustee shall invest and manage trust assets as a prudent investor would, by considering the purposes, terms, distribution requirements, and other circumstances of the trust. In satisfying this standard, the trustee shall exercise reasonable care, skill, and caution.

(b) A trustee's investment and management decisions respecting individual assets must be evaluated not in isolation but in the context of the trust portfolio as a whole and as a part of an overall investment strategy having risk and return objectives reasonably suited to the trust.

(c) Among circumstances that a trustee shall consider in investing and managing trust assets are such of the following as are relevant to the trust or its beneficiaries:

(1) General economic conditions;

(2) The possible effect of inflation or deflation;

(3) The expected tax consequences of investment decisions or strategies;

(4) The role that each investment or course of action plays within the overall trust portfolio, which may include financial assets, interests in closely held enterprises, tangible and intangible personal property, and real property;

(5) The expected total return from income and the appreciation of capital;

(6) Other resources of the beneficiaries;

(7) Needs for liquidity, regularity of income, and preservation or appreciation of capital; and

(8) An asset's special relationship or special value, if any, to the purposes of the trust or to one or more of the beneficiaries.

(d) A trustee shall make a reasonable effort to verify facts relevant to the investment and management of trust assets.

(e) A trustee may invest in any kind of property or type of investment consistent with the standards of this article.

(f) A trustee who has special skills or expertise, or is named trustee in reliance upon the trustee's representation that the trustee has special skills or expertise, has a duty to use those special skills or expertise.

§ 15-1.1-103. Diversification

A trustee shall diversify the investments of the trust unless the trustee reasonably determines that, because of special circumstances, the purposes of the trust are better served without diversifying.

§ 15-1.1-104. Duties at inception of trusteeship

Within a reasonable time after accepting a trusteeship or receiving trust assets, a trustee shall review the trust assets and make and implement decisions concerning the retention and disposition of assets, in order to bring the trust portfolio into compliance with the purposes, terms, distribution requirements, and other circumstances of the trust, and with the requirements of this article.

§ 15-1.1-105. Loyalty

A trustee shall invest and manage the trust assets solely in the interest of the beneficiaries.

§ 15-1.1-106. Impartiality

If a trust has two or more beneficiaries, the trustee shall act impartially in investing and managing the trust assets, taking into account any differing interests of the beneficiaries.

§ 15-1.1-107. Investment costs

In investing and managing trust assets, a trustee may only incur costs that are appropriate and reasonable in relation to the assets, the purposes of the trust, and the skills of the trustee.

§ 15-1.1-108. Reviewing compliance

Compliance with the prudent investor rule is determined in light of the facts and circumstances existing at the time of a trustee's decision or action and not by hindsight. um-they're always using hindsight

§ 15-1.1-109. Delegation of investment and management functions

(a) A trustee may delegate investment and management functions that a prudent trustee of comparable skills could properly delegate under the circumstances. The trustee shall exercise reasonable care, skill, and caution in:

> **(1) Selecting an agent;**
>
> **(2) Establishing the scope and terms of the delegation, consistent with the purposes and terms of the trust; and**
>
> **(3) Periodically reviewing the agent's actions in order to monitor the agent's performance and compliance with the terms of the delegation.**

(b) In performing a delegated function, an agent owes a duty to the trust to exercise reasonable care to comply with the terms of the delegation.

(c) A trustee who complies with the requirements of subsection (a)

of this section is not liable to the beneficiaries or to the trust for the decisions or actions of the agent to whom the function was delegated.

(d) By accepting the delegation of a trust function from the trustee of a trust that is subject to the law of this State, an agent submits to the jurisdiction of the courts of this State.

Now for some cases, to illustrate how some of these basic rules have been applied.

D. THE DUTY OF UNDIVIDED LOYALTY

Any trustee, or executor, has a duty of undivided loyalty to the beneficiaries. The fiduciary must never do anything that would put his or her own interests above the interests of the beneficiaries.

The following case is quite famous, partly because of the length of the trial involved, (extending over 8 months), and mainly because of the fame of the testator, the artist Mark Rothko. The litigation itself helped to make the general public more aware of the artist, Mark Rothko. As you read the case, try to imagine how Mark Rothko would have felt about this litigation. Would he have approved of the penalties inflicted on his closest friends, Bernard Reis, Theordoros Stamos, and Morton Levine? How could you have drafted the provisions of the will to give better instructions, and more protection, to the trustees?

Note that the lead plaintiff in the case, Rothko's daughter, Kate, had standing to sue only because of a special New York statute, since repealed, that gave standing to a residuary beneficiary under a will, or to an heir who would take by intestacy, IF the will gave more than one-half of the estate assets to charity. Kate and her younger brother would have been intestate takers if Rothko had had no will. So that gave Kate standing to object to everything.

Might this litigation have been driven by Kate's anger that her father left nearly all of his estate to the Rothko Foundation, to be managed by Reis, Stamos, and Levine and two others? Note that Levin, an anthropology professor, and his wife, had been named by Rothko as the guardians of Kate and her brother.

Before you read the case, it might be well to read the simple, two page will which was the foundation for all of this litigation.

LAST WILL AND TESTAMENT
of
MARK ROTHKO

I, MARK ROTHKO, of New York, N. Y. being of sound mind and memory, hereby make, publish and declare this to be my Last Will and Testament, hereby revoking all wills and other testamentary dispositions by me at any time heretofore made.

FIRST: I direct my Executors to pay all my just debts, funeral and administration expenses as soon after my decease as is convenient.

SECOND: I give and bequeath to the TATE GALLERY, London, England, five (5) paintings of their choice of those paintings which were created by me for the Seagram Building, New York in 1959.

THIRD: I give, devise and bequeath to my wife, MARY ALICE, the real estate owned by me at 118 East 95th Street, New York, together with all of the contents thereof.

FOURTH: I hereby bequeath to my wife, MARY ALICE, the sum of Two Hundred Fifty Thousand ($250,000) Dollars.

FIFTH: In the event of the death of my wife or the simultaneous death of myself and my wife, I give, devise and bequeath the sum of Two Hundred Fifty Thousand ($250,000) Dollars together with the real property at 118 East 95th Street, New York, and all the contents thereof, in equal shares to my children, KATE and CHRISTOPHER.

SIXTH: All the rest, residue and remainder of my property, I give and bequeath to the Mark Rothko Foundation, a non-profit organization, incorporated under the laws of the State of New York. The Directors of the Foundation are to be: WILLIAM RUBIN, ROBERT GOLDWATER, BERNARD J. REIS, THEODOROS STAMOS and MORTON LEVINE.

SEVENTH: In the event of the death of my wife or the simultaneous death of my wife and myself, I appoint as Guardians of my children, MR. and MRS. MORTON LEVINE, of New York.

EIGHTH: I hereby nominate, constitute and appoint MORTON LEVINE, BERNARD J. REIS and THEODOROS STAMOS as Executors of this will. I direct that my Executors shall not be required to furnish any bond, undertaking or security for the faithful performance of their duties. In the event of the death of either one or two of them, the remaining person or persons shall serve as Executor.

IN WITNESS WHEREOF, I have hereunto set my hand and seal this 13th day of September 1968.

Mark Rothko (L.S.)

On the 13th day of September, 1968, the above-named Testator, MARK ROTHKO, in our presence, subscribed and sealed the foregoing instrument, and at the time of such subscription, published and declared the same to be his Last Will and Testament, and thereupon we at such time, at the request of the above-named Testator, in his presence, and in the presence of each other, signed our names thereto as subscribing witnesses.

Louis Meyer, Mary Ann Harten, Ruth B.Miller, Witnesses

Court of Appeals of New York.
In the Matter of the ESTATE of Mark ROTHKO, Deceased.
Kate ROTHKO et al., Respondents,
v.
Bernard J. REIS et al., as Executors of Mark Rothko, Deceased, et al., Appellants-Respondents,
Attorney-General of the State of New York, Respondent-Appellant.
Nov. 22, 1977.

COOKE, Judge.

Mark Rothko, an abstract expressionist painter whose works through the years gained for him an international reputation of greatness, died testate on February 25, 1970. The principal asset of his estate consisted of 798 paintings of tremendous value, and the dispute underlying this appeal involves the conduct of his three executors in their disposition of these works of art. In sum, that conduct as portrayed in the record and sketched in the opinions was manifestly wrongful and indeed shocking.

Rothkos' will was admitted to probate on April 27, 1970 and letters testamentary were issued to Bernard J. Reis, Theodoros Stamos and Morton Levine. Hastily and within a period of only about three weeks and by virtue of two contracts each dated May 21, 1970, the executors dealt with all 798 paintings.

By a contract of sale, the estate executors agreed to sell to Marlborough A.G., a Liechtenstein corporation (hereinafter MAG), 100 Rothko paintings as listed for $1,800,000; $200,000 to be paid on execution of the agreement and the balance of $1,600,000 in 12 equal interest-free installments over a 12-year period. Under the second agreement, the executors consigned to Marlborough Gallery, Inc., a domestic corporation (hereinafter MNY), "approximately 700 paintings listed on a Schedule to be prepared", the consignee to be responsible for costs covering items such as insurance, storage restoration and promotion. By its provisos, MNY could sell up to 35 paintings a year from each of two groups, pre-1947 and post-1947, for 12 years at the best price obtainable but not less than the appraised estate value, and it would receive a 50% Commission on each painting sold, except for a commission of 40% on those sold to or through other dealers.

Petitioner Kate Rothko, decedent's daughter and a person entitled to share in his estate by virtue of an election under EPTL 5-3.3, instituted this proceeding to remove the executors, to enjoin MNY and MAG from disposing of the paintings, to rescind the aforesaid agreements between the executors and said corporations, for a return of the paintings still in possession of those corporations, and for damages. She was joined by the guardian of her brother Christopher Rothko, likewise interested in the estate. The Attorney-General of the State, as the representative of the ultimate beneficiaries of the Mark Rothko Foundation, Inc., a charitable corporation and the residuary legatee under decedent's will, joined in requesting relief substantially similar to that prayed for by petitioner.

On June 26, 1972 the Surrogate issued a temporary restraining order and on September 26, 1972 a preliminary injunction enjoining MAG, MNY, and the three executors from selling or otherwise disposing of the paintings referred to in the agreements dated May 21, 1970, except for sales or dispositions made with court permission. The Appellate Division modified the preliminary injunction order by increasing the amount of the bond and otherwise affirmed. By a 1974 petition, the Attorney-General, on behalf of the ultimate charitable beneficiaries of the Mark Rothko Foundation, sought the punishment of MNY, MAG, Lloyd and Reis for contempt and other relief.

Following a nonjury trial covering 89 days and in a thorough opinion, the Surrogate found: that Reis was a director, secretary and treasurer of MNY, the consignee art gallery, in addition to being a coexecutor of the estate; that the testator had a 1969 inter vivos contract with MNY to sell Rothko's work at a commission of only 10% and whether that agreement survived testator's death was a problem that a fiduciary in a dual position could not have impartially faced; that Reis was in a position of serious conflict of interest with respect to the contracts of May 21, 1970 and that his dual role and planned purpose benefited the Marlborough interests to the detriment of the estate; that it was to the advantage of coexecutor Stamos as a "not-too-successful artist, financially", to curry favor with Marlborough and that the contract made by him with MNY within months after signing the estate contracts placed him in a position where his personal interests conflicted with those of the estate, especially leading to lax contract enforcement efforts by Stamos; that Stamos acted negligently and improvidently in view of his own knowledge of the conflict of interest of Reis; that the third coexecutor, Levine, while not acting in self-interest or with bad faith, nonetheless failed to exercise ordinary prudence in the performance of his assumed fiduciary obligations since he was aware of Reis' divided loyalty, believed that Stamos was also seeking personal advantage, possessed personal opinions as to the value of the paintings and yet followed the leadership of his coexecutors without investigation of essential facts or consultation with competent and disinterested appraisers, and that the business transactions of the two Marlborough corporations were admittedly controlled and directed by Francis K. Lloyd.

It was concluded that the acts and failures of the three executors were clearly improper to such a substantial extent as to mandate their removal. The Surrogate also found that MNY, MAG and Lloyd were guilty of contempt in shipping, disposing of and selling 57 paintings in violation of the temporary restraining order dated June 26, 1972 and of the injunction dated September 26, 1972; that the contracts for sale and consignment of paintings between the executors and MNY and MAG provided inadequate value to the estate, amounting to a lack of mutuality and fairness resulting from conflicts on the part of Reis and Stamos and improvidence on the part of all executors; that said contracts were voidable and were set aside by reason of violation of the duty of loyalty and improvidence of the executors, knowingly participated in and induced by MNY and MAG; that the fact that these agreements were voidable did not revive the 1969 inter vivos agreements since the parties by their conduct evinced an intent to abandon and abrogate these compacts.

The Surrogate held that the present value at the time of trial of the paintings sold is the proper measure of damages as to MNY, MAG, Lloyd, Reis and Stamos. He imposed a civil fine of $3,332,000 upon MNY, MAG and Lloyd, same being the appreciated value at the time of trial of the 57 paintings sold in violation of the temporary restraining order and injunction.

It was held that Levine was liable for $6,464,880 in damages, as he was not in a dual position acting for his own interest and was thus liable only for the actual value of paintings sold MNY and MAG as of the dates of sale, and that Reis, Stamos, MNY and MAG, apart from being jointly and severally liable for the same damages as Levine for negligence, were liable for the greater sum of $9,252,000 "as appreciation damages less amounts previously paid to the estate with regard to sales of paintings."

The liabilities were held to be congruent so that payment of the highest sum would satisfy all lesser liabilities including the civil fines and the liabilities for damages were to be reduced by payment of the fine levied or by return of any of the 57 paintings disposed of, the new fiduciary to have the option in the first instance to specify which paintings the fiduciary would accept.

The Appellate Division affirmed.

The assertions that there were no conflicts of interest on the part of Reis or Stamos indulge in sheer fantasy. Besides being a director and officer of MNY, for which there was financial remuneration, however slight, Reis, as noted by the Surrogate, had different inducements to favor the Marlborough interests, including his own aggrandizement of status and financial advantage through sales of almost one million dollars for items from his own and his family's extensive private art collection by the Marlborough interests.

Similarly, Stamos benefited as an artist under contract with Marlborough and, interestingly, Marlborough purchased a Stamos painting from a third party for $4,000 during the week in May, 1970 when the estate contract negotiations were pending.

The conflicts are manifest. Further, as noted in Bogert, Trusts and Trustees (2d ed.), "The duty of loyalty imposed on the fiduciary prevents him from accepting employment from a third party who is entering into a business transaction with the trust. While he (a trustee) is administering the trust he must refrain from placing himself in a position where his personal interest or that of a third person does or may conflict with the interest of the beneficiaries."

Reis was employed and Stamos benefited in a manner contemplated by Bogert. In short, one must strain the law rather than follow it to reach the result suggested on behalf of Reis and Stamos.

Levine contends that, having acted prudently and upon the advice of counsel, a complete defense was established. Suffice it to say, an executor who knows that his coexecutor is committing breaches of trust and not only fails to exert efforts directed towards prevention but accedes to them is legally accountable even though he was acting on the advice of counsel.

When confronted with the question of whether to enter into the Marlborough contracts, Levine was acting in a business capacity, not a legal one, in which he was required as an executor primarily to employ such diligence and prudence to the care and management of the estate assets and affairs as would prudent persons of discretion and intelligence, accented by "not honesty alone, but the punctilio of an honor the most sensitive". Alleged good faith on the part of a fiduciary forgetful of his duty is not enough. He could not close his eyes, remain passive or move with unconcern in the face of the obvious loss to be visited upon the estate by participation in those business arrangements and then shelter himself behind the claimed counsel of an attorney.

Further, there is no merit to the argument that MNY and MAG lacked notice of the breach of trust. The record amply supports the determination that they are chargeable with notice of the executors' breach of duty.

The measure of damages was the issue that divided the Appellate Division. The contention of Reis, Stamos, MNY and MAG, that the award of appreciation damages was legally erroneous and impermissible, is based on a principle that an executor authorized to sell is not liable for an increase in value if the breach consists only in selling for a figure less than that for which the executor should have sold. For example, Scott states:

> "The beneficiaries are not entitled to the value of the property at the time of the decree if it was not the duty of the trustee to retain the property in the trust and the breach of trust consisted merely in selling the property for too low a price" (3 Scott, Trusts (3d ed.), (Emphasis added).
>
> "If the trustee is guilty of a breach of trust in selling trust property for an inadequate price, he is liable for the difference between the amount he should have received and the amount which he did receive. He is not liable, however, for any subsequent rise in value of the property sold".

However, employment of "merely" and "only" as limiting words suggests that where the breach consists of some misfeasance, other than solely for selling "for too low a price" or "for too little", appreciation damages may be appropriate. Under Scott and the Restatement, the trustee may be held liable for appreciation damages if it was his or her duty to retain the property, the theory being that the beneficiaries are entitled to be placed in the same position they would have been in had the breach not consisted of a sale of property that should have been retained. The same rule should apply where the breach of trust consists of a serious conflict of interest which is more than merely selling for too little.

The reason for allowing appreciation damages, where there is a duty to retain, and only date of sale damages, where there is authorization to sell, is policy oriented. If a trustee authorized to sell were subjected to a greater measure of damages he might be reluctant to sell (in which event he might run a risk if depreciation ensued). On the other hand, if there is a duty to retain and the trustee sells there is no policy reason to protect the trustee; he has not simply acted imprudently, he has violated an integral condition of the trust.

> "If a trustee in breach of trust transfers trust property to a person who takes with notice of the breach of trust, and the transferee has disposed of the property it seems proper to charge him with the value at the time of the decree, since if it had not been for the breach of trust the property would still have been a part of the trust estate" (4 Scott, Trusts (3d ed.).

This rule of law which applies to the transferees MNY and MAG also supports the imposition of appreciation damages against Reis and Stamos, since if the Marlborough corporations are liable for such damages either as purchaser or consignees with notice, from one in breach of trust, it is only logical to hold that said executors, as sellers and consignors, are liable also pro tanto.

Here, the executors, though authorized to sell, did not merely err in the amount they accepted but sold to one with whom Reis and Stamos had a self-interest. To make the injured party whole, in both instances the quantum of damages should be the same. In other words, since the paintings cannot be returned, the estate is therefore entitled to their value at the time of the decree, i. e., appreciation damages. These are not punitive damages in a true sense, rather they are damages intended to make the estate whole. Of course, as to Reis, Stamos, MNY and MAG, these damages might be considered by some to be exemplary in a sense, in that they serve as a warning to others. But their true character is ascertained when viewed in the light of overriding policy considerations and in the realization that the sale and consignment were not merely sales below value but inherently wrongful transfers which should allow the owner to be made whole.

The decree of the Surrogate imposed appreciation damages against Reis, Stamos, MNY and MAG in the amount of $7,339,464.72 computed as $9,252,000 (86 works on canvas at $90,000 each and 54 works on paper at $28,000 each) less the aggregate amounts paid the estate under the two rescinded agreements and interest. Appellants chose not to offer evidence of "present value" and the only proof furnished on the subject was that of the expert Heller whose appraisal as of January, 1974 (the month previous to that when trial commenced) on a painting-by-painting basis totaled $15,100,000. There was also testimony as to bona fide sales of other Rothkos between 1971 and 1974.

Under the circumstances, it was impossible to appraise the value of the unreturned works of art with an absolute certainty and, so long as the figure arrived at had a reasonable basis of computation and was not merely speculative, possible or imaginary, the Surrogate had the right to resort to reasonable conjectures and probable estimates and to make the best approximation possible through the exercise of good judgment and common sense in arriving at that amount.

This is particularly so where the conduct of wrongdoers has rendered it difficult to ascertain the damages suffered with the precision otherwise possible. Significantly, the Surrogate's factual finding as to the present value of these unreturned paintings was affirmed by the Appellate Division and, since that finding had support in the record and was not legally erroneous, it should not now be subjected to our disturbance.

We have considered the other alleged errors urged by the parties, and find those arguments to be without merit. In short, we find no basis for disturbing the result reached below.

Accordingly, the order of the Appellate Division should be affirmed, with costs to the prevailing parties against appellants.

Note: After this litigation, Stamos gave up all of his assets as part of an attempt to pay his part of the judgment, but the court did allow him to stay in his house until the end of his life.

E. DUTY OF IMPARTIALITY

No matter which statutory or common law standards are applied, any executor or trustee always has a duty to act impartially, for the benefit of all of the beneficiaries of the estate or trust. The duties of the trustee, normally, simply last for a longer time than the duties of the executor.

When the trust beneficiaries include different groups of beneficiaries, such as one group which is to receive the income, and another group which is to receive the remainder of the corpus, that duty of impartiality may be nearly impossible to achieve – since the two groups will have very different interests.

The following case illustrates some of the difficulties a trustee may face with regard to implementation of the duty of impartiality – and the temptation for a court to use hindsight when evaluating the actions of a trustee. Note that the last two income beneficiaries of the trust are also the remaindermen. Basically, now that the trust is nearing an end, they are claiming that the trustee favored the income beneficiaries (including plaintiffs), at the expense of the remaindermen (including the *same* people who are now suing the trustee as plaintiffs).

United States Court of Appeals, First Circuit.
Robert B. DENNIS, etc., et al., Plaintiffs, Appellants,
v.
RHODE ISLAND HOSPITAL TRUST NATIONAL BANK,
Defendant, Appellee.
Decided Sept. 28, 1984.

BREYER, Circuit Judge.

The plaintiffs are the great-grandchildren of Alice M. Sullivan and beneficiaries of a trust created under her will. They claimed in the district court that the Bank trustee had breached various fiduciary obligations owed them as beneficiaries of that trust. The trust came into existence in 1920. It will cease to exist in 1991 (twenty-one years after the 1970 death of Alice Sullivan's last surviving child). The trust distributes all its income for the benefit of Alice Sullivan's living issue; the principal is to go to her issue surviving in 1991. Evidently, since the death of their mother, the two plaintiffs are the sole surviving issue, entitled to the trust's income until 1991, and then, as remaindermen, entitled to the principal.

The controversy arises out of the trustee's handling of the most important trust assets, undivided interests in three multi-story commercial buildings in downtown Providence. The buildings (the Jones, Wheaton-Anthony, and Alice Buildings) were all constructed before the beginning of the century, in an area where the value of the property has declined markedly over the last thirty years. During the period that the trust held these interests the buildings were leased to a number of different tenants. Income distribution from the trust to the life tenants has averaged over $34,000 annually.

At the time of the creation of the trust in 1920, its interests in the three buildings were worth more than $300,000. The trustee was authorized by the will to sell real estate. When the trustee finally sold the buildings in 1945, 1970, and 1979, respectively, it did so at or near the lowest point of their value; the trust received a total of only $185,000 for its interests in them. These losses, in plaintiffs' view, reflect a serious mishandling of assets over the years.

The district court found that the trustee had failed to act impartially, as between the trust's income beneficiaries and the remaindermen; it had favored the former over the latter, and, in doing so, it had reduced the value of the trust assets. The court ordered a surcharge of $365,000, apparently designed to restore the real value of the trust's principal to its 1950 level.

I

The trustee first argues that the district court's conclusions rest on "hindsight." It points out that Rhode Island law requires a trustee to be "prudent and vigilant and exercise sound judgment," but "neither prophecy nor prescience is expected." It adds that a trustee can indulge a preference for keeping the trust's "inception assets," those placed in trust by the settlor and commended to the trustee for retention. How then, the trustee asks, can the court have found that it should have sold these property interests in 1950?

The trustee's claim might be persuasive had the district court found that it had acted *imprudently* in 1950, in retaining the buildings. If that were the case, one might note that every 1950 sale involved both a pessimistic seller and an optimistic buyer; and one might ask how the court could expect the trustee to have known then (in 1950) whose prediction would turn out to be correct. The trustee's argument is less plausible, however, where, as here, the district court basically found that in 1950 the trustee had acted not imprudently, but *unfairly,* between income beneficiaries and remaindermen.

Suppose, for example, that a trustee of farmland over a number of years overplants the land, thereby increasing short run income, but ruining the soil and making the farm worthless in the long run. The trustee's duty to take corrective action would arise from the fact that he knows (or plainly ought to know) that his present course of action will injure the remaindermen; settled law requires him to act impartially, "with due regard" for the "respective interests" of both the life tenant and the remainderman. The district court here found that a sale in 1950 would have represented one way (perhaps the only practical way) to correct this type of favoritism. It held that instead of correcting the problem, the trustee continued to favor the life tenant to the "very real disadvantage" of the remainder interests, in violation of Rhode Island law.

To be more specific, in the court's view the problem arose out of the trustee's failure to keep up the buildings, to renovate them, to modernize them, or to take other reasonably obvious steps that might have given the remaindermen property roughly capable of continuing to produce a reasonable income. This failure allowed the trustee to make larger income payments during the life of the trust; but the size of those payments reflected the trustee's acquiescence in the gradual deterioration of the property. In a sense, the payments ate away the trust's capital.

The trustee correctly points out that it did take certain steps to keep up the buildings; and events beyond its control made it difficult to do more. In the 1920's, the trustee, with court approval, entered into very long-term leases on the Alice and Wheaton-Anthony buildings. The lessees and the subtenants were supposed to keep the buildings in good repair; some improvements were made. The depression made it difficult during the 1930's to find tenants who would pay a high rent and keep up the buildings. After World War II the neighborhood enjoyed a brief renaissance; but, then, with the 1950's flight to the suburbs, it simply deteriorated.

Even if we accept these trustee claims, however, there is considerable evidence indicating that, at least by 1950, the trustee should have been aware of the way in which the buildings' high rents, the upkeep problem, the changing neighborhood, the buildings' age, the failure to modernize, all together were consuming the buildings' value. There is evidence that the trustee did not come to grips with the problem. Indeed, the trustee did not appraise the properties periodically, and it did not keep proper records. It made no formal or informal accounting in 55 years. There is no indication in the record that the trust's officers focused upon the problem or consulted real estate experts about it or made any further rehabilitation efforts. Rather, there is evidence that the trustee did little more than routinely agree to the *requests of the trust's income beneficiaries* that it manage the trust corpus to produce the largest possible income.

The district court also found that the trustee had at least one practical solution available. It might have sold the property in 1950 and reinvested the proceeds in other assets of roughly equivalent total value that did not create a "partiality" problem. The *Restatement of Trusts* foresees such a solution, for it says that "the trustee is under a duty to the beneficiary who is ultimately entitled to the principal not to retain property which is certain or likely to depreciate in value, although the property yields a large income, unless he makes adequate provision for amortizing the depreciation."

Rhode Island case law also allows the court considerable discretion, in cases of fiduciary breach, to fashion a remedy, including a remedy based on a hypothetical, earlier sale. In the absence of a showing that such a sale and reinvestment would have been impractical or that some equivalent or better curative steps might have been taken, the district court's use of a 1950 sale as a remedial measure of what the trustee ought to have done is within the scope of its lawful powers.

In reaching this conclusion, we have taken account of the trustee's argument that the buildings' values were especially high in 1950 (though not as high as in the late 1920's). As the trustee argues, this fact would make 1950 an unreasonable remedial choice, other things being equal.

But the record indicates that other things were not equal. For one thing, the district court chose 1950, not because of then-existing property values, but because that date marks a reasonable outer bound of the time the trustee could plead ignorance of the serious fairness problem. For another thing, the district court could properly understand plaintiffs' expert witness as stating that the suburban flight that led to mid-1950's downtown decline began before 1950; its causes (increased household income; more cars; more mobility) were apparent before 1950. Thus, the court might reasonably have felt that a brief (1948-52) downtown "renaissance" should not have appeared (to the expert eye) to have been permanent or long-lasting; it did not relieve the trustee of its obligation to do something about the fairness problem, nor did it make simple "building retention" a plausible cure. Finally, another expert testified that the trustee should have asked for power to sell the property "sometime between 1947 and 1952" when institutional investors generally began to diversify portfolios. For these reasons, we find that the choice of 1950 as a remedial base year is lawful.

Contrary to the trustee's contention, the case law it cites does not give it an absolute right under Rhode Island law to keep the trust's "inception assets" in disregard of the likely effect of retention on classes of trust beneficiaries. The district court's conclusion that the trustee should have sold the assets if necessary to prevent the trust corpus from being consumed by the income beneficiaries is reasonable and therefore lawful.

The trustee attacks the lawfulness of the district court's conclusion that it should have sold the Alice Building in 1950 on the ground that principles of res judicata require a finding that retention was lawful. In 1953, the Rhode Island Superior Court approved an application by the trust's beneficiaries to use trust assets to acquire an additional 1/32 interest in the Alice Building. A guardian *ad litem* represented the present plaintiffs (then minors) at that proceeding. The trustee states that explicit court approval of the *additional* acquisition in 1953 constituted implicit approval of its retaining its existing 1/4 interest.

The district court rejected this argument for sufficient reason. As a matter of pure logic, the two questions-additional purchase and retention-are not *necessarily* intertwined. It might at once be unreasonable to keep a 1/4 undivided interest in, say, a piece of land, but, at the same time, if one has ruled out the possibility of sale, it might then be wise to buy more. More important, as a practical matter, the two questions were, in the context of this litigation, quite separate. The particular question put to the 1953 court concerned the *prudence* of an additional purchase. The question of retention at issue here, however, does not concern the prudence of retention so much as it concerns the *fairness* of retention as between income recipients and remaindermen. This latter question was never presented to the court in 1953; there is no reason to believe the court would, or should, have considered the fairness issue as part of the question it decided. We therefore find no basis for overturning the district court.

The trustee challenges the district court's calculation of the surcharge. The court assumed, for purposes of making the trust principal whole, that the trustee had hypothetically sold the trust's interests in the Wheaton-Anthony and the Alice buildings in 1950, at their 1950 values (about $70,000 and $220,000, respectively). It subtracted, from that sum of about $290,000, the $130,000 the trust actually received when the buildings were in fact sold (about $40,000 for the Wheaton-Anthony interest in 1970 and about $90,000 for the Alice interest in 1979). The court considered the difference of $160,000 to be a loss in the value of the principal, suffered as a result of the trustee's failure to prevent the principal from eroding. The court then assumed that, had the trustee sold the buildings in 1950 and reinvested the proceeds, the trustee would have been able to preserve the real value of the principal. It therefore multiplied the $160,000 by 3.6 percent, the average annual increase in the consumer price index from 1950 to 1982, and multiplied again by 32, the number of full years since 1950. Finally, the court multiplied again by an annual 0.4 percent, designed to reflect an "allowance for appreciation." It added the result ($160,000 x 4 percent x 32), about $205,000, to the $160,000 loss and surcharged the trustee $365,000. We are aware of a number of mathematical problems with this calculation. (Why, for example, was no account taken of inflation when subtracting sale receipts from 1950 values?) But, in the context of this specific litigation, fairness as between the parties requires us to restrict our examination to the two particular challenges that the trustee raises.

First, the trustee claims that the court improperly ascertained the 1950 values of the trust's interests because it simply took a proportionate share of the buildings' values. That is to say, it divided the total value of the Alice Building by four to reflect the fact that the trust owned a 1/4 undivided interest. The trustee argues that the building's values should have been discounted further to reflect the facts that the trust owned a fractional interest in the buildings and that fractional interests (with their consequent problems of divided control) typically sell at a discount.

Second, the trustee argues that the district court should not have applied to the 1950 hypothetical sales value a 4 percent interest factor - a factor designed to compensate for 3.6 percent average annual inflation and for 0.4 percent "appreciation." We do not agree with the trustee in respect to the 3.6 percent.

Rhode Island law simply requires that the court's approach be reasonable and its calculations grounded in the record's facts. The trustee does not claim that it requires the court to follow any one particular calculation method, such as that, for example, contained in *Restatement (Second) of Trusts* § 241. And, we believe the inflation adjustment meets Rhode Island's broader requirements.

For one thing, it seems reasonable for the court - in devising a remedy for the trustee's violation of its duty of impartiality - to assume that a fair trustee would have maintained the property's *real* value from 1950 through 1982. Such an assumption is consistent with basic trust law policies of providing income to income beneficiaries while preserving principal for the remaindermen, and, consequently, of avoiding investment in wasting assets. Moreover, it is consistent with readily ascertainable general economic facts that wages and many asset values as well as prices have on average kept pace with inflation. While the value of long term bonds has fallen, the value of common stocks and much property has risen. Where a court is trying to create, not a measure of the trustee's duty, but simply a plausible reconstruction of what would have occurred to a hypothetical 1950 reinvestment, we see nothing unreasonable in assuming that the value of the corpus would have kept pace with inflation.

We reach a different conclusion, however, in respect to the additional 0.4 percent, designed to reflect "appreciation." Neither the court nor the parties have provided us with any reason to believe that the trustee would have outperformed inflation. We conclude that, in adding 0.4 percent interest for real appreciation, the district court exceeded its broad remedial powers. Our recalculation, omitting the 0.4 percent, reduces the surcharge from $365,781.67 to $345,246.56.

The trustee objects to the court's having removed it as trustee. The removal of a trustee, however, is primarily a matter for the district court. A trustee can be removed even if "the charges of his misconduct" are "not made out." The issue here is whether "ill feeling" might interfere with the administration of the trust. The district court concluded that the course of the litigation in this case itself demonstrated such ill feeling. Nothing in the record shows that the court abused its powers in reaching that conclusion.

II

The plaintiffs argue, on their cross appeal, that the district court should have awarded them prejudgment interest on the surcharge.

As the plaintiffs note, however, the purpose of this statute is "to compensate plaintiffs for waiting for the recompense to which they were legally entitled." That purpose would not be served by applying the statute here, for the district court calculated the surcharge in a way that made plaintiffs whole. The value of the corpus is maintained at its real 1950 level; that is the amount that the plaintiffs would (hypothetically) have received had the trustees fulfilled their obligations. Plaintiffs have lost nothing "for waiting for the recompense," as they can in no event receive the trust's corpus prior to 1991.

Plaintiffs also argue that the district court should have awarded them attorneys' fees to be paid by the trustee from its own pocket. The plaintiffs concede that in an action of this sort, the award of attorneys' fees at the expense of the trustees (not the trust) is an "exercise of the court's discretion."

The district court here found that plaintiffs succeeded in winning only a small part of the money that they claimed the trustee owed them. In its view, had the plaintiffs' claims been less extravagant, *eight years* of litigation might not have been necessary to obtain the surcharge that they won. The court also characterized the trustee's failing as a simple breach of fiduciary duty not reflecting willfully wrong or egregious conduct. It stated that there was "absolutely no evidence of malice or bad faith on the part of the Trustee." In addition, the court found evidence that plaintiffs' attorneys sought "inflated or unnecessary unsubstantiated charges." Under these circumstances, we believe the court did not abuse its powers in refusing to depart from the ordinary American rule requiring each party to pay its own attorneys' fees.

The judgment of the district court is modified and as modified affirmed.

So, some of the same people who benefited by a preference for the *income beneficiaries* are now suing the trustee for *preferring* the income beneficiaries - because these income beneficiaries will soon become *remaindermen.* The duty of impartiality may be tricky.

F. ALLOCATION OF INCOME AND PRINCIPAL (UPIA)

The Uniform Principal and Income Act, recently enacted in some states, attempts to give a trustee more specific guidance as to allocation of income and principal, and to set forth specific standards which the trustee must meet, and specific opportunities for the trustee to re-adjust allocation of principal and income between the lifetime beneficiaries and the remaindermen when that turns out to be necessary. The following case illustrates how some of the provisions of the Uniform Principal and Income Act have been applied.

As you will notice, the parties to this litigation, father and son, probably had plenty of money to spend on litigation of this sort.

Supreme Court of Nevada.
IN THE MATTER OF THE ORPHEUS TRUST.
Whittier Trust Company Special Trustee of The Orpheus Trust, Appellant, vs. Andrew R. Getty, Respondent.
March 27, 2008,

En banc.

In this appeal, we examine a question of first impression under Nevada law: whether a special trustee's power, under *NRS 164.795*, to adjust amounts of trust income and principal distributed to a trust income beneficiary and the trust corpus may be exercised with respect to principal and income accrued before the special trustee's appointment. Because the power to adjust is a corrective power, we conclude that, at a minimum, a special trustee may adjust between principal and income accrued in the year immediately preceding the special trustee's appointment. Because under *NRS 164.725(7)* the beneficiary challenging the propriety of any proposed adjustment bears the burden of demonstrating that the trustee did not appropriately comply with the requirements set forth in *NRS 164.795(1)* and *(2)*, we conclude that the district court in this case did not hold the challenging beneficiary to his appropriate burden. Accordingly, we remand this matter to the district court for further proceedings.

FACTS AND PROCEDURAL HISTORY

The Orpheus Trust is a nontestamentary trust domiciled in Nevada. It is one of several successor trusts to the historic John Paul Getty Family Trust created in California in 1934. Trustee Gordon Getty is the sole income beneficiary of the trust and controls 60 percent of the trustee votes. Respondent Andrew Getty, Gordon's son, is one of the four contingent remainder beneficiaries of the trust. Andrew is also the president and shareholder of A. Rork Investments, Inc., which is a co-trustee of the Orpheus Trust and controls 10 percent of the trustee votes.

Generally, the trustees of the Orpheus Trust are bound by the standards of the Uniform Prudent Investor Act, which Nevada adopted in 2003. Under the Prudent Investor Act, a trustee must impartially manage a trust in accordance with the standards of a prudent investor and may invest in a wide variety of property and investments. Traditionally, any income from these investments, such as interest or rents, would be paid to the income beneficiary, while any appreciation in principal would revert to the trust corpus for the benefit of the remainder beneficiaries.

However, in 2003, the Legislature enacted *NRS 164.795*, a provision of the Uniform Principal and Income Act, which provides that if a trustee is unable to otherwise comply with the statutory mandate that a trustee impartially administer a trust, the trustee may adjust between the amounts of income and principal distributed to the income beneficiary and the trust corpus. A primary purpose of this statute is to allow trustees to invest for total portfolio return and to take advantage of more lucrative investment opportunities that may not provide sufficient traditional trust income. Trustees who are also trust beneficiaries may not exercise the power to adjust, but they may seek appointment of a disinterested special trustee to do so.

In November 2004, over Andrew's objections, the trustees of the Orpheus Trust petitioned the district court to appoint a special trustee to adjust between principal and income. The district court appointed appellant Whittier Trust Company as special trustee in February 2005. In September 2005, Whittier filed a petition for approval of an adjustment between principal and income for the 2004 trust year. The petition indicated that, in 2004, the trust experienced a net return of 14.77 percent of the fair market value of trust assets, while income payable to Gordon amounted to only 2.59 percent of the trust assets. Therefore, Whittier proposed that Gordon receive a net adjustment of 1.20 percent of the fair market value of the trust assets.

Andrew objected to the adjustment, arguing that Whittier could not make a "retroactive" adjustment between principal and income for 2004. After hearing arguments, the district court denied Whittier's petition, reasoning that Whittier could only adjust between principal and income accrued from its date of appointment. In a subsequent order denying Whittier's motion for reconsideration, the district court also determined that Whittier did not comply with all requirements of *NRS 164.795(1)* and *(2)* in analyzing the proposed adjustment. Whittier has appealed.

DISCUSSION

NRS 164.795(1), enables trustees to "adjust" between the amounts of trust principal and income distributed to the income beneficiary and the trust corpus. This provision relieved trustees of their traditional obligation to devote a minimum threshold of trust assets to income-producing investments for the benefit of the trust income beneficiary. Instead, under this new regime, trustees are free to invest for total return, and then correct any unfair effect this may have on income paid to the income beneficiary, or the value of the trust corpus reserved for the remainder beneficiary.

Due to the corrective nature of the power to adjust, and the fact that trustees need not formally adopt any new investment strategy before seeking to exercise the power to adjust, we initially conclude that, at a minimum, a special trustee may adjust between principal and income accrued in the year immediately preceding its appointment. Thus, because the district court appointed Whittier as special trustee in early 2005, and Whittier sought an adjustment for the immediately preceding year, we determine that the proposed adjustment was not barred as a "retroactive" adjustment.

We remand this matter to the district court for a determination of whether Whittier appropriately analyzed the proposed adjustment using the factors set forth in *NRS 164.795(2)*.

Power to correctively adjust principal and income pursuant to NRS 164.795

A trustee is generally bound by a number of statutory guidelines when administering a trust. First, a trustee must act in accordance with the standards of a prudent investor, as defined in the Uniform Prudent Investor Act, adopted by Nevada in 2003. This act provides that a trustee may invest in a wide variety of property and investments and must evaluate these investments "not in isolation but in the context of the trust portfolio as a whole and as part of an overall strategy of investment having objectives for risk and return reasonably suited to the trust." When a trust has two or more beneficiaries, *NRS 164.720* dictates that a prudent investor must also "act impartially in investing and managing the trust property, taking into account any differing interests of the beneficiaries."

Any exercise of a discretionary power must also be impartial and "based on what is fair and reasonable to all the beneficiaries, except to the extent that the terms of the trust or the will clearly manifest an intention that the fiduciary shall or may favor one or more of the beneficiaries."

NRS 164.795(1) essentially provides that if a trustee is otherwise unable to impartially and fairly treat both principal and income beneficiaries, the trustee may make an adjustment between distributions of principal and income to trust beneficiaries. Because *NRS 164.795(3) (g)* prohibits trustees who are also trust beneficiaries from making an adjustment between principal and income, a special trustee must be appointed to make an adjustment when all trustees are also trust beneficiaries.[2]

Analysis of adjustment made under NRS 164.795(2)

Once a trustee determines that an adjustment between principal and income may be necessary pursuant to *NRS 164.795(1)*, *NRS 164.795(2)* requires a trustee to consider a wide variety of factors in determining the propriety and amount of any proposed adjustment. *NRS 164.795(2)* specifically provides as follows:

> In deciding whether and to what extent to exercise the power to adjust between principal and income, a trustee shall consider all factors relevant to the trust and its beneficiaries, including the following factors to the extent they are relevant:
>
> (a) The nature, purpose and expected duration of the trust;

[2] *See NRS 164.795(3)(g)* (prohibiting a trustee who is also a beneficiary from making an adjustment); *NRS 164.795(4)* (allowing a disinterested co-trustee to make an adjustment, even if the remaining trustees are not authorized to do so).

(b) The intent of the settlor;

(c) The identity and circumstances of the beneficiaries;

(d) The needs for liquidity, regularity of income, and preservation and appreciation of capital;

(e) The assets held in the trust, the extent to which the assets consist of financial assets, interests in closely held enterprises, tangible and intangible personal property, or real property, the extent to which an asset is used by a beneficiary, and whether an asset was purchased by the trustee or received from the settlor;

(f) The net amount allocated to income under the other provisions of this statute, and the increase or decrease in the value of the principal assets, which the trustee may estimate as to assets for which market values are not readily available;

(g) Whether and to what extent the terms of the trust give the trustee the power to invade principal or accumulate income or prohibit him from invading principal or accumulating income, and the extent to which he has exercised a power from time to time to invade principal or accumulate income;

(h) The actual and anticipated effect of economic conditions on principal and income and effects of inflation and deflation; and

The anticipated tax consequences of an adjustment.

Only after analyzing these factors can a trustee determine whether an adjustment is appropriate. Once the trustee has determined that an adjustment is necessary, *NRS 164.725(2)* provides that the trustee may provide notice of the proposed action to any interested beneficiary. If no beneficiary objects, the trustee may take the proposed action and "is not liable to any present or future beneficiary with respect to the proposed action."

If a beneficiary objects to the proposed action, the trustee may petition the district court for an order to take the proposed action. However, "the burden is on the beneficiary to prove that the proposed action should not be taken or should be modified."

Here, Andrew properly objected to Whittier's notice of proposed adjustment.

We reverse the district court's order and remand this matter to the district court for further proceedings to determine whether Whittier appropriately complied with the requirements of *NRS 164.795(2)*. [3]

---

[3] We note that in an unrelated dispute regarding the Getty Family Trust, the California Court of

CONCLUSION

We conclude that the power to adjust between trust principal and income set forth in *NRS 164.795* is a corrective power and may be exercised with respect to principal and income accrued in the year immediately preceding a special trustee's appointment. Thus, so long as the trustees are bound by the standards of the Uniform Prudent Investor Act, the terms of the trust require distribution of income to an income beneficiary, and a special trustee determines that an adjustment is necessary, the special trustee may adjust between principal and income accrued in the preceding year. Therefore, we conclude that Whittier's proposed adjustment was not barred as an impermissible "retroactive adjustment," and we reverse the district court's order denying Whittier's petition for approval of the proposed adjustment between principal and income for the 2004 trust year. We further note that in analyzing the propriety of any proposed adjustment, the challenging beneficiary bears the burden of demonstrating that the trustee did not appropriately comply with the requirements set forth in *NRS 164.795(1)* and *(2)*. Because the district court did not hold Andrew to his appropriate burden, we remand this matter to the district court for additional proceedings consistent with this opinion.

trustees have to foresee the future

G. DUTY TO EARMARK

It has always been important for a trustee to keep clear records, segregating the property of the trust from the personal assets of the trustee. This is described as the Duty to Earmark, and it is a duty which is rigorously applied. The basic rule is that if the trustee does not clearly separate the trust assets from the trustee's personal assets, then the trustee is personally liable for *any loss* resulting from a fall in value of the trust assets, even though the loss did *not result* from the fact that assets were held in the name of the trustee individually. The penalties are very severe against the trustee, because it is so dangerous for the trustee to fail to earmark – thus giving the trustee the chance to claim that assets which increased in value were the personal assets of the trustee, while the assets which fell in value were, unfortunately, the assets of the trust.

Appeal determined in 1972 that neither Sarah nor John Paul Getty had any intention to provide income for John Paul's children, including Gordon, by means of the trust. However, a later superior court order creating the successor Gordon Family Trust (a predecessor to the Orpheus Trust) specified that no provision of the 1972 decision in *Getty v. Getty* required trustees to favor either income or remainder beneficiaries in administering the trust. We anticipate that each of these decisions may be relevant in analyzing the nature, purpose, and duration of the trust, as well as the intent of the settlor, as required by *NRS 164.795(2)(a)* and *(b)*.

H. DUTY TO DIVERSIFY

There is a basic, fundamental rule, that a trustee has a duty to diversify the investments of the trust. In other words, the trustee is not to put all of the trust assets into Ford stock, even if, at the moment, Ford looks like a good investment. Because of the fluctuation of the value of all assets, it simply is not safe to put all of the trust assets in the same investment. The following case illustrates a serious breach of the duty to diversify – as well as several other serious breaches by the trustees of their fiduciary duties.

Court of Appeal, Second District, California.
Estate Of RALPH W. COLLINS, Deceased. CHARLES E. MILLIKAN, JR., As Trustee, Et Al., Petitioners And Respondents,
v.
MARGARET B. COLLINS HUGHES Et Al., Appellants
July 13, 1977.

lost almost everything

KAUS, P. J.

Objectors (plaintiffs) are beneficiaries under a testamentary trust established in the will of Ralph Collins, deceased. Carl Lamb and Charles E. Millikan, Jr., (defendants) were, respectively, Collins' business partner and lawyer. They were named in Collins' will as trustees. In 1973 defendants filed a petition for an order approving and settling the first and final account and discharging the trustees. Plaintiffs objected on grounds that defendants had improperly invested $50,000 and requested that defendants be surcharged. After a hearing, the trial court ruled in favor of defendants, and approved the account, terminated the trust, and discharged the trustees. Plaintiff beneficiaries have appealed.

Facts

The primary beneficiaries under the testamentary trust were Collins' wife and children; his mother and father were also named as beneficiaries. General support provisions were included; the will also specifically provided that the trustees pay his daughter $4,000 a year for five years for her undergraduate and graduate education.

Paragraph (d) of the declaration of trust recited the powers of the trustees in the usual, inclusive fashion.[4]

---

[4] Subparagraph (3) authorized the trustees to purchase "every kind of property, real, personal or mixed, and every kind of investment, specifically including, but not by way of limitation, corporate obligations of every kind, and stocks, preferred or common, irrespective of whether said investments are in accordance with the laws then enforced in the State of California pertaining to the investment of trust funds by corporate trustees."

Collins died in 1963 and his will was admitted to probate. In June 1965, the court ordered the estate to be distributed. After various other payments and distributions, defendant trustees received about $80,000 as the trust principal. After other distributions, such as the annual $4,000 payment for the education of Collins' daughter, the trustees had about $50,000 available for investment.

Defendant Millikan's clients included two real property developers, Downing and Ward. In March 1965, Millikan filed an action on behalf of Downing and Ward against a lender who refused to honor a commitment to carry certain construction loans. In June 1965, defendants learned that Downing and Ward wanted to borrow $50,000. Millikan knew that the builders wanted the loan because of their difficulties with the lender who had withdrawn its loan commitment.

The loan would be secured by a second trust deed to 9.38 acres of unimproved real property in San Bernardino County near Upland. This property was subject to a $90,000 first trust deed; the note which secured the first trust deed was payable in quarterly installments of interest only, and due in full in three years, that is, in July 1968. The $50,000 loan to be made by defendants would be payable in monthly installments of interest only, at 10 percent interest with the full amount due in 30 months, that is, in January 1968.

Defendants knew that the property had been sold two years earlier in 1963 for $107,000. Defendants checked with two real estate brokers in the area, one of whom said that property in that area was selling for $18,000 to $20,000 an acre. They did not have the property appraised, they did not check with the county clerk or recorder in either Los Angeles or San Bernardino County to determine whether there were foreclosures or lawsuits pending against the construction company. In fact, when defendants made the loan in July 1965, there were six notices of default and three lawsuits pending against Downing and Ward.

Defendants obtained and reviewed an unaudited company financial statement. This statement indicated that the Downing and Ward Company had a net worth in excess of $2 million.

Downing and Ward told defendants that they were not in default on any of their loans, that they were not defendants in any pending litigation, and that there had never been any liens filed on any of their projects. Defendants phoned the bank with whom Downing and Ward had a line of credit and learned that the bank had a satisfactory relationship with the builders.

Based on this information, on July 23, 1965, defendants lent Downing and Ward $50,000 on the terms described above. In addition to the second trust deed, Downing

---

Subparagraph (3) provided: "Unless specifically limited, all discretions conferred upon the Trustee shall be absolute, and their exercise conclusive on all persons interest[ed] in this trust. The enumeration of certain powers of the Trustee shall not limit its general powers, the Trustee, subject always to the discharge of its fiduciary obligations, being vested with and having all the rights, powers and privileges which an absolute owner of the same property would have."

and Ward pledged 20 percent of the stock in their company as security. However, defendants neither obtained possession of the stock, placed it in escrow, nor placed a legend on the stock certificates. Defendants also obtained the personal guarantees of Downing and Ward and their wives. However, defendants did not obtain financial statements from the guarantors.

When the loan was made in July 1965, construction in the Upland area was, as the trial court said, "enjoying boom times, although the bubble was to burst just a few months later." From July 1965 through September 1966, the builders made the monthly interest payments required by the note. In October 1966, Downing & Ward Construction Corporation was placed in involuntary bankruptcy and thereafter Mr. and Mrs. Ward and Mr. and Mrs. Downing declared personal bankruptcies. Defendants foreclosed their second trust deed in June 1967, and became the owners of the unimproved real property. They spent $10,000 in an unsuccessful effort to salvage the investment by forestalling foreclosure by the holder of the first trust deed. In September 1968, the holder of the first trust deed did foreclose. This extinguished the trustees' interest in the property and the entire investment. In short, about $60,000 of the trust fund was lost.

The trial court made findings of fact and drew conclusions of law. As relevant, the court found that defendant trustees "exercised the judgment and care, under the circumstances then prevailing, which men of prudence, discretion and intelligence exercised in the management of their own affairs, not in regard to speculation, but in regard to the disposition of their funds, considering the probable income, as well as the probable safety of their capital." In making the loan, "the co-trustees used reasonable care, diligence and skill. The co-trustees did not act arbitrarily or in bad faith."

Discussion

The trial court's finding that defendants exercised the judgment and care "which men of prudence, discretion and intelligence exercised in the management of their own affairs," reflects the standard imposed upon trustees by Civil Code section 2261.

Plaintiffs contend, and we agree, that contrary to the trial court's findings and conclusions, defendants failed to follow the "prudent investor" standard, first, by investing two-thirds of the trust principal in a single investment, second, by investing in real property secured only by a second deed of trust, and third, by making that investment without adequate investigation of either the borrowers or the collateral.

Although California does not limit the trustee's authority to a list of authorized investments, relying instead on the prudent investor rule, nevertheless, the prudent investor rule encompasses certain guidelines applicable to this case.

First, "the trustee is under a duty to the beneficiary to distribute the risk of loss by a reasonable diversification of investments, unless under the circumstances it is prudent not to do so." (Rest.2d Trusts, § 228)

Second, ordinarily, "second or other junior mortgages are not proper trust investments," unless taking a second mortgage is a reasonable method of settling a claim or making possible the sale of property. Stated more emphatically: "While loans secured by second mortgages on land are sometimes allowed, they are almost always disapproved by courts of equity. The trustee should not place the trust funds in a position where they may be endangered by the foreclosure of a prior lien In rare cases equity will sanction an investment secured by a second mortgage, but only when the security is adequate and unusual circumstances justify the trustee in taking this form of investment." (Bogert, Trusts and Trustees (2d ed.)

Third, in buying a mortgage for trust investment, the trustee should give careful attention to the valuation of the property, in order to make certain that his margin of security is adequate. He must use every reasonable endeavor to provide protection which will cover the risks of depreciation in the property and changes in price levels. And he must investigate the status of the property and of the mortgage, as well as the financial situation of the mortgagor. (Bogert)

We think it apparent that defendants violated every applicable rule. First, they failed totally to diversify the investments in this relatively small trust fund. Second, defendants invested in a junior mortgage on unimproved real property, and left an inadequate margin of security. As noted, the land had most recently sold for $107,000, and was subject to a first trust deed of $90,000. Thus, unless the land was worth more than $140,000, there was no margin of security at all. Defendants did not have the land appraised; the only information they had was the opinion of a real estate broker that property in the area - not that particular parcel - was going for $18,000 to $20,000 an acre. Thus, any assumption that the property was worth about $185,000 - and therefore the $140,000 in loans were well-secured - would have been little more than a guess.

Third, the backup security obtained by defendants was no security at all. The builders pledged 20 percent of their stock, but defendants never obtained possession of the stock, placed it in escrow or even had it legended. They accepted the personal guarantees of the builders and their wives without investigating the financial status of these persons. They accepted at face value the claimed $2 million value of the company shown in an unaudited statement. Defendant Millikan apparently ignored the fact that one lender had, for whatever reasons, reneged on a loan commitment to the builders.

Defendants contend that the evidence sustains the trial court's findings that they exercised the judgment and care under the circumstances then prevailing expected of men of prudence. They rely on the rule that the determination whether an investment was proper must be made in light of the circumstances existing at the time of the investment. That rule does not help defendants. Nothing that happened after the loan was made can change the fact that defendants invested two-thirds of the principal of the trust in a single second deed of trust on unappraised property, with no knowledge of the borrowers' true financial status, and without any other security.

We recognize, as did the trial court, that the loan was made in 1965, and defendants, some 10 years later, could not be expected to recall the specifics of their investigation. But that is the point of this case turned inside out: Defendants were required to rely on faded memories because their investigation was limited to casual conversations. No documentation existed, not because it was lost, but because it was never obtained. Further, it is defendants' own fault that they filed their "first and final account" more than eight years after assuming their duties.

Here defendants must be surcharged, not because they lacked prescience of what would happen, but because they both lacked and ignored information about what was happening at the time.

Plainly, defendants' conduct did not meet the prudent-investor standard. They claim, however, that the trust instrument conferred on them an "absolute discretion." Therefore, they argue, their sole obligation was not to act arbitrarily and to use their best judgment.

We leave aside that even a trustee with "absolute discretion" may not "neglect its trust or abdicate its judgment," or show a "reckless indifference" to the interests of the beneficiary. The record before us contains no evidence that defendants satisfied even the lesser standard of care for which they contend.

More fundamentally we do not agree with defendants' premise. While the declaration of trust may possibly enlarge the prudent-investor standard as far as the *type* of investment is concerned, it cannot be construed as permitting deviations from that standard in investigating the soundness of a specific investment. This distinction is well established.

The provisions on which defendants rely are subparagraphs (3) and (11) to paragraph (d). Neither supports their position.[5] Neither Civil Code section 2261 nor any other authority which we can locate authorizes different types of investments for "corporate trustees" as distinguished from amateurs. The difference is, rather, that the corporate trustee is held to a greater standard of care based on its presumed expertise.

In any event, even if the trust instrument permitted a type of investment generally frowned on under the prudent-investor rule, it did not authorize the trustees to make it blindly. Defendants might have a point, had they purchased a well-secured second trust deed after careful investigation. Clearly, however, the nature of their investment is the least of their problems.

Alternatively, defendants rely on the language in subparagraph (11) that "all discretions conferred upon the Trustee shall be absolute, ..." This reliance, too, is misplaced.

First, viewed as an exculpatory clause, subparagraph (11) is subject to the rule of strict construction.

Second, the "absolute discretion" is "specifically limited" by the requirement that the trustee is "subject always to the discharge of its fiduciary obligations ..."

Third, in context subparagraph (11) refers only to "discretions conferred on the Trustee" in paragraph (d) of the trust which, as noted, deals exclusively with powers, as

---

[5] Subparagraph (3) merely tracks section 2261 of the Civil Code and adds that the investments listed therein are permissible "irrespective of whether said investments are in accordance with the laws then in force in the State of California pertaining to the investment of trust funds by corporate trustees." This adds nothing.

distinguished from the degree of care with which they are to be exercised. Nor does any other part of the declaration of trust mention any relevant discretion which subparagraph (11) would make "absolute." Nowhere did the trustor say anything about a discretion not to diversify, a discretion to invest in a junior encumbrance without ability to protect against the foreclosure of a senior lien, a discretion not to make a businesslike investigation of the credit and net worth of the borrower, or a discretion not to insist on an appraisal of the security given by the borrower.

The orders are reversed with directions to determine the damages to which plaintiffs are entitled.

I. DUTY OF DISCLOSURE

Even in a case where the trustee may be given wide discretion on investment of trust assets, the trustee still has some duty to keep the beneficiaries informed as to how their assets are being managed, and in some situations the trustee may, in addition, have a duty to inform the beneficiaries before any large changes are made to trust investments. The following case illustrates one aspect of this duty of disclosure.

Supreme Court of Washington.
Freeman ALLARD and Evelyn Orkney, as beneficiaries of the trusts of J.T. Stone and Georgiana Stone *et al,* Appellants
v.
PACIFIC NATIONAL BANK, as trustee, Respondent, City of Seattle Credit Union and Seattle-First National Bank, Defendants.

July 21, 1983.

DOLLIVER, Justice.

Plaintiffs Freeman Allard and Evelyn Orkney are beneficiaries of trusts established by their parents, J.T. and Georgiana Stone. Defendant Pacific National Bank (Pacific Bank) is the trustee of the Stone trusts. Plaintiffs appeal a King County Superior Court decision dismissing their action against Pacific Bank for breach of its fiduciary duties as trustee of the Stone trusts.

We agree with the Superior Court that plaintiffs' claims are primarily equitable in nature and we affirm its decision that plaintiffs have no right to jury trial. We conclude, however, that Pacific Bank breached its fiduciary duties regarding management of the Stone trusts. We also find the Superior Court incorrectly awarded attorney fees and costs to Pacific Bank.

J.T. and Georgiana Stone, both deceased, established trusts in their wills conveying their property upon their deaths to Pacific Bank to be held for their children and the issue of their children. The Stones' children, Evelyn and Freeman, are life income beneficiaries of the Stone trusts. Upon the death of either life income beneficiary, the trustee is to pay the income from the trust to the issue of the deceased beneficiary. When all the children of the deceased beneficiary reach the age of 21 years, the trusts direct the trustee to distribute the trust corpus equally among the issue of that beneficiary.

In 1978 the sole asset of the Stone trusts was a fee interest in a quarter block located on the northwest corner of Third Avenue and Columbia Street in downtown Seattle. The trust provisions of the wills gave Pacific Bank "full power to ... manage, improve, sell, lease, mortgage, pledge, encumber, and exchange the whole or any part of the assets of the trust estate" and required Pacific Bank to

> "exercise the judgment and care under the circumstances then prevailing, which prudent men exercise in the management of their own affairs, not in regard to speculation but in regard to the permanent disposition of their funds, considering the probable income as well as the probable safety of their capital."

The Third and Columbia property was subject to a 99-year lease, entered into by the Stones in 1952 with Seattle-First National Bank (Seafirst Bank). The lease contained no rental escalation provision and the rental rate was to remain the same for the entire 99-year term of the lease. The right of first refusal to purchase the lessor's interest in the property was given to the lessee. The lease also contained several restrictive provisions. One paragraph required any repair, reconstruction, or replacement of buildings on the property by the lessee to be completed within 8 months from the date the original building was damaged or destroyed "from any cause whatsoever". Another paragraph provided that, upon termination of lease, the lessee had the option either to surrender possession of all improvements or to remove the improvements. The lease prohibited, without the lessor's consent, any encumbrance which would have priority over the lessor in case of the lessee's insolvency.

In June 1977 Seafirst Bank assigned its leasehold interest in the Third and Columbia property to the City Credit Union of Seattle (Credit Union). Eight months later, on February 14, 1978, Credit Union offered to purchase the property from Pacific Bank for $139,900. On April 25, 1978, Pacific Bank informed Credit Union it was interested in selling the property, but demanded at least $200,000. In early June 1978, Credit Union offered $200,000 for the Third and Columbia property. Pacific Bank accepted Credit Union's offer, and deeded the property to Credit Union on August 17, 1978. On September 26, 1978, Pacific Bank informed Freeman and Evelyn of the sale to Credit Union.

On May 1, 1979, plaintiffs commenced the present action against Pacific Bank for breach of its fiduciary duties regarding management of the Stone trusts, against Credit Union and Seafirst Bank for participation in the alleged breach, and against Credit Union for conversion. Plaintiffs' complaint requested money damages from Pacific Bank, Credit Union, and Seafirst Bank. The complaint also requested the imposition of a constructive trust on the Third and Columbia property and the removal of Pacific Bank as trustee.

The trial court granted motions by Credit Union and Seafirst Bank dismissing them from the case.

At trial, the primary dispute was over the degree of care owed by Pacific Bank to the Stone trusts and to the Stone trust beneficiaries.

At the culmination of the trial, the court entered judgment dismissing plaintiffs' action against Pacific Bank. It determined Pacific Bank acted in good faith and in conformance with its duties under the Stone trust instruments. The court concluded Pacific Bank neither had a duty to inform the trust beneficiaries prior to sale of the Third and Columbia property nor a duty to obtain an independent appraisal of the property or to place the property on the open market. Finally, the trial court awarded Pacific Bank $51,507.07 attorney fees and costs from the income and principal of the Stone trusts. From this judgment plaintiffs bring appeal.

I

The beneficiaries of the Stone trusts essentially allege Pacific Bank improperly depleted the trust assets by selling the Third and Columbia property for less than its fair market value. None of the beneficiaries have a present right to receive distribution of the trust corpus. Their only remedy for depletion of the trust corpus is restoration of the value of the corpus by the trustee, often referred to as a "surcharge" on the trustee. Since the trustee is under no duty to pay money besides the trust income to the beneficiaries, they have no action at law for breach of the trust agreement.

II

We now consider the crux of the case before us. Defendant contends it had full authority under the trust instrument to exercise its own judgment and impartial discretion in deciding how to invest the trust assets and a duty to use reasonable care and skill to make the trust property productive.

Plaintiffs' argument is twofold. First, Pacific Bank had a duty to inform them of the sale of the Third and Columbia property. Second, Pacific Bank breached its fiduciary duties by failing either to obtain an independent appraisal of the Third and Columbia property or to place the property on the open market prior to selling it to Seattle Credit Union. We agree with plaintiffs' position in both instances and hold defendant breached its fiduciary duty in its management of the trusts.

A

Initially, plaintiffs and amicus curiae the Attorney General of the State of Washington contend Pacific Bank should be held to a higher standard of care than the ordinary, prudent investor standard provided in RCW 30.24.020. Plaintiffs and amicus curiae argue the ordinary, prudent investor standard is inappropriate where the trustee represents that it has greater skill than that of a nonprofessional trustee. They fail to mention, however, the terms of the Stone trust agreements which specifically adopt the prudent investor standard of care provided in RCW 30.24.020.

Significantly, the statute recognizes the standard of care required of a trustee is "subject to any express provisions or limitations contained in any particular trust instrument". Furthermore, the terms of the trust instrument control as to the investments made by a trustee. Except where impossible, illegal, or where a change of circumstances occurs which would impair the purposes of the trust, the nature and extent of the duties and powers of a trustee are determined by the trust agreement. Although in some future case we may be called upon to determine if a corporate professional trustee should be held to a higher standard because of the language in the trust instruments, this issue need not be decided here.

B

The Stone trusts gave Pacific Bank "full power to ... manage, improve, sell, lease, mortgage, pledge, encumber, and exchange the whole or any part of the assets of [the] trust estate". Under such an agreement, the trustee is not required to secure the consent of trust beneficiaries before selling trust assets. The trustee owes to the beneficiaries, however, the highest degree of good faith, care, loyalty, and integrity.

Pacific Bank claims it was obligated to sell the property to Credit Union since Credit Union, as assignee of the lease agreement with Seafirst Bank, had a right of first refusal to purchase the property. Since it did not need to obtain the consent of the beneficiaries before selling trust assets, Pacific Bank argues it also was not required to inform the beneficiaries of the sale. We disagree. The beneficiaries could have offered to purchase the property at a higher price than the offer by Credit Union, thereby forcing Credit Union to pay a higher price to exercise its right of first refusal as assignee of the lease agreement. Furthermore, letters from the beneficiaries to Pacific Bank indicated their desire to retain the Third and Columbia property. While the beneficiaries could not have prevented Pacific Bank from selling the property, they presumably could have outbid Credit Union for the property. This opportunity should have been afforded to them.

On a previous occasion, we ruled the trustee's fiduciary duty includes the responsibility to inform the beneficiaries fully of all facts which would aid them in protecting their interests. We adhere to that view. That the settlor has created a trust and thus required the beneficiaries to enjoy their property interests indirectly does not imply the beneficiaries are to be kept in ignorance of the trust, the nature of the trust property, and the details of its administration. If the beneficiaries are able to hold the trustee to proper standards of care and honesty and procure the benefits to which they are entitled, they must know of what the trust property consists and how it is being managed. G. Bogert, *Trusts and Trustees.*

The duty to provide information is often performed by corporate trustees by rendering periodic statements to the beneficiaries, usually in the form of copies of the ledger sheets concerning the trust. For example, such condensed explanations of recent transactions may be mailed to the beneficiaries annually, semiannually, or quarterly. Ordinarily, periodic statements are sufficient to satisfy a trustee's duty to beneficiaries of informing the beneficiaries of transactions affecting the trust property. The trust provisions here, for example, provide the trustee

> "shall furnish on or before February 15 of each year to each person described in Section 1 of Article IV who is then a beneficiary ... a statement showing how the respective trust assets are invested and all transactions relating thereto for the preceding calendar year."

The trustee must also inform beneficiaries, however, of all material facts in connection with a nonroutine transaction which significantly affects the trust estate and the interests of the beneficiaries prior to the transaction taking place. The duty to inform is particularly required in this case where the only asset of the trusts was the property on the corner of Third and Columbia. Under the circumstances found in this case failure to inform was an egregious breach of fiduciary duty and defies the course of conduct any reasonable person would take, much less a prudent investor.

C

We also conclude Pacific Bank breached its fiduciary duties regarding management of the Stone trusts by failing to obtain the best possible price for the Third and Columbia property. Pacific Bank made no attempt to obtain a more favorable price for the property from Credit Union by, for example, negotiating to cancel the restrictive provisions in the lease originally negotiated with Seafirst Bank. The bank neither offered the property for sale on the open market, nor did it obtain an independent, outside appraisal of the Third and Columbia property to determine its fair market value.

We hold that a trustee may determine the best possible price for trust property either by obtaining an independent appraisal of the property or by "testing the market" to determine what a willing buyer would pay. The record discloses none of these actions were taken by the defendant. By its failure to obtain the best possible price for the Third and Columbia property, defendant breached its fiduciary duty as the prudent manager of the trusts.

III

Finally, we consider whether the trial court improperly awarded attorney fees to Pacific Bank. A trial court may allow and properly charge attorney fees to a trust estate for litigation that is necessary to the administration of the trust. The award of attorney fees against the trust estate is vested in the discretion of the trial court. A trial court's discretion to award attorney fees, however, is not absolute. The court must determine the litigation is indispensable to the proper administration of the trust; the issues presented are neither immaterial nor trifling; the conduct of the parties or counsel is not vexatious or litigious; and that there has been no unnecessary delay or expense. Furthermore, the trial court must consider the result of the litigation.

The court's underlying consideration must be whether the litigation and the participation of the party seeking attorney fees caused a benefit to the trust. A trustee who unsuccessfully defends against charges of breach of fiduciary duties obviously has not caused a benefit to the trust. Therefore, a trial court abuses its discretion when it awards attorney fees to a trustee for litigation caused by the trustee's misconduct.

A trustee may be awarded attorney fees and costs for litigation alleging breach of the trust agreement only if the trustee successfully defends against the action.

We also hold that since defendant breached its fiduciary duty plaintiffs should be granted their request to recover all attorney fees expended at both the trial and on appeal on behalf of the plaintiffs and all minor beneficiaries and unknown beneficiaries. Ordinarily, the trust estate must bear the general costs of administration of the trust, including the expenses of necessary litigation. Where litigation is necessitated by the inexcusable conduct of the trustee, however, the trustee individually must pay those expenses.

The case is remanded for a determination of the damages caused to plaintiffs by defendant's breach of its fiduciary duties as trustee of the Stone trusts and a determination of the amount of attorney fees to be awarded plaintiffs from the trustee individually.

J. RIGHTS OF BENEFICIARIES TO SEE TRUST RECORDS AND LEGAL ADVICE GIVEN TO TRUSTEES

In most situations, the beneficiaries have the right, upon proper notice to the trustee, to see all of the records of the trust. It is crucial, of course, for the beneficiaries to be able to see the records, if they are going to be able to hold the trustee to account if the trustee makes improper investments, or makes improper distributions, or makes any sort of improper allocation of trust funds.

An interesting situation arises, however, when the beneficiaries attempt to see the legal advice given to the trustees. The following recent U. S. Supreme Court case is an interesting illustration of the problem of how much of the legal advice given to the trustees must be disclosed to the beneficiaries – especially when the trustees and the beneficiaries have become adversaries. This case enunciates the usual standards for disclosure for private, irrevocable trusts.[6] It also sets forth an important exception to the general rule of disclosure.

Supreme Court of the United States.
UNITED STATES, Petitioner,
v.
JICARILLA APACHE NATION.
Decided June 13, 2011.

ALITO, J., delivered the opinion of the Court, in which ROBERTS, C.J., and SCALIA, KENNEDY, and THOMAS, JJ., joined. GINSBURG, J., filed an opinion concurring in the

[6] While a settlor retains full authority to revoke a trust, including the authority to remove the trustee, there is no duty of disclosure to other possible beneficiaries.

judgment, in which BREYER, J., joined. SOTOMAYOR, J., filed a dissenting opinion.

Justice ALITO delivered the opinion of the Court.

The attorney-client privilege ranks among the oldest and most established evidentiary privileges known to our law. The common law, however, has recognized an exception to the privilege when a trustee obtains legal advice related to the exercise of fiduciary duties. In such cases, courts have held, the trustee cannot withhold attorney-client communications from the beneficiary of the trust.

In this case, we consider whether the fiduciary exception applies to the general trust relationship between the United States and the Indian tribes. We hold that it does not. Although the Government's responsibilities with respect to the management of funds belonging to Indian tribes bear some resemblance to those of a private trustee, this analogy cannot be taken too far. The trust obligations of the United States to the Indian tribes are established and governed by statute rather than the common law, and in fulfilling its statutory duties, the Government acts not as a private trustee but pursuant to its sovereign interest in the execution of federal law. The reasons for the fiduciary exception—that the trustee has no independent interest in trust administration, and that the trustee is subject to a general common-law duty of disclosure—do not apply in this context.

I

The Jicarilla Apache Nation (Tribe) occupies a 900,000–acre reservation in northern New Mexico that was established in 1887. The land contains timber, gravel, and oil and gas reserves, which are developed pursuant to statutes administered by the Department of the Interior. Proceeds derived from these natural resources are held by the United States in trust for the Tribe.

In 2002, the Tribe commenced a breach-of-trust action against the United States in the Court of Federal Claims (CFC). The Tribe sued under the Tucker Act, and the Indian Tucker Act, § 1505, which vest the CFC with jurisdiction over claims against the Government that are founded on the Constitution, laws, treaties, or contracts of the United States. The complaint seeks monetary damages for the Government's alleged mismanagement of funds held in trust for the Tribe.

From December 2002 to June 2008, the Government and the Tribe participated in alternative dispute resolution in order to resolve the claim. During that time, the Government turned over to the Tribe thousands of documents but withheld 226 potentially relevant documents as protected by the attorney-client privilege, the attorney work-product doctrine, or the deliberative-process privilege.

In 2008, at the request of the Tribe, the case was restored to the active litigation docket. The CFC divided the case into phases for trial and set a discovery schedule. The first phase, relevant here, concerns the Government's management of the Tribe's trust accounts from 1972 to 1992. The Tribe alleges that during this period the Government failed to invest its trust funds properly. Among other things, the Tribe claims the Government failed to maximize returns on its trust funds, invested too heavily in short-term maturities, and failed to pool its trust funds with other tribal trusts. During discovery, the Tribe moved to compel the Government to produce the 226 withheld documents. In response, the Government agreed to withdraw its claims of deliberative-process privilege and, accordingly, to produce 71 of the documents. But the Government continued to assert the attorney-client privilege and attorney work-product doctrine with respect to the remaining 155 documents. The CFC reviewed those documents *in camera* and classified them into five categories: (1) requests for legal advice relating to trust administration sent by personnel at the Department of the Interior to the Office of the Solicitor, which directs legal affairs for the Department, (2) legal advice sent from the Solicitor's Office to personnel at the Interior and Treasury Departments, (3) documents generated under contracts between Interior and an accounting firm, (4) Interior documents concerning litigation with other tribes, and (5) miscellaneous documents not falling into the other categories.

The CFC granted the Tribe's motion to compel in part. The CFC held that communications relating to the management of trust funds fall within a "fiduciary exception" to the attorney-client privilege. Under that exception, which courts have applied in the context of common-law trusts, a trustee who obtains legal advice related to the execution of fiduciary obligations is precluded from asserting the attorney-client privilege against beneficiaries of the trust.

The Government sought to prevent disclosure of the documents by petitioning the Court of Appeals for the Federal Circuit for a writ of mandamus directing the CFC to vacate its production order. The Court of Appeals denied the petition.

We granted certiorari, and now reverse and remand for further proceedings.

II

The Federal Rules of Evidence provide that evidentiary privileges "shall be governed by the principles of the common law ... in the light of reason and experience." The attorney-client privilege "is the oldest of the privileges for confidential communications known to the common law." Its aim is "to encourage full and frank communication between attorneys and their clients and thereby promote broader public interests in the observance of law and administration of justice."

The objectives of the attorney-client privilege apply to governmental clients. The privilege aids government entities and employees in obtaining legal advice founded on a complete and accurate factual picture. Unless applicable law provides otherwise, the Government may invoke the attorney-client privilege in civil litigation to protect confidential communications between Government officials and Government attorneys.

The Tribe argues, however, that the common law also recognizes a fiduciary exception to the attorney-client privilege and that, by virtue of the trust relationship between the Government and the Tribe, documents that would otherwise be privileged must be disclosed. As preliminary matters, we consider the bounds of the fiduciary exception and the nature of the trust relationship between the United States and the Indian tribes.

A

English courts first developed the fiduciary exception as a principle of trust law in the 19th century. The rule was that when a trustee obtained legal advice to guide the administration of the trust, and not for the trustee's own defense in litigation, the beneficiaries were entitled to the production of documents related to that advice. The courts reasoned that the normal attorney-client privilege did not apply in this situation because the legal advice was sought for the beneficiaries' benefit and was obtained at the beneficiaries' expense by using trust funds to pay the attorney's fees.

The fiduciary exception quickly became an established feature of English common law, but it did not appear in this country until the following century.

The leading American case on the fiduciary exception is *Riggs Nat. Bank of Washington, D.C. v. Zimmer.* In that case, the beneficiaries of a trust estate sought to compel the trustees to reimburse the estate for alleged breaches of trust. The beneficiaries moved to compel the trustees to produce a legal memorandum related to the administration of the trust that the trustees withheld on the basis of attorney-client privilege. The Delaware Chancery Court, observing that "American case law is practically nonexistent on the duty of a trustee in this context," looked to the English cases. Applying the common-law fiduciary exception, the court held that the memorandum was discoverable.

B

In order to apply the fiduciary exception in this case, the Court of Appeals analogized the Government to a private trustee. We have applied that analogy in limited contexts, but that does not mean the Government resembles a private trustee in every respect. On the contrary, this Court has previously noted that the relationship between the United States and the Indian tribes is distinctive, "different from that existing between individuals whether dealing at arm's length, *as trustees and beneficiaries,* or otherwise." *Klamath and Moadoc Tribes v. United States,* (1935) (Emphasis added). "The *general* relationship between the United States and the Indian tribes is not comparable to a private trust relationship." *Cherokee Nation of Okla. v. United States,* (1990) (Emphasis added).

The Government, of course, is not a private trustee. Though the relevant statutes denominate the relationship between the Government and the Indians a "trust," that trust is defined and governed by statutes rather than the common law.

B/U The difference between a private common-law trust and the statutory Indian trust follows from the unique position of the Government as sovereign. The Government consents to be liable to private parties "and may yield this consent upon such terms and under such restrictions as it may think just." *Murray's Lessee v. Hoboken Land & Improvement.* waiving sov immun

Throughout the history of the Indian trust relationship, we have recognized that the organization and management of the trust is a sovereign function subject to the plenary authority of Congress. ("The United States retains plenary authority to divest the tribes of any attributes of sovereignty"); *United States v. Wheeler,* (1978).

Because the Indian trust relationship represents an exercise of that authority, we have explained that the Government "has a real and direct interest" in the guardianship it exercises over the Indian tribes; "the interest is one which is vested in it as a sovereign." This is especially so because the Government has often structured the trust relationship to pursue its own policy goals. Thus, while trust administration relates to the welfare of the Indians, the maintenance of the limitations which Congress has prescribed as a part of its plan of distribution is distinctly an interest of the United States.

III

The Court of Appeals concluded that the trust relationship between the United States and the Indian tribes, outlined in various statutes, is "sufficiently similar to a private trust to justify applying the fiduciary exception." We disagree.

As we have discussed, the Government exercises its carefully delimited trust responsibilities in a sovereign capacity to implement national policy respecting the Indian tribes. The two features justifying the fiduciary exception—the beneficiary's status as the "real client" and the trustee's common-law duty to disclose information about the trust—are notably absent in the trust relationship Congress has established between the United States and the Tribe.

A

Here, the Government attorneys are paid out of congressional appropriations at no cost to the Tribe. Courts look to the source of funds as a "strong indicator of precisely who the real clients were" and a "significant factor" in determining who ought to have access to the legal advice. We similarly find it significant that the attorneys were paid by the Government for advice regarding the Government's statutory obligations.

The payment structure confirms our view that the Government seeks legal advice in its sovereign capacity rather than as a conventional fiduciary of the Tribe. Undoubtedly, Congress intends the Indian tribes to benefit from the Government's management of tribal trusts. That intention represents "a humane and self imposed policy" based on felt "moral obligations." This statutory purpose does not imply a full common-law trust, however. Cf. Restatement 2d, § 25, Comment *b* ("No trust is created if the settlor manifests an intention to impose merely a moral obligation"). We have said that "the United States continues as trustee to have an active interest" in the disposition of Indian assets because the terms of the trust relationship embody policy goals of the United States.

In some prior cases, we have found that the Government had established the trust relationship in order to impose its own policy on Indian lands. In other cases, the Government has invoked its trust relationship to prevent state interference with its policy toward the Indian tribes. In this way, Congress has designed the trust relationship to serve the interests of the United States as well as to benefit the Indian tribes.

We cannot agree with the Tribe and its *amici* that "the government and its officials who obtained the advice have no stake in the substance of the advice, beyond their trustee role," or that "the United States' interests in trust administration were identical to the interests of the tribal trust fund beneficiaries," The United States has a sovereign interest in the administration of Indian trusts distinct from the private interests of those who may benefit from its administration. Courts apply the fiduciary exception on the ground that "management does not manage for itself."

But the Government is never in that position. While one purpose of the Indian trust relationship is to benefit the tribes, the Government has its own independent interest in the implementation of federal Indian policy. For that reason, when the Government seeks legal advice related to the administration of tribal trusts, it establishes an attorney-client relationship related to its sovereign interest in the execution of federal law. In other words, the Government seeks legal advice in a "personal" rather than a fiduciary capacity.

Moreover, the Government has too many competing legal concerns to allow a case-by-case inquiry into the purpose of each communication. When "multiple interests" are involved in a trust relationship, the equivalence between the interests of the beneficiary and the trustee breaks down. That principle applies with particular force to the Government. Because of the multiple interests it must represent, "the Government cannot follow the fastidious standards of a private fiduciary, who would breach his duties to his single beneficiary solely by representing potentially conflicting interests without the beneficiary's consent."

As the Court of Appeals acknowledged, the Government may be obliged "to balance competing interests" when it administers a tribal trust. The Government may need to comply with other statutory duties, such as environmental and conservation obligations. The Government may also face conflicting obligations to different tribes or individual Indians. Within the bounds of its "general trust relationship" with the Indian people, we have recognized that the Government has "discretion to reorder its priorities from serving a subgroup of beneficiaries to serving the broader class of all Indians nationwide." And sometimes, we have seen, the Government has enforced the trust statutes to dispose of Indian property contrary to the wishes of those for whom it was nominally kept in trust. The Government may seek the advice of counsel for guidance in balancing these competing interests. Indeed, the point of consulting counsel may be to determine whether conflicting interests are at stake.

The Court of Appeals sought to accommodate the Government's multiple obligations by suggesting that the Government may invoke the attorney-client privilege if it identifies "a specific competing interest" that was considered in the particular communications it seeks to withhold. But the conflicting interests the Government must consider are too pervasive for such a case-by-case approach to be workable.

We have said that for the attorney-client privilege to be effective, it must be predictable. If the Government were required to identify the specific interests it considered in each communication, its ability to receive confidential legal advice would be substantially compromised. The Government will not always be able to predict what considerations qualify as a "specific competing interest," especially in advance of receiving counsel's advice. Forcing the Government to monitor all the considerations contained in each communication with counsel would render its attorney-client privilege "little better than no privilege at all."

B

The Court of Appeals also decided the fiduciary exception properly applied to the Government because "the fiduciary has a duty to disclose all information related to trust management to the beneficiary." In general, the common-law trustee of an irrevocable trust must produce trust-related information to the beneficiary on a reasonable basis, though this duty is sometimes limited and may be modified by the settlor. [7]

The United States, however, does not have the same common-law disclosure obligations as a private trustee. Common-law principles are relevant only when applied to a "specific, applicable, trust-creating statute or regulation." The relevant statute in this case includes a provision that the Secretary of Interior must "supply account holders with periodic statements of their account performance" and must make "available on a daily basis" the "balances of their account." The Secretary has complied with these requirements by adopting regulations that instruct the Office of Trust Fund Management to provide each tribe with a quarterly statement of performance, that identifies "the source, type, and status of the trust funds deposited and held in a trust account; the beginning balance; the gains and losses; receipts and disbursements; and the ending account balance of the quarterly statement period.".

The common law of trusts does not override the specific trust-creating statute and regulations that apply here. Those provisions define the Government's disclosure obligation to the Tribe. The Tribe emphasizes that the statute identifies the list of trust responsibilities as nonexhaustive. Whatever Congress intended, we cannot read the clause to include a general common-law duty to disclose all information related to the administration of Indian trusts

By law and regulation, moreover, the documents at issue in this case are classed "the property of the United States" while other records are "the property of the tribe." Just as the source of the funds used to pay for legal advice is highly relevant in identifying the "real client" for purposes of the fiduciary exception, we consider ownership of the resulting records to be a significant factor in deciding who "ought to

---

7 We assume for the sake of argument that an Indian trust is properly analogized to an irrevocable trust rather than to a revocable trust. A revocable trust imposes no duty of the trustee to disclose information to the beneficiary. "While a trust is revocable, only the person who may revoke it is entitled to receive information about it from the trustee." Bogert § 962. The trustee of a revocable trust is not to provide reports or accountings or other information concerning the terms or administration of the trust to other beneficiaries without authorization either by the settlor or in the terms of the trust or a statute. **In many respects, Indian trusts resemble revocable trusts at common law because Congress has acted as the settlor in establishing the trust and retains the right to alter the terms of the trust by statute, even in derogation of tribal property interests.** (Emphasis added.)

have access to the document." In this case, that privilege belongs to the United States.

Courts and commentators have long recognized that "Not every aspect of private trust law can properly govern the unique relationship of tribes and the federal government." The fiduciary exception to the attorney-client privilege ranks among those aspects inapplicable to the Government's administration of Indian trusts. We therefore reverse the judgment of the Court of Appeals and remand the case for further proceedings consistent with this opinion.

It is so ordered.

CHAPTER 15 - MODIFICATION OR TERMINATION BY THE SETTLOR

The basic rule is that if a settlor does not specifically reserve the right to modify or terminate an inter vivos trust, then the trust becomes irrevocable, as soon as it is established. There may be some situations in which that would be appropriate, but in most situations it is probably more appropriate for the settlor to retain the power to amend and modify the trust, as circumstances change. When any trust is established it should be clearly stated who has the authority to amend or modify the trust, or terminate the trust early; what specific steps must be taken to make any such modification; and under what circumstances those modifications will be binding.

The following cases illustrate some of the problems which arise when a settlor attempts to modify a trust. Especially when a settlor sets up an inter vivos trust, naming the settlor as the initial trustee, and the sole present beneficiary, the settlor is likely to forget that the trust is a separate legal entity - and that the property in the trust is no longer subject to the unilateral control of the settlor - unless the settlor has specifically reserved such a right.

A. MODIFICATION OR REVOCATION BY WILL?

In the following case the settlor, perhaps, attempted to revoke a trust which she had previously established. Under the circumstances described in this case, if you had been the attorney for the settlor, what advice would you have given to her?

Colorado Court of Appeals.
In re the ESTATE OF Hazel I. McCREATH, Deceased.
Charlotte M. Ritchey, Appellant,
v.
Milford L. McCreath and Elton R. McCreath, Appellees.
Dec. 24, 2009. Rehearing Denied Jan. 28, 2010.

Opinion by Judge ROY.

Charlotte M. Ritchey (daughter) appeals the trial court's ruling that a last will and testament executed by Hazel I. McCreath (mother) did not presently revoke the Hazel I. McCreath Revocable Trust dated July 11, 1992; and that a quitclaim deed issued by mother alone as trustee of the trust on March 13, 2001, conveying the family farm and unrelated mineral interests was ineffective to transfer the real property out of the trust.

The Documents

Three documents are germane to the issues on appeal.

The first is a trust agreement dated July 11, 1992, which was executed by mother as settlor, and which designated both mother and daughter as trustees. The trust corpus consists of the family farm, including appurtenant mineral interests, and the trust agreement provides that upon termination, the trust estate is to be divided equally among mother's three children. The July 11, 1992 trust agreement amends a November 8, 1989 trust agreement for the apparent purpose of naming daughter as co-trustee replacing mother's husband, who was deceased.

As pertinent here, the trust provides:

> [Mother] reserves the right at any time or times to ... revoke ... this Trust, in whole or in part, or any provision thereof, by an instrument in writing signed by [mother] and delivered to Trustees.... If this Trust is revoked in its entirety, the revocation shall take effect upon the delivery of the required writing to Trustees. On the revocation of this Trust in its entirety, Trustees shall pay or transfer to [mother] as [mother] shall direct in the instrument of revocation, all of the trust estate. .... A majority of all fiduciaries in office at the time must concur in decisions except where Settlor has expressly placed discretion in one of them.

The second document is a recorded quitclaim deed dated March 13, 2001, executed by mother alone as a trustee of the trust, and conveying the family farm and unrelated mineral interests to daughter, individually, free and clear of the trust.

The third is a handwritten document (mother's will), which was executed May 25, 2005, and, which, for the purposes of this appeal, is presumed to be mother's last will and testament. Mother's will was handwritten by an attorney, was executed by mother, and was witnessed by the attorney and a nurse. It has mother's name at the top and has no characterization of the instrument, and the text consists of four bullet paragraphs, which state as follows:

> • revoke all prior wills and trusts
>
> • give personal property (contents of house) to children in equal shares. children choose what they want to take. all others sold and placed in the residuary.
>
> • residuary distributed. after expenses. debts + taxes, to:
>
> -Charlotte Mae Ritchy-80%
>
> -Elton Ray McCreath-10%
>
> -Milford Lee McCreath-10%
>
> • ~~trustee~~ [sic] Personal Representative (executor) shall be non-family member. if none can be found to appoint then Charlotte Mae Ritchy

Just looks like a list for the attorney

There is no dispute that mother's will was delivered to daughter, and there are allegations that a more formal document was prepared but never executed by mother.

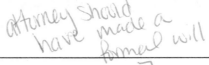

Mother passed away over a year after signing the will.

The Litigation

Milford and Elton McCreath (collectively, sons) commenced an action seeking declaratory judgment as to the validity and legal effect of certain documents, including those above-described, and alleging claims against daughter for breach of fiduciary duty, conversion, civil theft, an accounting, and constructive trust. Later, daughter filed for formal probate of mother's will. The sons subsequently entered the probate case as interested parties.

After consolidating the "estate plan" issues for trial, the trial court issued a modified case management order (MCMO) providing for a jury trial on the validity of mother's will, and a bench trial on the question of whether the will revoked the trust at the time it was executed and delivered to daughter. The remaining claims were stayed for future determination.

Effect of Mother's Will

Daughter first argues that mother's will was effective, at the time of its execution and delivery, as a matter of law, to revoke the trust. More specifically, she argues that mother's will revokes the trust: (1) pursuant to the trust agreement's explicit terms; and (2) because there is clear and convincing evidence of mother's intent to revoke the trust in her will. This is an issue of first impression in Colorado.

At the outset, we recognize that the validity of mother's will is an unresolved issue pending before the trial court. However, for the purposes of our analysis, we assume that the will is valid and probatable.

The general rule is that a trust may not be revoked by the settlor without the consent of all beneficiaries, unless the settlor has explicitly reserved to himself or herself the power to do so unilaterally. If a trust agreement provides a specific method for revocation, that method must be strictly adhered to in order revoke the trust.

Here, the trust provides for revocation "by an instrument in writing signed by [mother] and delivered to Trustees." It makes no provision for revocation by will. If a trust agreement reserves the power to revoke by giving notice to the trustee in a specified form or manner, the settlor may exercise that power only during his or her lifetime, and the power cannot be exercised through a will.

Attempts to modify or revoke by will, considered as wills, have all failed. The courts have held ineffective an attempted testamentary exercise of a reserved power to modify or revoke an inter vivos trust by deed or by written instrument delivered to the trustee. A reserved power to modify or revoke during the settlor's lifetime cannot be exercised by his will. This is a logical extension of the rule that a will does not become operable until the testator's death.

A noted treatise, 1 *Page on the Law of Wills* states:

> "The essential idea underlying the concept of the will is that though it is made by a person during his lifetime it does not become binding and has no legal force or operative effect until his death; nor does it pass any interest in

property or create rights in others until the death of the maker, at which time its dispositive effect operates upon the circumstances concerning the extent and the nature of the testator's property and the objects of his bounty existing at his death rather than at the time the will was executed. The two inherent characteristics of a will embodied within this concept, which distinguish it from other instruments affecting property, are expressed by saying that a will is revocable and ambulatory. The intent at the time of execution must be that the instrument take effect right at the time of death.

It follows that because of its ambulatory nature, a will does not have effect upon execution, or execution and delivery in this case.

Daughter also refers us to Restatement (Third) of Trusts section 63, and argues that the revocation can be enforced by the clear and convincing evidence of mother's revocatory intent. For our purposes, we presume mother subjectively intended to revoke the trust at the time she executed the will. The Restatement provides that an inter vivos trust may be revoked by a will as follows:

> "(1) The settlor of an inter vivos trust has power to revoke or modify the trust *to the extent the terms of the trust so provide.*
>
> ....
>
> (3) *Absent contrary provision in the terms of the trust,* the settlor's power to revoke or modify the trust can be exercised in any way that provides clear and convincing evidence of the settlor's intention to do so."

Restatement (Third) of Trusts § 63 (2003) (Emphasis added).

Comment i to section 63 further provides:

> "*Where method of revocation or amendment specified.* Although the terms of the trust provide a method for the exercise of a power of revocation or amendment, if the terms do not make that method exclusive, this is not a "contrary provision" for purpose of Subsection (3). Thus, the settlor's power can be exercised either in the specific manner or by a method described in Comment h, above [which includes revocation by a will]."

The trust agreement provides that the powers to revoke shall be exercised by delivering written, signed notice to the trustee. This is the explicit protocol for revocation. Consequently, because there is an exclusive method, comment i to section 63 is not applicable here.

The trust agreement's revocation clause makes clear that the settlor intended that the power should be exercised only during her lifetime by an instrument delivered to both trustees. Apart from the plain meaning of the revocation provision, the stated disposition of the trust estate following revocation is to mother, not mother's estate or any third party, which reinforces the conclusion that the trust must be revoked, if at all, during mother's lifetime. Had mother wished to retain the right to exercise the reserved powers to revoke by her last will and testament, the trust agreement should have so stated. This she failed to do and her intention with respect to termination during her lifetime is unmistakably drawn from a consideration of the entire instrument.

Mother's will was ineffective in revoking the trust, as a matter of law, at the time of its execution and delivery to daughter.

Quitclaim Deed

Daughter contends that mother, who was also the sole lifetime beneficiary of the trust, could convey the trust estate free of the trust to a co-trustee by quitclaim deed. We disagree.

Article III of the trust agreement states, in pertinent part:

> During [mother's] lifetime the net income and principal shall be distributed at least annually to [mother] or disposed of as [mother] may direct Trustees from time to time by an instrument in writing signed by [mother] and delivered to Trustees in the lifetime of [mother].

Relying on this clause, daughter contends mother complied fully with the trust's terms for disposition of the farm in executing the quitclaim deed. We disagree.

Mother, as trustee, signed the quitclaim deed purporting to transfer the trust estate to daughter, the co-trustee, free of the trust.[1] The effect of a trust is to separate legal ownership of property from the equitable or beneficial ownership. Though a settlor of a trust may maintain the right to receive proceeds from the property of the trust, he or she cannot concurrently maintain legal ownership of the trust property. Therefore, mother did not own the trust estate. And a quitclaim deed is ineffective to transfer a title not vested in the transferor at the time of its execution.

The trust agreement authorized the trustees, acting jointly, to convey the property. Where two or more persons hold title to property as trustees, any instrument purporting to convey that property must be executed by all of the trustees before a valid transfer of title will be accomplished. It is clear that the conveyance by one of the trustees, while the other trustee was acting as such, would not pass the legal title.

mother + daughter together could give a quitclaim deed

A settlor-co-trustee, who is also the sole lifetime beneficiary of trust income and principal, cannot, acting alone as trustee, transfer the trust estate to a third person or to another co-trustee free of the trust.

Constructive Revocation

Daughter next contends that the quitclaim deed of the trust's real property, if valid,

---

[1] While the issue is not before us here, we note that mother "revoked" or "terminated" father's trust following his death by the use of a quitclaim deed. We express no opinion whether that quitclaim deed may suffer from the same infirmity.

itself constitutes a constructive revocation of the trust, where such real property constituted the only asset of the trust. More specifically, she cites the Restatement (Third) of Trusts section 63 in support of the proposition that the quitclaim deed may serve to revoke, in part, the inter vivos trust. We disagree with the contention.

The quitclaim deed does nothing more than transfer to daughter the present interest of mother in the trust estate as trustee.

Reliance on Restatement (Third) of Trusts section 63 in this situation is also unavailing because mother specifically designated the method of termination - an instrument in writing signed by mother and delivered to the trustees. Section 63(3) provides, "Absent contrary provision in the terms of the trust, the settlor's power to revoke or modify the trust can be exercised in any way that provides clear and convincing evidence of the settlor's intention to do so." In this case, the trust provided an explicit protocol for revocation and, therefore, extrinsic evidence of the settlor's intent in drafting the quitclaim deed is not pertinent here.

The quitclaim deed of the trust's real property does not constitute a constructive revocation of the trust.

The cardinal rule in the interpretation of wills or other testamentary documents is that the testator's intent should be ascertained from the instrument itself and given effect. When the terms of a bequest are unambiguous, it is not permissible for a court to consider extrinsic evidence that casts doubt upon the meaning of the language used and renders such language susceptible of a different meaning. In other words, intent must be determined from the language itself, and an unambiguous document cannot be explained by extrinsic evidence so as to dispute its plain meaning. Neither party claims the terms of the will are ambiguous.

Consequently, the trial court did not need to conduct an evidentiary hearing, because mother's intent is not relevant here. We have presumed for the purposes of this opinion that the will is valid and that mother had a present intent to terminate the trust when she executed it. As harsh as it may sound, mother's intent does not make effective an otherwise ineffective means of transferring an interest or revoking a trust.

The trial court's order is affirmed.

B. ATTORNEY LIABILITY WHEN TRUST REVOKED?

What responsibility may an attorney have when a settlor revokes a trust? And to whom may the attorney have that responsibility?

When a beneficiary does not receive what he or she expected under a will or trust, it seems that one of the first reactions of the disappointed beneficiary may be to sue the attorney involved. What steps might an attorney take to try to decrease the likelihood of such litigation?

Supreme Court of Idaho.
Mary Killins SOIGNIER, Plaintiff-Appellant,
v.
W. Kent FLETCHER, Defendant-Respondent.
June 30, 2011.

W. JONES, Justice.

I. NATURE OF THE CASE

Mary K. Soignier appeals the district court's decision to grant summary judgment to W. Kent Fletcher, an attorney, on her claim for legal malpractice. She asserts that Fletcher negligently failed to ensure that a will he prepared conveyed to her the proceeds of a trust of which the decedent was a beneficiary until shortly before the decedent's death. Since Fletcher adequately effectuated the testator's intent as expressed in the will itself, the district court was correct to grant him summary judgment on the malpractice claim.

II. FACTUAL AND PROCEDURAL BACKGROUND

Attorney W. Kent Fletcher represented the decedent, Zachary A. Cowan, for several years until Cowan's death in October of 2006. During his lifetime, Cowan was the beneficiary of a trust that his mother provided for him, known as the Cowan Trust. The terms of the Cowan Trust provided that the trust would persist until Cowan reached age fifty, at which time it was to terminate and most of its assets were to be distributed to Cowan. Cowan's fiftieth birthday was in 2003, and on March 4, 2005, he signed a Final Release and Discharge agreement in which he terminated his interest in the trust. Cowan did not have any beneficial interests in any other trusts.

Shortly after terminating his interest in the Cowan Trust, Cowan instructed Fletcher to prepare his Last Will and Testament. The will provided that all of Cowan's remaining beneficial interests in any trusts be devised to Mary Killins Soignier, Appellant. It also referred to a written list of items and intended recipients that was never located. The American Cancer Society was named as the residual devisee for all of Cowan's other property.

Soignier filed a claim against Cowan's estate for the proceeds from the Cowan Trust, which the magistrate rejected. The magistrate found that, because the trust had terminated, the will unambiguously conveyed any assets that remained in Cowan's estate to the American Cancer Society.

Believing that Cowan intended to leave the trust assets to her, Soignier asserted this claim for legal malpractice against Fletcher in 2009. The district court granted summary judgment to Fletcher, ruling that there was no genuine issue of fact as to whether the will frustrated Cowan's intent.

Soignier appealed to this Court, contending that Fletcher negligently failed to carry out Cowan's wishes by inaccurately describing his trust assets. Fletcher responds that the will was not deficient in giving effect to Cowan's intent to leave any remaining trust interests to Soignier.

III. ANALYSIS

There are four elements to a legal-malpractice claim: (1) there is an attorney-client relationship between the plaintiff and defendant; (2) the defendant lawyer owed a duty of care to the plaintiff; (3) the lawyer breached the duty; and (4) the lawyer's negligence was a proximate cause of the client's damage. Here, the parties do not dispute that the first two elements are present in this case, as Idaho recognizes an exception to the traditional requirement that the plaintiff have been in privity with the defendant lawyer in order to expect the lawyer to owe him or her a professional duty of care. In Harrigfeld v. Hancock, (2004), this Court extended the attorney's duty to non-clients who are named or identified as beneficiaries in a testamentary instrument.

The pivotal issue in this appeal is whether Fletcher breached his duty of care to Soignier by drafting a will that leaves to her interests in trusts when the decedent had no such interests. Harrigfeld explained that the attorney's duty to a testamentary beneficiary requires the attorney to "effectuate the testator's intent *as expressed in the testamentary instruments.*" (Emphasis added). The attorney must properly draft and execute the will and other instruments, but only to effectuate the testator's intent as expressed within those documents.

As there is no genuine issue of material fact as to whether Fletcher breached a duty to Soignier, the district court properly granted summary judgment. The relevant portion of the will is entitled "Residue," and reads:

> "All of the rest, residue and remainder of my property which I own or have any interest in whatever at the time of my death, other than beneficial interests in trusts, I give, bequeath, and devise to the American Cancer Society. All beneficial interests that I have in any trusts I give, bequeath and devise to Mary Soignier. I exercise any power of appointment that I might hold and appoint Mary Soignier."

The parties agree that the will's language is unambiguous and that it was properly executed. The unambiguous intent of the testator, as it appears in the will, was to leave all beneficial interests in any trusts to Soignier if any so exist. The will does not mention the Cowan Trust, likely because it is a residuary clause not intended to bequeath any specific assets. Rather, it simply devises any trust assets to Soignier that have not already been disposed of in any other testamentary instrument. This clause effectuated the testator's expressed intent to make Soignier the residual devisee of any beneficial trust interests Cowan had at his death. The fact that no interests actually existed did not render the will deficient for its expressed purpose.

Soignier believes that Cowan intended to leave her the Cowan Trust assets. The main thrust of her appeal is that attorneys have an ongoing duty to monitor the status of the property that the testator includes in his or her will and notify their clients whenever it appears that the client may not understand the nature of their ownership interests. In her view, Fletcher was negligent by not checking the trust documents to see whether the Cowan Trust had already terminated before Cowan passed away. She also argues that Fletcher negligently failed to explain to Cowan that Cowan had no remaining beneficial interests in any trusts.

Soignier's arguments have already been rejected by this Court. First, Soignier presumes that Cowan intended to do something other than what was unambiguously expressed in his will. In Harrigfeld, however, this Court expressly held that attorneys have "no duty to see that the testator distributes his or her property among the named beneficiaries in any particular manner." In other words, lawyers have no duty to testamentary beneficiaries with regard to what share they receive from the testator's estate, if any. It is immaterial to Soignier's legal-malpractice claim whether she believes that Cowan intended to leave her assets that he did not identify in his will. Attorneys do not have to postulate whether a testator intended to do something other than what is expressed in the will.

Second, Soignier assumes that Cowan did not understand the nature of the assets he was leaving to Soignier. Again, Harrigfeld stated that "a testator who has sufficient mental capacity to make a valid will can also understand how his or her property will be distributed under the testamentary documents." Cowan is presumed to have understood that he was leaving a residuary interest to Soignier and not the specific assets he received as a distribution from the Cowan Trust. Thus, attorneys have no ongoing duty to monitor the legal status of the property mentioned in a testamentary instrument. The district court correctly granted summary judgment to Fletcher on Soignier's claim for legal malpractice.

IV. CONCLUSION

The district court correctly granted summary judgment to Fletcher on Soignier's claim for attorney malpractice. The judgment on that issue is affirmed.

Justice EISMANN, specially concurring.

I concur in the majority opinion, but write to add an additional comment.

If we were to expand Harrigfeld v. Hancock, as requested by Ms. Soignier, what amount of money would she be entitled to receive? That was a question she could not answer during oral argument.

Cowan had already received a distribution from the trust prior to making his final will. The money received was obviously no longer subject to the trust, and he made no attempt to bequeath that money to Ms. Soignier. Had he wanted to, he certainly could have done so either by making a specific bequest to her or granting her a portion of the residue of the estate other than "all beneficial interests that I have in any trusts." He did neither. Assuming that he wanted to give her a bequest, it was certainly not the money he had already received. So, what was it? How much money did he want her to receive? Any contention that Cowan intended for Ms. Soignier to receive some specific sum of money is certainly contrary to the provisions of his will because he did not bequeath her any specific sum. The need to speculate as to what he would supposedly have done had his attorney given different advice shows why Harrigfeld should not be expanded as Ms. Soignier requests.

C. CONFLICTS INVOLVING TRUST MODIFICATIONS – THE VICKERY SAGA

The following three brief cases, the Vickery saga, illustrate what may happen when family members involved in a dispute over trust modifications and probate go far beyond acceptable norms in attempting to cause injury to other family members. Lawyers doing probate work need to be alert to the necessity of trying to prevent their clients from engaging in such needless and costly behavior – if possible. Compensatory and exemplary damages of more than $400,000 are a high price to pay for irresponsible behavior.

As relevant to this segment of the book, the Vickery saga illustrates an unusual use of the power to modify a trust – and a warning to any lawyer dealing with a trust that is still subject to modification. Part I is the background story. Part II is the trust modification issue. Part III is the final result.

PART I OF THE VICKERY SAGA

This Part I of the Vickery saga tells the fairly dramatic background story of the Vickery saga, as set forth in the excerpt below.

Colorado Court of Appeals.
Monica David VICKERY, Plaintiff-Appellant,
v.
Merry Gayle VICKERY, Defendant-Appellee.
March 18, 2010.

Opinion by Judge LOEB.

I. Background and Procedural History

Plaintiff's husband, Donald, died of cancer on December 20, 2005. Defendant, Merry Gayle (sister), was Donald's sister. Evelyn Trumble (mother), was the mother of both Merry Gayle and Donald. Mother was also a co-defendant at trial, but is now deceased and is no longer a party to this appeal. During the period leading up to Donald's death, tensions mounted between Donald's wife, who is the plaintiff in this case, and Donald's mother and sister, the defendants, over rights to visit Donald, his medical care, and his property. The claims in this case arose out of sister's actions following Donald's death.

Initially, sister asserted in the probate court that a number of items of personal property associated with Donald's estate belonged to her or to mother. The probate court considered and rejected these challenges.

Then, sister challenged the validity of a codicil to Donald's will. The challenged codicil altered several devises in the will, and named wife as the devisee of oil and gas properties in Texas that had previously been bequeathed to sister and mother. Sister argued in the probate court that Donald's signature on the codicil was not genuine and was forged. The probate court considered this argument and concluded that Donald had signed the codicil and that the codicil was valid.

Having lost in the probate court, sister then sent letters to eleven different recipients (the Colorado Attorney General's office, the Denver District Attorney's office, the Denver Police Internal Affairs office, the United States Postal Service Postal Inspector, the Federal Bureau of Investigation, the Internal Revenue Service, the "Colorado State Revenue Service," American Express, Juno, the Navajo Nation, and the U.S. Department of Labor), claiming that wife, a sergeant with the Denver Police Department, had committed "murder, fraud, theft, and misuse of police authority." Later, sister also sent letters to American Express, Juno, and the United States Postal Service further accusing wife of fraud and other misdeeds. Sister also sent letters to two companies that managed the Texas oil and gas interests, stating that (1) wife submitted false evidence at the will contest, and that (2) the Internal Revenue Service, the Federal Trade Commission, and the Denver District Attorney's office were conducting criminal investigations into wife's behavior. The letters to the two companies requested that they not make any changes concerning the recipients of the royalties until presented with a court order to do so.

Wife then brought this action in district court, alleging that defendant committed malicious prosecution by claiming ownership of some of the personal property in Donald Vickery's possession and by challenging the codicil to Donald Vickery's will. She also alleged that defendant's letters defamed her.

During the pendency of the case in the trial court, wife discovered that in June 2008, sister had mailed two anonymous envelopes each to the Colorado Governor's office, the Denver Mayor's office, the Denver Police Department's Internal Affairs division, and the Fraternal Order of Police. These envelopes enclosed CDs or flash drives containing documents stating that plaintiff was under U.S. Treasury Department investigation, had used her position as a Denver police officer for personal gain, and had committed crimes of moral turpitude and public deception. With leave of the trial court, wife amended her complaint to allege that defendant sent these materials and that they were also defamatory. Wife also amended her complaint to request exemplary damages. Her prayer for relief also requested an award of prejudgment interest.

After a ten-day trial, the court submitted the case to the jury. The jury found that sister had not committed malicious prosecution in claiming ownership of Donald's personal property in the probate court. However, the jury concluded that sister had committed malicious prosecution in challenging the codicil to Donald's will, and awarded $59,000 in compensatory damages and $10,000 in exemplary damages on that claim.

The trial court then submitted plaintiff's defamation cause of action to the jury as nine separate claims. Prior to doing so, the trial court determined that, as a matter of law, defendant had defamed plaintiff on defamation claim number 5, but it left the determination of damages on that claim to the jury. The jury decided in favor of plaintiff on all of the remaining defamation claims and awarded damages, as summarized in the following table:

Defamation Claims	Compensatory Damages	Exemplary Damages
1. Letter dated February 2, 2006 to eleven recipients	$25,000	$25,000
2. Undated letter to American Express	$ 1	$ 2,000
3. Undated letter to postal inspector	$ 1,000	$ 5,000
4. Undated letter to Juno Online Services	$ 1	$ 1,000
5. Publication of letters to the oil and gas companies on May 14, 2007	$ 7,500	$15,000
6. Certain documents sent in June 2008	$25,000	$25,000
7. Statements on page 48 of documents sent to various parties in June 2008	$12,500	$25,000
8. Statements on page JIMD 00004 of the same documents	$12,500	$25,000
9. Statements on page JIMD 00005 of the same documents	$12,500	$25,000

On February 2, 2009, wife filed a motion requesting entry of judgment, including the addition of prejudgment interest.

The trial court then entered a final judgment on March 5, 2009, awarding compensatory damages on each of the defamation claims in the amounts determined by the jury plus statutory prejudgment interest. Then the court entered judgment for an award of exemplary damages on each of the claims, which was capped by the amount of compensatory damages assessed by the jury without the addition of prejudgment interest.

This appeal followed.

The judgment of the trial court in favor of wife is affirmed.

PART II OF THE VICKERY SAGA

Now for the trust modification part of the saga. After the jury had returned its verdict in Part I of the Vickery saga, above, but during the few days before the court actually entered the judgment, mother (Evelyn Trumble), who was suffering from a terminal illness, exercised her power to amend the Evelyn Trumble Living Trust, so that at mother's death the assets in the trust would not go to sister, (as they would have prior to the amendment), but would instead go directly to sister's daughter, Kelly. In that way mother attempted to insure that wife would not be able to collect anything from the trust assets in satisfying the award wife had just won against sister - yet the assets of the trust would still be available to sister's family.

So wife brought another suit joining as defendants sister, the trust itself, and the new trustee, Kelly. Part II of the Vickery saga, the Court of Appeals opinion in this second part of the Vickery Saga, is set forth in the excerpt below.

Colorado Court of Appeals.
Monica David VICKERY, Plaintiff–Appellant,
v.
EVELYN V. TRUMBLE LIVING TRUST; Kerry Vickery, individually and as Trustee of the Evelyn V. Trumble Living Trust; and Merry Gayle Vickery, Defendants-Appellees.
Aug. 18, 2011.

Opinion by Judge MILLER.

Plaintiff Monica Vickery (wife), appeals the district court's dismissal of her claims against defendants, the Evelyn V. Trumble Living Trust; Kerry Vickery, individually and as trustee of the trust; and Merry Gayle Vickery (sister), as well as its denial of plaintiff's motion for post-judgment relief.

I. Background

The principal question presented is whether the amendment of a revocable trust to change the contingent beneficiary from a judgment debtor to the debtor's daughter constitutes a violation of the Colorado Uniform Fraudulent Transfer Act. (CUFTA)

When Evelyn (mother) created her revocable trust, designating herself as settlor, trustee, and beneficiary, she named Merry Gayle (sister) as the successor trustee and sole beneficiary upon Evelyn's death.

In the earlier case of the Vickery saga, during discovery, Monica obtained a copy of the trust instrument. Monica investigated the assets held in the trust and learned that they were considerable. Monica prevailed at trial and obtained a $141,389 judgment against Evelyn, a $282,071 judgment against Merry Gayle, and an order awarding

$48,574 in costs against Evelyn and Merry Gayle, jointly and severally.[2]

After the jury returned its verdict but before judgment was entered [in Part I of the Vickery saga], Evelyn amended the trust instrument, designating her granddaughter, Kerry, as the successor trustee and sole beneficiary upon Evelyn's death. The court then entered judgment for Monica [in Part I of the Vickery saga], and Evelyn appealed. Evelyn died the following month.

Two days after Evelyn's death, Evelyn's counsel in the prior case offered to settle Monica's claims against Evelyn on the following terms: in exchange for dismissal of Evelyn's pending appeal, Monica would accept payment of the amount of the judgment against Evelyn and half the amount of the costs awarded jointly and severally against Evelyn and Merry Gayle, plus post-judgment interest. Evelyn's counsel did not advise Monica's counsel of the amendment to the trust instrument, and the complaint does not allege that Monica's counsel inquired regarding the status of the trust. Monica, [*probably expecting to recover the rest of the judgment from the trust assets*], accepted the offer to settle with Evelyn's estate, received payment in the amount of about $168,000, and filed a satisfaction of judgment with respect to her claims against Evelyn in that case. The appeal was withdrawn and dismissed.

In the instant case, [Part II of the Vickery saga], Monica asserted three claims: (1) that the amendment of the trust instrument constituted a fraudulent transfer under the CUFTA; (2) that Merry Gayle and Kerry committed fraudulent concealment by failing to disclose the amendment to the trust instrument before Monica entered the settlement agreement; and (3) that "two or more of the defendants" engaged in a civil conspiracy to defraud creditors. The complaint requests, among other things, damages, and orders "vacating" the amendment of the trust and allowing Monica to levy execution on the trust's assets.

In the lower court in this action Defendants moved to dismiss the complaint under C.R.C.P. 12(b)(1) and 12(b)(5). The lower court ruled that Monica failed to state a claim upon which relief could be granted, and dismissed the action.

The complaint in this case alleges, and it is undisputed, that Monica was a judgment creditor of both Merry Gayle and Evelyn at the time of the alleged fraudulent transfer. Monica's claims for fraudulent transfer and for conspiracy to defraud creditors rest on CUFTA, (the Colorado Uniform Fraudulent Transfer Act), which is intended to grant relief to creditors from fraudulent transfers. The complaint alleges that Evelyn amended the trust instrument with the specific purpose and intent of defrauding Monica as a judgment creditor by diverting to Kerry the assets Merry Gayle would otherwise have received, for the purpose of defeating Monica's efforts to collect her judgment; that Merry Gayle and Kerry participated in a common scheme to frustrate Monica's rights as a creditor; and that Monica's efforts to collect the judgment have been frustrated as a proximate result of defendants' actions. Thus, Monica has alleged that she was injured in fact by defendants' actions and that the injury was to her legally

---

[2] Because there was joint and several liability for the costs, Monica could have recovered the *full* amount of the costs against *either* Evelyn or Merry Gayle.

protected rights as a judgment creditor of Merry Gayle and Evelyn.

The complaint also alleges that Merry Gayle and Kerry, (the new trustee), fraudulently concealed a material fact from Monica; she acted upon that concealment by entering into the settlement agreement compromising the amount of her judgment; and that, as a result, Monica sustained damages.

1. The CUFTA Claim

Monica asserts her first claim under CUFTA. Section 38-8-105(1)(a), C.R.S.2010, provides, in pertinent part, as follows:

> A transfer made or obligation incurred by a debtor is fraudulent as to a creditor if the debtor made the transfer or incurred the obligation with actual intent to hinder, delay, or defraud any creditor of the debtor.
>
> The statute defines a "debtor" as "a person who is liable on a claim."

The complaint alleges that the amendment of the trust instrument constituted a "transfer" but does not specify whose conduct forms the basis of the claim. We consider the claims against each defendant in turn.

Monica's argument that she has asserted a valid fraudulent transfer claim against Merry Gayle fails because Evelyn, not Merry Gayle, amended the trust instrument. Although Monica argues that Merry Gayle participated in amending the trust instrument and that the amendment may be an "illusory sham," the complaint states that Evelyn "had sole and complete possession of and control over" the trust while she was alive. Thus, even assuming the amendment could constitute a transfer of an asset under CUFTA, Merry Gayle is not liable under CUFTA based on these allegations because she did not make the alleged transfer.

Monica next argues that she has stated a CUFTA claim against Evelyn and the trust because she collected only half of the judgment for costs entered jointly and severally against Evelyn and Merry Gayle. However, the complaint does not allege that Evelyn's amending the trust instrument hindered or delayed Monica's *ability* to collect what *Evelyn* owed her. To the contrary, the complaint states that the trust contained considerable assets and that a settlement was reached two days after Evelyn's death whereby the trust paid Monica about $168,000 and the pending appeal was dismissed. Thus, the amendment of the trust instrument did not deprive Evelyn of funds with which to satisfy her debt to Monica. Indeed, the amendment of the trust instrument did not alter in any way the assets available to pay Evelyn's debts.

Monica nonetheless contends that a CUFTA claim can be based on a transfer by a third party who is not a debtor, if the assets transferred recently belonged to the third party. However, because Merry Gayle never transferred any assets into the trust; the only assets in the trust were contributed by Evelyn. Thus, the amendment of the trust instrument by Evelyn did not "transfer" assets originally owned and transferred to the trust by Merry Gayle.

We therefore conclude that the complaint fails to state a CUFTA claim against Evelyn or Merry Gayle.

Monica's CUFTA claim against the trust and Kerry as trustee is derivative. For example, Monica's opening brief states that "Evelyn, acting as Trustee of the trust, thus perpetrated a fraud upon Monica by amending the Trust, and the Trust is liable for Evelyn's actions." The complaint does not allege that the trust itself made any transfer violating CUFTA. Therefore, because Monica's claim against Evelyn, as Trustee, fails, Monica has likewise failed to state a CUFTA claim against the trust or Kerry.

Thus, the trial court properly dismissed the CUFTA claim.

2. The Fraudulent Concealment Claim

The elements of a claim for fraudulent concealment are:

> (1) concealment of a material fact that in equity and good conscience should be disclosed; (2) knowledge on the part of the party against whom the claim is asserted that such a fact is being concealed; (3) ignorance of that fact on the part of the one from whom the fact is concealed; (4) the intention that the concealment be acted upon; and (5) action on the concealment resulting in damages.

To succeed on a claim for fraudulent concealment, a plaintiff must show that the defendant had a duty to disclose material information.

One party to a business transaction is under a duty to exercise reasonable care to disclose matters to the other party before the transaction is consummated, when there are:

> (a) matters known to him that the other is entitled to know because of a fiduciary or other similar relation of trust and confidence between them; and
> (b) matters known to him that he knows to be necessary to prevent his partial or ambiguous statement of the facts from being misleading; and if there is
> (c) subsequently acquired information that he knows will make untrue or misleading a previous representation that when made was true or believed to be so; and
> (d) the falsity of a representation not made with the expectation that it would be acted upon, if he subsequently learns that the other is about to act in reliance upon it in a transaction with him; and
> (e) facts basic to the transaction, if he knows that the other is about to enter into it under a mistake as to them, and that the other, because of the relationship between them, the customs of the trade or other objective circumstances, would reasonably expect a disclosure of those facts.

Whether such duty exists is a question of law.

Contrary to Monica's contention on appeal, the complaint alleges that Merry Gayle or Kerry—not Evelyn or her estate—had a duty to disclose that the trust instrument had been amended before Monica accepted the settlement offer. However, the complaint fails to allege circumstances under which such a duty would arise.

As a preliminary matter, we note that Merry Gayle did not have a duty to disclose anything because she was not a party to the settlement agreement, which pertained only to Monica's judgment against Evelyn.

Nor does the complaint allege facts that show that Kerry, as trustee, had such a duty under any of the tests articulated. The complaint does not allege a fiduciary relationship between Kerry and Monica, and neither Kerry nor the trust is alleged to have made any affirmative representations about the assets of the trust during the settlement negotiations or at any other time. Moreover, where the parties are in an adversarial relationship and each is represented by counsel, concealment by mere silence does not constitute fraud. "There must be some trick or contrivance intended to exclude suspicion and prevent inquiry."

Monica entered into a settlement of her claim against Evelyn, which included payment of half the costs for which Evelyn was jointly and severally liable in exchange for dismissal of a pending appeal. In this transaction, neither Kerry nor the trust had a duty to disclose information about the likelihood that Monica would be able to collect her judgment against Merry Gayle or the status or contents of any trust, will, or other instrument.

Therefore, the district court properly dismissed Monica's fraudulent concealment claim.

3. The Civil Conspiracy Claim

To establish a civil conspiracy in Colorado, a plaintiff must show: (1) two or more persons; (2) an object to be accomplished; (3) a meeting of the minds on the object or course of action; (4) an unlawful overt act; and (5) damages as to the proximate result. Civil conspiracy is a derivative cause of action that is not actionable per se. A transfer that violates CUFTA is a legal wrong that can support a claim of conspiracy. If, however, "the acts alleged to constitute the underlying wrong provide no cause of action, then there is no cause of action for the conspiracy itself."

Contrary to Monica's contention that she may pursue a common law claim for conspiracy to defraud a judgment creditor even if her other claims fail, Colorado case law clearly establishes that a conspiracy claim fails in the absence of a legal wrong to support it. Because the complaint did not allege facts supporting the underlying CUFTA and fraudulent concealment claims, or any other unlawful acts, we conclude that the district court properly dismissed Monica's claim for civil conspiracy.

The orders are affirmed, and the case is remanded to address the attorney fees issues.

Judge Terry specially concurring.

I concur in the majority's reasoning and the result reached. I write separately because the result in this case points to a potential flaw in the Colorado Uniform Fraudulent Transfer Act (CUFTA), which the General Assembly may wish to address.

CUFTA provides remedies to creditors of debtors who transfer property with the intent to defraud creditors.

Here, plaintiff Monica Vickery's complaint alleges the following facts pertinent to her claim, which we must assume are true for purposes of reviewing the dismissal of her complaint.

- The Evelyn V. Trumble Living Trust was created by Evelyn Trumble.
- As settlor and trustee, Evelyn had the sole possession and control over the trust.
- Before the trust was amended, Evelyn had designated her daughter, Merry Gayle Vickery, as the sole beneficiary and successor trustee, and the assets of the trust were to be distributed to Merry Gayle upon Evelyn's death.
- The jury returned a verdict for Monica and against Evelyn for $92,502 in compensatory damages plus $41,500 in punitive damages.
- The jury returned a verdict for Monica and against Merry Gayle for $155,002 in compensatory damages and $144,500 in punitive damages.
- Within about a month after these verdicts were returned against Evelyn and Merry Gayle, and shortly after Monica had filed a motion for award of costs jointly against Evelyn and Merry Gayle and a bill of costs, Evelyn, knowing of these events, amended the living trust.
- The amendment of the trust changed the sole beneficiary and successor trustee from Merry Gayle to Merry Gayle's daughter, Kerry.
- When Evelyn amended the trust to change the beneficiary and successor trustee, she knew that she had a serious illness, and she made the change with the specific purpose and intent of defrauding Monica as a judgment creditor by diverting to Kerry assets that Merry Gayle otherwise would have received from the trust upon Evelyn's death, and to defeat Monica's efforts to collect the judgment against Merry Gayle.
- Within a month after the trust amendment, the trial court entered judgment against Evelyn individually for $141,389; entered judgment against Merry Gayle individually for $282,071; and entered a costs judgment jointly and severally against Evelyn and Merry Gayle for $48,574.
- Within a month after entry of judgment, Evelyn died.
- Two days after Evelyn's death, counsel for Evelyn offered to settle Monica's claims against Evelyn in exchange for the full amount of the judgment against her, plus certain post judgment interest, and half the amount of the joint and several costs award, and Monica accepted the offer. Evelyn's counsel did not disclose the change in trust beneficiary prior to the settlement.
- Monica's complaint in the instant case stated that "Merry Gayle and/or Kerry, acting in concert with the Evelyn V. Trumble Living Trust, by express or tacit agreement, participated in a common plan, scheme or design to defeat and frustrate [Monica's]

legitimate rights as a creditor by concealing the existence of the Amended Trust and inducing [Monica] to accept [Evelyn's] offer of settlement."

• The amendment of the trust was a "transfer" under section 38-8-102(13), C.R.S.2010, and no value was given for the transfer, which was fraudulent.

• Merry Gayle has had access to the income and assets of the trust to pay for personal expenses, including her legal fees.

• Counsel for Merry Gayle has admitted that Evelyn amended the trust for the specific purpose of frustrating and defeating any attempt by Monica to collect the judgment from Merry Gayle.

These allegations contain many of the elements necessary to sustain a claim under CUFTA. Because of this court's resolution of the issues, we do not decide (1) whether the trust amendment was a transfer under section 38-8-102(13); or (2) whether the trust was an "asset" of Merry Gayle as defined in section 38-8-102(2) before the change of beneficiary—a prerequisite to finding a "transfer" under section 38-8-102(13).

Assuming that, as the complaint alleges, the trust amendment was a "transfer," a critical element is missing to sustain a CUFTA claim as it relates to the judgment owed by Merry Gayle: the complaint does not allege that *the debtor whose debt she now seeks to collect* (i.e., Merry Gayle) made the transfer, as required by the statute. *See* § 38-8-105 (imposing liability for fraudulent transfers made "by a debtor" under enumerated circumstances); *see also* § 38-8-106(1)-(2) (same).

Monica contends on appeal that because *Evelyn* was a debtor at the time she made the transfer, the statute applies to her conduct. That contention is unavailing. Because it is alleged that Evelyn knew that a jury verdict was pending against her when she made the transfer, we must assume she knew she was a "debtor" (defined in section 38-8-102(7) as "a person who is liable on a claim"). However, the complaint alleges that just after Evelyn's death, her estate entered into a settlement that resulted in her being fully released from her own liability to Monica. Thus, to the extent Evelyn is alleged to have tried to defraud Monica, she could not have defrauded her with respect to Evelyn's *own* debt.

Rather, the only relevant allegation pertaining to Evelyn is that she was trying to defraud Monica with respect to *Merry Gayle*'s debt. But Evelyn was not the debtor with respect to Merry Gayle's debt. To the extent that, on the date of the trust amendment, Evelyn knew she might soon be found jointly and severally liable with Merry Gayle as to the costs award, Evelyn could potentially have been viewed as attempting to defraud Monica with regard to Evelyn's own debt; however, the trial court correctly ruled that Monica's CUFTA claim for that conduct is barred by the terms of the settlement.

Again assuming the trust amendment could qualify as a transfer, it strikes me as anomalous that there is no CUFTA claim that could be sustained *against Merry Gayle, Kerry, or the trust* for the alleged conduct with respect to Merry Gayle's debt. Taking the complaint allegations as true, the trust, in concert with Merry Gayle or Kerry, conceived a scheme to defraud Monica as Merry Gayle's creditor; Merry Gayle was the intended beneficiary of the trust, and expected to receive it; Evelyn changed the beneficiary from Merry Gayle to Kerry, the daughter of Merry Gayle, specifically to ensure Monica would not be able to recover her judgment against Merry Gayle; and, despite the change in beneficiary, Merry Gayle received monetary benefits from the trust.

Again assuming this transaction could qualify as a transfer, it appears to have defeated a creditor's rights in a manner for which CUFTA was intended to provide a remedy, and resembles cases where a debtor has transferred assets to a spouse or other family member for the purpose of defrauding creditors, while the transferor continued to receive the benefit of those assets after the transfer. *See, e.g.,* Filip v. Bucurenciu, 129 Cal.App.4th 825,(2005) (transfers of real estate parcels among debtor, spouse, and family trust for purpose of defrauding creditors held to violate Uniform Fraudulent Transfers Act).

Assuming, as I must in reviewing the dismissal of Monica's claims, that the complaint allegations are true, then Evelyn and Merry Gayle appear to have found a valid loophole in section 38-8-105. Specifically, if a debtor does not actually make a transfer, but conspires with another party—who has control over assets that are expected to become the debtor's—to have that party execute the transfer in order to defraud a creditor, while the debtor still obtains the benefit of the transferred assets, such a transfer does not appear to violate the statute, even if all the other elements are met. I question whether the General Assembly would have intended such a loophole to be present, had that body been aware of its existence.

Nevertheless, because it exists, I must agree with the majority that the elements of a fraudulent transfer under CUFTA have not been alleged here, and that the trial court's judgment must therefore be affirmed.

PART III OF THE VICKERY SAGA

As might be expected, the litigation did not end here. Evidently there still was some money left for litigation, so the matter was taken to the Colorado Supreme Court on the issue of the amount of the exemplary damages.

Supreme Court of Colorado.
Monica David VICKERY, Petitioner
v.
Kerry Vickery EVANS as Personal Representative of the Estate of Marry Gayle Vickery, Respondent.
Dec. 12, 2011.

Justice COATS delivered the Opinion of the Court.

Monica Vickery petitioned for review of the court of appeals judgment affirming the district court's reduction of exemplary damages in her defamation suit against the mother and sister of her deceased husband. Both the district court and court of appeals understood section 13-21-102 of Colorado's revised statutes to limit Vickery's exemplary damages to an amount equal to the compensatory damages figure returned by the jury, before any adjustment for prejudgment interest.

Because "the amount of the actual damages awarded," to which "reasonable exemplary damages" are statutorily limited, refers not to the jury's assessment of total compensatory damages but to the compensatory damages awarded against the defendant as the direct result of that assessment, which necessarily include statutorily mandated prejudgment interest, the judgment of the court of appeals is reversed and the case is remanded for further proceedings consistent with this opinion.

The amount of compensatory damages ultimately awarded against the defendant is positively and invariably determined by the jury's assessment of total compensatory damages and its allocation of fault among the defendant, the victim, and any responsible third parties. It is inconsequential to the ultimate determination of this amount whether the statutorily mandated arithmetic calculations producing a final figure are made by the court or by the jury itself, after proper instruction. The award of compensatory damages against the defendant, as required by the application of statutorily mandated additions and reductions to the jury's assessment of total damages suffered by the victim, is the jury's award of actual damages as contemplated by section 13-21-102(1).

III.

Because "the amount of the actual damages awarded," to which "reasonable exemplary damages" are statutorily limited, refers not to the jury's assessment of total compensatory damages but to the compensatory damages awarded against the defendant as the direct result of that assessment, which necessarily include statutorily mandated prejudgment interest, the judgment of the court of appeals is reversed, and the case is remanded for further proceedings consistent with this opinion.

Reversed and remanded.

CHAPTER 16 – MODIFICATION OR TERMINATION BY OTHERS

The previous chapter covered some of the problems when various settlors attempted to modify or terminate their own trusts. In this chapter we will consider some of the potential dangers when a person or entity other than the settlor modifies or terminates a trust.

A. TERMINATION BY AGENT - POWER OF ATTORNEY

As a person becomes elderly, or for some other reason is not comfortable in handling his or her own financial affairs, the person may sign a Durable Power of Attorney, designating an agent to take over management of the financial affairs. Unless limits are specifically stated in the durable power of attorney, the agent normally has all of the powers the principal could have exercised over his or her own financial affairs. Needless to say, the potential for abuse under a Durable Power of Attorney is quite serious. Yet when an elderly person, or any other person, is no longer able to handle his or her own affairs, the three most realistic options available may be to delegate the financial powers under a Durable Power of Attorney; to go through what may be a difficult process to have the court appoint a conservator; or to have all of the elderly person's assets administered by a trust.

Because of the possibility that a settlor may live for some time after he or she no longer has the mental capacity to handle his or her own financial affairs, great care should be taken in the drafting of any inter vivos trust to insure that the provisions of the trust cannot be changed by an agent in ways which would be contrary to what the settlor would have wanted.

In the following case notice what actions the bank trustee could, and could not have taken in attempting to protect the beneficiary of the trust. How might a trust be drafted to anticipate, and prevent, what happened in the following case?

Supreme Court of Colorado.
In the Matter of the Trust of Franzen. FRANCES B. FRANZEN, Petitioner/Cross-Respondent, v. NORWEST BANK COLORADO, NATIONAL ASSOCIATION, TRUSTEE, Respondent/Cross-Petitioner.
April 13, 1998

JUSTICE SCOTT delivered the Opinion of the Court.

This case arises out of a disagreement over the disposition of assets in a trust created for the benefit of Frances Franzen by her late husband, James Franzen. The court of appeals held that James O'Brien, Mrs. Franzen's brother, was authorized to dissolve the trust by virtue of a power of attorney executed by Mrs. Franzen. The court of appeals also held, moreover, that the trustee was not liable for litigation expenses associated with challenging O'Brien's authority to dissolve the trust. We affirm the judgment of the court of appeals in its entirety.

I.

On February 4, 1992, James Franzen, the settlor, executed an instrument creating a trust designed to provide for himself and his wife, Frances Franzen, in their old age. The corpus of the trust initially consisted of three bank accounts containing a total of $74,251.19, but it did not include certain other assets held by Mr. and Mrs. Franzen as joint tenants, such as the family home. Norwest Bank, then known as United Bank of Denver, was named as the sole trustee in the trust agreement.

James Franzen was terminally ill when he created the trust, and he died four months later. Upon Mr. Franzen's death, a trust officer at the bank sent a letter to Frances Franzen, who was living in a nursing home, notifying her that she had "certain rights regarding the trust." A copy of the trust agreement was enclosed, and the letter referred to Article 5.1, which states:

> "At my death, if Frances survives me, she may direct the trustee in writing to deliver the residuary trust estate to her within three months of my death. If she does not so direct, this trust shall continue to be administered as provided in Article 3. If she so directs, the trust shall terminate on the date the trust estate is distributed to her."

The letter from the bank asked Mrs. Franzen for a decision in writing by August 1, 1992, "so that we have time to make arrangements for the transfer of assets if necessary." A handwritten note at the bottom of the letter, signed by Mrs. Franzen and dated July 14, 1992, says, "I wish to leave the trust intact for my lifetime."

The bank, concerned about the disposition of the vacant house and other assets not included in the trust, contacted Mrs. Franzen's nephews, who were named as remaindermen of the trust. The two nephews were reluctant to assume responsibility for Mrs. Franzen's affairs, though, and Mrs. Franzen's brother, James O'Brien, intervened. O'Brien moved Mrs. Franzen to a nursing home in Kentucky, where he lived, and asked the bank to turn over Mrs. Franzen's assets to him.

In the course of dealing with the bank, the nephews expressed concerns about O'Brien's motives. The bank declined to comply with O'Brien's request, and it filed a Petition for Instruction and Advice in the Denver Probate Court. Before the hearing, O'Brien sent the bank a copy of a power of attorney purporting to authorize him to act in Mrs. Franzen's behalf and a letter attempting to revoke the trust and to remove the bank as trustee, citing Article 6.2 and Article 8 of the trust agreement.

Article 6.2 of the trust provides that after the death of James Franzen, Frances Franzen "may remove any trustee," and that "any removal under this paragraph may be made without cause and without notice of any reason and shall become effective immediately upon delivery of written notice to the trustee" unless Frances Franzen and the trustee agree otherwise.

Article 8 of the trust agreement gives James Franzen "the right to amend or revoke this trust in whole or in part by a writing delivered to the trustee . . . . After my death, Frances may exercise these powers with respect to the entire trust estate."

The hearing was continued, and the bank filed a Petition for Appointment of a Conservator, asking the probate court to appoint someone to manage and protect Mrs. Franzen's assets. When the hearing on both petitions was held, the probate court ruled that the power of attorney had created a valid agency but that the trust had not been revoked and continued in existence. The probate court found that Mrs. Franzen needed protection, but a conservator was not available, so it appointed the bank as "special fiduciary" with responsibility for both trust and non-trust assets pursuant to *sections 15-14-408* and *15-14-409, C.R.S.* (1997). The probate court ordered the bank to use the assets to make payments for Mrs. Franzen's benefit.

Franzen appealed the probate court rulings. On appeal, the court of appeals reversed, holding that the power of attorney authorized O'Brien to remove the bank as trustee and to revoke the trust. The court of appeals also held, however, that the bank was not liable for expenditures made in good faith after receiving the removal and revocation letter, including the legal fees incurred in the course of opposing O'Brien's efforts.

II.

A.

A power of attorney is an instrument by which a principal confers express authority on an agent to perform certain acts or kinds of acts on the principal's behalf. In Colorado, the use and interpretation of such instruments is governed by statute. Under the power of attorney statute, the scope of an agent's authority to alter a trust is narrowly construed. "An agent may not revoke or amend a trust that is revocable or amendable by the principal without specific authority and specific reference to the trust in the agency instrument."

Norwest notes that the power of attorney executed by Mrs. Franzen did not refer specifically to the Franzen trust. Thus, Norwest argues, O'Brien was not authorized to remove the trustee or revoke the trust. The statutory specificity requirement, however, did not take effect until January 1, 1995, almost two years after the power of attorney was executed by Mrs. Franzen.

General principles of statutory construction lead us to conclude that the power of attorney statute is inapplicable to any agency instrument executed prior to its effective date. In addition, the general assembly expressly stated that the power of attorney statute does not "in any way invalidate any agency or power of attorney executed prior to January 1, 1995," conclusively demonstrating that no retroactive effect was intended.

Not retroactive

Norwest responds that the specificity requirement in *section 15-14-608(2)* merely restated the common law in effect prior to its adoption, so the same result should be reached even though the statute was not intended to be applied retroactively. The bank asserts that the common law would require the power of attorney to refer to the trust by name.

Unfortunately for Norwest, the cases it cites state no such common law rule. Instead, these cases stand for the unremarkable proposition that a power of attorney giving an agent broad authority to act on behalf of the principal should be construed in light of the surrounding circumstances. Where a broadly worded power of attorney arguably authorizes acts that may be inconsistent with the principal's interests or intent, the instrument should not be interpreted as allowing the agent to undertake such acts in the absence of specific authority.

For example, in *Estate of Casey v. Commissioner of Internal Revenue,* the Fourth Circuit applied Virginia law to hold that an agent acting under a power of attorney that conferred wide-ranging authority to act on the principal's behalf was not authorized to give away the principal's property. The court said, "The failure to enumerate a specific power, particularly one with the dangerous implications of the power to make unrestricted gifts of the principal's assets, reflects deliberate intention."

Similarly, in *Bryant v. Bryant*, the Supreme Court of Washington held that an agent acting under a broadly worded power of attorney was not authorized to make gifts of the principal's assets. The court noted the consensus view that "gift transfers or transfers without substantial consideration inuring to the benefit of the principal violate the scope of authority conferred by a general power of attorney to sell, exchange, transfer, or convey property for the benefit of the principal."

The principle recognized in these cases logically might extend by analogy to situations where a power of attorney gives an agent wide authority to make decisions on behalf of the principal but makes no mention of the power to alter the principal's rights under any trust. We are willing to assume, for the sake of argument, that the scope of the agent's authority under the common law in such circumstances would not extend to revocation of a trust established to benefit the principal.

Even so, we are not persuaded that under the common law, an agency instrument must expressly refer to a particular trust by name in order to confer authority on the agent to revoke it. Under the reasoning of the cases previously cited, the terms of the power of attorney need only evince an intention to authorize the agent to make decisions concerning the principal's interests in trusts generally, not necessarily a particular trust.

Section 1(c) of the power of attorney executed by Mrs. Franzen expressly authorizes O'Brien to manage "and in any manner deal with any real or personal property, tangible or intangible, or any interest therein in my name and for my benefit, upon such terms as [O'Brien] shall deem proper, including the funding, creation, and/or revocation of trusts or other investments."

We have little trouble concluding that the quoted language expressly authorizes O'Brien to revoke the Franzen trust, even though it does not mention the trust specifically by name.

B.

Mrs. Franzen contends that Norwest should be strictly liable for trustee and attorney fees spent after the removal and revocation letter was received from O'Brien. In essence, she argues that a trustee should be held liable for all expenses incurred after a trust it oversees is revoked, even if it incurs the expenses in reliance on a court ruling--later vacated on appeal--that the trust remains in effect.

Mrs. Franzen cites a host of authority in support of her contention that a trustee is liable for any act in excess of his or her authority, even if it was undertaken in good faith or in reliance on the advice of counsel.

She acknowledges that a trustee is entitled to indemnification for the expenses of prosecuting and defending actions on behalf of the trust, but notes that indemnification is available only if the need for litigation was not caused by the fault of the trustee.

Nowhere in the authorities cited by Mrs. Franzen can we find support for the view that a trustee is liable for acts in excess of his or her authority when the acts are undertaken in reliance on a court order, even when the ruling underlying the order is overturned on appeal. Both cases cited by Mrs. Franzen involved actions taken by fiduciaries in reliance on mistaken professional advice, not a court order. In fact, the reason why good faith reliance on the advice of counsel is not a defense to liability for a breach of duty is that a trustee has the option of seeking instruction from a court rather than depending on the potentially erroneous advice of a lawyer.

As for the propriety of Norwest's commencement of litigation to determine its responsibilities as trustee, we see no legal or equitable basis for imposing liability on the bank. At the time O'Brien sent the removal and revocation letter, the bank's representatives had reason to suspect that Frances Franzen might be incompetent and hence lack the capacity to execute a valid power of attorney authorizing O'Brien to act in her behalf. In addition, the remaindermen of the trust and others had expressed concerns about whether O'Brien was acting in Mrs. Franzen's interests. [1]

If the bank had turned over the trust assets as requested and Mrs. Franzen were

---

[1] We express no opinion concerning the motivations or credibility of Mrs. Franzen's friends and family members, some of whom claimed that O'Brien was attempting to gain control of the trust assets for personal benefit and was acting without Mrs. Franzen's knowledge or assent. The point is not whether O'Brien was in fact acting in Mrs. Franzen's best interests, but that the bank acted reasonably in light of the available information when it sought instructions from a neutral and detached judicial official rather than immediately complying with O'Brien's instructions.

later demonstrated to have been incompetent to execute the power of attorney, or if O'Brien had absconded with the money, then the bank would have faced liability for breach of its duty of care as a fiduciary. The remaindermen would likely have pointed out that they warned the bank about the possibility of irregularity in O'Brien's request.

Of course, to the extent that the bank was entitled to compensation for administering the trust only as long as the trust remained in existence and it remained the trustee, the bank's interests were served by challenging O'Brien's authority under the power of attorney and the terms of the trust agreement. However, the bank's interest in maintaining the trust with itself as trustee does not, ipso facto, demonstrate that the litigation did not benefit the trust estate.

Under the circumstances, then, the bank's decision to obtain a judicial determination of its responsibilities under the trust agreement was not only reasonable, but it appears to have been fully consistent with the bank's duty to protect the interests of the trust and its beneficiaries. Thus, we conclude that the need for litigation did not arise due to any fault on the part of Norwest, and the bank is entitled to indemnification.

III.

In conclusion, we hold that under the common law, a power of attorney that appears to give the agent sweeping powers to dispose of the principal's property is to be narrowly construed in light of the circumstances surrounding the execution of the agency instrument. However, the principal may confer authority to amend or revoke trusts on an agent without referring to the trusts by name in the power of attorney.

Moreover, a trustee is not liable for administration or related attorney fees incurred in reliance on an order of the probate court that is later vacated on appeal. Where the trustee acts in good faith to seek direction from a court concerning its responsibilities in relation to a trust it oversees, the trustee is entitled to indemnification for any associated legal expenses.

Accordingly, we affirm the judgment of the court of appeals in its entirety.

Now, after the trust is revoked, who will be the intestate taker of the property that was once in the trust? Does the court seem to be concerned that the nephews were the remainder beneficiaries under the trust, but that Mrs. Franzen's brother will be her heir if she dies intestate? How should this have been prevented?

B. MODIFICATION BY THE COURT

When the terms of a trust are not clearly spelled out in the trust instrument, the court has authority to supply the necessary missing terms, so that the trust will not fail for lack of sufficient details in the trust instrument. In the following case, the judge seems to have enjoyed the opportunity to re-write a trust, almost as if he were creating the trust from scratch. And he does a good job of it. It would have been much better, of course, if the issues now covered with such specificity by the judge had been discussed with the client, so that she could have made her own decisions on all of the details. And ideally, the original drafter, like the judge, should have been able to carry out the wishes of the testatrix without a violation of the Rule Against Perpetuities.

Circuit Court of Virginia, Rockingham County.
R. Keith RICHARDS, et al
v.
Mary Lantz MAIDEN, et al
Dec. 29, 2000.

DOHERTY, J.
Gentlemen:

Testatrix was survived by four adult children, both natural and adopted, and three infant grandchildren. The residuary clause of her will created a trust fund for the education of her grandchildren, using the following language:

> "I hereby give, devise, and bequeath all the rest, residue and remainder of my estate, both real and personal, of every nature, and wherever situate to my grandchildren, to be held in trust by my son, Thomas H. Lantz, and my daughter-in-law, Becky Lantz, and used for the educational benefit of all of my grandchildren."

The Executor filed a Bill of Complaint on behalf of himself and the Trustees, asking the Court to construe the educational trust. The Executor, the Trustees and the Guardian ad litem for the living infant grandchildren argue that it was the intent of the Testatrix to provide trust benefits only for her now living grandchildren. They believe that the Court merely needs to fix a termination date for the trust. The Guardian ad litem for any unknown and any unborn grandchildren claims, and the Court agrees, that the trust is void as it violates the rule against perpetuities.

RULE AGAINST PERPETUITIES

Upon the evidence presented, and upon having had the opportunity to observe the demeanor of the witnesses and to weigh their testimony accordingly, the Court finds that the language of the will is clear and unambiguous. The Testatrix intended to provide funds for the education of her present and future born grandchildren. Her method of doing so violated the rule against perpetuities, and therefore failed.

The interest given by the Testatrix to her grandchildren in her testamentary trust is an executory interest. This is so because an interval of time is required to lapse before vesting becomes possible. Any executory interest which, by possibility, may not take effect until after lives in being and twenty-one years and ten months, is *ipso facto and ab initio* void. In other words, the executory interest is void for remoteness if at its

springing executory interest

creation there exists a *possibility* that it may not take effect during any fixed number of now existing lives, nor within twenty-one years and ten months after the expiration of such lives, even though it is highly probable, or, indeed, almost certain, that it will take effect within the time prescribed.

Under the facts of this case it is possible that present grandchildren, or future grandchildren yet to be born, may not, either voluntarily or involuntarily, begin receiving education that requires funding from the trust until after the lapse of a life in being plus twenty-one years and ten months. The receipt of those funds are what causes the vesting, and not the birth of a grandchild into the class of beneficiaries. A contingent gift to a class must be so limited as to vest, if at all, in each member of the class within the period prescribed, or the gift will fail as to the whole class.

Under the facts of this case the possibility exists of a failure of vesting with any member of the class, thus the entire gift fails and the trust becomes void *ab initio.*

DISPOSITION OF TRUST CORPUS

But for the saving provision of the 1982 version of § 55-13.3, Code of Virginia as amended, which was in effect at all times pertinent to this case, upon the failure of the trust, its corpus would have reverted to the decedent's estate and been distributed as intestate property. Instead, in cases such as this, § 55-13.3 empowers the Court to dispose of the proceeds " in a manner which most closely effectuates the transferor's manifested plan of distribution, which is within the limits of the rule against perpetuities."

Having viewed the evidence, the appearance of the witnesses, their manner of testifying, their truthfulness and their interest in the outcome of the case, the Court finds that it was the transferor's manifest plan of distribution that all of the funds left in the residuary of her estate be used to provide, based on need and not equality, for the future education of as many of her grandchildren as possible. Accordingly, the Court directs that:

1. Thomas H. Lantz and Becky Lantz shall become trustees of the Josephine W. Lantz Education Trust. The funds currently held by them shall be placed in this trust.
2. All of the grandchildren of the Testatrix, whether presently in being or hereafter born, shall become beneficiaries of the trust. Their interest in the trust vests immediately for the current grandchildren, and at their birth for the future born grandchildren. The amount of each beneficiaries share will be determined as his or her school costs are progressively incurred.
3. The trust will terminate twenty-one years after the death of the last child of the Testatrix, or upon the depletion of its corpus, whichever first occurs, regardless of whether or not any or all of the grandchildren have received any benefits from the trust at the time of its termination. Any funds still remaining in the trust at its termination will be distributed, *per capita,* among the then surviving trust beneficiaries.
4. The trust funds will be used to pay any necessary private grade school or high

school tutoring needed by any of the beneficiaries, in order for them to ultimately complete grade school and high school in the public school system. The funds may not be used for private grade or high school costs.

5. The funds may also be used to provide the usual and normal costs of room and board on a college campus, college, post graduate, or vocational school tuition, and related expenses payable to the school, college, or post graduate school. The funds shall not be used for living expenses off the school or college campus, travel or automobile costs, clothing, spending money, supplies, computers or equipment.

6. All expenditures shall be at the discretion of the Trustees, who are admonished not to abuse that discretion.

7. The payments shall be based on the specific needs of the individual beneficiary, without any requirement of equality with the other beneficiaries.

8. The Trustees shall make prudent investments of the trust corpus, and report annually to the Commissioner of Accounts as any other fiduciary.

9. Upon their qualification before the Clerk of the Circuit Court for the County of Rockingham, the Trustees shall post bond, with corporate surety, in the amount of $150,000.00.[2]

ATTORNEY'S FEES AND COSTS

The Court fixes the attorney's fee of Thomas H. Howell, Guardian ad litem for the unknown grandchildren at $3,100.00, which fee includes his services for reviewing this letter opinion and for reviewing and endorsing the final decree in this matter. The Court fixes the attorney's fees of Timothy E. Cupp, Guardian ad litem for the known grandchildren at $2,350.00, which fee includes his services for reviewing this letter opinion and for reviewing and endorsing the final decree in this matter. Each of these fees shall be paid from the trust corpus by the trustees, in a timely manner. The Court finds that the attorney for the Plaintiffs shall not receive a fee or reimbursement of costs from the trust or from the decedent's estate for his services rendered in this chancery cause.

Counsel for Plaintiffs shall prepare an appropriate final decree in this matter, incorporating this letter opinion by reference, and present it for entry after first obtaining endorsement of all counsel.

C. BY THE BENEFICIARIES

In the following case, the circumstances of one of the great-grandchildren of the settlor are significantly different from what the settlor might have expected when he established the trust. The law has also changed significantly since that time. Now it might be beneficial for the family as a whole if there were some way for the present

[2] Note: The requirement for a trustee to post bond is highly unusual. It is interesting that a judge, who presumably has seen a great many disputes over estates and trusts, seems to feel that having the trustees post bond is a wise idea.

beneficiaries to modify the provisions of the trust. How might such provisions have been included in the original trust – without giving up all of the protections which were sought by putting the assets into a trust in the first place?

Court of Appeals of Oregon.
In the Matter of the Testamentary Trust under the Will of J. W. STUCHELL, Deceased. Edna E. Rogers HARRELL, Appellant
November 21, 1990
OPINION BY: BUTTLER

Petitioner appeals from the trial court's dismissal of her petition for approval of an agreement to modify a trust. The stated purpose of the proposed modification is to protect a retarded remainder beneficiary. We affirm.

Petitioner is one of two surviving life-income beneficiaries of a testamentary trust established by her grandfather, J.W. Stuchell, in his 1947 will. The trust will terminate on the death of the last income beneficiary, at which time the remainder is to be distributed equally to petitioner's children or their lineal descendants, *per stirpes*. One of petitioner's four children, John Harrell (Harrell), is a mentally retarded 25 year old who is unable to live independently without assistance. His condition is not expected to improve, and he will probably require care and supervision for the rest of his life. No guardian or conservator has been appointed for him. The Oregon Mental Health Division currently provides his basic care in the Eastern Oregon Training Center, a residential facility for mentally and physically disabled persons. He receives Medicaid and Social Security benefits, both of which have income and resource limitations for participants.

In December, 1989, petitioner requested the court to approve, on behalf of Harrell,[3] an agreement, which had been approved by the other income beneficiary and

---

[3] *ORS 126.227* provides:

"(1) If it is established that a basis exists as described in *ORS 126.157* for affecting the property and affairs of a person the court, without appointing a conservator, may authorize, direct or ratify: * * *

"(b) Any contract, trust or other transaction relating to the protected person's financial affairs or involving the estate of the person if the court determines that the transaction is in the best interests of the protected person.

"(2) Before approving a protective arrangement or other transaction under this section, the court shall consider the interests of creditors and dependents of the protected person and, in view of the disability of the person, whether the protected person needs the continuing protection of a conservator. The court may appoint a special conservator to assist in the accomplishment of any protective arrangement or other transaction authorized under this section who shall have the authority conferred by the order and serve until discharged by order after report to the court of all matters done under the order of appointment."

remaindermen, to modify the trust. If the trust is not modified, Harrell's remainder will be distributed directly to him if he survives the two life-income beneficiaries. If and when that happens, his ability to qualify for public assistance will be severely limited. The proposed modification provides for the continuation of the trust, if Harrell survives the two life-income beneficiaries, and contains elaborate provisions that are designed to avoid his becoming disqualified, in whole or in part, for any public assistance programs. The stated purpose is to ensure that the trust funds be used only as a secondary source of funds to supplement, rather than to replace, his current income and benefits from public assistance.

Petitioner emphasizes that the petition is uncontested. However, no one who might be opposed to the proposed modification is a party. The trustee has not consented, because it will be entitled to additional compensation if the modification is approved, which creates a conflict of interest. The other remaindermen, who have approved the proposed modification, also stand to benefit from it.

Petitioner relies on *ORS 128.135(2) (c)* as authority for court approval of the agreement to modify the trust or, if the statute does not authorize it, on the common law. The statute provides, in part:

> "(2) Any beneficiary of a trust may petition a court with jurisdiction to grant equitable remedies in any county where the trust assets are located or where the trustee resides for the purpose of any of the following:
>
> "(c) Obtaining authority, approval or instructions on any matter concerning the interpretation of the trust or the administration, settlement or distribution of the trust estate."

Petitioner contends that, because the statute authorizes the court to approve "any matter concerning the distribution of the trust estate," the court has authority to approve her proposed modification of the trust. Clearly, the statute does not go that far. There are many instances in which a beneficiary or a trustee might seek approval or instructions concerning a proposed distribution of the trust assets *under the terms of the trust.* Because the statute does not even mention the modification of a trust, we conclude that it does not authorize the court to approve an agreement to modify a trust, unless the modification is one that might be made without statutory authority, that is, at common law. We agree with petitioner that the statute does not limit or abrogate any right that she might have under common law principles.

That leaves petitioner to her reliance on the common law. She contends that *Clossett v. Burtchaell* is authority for allowing a court to approve her proposed modification. That case holds that a trust may be terminated, if (1) all of the beneficiaries agree, (2) none of the beneficiaries is under a legal disability and (3) the trust's purposes would not be frustrated by doing so. The court said:

> "It is a well-established rule that where the purposes for which a trust has been created have been accomplished and all of the beneficiaries are *sui juris,* a court will, on the application of all of the beneficiaries or of one possessing the entire beneficial interest declare a termination of the trust."
>
> *Restatement (Second) Trusts § 337* follows that rule.

By its terms, that rule applies only to the termination of a trust under very limited circumstances. Petitioner, relying on *Restatement (Second) Trusts § 167(1)* urges us to extend the rule to permit modification. That section provides:

> "The court will direct or permit the trustee to deviate from a term of the trust if owing to circumstances not known to the settlor and not anticipated by him compliance would defeat or substantially impair the accomplishment of the purposes of the trust; and in such case, if necessary to carry out the purposes of the trust, the court may direct or permit the trustee to do acts which are not authorized or are forbidden by the terms of the trust."
>
> *Comment b* to that section states:
>
> "The court will not permit or direct the trustee to deviate from the terms of the trust merely because such deviation would be more advantageous to the beneficiaries than a compliance with such direction."

Even assuming that the Restatement rule were to be adopted as the law in Oregon, it is clear that the limitation imposed by the comment would preclude permitting the proposed amendment, the only purpose of which is to make the trust more advantageous to the beneficiaries. The most obvious advantage would be to the three remaindermen who have consented to the amendment.

There being no statutory or common law authority for a court to approve the proposed agreement modifying the trust, the trial court did not err in dismissing the petition.[4]

Affirmed.

D. MODIFICATION FOR TAX PURPOSES

Under the Uniform Trust Code, there are various provisions authorizing a court to modify a trust for tax reasons, even though the trust was established as an

---

[4] We express no opinion as to whether the proposed modification would survive a challenge by state or federal agencies that are providing assistance to Harrell.

irrevocable trust. One of such provisions is UTC Section 4-416.

Sec. 4-416 Modification to Achieve Settlor's Tax Objectives.

To achieve the settlor's tax objectives, the court may modify the terms of a trust in a manner that is not contrary to the settlor's probable intention. The court may provide that the modification has retroactive effect.

There is, of course, no guarantee that the I.R.S. will accept a retroactive modification of the terms of a trust in order to avoid adverse tax consequences.

E. OTHER MODIFICATIONS ALLOWED

Here are a few other provisions regarding trust modification which are included in the Uniform Trust Code. Remember, of course, that the UTC itself is not law anywhere, but various provisions of the UTC may have been specifically adopted in various states.

§ 411. Modification or Termination of Noncharitable Irrevocable Trust by Consent.

[(a) [A noncharitable irrevocable trust may be modified or terminated upon consent of the settlor and all beneficiaries, even if the modification or termination is inconsistent with a material purpose of the trust.] [If, upon petition, the court finds that the settlor and all beneficiaries consent to the modification or termination of a noncharitable irrevocable trust, the court shall approve the modification or termination even if the modification or termination is inconsistent with a material purpose of the trust.] A settlor's power to consent to a trust's modification or termination may be exercised by an agent under a power of attorney only to the extent expressly authorized by the power of attorney or the terms of the trust; by the settlor's [conservator] with the approval of the court supervising the [conservatorship] if an agent is not so authorized; or by the settlor's [guardian] with the approval of the court supervising the [guardianship] if an agent is not so authorized and a conservator has not been appointed. [This subsection does not apply to irrevocable trusts created before or to revocable trusts that become irrevocable before [the effective date of this [Code] [amendment].]]

(b) A noncharitable irrevocable trust may be terminated upon consent of all of the beneficiaries if the court concludes that continuance of the trust is not necessary to achieve any material purpose of the trust. A noncharitable irrevocable trust may be modified upon consent of all of the beneficiaries if the court concludes that modification is not inconsistent with a material purpose of the trust.

(c) A spendthrift provision in the terms of the trust is not presumed to constitute a material purpose of the trust.

(d) Upon termination of a trust under subsection (a) or (b), the trustee shall distribute the trust property as agreed by the beneficiaries.

(e) If not all of the beneficiaries consent to a proposed modification or termination of the trust under subsection (a) or (b), the modification or termination may be approved by the court if the court is satisfied that:

(1) if all of the beneficiaries had consented, the trust could have been modified or terminated under this section; and

(2) the interests of a beneficiary who does not consent will be adequately protected.

§ 414. Modification or Termination of Uneconomic Trust.

(a) After notice to the qualified beneficiaries, the trustee of a trust consisting of trust property having a total value less than [$50,000] may terminate the trust if the trustee concludes that the value of the trust property is insufficient to justify the cost of administration.

(b) The court may modify or terminate a trust or remove the trustee and appoint a different trustee if it determines that the value of the trust property is insufficient to justify the cost of administration.

(c) Upon termination of a trust under this section, the trustee shall distribute the trust property in a manner consistent with the purposes of the trust.

§ 415. Reformation to Correct Mistakes.

The court may reform the terms of a trust, even if unambiguous, to conform the terms to the settlor's intention if it is proved by clear and convincing evidence that both the settlor's intent and the terms of the trust were affected by a mistake of fact or law, whether in expression or inducement.

CHAPTER 17 - EFFECT OF MURDER ON INTESTATE AND TESTATE SUCCESSION

Murder is not a recognized estate planning tool, of course, but it sometimes does happen. Virtually every state has some sort of provision to try to make sure that a murderer does not benefit from his or her crime. Two interesting cases follow.

The first involves a situation in which the decedent did not have a will, and the court discusses the possibility of using the equitable remedy of a constructive trust to be sure that justice is done.

The second case discusses the issue of whether or not relatives of the murderer should be permitted to take the gifts specifically devised to them in the will of the murdered person.

Supreme Court of Vermont.
In re ESTATE of Howard MAHONEY.
June 7, 1966.

SMITH, Justice.

The decedent, Howard Mahoney, died intestate on May 6, 1961, of gunshot wounds. His wife, Charlotte Mahoney, the appellant here, was tried for the murder of Howard Mahoney in the Addison County Court and was convicted by jury of the crime of manslaughter in March, 1962. She is presently serving a sentence of not less than 12 nor more than 15 years at the Women's Reformatory in Rutland.

Howard Mahoney left no issue, and was survived by his wife and his father and mother. His father, Mark Mahoney, was appointed administrator of his estate which at the present time amounts to $3,885.89. After due notice and hearing, the Probate Court for the District of Franklin entered a judgment order decreeing the residue of the Estate of Howard Mahoney, in equal shares, to the father and mother of the decedent. An appeal from the judgment order and decree has been taken here by the appellant widow. The question submitted is whether a widow convicted of manslaughter in connection with the death of her husband may inherit from his estate.

The general rules of descent provide that if a decedent is married and leaves no issue, his surviving spouse shall be entitled to the whole of decedent's estate if it does not exceed $8,000. Only if the decedent leaves no surviving spouse or issue does the estate descend in equal shares to the surviving father and mother. There is no statutory provision in Vermont regulating the descent and distribution of property from the decedent to the slayer. The question presented is one of first impression in this jurisdiction.

In a number of jurisdictions, statutes have been enacted which in certain instances, at least, prevent a person who has killed another from taking by descent or distribution from the person he has killed. A statute of this nature, carefully drawn, is considered by many authorities to be the best solution to the problems presented.

Courts in those states that have no statute preventing a slayer from taking by descent or distribution from the estate of his victim, have followed three separate and different lines of decision.

1. The legal title passed to the slayer and may be retained by him in spite of his crime. The reasoning for so deciding is that devolution of the property of a decedent is controlled entirely by the statutes of descent and distribution; further, that denial of the inheritance to the slayer because of his crime would be imposing an additional punishment for his crime not provided by statute, and would violate the constitutional provision against corruption of blood.

2. The legal title will not pass to the slayer because of the equitable principle that no one should be permitted to profit by his own fraud, or take advantage and profit as a result of his own wrong or crime. Decisions so holding have been criticized as judicially engrafting an exception on the statute of descent and distribution and being 'unwarranted judicial legislation.'

3. The legal title passes to the slayer but equity holds him to be a constructive trustee for the heirs or next of kin of the decedent. This disposition of the question presented avoids a judicial engrafting on the statutory laws of descent and distribution, for title passes to the slayer. But because of the unconscionable mode by which the property is acquired by the slayer, equity treats him as a constructive trustee and compels him to convey the property to the heirs or next of kin of the deceased.

The reasoning behind the adoption of this doctrine was well expressed by Mr. Justice Cardozo in his lecture on 'The Nature of the Judicial Process.' 'Consistency was preserved, logic received its tribute, by holding that the legal title passed, but it was subject to a constructive trust. A constructive trust is nothing but 'the formula through which the conscience of equity finds expression.' Property is acquired in such circumstances that the holder of legal title may not in good conscience retain the beneficial interest. Equity, to express its disapproval of his conduct, converts him into a trustee.'

The New Hampshire court was confronted with the same problem of the rights to the benefits of an estate by one who had slain the decedent, in the absence of a statute on the subject. *Kelley v. State*. Speaking for an unanimous court, Chief Justice Kenison said: 'But, even in the absence of statute, a court applying common law techniques can reach a sensible solution by charging the spouse, heir or legatee as a constructive trustee of the property where equity and justice demand it." We approve of the doctrine so expressed.

However, the principle that one should not profit by his own wrong must not be extended to every case where a killer acquires property from his victim as a result of the killing. One who has killed while insane is not chargeable as a constructive trustee, or if the slayer had a vested interest in the property, it is property to which he would have been entitled if no slaying had occurred. The principle to be applied is that the slayer should not be permitted to improve his position by the killing, but should not be compelled to surrender property to which he would have been entitled if there had been no killing. The doctrine of constructive trust is involved to prevent the slayer from profiting from his crime, but not as an added criminal penalty.

The appellant here was, as we have noted, convicted of manslaughter and not of murder. She calls to our attention that while the Restatement of Restitution, approves the application of the constructive trust doctrine where a devisee or legatee murders the testator, that such rules are not applicable where the slayer was guilty of manslaughter.

The cases generally have not followed this limitation of the rule but hold that the line should not be drawn between murder and manslaughter, but between voluntary and involuntary manslaughter.

We think that this is the proper rule to follow. Voluntary manslaughter is an intentional and unlawful killing, with a real design and purpose to kill, even if such killing be the result of sudden passion or great provocation. Involuntary manslaughter is caused by an unlawful act, but not accompanied with any intention to take life. It is the intent to kill, which when accomplished, leads to the profit of the slayer that brings into play the constructive trust to prevent the unjust enrichment of the slayer by reason of his intentional killing.

In Vermont, an indictment for murder can result in a jury conviction on either voluntary or involuntary manslaughter. The legislature has provided the sentences that may be passed upon a person convicted of manslaughter, but provides no definition of that offense, nor any statutory distinction between voluntary and involuntary manslaughter.

The cause now before us is here on a direct appeal from the probate court. Findings of fact were made below from which it appears that the judgment of the probate court decreeing the estate of Howard Mahoney to his parents, rather than to his widow, was based upon a finding of the felonious killing of her husband by Mrs. Mahoney. However, the appellees here have asked us to affirm the decree below by imposing a constructive trust on the estate in the hands of the widow.

But the Probate Court did not decree the estate to the widow, and then make her a constructive trustee of such estate for the benefit of the parents. The judgment below decreed the estate directly to the parents, which was in direct contravention of the statutes of descent and distribution. The Probate Court was bound to follow the statutes of descent and distribution and its decree was in error and must be reversed.

The Probate Court was without jurisdiction to impose a constructive trust on the estate in the hands of the appellant, even if it had attempted to do so. Probate courts are courts of special and limited jurisdiction given by statute and do not proceed according to common law. While probate courts possess a portion of equitable powers independent of statute, such powers do not extend to the establishment of purely equitable rights and claims. The claim of the parents here to the Estate of Howard

Bla

Bla

Bla

Mahoney is equitable in its origin, and in the extent of the rights in the estate claimed. The equity powers conferred upon the probate court do not extend to the establishment of purely equitable claims and equitable rights.

However, the jurisdiction of the court of chancery may be invoked in probate matters in aid of the probate court when the powers of that court are inadequate, and it appears that the probate court cannot reasonably and adequately handle the question. The jurisdiction of the chancery court in so acting on probate matters is special and limited only to aiding the probate court.

The Probate Court, in making its decree, used the record of the conviction of the appellant for manslaughter for its determination that the appellant had feloniously killed her husband. If the jurisdiction of the court of chancery is invoked by the appellees here it will be for the determination of that court, upon proof, to determine whether the appellant willfully killed her late husband, as it will upon all other equitable considerations that may be offered in evidence, upon charging the appellant with a constructive trust. 'The fact that he is convicted of murder in a criminal case does not dispense with the necessity of proof of the murder in a proceedings in equity to charge him as a constructive trustee.'

The jurisdiction over charging the appellant with a constructive trust on the estate of Howard Mahoney lies in the court of chancery, and not in the probate court.

Decree reversed and cause remanded, with directions that the proceedings herein be stayed for sixty days to give the Administrator of the Estate of Howard Mahoney an opportunity to apply to the Franklin County Court of Chancery for relief. If application is so made, proceedings herein shall be stayed pending the final determination thereof. If application is not so made, the Probate Court for the District of Franklin shall assign to Charlotte Mahoney, surviving wife, the right and interest in and to the estate of her deceased husband which the Vermont Statutes confer.

In 2012 the Rhode Island Supreme Court had to decide the issue of whether or not the children of the murderer, the step-children of the decedent, should also be prevented from taking under the decedent's will.

Supreme Court of Rhode Island.
Jennifer SWAIN et al.
v.
ESTATE OF Shelley TYRE by and through James H. REILLY as Administrator d.b.n, c.t.a.[1]
Dec. 13, 2012.

Justice INDEGLIA, for the Court.

Before this Court is a question of first impression. We are called upon to determine

[1] This just stands for *de bonus nom, cum testament annexo*, in other words someone with a good name who was not named in the will, but is administering the estate *cum testament annexo*, with the will annexed.

whether the Rhode Island Slayer's Act, G.L.1956 chapter 1.1 of title 33 (Slayer's Act, or Act), prohibits the testatrix's stepchildren, Jennifer and Jeremy Swain (plaintiffs), from inheriting as named contingent testamentary beneficiaries (contingent beneficiaries) because this inheritance would confer a benefit on their father, David Swain (David). David, a slayer pursuant to the Act, has been adjudicated responsible for intentionally causing the death of the testatrix, Shelley Arden Tyre (Shelley).

The plaintiffs appeal from a grant of summary judgment in favor of defendant, Estate of Shelley A. Tyre (Estate or defendant), holding that they were barred as a matter of law from inheriting under the Slayer's Act. For the reasons set forth in this opinion, we affirm the judgment of the Superior Court.

I

Facts

The essential facts of this case are not in dispute. Shelley executed the will in question on October 5, 1993, in contemplation of her marriage to David. She married David shortly thereafter. Her will named David as the sole beneficiary of her estate. She also specifically named both Jennifer and Jeremy Swain as the only contingent beneficiaries under her will.[2] They stood to inherit in the event that David predeceased her.

Shelley's untimely death by drowning in 1999 triggered the administration of her estate.[3] Pursuant to her will, David was named as the executor. However, this role was short-lived.

On March 5, 2002, Shelley's parents brought a wrongful-death action against David alleging that he (1) was a slayer pursuant to § 33–1.1–1(3); (2) caused Shelley's wrongful death; and (3) should be subject to civil liability for a criminal act, pursuant to G.L.1956 § 9–1–2.

On May 1, 2002 Shelley's parents filed a petition in the Jamestown Probate Court to remove David as executor. The probate judge granted the petition on July 3, 2002, removed David as executor, and then appointed James H. Reilly as the administrator d.b.n., c.t.a., of Shelley's estate. Additionally, the probate judge ordered David to return the sum of $152,568.19, which the probate court deemed he had wrongfully taken from the estate.

After a trial in the wrongful death case was held in February of 2006, a jury returned a verdict in favor of Shelley's parents on all three counts, finding that David "intentionally killed Shelley with malice aforethought" and that he therefore met the definition of slayer set forth in the Slayer's Act. Shelley's parents were awarded

---

[2] Clause III of Shelley's Last Will and Testament reads as follows: "I give all my tangible personal property to my husband, or if he is not living thirty (30) days after my death, then in substantially equal shares to such of my husband's children, Jennifer Swain and Jeremy Swain (hereinafter 'my husband's children'), as are then living."

[3] On March 12, 1999, Shelley died while scuba diving with David off the coast of Tortola in the British Virgin Islands.

compensatory damages in the amount of $2,815,085.46, as well as punitive damages totaling $2 million. After the trial justice denied his motion for a new trial, David appealed to this Court. On May 13, 2008, we affirmed the lower court ruling, holding that "once the Superior Court has made a declaration with respect to whether a defendant is a slayer it is then within the province of the probate court to determine what effect, if any, that declaration has on the distribution of the decedent's assets under a will or other instrument."

Thereafter, on May 20, 2008, Reilly filed a petition in the Jamestown Probate Court to construe the will in light of this Court's decision. On June 27, 2008, the probate judge issued a written order declaring that "neither David A. Swain, nor his heirs at law, shall receive directly or indirectly from the Estate of Shelley Arden Tyre." Accordingly, based on that order, Jennifer and Jeremy were precluded from inheriting under Shelley's will as contingent beneficiaries.

The plaintiffs timely appealed the probate order to the Newport County Superior Court. On cross-motions for summary judgment, the hearing justice found in favor of the Estate, holding that the Slayer's Act barred Jennifer and Jeremy from inheriting under Shelley's will.

The hearing justice based his decision to bar plaintiffs' taking under Shelley's will on the undisputed facts that: (1) Jeremy had personally contributed and raised money to finance his father's defense;[4] and (2) Jennifer and Jeremy had both stated that they would use any proceeds they inherited from Shelley's estate for their father's criminal defense, if necessary.

The plaintiffs then filed a notice of appeal to this Court.

At the oral argument held on October 3, 2011, issues concerning mootness emerged. This Court deferred consideration of the merits of the appeal and issued an order directing the parties to file a joint statement as to whether the judgment of the Jamestown Probate Court (holding David responsible for paying the Estate $152,568.19) had been discharged in bankruptcy. Pursuant to our order, the parties submitted a joint statement confirming that the entire judgment had, in fact, been discharged in bankruptcy by the United States Bankruptcy Court for the District of Rhode Island. In this joint statement, the parties also indicated that approximately $5,571.99 remained in the estate for distribution.

Thereafter, on October 21, 2011, we issued an order referring this matter to the Supreme Court Appellate Mediation Program for resolution. In the event that mediation failed, the order directed the parties to file additional briefs with this Court as to whether a justiciable controversy remained.

After an unsuccessful attempt to resolve this case through mediation, the parties submitted additional briefs addressing the issue of mootness, pursuant to our order. On

---

[4] At the time, David was convicted of murder for Shelley's death in the British Virgin Islands. This conviction has since been overturned. *David Swain and the Queen,* HCRAP 2008/09, (B.V.I. Sept. 29, 2011).

May 2, 2012, we issued a subsequent order assigning the case to the show-cause calendar, and we indicated that the parties "may file additional memoranda, if so desired, in order to address any *supplementary issues that may have arisen* since the date of their last appearance before this Court."[5] (Emphasis added.)

II

Standard of Review (omitted)

III

Discussion

A

Justiciability (omitted)

B

The History and Policy Rationale of the Slayer's Act

To aid in our analysis, we briefly examine the history and policy rationale of the Slayer's Act. The notion that a person should not profit or benefit from his or her own wrong derives from the common law. The axiom was incorporated in the doctrines of attainder, forfeiture of estate, and corruption of blood.[6] Together, these doctrines prohibited a slayer and his or her heirs from receiving property under the distribution of a victim's estate.

The United States Constitution later substantially abolished these common-law doctrines; however, the premise that no person shall benefit from his or her own wrongdoing endured. In the late nineteenth century, the United States Supreme Court addressed the inheritance rights of a slayer and his issue. In that case, an insurance company refused to pay the victim's policy proceeds to the slayer's estate, even though the victim's policy explicitly stated that the policy proceeds were payable to the slayer. Relying on the maxim that no person shall benefit from his own wrong, the Court held that the slayer's estate was barred from collecting the proceeds of the victim's insurance policy, even though the estate's beneficiaries consisted of potentially innocent heirs. The Court stated:

> "[I]ndependently [*sic*] of any proof of the motives of [the slayer] in obtaining the policy, and even assuming that they were just and proper, he forfeited all rights under it when, to secure its immediate payment, he murdered the assured. It would be a reproach to the jurisprudence of the country, if one could

[5] In its supplemental brief, the Estate raises the novel issue of whether Shelley's publicity rights, if any, survive her death and therefore are inheritable. However, the Estate could have raised this issue below and failed to do so. It is well settled that "this Court's 'raise-or-waive' rule precludes our consideration of an issue that has not been raised and articulated below.

[6] "Attainder" is "the act of extinguishing a person's civil rights when sentenced to death or declared an outlaw for committing a felony or treason." Black's Law Dictionary 123 (7th ed.1999). "Forfeiture" is "the loss of a right, privilege, or property because of a crime, breach of obligation, or neglect of duty." *Id.* at 661. "Corruption of blood" is a doctrine pursuant to which "a person loses the ability to inherit or pass property as a result of an attainder or of being declared civilly dead." *Id.* at 348.

> recover insurance money payable on the death of a party whose life he had feloniously taken. As well might he recover insurance money upon a building that he had willfully fired."

Later, New York's highest court disqualified a slayer from inheriting under the decedent's will, declaring:

> "What could be more unreasonable than to suppose that it was the legislative intention in the general laws passed for the orderly, peaceable, and just devolution of property that they should have operation in favor of one who murdered his ancestor that he might speedily come into the possession of his estate?"

Today, the vast majority of states have adopted some form of a slayer statute, thereby further entrenching the principle that no person shall benefit from the killing of another. Having enacted its own slayer statute in 1962, Rhode Island is no exception.

The Slayer's Act provides in part that "neither the slayer nor any person claiming through him or her shall in any way acquire any property or receive any benefit as the result of the death of the decedent, but the property shall pass as provided in this chapter." A slayer is defined under the statute as "any person who willfully and unlawfully takes or procures to be taken the life of another." When the slayer is named as a beneficiary in the decedent's will, "the slayer shall be deemed to have predeceased the decedent as to property which would have passed to the slayer by devise or legacy from the decedent, except that the provisions of the anti-lapse statute shall not apply." Additionally, the Act precludes a slayer from inheriting an intestate or spousal share, thereby also precluding the slayer's issue from such inheritance.

C

Arguments of the Parties

The plaintiffs contend that the Slayer's Act does not preclude them from inheriting under Shelley's will as named contingent beneficiaries. The language of the Slayer's Act explicitly states that a person "*claiming through* " the slayer is prohibited from "acquiring any property or receiving any benefit as a result of the death of the decedent." Here, it is clear that plaintiffs are not claiming through the slayer. Rather, they seek their share explicitly under the terms of Shelley's will. They maintain that applying the Slayer's Act to preclude their inheritance directly contravenes Shelley's testamentary intent. They note that the Estate has never refuted plaintiffs' assertion that Shelley valued her relationship with them and that they shared a strong familial bond.

Further, plaintiffs emphasize that there is no language in the Slayer's Act specifically precluding a slayer's issue from inheriting as named contingent beneficiaries. Thus, according to plaintiffs, the Slayer's Act only applies to disinherit a slayer's issue when they have not been named as beneficiaries in the decedent's will.

Additionally, they contend that the Legislature carefully drafted the Slayer's Act to strike a balance between two competing interests: the interest in prohibiting a slayer from benefitting from his or her wrongs, and the interest in carrying out the wishes of testators under the terms of their wills. As such, then, the Slayer's Act explicitly carves out language to preclude a slayer's issue from inheriting under the anti-lapse statute or through intestacy, while otherwise allowing a slayer's issue to inherit as named beneficiaries of the testator. Furthermore, plaintiffs contend that the Legislature did not intend to bar contingent beneficiaries from inheriting when such inheritance may only "indirectly" benefit a slayer.

The Estate maintains, however, that the broad language and construction of the Slayer's Act bar plaintiffs from taking under Shelley's will. The Act explicitly prohibits a slayer from "*in any way* acquiring any property or receiving any benefit as the result of the death of the decedent." Moreover, the Act states that it "shall be construed broadly in order to effect the policy of this state that no person shall be allowed to profit by his or her own wrong."

Therefore, the Estate argues, plaintiffs' taking under Shelley's will would directly contravene the Slayer's Act by conferring a benefit on David. Since the Act does not define what a benefit is, the Estate cites various dictionary definitions, which all generally define "benefit" as an advantage or a gain. The Estate points out the undisputed facts that both Jennifer and Jeremy deny their father's involvement in Shelley's death. Jeremy has contributed financially to his father's criminal defense; and both siblings have stipulated that if they are successful in this appeal, they would use any assets obtained for their father's defense, if necessary. Thus, the inclusion of the language precluding a slayer from benefiting "in any way," together with the broad construction required by the Act, operates to bar plaintiffs from inheriting as contingent beneficiaries.

Additionally, the Estate maintains that, "it is clear that Shelley's will was made without the benefit of knowing that David would kill her, and the legal fiction that he predeceased her, despite not being dead, would result in his children taking her estate." Thus, the Estate asserts that, although Jennifer and Jeremy stood to inherit under Shelley's will as contingent beneficiaries in the event that David predeceased her, she did not intend for them to inherit if David otherwise "predeceased" her by virtue of the Slayer's Act.

D

Analysis

In reviewing the language of the Slayer's Act, we repeat that a statute may not be construed in a way that "would defeat the underlying purpose of the enactment." "Our ultimate goal is to give effect to the purpose of the act as intended by the Legislature."

The Slayer's Act explicitly states that it "shall be construed broadly in order to effect the policy of this state that no person shall be allowed to profit by his or her own wrong." We consider this language mandating a broad construction of the Act to be crucial to our analysis. It is axiomatic that 'this Court will not broaden statutory provisions by judicial interpretation *unless such interpretation is necessary and appropriate in carrying out the clear intent or defining the terms of the statute.*" Here, the clear intent of the Slayer's Act is to ensure that a slayer does not benefit from his or her wrongdoing. Thus, although the Slayer's Act does not specifically include language barring the slayer's issue from inheriting as contingent beneficiaries, the clear and unequivocal direction of the Act requires this Court, based on the facts before us,[7] to interpret it so as to prevent the slayer from benefitting.[8]

Here, it is undisputed that David will benefit from murdering Shelley if Jennifer and Jeremy are allowed to inherit under her will. The plaintiffs have put on the record that they would use any money from their share of the estate to finance their father's defense, if necessary. They vigorously maintain that their father was not involved in Shelley's tragic death. Further, although the probate judgment of $152,568.19 against David has been discharged in bankruptcy, the outstanding multimillion-dollar civil judgment in favor of Shelley's parents remains against David for Shelley's wrongful death. It is foreseeable to conclude that plaintiffs would use assets obtained from Shelley's estate to help relieve their father's burden of satisfying this obligation.

Such a benefit to David would directly contravene both the language and the intent of the Slayer's Act. Indeed, on the facts presented, allowing plaintiffs to inherit under Shelley's will would allow David to obtain a benefit in direct contravention of the Act. Therefore, we hold that the Slayer's Act bars plaintiffs from inheriting as contingent beneficiaries.

We pause to respond to the dissent's suggestion that we have created a third category of prohibited beneficiaries not contemplated by the Slayer's Act. We have done no such thing. As stated above, § 33–1.1–2 provides that, "neither the slayer nor any person claiming through him or her shall in any way acquire any property or receive any benefit as the result of the death of the decedent" Thus, the Act explicitly forbids a slayer from obtaining a benefit. Here, both plaintiffs have stated that they would use the assets to pay for their father's defense, if necessary. Thus, on the facts presented, there is no question that David will obtain a benefit if plaintiffs are permitted to take under Shelley's will—a result directly at odds with the express

[7] We note that although David's murder conviction has since been overturned thereby nullifying the need for any additional funds to be spent on his criminal defense, plaintiffs have already contributed financially to their father's defense. Therefore, any share they obtain from the estate could be reimbursement for money already spent for David's benefit.

[8] We acknowledge that there may be situations in which the Slayer's Act does not apply to bar the slayer's issue from inheriting as contingent testamentary beneficiaries. For example, in the situation of a murder-suicide, the slayer is no longer living to reap the benefit of his wrongdoing. Thus, the Slayer's Act would not preclude the slayer's issue from inheriting, since such inheritance would not confer any benefit on the slayer. Similarly, there might be a factual question as to whether estranged children of the slayer, also named as contingent testamentary beneficiaries, would use such inheritance to the slayer's benefit.

language of the Act.

The dissent concedes that the Slayer's Act "shall be construed broadly," in accordance with the Legislature's intent. However, the dissent's own analysis applies a narrow construction of the Act. Indeed, the dissent restricts the Act's reach by concluding that it does not prohibit a slayer from receiving a benefit, provided that such benefit is "one step removed" from the death of the decedent. In so doing, the dissent ignores the explicit language of the Act which forbids a slayer from benefitting or acquiring property "*in any way* as a result of the death of the decedent." Thus, the dissent's reading of the Slayer's Act is incompatible with the Legislature's mandate that the Act be construed broadly.

The dissent suggests that we have construed the Act "limitlessly" rather than broadly. We respectfully disagree with this characterization of our holding. As stated earlier in this opinion, we acknowledge that there may indeed be factual situations in which contingent beneficiaries will not confer a benefit on a slayer, and therefore are not precluded from inheriting. Noting this, we expressly limited our holding to the facts of this case, in which there is no dispute that the plaintiffs' taking under Shelley's will unquestionably would confer a benefit upon David, in direct contravention of the Slayer's Act.

IV

Conclusion

For the reasons set forth in this opinion, we affirm the judgment of the Superior Court, to which we remand the record in this case.

CHAPTER 18 - DISCLAIMER AND ACCELERATION

A. DISCLAIMER – STATUTORY PROVISIONS

Occasionally there are times when it is beneficial for a family member to renounce, or disclaim, gifts provided in a will or trust. Sometimes this is done because an older member of the family really does not need the money, and prefers to have it go directly to a younger generation. Sometimes this is done for tax reasons, when an older member of the family, for example, will disclaim his or her gift so that the money will pass to a younger generation, and be less likely to end up as taxable in the estate of the older family member. Such disclaimers must be done within a short time, roughly six to nine months, or the IRS will count the disclaimer as a taxable gift.

Sometimes a person may disclaim property in an attempt to avoid creditors, or in an attempt to prevent an ex-spouse from getting the money, or for an assortment of other reasons. No beneficiary is ever required to accept any gift.

First, it should be noted that by statute, property automatically devolves, at death *subject to* various necessities of probate.

Here is a sample statutory provision.

> C.R.S.§ 15-12-101. Devolution of estate at death; restrictions
> The power of a person to leave property by will and the rights of creditors, devisees, and heirs to his property are subject to the restrictions and limitations contained in this code to facilitate the prompt settlement of estates. Upon the death of a person, his real and personal property devolves to the persons to whom it is devised by his last will or to those indicated as substitutes for them in cases involving lapse, renunciation, or other circumstances affecting the devolution of the testate estate or, in the absence of testamentary disposition, to his heirs or to those indicated as substitutes for them in cases involving renunciation or other circumstances affecting devolution of intestate estates, subject to exempt property and family allowances, rights of creditors, elective share of the surviving spouse, and administration.

Despite this provision for automatic devolution of property, a disclaimer is still always possible. A typical disclaimer statute follows.

Notice that in section 15-11-1213(b), anyone who <u>contracts</u> to make a disclaimer, has <u>lost</u> the right to make the disclaimer, because of that very contract.

Especially important provisions of the following statute have been printed in bold.

C.R.S. § 15-11-1205. Power to disclaim--general requirements—when irrevocable

(1) A person may disclaim, in whole or in part, any interest in or power over property, including a power of appointment. **A person may disclaim the interest or power even if its creator imposed a spendthrift provision or similar restriction on transfer or a restriction or limitation on the right to disclaim.**

(2) Except to the extent a fiduciary's right to disclaim is expressly restricted or limited by another statute of this state or by the instrument creating the fiduciary relationship, a fiduciary may disclaim, in whole or in part, any interest in or power over property, including a power of appointment, whether acting in a personal or representative capacity.

(3) To be effective, a disclaimer shall be in writing or other record, declare the disclaimer, describe the interest or power disclaimed, be signed by the person making the disclaimer, and be delivered or filed, and, with regard to an interest in real property, be recorded in the manner provided for in section 15-11-1212.

(4) A partial disclaimer may be expressed as a fraction, percentage, monetary amount, term of years, limitation of a power, or any other interest or estate in the property.

(5) A disclaimer becomes irrevocable when it is delivered or filed and, with regard to an interest in real property, recorded.

(6) A disclaimer made pursuant to this part 12 is not a transfer, assignment, or release.

§ 15-11-1206. Disclaimer of interest in property

(a) The disclaimer takes effect as of the time the instrument creating the interest becomes irrevocable, or, if the interest arose under the law of intestate succession, as of the time of the intestate's death.

(b) The disclaimed interest passes according to any provision in the instrument creating the interest, providing for the disposition of the interest, should it be disclaimed, or of disclaimed interests in general.

(c) If the instrument does not contain a provision described in paragraph (b) of this subsection, the following rules apply:

(I) If the disclaimant is not an individual, the disclaimed interest passes as if the disclaimant had ceased to exist immediately before the time of distribution.

(II) If the disclaimant is an individual, except as otherwise provided for in subparagraphs (III) and (IV) of this paragraph (c), the disclaimed interest passes as if the disclaimant had died

immediately before the time of distribution. ...

(d) Upon the disclaimer of a preceding interest, a future interest held by a person other than the disclaimant takes effect as if the disclaimant had died or ceased to exist immediately before the time of distribution, but a future interest held by the disclaimant is not accelerated in possession or enjoyment.

§ 15-11-1207. Disclaimer of rights of survivorship in jointly held property

(1) Upon the death of a holder of jointly held property, a surviving holder may disclaim, in whole or in part, the incremental portion of the jointly held property devolving to the surviving holder by right of survivorship.

(a) The disclaimer does not sever the joint tenancy with respect to the jointly held property as among the surviving holders;

(b) The incremental portion disclaimed shall, as a consequence of a disclaimer, devolve to the surviving holders in proportion to their respective interests in the jointly held property excluding the disclaimant.

§ 15-11-1209. Disclaimer of power of appointment or other power not held in fiduciary capacity

(1) If a holder disclaims a power of appointment or other power not held in a fiduciary capacity, the disclaimer applies only to that holder, and the following rules apply:

(a) If the holder has not exercised the power, the disclaimer takes effect as of the time the instrument creating the power becomes irrevocable;

(b) If the holder has exercised the power and the disclaimer is of a power other than a presently exercisable general power of appointment, the disclaimer takes effect immediately after the last exercise of the power; and

(c) The instrument creating the power is construed as if the power expired when the disclaimer became effective.

§ 15-11-1210. Disclaimer by appointee, object, or taker in default of exercise of power of appointment

(1) A disclaimer of an interest in property by an appointee of a power of appointment takes effect as of the time the instrument by which the holder exercises the power becomes irrevocable.

(2) A disclaimer of an interest in property by an object or taker in default of an exercise of a power of appointment takes effect as of the time the instrument creating the power becomes irrevocable.

§ 15-11-1212. Delivery or filing

...

(3) In the case of an interest created under the law of intestate succession or an interest created by will, other than an interest in a testamentary trust:

(a) A disclaimer shall be delivered to the personal representative of the decedent's estate; or

(b) If no personal representative is then serving, a disclaimer shall be filed with a court having jurisdiction to appoint a personal representative.

(4) In the case of an interest in a testamentary trust:

(a) A disclaimer shall be delivered to the trustee then serving or, if no trustee is then serving, to the personal representative of the decedent's estate; or

(b) If no personal representative is then serving, the disclaimer shall be filed with a court having jurisdiction to enforce the trust.

§ 15-11-1213. When disclaimer barred or limited

(1) A disclaimer is barred by a written waiver of the right to disclaim.

(2) A disclaimer of an interest in property is barred if any of the following events occur before the disclaimer becomes effective:

(a) The disclaimant accepts the interest sought to be disclaimed;

(b) The disclaimant voluntarily assigns, conveys, encumbers, pledges, or transfers the interest sought to be disclaimed or contracts to do so; or ...

(7) Notwithstanding any other provision in this part 12, this part 12 shall not modify the construction of law or application of law with respect to:

(a) A disqualification of medical assistance benefits to a disclaimant who is or was an applicant for or recipient of such benefits; or

(b) A recovery from the estate of a deceased recipient of such medical assistance benefits.

§ 15-11-1214. Tax-qualified disclaimer

Notwithstanding any other provision of this part 12, if, as a result of a disclaimer or transfer, the disclaimed or transferred interest is treated pursuant to the provisions of title 26 of the United States internal revenue code, as now or hereafter amended, or any successor statute thereto, and the regulations promulgated thereunder, as never having been transferred to the disclaimant, then the disclaimer or transfer is effective as a disclaimer pursuant to this part 12.

Now for some interesting cases involving disclaimers.

B. DISCLAIMER IN TIME OF WAR

Circuit Court of Appeals, Second Circuit.
STOEHR
v.
MILLER.
December 17, 1923.

ROGERS, Circuit Judge.

The evidence discloses that the complainant came to the United States in 1900, and that he has resided here ever since with the exception that he was absent from the country between 1903 and 1907 which years were spent in Germany, France, South America, and Australia. In May, 1911, he became a citizen of the United States, having previously married an American wife. His father had established in 1879 or 1880 a firm under his own name to engage in the woolen business, and in 1910 or 1911 the firm was changed into an Aktiengesellschaft which answers to our corporation. In 1889 the father organized and incorporated in this country the Botany Worsted Mills of Passaic, N.J. The German and the American corporations both prospered, and it appears that before the World War Eduard Stoehr was the highest taxpayer in Leipsig.

It appears that in 1912 Eduard had fully worked out and announced to his associates in the German corporation a plan which had been adopted as a family understanding for the division of his fortune among his children. His son Georg was to remain in the management of his German corporation, and the management and ownership of his American interests were to be vested in Max, the complainant.

Early in 1917 war between Germany and the United States appeared imminent and Hans and Max thought that they should no longer postpone carrying out their father's wishes. Hans instructed the family lawyer in this country to take the necessary legal steps to incorporate the company.

Action in turning over the property of the partnership to the corporation was taken by Hans, who personally directed the issuance of the stock to Max. The latter then realizing that he held the American shares and also held the title to his German properties which were to be turned over to his brother Georg who was to live in Germany, fully discussed the situation with the family attorney who presented him the declarations of trust which he signed. Max put them in his safe, where they remained until he surrendered them to the Alien Property Custodian, and did not make them known to his father or to Georg until the winter of 1922.

The declarations were not mentioned by Max either to his father or to Georg, until Max arrived in Germany again in December, 1921. At his request they then signed what are referred to as 'renunciations.' That signed by the father is found in the margin.[1] That signed by Georg is similar

As a result of the transactions above set forth, the complainant Max, an American citizen, finds himself deprived of all his property. He turned over his German properties to his father and his brother Georg in accordance with the understanding he had with them. And the Alien Property Custodian has seized and taken possession of the property held by him as trustee under the circumstances already set forth.

We have examined this record with care. It satisfies us that prior to the entry of the United States into the war with Germany and as early as 1915 a family understanding existed between Eduard Stoehr and his sons, Georg, Hans, and Max, and that the American properties were to belong to Max, and that the latter's interests in the European properties were to be made over to Eduard and Georg Stoehr. That such an understanding existed is incontrovertibly established. And it existed long before America's entrance into the war was expected.

In an attempt to carry this understanding into effect, the declarations of trust were signed. Neither Eduard nor Georg had any knowledge that such declarations were to be signed or had been signed until some years after the seizure complained of herein. That the legal title to the trust property is in Max is not denied. The question is whether the equitable title is in Eduard and Georg. If it is not, then there was no alien interest which the Alien Property Custodian could seize.

The record shows that in executing the declarations of trust Max acted upon the advice of the family attorney, and that he was influenced solely by the fact that he was at that time owning both the German and American stock, although he was under obligations to transfer the German stock to his father and brother in Germany and it was in the hope that if anything happened to him before the transfer could be made his father and brother would be protected.

With this statement as to the facts we are brought to a consideration of the legal questions involved.

It is undoubted that a person intending to make a voluntary disposition of property for the benefit of another may accomplish his purpose in either of the following modes: (1) By a direct conveyance or assignment of it to the donee. (2) By a transfer of the

---

[1] 'The undersigned deposes under oath the following: It became known to me that my son Max Stoehr has signed a deed of trust at the incorporation of the partnership of Stoehr & Sons, in which he declared 1,875 shares, which are standing in his name on the books of the firm, as my property. I herewith declare that I do not consider these 1,875 shares as my property, as they should belong to my son Max in accordance with former arrangements in our family, and that if these shares seized by the Alien Property Custodian, should be returned by him to me, I would feel myself obliged to return them to my son Max as his rightful property.
'Eisenach, January 13, 1922.
'(Signed) Paul Rudolph Eduard Stoehr.'

property to a third person upon a trust for the donee. (3) By declaring himself a trustee for the donee. And we do not doubt that where the third mode has been adopted it is not essential that the declaration of trust should be delivered to a third person or that the cestui que trust should have been informed of the trust.

It is also well established that if a trust is one perfectly created, although it is voluntary, it is irrevocable, and is not affected by the subsequent acts of the settlor or the trustee.

It is our understanding that if one signs a written declaration of trust which he never delivers, but retains in his own possession, and never discloses to the person designated as cestui que trust or to any one for him, while the document prima facie creates a trust, evidence aliunde may be received to determine the intent and effect of the instrument.

In the case of a voluntary declaration of trust not delivered or announced, the court may look into the surrounding circumstances and receive evidence bearing upon intent.

In the instant case it is not left to inference what the intention of Max W. Stoehr, the complainant, was in signing the declaration of trust. The sworn testimony of the complainant, which we have no reason for believing untrue, is in the record. The reason for the document was the protection of the complainant's father and brother, who had transferred to him their American interests, in case anything happened to the complainant before he succeeded in transferring to them his interests in the properties in Germany in return for their transfer to him of their interests in the American properties of which he was already in possession.

There is another aspect of this case which must now be stated, and which is fatal in our opinion to the claim that the property represented by the trust certificates was the property of Eduard and Georg Stoehr, alien enemies. In the case of a trust the creator of the trust cannot compel a third person to be the trustee against his consent, but his acceptance of the office is necessary to constitute him trustee and to vest the title in him. It is equally true that property cannot be forced upon a cestui que trust against his will, and a valid trust does not exist if the cestui que trust when informed of it clearly and unequivocably rejects or renounces its benefits.

Any equitable rights arising from a declaration of trust are at an end after the renunciation, and the settlor holds the title to the res free and clear of the trust. If the cestui que trust when he learns of the trust accepts it, his acceptance relates back to the date of the declaration. If he repudiates it when he learns of it, his repudiation relates back in the same manner and the title must be regarded as having been in the settlor all of the time.

The record in this case discloses that the cestuis que trustent under the declarations herein involved renounced their rights in them when they learned of their existence, which was not until January, 1922.

This court is not concerned with the motive which may have induced the renunciation. The cestuis que trustent were in honor and in all good faith bound to renounce. But if their renunciation had been made in order to defeat the seizure which the Alien Property Custodian had made it would be quite immaterial. They owed no duty to the United States, and the seizure of the property by the Alien Property Custodian did not deprive them of their right to renounce. We fail to see how their renunciation defeated any lawful purposes of the Trading with the Enemy Act. If the consequence of the renunciation is to revest the property in the hands of an American citizen no wrong to the United States is done.

The Trading with the Enemy Act gave to the Alien Property Custodian no authority to seize property other than 'property in the United States due or belonging to an enemy, or ally of an enemy.' And as the property which he seized and which is the subject of this suit was not such property, he had no authority to seize it and has no right to retain it.

The decree is reversed, with directions to reinstate the bill and grant the relief prayed for therein.

C. DISCLAIMER AND ACCELERATION

There are probably few people who would consciously renounce or disclaim wealth simply because they did not want to accept the money. But sometimes it happens, as illustrated by the following case. What could have been done in drafting the trust in the following case to be sure that when Luther renounced the wealth intended for him by his father, Luther did not also cut off the rights of any future children he might have, grandchildren of the testator, from someday sharing in the family wealth?

Surrogate's Court, New York County, New York.
Proceeding by Martin A. Coleman, as Executor of the
ESTATE OF Peter GILBERT, Deceased,
for Advice and Direction Pertaining to a Notice of Renunciation.
Nov. 25, 1992.

RENEE R. ROTH, Surrogate.

The executor of the estate of Peter Gilbert asks the court to declare null and void a renunciation by Mr. Gilbert's son, Lester, of his interest in two wholly discretionary trusts under decedent's will.

Mr. Gilbert died on March 26, 1989, leaving an estate of over $40,000,000. He was survived by his wife and four children. Under his will, testator, after making certain pre-residuary legacies, created an elective share trust for the life income benefit of his wife. The amount of decedent's generation-skipping transfer (GST) tax exemption was divided into four discretionary trusts, one for the primary benefit of each of his children. The residue of Mr. Gilbert's estate was similarly divided. Upon the death of the widow, the remainder of her trust is to be added in equal shares to the residuary trusts for decedent's children. The trusts are wholly discretionary. Decedent's son, Lester, is therefore a discretionary income beneficiary of two testamentary trusts, one of which will be augmented at the widow's death. Decedent's issue, including Lester's sisters, nieces and nephews as well as Lester's issue (should he have any), are also discretionary beneficiaries of both of Lester's trusts.

Lester, who has no issue, timely served on the executor a notice of renunciation of his "dispositive share in the estate of Peter Gilbert".

The executor, supported by the guardian ad litem for decedent's minor grandchildren, takes the position that Lester's renunciation should be declared invalid. Blu First, he states that permitting the renunciation would violate the testator's intention to provide for Lester. Second, the executor argues that Lester possesses no current property interest and therefore has nothing to renounce. The executor maintains that Lester's renunciation is premature and may be made only if, and at such time as, the trustees exercise their discretion to distribute income or principal to him.

The executor explains decedent's intention as follows:

> Lester, who is approximately 32 years of age, ... has left the religion of his birth and has for some time lived in Virginia with a small group of people who share a similar religious doctrine. Some months ago he phoned your petitioner and announced that he planned to renounce whatever bequest was left for him. When asked what he planned to do if he were ever taken seriously ill and needed expensive medical care, he responded "Jesus will provide for me".

The fact that Lester had chosen to alienate himself from his family did not stop the decedent from loving his son or worrying about his future needs. The decedent wanted to know that funds would be available if the Trustees, acting in the manner that they thought the decedent would have acted had he then been living, should ever decide, for example, to pay a medical bill for Lester.

In effect, the executor argues that if the beneficiary of a wholly discretionary trust is permitted to renounce his or her interest, then no trust can ever be created to protect someone who is now disdainful of financial assistance but may in the future be in dire need, or simply have a change of heart.

However, under these circumstances, decedent's intention is not controlling. With respect to every renunciation, the intent to make a transfer is thwarted by the beneficiary who refuses to accept it. But clearly, "the law does not compel a man to accept an estate, either beneficial or in trust, against his will."

The executor suggests in his memorandum that he might be forced "to inquire into the mental capacity of Lester, since there is no rational reason which explains Lester's conduct." However, the desire to renounce wealth is not necessarily irrational. Presumably, the executor would not argue that a nun who takes a vow of poverty is mentally incompetent. Here, the acceptance of a monetary benefit apparently conflicts

G

with Lester's religious beliefs. It would not be appropriate for the court to determine the validity of those beliefs, even if requested to do so. Furthermore, even if Lester's renunciation were purely whimsical, this would not in itself be sufficient reason either to reject the renunciation or to find him incompetent. In any event, the question of Lester's mental capacity has not been raised. There is no allegation in the petition or in any affidavit that Lester is a person under disability. The court must therefore proceed on the assumption that Lester is competent to make an effective renunciation.

The executor's second argument is that Lester has no current property interest which he can renounce. Rather, the executor maintains that Lester must wait until the trustees exercise their discretion to distribute income or principal to him, at which time, the executor asserts, Lester can renounce the property subject to such exercise of discretion. There appears to be no decision in New York with respect to the renunciation of a discretionary interest.

Renunciations are governed by EPTL 2-1.11. Paragraph (b)(1) of such statute provides that "any beneficiary of a disposition may renounce all or part of his interest ". EPTL 1-2.4 defines "disposition" as "a transfer of property by a person during his lifetime or by will." "Property" is defined in EPTL 1-2.15 as "anything that may be the subject of ownership." Therefore, under the statute, a renunciation may be made only with respect to a transfer of something which may be the subject of ownership. The statute, however, does not require that property be transferred *to* the beneficiary. Instead, the property may be transferred to a trustee *for the benefit of* a beneficiary. Furthermore, the statute does not require that the beneficiary renounce the disposition itself; rather, he may renounce "all or part of his *interest*" in the disposition (EPTL 2-1.11[b][1]) [Emphasis added].

In this case, decedent by his will transferred property to trusts of which Lester is a beneficiary, albeit a discretionary beneficiary. Similarly, the subject of Lester's renunciation is his interest in the trusts, although that interest is discretionary. The renunciation, therefore, appears to satisfy the terms of the statute.

The executor, however, contends that Lester's interest in the trusts does not rise to the level contemplated by the statute. He argues that for a renunciation to be effective, the renounced interest must be in the nature of property. Claiming that Lester's interest is not property, the executor cites Hamilton v. Drogo, where the Court of Appeals held that a judgment creditor was not entitled to levy on the interest of one of the beneficiaries of a discretionary trust. Holding that the judgment creditor could attach the income if and when the trustee distributed it to the beneficiary, the court observed:

> "In the present case no income may ever become due to the judgment debtor. We may not interfere with the discretion which the testatrix has vested in the trustee any more than her son may do so. But if it is exercised in favor of the duke then at least for some appreciable time, however brief, the award must precede the delivery of the income he is to receive and during that time the lien

of the execution attaches."

Similarly, in Matter of Duncan, the court held that a beneficiary of a discretionary trust possesses no property reachable by creditors until distribution is made.

But the cases relied upon by the executor are clearly distinguishable from the instant case in that they deal with the rights of creditors and not with those of beneficiaries. More closely analogous are those decisions which determine the rights of beneficiaries to compel distribution by trustees. Although in this case Lester's creditors cannot reach the trusts, Lester may nonetheless have the right to force the trustees to distribute income or principal to him under certain circumstances.

Although our courts cannot ordinarily interfere with the exercise of a trustee's discretion, they can ensure that such discretion is exercised fairly and honestly.

In the present case, the trustees' discretion is absolute and not limited by any standard. However, even in such a case, the trustees may be compelled to distribute funds to the beneficiary if they abuse their discretion in refusing to make distribution.

Thus, Lester may have the right to compel the trustees to distribute trust property to him under certain circumstances. Therefore, even if the court accepts the executor's interpretation of the statute, Lester arguably has a current interest which could be deemed "property" for the purpose of an effective renunciation.

Lester's renunciation also applies to his remainder interest in the elective share trust, which is contingent upon his surviving the widow. As discussed above, any interest, whether or not contingent, is within the scope of the statute. Even if the executor's interpretation is correct and a renunciation must relate to an interest in property, a contingent remainder has historically been recognized as a property interest.

Finally, the guardian ad litem argues that if Lester's renunciation is allowed, the remainder interests in his trusts should not be accelerated. The remainder of Lester's trusts would be payable to his issue. As mentioned earlier, Lester has no issue. If the interests are accelerated, Lester's unborn issue would be cut off and decedent's living grandchildren would lose certain present interests in these trusts. It is noted that acceleration of the trust remainders would have no direct tax consequences and any indirect effects would be relatively minor.

The question is whether under EPTL 2-1.11(d) this court has any discretion to suspend acceleration. Such statute, in relevant part, provides that:

> Unless the creator of the disposition has otherwise provided, the filing of a renunciation, as provided in this section, has the same effect with respect to the renounced interest as though the renouncing person had predeceased the creator or the decedent and shall have the effect of accelerating the possession and enjoyment of subsequent interests.

Thus, it appears that under the language of the statute, the remainder interests in

Lester's trusts will be accelerated unless the decedent has "otherwise provided". There is no explicit "otherwise provision" in testator's will, but the guardian ad litem argues that the court should infer an "otherwise provision" from the general language of the will and the circumstances surrounding its execution.

When EPTL 2–1.11 was enacted in 1977, the language regarding acceleration was added to resolve the dispute reflected in a number of conflicting decisions. Those cases looked to testator's intent as the appropriate guideline and determined acceleration on a case-by-case basis, with unpredictable results. It is clear the addition of this language was intended to provide uniformity. To engage in the type of analysis suggested by the guardian ad litem would mean a return to the approach rejected by the Legislature.

Based upon the foregoing, it is concluded that Lester's renunciation is valid as to any and all interests in his father's estate. Lester is thus to be treated as if he predeceased his father without issue.

It is so Ordered.

CHAPTER 19 - REVOCATION OR REVIVAL OF WILLS

A. REVOCATION BY TESTATOR

After a will has been properly executed, then issues may arise as to how the will may be revoked. A will may always be revoked by a subsequent will, executed with the proper formalities – unless the will is a contract will. The special rules applicable to contract wills are covered in section B of this chapter.

A typical state statute on revocation follows.

C.R.S.§ 15-11-507. REVOCATION BY WRITING OR BY ACT

(1) A will or any part thereof is revoked:

(a) By executing a subsequent will that revokes the previous will or part expressly or by inconsistency; or

(b) By performing a revocatory act on the will, if the testator performed the act with the intent and for the purpose of revoking the will or part of it or if another individual performed the act in the testator's conscious presence and by the testator's direction. For purposes of this paragraph (b), "revocatory act on the will" includes burning, tearing, canceling, obliterating, or destroying the will or any part of it. A burning, tearing, or canceling is a "revocatory act on the will," whether or not the burn, tear, or cancellation touched any of the words on the will.

(2) If a subsequent will does *not expressly revoke* a previous will, the execution of the subsequent will wholly revokes the previous will by *inconsistency* if the testator intended the subsequent will to replace rather than supplement the previous will.

(3) The testator is presumed to have intended a subsequent will to *replace* rather than supplement a previous will if the subsequent will makes a *complete* disposition of the testator's estate. If this presumption arises and is not rebutted by clear and convincing evidence, the previous will is revoked; only the subsequent will is operative on the testator's death.

(4) The testator is presumed to have intended a subsequent will to *supplement* rather than replace a previous will if the subsequent will does *not make* a complete disposition of the testator's estate. If this presumption arises and is not rebutted by clear and convincing evidence, the subsequent will revokes the previous will *only* to the extent the subsequent will is *inconsistent with the previous will; each will is fully operative on the testator's death to the extent they are not inconsistent.* (Emphasis added.)

Needless to say, it is important at the beginning of every will to state specifically that the current will revokes all previous wills and codicils. The statute above makes it look as if it is fairly easy to revoke a will, which it is. Nevertheless, the provisions of the statute must be properly complied with, in order to make the revocation effective. Do not be tempted to take the shortcuts attempted by the judge in the classic case which follows.

Supreme Court of Virginia.
SALLY J. THOMPSON, ET AL. v. JENNIE BOWEN ROYALL
September 20, 1934

HUDGINS, J., delivered the opinion of the court.

The only question presented by this record is whether the will of Mrs. M. Lou Bowen Kroll had been revoked shortly before her death.

The uncontroverted facts are as follows: On the 4th day of September, 1932, Mrs. Kroll signed a will, typewritten on five sheets of legal cap paper; the signature appeared on the last page duly attested by three subscribing witnesses. H. P. Brittain, the executor named in the will, was given possession of the instrument for safe-keeping. A codicil typed on the top third of one sheet of paper dated September 15, 1932, was signed by the testatrix in the presence of two subscribing witnesses. Possession of this instrument was given to Judge S. M. B. Coulling, the attorney who prepared both documents.

On September 19, 1932, [15 days after signing the will], at the request of Mrs. Kroll, Judge Coulling, and Mr. Brittain took the will and the codicil to her home where she told her attorney, in the presence of Mr. Brittain and another, to destroy both. But instead of destroying the papers, at the suggestion of Judge Coulling, she decided to retain them as memoranda, to be used as such in the event she decided to execute a new will. Upon the back of the manuscript cover, which was fastened to the five sheets by metal clasps, in the handwriting of Judge Coulling, signed by Mrs. Kroll, there is the following notation: "This will null and void and to be only held by H. P. Brittain, instead of being destroyed, as a memorandum for another will if I desire to make same. This 19 Sept 1932 M. LOU BOWEN KROLL."

The same notation was made upon the back of the sheet on which the codicil was written, except that the name, S. M. B. Coulling, was substituted for H. P. Brittain; this was likewise signed by Mrs. Kroll.

Mrs. Kroll died October 2, 1932, [less than a month after signing the will], leaving numerous nephews and nieces, some of whom were not mentioned in her will, and an estate valued at approximately $200,000. On motion of some of the beneficiaries, the will and codicil were offered for probate. All the interested parties including the heirs at law were convened, and the jury found that the instruments dated September 4th and 15, 1932, were the last will and testament of Mrs. M. Lou Bowen Kroll. From an order sustaining the verdict and probating the will this writ of error was allowed.

For more than one hundred years, the means by which a duly executed will may be revoked, have been prescribed by statute. The statute provides that: "No will or codicil, or any part thereof, shall be revoked, unless by a subsequent will or codicil, or by some writing declaring an intention to revoke the same, and executed in the manner in which a will is required to be executed, or by the testator, or some person in his presence and by his direction, cutting, tearing, burning, obliterating, canceling, or destroying the same, or the signature thereto, with the intent to revoke."

The notations, dated September 19, 1932, are not wholly in the handwriting of the testatrix, nor are her signatures thereto attached attested by subscribing witnesses; hence under the statute they are ineffectual as "some writing declaring an intention to revoke." The faces of the two instruments bear no physical evidence of any cutting, tearing, burning, obliterating, canceling, or destroying. The only contention made by appellants is, that the notation written in the presence, and with the approval, of Mrs. Kroll, on the back of the manuscript cover in the one instance, and on the back of the sheet containing the codicil in the other, constitute "canceling" within the meaning of the statute.

Both parties concede that to effect revocation of a duly executed will, in any of the methods prescribed by statute, two things are necessary: (1) The doing of one of the acts specified, (2) accompanied by the intent to revoke -- the animo revocandi. Proof of either, without proof of the other, is insufficient.

The proof established the intention to revoke. The entire controversy is confined to the acts used in carrying out that purpose. The testatrix adopted the suggestion of her attorney to revoke her will by written memoranda, admittedly ineffectual as revocations by subsequent writings. But appellants contend the memoranda, in the handwriting of another, and testatrix's signatures, are sufficient to effect revocation by cancellation.

The authorities hold that revocation of a will by cancellation within the meaning of the statute, contemplates marks or lines across the written parts of the instrument, or a physical defacement, or some mutilation of the writing itself, with the intent to revoke. If written words are used for the purpose, they must be so placed as to physically affect the written portion of the will, not merely on blank parts of the paper on which the will is written. If the writing intended to be the act of cancelling, does not mutilate, or erase, or deface, or otherwise physically come in contact with any part of written words of the will, it cannot be given any greater weight than a similar writing on a separate sheet of paper, which identifies the will referred to, just as definitely, as does the writing on the back. If a will may be revoked by writing on the back, separable from the will, it may be done by a writing not on the will. This the statute forbids.

The learned trial judge, A. C. Buchanan, in his written opinion, pertinently said:

> "The statute prescribes certain ways of executing a will, and it must be so executed in order to be valid, regardless of how clear and specific the intent. It also provides certain ways of revoking and it must be done so in order to be a valid revocation, regardless of intent."

The same reasoning led the Illinois court to the same conclusion in Dowling v. Gilliland, where it is said:

> "The great weight of authority is to the effect that the mere writing upon a will which does not in any wise physically obliterate or cancel the same is insufficient to work a destruction of a will by cancellation, even though the writing may express an intention to revoke and cancel. This appears to be the better rule. To hold otherwise would be to give to words written in pencil, and not attested to by witnesses nor executed in the manner provided by the statute, the same effect as if they had been so attested."

The attempted revocation is ineffectual, because testatrix intended to revoke her will by subsequent writings not executed as required by statute, and because it does not in any wise physically obliterate, mutilate, deface, or cancel any written parts of the will.

For the reasons stated, the judgment of the trial court is affirmed.

Affirmed.

Because it is important that the revocatory acts be performed on the will itself, virtually never should wills be executed as duplicate originals. There should be only one original will – only one will which has legal significance, so that the revocatory acts performed on that will clearly revoke the will.

A lawyer will always keep a Xerox copy, or an electronic copy, of every will executed by a client of the attorney. These copies kept by the lawyer might be useful for proving the contents of the will if the will itself were destroyed by some catastrophic event, such as the client's whole house being burned down. Electronic copies are also very handy when a client comes in to make a few changes to a pre-existing will. However, the basic rule is that it is only the one, original, properly executed will which has any legal significance. If the original will cannot be found, then legally, there is a very strong presumption that the testator revoked the will. The following case illustrates one reason why there should never be more than one original version of a will.

Supreme Court of Alabama.
Katherine Crapps Harrison v. Mae S. Bird, as administratrix of the Estate of Daisy Virginia Speer, deceased
May 28, 1993

HOUSTON, JUSTICE.

The proponent of a will appeals from a judgment of the Circuit Court of Montgomery County holding that the estate of Daisy Virginia Speer, deceased, should be administered as an intestate estate and confirming the letters of administration granted by the probate court to Mae S. Bird.

The following pertinent facts are undisputed:
Daisy Virginia Speer executed a will in November 1989, in which she named Katherine Crapps Harrison as the main beneficiary of her estate. The original of the will was retained by Ms. Speer's attorney and a duplicate original was given to Ms. Harrison. On March 4, 1991, Ms. Speer telephoned her attorney and advised him that she wanted to revoke her will. Thereafter, Ms. Speer's attorney or his secretary, in the presence of each other, tore the will into four pieces. The attorney then wrote Ms. Speer a letter, informing her that he had "revoked" her will as she had instructed and that he was enclosing the pieces of the will so that she could verify that he had torn up the original. In the letter, the attorney specifically stated, "As it now stands, you are without a will."

Ms. Speer died on September 3, 1991. Upon her death, the postmarked letter from her attorney was found among her personal effects, but the four pieces of the will were not found. Thereafter, on September 17, 1991, the Probate Court of Montgomery County granted letters of administration on the estate of Ms. Speer, to Mae S. Bird, a cousin of Ms. Speer. On October 11, 1991, Ms. Harrison filed for probate a document purporting to be the last will and testament of Ms. Speer and naming Ms. Harrison as executrix. Thereafter, Ms. Bird filed an answer contesting the will on the grounds that Ms. Speer had revoked her will.

The circuit court ruled in part that Ms. Speer's will was not lawfully revoked when it was destroyed by her attorney at her direction and with her consent, but not in her presence; and that, based on the fact that the pieces of the destroyed will were delivered to Ms. Speer's home but were not found after her death, there arose a presumption that Ms. Speer thereafter revoked the will herself.

The circuit court held that the estate should be administered as an intestate estate and confirmed the letters of administration issued by the probate court to Ms. Bird. The case is here on appeal.

If the evidence establishes that Ms. Speer had possession of the will before her death, but the will is not found among her personal effects after her death, a presumption arises that she destroyed the will. Furthermore, if she destroys the copy of the will in her possession, a presumption arises that she has revoked her will and all duplicates, even though a duplicate exists that is not in her possession. However, this presumption of revocation is rebuttable and the burden of rebutting the presumption is on the proponent of the will.

Based on the foregoing, we conclude that under the facts of this case there existed a presumption that Ms. Speer destroyed her will and thus revoked it. Therefore, the burden shifted to Ms. Harrison to present sufficient evidence to rebut that presumption -- to present sufficient evidence to convince the trier of fact that the absence of the will from Ms. Speer's personal effects after her death was not due to Ms. Speer's destroying and thus revoking the will.

From a careful review of the record, we conclude, as did the trial court, that the

evidence presented by Ms. Harrison was not sufficient to rebut the presumption that Ms. Speer destroyed her will with the intent to revoke it. We, therefore, affirm the trial court's judgment.
Affirmed.

Generally speaking, clients should never attempt to make any changes to a will by making any marks on the original will, or by crossing out any provisions in the original will. Although the cross-outs might work as a partial revocation, that partial revocation is likely to have the effect of increasing the size of some other gift, and that new gift would not be made with the proper attestation by two witnesses. So partial revocations should never be attempted by marks on an existing will.

More importantly, if a will is found with some marks on it, there is almost no way of ascertaining who actually made the marks. Were the marks made by the testator? Or by some disappointed beneficiary, who found the will and decided to try to change the provisions of the will after the death of the testator?

The serious lack of safeguards is why the result in the following case came as such a surprise in 2011 to most of the members of the probate bar.

Colorado Court of Appeal.
In re the ESTATE OF David SCHUMACHER, deceased.
Maria Caldwell, Petitioner–Appellant,
v.
Deborah Caldwell, Respondent–Appellee.
April 14, 2011.

Opinion by Judge MÁRQUEZ.

Petitioner, Maria Caldwell, appeals the probate court's order giving testamentary effect to words crossed out on decedent's holographic will. We affirm.

I. Background

On December 1, 2004, David Schumacher (decedent) executed a holographic will, which contained a clause devising shares of Meyers Land & Cattle stock to decedent's cousins, petitioner, Maria Caldwell, Cheryl Smart, and respondent, Deborah Caldwell.

On January 12, 2006, decedent met with his attorney, Michael Gilbert, to create a typed will. In a later hearing, attorney Gilbert testified he had no specific recollection whether he saw the original will or only the photocopy. Attorney Gilbert's copy of the will included lines crossing out the names of petitioner and Cheryl as remainder devisees of all the shares of the stock. Attorney Gilbert testified:

> "What decedent told me was that he had prepared a holographic will and subsequent to preparing it he had decided that he did not want his stock to be

given to two of his three cousins, and those names had been crossed out on the copy of the will which I had. Decedent told me that, except for those deletions, he wanted me to prepare a will that contained the same dispositive provisions as in his original will from December of 2004.

I asked decedent about the change, why Maria and Cheryl's names had been deleted and essentially what he told me was that he felt closest to his cousin, Deborah, and he had changed his mind and he wanted the stock after the death of his mother to go to Deborah alone."

However, attorney Gilbert did not ask decedent who made the cross-outs.

Attorney Gilbert then drafted a typed will pursuant to decedent's instructions and transmitted it to decedent. Decedent died on July 3, 2007 without ever executing the typed will. After decedent's death, attorney Gilbert tendered the copy of the holographic will to the probate court.

Approximately six months prior to his death, decedent had sent several boxes of his personal records to his secretary with instructions that she store them in her garage and sort them out. When decedent died, decedent's secretary, her sister, and decedent's personal representative found, in an unopened box, the original holographic will signed by decedent and containing the lines crossing out the names of Maria and Cheryl as devisees of the stock. The personal representative took the original holographic will to attorney Gilbert, who tendered it to the probate court.

On April 14, 2008, the personal representative filed a petition for determination of validity of decedent's holographic will dated December 1, 2004. Petitioner and Cheryl later filed a petition for construction of the holographic will to determine the validity of the markings on the will.

The probate court held a hearing in June 2009 in which attorney Gilbert and a handwriting expert testified. The probate court later issued a written order, finding that decedent performed a "revocatory act" on the will by crossing out petitioner's and Cheryl's names, with the intent and for the purpose of revoking part of his holographic will. The court ordered that "the strikethroughs in the Holographic Will can and must be given effect in probate."

Both Cheryl and Maria appealed the probate court's order. Petitioner does not challenge the validity of the will without the cross-outs, but contends that the probate court erred in giving testamentary effect to the cross-outs when it probated the will.

II. Sufficiency of the Evidence

Prior to 1995, section 15–11–507 only allowed for total revocation of a will. However, in 1995 the General Assembly revised the statute to allow part of a will to be revoked if certain formalities have been satisfied. Accordingly, now, under C.R.S. 15–11–507(1), C.R.S.2010:

"A will *or any part thereof* is revoked:

...

> (b) By performing a revocatory act on the will, if the testator performed the act with the intent and for the purpose of revoking the will *or part of it* or if another individual performed the act in the testator's conscious presence and by the testator's direction. For purposes of this paragraph (b), "revocatory act on the will" includes burning, tearing, canceling, obliterating, or destroying the will or any part of it." (Emphasis added.)

Here, the probate court found that decedent made the cross-outs with the intent and purpose to effectuate a partial revocation of the devise of the stock to petitioner and Cheryl. It based its decision primarily upon the testimony and affidavit of attorney Gilbert.

Petitioner's expert handwriting analyst, whose testimony was based on a comparison of the photocopy of the will and the original, opined that "it was not possible to determine who wrote the cross-outs" on the will.

III. Performance of Act

Attorney Gilbert's testimony, together with the evidence, as discussed below, that the original will with the crossed-out portions was found in decedent's possession, is sufficient evidence to demonstrate that decedent made the cross-outs.

IV. Possession

Neither petitioner nor respondent disputes that if a properly executed will containing tears or cancellations is known to be in the possession of the testator at the time of death, the testator is presumed to have revoked all or some of it. Rather, what is contested is whether the original holographic will was in fact in decedent's possession upon his death.

Here, the probate court found that the will was in decedent's possession when it was at his secretary's house "because he employed the secretary." Petitioner, however, contends that the decedent must have been in exclusive possession of the will for the presumption to apply, and because the will was found at decedent's secretary's house, it was not in his exclusive possession. We conclude petitioner views possession too narrowly.

Other Colorado cases addressing the last known possession of a missing will have not used the word "exclusive." Thus, we conclude the will need only be found in testator's possession upon death.

The evidence necessary to find possession is contingent on the factual circumstances of each case.

Moreover, even when others have had access to the will, "the law will not presume fraud, commission of a crime or compulsion." Thus, the presumption is not overcome when other persons who had access to the will, who may have had a motive or an opportunity to perform the revocatory act, did not know of its existence or would not benefit from the revocation. See, e.g., In re Hildebrand's Estate, Pa. (1950) (evidence that beneficiary had access to safe deposit box with will in it, but did not know it was in the box, did not overcome presumption of possession).

The record contains evidence that decedent had given the boxes of his own effects to his secretary to organize and keep on his behalf, and the will was found among many of his other personal items. Unbeknownst to the secretary, the boxed items included the will. There is no evidence that anyone but the secretary, her sister, and the personal representative had access to the will. Additionally, none of them benefited under the will, and all three signed affidavits averring that at no point did they alter the will. Thus, the record supports the court's finding that it was in decedent's possession upon death.

The probate court also properly concluded that "decedent hired the secretary and as such, the decedent was still in possession and/or control of the will because he employed the secretary." An employee acts on behalf of his or her employer when the employee is acting within the scope of his or her employment. Here, the probate court determined the secretary stored decedent's effects based on his instructions and her position as his employee, and because the question whether an employee is acting within the scope of the employment is a question of fact for the trial court, we must accept its determination.

Based on the facts of this case, we are satisfied that the probate court did not err in finding the will was still in decedent's possession upon his death.

V. Intent and Purpose

Petitioner also contends that there is no evidence to prove that decedent made the cross-outs with the intent and purpose to revoke the devise of stocks to her. We disagree.

Extrinsic evidence is admissible to establish the testator's intent.

Here, the court determined that clear and convincing evidence established decedent's intent and purpose to revoke the devise of stock through the cross-outs. The court's determination was based on attorney Gilbert's testimony.

We conclude that the court's finding is adequately supported by sufficient evidence in the record. The court's finding that decedent was in possession of the will at the time of his death also establishes a presumption the he made the cross-outs with the intent and purpose of partial revocation.

We also reject petitioner's contention that the totality of the evidence demonstrates that the "cross-outs were so that attorney Gilbert could draft a new will." Petitioner cites the lack of a signature by the cross-outs as evidence that decedent did not intend the partial revocation to be final. However, it was the court's prerogative to give the most weight to attorney Gilbert's testimony that the cross-outs represented decedent's then current intent and purpose to revoke that portion of his will, and we will not disturb that choice on appeal.

Because both elements of partial revocation as required by section 15-11-507 have been met and are adequately supported by the record, the probate court's decision to give the cross-outs testamentary effect was not erroneous.

VI. Section 15–11–503

Petitioner contends that the probate court erred in applying section 15–11–503, C.R.S.2010, because (1) the changes were not signed by decedent as his will and (2) there is no showing "by clear and convincing evidence" that decedent intended the cross-outs to be a partial revocation of his will. We perceive no reversible error.

Section 15–11–503, [the Harmless Error provision] provides that:

> (1) Although a document, or writing added upon a document, was not executed in compliance with section 15–11–502, the document or writing is treated as if it had been executed in compliance with that section if the proponent of the document or writing establishes by clear and convincing evidence that the decedent intended the document or writing to constitute:
>
> ...
>
> (b) A partial or complete revocation of the will.
>
> ...
>
> (2) Subsection (1) of this section shall apply only if the document is signed or acknowledged by the decedent as his or her will....

The purpose of section 15–11–503 is to give probate courts a mechanism to cure minor errors in the formal requirements of will execution established by section 15–11–502.

Here, petitioner is not challenging the probate of the entire holographic will, but rather only whether the cross-outs should be given testamentary effect. And, as stated above, the court correctly found attorney Gilbert's testimony to be clear and convincing evidence of decedent's intent to revoke part of his will. Petitioner argues that there is no signature by the cross-outs, but does not explain how the lack of a signature fails to comply with section 15–11–502, and to the extent she broadly contends that the will fails to comply with statutory formalities and therefore the cross-outs should not be entitled to probate, she does not identify the formalities to which she is referring.

Section 15–11–503(1) permits courts to probate wills and documents that are not in compliance with section 15–11–502 so long as the testator's intent has been proved through clear and convincing evidence. Although section 15–11–503(2) requires that the document be signed by the testator as his or her will in order for the document to be probated, we find nothing in section 15–11–502 or section 15–11–503(2) that requires a signature by a cross-out in order to effectuate a partial revocation. Rather, the statutes require that the document be acknowledged or signed by the testator as his or her will, but not that a revocation have an additional acknowledgement or signature.

In addition, section 15–11–507, which governs the formalities of an effective partial revocation, does not require additional signatures. Therefore, we cannot see how the probate court's citation to section 15–11–503 here requires reversal, and thus, we uphold the probate of the will.

The order is affirmed.

What will the impact of this decision be on later cases? How much proof will be required to insure that a *beneficiary* has not increased his or her share by means of cross-outs? Is it possible to open a will which was in a sealed envelope, make a few cross-outs, and then reseal the will in a new envelope? Does a partial revocation actually create new gifts, or enlarge existing gifts, without any of the formalities required for executing a will?

B. REVOCATION BY DIVORCE

In many jurisdictions there may be a statute that specifically revokes various provisions of a will when the testator gets a divorce. Statutes may revoke the whole will upon the entry of a decree of divorce. Or the statute may say that only the provisions for the ex-spouse are revoked, leaving gifts to various relatives of the ex-spouse as valid parts of the will. Or the statute may state that all the provisions for the ex-spouse, and the relatives of the ex-spouse, are automatically revoked. Virtually always it would be possible to draft around such statutes – to state, for example, that the gifts to the nieces and nephews by marriage are intended to survive any divorce.

But whenever a testator becomes divorced from a former spouse, the applicable statute should be consulted – and a new will should be written.

An example of a typical divorce statute follows.

C.R.S.§ 15-11-804. Revocation of probate and nonprobate transfers by divorce; no revocation by other changes of circumstances

(1) Definitions. As used in this section, unless the context otherwise requires:

(a) "Disposition or appointment of property" includes a transfer of an item of property or any other benefit to a beneficiary designated in a governing instrument.

(b) "Divorce or annulment" means any divorce or annulment, or any dissolution or declaration of invalidity of a marriage, that would exclude the spouse as a surviving spouse within the meaning of section 15-11-802. A decree of separation that does not terminate the status of husband and wife is not a divorce for purposes of this section.

(c) "Divorced individual" includes an individual whose marriage has been annulled.

(d) "Governing instrument" refers to a governing instrument executed by the divorced individual before the divorce or annulment of his or her marriage to his or her former spouse.

(e) "Relative of the divorced individual's former spouse" means an individual who is related to the divorced individual's former spouse by blood, adoption, or affinity and who, after the divorce or annulment, is not related to the divorced individual by blood, adoption, or affinity.

(f) "Revocable" with respect to a disposition, appointment, provision, or nomination, means one under which the divorced individual, at the time of the divorce or annulment, was alone empowered, by law or under the governing instrument, to cancel the designation in favor of his or her former spouse or former spouse's relative, whether or not the divorced individual was then empowered to designate himself or herself in place of his or her former spouse or in place of his or her former spouse's relative and whether or not the divorced individual then had the capacity to exercise the power.

(2) Revocation upon divorce. Except as provided by the express terms of a governing instrument, a court order, or a contract relating to the division of the marital estate made between the divorced individuals before or after the marriage, divorce, or annulment, the divorce or annulment of a marriage:

(a) Revokes any revocable (i) disposition or appointment of property made by a divorced individual to his or her former spouse in a governing instrument and any disposition or appointment created by law or in a governing instrument to a relative of the divorced individual's former spouse, (ii) provision in a governing instrument conferring a general or nongeneral power of appointment on the divorced individual's former spouse or on a relative of the divorced individual's former spouse, and (iii) nomination in a governing instrument nominating a divorced individual's former spouse or a relative of the divorced individual's former spouse to serve in any fiduciary or representative capacity, including a personal representative, executor, trustee, conservator, agent, or guardian; and

(b) Severs the interests of the former spouses in property held by them at the time of the divorce or annulment as joint tenants with the right of survivorship or as community property with the right of survivorship, transforming the interests of the former spouses into tenancies in common. ...

(4) Effect of revocation. Provisions of a governing instrument are given effect as if the former spouse and relatives of the former spouse disclaimed all provisions revoked by this section or, in the case of a revoked nomination in a fiduciary or representative capacity as if the former spouse and relatives of the former spouse died immediately before the divorce or annulment.

(5) Revival if divorce nullified. Provisions revoked solely by this section are revived by the divorced individual's remarriage to the former spouse or by a nullification of the divorce or annulment.

(6) No revocation for other change of circumstances. No change of

circumstances other than as described in this section and in section 15-11-803 effects a revocation.

Note: Part (8)(b) of this statute is at the end of the following case. Once you have read the case, you will understand why that part of the statute is far more meaningful after you have read the case.

Supreme Court of the United States.
DONNA RAE EGELHOFF, PETITIONER v. SAMANTHA EGELHOFF, A MINOR, BY AND THROUGH HER NATURAL PARENT KATE BREINER, AND DAVID EGELHOFF
March 21, 2001

JUSTICE THOMAS delivered the opinion of the Court.

A Washington statute provides that the designation of a spouse as the beneficiary of a nonprobate asset is revoked automatically upon divorce. We are asked to decide whether the Employee Retirement Income Security Act of 1974 (ERISA), pre-empts that statute to the extent it applies to ERISA plans. We hold that it does.

I

Petitioner Donna Rae Egelhoff was married to David A. Egelhoff. Mr. Egelhoff was employed by the Boeing Company, which provided him with a life insurance policy and a pension plan. Both plans were governed by ERISA, and Mr. Egelhoff designated his wife as the beneficiary under both. In April 1994, the Egelhoffs divorced. Just over two months later, Mr. Egelhoff died intestate following an automobile accident. At that time, Mrs. Egelhoff remained the listed beneficiary under both the life insurance policy and the pension plan. The life insurance proceeds, totaling $ 46,000, were paid to her.

Respondents Samantha and David Egelhoff, Mr. Egelhoff's children by a previous marriage, are his statutory heirs under state law. They sued petitioner in Washington state court to recover the life insurance proceeds. Respondents relied on a Washington statute that provides:

> "If a marriage is dissolved or invalidated, a provision made prior to that event that relates to the payment or transfer at death of the decedent's interest in a nonprobate asset in favor of or granting an interest or power to the decedent's former spouse is revoked. A provision affected by this section must be interpreted, and the nonprobate asset affected passes, as if the former spouse failed to survive the decedent, having died at the time of entry of the decree of dissolution or declaration of invalidity." Wash. Rev. Code.

That statute applies to "all nonprobate assets, wherever situated, held at the time of entry by a superior court of this state of a decree of dissolution of marriage or a declaration of invalidity." It defines "nonprobate asset" to include "a life insurance policy, employee benefit plan, annuity or similar contract, or individual retirement account."

Respondents argued that they were entitled to the life insurance proceeds because the Washington statute disqualified Mrs. Egelhoff as a beneficiary, and in the absence of a qualified named beneficiary, the proceeds would pass to them as Mr. Egelhoff's heirs. In a separate action, respondents also sued to recover the pension plan benefits. Respondents again argued that the Washington statute disqualified Mrs. Egelhoff as a beneficiary and they were thus entitled to the benefits under the plan.

The trial courts, concluding that both the insurance policy and the pension plan "should be administered in accordance" with ERISA, granted summary judgment to petitioner in both cases. The Washington Court of Appeals consolidated the cases and reversed. It concluded that the Washington statute was not pre-empted by ERISA. Applying the statute, it held that respondents were entitled to the proceeds of both the insurance policy and the pension plan.

The Supreme Court of Washington affirmed. ...

To resolve the conflict, we granted certiorari.

II

Petitioner argues that the Washington statute falls within the terms of ERISA's express pre-emption provision and that it is pre-empted by ERISA under traditional principles of conflict pre-emption. Because we conclude that the statute is expressly pre-empted by ERISA, we address only the first argument.

ERISA's pre-emption section, 29 U.S.C. § 1144(a), states that ERISA "shall supersede any and all State laws insofar as they may now or hereafter relate to any employee benefit plan" covered by ERISA. We have observed repeatedly that this broadly worded provision is "clearly expansive." But at the same time, we have recognized that the term "relate to" cannot be taken "to extend to the furthest stretch of its indeterminacy," or else "for all practical purposes pre-emption would never run its course."

We have held that a state law relates to an ERISA plan "if it has a connection with or reference to such a plan." Petitioner focuses on the "connection with" part of this inquiry. Acknowledging that "connection with" is scarcely more restrictive than "relate to," we have cautioned against an "uncritical literalism" that would make preemption turn on "infinite connections." Instead, "to determine whether a state law has the forbidden connection, we look both to 'the objectives of the ERISA statute as a guide to the scope of the state law that Congress understood would survive,' as well as to the nature of the effect of the state law on ERISA plans."

Applying this framework, petitioner argues that the Washington statute has an impermissible connection with ERISA plans. We agree. The statute binds ERISA plan administrators to a particular choice of rules for determining beneficiary status. The administrators must pay benefits to the beneficiaries chosen by state law, rather than to those identified in the plan documents. The statute thus implicates an area of core ERISA concern. In particular, it runs counter to ERISA's commands that a plan shall "specify the basis on which payments are made to and from the plan," and that the fiduciary shall administer the plan "in accordance with the documents and instruments governing the plan," making payments to a "beneficiary" who is "designated by a participant, or by the terms of the plan." In other words, unlike generally applicable laws regulating "areas where ERISA has nothing to say," which we have upheld notwithstanding their incidental effect on ERISA plans, this statute governs the payment of benefits, a central matter of plan administration.

The Washington statute also has a prohibited connection with ERISA plans because it interferes with nationally uniform plan administration. One of the principal goals of ERISA is to enable employers "to establish a uniform administrative scheme, which provides a set of standard procedures to guide processing of claims and disbursement of benefits." Uniformity is impossible, however, if plans are subject to different legal obligations in different States.

The Washington statute at issue here poses precisely that threat. Plan administrators cannot make payments simply by identifying the beneficiary specified by the plan documents. Instead they must familiarize themselves with state statutes so that they can determine whether the named beneficiary's status has been "revoked" by operation of law. And in this context the burden is exacerbated by the choice-of-law problems that may confront an administrator when the employer is located in one State, the plan participant lives in another, and the participant's former spouse lives in a third. In such a situation, administrators might find that plan payments are subject to conflicting legal obligations.

To be sure, the Washington statute protects administrators from liability for making payments to the named beneficiary unless they have "actual knowledge of the dissolution or other invalidation of marriage," and it permits administrators to refuse to make payments until any dispute among putative beneficiaries is resolved. But if administrators do pay benefits, they will face the risk that a court might later find that they had "actual knowledge" of a divorce. If they instead decide to await the results of litigation before paying benefits, they will simply transfer to the beneficiaries the costs of delay and uncertainty. Requiring ERISA administrators to master the relevant laws of 50 States and to contend with litigation would undermine the congressional goal of "minimizing the administrative and financial burdens" on plan administrators -- burdens ultimately borne by the beneficiaries.

We recognize that all state laws create some potential for a lack of uniformity. But differing state regulations affecting an ERISA plan's "system for processing claims and paying benefits" impose "precisely the burden that ERISA pre-emption was intended to avoid." And as we have noted, the statute at issue here directly conflicts with ERISA's requirements that plans be administered, and benefits be paid, in accordance with plan documents. We conclude that the Washington statute has a "connection with" ERISA plans and is therefore pre-empted.

III

Respondents emphasize that the Washington statute involves both family law and probate law, areas of traditional state regulation. There is indeed a presumption against pre-emption in areas of traditional state regulation such as family law. But that presumption can be overcome where, as here, Congress has made clear its desire for pre-emption. Accordingly, we have not hesitated to find state family law pre-empted when it conflicts with ERISA or relates to ERISA plans. See, e.g., Boggs v. Boggs, 520 U.S. 833 (1997) (holding that ERISA pre-empts a state community property law permitting the testamentary transfer of an interest in a spouse's pension plan benefits).

Finally, respondents argue that if ERISA pre-empts this statute, then it also must pre-empt the various state statutes providing that a murdering heir is not entitled to receive property as a result of the killing. In the ERISA context, these "slayer" statutes could revoke the beneficiary status of someone who murdered a plan participant. Those statutes are not before us, so we do not decide the issue. We note, however, that the principle underlying the statutes -- which have been adopted by nearly every State -- is well established in the law and has a long historical pedigree predating ERISA. And because the statutes are more or less uniform nationwide, their interference with the aims of ERISA is at least debatable.

The judgment of the Supreme Court of Washington is reversed, and the case is remanded for further proceedings not inconsistent with this opinion.

It is so ordered.

Final part of the sample revocation statute quoted before this case.

C.R.S. 15-11-804(8)

(b) If this section or any part of this section *is preempted by federal law* with respect to a payment, an item of property, or any other benefit covered by this section, *a former spouse*, relative of the former spouse, or any other person *who*, not for value, *received a payment*, item of property, or any other benefit *to which that person is not entitled under this section is obligated to return that payment*, item of property, or benefit, or is personally liable for the amount of the payment or the value of the item of property or benefit, *to the person who would have been entitled to it were this section or part of this section not preempted.* (Emphasis added.)

Wow! Is this an attempt by the Colorado legislature to nullify the preceding U.S. Supreme Court case? Does a state legislature have authority to do such a thing?

C. REVOCATION BY MARRIAGE OR BIRTH OF CHILD

(1) OMITTED SPOUSE

In some jurisdictions a will may be revoked by the subsequent marriage of the testator. In all jurisdictions there is likely to be some sort of statutory provision for an "omitted spouse," a person who married the testator after the will was signed, and was thus omitted from the testator's will.

The following statute is a typical statute protecting an omitted spouse.

C.R.S. § 15-11-301. Entitlement of spouse; premarital will

(1) If a testator's surviving spouse married the testator after the testator executed his or her will, the surviving spouse is entitled to receive, as an intestate share, no less than the value of the share of the estate he or she would have received if the testator had died intestate as to that portion of the testator's estate, if any, that neither is devised outright to nor in trust for the benefit of a child of the testator who was born before the testator married the surviving spouse and who is not a child of the surviving spouse nor is so devised to a descendant of such a child, or passes under section 15-11-603 or 15-11-604 to such a child or to a descendant of such a child, unless:

(a) It appears from the will or other evidence that the will was made in contemplation of the testator's marriage to the surviving spouse;

(b) The will expresses the intention that it is to be effective notwithstanding any subsequent marriage; or

(c) The testator provided for the spouse by transfer outside the will and the intent that the transfer be in lieu of a testamentary provision is shown by the testator's statements or is reasonably inferred from the amount of the transfer or other evidence.

(2) In satisfying the share provided by this section, devises made by the will to the testator's surviving spouse, if any, are applied first, and other devises, other than a devise outright to or in trust for the benefit of a child of the testator who was born before the testator married the surviving spouse and who is not a child of the surviving spouse or a devise or substitute gift under section 15-11-603 or 15-11-604 to a descendant of such a child, abate as provided in section 15-12-902.

Kids protected

Court of Appeal of California.
Estate of RUSSELL DONOVAN SHANNON, Deceased.
GILBERT A. BROWN, as Executor, Petitioner and Appellant, v. BEATRICE MARIE SALESKI, Objector and Respondent
October 24, 1990

OPINION BY: HUFFMAN

Gilbert A. Brown, executor of the will of Lila Demos Shannon (also known as Lila King Demos), appeals on behalf of Lila's estate from an order of the probate court denying her petition for determination of heirship as an omitted spouse under Probate Code section 6560 in the estate of Russell Donovan Shannon. We reverse.

Factual and Procedural Background

On January 25, 1974, Russell, an unmarried widower, executed his last will and testament, naming his daughter, Beatrice Marie Saleski, executrix and sole beneficiary. The will also provided his grandson, Donald Saleski, would inherit his estate in the event Beatrice did not survive him for thirty days and contained a disinheritance clause which provided as follows:

> "Seventh: I have intentionally omitted all other living persons and relatives. If any devisee, legatee, beneficiary under this Will, or any legal heir of mine, person or persons claiming under any of them, or other person or persons shall contest this Will or attack or seek to impair or invalidate any of its provisions or conspire with or voluntarily assist anyone attempting to do any of those things mentioned, in that event, I specifically disinherit such person or persons. If any Court finds that such person or persons are lawful heirs and entitled to participate in my estate, then in that event I bequeath each of them the sum of one ($ 1.00) dollar and no more."

On April 27, 1986, Russell married Lila. On February 22, 1988, Russell died. He did not make any changes in his will after his marriage to Lila and before his death. His 1974 will was admitted to probate May 9, 1988, and Beatrice was named executrix of his estate.

On September 27, 1988, Lila filed a petition for family allowance, to set apart probate homestead and or determination of entitlement to estate distribution as an omitted surviving spouse. The court denied the petition for family allowance and Lila withdrew her petition to set apart probate homestead. The remaining issue of Lila's entitlement to share in Russell's estate was heard December 14, 1988.

On March 24, 1989, the probate court issued its order denying Lila's petition to determine heirship. She timely appealed . During the pendency of this appeal, Lila died and her son Brown was named executor of her estate and substituted in her place as appellant.

Discussion

On appeal, Lila contends she was a pretermitted spouse within the meaning of section 6560 and does not fall under any of the exceptions under section 6561 which would preclude her from sharing in Russell's estate as an omitted spouse. We agree and reverse.

> Section 6560 states: "Except as provided in Section 6561, if a testator fails to provide by will for his or her surviving spouse who married the testator after the execution of the will, the omitted spouse shall receive a share in the estate consisting of the following property in the estate: (a) The one-half of the community property that belongs to the testator; (b) The one-half of the quasi-community property that belongs to the testator; and (c) A share of the separate property of the testator equal in value to that which the spouse would have received if the testator had died intestate, but in no event is the share to be more than one-half the value of the separate property in the estate."

> Section 6561 states: "The spouse does not receive a share of the estate under Section 6560 if any of the following is established: (a) The testator's failure to provide for the spouse in the will was intentional and that intention appears from the will; (b) The testator provided for the spouse by transfer outside the will and the intention that the transfer be in lieu of a testamentary provision is shown by statements of the testator or from the amount of the transfer or by other evidence.; or (c) The spouse made a valid agreement waiving the right to share in the testator's estate."

It is well established section 6560 reflects a strong statutory presumption of revocation of the will as to the omitted spouse based upon public policy. Such presumption is rebutted only if circumstances are such as to fall within the literal terms of one of the exceptions listed in section 6561. The burden of proving that the presumption is rebutted is on the proponents of the will.

Here, Russell failed to provide for Lila in his will. Under the language of section 6560, she is thus an omitted spouse and the crucial inquiry becomes whether Beatrice met the burden of rebutting this presumption. Specifically, the issues are whether the will shows a specific intent to exclude Lila pursuant to section 6561, subdivision (a) and whether Beatrice presented sufficient evidence to show Russell had intended to otherwise provide for Lila outside of his will in lieu of her taking under it pursuant to section 6561, subdivision (b), or to show Lila waived her rights to share in his estate under section 6561, subdivision (c).

The will on its face does not evidence an intent on Russell's part to disinherit Lila. As the presumption under section 6560 is only rebutted by a clear manifestation of such intent on the face of the will, "regardless of what may have been the wishes of the decedent," the section 6561, subdivision (a) exception has not been established.

Estate of Axcelrod, held that a general provision in a will, that the testator "intentionally omitted all of my heirs who are not specifically mentioned herein, intending thereby to disinherit them," may not be construed as mentioning a subsequently acquired spouse in such a way as to show an intention not to make provision for the spouse, where the testator at the time the will was executed had no spouse who could become "an heir."

Case law has also held exclusionary clauses in wills which fail to indicate the testator contemplated the possibility of a future marriage are insufficient to avoid the statutory presumption. Even testamentary clauses specifically disinheriting a named individual whom the testator planned to marry and a clause stating "any other person not specifically mentioned in this Will, whether related by marriage or not" have been held insufficient to disclose the explicit intention of a testator to omit provision for another woman the testator married after executing the will either as a member of the designated disinherited class or as a contemplated spouse. As there is no mention of Lila or the fact of a future marriage in the disinheritance clause of the will, it does not manifest Russell's intent to specifically disinherit Lila as his surviving spouse.

Nor have the circumstances of section 6561, subdivisions (b) or (c) been established. Beatrice asserts a retired California Highway Patrolmen Widow's and Orphan's Fund from which $ 2,000 was paid to Lila as Russell's beneficiary, coupled with a declaration of Russell's attorney "that in the twelve months immediately preceding Russell's death, he informed this declarant that he had remarried and that his wife was independently wealthy and that she had more than he had and that he wanted his daughter to have his estate upon his death," evidence Russell's intent to provide for Lila outside the will in lieu of a testamentary provision and satisfy the requirements of section 6561, subdivision (b).

However, as Lila notes, the evidence of the widows' and orphans' trust fund benefits and Beatrice's attorney's declaration were excluded from evidence at the court hearing on the probate heirship matter making it impossible for the court to base its determination on such claimed transfer.

Even assuming the evidence were properly before the probate court at the time of the hearing, such was insufficient to rebut the presumption of section 6560 because it does not show Russell provided the trust fund benefits for Lila in lieu of sharing in his estate.

Moreover, the facts presented at the probate hearing that Russell and Lila kept their property separate during the course of their marriage is not sufficient to show "a valid agreement waiving the right to share" in each other's estate pursuant to section 6561, subdivision (c).

Beatrice has simply not met her burden of proving Russell's intent to disinherit Lila and rebut the presumption of revocation under section 6560. The probate court therefore erred in denying Lila's petition to determine heirship.

The order denying Lila's petition for heirship is reversed and remanded for further proceedings consistent with this opinion.

Is there any potential liability against the attorney who, knowing the situation and the client's intent, still failed to re-draft the will after the marriage?

(2) Pretermitted Child

There is usually some statutory provision to protect any child who is born to the testator after the testator has signed his or her will. Although there is almost never any statutory requirement that a parent leave anything to a child, the law protects a child who may have been left out of a will by accident. A typical statue follows. Is this statute consistent with what most people would want in the various situations covered by the statute?

C.R.S.§ 15-11-302. Omitted children

(1) Except as provided in subsection (2) of this section, if a testator fails to provide in his or her will for any of his or her children born or adopted after the execution of the will, the omitted after-born or after-adopted child receives a share in the estate as follows:

(a) If the testator had no child living when he or she executed the will, an omitted after-born or after-adopted child receives a share in the estate equal in value to that which the child would have received had the testator died intestate, unless the will devised all or substantially all the estate to the other parent of the omitted child and that other parent survives the testator and is entitled to take under the will.

(b) If the testator has one or more children living when he or she executed the will, and the will devised property or an interest in property to one or more of the then living children, an omitted after-born or after-adopted child is entitled to share in the testator's estate as follows:

(I) The portion of the testator's estate in which the omitted after-born or after-adopted child is entitled to share is limited to devises made to the testator's then living children under the will.

(II) The omitted after-born or after-adopted child is entitled to receive the share of the testator's estate, as limited in subparagraph (I) of this paragraph (b), that the child would have received had the testator included all omitted after-born and after-adopted children with the children to whom devises were made under the will and had given an equal share of the estate to each child.

(III) To the extent feasible, the interest granted an omitted after-born or after-adopted child under this section shall be of the same character, whether equitable or legal, present or future, as that devised to the testator's then living children under the will.

(IV) In satisfying a share provided by this paragraph (b), devises to the testator's children who were living when the will was executed abate ratably. In abating the devises of the then living children, the court shall preserve to the maximum extent possible the character of the testamentary plan adopted by the testator.

(2) Neither paragraph (a) nor (b) of subsection (1) of this section applies if:

(a) It appears from the will that the omission was intentional; or

(b) The testator provided for the omitted after-born or after-adopted child by transfer outside the will and the intent that the transfer be in lieu of a testamentary provision is shown by the testator's statements or is reasonably inferred from the amount of the transfer or other evidence.

(3) If at the time of execution of the will the testator fails to provide in his or her will for a living child solely because he or she believes the child to be dead, the child is entitled to share in the estate as if the child were an omitted after-born or after-adopted child.

The following two cases illustrate the problem of a pretermitted child in states where the statutes are not as detailed as the sample statute above. But would this statute really have changed the result in the following case? Why, or why not?

District Court of Appeal of Florida,
Patricia AZCUNCE, as a beneficiary of the Estate of Rene R. Azcunce, Deceased, Appellant,
v.
ESTATE OF Rene R. AZCUNCE, Deceased, et al., Appellees.
Sept. 17, 1991.

HUBBART, Judge.

The central issue presented by this appeal is whether a child who is born after the execution of her father's will but before the execution of a codicil to the said will is entitled to take a statutory share of her father's estate under Florida's pretermitted child statute-when the will and codicils fail to provide for such child and all the other statutory requirements for pretermitted-child status are otherwise satisfied. We hold that where *inter alia* the subject codicil expressly republishes the original will, as here, the testator's child who is living at the time the codicil is executed is not a pretermitted child within the meaning of the statute. We, accordingly, affirm the final order under review which denies the child herein a statutory share of her father's estate as a pretermitted child.

I

The facts of this case are entirely undisputed. On May 4, 1983, the testator Rene R. Azcunce executed a will which established a trust for the benefit of his surviving spouse and his then - born children: Lisette, Natalie, and Gabriel; the will contained no provision for after-born children. On August 8, 1983, and June 25, 1986, the testator executed two codicils which did not alter in any way this testamentary disposition and also made no provision for after-born children.

On March 14, 1984, the testator's daughter Patricia Azcunce was born - after the first codicil was executed, but before the second codicil was executed. The first codicil expressly republished all the terms of the original will; the second codicil expressly republished all the terms of the original will and first codicil.

On December 30, 1986, the testator, who was thirty-eight (38) years old, unexpectedly died of a heart attack - four months after executing the second codicil. After the will and codicils were admitted to probate, Patricia filed a petition seeking a statutory share of her father's estate as a pretermitted child; the trial court denied this petition. Patricia appeals.

II

The statute on which Patricia relies for a share of her father's estate provides:

> "When a testator omits to provide in his will for any of his children *born or adopted after making the will* and the child has not received a part of the testator's property equivalent to a child's part by way of advancement, the child shall receive a share of the estate equal in value to that he would have received if the testator had died intestate, unless:
>
> (1) It appears from the will that the omission was intentional; or
>
> (2) The testator had one or more children when the will was executed and devised substantially all his estate to the other parent of the pretermitted child.

Without dispute, Patricia was a pretermitted child both at the time the testator's will and the first codicil thereto were executed, as, in each instance, the testator "omitted to provide in his will or codicil for Patricia who was born after the will or codicil was executed"; moreover, Patricia at no time received a part of the testator's property by way of advancement, the will and first codicil do not expressly disinherit Patricia, and the testator did not substantially devise all of his estate to Patricia's mother. The question in this case is whether the testator's execution of the *second* codicil to the will *after* Patricia had been born destroyed her prior statutory status as a pretermitted child.

It is well settled in Florida that, as a general rule, the execution of a codicil to a will has the effect of republishing the prior will as of the date of the codicil. Although this is not an inflexible rule and must at times give way to a contrary intent of the testator, it always applies where, as here, the codicil expressly adopts the terms of the prior will; this is so for the obvious reason that such a result comports with the express intent of the testator.

III

Turning to the instant case, it is clear that the testator's second codicil republished the original will and first codicil because the second codicil expressly so states. This being so, Patricia's prior status as a pretermitted child was destroyed inasmuch as Patricia was alive when the second codicil was executed and was not, as required by Florida's pretermitted child statute, born after such codicil was made. Presumably, if the testator had wished to provide for Patricia, he would have done so in the second codicil as she had been born by that time; because he did not, Patricia was, in effect, disinherited which the testator clearly had the power to do. Indeed, the result we reach herein is in full accord with the results reached by courts throughout the country based on identical circumstances.

To avoid this inevitable result, Patricia argues that the will and two codicils are somehow ambiguous and that, accordingly, the court should have accepted the parol evidence adduced below that the testator intended to provide for Patricia; Patricia also urges that the will should have been voided because the draftsman made a "mistake" in failing to provide for Patricia in the second codicil. These arguments are unavailing. First, there is utterly no ambiguity in the subject will and codicils which would authorize the taking of parol evidence herein, and the trial court was entirely correct in rejecting same. Second, the mistake of which Patricia complains amounts, at best, to the draftsman's alleged professional negligence in failing to apprise the testator of the need to expressly provide for Patricia in the second codicil; this is not the type of mistake which voids a will under Florida statutes.

For the above-stated reasons, the final order under review is, in all respects,

Affirmed.

Levy, Judge (specially concurring).

I write separately only to express my frustration with the apparent inability of the justice system of this State to be in a position to provide relief to someone who is clearly entitled to it, to-wit: Patricia Azcunce, the appellant herein who was the daughter of Rene R. Azcunce.

Rene R. Azcunce (decedent) executed his Last Will and Testament on May 4, 1983. His will established a trust for the benefit of his then born children defined in article Twelfth, Paragraph (a) as "my daughters Lisette and Natalie Azcunce, and my son Gabriel Azcunce". Article Twelfth defined "issue" as "my children [as defined in Paragraph (a) above] and their legitimate natural born and legally adopted lineal decedents (sic)." There was no provision in the will of decedent for after-born children.

On August 8, 1983, the decedent executed a first codicil to his will. The first codicil stated that upon the death of the surviving spouse, accrued income and corpus of the Residuary Estate (Marital Trust) were to be paid to the surviving issue, per stirpes. Furthermore, the first codicil republished all other terms of the will. Thereafter, decedent and his wife had a fourth child, Patricia, who was born on March 14, 1984.

On June 25, 1986, decedent executed a second codicil which removed a certain person as a Trustee in order to qualify for a marital deduction under the federal and state tax laws. Testimony from the attorney who prepared the second codicil revealed that the decedent had contacted him and mentioned that he (the decedent) and his wife had another child. At the request of the decedent, the attorney prepared a new will which included that child, Patricia, as a beneficiary. A copy of the new will was mailed to the decedent on April 4, 1986, for the decedent to review. The new will, however, was not executed due to a disagreement that the attorney had with the decedent over the worth of decedent's assets. The disagreement between the decedent and the attorney, which caused the decedent not to sign the new will, was totally unrelated to the provision in the new will relating to Patricia. Based upon decedent's concern that a change in the marital trust, contained in the original will, had to be effected expeditiously, the second codicil was prepared by the attorney, and signed by decedent, so that the marital trust change could be effectuated immediately, rather than waiting for the preparation of another draft of a new will. The second codicil contained language that specifically republished the terms of the original will and the first codicil. Not long thereafter, decedent died.

The lower court held there was no ambiguity between the will and the first and second codicils as to the definition of issue or children and, thus, there was no ambiguity as to the testator's intent. Because the second codicil made no reference to Patricia, but did specifically republish the original will, her status as a pretermitted child was destroyed, pursuant to Section 732.302, Florida Statutes , and she was no longer able to share in her father's estate.

What makes this case so troubling is that, beyond the fact that she is being denied the opportunity to share in her deceased father's assets, the record in this case, as well as in the companion case of *Espinosa v. Sparber, Shevin,* clearly reflects that it is virtually uncontroverted that Rene R. Azcunce intended that his daughter, the appellant herein, share in his assets after his death. Based upon the evidence presented before the trial court, it is clear that her apparent inability to receive that which her father clearly wanted her to have is the result of the current state of the case law in the State of Florida.

Lest there be any misunderstanding, I hasten to add that I understand that the majority opinion has correctly interpreted and applied the current law of this State that relates to the facts of this case. The majority opinion reflects that the current posture of the law in this area is designed to give effect to the testator's wishes and to deny any relief to false or fraudulent claimants. However, the fear of false or fraudulent claims should never be allowed to be used as the reason to bar claimants from filing their claims with the courts of this State. Rather, the courthouse doors must always remain open in the hope that the justice system will do what it is supposed to do - render justice. In furtherance of that end, hopefully, valid claims will prevail and false claims will fail. If, however, courthouse doors are barred to any type of claimant, then we all, as members of a supposedly free and just society, suffer from such a denial of access to the courts.

As I indicated above, the unrefuted evidence in this case reflects that Patricia's father, the decedent herein, intended Patricia to receive her fair share. It is only through an unfortunate series of circumstances, and the legal implications springing therefrom, that Patricia is being denied what her father wanted her to receive.

The next to last paragraph of the majority opinion seems to suggest the possibility that Patricia might find relief in a professional malpractice action against the professional draftsman who prepared the second codicil knowing, according to the undisputed evidence, that Patricia's father wanted Patricia to receive her fair share of his estate, but still allowed Patricia's father to sign it (thereby extinguishing Patricia's right to receive her share as a "pretermitted child") without either advising her father of the legal consequences of signing the second codicil (to-wit: that Patricia would lose her status as a pretermitted child) or providing for her in the second codicil, or some other such document, so as to give life and vitality to her father's (the testator's) wishes. However, this flicker of light of possible relief, that might appear to offer hope to Patricia, is soon doused as one reads the majority opinion of this Court in *Espinosa v. Sparber, Shevin,* which is the appeal growing out of the trial court's dismissal of the professional malpractice case filed, on behalf of Patricia, against the draftsman of the codicil. For the reasons stated in my concurring opinion in the case of *Espinosa v. Sparber, Shevin,* and the cases that I refer to therein, it would appear that the case law of this State has "missed the boat" in its efforts to make sure that there is "a remedy for every wrong".

After the result in this case, the family decided to sue the attorneys, with the following result. How difficult would it have been for the attorney to have included the possibility of after-born children in the original will? Is there any way to hold the attorney accountable for poor drafting?

Supreme Court of Florida.
Marta ESPINOSA, et al., Petitioners,
v.
SPARBER, SHEVIN, et al., Respondents.
Feb. 4, 1993.

McDONALD, Justice.

We review Espinosa v. Sparber, Shevin, which involves the following question of great public importance certified in an unpublished order dated September 17, 1991:

> UNDER THE FACTS OF THIS CASE ... MAY A LAWSUIT ALLEGING PROFESSIONAL MALPRACTICE BE BROUGHT, ON BEHALF OF PATRICIA AZCUNCE, AGAINST THE DRAFTSMAN OF THE SECOND CODICIL?

Howard Roskin, a member of the Sparber, Shevin law firm, drafted a will for Rene Azcunce, the testator. At the time he signed his will, Rene and his wife, Marta, had three children, Lisette, Natalie, and Gabriel.

Neither the will nor the first codicil to the will, executed on August 8, 1983, made any provisions for after-born children. On March 14, 1984, Patricia Azcunce was born as the fourth child of Rene and Marta. Rene contacted Roskin and communicated his desire to include Patricia in his will. In response, Roskin drafted a new will that provided for Patricia and also restructured the trust. However, due to a disagreement between Rene and Roskin on the amount of available assets, Rene never signed the second will. Instead, on June 25, 1986, he executed a second codicil drafted by Roskin that changed the identity of the co-trustee and co-personal representative, but did not provide for the after-born child, Patricia. When Rene died on December 30, 1986, he had never executed any document that provided for Patricia.[1]

Marta brought a malpractice action on behalf of Patricia and the estate against Roskin and his law firm. The trial court dismissed the complaint with prejudice for lack of privity and entered final summary judgment for Roskin and his firm. The Third District Court of Appeal reversed the dismissal with regard to the estate, affirmed it with regard to Patricia, and certified the question of whether Patricia has standing to bring a legal malpractice action under the facts of this case.

An attorney's liability for negligence in the performance of his or her professional duties is limited to clients with whom the attorney shares privity of contract. To bring a legal malpractice action, the plaintiff must either be in privity with the attorney, wherein one party has a direct obligation to another, or, alternatively, the plaintiff must be an intended third-party beneficiary. In the instant case, Patricia Azcunce does not fit into either category of proper plaintiffs.

In the area of will drafting, a limited exception to the strict privity requirement has been allowed where it can be demonstrated that the apparent intent of the client in engaging the services of the lawyer was to benefit a third party. Because the client is no longer alive and is unable to testify, the task of identifying those persons who are intended third-party beneficiaries causes an evidentiary problem closely akin to the problem of determining the client's general testamentary intent. To minimize such

---

[1] Patricia brought suit in probate court to be classified as a pretermitted child, which would have entitled her to a share of Rene's estate. Her mother and adult sibling consented to Patricia's petition being granted. The probate court judge appointed a guardian ad litem for Patricia's two minor siblings, and the guardian opposed the petition.

We are not privy to the factors that the guardian ad litem considered in deciding not to consent to Patricia's classification as a pretermitted child, a decision that deprived Patricia of a share in the estate and ultimately led to costly litigation. We hope, however, that a guardian evaluating the facts of this case would not focus strictly on the financial consequences for the child, but would also consider such important factors as family harmony and stability.

evidentiary problems, the will was designed as a legal document that affords people a clear opportunity to express the way in which they desire to have their property distributed upon death. To the greatest extent possible, courts and personal representatives are obligated to honor the testator's intent in conformity with the contents of the will.

If extrinsic evidence is admitted to explain testamentary intent, as recommended by the petitioners, the risk of misinterpreting the testator's intent increases dramatically. Furthermore, admitting extrinsic evidence heightens the tendency to manufacture false evidence that cannot be rebutted due to the unavailability of the testator. For these reasons, we adhere to the rule that standing in legal malpractice actions is limited to those who can show that the testator's intent *as expressed in the will* is frustrated by the negligence of the testator's attorney. Although Rene did not express in his will and codicils any intention to exclude Patricia, his will and codicils do not, unfortunately, express any affirmative intent to provide for her. Because Patricia cannot be described as one in privity with the attorney or as an intended third-party beneficiary, a lawsuit alleging professional malpractice cannot be brought on her behalf.

Rene's estate, however, stands in the shoes of the testator and clearly satisfies the privity requirement. Therefore, we agree with the district court's decision that the estate may maintain a legal malpractice action against Roskin for any acts of professional negligence committed by him during his representation of Rene. Because the alleged damages to the estate are an element of the liability claim and are not relevant to the standing question in this particular case, we do not address that issue.

For the reasons stated above, we answer the certified question in the negative and approve the decision of the district court.

It is so ordered.

D. CONTRACT WILLS

There are some situations in which it may turn out to be impossible for a testator to revoke a will during the life of the testator. That may be the case when a husband and wife have executed a joint will, which is considered to be a contract will. As the following case illustrates, different states have different rules as to what sort of will is considered to be a contract will.

Although it is the basic rule that a will is always revocable by the testator until the moment of death, the following case illustrates that in some situations that may not be the law.

Court of Appeals of Colorado.
In the Matter of the Estate of Lois Maude Loflin, Deceased. Margaret Vandever, Mary Brammer, and Calvin F. Lorentz, Petitioners-Appellants, v. Geneva Smith Emery, Noel Adam, Raymond Adam, Gregory Emery, Jan Bartlett Emery, Gail Emery, Leland Smith, Stephen Ray Smith, and Robert Wayne Cox, Respondents-Appellees.
August 14, 2003

JUDGES: Opinion by JUDGE ROY.

Petitioners, Margaret Vandever, Mary Brammer, and Calvin F. Lorentz (husband's family) appeal the trial court's order probating the will of Lois Maude Loflin (wife). The respondents Geneva Smith Emery, Noel Adam, Raymond Adam, Gregory Emery, Jan Bartlett Emery, Gail Emery, Leland Smith, Stephen Ray Smith, and Robert Wayne Cox, are members of wife's family. We reverse.

In 1975, while living in Kansas, wife and her husband, Kenneth Loflin (husband), executed a single "Joint and Mutual Last Will and Testament of Kenneth Jackson Loflin and Lois Maude (Smith) Loflin, Husband and Wife" (the Kansas Will). Husband and wife had no descendants.

The Kansas Will provides that upon the death of the first to die the entire estate would pass to the survivor, and, upon the death of the survivor the estate was to be distributed equally among several devisees including wife's brothers and sisters and husband's nieces and nephews. The effect of this distribution at wife's death was to divide the estate equally between the two families.

The couple later moved to Oklahoma, where the husband died. Wife submitted the Kansas Will to probate in Oklahoma, and the entire estate of husband passed to wife in accordance with the Kansas Will.

Wife then moved to Colorado and executed a new Last Will and Testament (the Colorado Will). The Colorado Will revoked all prior wills and codicils and distributed the estate one half in equal shares to her sisters and one-half in equal shares to seven of her nieces and nephews and one of husband's nephews. The Colorado Will substantially increased the distribution to wife's family at the expense of husband's family which was reduced to one-sixteenth of the estate.

Following wife's death in Colorado, the personal representative named in the Colorado Will filed for informal probate and submitted both wills. Husband's family petitioned for probate of the Kansas Will and argued that it was a contract will and thus irrevocable by wife following husband's death. Wife's family took the contrary position.

After a hearing, the trial court concluded that Colorado law applied and that the Kansas Will was not a contract will under either Kansas or Colorado law and accordingly admitted the Colorado Will to probate. The son of one of husband's nephews, a lawyer and judge in Kansas who prepared the Kansas Will, testified that he advised husband and wife that the Kansas Will was a contract will which could not be unilaterally revoked. Wife's family objected to this testimony.

I.

We must first determine what law controls the determination of whether the Kansas Will is a contract will. Husband's family argues that Kansas law controls because the Kansas Will was executed in Kansas in accordance with the laws of that state. Wife's family argues that Colorado law should control because Colorado is where the deceased died and where the estate is located. We conclude that Kansas law applies.

A contract will is an agreement between two persons to devise property according to a "common plan" by means of a contract that cannot be unilaterally revoked. At the time of the execution of the Kansas Will, both Colorado and Kansas recognized the validity of contract wills.

However, the two states differ on the requirements to create a binding contract will. By statute, Colorado requires express language in the will evidencing a contract, another writing signed by the decedent that evidences a contract, or material provisions of the contract appear in the will. See C.R.S. § 15-11-514. In contrast, Kansas has no similar statute and does not require express contract language or another document evidencing a contract, instead, its courts have held that a binding contract will exists if the will evidences that a contract was made. Thus, the laws of Kansas and Colorado conflict.

With respect to the construction, validity, and effect of contracts, Colorado applies the law of the state in which the contract was made. Those courts that have applied conflict of laws principles to determine whether a will is a contract will have applied the contract choice of law rules and looked to the law of the jurisdiction in which the will was, or wills were, executed.

In today's mobile society, the law should not require testators and their counsel to comply with the laws of every state in attempting to enter a contract will. Moreover, the choice of law should not impair the important feature of a contract will that it is not unilaterally revocable, and thus one spouse may not change the will after his or her spouse is deceased.

In determining whether a will is a contract will, using the law of the state of residence (domicile) of the second to die at the time of death, would be contrary to the original purpose and intent of the contract will. It would allow surviving spouses to move to a state where contract wills are not recognized, or where more stringent requirements are imposed, and thereafter unilaterally revoke the contract will. Or, alternatively, using domicile law would unnecessarily introduce instability in the expectations of the first to die.

Thus, we conclude that whether a will is a contract will must be determined under the laws of the state in which the will was drafted, in this case, Kansas law.

II.

Having concluded that Kansas law applies, we now must determine whether the Kansas Will is a valid contract will under Kansas law. We conclude that it is.

Here, the Kansas Will contains no clearly expressed intent of the parties to be bound. Further, there is no presumption that a joint and mutual will is a contract will in the absence of evidence to support a finding that the testators intended to contract and be bound. However, the intent of the testators to be bound by a joint and mutual will may be determined circumstantially by other expressions used in the will.

The factors to be considered under Kansas law in determining whether a will is a contract will are set forth in In re Zahradnik's Estate. They are as follows:

> (1) A provision in the will for a distribution of property on the death of the survivor;
> (2) a carefully drawn provision for the disposition of any share in case of a lapsed residuary bequest;
> (3) the use of plural pronouns;
> (4) joinder and consent language;
> (5) the identical distribution of property upon the death of the survivor;
> (6) joint revocation of former wills; and
> (7) consideration, such as mutual promises.

Here, the parties agree that the Kansas Will exhibits five of the seven Zahradnik factors. The will provides for distribution to the survivor, provides for disposition of a share in case of a lapsed residuary bequest, uses plural first person pronouns, makes identical distributions of property upon the death of the survivor, and revokes the former wills of both testators. However, the parties disagree whether consideration was given and whether the Kansas Will contains joinder and consent language.

The Kansas Will states, in pertinent part, as follows:

> "In the event either of us shall predecease the other, it is our respective desire and request that all of the property of the deceased, be it real, personal or mixed, and wherever located, shall pass to the survivor.
> "A. Upon the death of the survivor of us, or in the event we both die as the result of a common disaster, within 30 days of one another, then in that event we hereby give, devise, and bequeath all of our property, be it real, personal or mixed, and wherever located, to the following individuals in shares as set out by their respective names. [Seven names with equal shares follow.]
> "B. We want it to be clear that we have other good friends and relatives, but it is our desire to leave our estate as set forth herein, and any name not mentioned herein is intentional.
> "C. For the purpose of carrying out the provisions of Paragraph A we hereby direct the executor of our estate to liquidate our assets as soon as is practical after the death of the survivor of us."

Kansas courts have found consideration sufficient to support an agreement when there is evidence of mutual promises made between the testators regarding the disbursement of property to each testator's family.

Here, the parties clearly made mutual promises. The testators divided their property equally among members of both of their families. In addition, neither having descendants, they mutually promised one another to devise their estate in total to the survivor and not to their separate families. These provisions are, in our view, sufficient consideration and evidence of an agreement.

Further, although exactly what constitutes joinder and consent language has not been fully determined in Kansas, Kansas courts have found that language such as "in consideration of the mutual testamentary provisions herein contained for the benefit of each other" qualifies as joinder and consent language. Here, although there is no language in the Kansas Will stating that the parties drafted it with the consent of the other, the will is entitled "Joint and Mutual Last Will and Testament," is signed by both parties, and refers to their property, estate, or desires in joint terms, such as "our" and "we." That, in our view, is evidence of joinder and consent language.

Moreover, Kansas law does not require that the will meet all seven factors in order to be recognized as a contract will. Thus, even if the evidence of joinder and consent language or consideration were insufficient, there is nonetheless sufficient evidence that the parties intended a contract will.

Respondents argue that because the Kansas Will contains no contract language and does not contain the key words of "absolute" and "forever," the will is not a contract will. However, Kansas law does not require that the will contain express contract language. Nor is there a requirement that the will state that it is "absolute" or "forever." In fact, the Kansas courts have found the existence of such words to be evidence that the will is not a contract will.

Therefore, we conclude that the Kansas Will is a contract will. It follows then that the heirs of the Kansas Will will have an interest in the distribution of the estate, including the after-acquired property. See Bell v. Brittain, (a joint and mutual will includes all after-acquired property of the survivor unless a different intention appears from the will).

The Colorado Will may, however, determine the deceased's other wishes, such as burial and the selection of a personal representative because it properly revoked the Kansas Will with respect to those matters. See Reznik v. McKee, (a single instrument may be both a will, and a contract testamentary in nature; as a will it is revocable but as a contract it is enforceable).

Accordingly, the trial court erred in finding that the Colorado Will revoked the contract of the Kansas Will designating and defining the interests of the devisees.

The order is reversed.

E. DEPENDENT RELATIVE REVOCATION & REVIVAL

One of the most complex areas of the laws regarding wills is the topic of Dependent Relative Revocation. Basically, the idea is that if a person attempts to revoke a will, but would not have done so, if he or she understood all of the consequences, then the attempted revocation is not legally effective, and the will is revived.

As you read the following case, notice which will is actually probated, and which state's law is applied.

Supreme Court of Wisconsin.
In re ESTATE of Ottilie L. ALBURN, Deceased.
Adele RUEDISILI, Appellant,
v.
Viola HENKEY et al., Respondents.
Jan. 8, 1963.

CURRIE, Justice.

This court is committed to the doctrine of dependent relative revocation. The usual situation for application of this doctrine arises where a testator executes one will and thereafter attempts to revoke it by making a later testamentary disposition which for some reason proves ineffective. In other cases, however, the doctrine has been applied to the unusual situation in which a testator revokes a later will under the mistaken belief that by so doing he is reinstating a prior will. In this unusual situation, the doctrine of dependent relative revocation is invoked to render the revocation ineffective. The basis of the doctrine is stated in Estate of Callahan, (Wis.) as follows:

> 'The doctrine of dependent relative revocation is based upon the testator's inferred intention. It is held that as a matter of law the destruction of the later document is intended to be conditional where it is accompanied by the expressed intent of reinstating a former will and where there is no explanatory evidence. Of course if there is evidence that the testator intended the destruction to be absolute, there is no room for the application of the doctrine of dependent revocation.'

The sole question raised by appellant on this appeal is whether the finding of the trial court that deceased revoked the Kankakee will under the mistaken belief that she was thereby reinstating the prior Milwaukee will is against the great weight and clear preponderance of the evidence. This requires that we review the pertinent evidence.

Testatrix was born in Wisconsin. For about thirty years she had resided in San Francisco, California, and later in Cleveland, Ohio. As a widow without children, she came to Milwaukee in the fall of 1954 and lived there with Viola Henkey, her grandniece. While so residing she executed the Milwaukee will on August 12, 1955. The original of this will was left with Attorney George R. Affeldt of Milwaukee, who had drafted it, where it remained until the death of testatrix. Sometime shortly prior to May

22, 1959, testatrix moved to Kankakee, Illinois, and resided there with her brother, Robert Lehmann. On May 22, 1959, she executed the Kankakee will.

On June 28, 1960, testatrix left Kankakee and came to Fort Atkinson, Wisconsin, and lived there with another brother, Edwin Lehmann, until her death in November of 1960. Testatrix was a patient at a hospital in Fort Atkinson during part of October and November of that year. Edwin testified that he had learned of the execution of the Kankakee will prior to the arrival of testatrix on June 28, 1960. On the evening of her arrival, he asked her what she had done with that will, and she replied, 'What do you suppose, I got rid of it.' The next morning testatrix came downstairs with the torn pieces of the Kankakee will tied up in a handkerchief. Edwin provided her with a paper sack in which she deposited the pieces of the will. Edwin then took the sack with the garbage to the dump. There he opened the sack and let the pieces fly in the wind as testatrix had directed him to do.

Edwin was not questioned about any statement regarding the Milwaukee will which testatrix might have made in his presence at Fort Atkinson. He did testify that after her death he searched through her effects for a will but failed to find one. In view of the following testimony given by Olga Lehmann, his wife, this gives rise to an inference that Edwin was searching for the Milwaukee will.

Olga Lehmann was called as a witness by counsel for proponents of the Kankakee will and proved to be a reluctant if not a hostile witness. She was shown a letter dated January 25, 1961, which she had written to Olga Olson, a resident of San Francisco and an old friend of testatrix, and asked if this letter refreshed her memory regarding a statement made by testatrix, about the time of her arrival in Fort Atkinson, in the witness's presence that testatrix wished her Milwaukee will to stand. The witness stated that her memory was not refreshed by this letter although she admitted that the letter bore her signature. The letter of Olga Lehmann to Olga Olson was offered in evidence by counsel for proponents of the Kankakee will but, objection having been made to its admission, the trial court ruled it inadmissible.

Olga Lehmann then testified that the matter of the Milwaukee will was not discussed by testatrix until during a conversation with Viola Henkey after June 29, 1960, when the witness was also present. Olga Lehmann was then asked the following questions and gave the following answers thereto:

> 'Q. Did the deceased ever discuss in your presence the matter of the Milwaukee will at any other time other than the time we are just now referring to?
> 'A. Yes.
> 'Q. Who was present at that time?
> 'A. Just myself.
> 'Q. What did she tell you concerning the Milwaukee will?
> 'A. That was the one she wanted to stand.
> 'Q. Can you tell me in point of time when this might have been?
> 'A. No, we talked often.'

We deem it significant that counsel for appellant did not cross-examine Olga Lehmann with respect to her testimony that testatrix said she wanted the Milwaukee will to stand. Therefore, Olga Lehmann's testimony was not qualified or limited in any way.

This statement by testatrix clearly occurred after her destruction of the Kankakee will. Appellant now attacks this statement on the ground that it was not made contemporaneously with such destruction. In Estate of Callahan, however, the only evidence regarding the intent of testatrix when she destroyed her 1944 will was her husband's statement in her presence after the destruction and her silence indicating acquiescence.

The plan of testamentary disposition under the two wills at issue in this case was in part as follows:

The Milwaukee will contained specific bequests of jewelry and household furnishings to Viola Henkey, the grandniece of testatrix, and directed that any indebtedness owing deceased by Viola Hekey and her husband be deemed satisfied. The residuary clause bequeathed one fourth of the estate to her friend Olga Olson, one fourth to Doris Alburn, one fourth to Lulu Alburn, and one fourth to Viola Henkey.

The Kankakee will included a bequest to Olga Olson of 38 shares of stock in the Bank of America National Trust & Savings Association and bequests of jewelry to Lulu and Addie Alburn. The remainder of the estate was bequeathed as follows: four tenths to Lulu Alburn, five tenths to Doris Alburn, and one tenth to Robert Lehmann, brother of testatrix. The Alburns are not related to testatrix but are relatives of her deceased husband. Viola Henkey, although a blood relative of testatrix, is not one of her next-of-kin who would inherit in the event testatrix had died intestate.

The next-of-kin consist of four surviving brothers and one sister plus a large number of nieces and nephews of testatrix, the children of four deceased sisters and one deceased brother. Thus under the Milwaukee will, none of the next-of-kin were named as legatees, whereas under the Kankakee will, the only next-of-kin named a legatee was Robert, her brother. His share under the Kankakee will is somewhat less than the one-tenth share of the entire estate which he would receive if testatrix had died intestate. The bulk of the estate under both wills was bequeathed to the Alburns and Olga Olson. This plan of testamentary disposition extended as late as May, 1959.

There is no evidence of any change of circumstances occurring thereafter that would indicate any reason why testatrix should die intestate and nine tenths of her estate go to next-of-kin not named in either will. The one change in circumstance was her leaving the home of her brother Robert and moving in with her brother Edwin. This move might provide a reason for her desiring to revoke the Kankakee will, but certainly not for her wishing to die intestate.

The learned trial judge stated, 'I have a strong conviction that decedent did not want to die intestate.' The evidence fully supports this conclusion despite the fact that testatrix took no steps between June 29, 1960, and her death nearly five months later to draft a new will.

We deem that a reasonable inference to be drawn from the competent evidence in this case is that her failure to make a new will indicated her evident belief that her Milwaukee will was still operative. Testatrix must have known that the original of the Milwaukee will was still in possession of Attorney Affeldt and believed that the only impediment to this will was the revocation clause of the Kankakee will. She also knew that the Kankakee will had been destroyed by tearing it in pieces and scattering the pieces so that they could not be found.

We are constrained to conclude that the statement made to Olga Lehmann that testatrix wished her Milwaukee will to stand, the inference that she did not wish to die intestate, and the fact that she took no steps following the destruction of the Kankakee will to make a new will are sufficient evidence to support the finding that she destroyed the Kankakee will under the mistaken belief that the Milwaukee will would control the disposition of her estate.

Therefore, the Kankakee will, having been destroyed under a mistaken belief as to the law, is entitled to probate.

Judgment affirmed.

Does the following Colorado statute make anything easier?

§ 15-11-509. Revival of revoked will

(1) If a subsequent will that wholly revoked a previous will is thereafter revoked by a revocatory act under section 15-11-507(1)(b), the previous will remains revoked unless it is revived. The previous will is revived if it is evident from the circumstances of the revocation of the subsequent will or from the testator's contemporary or subsequent declarations that the testator intended the previous will to take effect as executed.

(2) If a subsequent will that partly revoked a previous will is thereafter revoked by a revocatory act under section 15-11-507(1)(b), a revoked part of the previous will is revived unless it is evident from the circumstances of the revocation of the subsequent will or from the testator's contemporary or subsequent declarations that the testator did not intend the revoked part to take effect as executed.

(3) If a subsequent will that revoked a previous will in whole or in part is thereafter revoked by another, later will, the previous will remains revoked in whole or in part, unless it or its revoked part is revived. The previous will or its revoked part is revived to the extent it appears from the terms of the later will that the testator intended the previous will to take effect.

CHAPTER 20 - TORTIOUS INTERFERENCE WITH EXPECTANCY

In addition to trying to sue the lawyer involved in drafting a will, disappointed relatives may also try to sue the beneficiaries who took under the provisions of the will. A relatively new legal theory for such a suit is called tortious interference with expectancy. Because this is a tort remedy, that means that damages, possibly including punitive damages, are available. Therefore, it might turn out that a disappointed relative might actually get more, under the theory of tortious interference with expectancy, than the relative would have gotten if the decedent had left his or her entire estate to the disappointed relative.

The most famous case alleging tortious interference with an expectancy is the case of *Stern v. Marshall,* below. It is unusual for the United States Supreme Court to have heard a case of this kind. This controversy, however, has made it to the U.S. Supreme Court twice – so far. What has contributed most to the fame of *Stern v. Marshall* is the identity of the parties.

Jeffry Toobin's recent book, THE OATH, THE OBAMA WHITE HOUSE AND THE SUPREME COURT, Jeffrey Toobin, Doubleday, © 2012 by Jeffrey Toobin, describes the story at pages 55-56.

> "Her name at birth was Vickie Lynn Hogan, and she was the second child born to her sixteen-year-old mother. At the age of nineteen, with a child of her own, she became an exotic dancer (not a stripper, exactly) in one of Houston's lesser clubs. To add to her appeal, according to a biographer, she had several rounds of plastic surgery "to create her infamous 42DD bra size, the product finally of two implants on each side and a total of three pints of fluid." She also began using the name Anna Nicole Smith.
>
> One day a man in a wheelchair named J. Howard Marshall II stopped in to watch her at a place called Gigi's. Many years earlier, Marshall had been a professor at Yale Law School, where he had co-written scholarly articles with his faculty colleague William O. Douglas. Marshall left academia for the oil business and became an early investor in the company later known as Koch Industries (which would later have its own place in Supreme Court history). At the time he was wheeled into Gigi's, Marshall was worth as much as $1.6 billion.
>
> The first time they met, Marshall and Anna Nicole spent the night together, and they married two years later, on June 27, 1994. Marshall was eighty-nine, and Anna Nicole twenty-six. He died thirteen months later, on August 4, 1995. In

> the meantime, Anna Nicole had become famous as a model and an actress of sorts as well as the subject of an early reality television series.
>
> Marshall did not mention Anna Nicole in his will, and he left virtually his entire fortune to his son E. Pierce Marshall. (Another son, J. Howard Marshall III, was also excluded from the will.) A protracted legal struggle over the estate ensued in courts all over the United States. Notwithstanding the omission in the will, one court awarded Anna Nicole $474 million, which another knocked down to $88 million, which still another reduced to zero. Five years after Marshall's death, a federal court in California and a state court in Texas both asserted jurisdiction over the will, and it was this dispute that eventually wound up before the justices. When they heard arguments in this arcane matter of federal jurisdiction, the courtroom was nearly as crowded as it had been for Bush v. Gore."

An excerpt from that most recent U.S. Supreme Court case involving Anna Nicole Smith follows.

Supreme Court of the United States.
Howard K. STERN, Executor of the Estate of Vickie Lynn Marshall, Petitioner,
v.
Elaine T. MARSHALL, Executrix of the Estate of E. Pierce Marshall.
Decided June 23, 2011.

CHIEF JUSTICE ROBERTS delivered the opinion of the Court.

This "suit has, in course of time, become so complicated, that ... no two ... lawyers can talk about it for five minutes, without coming to a total disagreement as to all the premises. Innumerable children have been born into the cause: innumerable young people have married into it;" and, sadly, the original parties "have died out of it." A "long procession of [judges] has come in and gone out" during that time, and still the suit "drags its weary length before the Court."

Those words were not written about this case, see C. Dickens, Bleak House, in 1 Works of Charles Dickens 4–5 (1891), but they could have been. This is the second time we have had occasion to weigh in on this long-running dispute between Vickie Lynn Marshall and E. Pierce Marshall over the fortune of J. Howard Marshall II, a man believed to have been one of the richest people in Texas. The Marshalls' litigation has worked its way through state and federal courts in Louisiana, Texas, and California, and two of those courts—a Texas state probate court and the Bankruptcy Court for the Central District of California—have reached contrary decisions on its merits.

Although the history of this litigation is complicated, its resolution ultimately turns on very basic principles. Article III, § 1, of the Constitution commands that "[t]he judicial Power of the United States, shall be vested in one supreme Court, and in such inferior Courts as the Congress may from time to time ordain and establish." That Article further provides that the judges of those courts shall hold their offices during good behavior, without diminution of salary. Those requirements of Article III were not honored here. The Bankruptcy Court in this case exercised the judicial power of the United States by entering final judgment on a common law tort claim, even though the judges of such courts enjoy neither tenure during good behavior nor salary protection. We conclude that, although the Bankruptcy Court had the statutory authority to enter judgment on Vickie's counterclaim, it lacked the constitutional authority to do so.

I

Of current relevance are two claims Vickie filed in an attempt to secure half of J. Howard's fortune. Known to the public as Anna Nicole Smith, Vickie was J. Howard's third wife and married him about a year before his death. Although J. Howard bestowed on Vickie many monetary and other gifts during their courtship and marriage, he did not include her in his will. Before J. Howard passed away, Vickie filed suit in Texas state probate court, asserting that Pierce - J. Howard's younger son - fraudulently induced J. Howard to sign a living trust that did not include her, even though J. Howard meant to give her half his property.

After J. Howard's death, Vickie filed a petition for bankruptcy in the Central District of California. Pierce filed a complaint in that bankruptcy proceeding, contending that Vickie had defamed him by inducing her lawyers to tell members of the press that he had engaged in fraud to gain control of his father's assets.

Vickie responded to Pierce's initial complaint by asserting truth as a defense to the alleged defamation and by filing a counterclaim for tortious interference with the gift she expected from J. Howard.

On November 5, 1999, the Bankruptcy Court issued an order granting Vickie summary judgment on Pierce's claim for defamation. On September 27, 2000 the Bankruptcy Court issued a judgment on Vickie's counterclaim in her favor. The court later awarded Vickie over $400 million in compensatory damages and $25 million in punitive damages.

When the case reached the U.S. District Court the District Court determined that it was required to treat the Bankruptcy Court's judgment as "proposed, rather than final," and engage in an "independent review" of the record. Although the Texas state court had by that time conducted a jury trial on the merits of the parties' dispute and entered a judgment in Pierce's favor, the District Court declined to give that judgment preclusive effect and went on to decide the matter itself. Like the Bankruptcy Court, the District Court found that Pierce had tortuously interfered with Vickie's expectancy of a gift from J. Howard. The District Court awarded Vickie compensatory and punitive damages, each in the amount of $44,292,767.33.

The Court of Appeals reversed. We again granted certiorari.

Although we conclude that § 157(b) (2) (C) permits the Bankruptcy Court to enter final judgment on Vickie's counterclaim, Article III of the Constitution does not.

Article III, § 1, of the Constitution mandates that "the judicial Power of the United

States, shall be vested in one supreme Court, and in such inferior Courts as the Congress may from time to time ordain and establish." The same section provides that the judges of those constitutional courts "shall hold their Offices during good Behavior" and "receive for their Services a Compensation that shall not be diminished" during their tenure.

As its text and our precedent confirm, Article III is "an inseparable element of the constitutional system of checks and balances" that "both defines the power and protects the independence of the Judicial Branch." Under "the basic concept of separation of powers... that flows from the scheme of a tripartite government" adopted in the Constitution, "the 'judicial Power of the United States' can no more be shared" with another branch than "the Chief Executive, for example, can share with the Judiciary the veto power, or the Congress share with the Judiciary the power to override a Presidential veto."

In establishing the system of divided power in the Constitution, the Framers considered it essential that "the judiciary remain truly distinct from both the legislature and the executive." The Federalist No. 78, (A. Hamilton). As Hamilton put it, quoting Montesquieu, "'there is no liberty if the power of judging be not separated from the legislative and executive powers.' "

Article III of the Constitution provides that the judicial power of the United States may be vested only in courts whose judges enjoy the protections set forth in that Article. We conclude today that Congress, in one isolated respect, exceeded that limitation in the Bankruptcy Act of 1984. The Bankruptcy Court below lacked the constitutional authority to enter a final judgment on a state law counterclaim that is not resolved in the process of ruling on a creditor's proof of claim. Accordingly, the judgment of the Court of Appeals is affirmed.

It is so ordered.

While *Stern v. Marshall* is certainly the most famous case on tortious interference with an expectancy, the following cases actually give a better description of the legal theory, and when the theory may, or may not, be a successful method of litigation.

Supreme Court of Illinois.
In re ESTATE OF Grace ELLIS, Deceased
Shriners Hospitals for Children, Appellant,
v.
James G. Bauman, Indiv. & as Ex'r of the Estate of Grace Ellis, Appellees).
Oct. 29, 2009. Rehearing Denied Jan. 25, 2010.

Justice BURKE delivered the judgment of the court, with opinion.

Grace Ellis executed a will in 1964 naming Shriners Hospitals for Children

(Shriners) as beneficiary of her estate if she died without direct descendants. In 1999, she executed a new will naming James G. Bauman as sole beneficiary. Bauman was the pastor of the church of which Ellis was a member. When Ellis died in 2003, the 1999 will was admitted to probate. It was not until 2006 that Shriners became aware of its interest in the 1964 will. Shriners filed the instant action to contest the 1999 will based on theories of undue influence and fraud and included a tort count for intentional interference with an expectancy of inheritance. The circuit court of Cook County dismissed all counts as untimely pursuant to section 8–1 of the Probate Act. On appeal, Shriners challenged only the dismissal of the tort claim. The appellate court affirmed the trial court's judgment.

We allowed Shriners' petition for leave to appeal and now hold that Shriners' tort claim for intentional interference with an expectancy of inheritance is not limited by the six-month limitation period in section 8–1. Accordingly, we reverse the appellate court's judgment and remand to the trial court for further proceedings.

BACKGROUND

On December 3, 1964, Ellis executed a will designating her elderly parents as the primary beneficiaries of her estate, and designating her descendants and petitioner Shriners as contingent beneficiaries. On August 9, 1999, Ellis executed a new will designating Bauman as sole primary beneficiary and Ellis' surviving heirs at law as contingent beneficiaries of her estate.

Ellis died on October 8, 2003, at the age of 86, leaving no direct descendants. Her estate was worth more than $2 million dollars. The 1999 will was filed with the clerk of the circuit court of Cook County on October 9, 2003, and admitted to probate on October 29, 2003. Bauman was named independent executor of the estate.

Shriners first became aware of its interest in the 1964 will when Bauman filed the will with the circuit court in 2006 as part of a separate will contest brought by several of Ellis' heirs at law. Shriners filed its "Petition to Contest Will and For Other Relief" on August 8, 2006. Shriners alleged that Ellis met Bauman in 1994 and became a member of St. John's Lutheran Church in Glenview, Illinois, where Bauman was a pastor. Ellis subsequently gave Bauman powers of attorney over her health care and property, changed title to more than $1 million of her assets to Bauman, and purchased gifts and an automobile for Bauman. Counts I and II of the petition contested the validity of the 1999 will based on theories of undue influence and mental incapacity. Both counts requested the vacation of the order admitting the 1999 will to probate, and requested the admission to probate of the 1964 will.

Count III, the count that is at issue in this appeal, set forth a tort claim for intentional interference with an expectancy of inheritance. It alleged that: (1) but for the 1999 will obtained by Bauman, Shriners would have received Ellis' entire estate; (2) with knowledge of the 1964 will, Bauman set forth on an intentional scheme to interfere with Shriners' expectancy for his personal benefit; (3) Bauman interfered with Shriners' expectancy by abusing his position of trust, unduly influencing Ellis to execute a new will and to buy him gifts, violating his fiduciary duty to Ellis, taking advantage of her age and diminished capacity, and failing to notify beneficiaries and interested parties after her death; and (4) but for Bauman's actions, the bequest to Shriners would have been received. Shriners asked that the circuit court enter judgment against Bauman. In its prayer for relief, it requested compensatory damages in excess of $2 million dollars, an accounting of all *inter vivos* transfers and gifts, and punitive damages.

Bauman filed a motion to dismiss the petition, asserting that it was filed more than six months after admission to probate of the 1999 will, in violation of section 8–1 of the Probate Act.

> Section 8–1 provides, in relevant part:
> "Within 6 months after the admission to probate of a domestic will, any interested person may file a petition in the proceeding for the administration of the testator's estate or, if no proceeding is pending, in the court in which the will was admitted to probate, to contest the validity of the will."

ANALYSIS

The sole issue in this appeal is the timeliness of Shriners' tort claim. As noted, the appellate court applied the six-month limitation period for filing a will contest set forth in section 8–1. This six-month limitation period is jurisdictional and not subject to tolling by fraudulent concealment or any other fact not expressly provided for by the Probate Act. If a challenger to a will fails to initiate a direct proceeding to contest the will within the six-month statutory time period, the validity of the will is established for all purposes.

Shriners contends that the appellate court's application of section 8–1 of the Probate Act of 1975 to a tort claim for intentional interference with expectancy of inheritance contradicts the clear and unambiguous language of the statute and confuses the tort with a will contest. We agree. Under the plain language of section 8–1, the six-month statutory limitation period applies to a "petition to contest the validity of the will." A tort action for intentional interference with inheritance is distinct from a petition to contest the validity of a will, in several important respects. The single issue in a will contest is whether the writing produced is the will of the testator. Any ground which, if proved, would invalidate the will, including undue influence, incapacity, fraud, or revocation, may state a cause of action. The object of a will contest proceeding is not to secure a personal judgment against an individual defendant but is a *quasi in rem* proceeding to set aside a will.

By contrast, in a tort claim for intentional interference with inheritance, "one who by fraud, duress or other tortious means intentionally prevents another from receiving from a third person an inheritance or gift that he would otherwise have received is subject to liability to the other for loss of the inheritance or gift." Restatement (Second) of Torts § 774B (1979). The "widely recognized tort" does not contest the validity of the will; it is a personal action directed at an individual tortfeasor. See Marshall v.

Marshall, 547 U.S. 293 (2006). Although some of the evidence may overlap with a will contest proceeding, a plaintiff filing a tort claim must establish the following distinct elements: (1) the existence of an expectancy; (2) defendant's intentional interference with the expectancy; (3) conduct that is tortious in itself, such as fraud, duress, or undue influence; (4) a reasonable certainty that the expectancy would have been realized but for the interference; and (5) damages. The remedy for a tortious interference action is not the setting aside of the will, but a judgment against the individual defendant, and, where the defendant has himself received the benefit of the legacy, a constructive trust, an equitable lien, or "a simple monetary judgment to the extent of the benefits thus tortiously acquired." Restatement (Second) of Torts § 774B(e) (1979). Thus, a tort claim for intentional interference with an expectancy is not a "petition to contest the validity of the will" under the plain statutory language of section 8–1.

Although section 8–1 does not expressly limit a tort action, Illinois courts nevertheless have restricted the tort in certain circumstances where a plaintiff forgoes an opportunity to file a tort claim within the six-month period for a will contest. If a will contest is available and would provide an adequate remedy to the petitioner, no tort action will lie.

In the instant case, we cannot say that a will contest was "available" to Shriners, nor that a successful will contest would have furnished the relief sought by Shriners in its tort action. The parties agree that Shriners was unaware of its bequest in the 1964 will until more than two years after the 1999 will had been admitted to probate. Shriners did not choose to forgo an opportunity to contest the probated will. It never had that opportunity. Once the 1999 will was admitted to probate, and the six-month jurisdictional period had passed with no will contest having been filed, the validity of the will was established for all purposes.

The facts in the case at bar are similar to Schilling v. Herrera, 952 So.2d 1231 (Fla.App.2007), where a Florida appellate court permitted the plaintiff's tortious interference with expectancy claim to go forward. The plaintiff was the decedent's only heir-at-law and was named the sole beneficiary in a 1996 will. In 2003, the defendant convinced the decedent to execute a new will naming the defendant as the sole beneficiary of her estate. The plaintiff did not learn of the decedent's death until after the defendant had petitioned the probate court for discharge of probate on the 2003 will.

Shortly thereafter, in *Schilling* the final order of discharge was entered by the probate court. The plaintiff subsequently filed his complaint for intentional interference with an expectancy of inheritance.

The Schilling court held, however, that because the defendant's fraud was not discovered until after probate, the plaintiff was allowed to bring a later action for damages because relief in probate was impossible. Similarly, Shriners did not have a fair opportunity to pursue a remedy in probate because it was not aware of its expectancy under the earlier will, nor was it aware of Bauman's allegedly fraudulent conduct, until after the 1999 will was admitted to probate and the six-month deadline for a will contest had expired.

Furthermore, a will contest would not have provided sufficient relief to Shriners because it would not have extended to the alleged *inter vivos* transfers of property. Shriners alleged that Bauman depleted Ellis' estate by inducing her to transfer assets worth more than $1 million to him prior to her death. In a successful will contest, Shriners could have recovered only assets that were part of the estate upon Ellis' death but could not have reached the assets transferred during her lifetime.

The court allowed the entire complaint to proceed in the probate division. The court rejected the defendants' contention that the will contest proceeding was sufficient to protect the parties' expectancies because, even if the plaintiffs had prevailed in a will contest proceeding, it would not have provided them the relief which they were seeking. Jeziorski. Similarly, in the case at bar, had Shriners filed a timely will contest, it would not have provided a remedy for the alleged *inter vivos* transfers.

Accordingly, we find that section 8–1 does not apply to the tort action filed by Shriners against Bauman.

Reversed and remanded.

Note: The facts in the Schilling case mentioned above are dramatic, and unfortunately, may not be too unusual. Here is a short excerpt from the 2007 Florida case.

The plaintiff in that case alleged that he had not known of his sister's death earlier because of the actions of the caregiver. "Mr. Schilling alleged that, 'In December 1996, Mignonne Helen Schilling (the decedent) executed her Last Will and Testament, naming her brother and only heir- at-law, Mr. Schilling, as her personal representative and sole beneficiary, and in May 1997, she executed a Durable Power of Attorney, naming Mr. Schilling as her attorney-in-fact.

In December 1999, the decedent was diagnosed with renal disease, resulting in several hospitalizations. During this period, Mr. Schilling, who resides in New Jersey, traveled to Florida to assist the decedent. In January 2000, the decedent executed a Power of Attorney for Health Care, naming Mr. Schilling as her attorney-in-fact for health care decisions.

On January 12, 2001, when the decedent was once again hospitalized, Mr. Schilling traveled to Florida to make arrangements for the decedent's care. After being released from the hospital, the decedent was admitted to a rehabilitation hospital, then to a health care center, and then to the Clairidge House for rehabilitation. While at the Clairidge House, Ms. Herrera became involved in the decedent's care, and when the decedent was discharged from the Clairidge House on December 16, 2001, Ms. Herrera notified Mr. Schilling.

After being discharged from the Clairidge House, the decedent returned to her apartment, and Ms. Herrera began to care for her on an "occasional, as needed basis." In

2003, when the decedent's condition worsened and she was in need of additional care, Ms. Herrera converted her garage into a bedroom, and the decedent moved in. The decedent paid Ms. Herrera rent and for her services as caregiver.

When Mr. Schilling spoke to Ms. Herrera over the phone, Ms. Herrera complained that she was not getting paid enough to take care of the decedent, and on April 10, 2003, Mr. Schilling sent Ms. Herrera money. While living in the converted garage, the decedent became completely dependent on Ms. Herrera. In September 2003, without Mr. Schilling's knowledge, Ms. Herrera convinced the decedent to prepare and execute a new Power of Attorney, naming Ms. Herrera as attorney-in-fact, and to execute a new Last Will and Testament naming Ms. Herrera as personal representative and sole beneficiary of the decedent's estate.

Mr. Schilling visited the decedent in March of 2004. On August 6, 2004, the decedent died at Ms. Herrera's home.

On August 24, 2004, Ms. Herrera filed her Petition for Administration. On December 2, 2004, following the expiration of the creditor's period, Ms. Herrera petitioned for discharge of probate. On December 6, 2004, **after the expiration of the creditor's period and after Ms. Herrera had petitioned the probate court for discharge of probate, Ms. Herrera notified Mr. Schilling for the first time that the decedent, his sister, had passed away on August 6, 2004.** (Emphasis in original.)

Shortly thereafter, in late December 2004, the Final Order of Discharge was entered by the probate court. Mr. Schilling alleges that prior to being notified of his sister's death on December 6, 2004, he attempted to contact the decedent through Ms. Herrera, but Ms. Herrera did not return his calls until the conclusion of probate proceedings and did not inform him of his sister's death, thereby depriving him of both the knowledge of the decedent's death and the opportunity of contesting the probate proceedings.

Mr. Schilling further alleges that prior to the decedent's death, Ms. Herrera regularly did not immediately return his phone calls, and that Ms. Herrera's "intentional silence was part of a calculated scheme to prevent [Mr.] Schilling from contesting the Estate of Decedent, and was intended to induce [Mr.] Schilling to refrain from acting in his interests to contest the probate proceedings in a timely fashion, as [Mr.] Schilling was used to long delays in contact with [Ms.] Herrera, and did not suspect that the delay was intended to fraudulently induce [Mr.] Schilling to refrain from acting on his own behalf."

Finally, Mr. Schilling alleges that he expected to inherit the decedent's estate because he was the decedent's only heir-at-law and because he was named as the sole beneficiary in the 1996 will; Ms. Herrera's fraudulent actions prevented him from receiving the decedent's estate, which he was entitled to; and but for Ms. Herrera's action of procuring the will naming her as sole beneficiary, he would have received the benefit of the estate.

After Mr. Schilling filed his amended complaint, Ms. Herrera filed a renewed motion to dismiss, arguing the same issues that she had raised in her previous motion to dismiss. The trial court granted the motion to dismiss with prejudice, finding that Ms.

Herrera had no duty to notify Mr. Schilling of the decedent's death as Mr. Schilling did not hire Ms. Herrera to care for the decedent, and therefore, there was "no special relationship giving rise to a proactive responsibility to provide information...." The trial court also found that Mr. Schilling was barred from filing a claim for intentional interference with an expectancy of inheritance because he failed to exhaust his probate remedies. That judgment was reversed.

The following 2012 case, in which California adopted the theory of Intentional Interference with and Expected Inheritance (IIEI) for the first time, provides a thoughtful analysis of the pros and cons of the tort of IIEI. Note the difficulties that there may be in obtaining the required proof.

Court of Appeal, Fourth District, California.
Brent BECKWITH, Plaintiff and Appellant,
v.
Susan DAHL, Defendant and Respondent.
May 3, 2012.

O'LEARY, P.J.

Brent Beckwith appeals from a judgment of dismissal entered after the trial court sustained without leave to amend Susan Dahl's demurrer to his complaint alleging intentional interference with an expected inheritance (IIEI) and deceit by false promise. Beckwith argues we should join the majority of other states in recognizing the tort of IIEI as a valid cause of action. We agree it is time to officially recognize this tort claim. Given the unique circumstances of this case, Beckwith must be afforded an opportunity to amend the complaint if he believes he can allege the facts necessary to support an IIEI claim as delineated in this opinion. The matter is remanded for further proceedings.

FACTS & PROCEDURE

1. Marc Christian MacGinnis

Beckwith and his partner, Marc Christian MacGinnis (MacGinnis), were in a long-term, committed relationship for almost 10 years. They leased an apartment together and were occasional business partners. MacGinnis had no children and his parents were deceased. His sister, Susan Dahl, with whom he had an estranged relationship, was his only other living family. At some point during their relationship, MacGinnis showed Beckwith a will he had saved on his computer. The will stated that upon MacGinnis's death, his estate was to be divided equally between Beckwith and Dahl. MacGinnis never printed or signed the will.

In May 2009, MacGinnis's health began to decline. On May 25, 2009, MacGinnis was in the hospital awaiting surgery to repair holes in his lungs. He asked Beckwith to locate and print the will so he could sign it. Beckwith went to their home and looked for the will, but he could not find it. When Beckwith told MacGinnis that he could not locate the will, MacGinnis asked Beckwith to create a new will so he could sign it the next day. That night, Beckwith created a new will for MacGinnis using forms downloaded from the Internet. The will stated: " 'I [MacGinnis] give all the rest, residue and remainder of my property and estate, both real and personal, of whatever kind and wherever located, that I own or to which I shall be in any manner entitled at the time of my death (collectively referred to as my "residuary estate"), as follows: (a) If Brent Beckwith and Susan Dahl survive me, to those named in clause (a) who survive me in equal shares.' "

Before Beckwith presented the will to MacGinnis, he called Dahl to tell her about the will and e-mailed her a copy. Later that night, Dahl responded to Beckwith's e-mail stating: "'I really think we should look into a Trust for [MacGinnis]. There are far less regulations and it does not go through probate. The house and all property would be in *our names* and if something should happen to [MacGinnis] *we* could make decisions without it going to probate and the taxes are less on a trust rather than the normal inheritance tax. I have [two] very good friends [who] are attorneys and I will call them tonight." [Emphasis added.] After receiving the e-mail, Beckwith called Dahl to discuss the details of the living trust. Dahl told Beckwith not to present the will to MacGinnis for signature because one of her friends would prepare the trust documents for MacGinnis to sign "in the next couple [of] days." Beckwith did not present the will to MacGinnis.

Two days later, on May 27, MacGinnis had surgery on his lungs. Although the doctors informed Dahl there was a chance MacGinnis would not survive the surgery, the doctors could not discuss the matter with Beckwith since he was not a family member under the law. Nor did Dahl tell Beckwith about the risks associated with the surgery. Dahl never gave MacGinnis any trust documents to sign. After the surgery, MacGinnis was placed on a ventilator and his prognosis worsened. Six days later, Dahl, following the doctors' recommendations, removed MacGinnis from the ventilator. On June 2, 2009, MacGinnis died intestate. He left an estate worth over $1 million.

2. The Probate Proceedings

Following MacGinnis's death, Beckwith and Dahl met to discuss the disposition of MacGinnis's personal property. After Beckwith suggested they find the will that MacGinnis prepared, Dahl told Beckwith "we don't need a will." Two weeks after MacGinnis' death, on June 17, 2009, Dahl opened probate in Los Angeles Superior Court. Dahl verbally informed Beckwith that she had opened probate, but she did not send him any copies of the probate filings. In the filing, she did not identify Beckwith as an interested party. Dahl also applied to become the administrator of the estate.

In September 2009, Beckwith began to ask Dahl for details of the probate case. Dahl informed Beckwith that she had not had any contact with the probate attorney so she did not know anything. On October 2, 2009, Beckwith looked up the probate case online. He then sent Dahl an e-mail stating: "'In case you hadn't had a chance to talk to speak [*sic*] with the probate attorney, I looked up [MacGinnis's] probate case on-line http:// www. la superior court. org/ Probate/ and the next hearing date is not until 8/27/10, so unfortunately as expected it is going to take over a year from [MacGinnis's] passing until we get *our proceeds* from the estate." [Emphasis added.] When Dahl did not respond, Beckwith sent her another e-mail on December 2, 2009, asking if she needed any information from him regarding the distribution of MacGinnis's assets. Again, Dahl did not respond. Beckwith then e-mailed Dahl again on December 18, 2009, asking about the probate proceedings. This time Dahl responded by e-mail, stating: "Because [MacGinnis] died without a will, and the estate went into probate, I was made executor of his estate. The court then declared that his assets would go to his only surviving family member which is me." A few weeks later, in January 2010, Dahl filed a petition with the probate court for final distribution of the estate. Beckwith filed an opposition to Dahl's petition in March 2010. After a hearing, at which Beckwith appeared *pro se*, the probate judge found that Beckwith had no standing because he was "not a creditor of the estate" and he had "no intestate rights" with regard to MacGinnis's estate.

3. The Civil Action and Demurrer

On July 30, 2010, while the probate case was still pending, Beckwith filed the instant civil action against Dahl alleging IIEI, deceit by false promise, and negligence. In the complaint, Beckwith asserted Dahl interfered with his expected inheritance of one half of MacGinnis's estate by lying to him about her intention to prepare a living trust for MacGinnis to sign. Beckwith further alleged Dahl made these false promises in order to "caus[e] a sufficient delay to prevent [MacGinnis] from signing his will before his surgery" because she knew that if MacGinnis died without a will, she would inherit the entire estate. Finally, Beckwith claimed that as a result of his reliance on Dahl's promises, "he was deprived of his ... share of [MacGinnis's] estate," and because he had no standing in probate court, a civil action against Dahl was his only remedy.

Dahl demurred to all three causes of action. ...

4. Intentional Interference with Expectation of Inheritance

The trial court sustained without leave to amend Dahl's demurrer to Beckwith's first cause of action, IIEI, because the tort had not been officially recognized as valid in California. However, "[t]he law of torts is anything but static, and the limits of its development are never set. When it becomes clear that the plaintiff's interests are entitled to legal protection against the conduct of the defendant, the mere fact that the claim is novel will not of itself operate as a bar to a remedy." (Prosser & Keeton, Torts (5th ed. 1984).)

a. Background of the Tort

The parties are in agreement that California has not yet recognized the tort of IIEI. However, "Twenty-five of the forty-two states that have considered it have validated it."

In general, most states recognizing the tort adopt it with the following elements: (1) an expectation of receiving an inheritance; (2) intentional interference with that expectancy by a third party; (3) the interference was independently wrongful or tortious; (4) there was a reasonable certainty that, but for the interference, the plaintiff would have received the inheritance; and (5) damages. Most states prohibit an interference action when the plaintiff already has an adequate probate remedy.

b. Policy Considerations

In order to decide whether a new tort cause of action should be recognized, we must consider the relevant policy considerations and balance the benefits of such recognition against any potential burdens and costs that recognition of the tort would bring.

The tort of IIEI developed under the "general principle of law that whenever the law prohibits an injury it will also afford a remedy." Similarly, it is a maxim of California jurisprudence that, "for every wrong there is a remedy." In addition, in California, "[e]very person is bound, without contract, to abstain from injuring the person or property of another, or infringing upon any of his or her rights." "We cannot let the difficulties of adjudication frustrate the principle that there be a remedy for every substantial wrong." See Lucas v. Hamm (1961) holding that intended beneficiaries of wills can recover in tort against a negligent draftsman even though there was a lack of privity because if such plaintiffs were precluded from bringing a tort claim, "no one would be able to do so and the policy of preventing future harm would be impaired." Recognition of the IIEI tort in California is consistent with and advances these basic principles.

One policy concern that stands out is the effect that recognition of the tort could have on the probate system. The probate system was created to protect a decedent's testamentary intent by imposing very stringent requirements on a will contest. Recognition of the IIEI tort could enable plaintiffs to usurp a testator's true intent by bypassing these stringent probate requirements. If we were to permit, much less encourage, dual litigation tracks for disgruntled heirs, we would risk destabilizing the law of probate and creating uncertainty and inconsistency in its place. We would risk undermining the legislative intent inherent in creating the Probate Code as the preferable, if not exclusive, remedy for disputes over testamentary documents. These are very valid concerns that warrant this court's attention.

A majority of the states which have adopted the tort of interference with an inheritance have achieved such a balance by prohibiting a tort action to be brought where the remedy of a will contest is available and would provide the injured party with adequate relief. By applying a similar last recourse requirement to the tort in California, the integrity of the probate system is protected because where a probate remedy is available, it must be pursued. In addition, the only plaintiffs who will be able to utilize the tort are those who lack an adequate probate remedy *because of the interference of another.* In a sense, the interfering tortfeasor has "obtained the benefit of the testamentary intent rule by committing a tort against a third party." Allowing those so harmed to bring a tort action still would give defendants all the benefits that the testamentary intent rule calls for them to receive. Once possessed of those benefits, however, defendants would be liable to respond in damages for torts that they may have committed—a separate legal inquiry with its own societal justifications.

Another common reason cited against recognition is that the IIEI tort is contrary to the principle that gratuitous promises are generally not enforceable. In California, a will is generally revocable by the testator at any time and for any reason prior to his or her death. Likewise, a bare promise to make a gift in the future, in the absence of consideration, is not legally enforceable. Therefore, the argument goes, it would be inconsistent to allow a prospective beneficiary to recover against a third party for interfering with an expectancy when the prospective beneficiary could not legally enforce the same promise against the testator. However, California already recognizes other interference torts that protect only *expectancies* of future economic benefits that could not be enforced directly.

For example, interference with an at-will contract is actionable even though there is only an expectation of future contractual relations because "it is the contractual relationship, not any term of the contract, which is protected against outside interference." Likewise, interference with an employment relationship is actionable even if the relationship is terminable at-will because "the fact that the employer was privileged to discharge plaintiff at any time does not necessarily privilege a third party unjustifiably to induce the termination."

Closely related is the concern that expectancy in an inheritance is too speculative to warrant a tort remedy because the testator may have changed his mind notwithstanding any interference from a third party. However, where there is a strong probability that an expected inheritance would have been received absent the alleged interference, whether or not the decedent changed his mind is a question of fact necessary to prove an element of the tort and is not a reason to refuse to recognize the existence of the tort altogether. Courts have dealt with this issue with respect to other interference torts by developing "a threshold causation requirement for maintaining a cause of action namely, proof that it is reasonably *probable* that the lost economic advantage would have been realized but for the defendant's interference." As discussed above, a similar threshold requirement is built into the IIEI tort because one of the tort's required elements is that there exists a reasonable certainty that, but for the interference, the plaintiff would have received the inheritance.

As Prosser & Keeton points out, there is no essential reason for "refusing to protect such non-commercial expectancies, at least *where there is a strong probability that they would have been realized.*" Accordingly, many sister states considering the issue have recognized the tort because "if the law protects a person from interference with an opportunity to receive a benefit by entering into contractual relations in the future, the same protection should be accorded to a person's opportunity to receive a benefit as a prospective legatee. The uncertainty attendant upon the expectancy is equivalent. Neither the employee nor the prospective legatee has any enforceable right to his likely benefit."

Synthesizing the above, we conclude that a court should recognize the tort of IIEI if it is necessary to afford an injured plaintiff a remedy. The integrity of the probate system and the interest in avoiding tort liability for inherently speculative claims are very important considerations. However, a court should not take the "drastic consequence of an absolute rule which bars recovery in all cases" when a new tort cause of action can be defined in such a way so as to minimize the costs and burdens associated with it. California case law in analogous contexts shields defendants from tort liability when the expectancy is too speculative. In addition, case law from other jurisdictions bars IIEI claims when an adequate probate remedy exists. By recognizing similar restrictions in IIEI actions, we strike the appropriate balance between respecting the integrity of the probate system, guarding against tort liability for inherently speculative claims, and protecting society's interest in providing a remedy for injured parties.

Further, California courts have frequently rejected the contention that the rule permitting the maintenance of the action would be impractical to administer and would flood the courts with litigation as being but an argument that the courts are incapable of performing their appointed tasks. Indubitably juries and trial courts, constantly called upon to distinguish the frivolous from the substantial and the fraudulent from the meritorious, reach some erroneous results. But such fallibility, inherent in the judicial process, offers no reason for substituting for the case-by-case resolution of causes an artificial and indefensible barrier. Courts not only compromise their basic responsibility to decide the merits of each case individually but destroy the public's confidence in them by using the broad broom of 'administrative convenience' to sweep away a class of claims a number of which are admittedly meritorious.

Having decided we can recognize a cause of action for IIEI, we turn to whether Beckwith sufficiently stated the cause of action in his complaint. To state a claim for IIEI, a plaintiff must allege five distinct elements. First, the plaintiff must plead he had an expectancy of an inheritance. It is not necessary to allege that "one is in fact named as a beneficiary in the will or that one has been devised the particular property at issue. That requirement would defeat the purpose of an expectancy claim. Second, as in other interference torts, the complaint must allege causation. "This means that, as in other cases involving recovery for loss of expectancies there must be proof amounting to a reasonable degree of certainty that the bequest or devise would have been in effect at the time of the death of the testator if there had been no such interference." (Rest.2d Torts, § 774B.) Third, the plaintiff must plead intent, i.e., that the defendant had knowledge of the plaintiff's expectancy of inheritance and took deliberate action to interfere with it. Fourth, the complaint must allege that the interference was conducted by independently tortious means, i.e., the underlying conduct must be wrong for some reason other than the fact of the interference. Finally, the plaintiff must plead he was damaged by the defendant's interference.

Additionally, an IIEI defendant must direct the independently tortious conduct at someone other than the plaintiff. The cases firmly indicate a requirement that "the fraud, duress, undue influence, or other independent tortious conduct required for this tort is directed at the testator. *The beneficiary is not directly defrauded* or unduly influenced; the testator is. In other words, the defendant's tortious conduct must have induced or caused the testator to take some action that deprives the plaintiff of his expected inheritance. Even in the relatively few IIEI cases we found where the defendant's wrongful conduct was directed at someone other than the testator, the defendant's interference was never directed only at the plaintiff.

We must also emphasize the tort of IIEI is one for wrongful interference with an expected inheritance and not an independent action for the underlying tortious conduct such as fraud or undue influence. The underlying tort is only the means by which the interference occurs. This distinction explains the development of the tort as one designed to provide a remedy for disappointed legatees. In the absence of an IIEI cause of action, when tortious conduct causing injury to an expected legatee is directed at the testator, the injured party has no independent action in tort. Thus, probate remedies developed to provide a remedy and method of challenging a tortiously induced bequest even when no independent tort action was available. (See Prob.Code, § 6104 ["The execution or revocation of a will or a part of a will is ineffective to the extent the execution or revocation was procured by duress, menace, fraud, or undue influence"].) Similarly, the tort of IIEI developed to provide a remedy when both of these avenues failed, i.e., when the plaintiff had no independent tort action because the underlying tort was directed at the testator and when the plaintiff had no adequate remedy in probate. The common law court has created this cause of action not primarily to protect the beneficiary's inchoate rights, but to protect the deceased testator's former right to dispose of property freely and without improper interference. In a sense, the beneficiary's action is derivative of the testator's rights. Thus, when the defendant's tortious conduct is directed at the plaintiff, rather than at the testator, the plaintiff has an independent tort claim against the defendant and asserting the IIEI tort is unnecessary and superfluous.

Here, Beckwith alleged he had an expectancy in MacGinnis's estate that would have been realized but for Dahl's intentional interference. However, Beckwith did not allege Dahl directed any independently tortious conduct *at MacGinnis*. The only wrongful conduct alleged in Beckwith's complaint was Dahl's false promise to *Beckwith*. Accordingly, Beckwith's complaint failed to sufficiently allege the IIEI tort.

We must still decide whether there is a reasonable possibility that the defect can be cured by amendment. Under the circumstances here, Beckwith did not have a fair opportunity to correct the deficiencies with regard to his IIEI cause of action. The trial court found Beckwith's IIEI cause of action insufficient on its face, based on its conclusion the tort was not legally recognized in California. Accordingly, the court did not inquire into the sufficiency of the factual allegations supporting the IIEI claim. In light of the subsequent guidance provided by this opinion, we think it is appropriate Beckwith be given an opportunity to amend his complaint to address, if possible, the defects we have pointed out.

The judgment of dismissal is reversed and the matter remanded. The trial court is directed to overrule the demurrer to the promissory fraud cause of action and grant leave to amend the IIEI cause of action.

The final case in this section, *Baillis v. Ross*, demonstrates that the theory of tortious interference with expectancy is not always successful. It is also a rather amazing demonstration of friends and relatives attempting to divide up a person's assets while the person is still alive! Such behavior of friends and relatives, of course, is entirely improper.

Court of Appeals of Ohio.
Eighth District, Cuyahoga County.
Kevin BAILLIS, et al., Plaintiffs-Appellants
v.
Laura ROSS, et al., Defendants-Appellees.
Feb. 23, 2012.

MARY EILEEN KILBANE, J.

Plaintiffs-appellants, Kevin Baillis ("Baillis") and Patricia Novak ("Novak") (collectively referred to as plaintiffs), appeal the trial court's judgment granting the motion to dismiss of defendants-appellees Laura Ross ("Laura") and Daniel Beears ("Daniel") (collectively referred to as defendants). Finding no merit to the appeal, we affirm.

In April 2011, plaintiffs filed a complaint against defendants, asserting five causes of action. Plaintiffs alleged that a settlement agreement between plaintiffs, and defendants provided that the plaintiffs were to receive certain bank accounts and 15 percent of Donald Beears's ("Donald") Trust upon his death, which was in January 2011. Baillis was friends with the decedent, Donald, for approximately 12 years before Donald's death. Novak lives with Baillis and was friends with Donald for approximately 12 years before Donald's death. Laura and Daniel are Donald's children and trustees and co-executors of Donald's estate. The plaintiffs allege that despite due demand, Laura and Daniel have refused to comply with the agreement. None of the parties signed this agreement before Donald's death.

Trust Reformation

The plaintiffs, relying on R.C. 5804.15, argue that they stated a claim for reformation because Donald intended to amend his trust to provide a distribution for them.

R.C. 5804.15 provides that "the court may reform the terms of a trust, even if they are unambiguous, to conform the terms to the settlor's intention if it is proved by clear and convincing evidence that both the settlor's intent and the terms of the trust were affected by a mistake of fact or law, whether in expression or inducement." Thus, R.C. 5804.15 requires clear and convincing proof of both the settlor's intent and that the terms of the trust were affected by a mistake of fact or law, whether in expression or inducement.

In *Holdren v. Garrett,* Tenth District Court of Appeals stated:

> "A mistake of fact exists when one understands a fact to be different than it actually is. A mistake of law occurs where a person is truly acquainted with the existence or nonexistence of facts, but is ignorant of, or comes to an erroneous conclusion as to, their legal effect."

In the instant case, plaintiffs' complaint fails to allege facts indicating there was a mistake of fact or law in Donald's Trust. Rather, the complaint alleges that the settlement agreement allowed Donald to give plaintiffs 15 percent of the Trust residue and transfer certain bank accounts upon death to plaintiffs. Moreover, the language of the unsigned agreement did not require Donald to provide any benefit to plaintiffs except possible future compensation for services rendered.

Thus, the trial court properly dismissed plaintiffs' reformation claim.

Tortious Interference with Inheritance

Fourth, plaintiffs argue their tortious interference with inheritance cause of action was properly pled because they alleged that they had an expectancy based upon the language of the agreement and defendants interfered with that expectancy by instituting guardianship proceedings over Donald.

In Firestone v. Galbreath (1993), the Ohio Supreme Court set forth the elements of the tort of intentional interference with expectancy of inheritance as follows:

> (1) an expectancy of inheritance in the plaintiff; (2) an intentional interference by a defendant(s) with that expectancy of inheritance; (3) conduct by the defendant involving the interference which is tortious, such as fraud, duress or undue influence, in nature; (4) a reasonable certainty that the expectancy of inheritance would have been realized, but for the interference by the defendant; and (5) damage resulting from the interference.

In the instant case, the guardianship proceedings were instituted before the parties began negotiating the settlement agreement. As a result, the defendants did not interfere with plaintiffs' expectancy of inheritance. Furthermore, Donald never exercised his discretion to disburse gifts to the plaintiffs. Therefore, plaintiffs failed to demonstrate that they had a reasonable expectation of inheritance and that the expectancy of inheritance would have been realized, but for the interference by defendants.

Thus, the trial court properly dismissed plaintiffs' tortious interference with inheritance claim.

Constructive Trust

Lastly, plaintiffs argue that the trial court should have allowed their claim for constructive trust because they alleged the terms of the settlement agreement provided that Donald intended to give them certain funds, but the agreement could not be executed prior to Donald's death.

The Ohio Supreme Court in Estate of Cowling (2006) found that

> "A constructive trust is a trust by operation of law which arises contrary to intention and in invitum, against one who, by fraud, actual or constructive, by duress or abuse of confidence, by commission of wrong, or by any form of unconscionable conduct, artifice, concealment, or questionable means, or who in any way against equity and good conscience, either has obtained or holds the legal right to property which he ought not, in equity and good conscience, hold and enjoy. It is raised by equity to satisfy the demands of justice. A constructive trust is considered a trust because "when property has been acquired in such circumstances that the holder of the legal title may not in good conscience retain the beneficial interest, equity converts him into a trustee."

A constructive trust is an equitable remedy to unjust enrichment and fraud. In the instant case, the plaintiffs failed to raise these claims, and as such, they are not entitled to equitable relief. As previously stated, Donald retained the sole discretion, at all times, to amend his Trust, retitle his assets, or make distributions, but did not do so prior to his death. Consequently, nothing is owed to plaintiffs, even on an equitable basis.

Thus, the trial court properly dismissed plaintiffs' constructive trust claim.

Judgment is affirmed.

CHAPTER 21 - STATUTES WHICH OVERRIDE WILLS, TRUSTS, JOINT TENANCIES AND GIFTS!

In virtually every state the legislature has provided some statutory protection for a surviving spouse – even though the spouse might have been intentionally omitted from the decedent's estate plan. There is simply a very strong legislative concern that no spouse be left penniless – (and thus perhaps a charge on the state). Usually these protections are just provided for the surviving spouse, not the decedent's children, evidently because it is so rare that someone intentionally excludes his or her children.

Hopefully you will notice, however, that some of the following statutes may be available for children of the decedent, as well as the surviving spouse of the decedent. All of the following statutes apply regardless of the intent of the decedent. The first three statutes protect the decedent's family – even if that means that decedent's creditors will not be paid. The last statute discussed, involving the right of the surviving spouse to elect to take a share of the augmented estate, overrides both joint tenancy and completed inter vivos gifts, in some situations!

The specific dollar amounts available under these various statutes vary from state to state, and in some statutes are pegged to an automatic adjustment based on some factor such as the cost of living.

A. EXEMPT PROPERTY

A sample of an exempt property statute follows.

C.R.S. § 15-11-403. Exempt property
On and after January 1, 2012, the decedent's surviving spouse is entitled to exempt property from the estate in the form of cash in the amount of or other property of the estate in the value of thirty thousand dollars in excess of any security interests therein. If there is no surviving spouse, the decedent's dependent children are entitled jointly to the same exempt property. Rights to exempt property have priority over all claims against the estate, except claims for the costs and expenses of administration, and reasonable funeral and burial, interment, or cremation expenses, which shall be paid in the priority and manner set forth in section 15-12-805. The right to exempt property shall abate as necessary to permit payment of the family allowance. These rights are in addition to any benefit or share passing to the surviving spouse or dependent children by the decedent's will, unless otherwise provided, by intestate succession, or by way of elective-share.

The next case illustrates how an election to take exempt property may be used to keep assets away from the creditors of a decedent, for the benefit of decedent's family. Whether you are representing a valid creditor of a decedent or a member of the family, it may be important to understand exempt property elections.

Supreme Court of Colorado.
Larry FOILES, Petitioner
v.
Deanna WHITTMAN, as P. R. for the Estate of Lily Whittman, Respondent.
June 28, 2010.

Justice MARTINEZ delivered the Opinion of the Court.

I. Introduction

Petitioner Larry Foiles ("Foiles") appeals the court of appeals' judgment which held that the trial court erred by not permitting respondent Deanna Whittman to make a claim for an exempt property allowance in her capacity as personal representative for the estate of her mother, Lily Whittman. We agree with the court of appeals that the right to an exempt property allowance automatically vested in Lily Whittman when she survived her husband, and thus the right passed to her estate when she died. We therefore affirm the judgment of the court of appeals.

II. Facts and Procedural History

This case is a consolidated action involving a civil suit and several probate matters. It began when Foiles sued Dean Allen Whittman for breach of contract. Before trial, Mr. Whittman died and his wife, Lily Whittman, was substituted as a party in her capacity as personal representative of her husband's estate. Then ten months later, but before the trial could take place, Lily Whittman died. As a result, the probate court appointed a special administrator for Mr. Whittman's estate, who was substituted as a party in the civil action. The Whittmans' daughter, Deanna, was appointed personal representative for her mother's estate. Foiles then timely filed probate claims against both Whittmans' estates in light of the pending civil suit. As representative for her mother's estate, Deanna Whittman filed timely claims against her father's estate for exempt property and family allowances.

Pertinent to this appeal, the trial court granted the claim for a family allowance against Mr. Whittman's estate but denied the claim for an exempt property allowance because the request was not made until after Lily Whittman's death. On appeal, the court of appeals held that Lily Whittman's estate was permitted to assert the claim for an exempt property allowance on her behalf and directed the trial court to allow the claim. Foiles then petitioned for certiorari, which we granted on the issue of whether the court of appeals erred when it held that the personal representative of the surviving spouse's estate can rightfully claim an exempt property allowance in the decedent spouse's estate.

III. Analysis

1. Standard of Review (omitted)

B. The Exempt Property Allowance

Under section 15-11-403, a decedent's "surviving spouse" is entitled to exempt property from the decedent's estate in the value of $26,000.[65] The decedent's dependent children are entitled to the same exempt property allowance if there is no surviving spouse. Even though Lily Whittman died ten months after her husband died, she is a surviving spouse for purposes of the exempt property statute.

The Probate Code defines the term "survive," or its derivatives, to mean that "an individual has neither predeceased an event, including the death of another individual, nor is deemed to have predeceased an event. Of particular importance here, section 15-11-104, states that "an individual who fails to survive the decedent by one hundred twenty hours is deemed to have predeceased the decedent for the purposes of *exempt property*, and intestate succession." (Emphasis added). Thus, based on a plain reading of the relevant statutory language, the only qualification for making a claim under the exempt property statute is that the spouse must survive the decedent by at least five days. Because Lily Whittman survived her husband by ten months, she was a surviving spouse entitled to the exempt property allowance.

Foiles argues that, although Lily Whittman may have been entitled to assert her claim for exempt property while she was still living, her right to assert the claim for exempt property was extinguished when she died. Thus, according to Foiles, her estate was not permitted to make the claim on her behalf. We disagree. Nothing in the plain language of the exempt property statute demonstrates that the General Assembly intended to limit the allowance to a *living* surviving spouse. Indeed, as noted by the court of appeals in this case, the silence of the exempt property statute regarding termination of the right is in marked contrast to other similar statutes. First, the family allowance statute, located in the Probate Code just one section away from the exempt property statute, expressly states that the allowance is "payable to the surviving spouse, *if living*." § 15-11-404(1), The family allowance statute further clarifies that "the death of any person entitled to a family allowance terminates the right to receive an allowance." Likewise, elsewhere in the Probate Code, the elective share statute expressly provides that a right of election "may be exercised only by a surviving spouse *who is living* when the petition for the elective-share is filed in the court."

Thus, it is apparent that where the General Assembly intended to limit statutory benefits under the Probate Code to living persons, it did so in a clear and express manner. When considering the plain language of the exempt property statute in contrast with the plain language of the family allowance and elective share statutes, it is evident that the General Assembly did not intend to limit claims for exempt property to living persons; rather, it only intended to limit the claim to spouses who survive the decedent by five or more days. As such, the moment Lily Whittman survived one

[65] This amount was increased to $30,000 in 2012, after this case was decided.

hundred and twenty hours past her husband's death she was a "surviving spouse" under the exempt property statute, and once the right to an exempt property allowance vested, she could not lose the right upon her death.[66] Thus, we agree with the court of appeals that the trial court should have granted Lily Whittman's estate's request for an exempt property allowance.

Foiles asks us to ignore the clear and unambiguous statutory language and instead look to the purpose of the exempt property allowance, which he argues would be undermined by a strict reading of the statute's language. Our inquiry into the meaning of a statute ends, however, where a plain reading of the statutory language renders clear the statute's meaning. Furthermore, we do not see that a plain reading of the statute is inconsistent with the purpose underlying the exempt property allowance. If the General Assembly intended a different result, it has demonstrated that it can make its meaning clear through precise limiting language, which it did not do here.

IV. Conclusion

We agree with the court of appeals that the right to an exempt property allowance automatically vested in Lily Whittman when she survived her husband's death by more than one hundred twenty hours, and thus the right passed to her estate following her death. Because Lily Whittman's estate timely filed for an exempt property allowance, the trial court should have permitted the claim. We therefore affirm the judgment of the court of appeals.

B. FAMILY ALLOWANCE

In addition to the exempt property allowance, the statute also provides for a family allowance. Note that the amount of the family allowance may be larger or smaller than the amount set forth in the statute, at the discretion of the judge. Thus if a wealthy person made inadequate provisions for his minor children, for example, a court might be able to readjust the decedent's estate plan by means of a generous family allowance, which could continue for the full time the estate is being administered in probate – if the estate has sufficient assets. What might Kate Rothko have done with a provision like this? (See Rothko case in Chapter 14)

C.R.S. § 15-11-404. Family allowance

(1) In addition to the right to exempt property, the decedent's surviving spouse

[66] Although a surviving spouse is entitled to an exempt property allowance, the claim must be filed within the statutory period. Section 15-11-405(3), C.R.S. (2009), states that a "person entitled to payment" of an exempt property allowance must file a request for such payment within "six months after the first publication of notice to creditors for filing claims which arose before the death of the decedent, or within one year after the date of death, whichever time limitation first expires." According to the record in this case, Lily Whittman's claim was timely filed by Deanna Whittman as personal representative for her mother's estate.

and minor children who the decedent was obligated to support and children who were in fact being supported by the decedent are entitled to a reasonable allowance in money out of the estate for their maintenance *during the period of administration,* which allowance may not continue for longer than one year *if the estate is inadequate to discharge allowed claims.* The allowance may be paid as a lump sum or in periodic installments. It is payable to the surviving spouse, if living, for the use of the surviving spouse and minor and dependent children; otherwise to the children, or persons having their care and custody. If a minor child or dependent child is not living with the surviving spouse, the allowance may be made partially to the child or his or her guardian or other person having the child's care and custody, and partially to the spouse, as their needs may appear. The family allowance is exempt from and has priority over all claims except claims for the costs and expenses of administration, and reasonable funeral and burial, interment, or cremation expenses. (Emphasis added.)

(2) The family allowance is not chargeable against any benefit or share passing to the surviving spouse or children by the will of the decedent, unless otherwise provided, by intestate succession, or by way of elective-share. The death of any person entitled to a family allowance terminates the right to receive an allowance for any period arising after his or her death, but does not affect the right of his or her estate to recover the unpaid allowance for periods prior to his or her death.

§ 15-11-405. Source, determination, and documentation

(1) If the estate is otherwise sufficient, property specifically devised or disposed of by memorandum under section 15-11-513 to any person other than a person entitled to exempt property may not be used to satisfy rights to exempt property. Subject to this restriction, the surviving spouse, the guardians of minor children, or dependent children who are adults may select property[67] of the estate as their exempt property. The personal representative may make these selections if the surviving spouse, the dependent children, or the guardians of the minor children are unable or fail to do so within a reasonable time or there is no guardian of a minor child. The personal representative may execute an instrument or deed of distribution to establish the ownership of property taken as exempt property allowance. On and after January 1, 2012, the personal representative may determine the family allowance in a lump sum not

[67] In order to maximize the value of the exempt property to the family it is usually wise to select specific items of property, such as furniture, rather than taking cash for the exempt property allowance. A used sofa, for example, probably has a value of about $10. Purchasing a new sofa would cost about $700. So the family can protect far more property from creditors if it takes specific items, at the "garage sale" value, rather than taking cash, and then having to replace the items at the price of new items.

exceeding thirty thousand dollars or periodic installments not exceeding two thousand five hundred dollars per month for one year and may disburse funds of the estate in payment of the family allowance. The personal representative or *an interested person aggrieved by any selection, determination, payment, proposed payment,* or failure to act under this section *may petition the court for appropriate relief, which may provide a family allowance other than that which the personal representative determined or could have determined.*[68]

(2) If the right to an elective-share is exercised on behalf of a surviving spouse who is an incapacitated person, the personal representative may add any unexpended portions payable under the exempt property and family allowance to the trust established under section 15-11-206(2).

(3) No exempt property or family allowance shall be payable unless the person entitled to payment thereof requests such payment within six months after the first publication of notice to creditors for filing claims which arose before the death of the decedent, or within one year after the date of death, whichever time limitation first expires. The court may extend the time for presenting such request as it sees fit for cause shown by the person entitled to payment before the time limitation has expired; except that the time for presenting the request shall not be extended beyond two years after the date of death. The request shall be made to the personal representative, or, if none is appointed, to any other person having possession of the decedent's assets. A request on behalf of a minor or dependent child may be made by the child's guardian or other person having his or her care and custody.

C. HOMESTEAD EXEMPTION

The homestead exemption is available outside of probate. It is also recognized in probate, as an exemption that survives the death of the decedent in certain circumstances. It may be used to protect the family home from claims of creditors – *unless* when the debt was incurred the protections of the homestead exemption were waived as to that creditor. The amount of the homestead exemption varies widely from state to state, sometimes including the entire value of the family home. The sample below is a much more modest exemption.

§ 38-41-201. Homestead exemption--definitions

(1) Every homestead in the state of Colorado shall be exempt from execution and attachment arising from any debt, contract, or civil obligation not

[68] This is the statutory provision that allows the court to order a larger – or smaller – family allowance than the specific amount specified in the statute.

exceeding in actual cash value in excess of any liens or encumbrances on the homesteaded property in existence at the time of any levy of execution thereon:

(a) The sum of sixty thousand dollars if the homestead is occupied as a home by an owner thereof or an owner's family; or

(b) The sum of ninety thousand dollars if the homestead is occupied as a home by an elderly or disabled owner, an elderly or disabled spouse of an owner, or an elderly or disabled dependent of an owner.

(2) As used in this section, unless the context otherwise requires:

(a) "Disabled owner", "disabled spouse", or "disabled dependent" means an owner, spouse, or dependent who has a physical or mental impairment that is disabling and that, because of other factors such as age, training, experience, or social setting, substantially precludes the owner, spouse, or dependent from engaging in a useful occupation, as a homemaker, a wage earner, or a self-employed person in any employment that exists in the community and for which he or she has competence.

(b) "Elderly owner", "elderly spouse", or "elderly dependent" means an owner, spouse, or dependent who is sixty years of age or older.

D. ELECTIVE SHARE – AUGMENTED ESTATE

The greatest protection for the surviving spouse is provided by the elective share, which is a share the surviving spouse is allowed to elect from the decedent's estate – regardless of any provisions the decedent may have made – or failed to make – for the surviving spouse. The terms of the elective share vary from state to state. The newest, and most comprehensive elective share statute is found in the Uniform Probate Code (UPC). The UPC gives the surviving spouse a right to an elective share in the Augmented Estate. The basic concept of the augmented estate is that the assets of *both* team members, *both* husband and wife, are combined into one big "box," figuratively speaking. Then the surviving spouse, either H or W, is entitled to a certain percentage of the total assets in the "box." The applicable percentage varies with the length of the marriage – perhaps 5% for a one-year marriage, and 50% for a marriage that has lasted for ten years or more. So up to a certain point, maybe ten or fifteen years, the longer the marriage, the more the surviving spouse is able to take as an elective share. But the surviving spouse is never entitled to take more than 50% of the total augmented estate.

All elective shares, including the election to take part of the augmented estate, are *elections.* So if the surviving spouse already owns more than 50% of the "team" assets, (all of the assets of both husband and wife that are included in the big "box" of the augmented estate, for example), then the surviving spouse will not elect. The surviving spouse is already better off than he or she would be after an election. So the surviving spouse will simply keep what he or she already has – with no obligation to contribute anything to the decedent's estate. The attorney for the surviving spouse will be expected to be able to advise the surviving spouse on whether or not it would be beneficial to make the election.

To avoid past abuses,[69] when the surviving spouse's election was just against the *probate* estate of the decedent, the new UPC's Augmented Estate is quite complex. It *pulls back into* the augmented estate various *gifts* made during the marriage, including outright gifts made within two years of death[70] and property which the decedent had placed in the names of himself and another as joint tenants![71] Thus it is important to realize that the augmented estate statute overrides joint tenancy, and some valid, completed, inter vivos gifts!

For more details on exactly what is included in the augmented estate, and a practical way to calculate how much of each inter vivos gift, for example, must be returned to the surviving spouse, see Drafting Wills & Trusts, Lucy A. Marsh, Chapter 9, "Protection of the Surviving Spouse – The Augmented Estate – UPC II," Vandeplas Publishing (2009).

For now, the following three cases will demonstrate some of the basic rules applicable to the UPC Augmented Estate.

Supreme Court of Montana.
IN THE MATTER OF THE ESTATE OF ALCORN
February 11, 1994
OPINION BY: HARRISON

This is an appeal from the Eighth Judicial District Court, Cascade County. Appellant Robert A. Alcorn (Robert), as personal representative of his father's estate, appeals the District Court's determination that a common-law marriage existed between respondent Kathee Melinda Young (Kathee) and Fred "Fritz" Alcorn (Fred), the decedent. In this matter of probate, Kathee asserted rights to an elective share of the augmented estate, a homestead allowance, an exempt property allowance and a family allowance. Robert appeals.

Fred and Kathee met on August 27, 1981, at Metra Park, a horse racetrack in Billings, Montana. At the time of their meeting, Kathee was separated from her husband, Fred Young (Young). Kathee's divorce from Young was complete in May

[69] When the election was only against the probate estate of the decedent, for example, one spouse might put all of his or her assets into an inter vivos trust, so that there would be virtually nothing left in the probate estate. Or a person with a terminal illness might make very large inter vivos gifts, to leave as little as possible in the probate estate.
[70] UPC 2-205(3)The augmented estate now included property that passed during the marriage and during the two-year period next preceeding the decedent's death if the transfer was ...(C) Any transfer of property... made to or for the benefit of a person other than the decedent's surviving spouse. The amount included is the value of the transferred property to the extent the transfers to any one donee in either of the two years exceeded [$12,000].
[71] UPC 2-205 (B) "The decedent's fractional interest in property held by the decedent in joint tenancy with right of survivorship."

1985. From the day they met in August 1981, Fred and Kathee cohabited until Fred died on May 10, 1991. The couple first lived together in Great Falls, but soon moved to Fred's ranch house in Vaughn, Montana.

Kathee, 46, has been a Delta Airlines flight attendant for seventeen years. Fred, who died at age 59, owned and operated an automobile dealership in Great Falls. The couple shared a common interest in horses and in horse racing. In fact, they jointly owned race horses and regularly attended horse races together. Throughout her relationship with Fred, Kathee retained her last name and filed her tax returns as a single person; however, the couple did share joint bank accounts at First Liberty Credit Union in Great Falls.

During the time Kathee and Fred were together, Fred was plagued with physical ailments -- including heart problems, back problems which required surgery, throat cancer which required surgery, and a lung removal which required related surgeries. Fred died of a heart attack on May 10, 1991.

In his will, Fred designated his son, Robert, as the personal representative of his estate. On October 1, 1991, Kathee filed a Notice of Election Against Will by Surviving Spouse. Kathee contends that she and Fred had a common-law marriage from the day they met until the day Fred died. Robert challenges this assertion.

By will, Fred devised to Kathee one-half of the net value of his ranch and all of his household furniture and household goods. Kathee additionally sought the following entitlements: one third of the augmented estate; a homestead allowance of $ 20,000; an exempt property allowance not to exceed $ 3,500; and a family allowance.

The District Court conducted a non-jury trial in July and August 1992, and concluded that Kathee was Fred's common-law wife and, therefore, granted her the entitlements she sought as Fred's surviving spouse.

The sole issue before this Court is whether the District Court properly determined that a common-law marriage was established by Kathee Young.

Montana recognizes the validity of common-law marriages. A rebuttable presumption exists in favor of a valid marriage when "a man and a woman deporting themselves as husband and wife have entered into a lawful contract of marriage." In order to establish the existence of a common law marriage, the party asserting the marriage must show 1) the parties are competent to enter into a marriage; 2) the assumption of such a relationship by mutual consent and agreement; and 3) cohabitation and repute.

Robert argues that Kathee failed to prove that she and Fred were ever married. Robert contends that Kathee was not competent to marry Fred until May 1, 1985, when her divorce with Young was finalized. According to Robert, Kathee failed to introduce evidence that she and Fred agreed to marry one another after her divorce in 1985. Robert asserts that "marriage cannot occur in a piecemeal fashion, but rather comes instantly into being or does not come at all."

The following exchange occurred at the August 17, 1992, hearing:

> Q. [By Donald Ostrem, Kathee's attorney] Okay. Now there are several items that you and I have talked about involving common law marriage. Did you feel that you were married to Fritz Alcorn?
>
> A. Yes, I did.
>
> Q. And did you during the entirety of your relationship feel that you were married to Fritz Alcorn?
>
> A. Yes, I did. ...
>
> Q. Now, did you state that you -- when you first started living together, you were in the process of getting a divorce from your previous husband. And you did get that divorce?
>
> A. Yes.
>
> Q. So you also had the capability of consent at the time that you got that divorce is that correct?
>
> A. Yes.

Kathee testified that she and Fred were capable to consent to marriage. She also testified that neither she nor Fred were incompetent or suffering from any disabilities.

We determine, as a matter of law, that Kathee and Fred were incapable of consenting to marriage until Kathee's divorce with Young became final on May 1, 1985. However, persons who cohabit after the removal of the impediment may become lawfully married as of the date of the removal of the impediment. Therefore, when Kathee's divorce to Young became final, the impediment to her common-law marriage to Fred was removed.

Having determined that Kathee and Fred were competent to marry after May 1, 1985, we turn our discussion to whether Kathee and Fred assumed a common-law marriage by mutual consent and agreement. In support of her contention that she and Fred mutually consented and agreed to marriage, Kathee claims to have a wedding ring given to her by Fred. The ring, which she wore to the August 17, 1992, hearing, contains two intertwining horseshoes made with Yogo sapphires. According to Kathee, "Fritz had it designed and had it made. And the bracelet -- he got a bracelet for me to match."[72] In addition to the ring and bracelet, Kathee and Fred incorporated the intertwining horseshoe design into their home in Vaughn. The couple had horseshoes

---

[72] Have you ever seen a *wedding ring* that comes with a matching bracelet? Certainly standard jewelry, that does *not* indicate any marital relationship, frequently comes with matching bracelets and rings.

cemented into the concrete walkway leading to their house, with their names etched into the concrete beneath the horseshoes.

At the August 17th hearing, the following question was asked: "Did you both agree that you were married, that you were husband and wife?" Kathee responded, "Yes, we did." The combination of Kathee's wedding ring, the concrete design at the couple's home in Vaughn, and Kathee's testimony indicates that Kathee and Fred mutually consented and agreed to a common-law marriage.

We look finally to cohabitation and repute. It is clear from the record, and Robert agrees, that Kathee and Fred cohabited for about nine years -- from the day they met until the day Fred passed away. They lived together for a short time in Great Falls before moving to Fred's house in Vaughn. In fact, it is apparent that the couple invested a great deal of time and money in decorating and refurbishing their home. However, as Robert correctly asserts, marriage "does not result from mere cohabitation alone." Therefore, we now turn our attention to repute.

Robert contends that Kathee and Fred admitted in writing that they were not married after May 1, 1985. In support of his contention, Robert presented evidence that Kathee: 1) never changed her last name from "Young" to "Alcorn;" 2) did not list Fred as a beneficiary on her employee life insurance, health insurance or retirement forms; and 3) filed her tax returns as a single person throughout her entire relationship with Fred. Moreover, *Fred stated in his will that he was a single man.*

Kathee testified that she chose to keep the last name "Young" for professional reasons. Kathee testified that her mother was listed as beneficiary on her insurance, health and retirement forms. Kathee also testified that she filed her tax returns as a single person because she thought she could not file as "married" unless the marriage was a matter of record and because her accountants "told [her] to file it that way."

This Court is unaware of any legal requirement that a wife assume the last name of her husband or that she list her husband as beneficiary on her insurance, retirement or health forms. The District Court accepted Kathee's explanations -- including her rationale for filing her tax returns individually rather than as a married person -- as valid. The District Court was in the best position to observe Kathee and her demeanor. We determine that the District Court's finding as to this issue is not clearly erroneous.

Robert next contends that each witness testified either that Fred and Kathee were not married or that they merely assumed or considered the couple as married. According to Robert, the fact that people assumed or considered the couple as married does not demonstrate that Kathee ever held herself out to be Fred's wife.

The record, however, is replete with evidence and testimony that Kathee and Fred held themselves out to be husband and wife. Kathee and Fred shared joint checking accounts at First Liberty Credit Union. Kathee wore a wedding ring designed and made especially for her, compliments of Fred. The record indicates that Kathee and Fred spent all of their time -- excepting work -- together for nine years. Because the couple had a large home, they regularly hosted members from both Fred and Kathee's families for holidays. Christmas at the Vaughn ranch became a tradition. The couple hosted barbecues and pool parties in the summer for family and friends. Kathee's family members referred to Fred as "Uncle Fritz."

Fred spent about eight years of his time with Kathee in poor health. Throughout Fred's illnesses, Kathee was by his side. The record indicates that Kathee cared for Fred through chemotherapy and through visits to Seattle for treatment.

Robert's daughter and Fred's granddaughter, Kara Alcorn, testified that she and her brother, Robert, who live in Washington, would visit Fred and Kathee in Vaughn. Kara testified that she considered Kathee and Fred to be married, that she received Christmas cards from the couple, and that she received information concerning changes in Fred's medical condition from Kathee.

Robert Layton, Kara's brother and Fred's grandson, testified that the relationship between Kathee and Fred was always portrayed to him as that of husband and wife. He further testified that he visited them every summer, that they "always were together" and that he considered them to be married. On occasion, Robert would go to the horse racetrack with Fred, who would introduce Robert as his "grandson" and Kathee as his "wife."

Judge John McCarvel, a district court judge in Cascade County, was a long-time friend of Fred's. Judge McCarvel used to see Fred run his horses at racetracks in Spokane, Billings and Great Falls. The Judge testified that he considered Fred and Kathee to be married, that Fred always introduced Kathee as his wife, and that he "thought they were married all the time." On one occasion, as he left the Great Falls Airport, Kathee was waiting in the truck to pick up Fred. The Judge testified that "Kathee hollered to me, 'Is my husband on that plane?'"

Janice Mountan, Kathee's sister, testified that "Fritz introduced us as his in-laws. Everyone knew Fritz as being Kathee's husband and Kathee as Fritz's wife." We need not belabor the record. It is abundantly clear that Kathee and Fred cohabited and held themselves out to the community as being husband and wife.

Robert challenges the District Court's findings of fact as erroneous and contradicted by the record. Robert contends that the court omitted from its findings references to testimony which indicated that Fred and Kathee were not married. Specifically, Robert points to the testimony of Donna and Chuck Plant -- friends of Fred -- who stated that Fred had told them after 1985 that he was not married to Kathee. Robert also notes the absence of Robert Emmons' testimony from the findings. *Emmons, an attorney, testified that Fred represented that he was a single man in each of the three wills Emmons drafted for Fred.*

It cannot be said that the District Court failed to consider all the testimony merely because it chose not to reference all the testimony it heard in its findings of fact and conclusions of law. The court heard testimony from fifteen witnesses. It found capability of consent to a common-law marriage between Fred and Kathee, mutual assent and agreement to a common-law marriage, cohabitation, and repute in the community as husband and wife.

The court was in the best position to judge the credibility of the witnesses. We will not substitute our judgment for that of the District Court even where there is evidence in the record to support contrary findings.

After a careful review of the record, we determine that the District Court's findings of fact were not clearly erroneous. We hold that the District Court correctly interpreted the law when it concluded 1) that the relationship between Kathee Young and Fred Alcorn constituted a valid common-law marriage; and 2) that Kathee is entitled to claim the elections set forth in her Notice of Election Against the Will filed with the District Court on October 1, 1991.

Affirmed.

If two people are living together and do *not* intend that relationship to constitute a common law marriage, what steps should they take to document that intent? Would a statement signed by both parties today, stating that they do not consider themselves to be married, today, prevent them from changing their minds tomorrow, and both consenting to enter into a common law marriage? Is there anything that Fred could have done to avoid finding, after his death, that he had been married to Kathy?

The next case clearly illustrates that the right to a portion of the augmented estate is *not* affected by the behavior of the surviving spouse during the marriage.

Supreme Court of Alaska.
ROBERT J. RIDDELL, Appellant, v. IRVIN H. EDWARDS, Appelee.
September 5, 2003, Decided
OPINION BY: BRYNER

I. INTRODUCTION

In a probate proceeding involving the estate of his deceased wife, Robert J. Riddell petitioned as a surviving spouse to receive his statutory homestead allowance, family allowance, and elective share. Despite finding that Riddell had "ingratiated himself" to his wife before their marriage "for the purpose of obtaining her assets" and that his wife had suffered from dementia for the majority of their relationship, the superior court ruled that Riddell and his wife had been validly married and that the estate had no standing to argue that the marriage was voidable. The court nonetheless concluded that Riddell's unconscionable conduct warranted establishing a constructive trust to give the estate Riddell's statutory benefits. Because the superior court's finding that the marriage was valid is not disputed and because Alaska law unconditionally gives the surviving spouse of a valid marriage the right to marital allowances and a share of the estate based solely on the existence of a valid marriage, we hold that the necessary elements for a constructive trust are lacking and that establishing the trust exceeded the court's equitable powers. We thus vacate the trust and remand with directions to fix the amount of Riddell's statutory benefits.

II. FACTS AND PROCEEDINGS

In December 1993 Lillie Rahm-Riddell, who was in her early nineties, met Robert J. Riddell, who was in his mid-sixties. Riddell ingratiated himself to Lillie and became her handyman. He soon moved in with her and started to isolate her from her family and friends. Riddell married Lillie in Ketchikan in May 1995, while guardianship proceedings were pending to determine Lillie's competency to manage her personal and financial affairs. Those proceedings resulted in the appointment of the Public Guardian as Lillie's primary conservator; several months later, prompted by reports of domestic violence, the superior court entered an order restraining Riddell from contacting Lillie. Lillie moved to an assisted-living home in Washington state. Riddell spirited her away from the home and took her to Oregon, where they lived together until Lillie died in September 1997. The entire time that Lillie knew Riddell, she suffered from Alzheimer's disease and/or senile dementia.

Lillie's brother, Irvin H. Edwards, accepted the superior court's appointment as personal representative of her estate. Ensuing litigation between the estate and Riddell generated three appeals. In the first appeal, we affirmed the superior court's order invalidating for lack of testamentary capacity a will that Lillie executed shortly before her death leaving her entire estate to Riddell. In the second, we affirmed the superior court's order denying creditor claims that Riddell filed against the estate seeking compensation for alleged premarital and marital services to Lillie.

The third appeal, which we now consider, arises from two related superior court orders: (1) an order declaring Lillie's marriage to Riddell valid and finding Riddell eligible as Lillie's surviving spouse to claim his statutory rights to allowances and share; and (2) a subsequent order, based on a finding of fraudulent conduct by Riddell toward Lillie, establishing a constructive trust in the estate's favor to receive Riddell's payments of allowances and share. Our decision requires us to describe these orders in considerable detail.

In the course of the probate proceedings, after Riddell petitioned for his statutory allowances and share, the superior court ordered briefing and conducted a hearing to determine the validity of the marriage. The estate sought to invalidate the marriage, arguing that it was voidable because Lillie had been incompetent and Riddell had fraudulently induced her to enter into the marriage. Following the hearing, the court issued a thoughtful and carefully reasoned decision that found clear and convincing evidence of Riddell's fraudulent conduct toward Lillie but nevertheless rejected the estate's challenge to the marriage and declared Riddell eligible to claim allowances and elective share.

The superior court began its decision by unequivocally recognizing the compelling evidence of Riddell's misconduct toward Lillie:

A review of the prior evidence and the new evidence leaves no question to any objective observer that by clear and convincing evidence Mr. Riddell ingratiated himself to Lillie for the purposes of obtaining her assets. She was suffering from dementia, was alone and lonely and he did small things for her in a way that kept her from making decisions that she would have made when she was fully competent. He isolated her by changing her phone, bullying family and friends that were old and frail themselves in such a way that they were not able to be supportive of her.

Three separate court actions involving injunctions under the Domestic Violence law, a conservatorship and a guardianship were filed. Lawyers, a conservator, a temporary guardian and a guardian ad litem were appointed for Lillie. Mr. Riddell defeated them all. In his own words, he and Lillie sneaked to Juneau to get a marriage license and got married secretly in Ketchikan while conservator proceedings were pending.

Mr. Riddell physically intimidated friends, family, lawyers and caregivers. He spirited Lillie away from the nursing home in Washington and kept her from authorities despite attempts to locate her by lawyers, a private investigator and court orders that he disclose her whereabouts.

Mr. Riddell provided Lillie with the attention she craved and did small things for her that made her life better. He also abused her physically and cut her off from her friends and family so that she was utterly dependent upon him for all her needs.

But the court also recognized that this evidence did not necessarily render Lillie's marriage invalid. Noting that "persons suffering from dementia have fluctuating periods of more contact with reality and ability to cope," the court reviewed the evidence and found credible testimony indicating that Lillie was competent and understood the consequences of her actions at the time that she married Riddell. In the court's view, then, the evidence did not convincingly prove Lillie's incompetence when she entered into the marriage: "This court cannot say that at the time she applied for the marriage license or when she actually participated in the ceremony she did not understand that she was getting married."

The superior court then proceeded to consider the legal significance of this finding; in so doing, it drew an important distinction between marriages that are void and those that are merely voidable. The court noted that, in AS 25.24.020, the Alaska Legislature defined a narrow class of marriages as legally void. That statute provides:

"A marriage which is prohibited by law on account of consanguinity between the persons, or a subsequent marriage contracted by a person during the life of a former husband or wife which marriage has not been annulled or dissolved is void."

In contrast, the court pointed out, AS 25.24.030 defines a broader class of marriages as voidable. Alaska Statute 25.24.030 provides:

> "A marriage may be *declared* void for any of the following causes existing at the time of the marriage:
>
> (1) [under the age of legal consent];
>
> (2) that either party was of unsound mind, unless that party, after coming to reason, freely cohabited with the other as husband and wife;
>
> (3) that the consent of either party was obtained by fraud, unless that party afterwards, with full knowledge of the facts constituting the fraud, freely cohabited with the other as husband and wife;
>
> (4) that the consent of either party was obtained by force, unless that party afterwards freely cohabited with the other as husband and wife;
>
> (5) [failure to consummate]."

If either party to a marriage is incapable of consenting to it at the time of the marriage for want of marriageable age of consent or sufficient understanding, or if the consent of either party is obtained by force or fraud, or if either party fails to consummate the marriage, the marriage is voidable but only at the suit of the party under the disability or upon whom the force or fraud is imposed.

Applying this analysis, the superior court examined the circumstances of the case at issue here to determine whether they established that Lillie's marriage was either void (as opposed to being merely voidable) or involved the kind of gross fraud that led other jurisdictions to entertain post-mortem claims of invalidity by personal representatives. Because the court found the evidence as a whole to show that Lillie "understood the nature of her decision to marry Mr. Riddell," it declined to find the marriage void. The court went on to consider whether the case fell within the gross-fraud exception, which allows post-mortem challenges to a valid marriage upon proof of gross fraud arising from "a combination of incompetence and egregious behavior. " Though it noted that "Mr. Riddell did isolate Lillie from her family and friends and he may have married her to obtain her property," the court found that "his conduct did not rise to the level of gross fraud."

Accordingly, the superior court's order declared the marriage valid and precluded the estate from challenging it under provisions describing voidable marriages; on this basis the court ruled that Riddell was Lillie's surviving spouse and was therefore eligible to claim a surviving spouse's statutory allowances and share.

But the court's first order merely declared that Riddell was eligible to claim his statutory allowances and share; it did not actually direct the estate to pay.

After receiving the order declaring him eligible to receive the statutory marital allowances and share, Riddell filed a motion seeking to enforce that order. In response, the estate cross-moved to establish a constructive trust requiring Riddell's allowances and share to be paid to the estate. The superior court's second order granted the estate's cross-motion for a constructive trust. The court preliminarily observed that "A constructive trust can be imposed in any case where a wrongful acquisition or detention of property to which another is entitled has occurred."

Although this court was unable to find the type of gross fraud needed to invalidate the marriage in its previous findings, that does not mean the "exercise of equity jurisdiction to impose a constructive trust with respect to property acquired from the decedent" is not warranted here. This court finds clear and convincing evidence that a constructive trust is warranted."

Riddell appeals.

III. DISCUSSION

A. Standard of Review

Although we generally defer to the trial court's broad discretion in balancing equitable principles, we use our independent judgment for legal issues and review de novo the court's interpretation of the law and its application of law to facts.

B. The Elements of a Constructive Trust

A constructive trust is an equitable remedy that becomes available upon clear and convincing proof that the party against whom the trust will be imposed has been unjustly enriched by receiving assets that rightly belong to the party in whose favor the trust will be created. We have said that a constructive trust may be defined as a device used by chancery to compel one who unfairly holds a property interest to convey that interest to another to whom it justly belongs; the trust arises to prevent the property holder from retaining property obtained "by reason of unjust, unconscionable, or unlawful means." At a minimum, then, a constructive trust presupposes a transfer or holding of property in which the equitable beneficiary has a legal interest and unconscionable conduct by the property's holder in connection with its acquisition.

The estate has not challenged the superior court's decision upholding the validity of the marriage despite Lillie's vulnerable mental condition and Riddell's fraudulent conduct. Because that decision turned on the trial court's evaluation of competing evidence and has not been disputed, we have no occasion to question it here. A prospective heir generally has no recognized right to a living relative's property: we have held that a decedent's property interests devolve to heirs and devisees only upon death; and even then the heirs and devisees receive their interests only "subject to" the surviving spouse's statutory allowances and share, [73] which similarly vest upon death

[73] In this regard, AS 13.16.005 expressly provides:

and depend solely on the surviving spouse's marital status -- that is, on the existence of a valid marriage.

By ruling that Riddell's marriage was valid and could not be set aside by the estate, the superior court effectively determined that Riddell's statutory entitlements to allowances and share had vested upon Lillie's death -- before Lillie's estate ever received any cognizable interest or right to the portion of Lillie's estate that vested in Riddell. As a matter of law, then, the court's order validating the marriage ruled out the existence of an element necessary to support the court's subsequent decision to impose a constructive trust: a finding that the portion of Lillie's estate passing to Riddell "justly belonged" to the estate.

Moreover, even if we assume that the estate had a cognizable interest in these funds, the superior court's declaration of a valid marriage would still rule out the second prerequisite for a constructive trust: a finding that Riddell obtained his statutory rights "by reason of unjust, unconscionable, or unlawful means." As already explained, Riddell acquired his statutory right to allotments and share solely because he married Lillie and survived her with their marriage intact. We conclude that the superior court's order declaring the marriage to be valid *despite* Riddell's unconscionable premarital conduct precludes a finding that he acquired his statutory rights because of that conduct.

To be sure, as the superior court noted in its order validating the marriage, Riddell's fraudulent conduct persisted after he married Lillie; and as this court made clear in *Riddell I*, Riddell's continuing misconduct ultimately caused Lillie to execute a new will shortly before her death, naming Riddell as her sole beneficiary. But the superior court's earlier decision invalidating that will for lack of testamentary capacity -- the decision we affirmed in *Riddell I* -- directly addressed the harm caused by that ongoing misconduct. And neither the new will nor the unconscionable postmarital conduct that led to its execution had any effect on Riddell's right to the statutory benefits, since his right to those benefits depended solely on the validity of the

---

The power of a person to leave property by will, and the rights of creditors, devisees, and heirs to the property are subject to the restrictions and limitations contained in AS 13.06 -- AS 13.36 to facilitate the prompt settlement of estates. Upon the death of a person, that person's real and personal property devolves to the persons to whom it is devised by the last will or to those indicated as substitutes for them in cases involving lapse, renunciation, or other circumstances affecting the devolution of testate estates, or in the absence of testamentary disposition, to the heirs, or to those indicated as substitutes for them in cases involving renunciation or other circumstances affecting devolution of intestate estates, *subject to homestead allowance*, exempt property and *family allowance*, to rights of creditors, *elective share of the surviving spouse*, and to administration. (Emphasis added.)

AS 13.12.202(a) provides: "The surviving spouse of a decedent who dies domiciled in this state has a right of election . . . to take an elective share amount equal to one-third of the augmented estate."

marriage at its inception and on his survival of Lillie while still her spouse. The estate did not assert, nor did the superior court find, that Riddell's misconduct during the marriage brought about or hastened Lillie's death, thereby causing his statutory benefits to vest sooner, or that it had any other causal connection to the timing or ultimate vesting of his right to the benefits.

The absence of a causal link between Riddell's unconscionable postmarital conduct and his right to receive the statutory benefits of marriage thus readily distinguishes his case from cases involving constructive trusts imposed against murderers. The constructive trust principle applies in those cases because "the title to property *is acquired by* murder as it is where the title *is acquired by* fraud, duress, or undue influence." Thus, in the present case, the causal link that justifies imposing a constructive trust in cases of spousal murder -- and that certainly would have justified a constructive trust had it been found to exist here -- is missing.

C. General Principles Governing Equitable Relief

A consideration of generally recognized principles governing equitable relief confirms the conclusion that a constructive trust was improper under these circumstances. Two equitable principles are relevant here.

First, a court acting in equity ordinarily cannot intrude in matters that are plain and fully covered by a statute. Here, the Alaska Legislature has explicitly set out the property interests that vest upon death in a surviving spouse: homestead allowance, family allowance, and elective share; the legislature has specified the circumstance that makes them vest: the existence of a "surviving spouse" -- that is, a spouse who remained legally married at the time of death; and the legislature has attached no other prerequisite to the surviving spouse's statutory right. Similarly, by specifying the requirements for a valid marriage and limiting the ways in which a marriage may be invalidated, the legislature has fully covered the manner in which courts may determine whether a person qualifies as a "surviving spouse" for purposes of acquiring a vested statutory right to allowances and share. As the superior court recognized in upholding the validity of Riddell's marriage, the legislature deliberately limited the right to challenge the validity of a marriage that is voidable on grounds of disability, force, or fraud, extending that right exclusively to "the party under the disability or upon whom the force or fraud is imposed." Given the superior court's findings that Riddell's marriage was neither void ab initio because of Lillie's incapacity nor voidable after her death for gross fraud arising from a combination of Lillie's incompetence and Riddell's egregious behavior," it follows that the statutory provisions governing a surviving spouse's automatic entitlements to allotments and share "fully covered" Riddell's situation.

A second, closely related equitable principle that controls these circumstances is that a court must not apply equity to do indirectly "what the law or its clearly defined policy forbids to be done directly." Here, the superior court recognized that Lillie, despite her incapacity, understood the consequences of her actions when she accepted Riddell in marriage; the court further held that, even when combined with Lillie's incapacity, Riddell's fraudulent actions were not sufficiently gross to allow a post-mortem claim that the marriage was voidable. In consequence, the law required the court to declare Riddell eligible to receive the statutory benefits of a surviving spouse; indeed, the court's first order recognized that requirement. Yet by subsequently invoking the same factual findings of fraud and incompetence to trigger the equitable mechanism of a constructive trust, the court did indirectly what the law specifically forbade it to do directly: in nullifying Riddell's already vested right to allotments and share and awarding the money to the estate, the court effectively allowed the estate to avoid on equitable grounds the direct legal consequences of the court's earlier legal conclusion that Lillie had made "a competent decision about her marriage" and had "understood the nature of her decision to marry Mr. Riddell."

D. Other Considerations

We further recognize that Alaska's Uniform Probate Code generally gives trial courts broad latitude to supplement statutory provisions with equitable principles: AS 13.06.015 specifies that "unless displaced by the particular provisions of the code, the principles of law and equity supplement those provisions." Yet nothing in this opinion discourages the use of these broad supplemental powers; we merely hold that the factual circumstances the trial court found here did not leave room for equitable supplementation: the "particular provisions" of statutory law governing void and voidable marriages and accrual of allowances and share fully covered this situation and affirmatively "displaced" the equitable remedy of constructive trust. We apply no broad limitations on the use of equitable measures in probate cases; instead, we merely hold that the selected measure of a constructive trust did not apply here.

The facts in this case obviously make it tempting to deny Riddell any benefit from his fraudulent conduct; this makes the recourse of a constructive trust seem alluringly sensible. But allowing offensive factual circumstances to dictate an unauthorized legal remedy can have a pernicious effect in the long-run by upsetting the complex and delicate balance that our system of government strives to maintain between the legislature's lawmaking powers and the courts' traditional equitable powers. The superior court here carefully examined all relevant evidence and declared Riddell to be the surviving spouse of a valid marriage. The legislature has spelled out the rights that Riddell acquires by virtue of his status. To dilute these plain and complete legislative directives with a legally inappropriate equitable remedy would impermissibly expand the court's equitable powers at the expense of established positive law.

We must therefore vacate the order imposing a constructive trust and remand this case to allow the superior court to determine the amount of Riddell's allowances and share. In remanding the case, however, we note that the applicable statutes specify the amount of both the homestead allowance and elective *share but leave the amount of the family allowance in the court's discretion. To this extent, the statutes allow the superior court to factor equitable considerations into its decision on remand.*

IV. CONCLUSION

We REVERSE the order imposing a constructive trust and REMAND for further proceedings to establish the amount of the statutory allowances and share.

Clearly the right of a surviving spouse to take part of the augmented estate is *not* affected by the conduct of the spouse before or during the marriage.

The next case illustrates the complexity of making an election for a share of the augmented estate when the surviving spouse is mentally incompetent at the time of the election. There are a number of special rules for situations of this type – and the rules within a particular state may be inconsistent with each other.

Colorado Court of Appeals.
In the Matter of the ESTATE OF John G. FALLER
Iris L. Fisher, Trustee, Petitioner-Appellee,
v.
Colorado Department of Health Care Policy and Financing, Respondent-Appellant.
July 18, 2002.
Certiorari Denied April 14, 2003

Opinion by Judge Ney.

The Colorado Department of Health Care Policy and Financing (Department) appeals from the Denver Probate Court's order establishing an elective-share trust for the benefit of Ruby Faller, the surviving spouse of the decedent, John G. Faller. We reverse.

In 2000, petitioner, Iris L. Fisher, filed a Petition for Elective-Share and Allowances on surviving spouse's behalf, requesting that any award of assets to the surviving spouse from the decedent's estate be placed in trust. Additionally, the petitioner requested that distributions from the trust be restricted to maintain the surviving spouse's eligibility for benefits under the Colorado Medicaid Program.

The probate court granted the petition. The court determined that the surviving spouse's elective share and allowances of the decedent's estate was $96,133.56. The court then placed these funds in a trust, and further required that the assets "must be distributed in such a manner as to protect surviving spouse's eligibility for Medicaid benefits." The court also ruled that the assets in the trust were not the property of the surviving spouse because the trust was funded with the decedent's property, and thus it was not available to pay for the costs of her care that are otherwise provided for by Medicaid.

On appeal, the Department asserts that the assets in the elective share trust created here are "available assets" to be used to determine Medicaid eligibility, and it contends that the probate court thus erred in requiring that the trust be distributed in such a manner as to protect the surviving spouse's eligibility for Medicaid benefits. We agree.

The Colorado General Assembly has established three different types of trusts for the specific purpose of establishing or maintaining income eligibility for nursing home care or home- and community-based services: income trusts, disability trusts, and pooled trusts.

Each of these trust provisions states that "no person is entitled to payment from the remainder of the trust until the state medical assistance agency has been fully reimbursed for the assistance rendered to the person for whom the trust was created."

The elective-share trust in this case was created pursuant to the augmented estate statute, § 15-11-206(2), which provides:

> "If the election is exercised on behalf of a surviving spouse who is an incapacitated person, the court shall set aside the appropriate portion of the elective-share and supplemental elective-share amounts due from the decedent's probate estate ... and shall appoint a trustee to administer that property for the support of the surviving spouse.
>
> Expenditures of income and principal may be made in the manner, when, and to the extent that the trustee determines suitable and proper for the surviving spouse's support, ... *with regard to* other support, income, and property of the surviving spouse and *benefits of medical or other forms of assistance from any state or federal government or governmental agency for which the surviving spouse must qualify on the basis of need.*
>
> The assets remaining in the elective-share trust at the death of the surviving spouse will pass in accordance with the decedent's *will* or to the decedent's heirs *under the laws of intestacy."* (Emphasis added.)

On appeal, petitioner argues that the elective-share trust is funded with assets that are not owned by either the surviving spouse or the decedent because the remainder of the trust will pass to the decedent's heirs pursuant to § 15-11-206(2)(c). Thus, she asserts that the trust assets are not actually available to the incapacitated surviving spouse, for the purpose of determining her Medicaid eligibility.

However, § 15-14-412.6(2) limits the types of trusts that may be used to establish or maintain Medicaid eligibility:

> "Notwithstanding any statutory provision to the contrary, a court shall not authorize, direct, or ratify any trust established by an individual that has the effect of qualifying or purports to qualify the trust beneficiary for public assistance unless the trust meets the criteria set forth in [various] sections of this statute."

This provision specifically prohibits the authorization of a trust that has the effect of qualifying the trust beneficiary, here, the incapacitated surviving spouse, for public assistance unless it meets the criteria set forth for income trusts, disability trusts, or pooled trusts, which all provide that any funds remaining in the trust shall be available for reimbursement to Medicaid.

The elective-share trust at issue does not meet the criteria set forth in those statutes.

We conclude that the court erred in attempting to shield the assets of the trust here for the purpose of determining Medicaid eligibility.

The order is reversed, and the case is remanded for further proceedings consistent with this opinion.

It is thus impossible to set up an elective share trust for an incompetent surviving spouse that will shield the assets from Medicaid until the death of the surviving spouse. The elective share statute requires that any expenditures from the elective share trust be made after considering the money available from Medicaid, and that any remainder of the assets in the elective share trust on the death of the surviving spouse shall be returned to the estate of the deceased spouse. The Medicaid statute requires that any remaining assets in any authorized trust be first available for reimbursement to Medicaid. So it is impossible to create a trust which is in compliance with both statutes.

CHAPTER 22 - OUTLINE OF PROBATE

When someone dies, there normally is probate of the estate, unless some of the will substitutes discussed in previous chapters have been used. Particularly if land is involved, there needs to be some way to provide a record in the land records as to how the ownership of a piece of land got from the decedent to the next person who became the owner. Probate provides that record.

On the other hand, if land was held in joint tenancy, there would be no need for probate of that land. Instead, someone would just file a copy of the decedent's death certificate in the land records, and in many jurisdictions would also file an affidavit, basically stating that one of the joint tenants had died - therefore leaving the other joint tenant as the sole owner.

Probate is also an effective way of collecting all the property of the decedent, paying all the legally enforceable debts of the decedent, and then properly distributing the remaining assets of the decedent, in accordance with the terms of the will, or the terms of the intestate statute, if there is no will.

Prior to 1975 it was standard practice for the attorney handling the probate of an estate to charge a fee based on a percentage of the value of the estate. Understandably, that helped to give probate a bad name. In addition, probate could be a long, rather complex process. That was another reason that a number of people tried to find ways of avoiding probate when passing their property on to relatives or friends at death.

Partly in response to strong objections by the public, the probate process has now been significantly reformed. In most jurisdictions attorneys are no longer allowed to charge a percentage of the estate. Instead, probate attorneys just charge on the basis of an hourly fee, for the work actually performed. And the probate process has been greatly simplified, so that the whole process should take no more than about a year - unless fights break out among various beneficiaries and creditors. In most jurisdictions probate can now be handled by a normally intelligent person, filling out the appropriate forms, without the assistance of an attorney. However, an experienced attorney still can make the whole process go much more smoothly.

In a few states, attorneys are still allowed to set their fees as a percentage of the probate estate. In such jurisdictions there is still a motivation for people to try to avoid probate - but that is mainly just to try to avoid unfairly high fees authorized to be charged by attorneys.

One of the great benefits of probate is that it provides a definite cut-off for all claims against the decedent. The goal of probate is to collect the property, pay the legally enforceable claims against the decedent, distribute the remaining property, and then let everyone go on with life.

The following case gives a very good outline of the basic probate process. It also made a major change in how the creditors of a decedent must be notified of the death of the decedent, and their of opportunity to file their claims in probate.

A. PAYMENT OF CREDITORS

(1) REQUIRED NOTICE TO CREDITORS

In 1988 the U. S. Supreme Court announced an opinion that significantly changed the probate process in most states in the country. That opinion follows.

Supreme Court of the United States.
TULSA PROFESSIONAL COLLECTION SERVICES, INC., Appellant
v.
JoAnne POPE, Executrix of the Estate of H. Everett Pope, Jr., Deceased.
Decided April 19, 1988.

Justice O'CONNOR delivered the opinion of the Court.

This case involves a provision of Oklahoma's probate laws requiring claims "arising upon a contract" generally to be presented to the executor or executrix of the estate within two months of the publication of a notice advising creditors of the commencement of probate proceedings. The question presented is whether this provision of notice solely by publication satisfies the Due Process Clause.

I

Oklahoma's Probate Code requires creditors to file claims against an estate within a specified time period, and generally bars untimely claims. Such "nonclaim statutes" are almost universally included in state probate codes. Giving creditors a limited time in which to file claims against the estate serves the State's interest in facilitating the administration and expeditious closing of estates. Nonclaim statutes come in two basic forms. Some provide a relatively short time period, generally two to six months, that begins to run after the commencement of probate proceedings. Others call for a longer period, generally one to five years, that runs from the decedent's death. Most States include both types of nonclaim statutes in their probate codes, typically providing that if probate proceedings are not commenced and the shorter period therefore never is triggered, then claims nonetheless may be barred by the longer period. Most States also provide that creditors are to be notified of the requirement to file claims imposed by the nonclaim statutes solely by publication. See Uniform Probate Code § 3-801. Indeed, in most jurisdictions it is the publication of notice that triggers the nonclaim statute. The Uniform Probate Code, for example, provides that creditors have four months from publication in which to file claims.

The specific nonclaim statute at issue in this case, Okla.Stat., Tit. 58, § 333 (1981), provides for only a short time period and is best considered in the context of Oklahoma probate proceedings as a whole. Under Oklahoma's Probate Code, any party interested in the estate may initiate probate proceedings by petitioning the court to have the will proved. The court is then required to set a hearing date on the petition, and to mail notice of the hearing "to all heirs, legatees and devisees, at their places of residence." If no person appears at the hearing to contest the will, the court may admit the will to probate on the testimony of one of the subscribing witnesses to the will. After the will is admitted to probate, the court must order appointment of an executor or executrix, issuing letters testamentary to the named executor or executrix if that person appears, is competent and qualified, and no objections are made.

Immediately after appointment, the executor or executrix is required to "give notice to the creditors of the deceased." Proof of compliance with this requirement must be filed with the court. This notice is to advise creditors that they must present their claims to the executor or executrix within two months of the date of the first publication. As for the method of notice, the statute requires only publication: "Such notice must be published in some newspaper in [the] county once each week for two (2) consecutive weeks." A creditor's failure to file a claim within the 2-month period generally bars it forever. The nonclaim statute does provide certain exceptions, however. If the creditor is out of State, then a claim "may be presented at any time before a decree of distribution is entered." Mortgages and debts not yet due are also excepted from the 2-month time limit.

This shorter type of nonclaim statute is the only one included in Oklahoma's Probate Code. Delays in commencement of probate proceedings are dealt with not through some independent, longer period running from the decedent's death, but by shortening the notice period once proceedings have started. Section 331 provides that if the decedent has been dead for more than five years, then creditors have only 1 month after notice is published in which to file their claims. A similar one-month period applies if the decedent was intestate.

II

H. Everett Pope, Jr., was admitted to St. John Medical Center, a hospital in Tulsa, Oklahoma, in November 1978. On April 2, 1979, while still at the hospital, he died testate. His wife, appellee JoAnne Pope, initiated probate proceedings in the District Court of Tulsa County in accordance with the statutory scheme outlined above. The court entered an order setting a hearing. After the hearing the court entered an order admitting the will to probate and, following the designation in the will, named appellee as the executrix of the estate. Letters testamentary were issued, and the court ordered appellee to fulfill her statutory obligation by directing that she "immediately give notice to creditors." Appellee published notice in the Tulsa Daily Legal News for two consecutive weeks beginning July 17, 1979. The notice advised creditors that they must file any claim they had against the estate within two months of the first publication of the notice.

Appellant Tulsa Professional Collection Services, Inc., is a subsidiary of St. John Medical Center and the assignee of a claim for expenses connected with the decedent's long stay at that hospital. Neither appellant, nor its parent company, filed a claim with appellee within the 2-month time period following publication of notice. In October 1983, however, appellant filed an Application for Order Compelling Payment of Expenses of Last Illness. In making this application, appellant relied on Okla.Stat., Tit. 58, § 594 (1981), which indicates that an executrix "must pay the expenses of the last sickness." Appellant argued that this specific statutory command made compliance with the 2-month deadline for filing claims unnecessary. The District Court of Tulsa County rejected this contention, ruling that even claims pursuant to § 594 fell within the general requirements of the nonclaim statute. Accordingly, the court denied appellant's application.

The District Court's reading of § 594's relationship to the nonclaim statute was affirmed by the Oklahoma Court of Appeals. Appellant then sought rehearing, arguing for the first time that the nonclaim statute's notice provisions violated due process. In a supplemental opinion on rehearing the Court of Appeals rejected the due process claim on the merits.

Appellant next sought review in the Supreme Court of Oklahoma. That court granted certiorari and, after review of both the § 594 and due process issues, affirmed the Court of Appeals' judgment.

We noted probable jurisdiction, and now reverse and remand.

III

Mullane v. Central Hanover Bank & Trust Co. established that state action affecting property must generally be accompanied by notification of that action: "An elementary and fundamental requirement of due process in any proceeding which is to be accorded finality is notice reasonably calculated, under all the circumstances, to apprise interested parties of the pendency of the action and afford them an opportunity to present their objections." In the years since *Mullane* the Court has adhered to these principles, balancing the "interest of the State" and "the individual interest sought to be protected by the Fourteenth Amendment." The focus is on the reasonableness of the balance, and, as *Mullane* itself made clear, whether a particular method of notice is reasonable depends on the particular circumstances.

Applying these principles to the case at hand leads to a similar result. Appellant's interest is an unsecured claim, a cause of action against the estate for an unpaid bill. Little doubt remains that such an intangible interest is property protected by the Fourteenth Amendment.

The Fourteenth Amendment protects this interest, however, only from a deprivation by state action. Private use of state-sanctioned private remedies or procedures does not rise to the level of state action. Nor is the State's involvement in the mere running of a general statute of limitations generally sufficient to implicate due process. But when private parties make use of state procedures with the overt, significant assistance of state officials, state action may be found. The question here is whether the State's involvement with the nonclaim statute is substantial enough to implicate the Due Process Clause.

It is true that nonclaim statutes generally possess some attributes of statutes of limitations. They provide a specific time period within which particular types of claims must be filed and they bar claims presented after expiration of that deadline.

The State's interest in a self-executing statute of limitations is in providing repose for potential defendants and in avoiding stale claims. The State has no role to play beyond enactment of the limitations period. While this enactment obviously is state action, the State's limited involvement in the running of the time period generally falls short of constituting the type of state action required to implicate the protections of the Due Process Clause.

Here, in contrast, there is significant state action. The probate court is intimately involved throughout, and without that involvement the time bar is never activated. The nonclaim statute becomes operative only after probate proceedings have been commenced in state court. The court must appoint the executor or executrix before notice, which triggers the time bar, can be given. Only after this court appointment is made does the statute provide for any notice; § 331 directs the executor or executrix to publish notice "immediately" after appointment. Indeed, in this case, the District Court reinforced the statutory command with an order expressly requiring appellee to "immediately give notice to creditors." The form of the order indicates that such orders are routine. Finally, copies of the notice and an affidavit of publication must be filed with the court. It is only after all of these actions take place that the time period begins to run, and in every one of these actions, the court is intimately involved. This involvement is so pervasive and substantial that it must be considered state action subject to the restrictions of the Fourteenth Amendment.

Where the legal proceedings themselves trigger the time bar, even if those proceedings do not necessarily resolve the claim on its merits, the time bar lacks the self-executing feature necessary to remove any due process problem. Rather, in such circumstances, due process is directly implicated and actual notice generally is required. Our conclusion that the Oklahoma nonclaim statute is not a self-executing statute of limitations makes it unnecessary to consider appellant's argument that a 2-month period is somehow unconstitutionally short. We also have no occasion to consider the proper characterization of nonclaim statutes that run from the date of death, and which generally provide for longer time periods, ranging from one to five years. In sum, the substantial involvement of the probate court throughout the process leaves little doubt that the running of Oklahoma's nonclaim statute is accompanied by sufficient government action to implicate the Due Process Clause.

Nor can there be any doubt that the nonclaim statute may "adversely affect" a protected property interest. In appellant's case, such an adverse effect is all too clear. The entire purpose and effect of the nonclaim statute is to regulate the timeliness of such claims and to forever bar untimely claims, and by virtue of the statute, the probate proceedings themselves have completely extinguished appellant's claim. Thus, it is irrelevant that the notice seeks only to advise creditors that they may become parties rather than that they are parties, for if they do not participate in the probate proceedings, the nonclaim statute terminates their property interests. It is not necessary for a proceeding to directly adjudicate the merits of a claim in order to "adversely affect" that interest.

In assessing the propriety of actual notice in this context consideration should be given to the practicalities of the situation and the effect that requiring actual notice may have on important state interests. As the Court noted in *Mullane,* "Chance alone brings to the attention of even a local resident an advertisement in small type inserted in the back pages of a newspaper." Creditors, who have a strong interest in maintaining the integrity of their relationship with their debtors, are particularly unlikely to benefit from publication notice. As a class, creditors may not be aware of a debtor's death or of the institution of probate proceedings. Moreover, the executor or executrix will often be, as is the case here, a party with a beneficial interest in the estate. This could diminish an executor's or executrix's inclination to call attention to the potential expiration of a creditor's claim. There is thus a substantial practical need for actual notice in this setting.

B/U

At the same time, the State undeniably has a legitimate interest in the expeditious resolution of probate proceedings. Death transforms the decedent's legal relationships and a State could reasonably conclude that swift settlement of estates is so important that it calls for very short time deadlines for filing claims. As noted, the almost uniform practice is to establish such short deadlines, and to provide only publication notice.

Providing actual notice to known or reasonably ascertainable creditors, however, is not inconsistent with the goals reflected in nonclaim statutes. Actual notice need not be inefficient or burdensome. We have repeatedly recognized that mail service is an inexpensive and efficient mechanism that is reasonably calculated to provide actual notice. In addition, *Mullane* disavowed any intent to require "impracticable and extended searches in the name of due process." As the Court indicated, all that the executor or executrix need do is make "reasonably diligent efforts," to uncover the identities of creditors. For creditors who are not "reasonably ascertainable," publication notice can suffice. Nor is everyone who may conceivably have a claim properly considered a creditor entitled to actual notice. Here, as in *Mullane,* it is reasonable to dispense with actual notice to those with mere "conjectural" claims.

On balance then, a requirement of actual notice to known or reasonably ascertainable creditors is not so cumbersome as to unduly hinder the dispatch with which probate proceedings are conducted. Notice by mail is already routinely provided at several points in the probate process. In Oklahoma, for example, § 26 requires that "heirs, legatees, and devisees" be mailed notice of the initial hearing on the will. Indeed, a few States already provide for actual notice in connection with short nonclaim statutes. We do not believe that requiring adherence to such a standard will be so burdensome or impracticable as to warrant reliance on publication notice alone.

Whether appellant's identity as a creditor was known or reasonably ascertainable by appellee cannot be answered on this record. Neither the Oklahoma Supreme Court nor the Court of Appeals nor the District Court considered the question. Appellee of course was aware that her husband endured a long stay at St. John Medical Center, but it is not clear that this awareness translates into a knowledge of appellant's claim. We therefore must remand the case for further proceedings to determine whether "reasonably diligent efforts," would have identified appellant and uncovered its claim. If appellant's identity was known or "reasonably ascertainable," then termination of appellant's claim without actual notice violated due process.

IV

We hold that Oklahoma's nonclaim statute is not a self-executing statute of limitations. Rather, the statute operates in connection with Oklahoma's probate proceedings to "adversely affect" appellant's property interest. Thus, if appellant's identity as a creditor was known or "reasonably ascertainable," then the Due Process Clause requires that appellant be given "Notice by mail or other means as certain to ensure actual notice." Accordingly, the judgment of the Oklahoma Supreme Court is reversed and the case is remanded for further proceedings not inconsistent with this opinion.

It is so ordered.

(2) AVOIDING NOTICE TO CREDITORS

Twelve years after *Tulsa v. Pope* was announced, the Colorado Supreme Court came out with an opinion which looked, at first, as if the court had not yet heard about *Tulsa v. Pope.* As you read the following opinion, try to decide what impact this opinion would have on your legal and ethical responsibilities in a similar situation. Is it true that this state court opinion is consistent with the dictates of the U.S. Supreme Court in the prior opinion? Does this opinion put a new burden on creditors of a decedent?

Like the preceding case, this case will give you a good idea of how the probate process actually works.

Supreme Court of Colorado.
In the Matter of the ESTATE OF Veronica C. ONGARO, Deceased.
Denver Water Department Credit Union, Petitioner,
v.
The Estate of Veronica C. Ongaro Respondent.
March 13, 2000

Chief Justice MULLARKEY delivered the Opinion of the Court.

The Denver Water Department Credit Union (the Credit Union) appeals the court of appeals' decision affirming the probate court's dismissal of the Credit Union's claim against the estate (Estate) of Veronica Ongaro (Decedent). We granted certiorari to determine whether the court of appeals erred by determining that the Credit Union's claim against the Estate is barred because the Credit Union failed to comply with the reasonable notice and proper presentation requirements of section 15-12-803(1)(a)(III), 5 C.R.S. We now affirm the court of appeals' decision.

I.

This case arises from a loan transaction that occurred prior to the Decedent's death.

In October 1992, Arthur Watson (Watson), an employee of the Denver Water Department and member of the Credit Union, applied for a loan to purchase a 1990 Plymouth Voyager station wagon. Based on Watson's credit history, the Credit Union denied the loan application. Thereafter, Watson's wife, Mary Ongaro-Watson (Ongaro-Watson), attempted to co-sign the loan on behalf of her mother, the Decedent, pursuant to authority granted in several powers of attorney. The Credit Union, however, declined to recognize Ongaro-Watson as the Decedent's authorized agent.

The Decedent eventually appeared in person at the Credit Union to help her son-in-law obtain the loan. In exchange for the loan, the Decedent and Watson signed and delivered a promissory note in the amount of $14,881.45 to the Credit Union. The note was payable in semimonthly installments of $190.51 and was secured by the 1990 Plymouth Voyager station wagon that Watson purchased with the loan.

Payments on the note were deducted from Watson's paycheck until the summer of 1993, when he ended his employment with the Denver Water Department. Thereafter, Watson fell behind on his payments, and on March 23, 1994, the Credit Union sent notices of default to Watson and the Decedent.

On March 31, 1994, the Decedent tendered enough money to the Credit Union to bring the payments on the note current. Subsequent payments were made by Ongaro-Watson from a joint checking account owned with the Decedent. After each payment, the Credit Union sent identical receipts to Watson and the Decedent.

On May 13, 1994, the Decedent died, survived by Ongaro-Watson and her other daughter, Elizabeth Ongaro-Ruhl (Ongaro-Ruhl). The Moffat County District Court (probate court) admitted the Decedent's estate to probate and appointed Ongaro-Watson personal representative of the Estate.

Ongaro-Watson advised the Estate's attorney of the Decedent's liability on the note but was informed that she did not need to notify the Credit Union of the Decedent's death or of the deadline for presenting claims against the Estate. Ongaro-Watson published a notice in the Northwest Colorado Daily Press providing creditors an October 11, 1994 deadline for filing claims against the Estate but did not provide the Credit Union with actual notice of the Decedent's death or of the deadline for filing claims.

In November 1994, Joseph Janosec (Janosec) replaced Ongaro-Watson as the Estate's personal representative. At that time Janosec had no knowledge of the Decedent's liability on the note.

Ongaro-Watson continued to make payments on the note from the joint account until January 1995. In April 1995, the Credit Union repossessed Watson's station wagon. The Credit Union subsequently sold the station wagon for $6,000. The proceeds from the sale only partially satisfied the debt remaining on the note.

On May 24, 1995, the Credit Union first learned of the Decedent's death. The following day, a year and twelve days after the Decedent's death, the Credit Union presented a formal claim against the Estate for the amount remaining on the note.

On June 9, 1995, Janosec notified the Credit Union that the Estate was disallowing the claim. The Credit Union responded by submitting a second formal claim to Janosec and filing a petition for allowance of claim in the probate court.

The probate court interpreted section 15-12-803(1) (a) (III) as a nonclaim statute that required all creditors to present claims against the Estate within one year of the Decedent's death. Finding that the Credit Union had failed to present its claim against the Estate within one year of the Decedent's death, the probate court dismissed the Credit Union's claim as time-barred. The probate court rejected the Credit Union's arguments that Ongaro-Watson had wrongfully concealed the fact of the Decedent's death and that the one-year period for presenting claims under section 15-12-803(1)(a)(III) was tolled by Ongaro-Watson's conduct. The probate court further rejected the Credit Union's assertions that Ongaro-Watson's personal knowledge of the Decedent's liability on the note excused the Credit Union's duty to present its claims against the Estate.

The court of appeals affirmed the probate court's decision. This appeal followed.

II.

Section 15-12-804 sets forth three methods of presenting a claim against an estate. First, a claimant may mail or deliver a written statement to the estate's personal representative. Second, a claimant may file its written claim with the clerk of the court where the estate is being probated. Third, a claimant may commence litigation against the personal representative to obtain payment of its claim against the estate.

The Credit Union maintains that under Colorado law a claimant need not file a formal claim against an estate when the estate's personal representative has knowledge of the claim. The Credit Union urges us to consider the totality of the circumstances when analyzing whether the Credit Union provided Ongaro-Watson with reasonable notice of its claim against the Estate. According to the Credit Union, Ongaro-Watson's participation in the loan application process, the payments on the note made by Ongaro-Watson from the joint checking account, and a single payment receipt addressed to the Decedent and mailed to Ongaro-Watson's residence provided sufficient notice of the Credit Union's claim against the Estate. Thus, the Credit Union argues that it is excused from the formal presentation requirements of section 15-12-804.

We agree with the Credit Union that a creditor need not comply strictly with each of the formal requirements of section 15-12-804. The General Assembly has not required creditors to describe their claims with absolute precision. "Failure to describe correctly the security, the nature of any uncertainty, and the due date of a claim not yet due does not invalidate the presentation made." § 15-12-804(1).

Nevertheless, we find that section 15-12-804 does require that a creditor provide a personal representative with reasonable notice that it is making a claim against an estate. Notice to a personal representative that a creditor could bring a claim against an estate is different from notice that the creditor in fact is bringing that claim. At a minimum a written claim must contain (1) a request or demand for payment from the estate, and (2) sufficient information to allow the personal representative to investigate and respond to the claim.

Ongaro-Watson's mere knowledge that the Credit Union could demand payment from the Estate does not excuse the Credit Union's failure to demand such payment.

Furthermore, we cannot construe the payment receipt addressed to the Decedent and mailed to Ongaro-Watson's residence as a written statement by which the Credit Union presented its claim against the Estate. Although the receipt indicated the Credit Union's name and address, an account number, and an account balance, it did not request or demand payment of that balance by the Decedent or the Estate. Because the receipt did not indicate that the Credit Union was asserting a claim against the Estate rather than merely acknowledging the Decedent's payment, it failed to satisfy the requirements for presentation of claims prescribed by section 15-12-804(1).

IV.

A.

Section 15-12-803(1) establishes the deadline for presenting a personal representative with claims against a decedent's estate for debts that arose prior to the decedent's death. Claimants that receive publication notice that they must present claims against an estate must do so within the time set forth in the publication. Claimants receiving written notice must present claims within the time set forth in the written notice. All creditors must present claims within one year after a decedent's death.

Neither party disputes that the Credit Union did not receive written notice to present its claims against the Estate. Further, the probate court held publication notice to be ineffective as to known creditors such as the Credit Union. *See generally Tulsa Prof'l Collection Servs. v. Pope.*

The Credit Union argues that the probate court and court of appeals incorrectly interpreted section 15-12-803(1) (a) (III) as a nonclaim statute and not an ordinary statute of limitations. The Credit Union maintains that section 15-12-803(1) (a) (III), as a statute of limitations, is subject to tolling in appropriate circumstances. The Credit Union urges that, given Ongaro-Watson's decision not to mail the Credit Union notice of the Decedent's death notwithstanding her knowledge of the Decedent's liability on the note, equity requires that the one-year period for filing claims be tolled.

In In re Estate of Randall we interpreted the predecessor of section 15-12-803(1) to be a nonclaim statute, not an ordinary statute of limitations. We held that the particular language of the statute providing that claims "if not so filed, shall be forever *barred*" was not the language of a statute of limitations. Rather, the statute created "an absolute bar" against the enforcement of late-filed claims. We noted that, otherwise,

> "The settlement of an estate might be deferred indefinitely, and the heirs and legatees, the rightful owners of the property of the estate, or the beneficiaries of the will of the decedent kept out of the enjoyment of their possessions and deprived of the benefits secured to them by the laws of the state for such an unreasonable time as to practically deprive them of their property."

Applying the reasoning of our decision in *Estate of Randall*, we find section 15-12-803(1) to be a nonclaim statute, not a statute of limitations. The statute states that claims not filed within the applicable time period "are *barred* against the estate, the personal representative, and the heirs and devisees of the decedent." §15-12-803(1) (Emphasis added.) The General Assembly's use of the term "barred" indicates its intent to render concepts of waiver or tolling, which are applicable to statutes of limitations, generally inapplicable to section 15-12-803(1).

Interpreting section 15-12-803(1) as a nonclaim statute furthers the purposes of the Colorado Probate Code. Among these purposes is the promotion of "a speedy and efficient system for settling the estate of the decedent and making distributions to his successors." Allowing creditors to toll claims against estates would frustrate the speedy and efficient settlement of estates and distribution of assets.

B.(omitted)

C.

Unlike a statute of limitations, the deadline for filing claims established by section 15-12-803(1) generally cannot be waived or tolled. The rationale behind not permitting an estate's personal representative to waive the requirement that creditors present claims within one year is "that the personal representative is a trustee of the estate for the benefit of its creditors and heirs, and as such cannot by his conduct waive any provision of a statute affecting their substantial rights." Likewise, courts generally have refused to toll the one-year nonclaim period in order to "expedite the orderly and exact settlement of estates of decedents." Our cases consistently have recognized the policy in favor of dismissing untimely claims brought against an estate where addressing the merits of the claims would delay the settlement of the estate and the distribution of assets to the estate's devisees, legatees, and other claimants.

In this case, permitting the Credit Union's claim to go forward would impair the speedy and efficient settlement of the Estate. The record reflects that the probate court found the Decedent's two daughters, Ongaro-Watson and Ongaro-Ruhl, to be her heirs. The record further reflects that the Decedent's will leaves half of the residuary of the Estate to Ongaro-Watson and the other half to be kept in trust for Ongaro-Ruhl and her son. Permitting the Credit Union to litigate its claim would delay the distribution of these parties' shares of the Estate and undermine the policy behind section 15-12-803(1). Accordingly, we reject the Credit Union's argument that Ongaro-Watson's conduct tolled the one-year period for presenting claims against the Estate and conclude that the trial court properly dismissed the Credit Union's claim.

We are aware that the firm deadline for presenting claims under section 15-12-803(1) occasionally will work a hardship on claimants who do not receive actual notice of a decedent's death. The General Assembly, however, has determined that the burden on those claimants is outweighed by the interest in the speedy and efficient settlement of estates.

We also recognize that our holding today may appear to provide an incentive to some personal representatives not to provide known creditors with written notice of the deadline for presenting claims. There is, however, a statutory disincentive. A personal representative who decides not to provide known creditors with written notice of a decedent's death and of the deadline for filing claims must forfeit the shorter nonclaim periods under sections 15-12-803(1)(a)(I) and (II) in favor of the one-year period under section 15-12-803(1)(a)(III). We also note that, should a personal representative's conduct rise to the level of fraud, section 15-10-106, 5 C.R.S., provides a remedy to injured claimants.

V.

Lastly, the Credit Union argues that dismissal of its claim pursuant to section 15-12-803(1) (a) (III) violates the Due Process Clause of the Fourteenth Amendment to the United States Constitution. In support of this argument, the Credit Union cites Tulsa Professional Collection Services, Inc. v. Pope, 485 U.S. 478, (1988).

The Due Process Clause of the Fourteenth Amendment requires states to provide a party with notice and an opportunity to be heard prior to taking action that will affect that party's property interests. *See* Tulsa. Such notice must be "'reasonably calculated to apprise interested parties of the pendency of the action and afford them the opportunity to present their objections." If an interested party's name and address are reasonably ascertainable, the state must provide the party with actual notice of the pending action.

In *Tulsa,* the United States Supreme Court concluded that the period for presenting claims under the statute did not begin to run without significant state action and, therefore, the statute was not self-executing. Specifically, the Supreme Court noted that appointing an executor or executrix and filing copies of the publication notice and an affidavit with the court were preconditions to the running of the limitations period under the nonclaim statute. The Supreme Court held that this significant state action implicated the actual notice requirements of the Due Process Clause of the Fourteenth Amendment. Thus, the statute was unconstitutional as to known creditors entitled to receive actual notice - not merely publication notice - of deadlines for filing claims against estates.

Unlike the Oklahoma nonclaim statute declared unconstitutional in *Tulsa,* section 15-12-803(1) (a) (III) is self-executing. The one-year period for presenting claims begins to run on the day of the decedent's death, not on the occurrence of an event requiring action by the state. *See* § 15-12-803(1) (a) (III). Accordingly, we find

Tulsa inapposite to the case presently before us.

The only remaining question, then, is whether the Credit Union was denied due process because section 15-12-803(1) (a) (III) required that it file its claim against the Estate within one year of the Decedent's death. Ordinarily, a state's mere involvement in the running of a statute of limitations will not constitute a deprivation of a claimant's constitutional rights to due process.

We previously have held that a statute of limitations does not deprive a claimant of its rights to due process unless the time for bringing the claim is so limited as to amount to a denial of justice. The legislature is the primary judge of what amount of time is reasonable.

The General Assembly has determined that a one-year period for presenting claims is necessary to promote the speedy and efficient settlement of estates. We cannot conclude that the one-year period for bringing a claim against an estate under section 15-12-803(1) (a) (III) is so limited as to amount to a denial of justice. Consequently, we find that the Credit Union was not deprived of its right to due process by application of the one-year limitation.

The judgment of the court of appeals is affirmed.

B. CHOICE OF PERSONAL REPRESENTATIVE

In most cases, the choice of who should serve as the personal representative of an estate is fairly clear. The will normally nominates a personal representative, and also names one or two additional people who might serve as the personal representative, if the first person named "fails to qualify or ceases to serve."

If no personal representative is named in the will, or if the decedent dies without a valid will, then the statute lists the priority of persons who should be named by the court to handle the estate.

In some situations, however, there may be a dispute as to the person who should serve as personal representative. The following case illustrates some of the rules in a situation of that sort, in which two people, who had previously been involved in litigation against each other, are fighting over which of them shall be named as personal representative.

Colorado Court of Appeals.
In re the ESTATE OF Kathryn E. NEWTON, deceased.
Mojo Properties, LLC, Claimant–Appellant,
v.
Patrick J. Woods, Personal Representative–Appellee.
Aug. 4, 2011.
Cert. Denied by Colorado Supreme Court December 12, 2011

Opinion by Judge BERNARD.

In this appeal, we resolve a question involving Colorado's statute establishing the priorities of those persons who seek appointment as a personal representative to administer the estate of a deceased. Specifically, we are asked to determine whether the nominee of one with a prior right to appointment stands in the shoes of his or her nominator with regard to that priority. We hold that the answer to this question is "yes." As a result, we affirm the district court's order.

I. Background

Mojo Properties, LLC (creditor), appeals the district court's order appointing Patrick J. Woods (nominee), as personal representative of the estate of Kathryn E. Newton (decedent).

Decedent died in December 2009. She was survived by two daughters, and by Patrick J. Woods, the nominee, who had lived with decedent for approximately ten years. Decedent did not leave a will.

In March 2010, both daughters nominated Woods, the nominee, to act as personal representative of decedent's estate.

Creditor had been involved in business dealings with a construction company owned by nominee and decedent before her death. A dispute ensued, and creditor sued decedent, nominee, and the construction company in Denver District Court.

After decedent died, creditor requested, in May 2010, to be appointed as personal representative of the estate, identifying itself as one of the estate's creditors. The district court rejected creditor's argument that it had statutory priority to serve as personal representative of the estate and appointed nominee.

II. Discussion

A. General Principles of Statutory Construction (omitted)

B. Relevant Sections of Colorado's Probate Code

Section 15–12–203, C.R.S.2010, establishes the order of priority among persons seeking appointment as personal representative of an estate. Subsection (1) provides:

> "Whether the proceedings are formal or informal, persons who are not disqualified have priority for appointment in the following order:
> (a) The person with priority as determined by a probated will including a person nominated by a power conferred in a will;

(b) The surviving spouse of the decedent who is a devisee of the decedent;

(b.5) A person given priority to be a personal representative in a designated beneficiary agreement made pursuant to article 22 of this title;

(c) Other devisees of the decedent;

(d) The surviving spouse of the decedent;

(e) Other heirs of the decedent;

(f) Forty-five days after the death of the decedent, any creditor."

Thus, where, as here, an unmarried person dies intestate, his or her heirs have priority over creditors. An heir or group of heirs may also nominate a person to serve as personal representative:

> "A person entitled to letters under paragraphs (b) to (e) of subsection (1) of this section may nominate a qualified person to act as personal representative. When two or more persons share a priority, those of them who do not renounce must concur in nominating another *to act for them* or in applying for appointment." (Emphasis added.)

As pertinent here, subsection (5) states:

> "Appointment of a person who is nominated pursuant to subsection (3) of this section may be made in an informal proceeding. Before formal appointment of one without priority, the court must determine that those having priority, although given notice of the proceedings, have failed to request appointment or to nominate another for appointment and that administration is necessary."

C. Nominee's Priority over Creditor

It is undisputed here that, under section 15-12-203(1) (e), decedent's daughters, as her heirs, had priority to be appointed personal representative over creditor, whose priority is next in line under section 15-12-203(1) (f). However, nominee, absent his status as a nominee, has no statutory priority in his own right. Therefore, unless the daughters' priority was conferred to nominee, creditor had a prior right to appointment as personal representative.

We conclude that the plain language of the foregoing statutes provides nominee with the daughters' priority. We reach this conclusion for the following reasons.

First, subsection (1) establishes priorities, and subsection (5) adds that any nomination may be made informally. Subsection (3) states that a nominee "acts for" his or her nominators.

As relevant here, the verb "to act" means to "take action," and the preposition "for" means "in behalf of." Thus, a nominee takes action in behalf of his or her nominator.

When read together, the language of these subsections leads us to conclude that a nominee, by *acting for* a person enumerated in paragraphs (b) to (e) of subsection (1), is the nominator's agent.

Because an agent generally represents a principal contractually, he or she may take authorized actions on the principal's behalf that bind the principal. The existence of this authority leads us to conclude that a nominee, as the nominator's agent, stands in the nominator's shoes, and, thus, assumes the priority of the nominator.

Further, subsection (5) conditions a court's power to appoint a person without statutory priority on a determination that all persons who have priority have not requested such an appointment, and that they have not *nominated* another person for appointment. This language implies that nominees have the priority of their nominators.

Second, our interpretation is consistent with the general policies of the Colorado Probate Code set forth by the legislature. The General Assembly has declared that the Colorado Probate Code shall be construed liberally and "applied to promote its underlying purposes and policies." Those purposes and policies include "promoting a speedy and efficient system for settling the estate of the decedent and making distribution to his successors."

Third, although statutes in other states are somewhat different, courts from other jurisdictions have reached the same result.

We recognize that some states have statutes that expressly provide nominees with the same priority as their nominators. *See, e.g.,* Cal. Prob.Code § 8465 (establishing priority of nominee based on class of nominator); Me.Rev.Stat. tit. 18–A, § 3–203(e) ("Appointment of one who has priority resulting from renunciation or nomination ... may be made in informal proceedings."); Neb. Rev. St. § 30–2412(e) ("Appointment of one having priority resulting from renunciation or nomination may be made in informal proceedings."); N.M. Stat. Ann. § 45–3–203(C) ("A person entitled to letters may nominate a qualified person to act as personal representative and thereby confer the person's relative priority for appointment on the person's nominee."); S.C.Code Ann. § 62–3–203(a)(8) (subject to certain exceptions, "a person with priority may nominate another, who shall have the same priority as the person making the nomination"). However, in light of the preceding statutory analysis, the absence of such express language in Colorado's statute does not lead us to the conclusion that nominees do not assume their nominators' priority.

Fourth, accepting the interpretation proposed by creditor—that nomination by one with priority does not confer that priority on the nominee—would lead to an absurd result. The nominator would, in effect, relinquish his or her priority by naming a person to act on his or her behalf. Such a result would vitiate section 15–12–203(3), because a person entitled to letters would be required to fulfill the role of personal representative personally to avoid ceding control of an estate to one with a junior enumerated right to appointment. Creditor has not provided us with any authority supporting its position, and our research has not discovered any.

We note that creditor and nominee appear to equate nomination of a personal representative with renunciation of rights. These acts are clearly different, as subsection (3) recognizes that a person with a statutory priority may "renounce his right to nominate or to an appointment." Here, the daughters did not renounce; they nominated. Although the form each signed is entitled "Renunciation and/or Nomination of Personal Representative," each daughter checked only the box on the form stating, "Having the right to nominate a qualified person to act as personal representative, I nominate [nominee]." Contrary to the assertion of both parties on appeal, the record does not indicate that either daughter renounced her right to appointment as personal representative.

We conclude that nominee assumed the priority of his nominators, the daughters. The daughters, as heirs, had priority of appointment over creditor. Thus, the probate court properly appointed nominee as personal representative.

The order is affirmed.

C. SMALL ESTATES – $100,000

In every jurisdiction there is probably some "small estates" statute, which provides that for estates under a certain amount, no probate will be required. Generally, these statutes apply only where no land is involved, because of the necessity for some official documentation to be recorded in the land records, documenting how the ownership of land got from the decedent to the next owner.

Here are the applicable provisions from the Uniform Probate Code.

§ 3-1201. Collection of Personal Property by Affidavit.

(a) Thirty days after the death of a decedent, any person indebted to the decedent or having possession of tangible personal property or an instrument evidencing a debt, obligation, stock or chose in action belonging to the decedent shall make payment of the indebtedness or deliver the tangible personal property or an instrument evidencing a debt, obligation, stock or chose in action to a person claiming to be the successor of the decedent upon being presented an affidavit made by or on behalf of the successor stating that:

(1) the value of the entire estate, wherever located, less liens and encumbrances, does not exceed $25,000; and

(2) 30 days have elapsed since the death of the decedent; and

(3) no application or petition for the appointment of a personal representative is pending or has been granted in any jurisdiction; and

(4) the claiming successor is entitled to payment or delivery of the property.

(b) A transfer agent of any security shall change the registered ownership on the books of a corporation from the decedent to the successor or successors upon the presentation of an affidavit as provided in subsection (a).

§ 3-1202. Effect of Affidavit.

The person paying, delivering, transferring, or issuing personal property or the evidence thereof pursuant to affidavit is discharged and released to the same extent as if he dealt with a personal representative of the decedent. He is not required to see to the application of the personal property or evidence thereof or to inquire into the truth of any statement in the affidavit. If any person to whom an affidavit is delivered refuses to pay, deliver, transfer, or issue any personal property or evidence thereof, it may be recovered or its payment, delivery, transfer, or issuance compelled upon proof of their right in a proceeding brought for the purpose by or on behalf of the persons entitled thereto. Any person to whom payment, delivery, transfer or issuance is made is answerable and accountable therefor to any personal representative of the estate or to any other person having a superior right.

§ 3-1203. Small Estates; Summary Administration Procedure.

If it appears from the inventory and appraisal that the value of the entire estate, less liens and encumbrances, does not exceed homestead allowance, exempt property, family allowance, costs and expenses of administration, reasonable funeral expenses, and reasonable and necessary medical and hospital expenses of the last illness of the decedent, the personal representative may, without giving notice to creditors, immediately disburse and distribute the estate to the persons entitled thereto, and file a closing statement as provided in Section 3-1204.

§ 3-1204. Small Estates; Closing by Sworn Statement of Personal Representative.

(a) Unless prohibited by order of the court and except for estates being administered by supervised personal representatives, a personal representative may close an estate administered under the summary procedures of Section 3-1203 by filing with the court, at any time after disbursement and distribution of the estate, a verified statement stating that:

(1) to the best knowledge of the personal representative, the value of the entire estate, less liens and encumbrances, did not exceed homestead allowance, exempt property, family allowance, costs and expenses of administration, reasonable funeral expenses, and reasonable, necessary medical and hospital expenses of the last illness of the decedent;

(2) the personal representative has fully administered the estate by disbursing and distributing it to the persons entitled thereto; and

(3) the personal representative has sent a copy of the closing statement to all distributees of the estate and to all creditors or other claimants of whom he is aware whose claims are neither paid nor barred, and has furnished a full account in writing of his administration to the distributees whose interests are affected.

(b) If no actions or proceedings involving the personal representative are pending in the court one year after the closing statement is filed, the appointment of the personal representative terminates.

(c) A closing statement filed under this section has the same effect as one filed under Section 3-1003.

Standard forms are available for use in small estates.

D. INFORMAL PROBATE

When the small estates procedures are not appropriate, the default rule for a Uniform Probate Code jurisdiction is that any estate should be probated by Informal Probate, which is basically just filing the necessary papers with the Registrar, not the Judge. If there are no fights among the heirs and devisees, informal probate is a very simple, efficient, and expeditious process.

However, the Registrar has no authority to decide contested issues. Thus, for anything that requires a judicial decision, formal probate must be used. Within a particular estate, most of the work may be done in informal probate, with formal probate used just for specific issues.

The closing of the probate process may be done either informally or formally, even when all of the prior actions have been done in informal probate. The advantage of a formal closing is that the personal representative is discharged more quickly under a formal closing.

For example, in Colorado, if formal closing is used, then C.R.S. § 15-12-1001(1) provides that:

> After notice to all interested persons and hearing, the court may enter an order or orders, on appropriate conditions, determining the persons entitled to distribution of the estate, and, as circumstances require, approving settlement and directing or approving distribution of the estate and **discharging the personal representative from further claim or demand of any interested person.**

By contrast, if **informal** closing is used, then C.R.S. § 15-12-1003(2)) provides that:

> If no proceedings involving the personal representative are pending in the court **one year after the closing statement is filed**, the appointment of the personal representative terminates.

So it is far better, for the personal representative, to have a formal closing.

E. FORMAL PROBATE

Formal probate is used whenever there may be disputes that must be settled by a judge. It is possible to switch back and forth between informal and formal probate, as the needs arise. Because of the necessity to involve the judge, formal probate usually takes a bit longer, and may be more expensive. But it is always available when it is necessary to have a judge decide a disputed matter.

F. SUPERVISED ADMINISTRATION

One step beyond formal probate is **supervised administration**, which is rarely used, and is usually reserved for cases in which the involvement of certain "high risk" people, or certain "high risk" assets may suggest the need for very close judicial supervision of every step of the process.

G. AGREEMENT OF THE PARTIES MAY CHANGE EVERYTHING!

Note that it is possible, under case law, and under the provisions of some state statutes, for the interested parties to get together and agree to re-write a will, or a testamentary trust! Normally the parties must first create some sort of controversy among themselves, and then when they settle the "controversy" the agreement must be approved by the court.

The relevant Uniform Probate Code provision states:

> **§ 3-1101. Effect of Approval of Agreements Involving Trusts, Inalienable Interests, or Interests of Third Persons.**
> A compromise of any controversy as to admission to probate of any instrument offered for formal probate as the will of a decedent, the construction, validity, or effect of any governing instrument, the rights or interests in the estate of the decedent, of any successor, or the administration of the estate, if approved in a formal proceeding in the court for that purpose, is binding on all the parties thereto including those unborn, unascertained or who could not be located. An approved compromise is binding even though it may affect a trust or an inalienable interest. A compromise does not impair the rights of creditors or of taxing authorities who are not parties to it.

H. ENTRY INTO SAFE DEPOSIT BOX

* know this

One issue which frequently arises after the death of a person is access to the safe deposit box of the decedent. State statutes vary widely on this point. In some states, it is extremely difficult for anyone to get into the decedent's safe deposit box after the decedent's death. For that reason, in those jurisdictions, the last place a will should be stored is in the safe deposit box of the testator. It is simply too difficult for anyone to get into the safe deposit box, after the death of the decedent, to see if the decedent left a will.

In other states a safe deposit box may be a perfectly appropriate place to store a will. The following Colorado statute is an illustration of the rules in the states in which access to the decedent's safe deposit box is relatively easy.

C.R.S. § 15-10-111. Entry into safe deposit box of decedent--definitions

(1)(a) Whenever a decedent at the time of his or her death was a sole or joint lessee of a safe deposit box, the custodian shall, prior to notice that a personal representative or special administrator has been appointed, allow access to the box by:

(I) A successor of the decedent, if such decedent was the sole lessee of the box, upon presentation of an affidavit made pursuant to section 15-12-1201 for the purpose of delivering the contents of the box in accordance with said section; or

(II) A person who is reasonably believed to be an heir at law or devisee of the decedent, a person nominated as a personal representative, or the agent or attorney of such person for the purpose of determining whether the box contains an instrument that appears to be a will of the decedent, deed to a burial plot, or burial instructions. *

(b) If a person described in subparagraph (I) or (II) of paragraph (a) of this subsection (1) desires access to a safe deposit box but does not possess a key to the box, the custodian shall drill the safe deposit box at the person's expense. In the case of a person described in subparagraph (I) of paragraph (a) of this subsection (1), the custodian shall deliver the contents of the box, other than a purported will, deed to a burial plot, and burial instructions, to the person in accordance with section 15-12-1201. In the case of a person described in subparagraph (II) of paragraph (a) of this subsection (1), the custodian shall retain, in a secure location at the person's expense, the contents of the box other than a purported will, deed to a burial plot, and burial instructions. A custodian shall deliver a purported will as described in paragraph (c) of subsection (2) of this section. A deed to a burial plot and burial instructions that are not part of a purported will may be removed by a person described in subparagraph (I) of paragraph (a) of this subsection (1) pursuant to paragraph (d) of subsection (2) of this section, and the custodian shall not prevent the removal. Expenses incurred by a custodian pursuant to this section shall be considered an estate administration expense.

(c) A representative of the custodian shall be present during the entry of a safe deposit box pursuant to this section.

(1.5) As used in this section, unless the context otherwise requires:

(a) "Custodian" means a bank, savings and loan association, credit union, or other institution acting as a lessor of a safe deposit box.

(b) "Representative of a custodian" means an authorized officer or employee of a custodian.

(2)(a) If an instrument purporting to be a will is found in a safe deposit box as the result of an entry pursuant to subsection (1) of this section, the purported will shall be removed by the representative of the custodian.

(b) At the request of the person or persons authorized to have access to the safe deposit box under the provisions of subsection (1) of this section, the representative of the custodian shall copy each purported will of the decedent, at the expense of the requesting person, and shall deliver the *copy* of each purported will to the person, or if directed by the person, to the person's agent or attorney. In copying any purported will, the representative of the custodian *shall not remove any staples or other fastening devices or disassemble the purported will in any way.*

Staple rule :)

[Note that the bank employee must NOT remove the staples! This is to try to insure that no one, later, can claim that a different page 2 was substituted for the original page 2, for example.]

(c) The *custodian* shall mail the purported will by registered or certified mail or deliver the purported will in person to the clerk of the district or probate court of the county in which the decedent was a resident. If the custodian is unable to determine the county of residence of the decedent, the custodian shall mail the purported will by registered or certified mail or deliver the purported will in person to the office of the clerk of the proper court of the county in which the safe deposit box is located.

(d) If the safe deposit box contains a deed to a burial plot or burial instructions that are not a part of a purported will, the person or persons authorized to have access to the safe deposit box under the provisions of subsection (1) of this section may remove these instruments.

(3) After the appointment of a personal representative or special administrator for the decedent, the personal representative or special administrator shall be permitted to enter the safe deposit box upon the same terms and conditions as the decedent was permitted to enter during his or her lifetime.

(4) If at the time of the decedent's death one or more other persons were

legally permitted to enter the safe deposit box, *their permission to enter shall continue,* notwithstanding the death of the decedent.

(5) A custodian shall not be liable to a person for an action taken pursuant to this section or for a failure to act in accordance with the requirements of this section unless the action or failure to act is shown to have resulted from the custodian's bad faith, gross negligence, or intentional misconduct. (Emphasis added.)

I. ADVANCEMENTS

An additional issue that may come up in probate is that one child claims that another child, C, should get a smaller share of the estate, either because C had already been given lots of gifts while the decedent was alive, or because C still owed money to the decedent at the time of the decedent's death.

When a parent gives a large gift to one child, prior to the parent's death, that gift may have been intended by the parent to be an advance payment to the child of part or all of the amount that the child would have inherited. In any case, the other, less favored children, are likely to argue that the inter vivos gift was an advancement, and should be deducted from the share that the favored child, C, gets from the parent's estate.

The following section of the Uniform Probate Code sets forth the rules for advancements.

§ 2-109. Advancements.

(a) If an individual dies *intestate* as to all or a portion of his or her estate, property the decedent gave during the decedent's lifetime to an individual who, at the decedent's death, is an heir is treated as an *advancement* against the heir's intestate share *only* if:

(i) the decedent declared in a contemporaneous writing or the heir acknowledged in writing that the gift is an advancement, or

(ii) the decedent's contemporaneous writing or the heir's written acknowledgment otherwise indicates that the gift is to be taken into account in computing the division and distribution of the decedent's intestate estate.

(b) For purposes of subsection (a), property advanced is valued as of the time the heir came into possession or enjoyment of the property or as of the time of the decedent's death, whichever first occurs.

(c) If the recipient of the property fails to survive the decedent, the property is not taken into account in computing the division and distribution of the decedent's intestate estate, unless the decedent's contemporaneous writing provides otherwise.

J. DEBTS OWED <u>TO</u> THE DECEDENT BY AN HEIR

A similar dispute may arise among siblings if one child had borrowed money from the parent, and had not paid it back at the time of the parent's death. The applicable Uniform Probate Code provision for that situation is below.

§ 2-110. Debts to Decedent.
A debt owed to a decedent is not charged against the intestate share of any individual except the debtor. If the debtor fails to survive the decedent, the debt is not taken into account in computing the intestate share of the debtor's descendants.

K. DEBTS <u>OF</u> THE DECEDENT

Always remember that if there are not enough assets in the decedent's estate to pay all of the creditors of the decedent, then the debts of the decedent simply do not get paid. The decedent's debts die with the decedent. No family member is ever required to pay the debts of another family member who died with more debts than could be paid by the assets of the decedent.

estate has to pay, but heirs do not!

CONCLUSION

Having read a variety of cases and statutes, you should now have a very good understanding of the basic issues in contemporary estate planning – what happens without a will or trust, and what can be done with a variety of estate planning documents. Specific laws will of course continue to evolve and change. However, having now considered various issues and possibilities, you should be in a good position to help clients draft the appropriate documents to provide for thoughtful and effective distribution of the property that is most important to them. Enjoy!

And if litigation becomes necessary, you should now have a good idea of the various techniques available for solving disputes involving wills, trusts, and intestate succession.

APPENDIX

THE COMPLETE WILL OF ELVIS PRESLEY

LAST WILL AND TESTAMENT

OF

ELVIS A. PRESLEY

I, ELVIS A. PRESLEY, a resident and citizen of Shelby County, Tennessee, being of sound mind and disposing memory, do hereby make publish and declare this instrument to be my last will and testament, hereby revoking any and all wills and codicils ~~by me at any time heretofore made~~.

ITEM I

Debts. Expenses and Taxes

~~I direct my Executor~~, hereinafter named, to pay all of my ~~matured debts~~ and my funeral expenses, as well as the costs and expenses of the administration of my estate, as soon after my death as practicable. I further direct that all estate, inheritance, transfer and succession taxes which are payable by reason of my death, whether or not with respect to property passing under this will, be paid out of my residuary estate; and I hereby waive on behalf of my estate any right to recover from any person any part of such taxes so paid. My ~~Executor,~~ in his sole discretion, may pay from my domiciliary estate all or any portion of the costs of ancillary administration and similar proceedings in other jurisdictions.

ITEM II

Instructions Concerning Personal Property: Enjoyment in Specie

I anticipate that included as a part of my property and estate at the time of my death will be tangible personal property of various kinds, characters and values, including trophies and other items accumulated by me during my professional career. I hereby specifically instruct all concerned that my Executor, herein appointed, shall have complete freedom and discretion as to disposal of any and all such property so long as he shall act in good faith and in the best interest of my estate and my beneficiaries, and his discretion so exercised shall not be subject to question by anyone whomsoever.

I hereby expressly authorize my Executor and my Trustee, respectively and successively, to permit any beneficiary of any and all trusts created hereunder to enjoy in specie the use or benefit of any household goods, chattels, or other tangible personal property (exclusive of choses in action, cash, stocks, bonds or other securities) which either my Executor or my Trustee may receive in kind, and my Executor and my Trustee shall not be liable for any consumption, damage, injury to or loss of any tangible property so used, nor shall the beneficiaries of any trusts hereunder or their executors or administrators be liable for any consumption, damage, injury to or loss of any tangible personal property so used.

ITEM III

Real Estate

If I am the owner of any real estate at the time of my death, I instruct and empower my Executor and my Trustee (as the case may be) to hold such real estate for investment, or to sell same, or any portion thereof, as my Executor or my Trustee (as the case may be) shall in his sole judgment determine to be for the best interest of my estate and the beneficiaries thereof.

ITEM IV ← she likes numbers not roman numeral

don't ever do internal references!

Residuary Trust

After payment of all debts, expenses and taxes as directed under ITEM I hereof, I give, devise, and bequeath all the rest, residue, and remainder of my estate, including all lapsed legacies and devises, and any property over which I have a power of appointment, to my Trustee, hereinafter named, in trust for the following purposes:

(a) The Trustee is directed to take, hold, manage, invest and reinvest the corpus of the trust and to collect the income therefrom in accordance with the rights, powers, duties, authority and discretion hereinafter set forth. The Trustee is directed to pay all the expenses, taxes and costs incurred in the management of the trust estate out of the income thereof.

(b) After payment of all expenses, taxes and costs incurred in the management of the trust estate, the Trustee is authorized to accumulate the net income or to pay or apply so much of the net income and such portion of the principal at any time and from time to time for the health, education, support, comfortable maintenance and welfare of: (1) my daughter, Lisa Marie Presley, and any other lawful issue I might have, (2) my grandmother, Minnie Mae Presley, (3) my father, Vernon E. Presley, and (4) such other relatives of mine living at the time of my death who in the absolute discretion of my Trustee are in need of emergency assistance for any of the above mentioned purposes and the Trustee is able to make such distribution without affecting the ability of the trust to meet the present needs of the first three numbered categories of beneficiaries herein mentioned or to meet the reasonably expected future needs of the first three classes of beneficiaries herein mentioned. Any decision of the Trustee as to whether or not distribution shall be made, and also as to the amount of such distribution, to any of the persons described hereunder shall be final and conclusive and not subject to question by any legatee or beneficiary hereunder.

(c) Upon the death of my father, Vernon E. Presley, the Trustee is instructed to make no further distributions to the fourth category of beneficiaries and such beneficiaries shall cease to have any interest whatsoever in this trust. Um-interesting

(d) Upon the death of both my said father and my said grandmother, the Trustee is directed to divide the Residuary Trust into separate and equal trusts, creating one such equal trust for each of my lawful children then surviving and one such equal trust for the living issue collectively, if any, of any deceased child of mine. The share, if any, for the issue of any such deceased child, shall immediately vest in such issue in equal shares but shall be subject to the provisions of ITEM V herein. Separate books and records shall be kept for each trust, but it shall not be necessary that a physical division of the assets be made as to each trust.

The Trustee may from time to time distribute the whole or any part of the net income or principal from each of the aforesaid trusts as the Trustee, in its uncontrolled discretion, considers necessary or desirable to provide for the comfortable support, education, maintenance, benefit and general welfare of each of my children. Such distributions may be made directly to such beneficiary or to any person standing in the place of a parent or the guardian of the person of such beneficiary and without responsibility on my Trustee to see to the application of any such distributions and in making such distributions, the Trustee shall take into account all, other sources of funds known by the Trustee to be available for each respective beneficiary for such purpose,

(e) As each of my respective children attains the age of twenty-five (25) years and provided that both my father and grandmother then be deceased, the trust created hereunder for such child shall terminate, and all the remainder of the assets then contained in said trust shall be distributed to such child so attaining the age of twenty-five (25) years outright and free of further trust.

(f) If any of my children for whose benefit a trust has been created hereunder should die before attaining the age of twenty-five (25) years, then the trust created for such child shall terminate on his death, and all remaining assets then contained in said trust shall be distributed outright and free of further trust and in equal shares to the surviving issue of each deceased child but subject to the provisions of ITEM V herein; but if there be no such surviving issue, then to the brothers and sisters of such deceased child in equal shares, the issue of any other deceased child being entitled collectively to their deceased parent's share. Nevertheless, if any distribution otherwise becomes payable outright and free of trust under the provisions of this paragraph (f) of this ITEM IV of my will to a beneficiary for whom the Trustee is then administering a trust for the benefit of such beneficiary under the provisions of this last will and testament, such distribution shall not be paid outright to such beneficiary but shall be added to and become a part of the trust so being administered for such beneficiary by the Trustee.

ITEM V

Distribution to Minor Children

If any share of corpus of any trust established under this will becomes distributable outright and free of trust to any beneficiary before said beneficiary has attained the age of eighteen (18) years, then said share shall immediately vest in said beneficiary, but the Trustee shall retain possession of such share during the period in which such beneficiary is under the age of eighteen (18) years, and, in the meantime, shall use and expend so much of the income and principal of each share as the trustee deems necessary and desirable for the care, support and education of such beneficiary, and any income not so expended shall be added to the principal. The Trustee shall have with respect to each share so retained all the power and discretion had with respect to such trust generally.

ITEM VI

Alternate Distributees

In the event that all of my descendants should be deceased at any time prior to the time for the termination of the trusts provided for herein, then in such event all of my estate and all the assets of every trust to be created hereunder (as the case may be) shall then be distributed outright in equal shares to my heirs at law per stirpes.

ITEM VII

Unenforceable Provisions

If any provisions of this will are unenforceable, the remaining provisions shall, nevertheless, be carried into effect.

ITEM VIII

Life Insurance

If my estate is the beneficiary of any life insurance on my life at the time of my death, I direct that the proceeds therefrom will be used by my Executor in payment of the debts, expenses and taxes listed in ITEM I of this will, to the extent deemed advisable by the Executor. All such proceeds not so used are to be used by my Executor for the purpose of satisfying the devises and bequests contained in ITEM IV herein.

ITEM IX

Spendthrift Provision

I direct that the interest of any beneficiary in principal or income of any trust created hereunder shall not be subject to claims of creditors or others, nor to legal process, and may not be voluntarily or involuntarily alienated or encumbered except as herein provided. Any bequests contained herein for any female shall be for her sole and separate use, free from the debts, contracts and control of any husband she may ever have.

ITEM X

Proceeds From Personal Services

All sums paid after my death (either to my estate or to any of the trusts created hereunder) and resulting from personal services rendered by me during my lifetime, including, but not limited to, royalties of any nature, concerts, motion picture contracts, and personal appearances shall be considered to be income, notwithstanding the provisions of estate and trust law to the contrary.

ITEM XI

Executor and Trustee

I appoint as Executor of this, my last will and testament, and as Trustee of every trust required to be created hereunder, my said father.

I hereby direct that my said father shall be entitled by his last will and testament, duly probated, to appoint a successor Executor of my estate, as well as a successor Trustee or Trustees of all trusts to be created under my last will and testament.

If, for any reason, my said father be unable to serve or to continue to serve as Executor and/or as Trustee, or if he be deceased and shall not have appointed a successor Executor or Trustee, by virtue of his last will and testament as stated above, then I appoint National Bank of Commerce, Memphis, Tennessee, or its successor or the institution with which it may merge, as successor Executor and/or as successor Trustee of all trusts required to be established hereunder.

None of the appointees named hereunder, including any appointment made by virtue of the last will and testament of my said father, shall be required to furnish any bond or security for performance of the respective fiduciary duties required hereunder, notwithstanding any rule of law to the contrary.

ITEM XII

Powers, Duties, Privileges and Immunities of the Trustee

Except as otherwise stated expressly to the contrary herein, I give and grant to the said Trustee (and to the duly appointed successor Trustee when acting as such) the power to do everything he deems advisable with respect to the administration of each trust required to be established under this, my last will and testament, even though such powers would not be authorized or appropriate for the Trustee under statutory or other rules of law. By way of illustration and not in limitation of the generality of the foregoing grant of power and authority of the Trustee, I give and grant to him plenary power as follows:

(a) To exercise all those powers authorized to fiduciaries under the provisions of the Tennessee Code Annotated, Sections 35-616 to 35-618, inclusive, including any amendments thereto in effect at the time of my death, and the same are expressly referred to and incorporated herein by reference.

(b) Plenary power is granted to the Trustee, not only to relieve him from seeking judicial instruction, but to the extent that the Trustee deems it to be prudent, to encourage determinations freely to be made in favor of persons who are the current income beneficiaries. In such instances the rights of all subsequent beneficiaries are subordinate, and the Trustee shall not be answerable to any subsequent beneficiary for anything done or omitted in favor of a current income beneficiary, but no current income beneficiary may compel any such favorable or preferential treatment. Without in anywise minimizing or impairing the scope of this declaration of intent, it includes investment policy, exercise of discretionary power to pay or apply principal and income, and determination of principal and income questions;

(c) It shall be lawful for the Trustee to apply any sum that is payable to or for the benefit of a minor (or any other person who in the judgment of the Trustee, is incapable of making proper disposition thereof) by payments in discharge of the costs and expenses of educating, maintaining and supporting said beneficiary, or to make payment to anyone with whom said beneficiary resides or who has the care or custody of the beneficiary, temporarily or permanently, all without intervention of any guardian or like fiduciary. The receipt of anyone to whom payment is so authorized to be made shall be a complete discharge of the Trustee without obligation on his part to see to the further application thereof, and without regard to other resources that the beneficiary may have, or the duty of any other person to support the beneficiary;

(d) In dealing with the Trustee, no grantee, pledgee, vendee, mortgagee, lessee or other transferee of the trust properties, or any part thereof, shall be bound to inquire with respect to the purpose or necessity of any such disposition or to see to the application of any consideration therefore paid to the Trustee.

ITEM XIII

Concerning the Trustee And the Executor

(a) If at any time the Trustee shall have reasonable doubt as to his power, authority or duty in the administration of any trust herein created, it shall be lawful for the Trustee to obtain the advice and counsel of reputable legal counsel without resorting to the courts for instructions; and the Trustee shall be fully absolved from all liability and damage or detriment to the various trust estates or any beneficiary thereunder by reason of anything done, suffered or omitted pursuant to advice of said counsel given and obtained in good faith, provided that nothing contained herein shall be construed to prohibit or prevent the Trustee in all proper cases from applying to a court of competent jurisdiction for instructions in the administration of the trust assets in lieu of obtaining advice of counsel.

(b) In managing, investing, and controlling the various trust estates, the Trustee shall exercise the judgment and care under the circumstances then prevailing, which men of prudence, discretion and judgment exercise in the management of their own affairs, not in regard to speculation, but in regard to the permanent disposition of their funds, considering the probable income as well as probable safety of their capital, and, in addition, the purchasing power of income distribution to beneficiaries.

(c) My Trustee (as well as my Executor) shall be entitled to reasonable and adequate compensation for the fiduciary services rendered by him.

(d) My Executor and his successor Executor shall have the same rights, privileges, powers and immunities herein granted to my Trustee wherever appropriate.

(e) In referring to any fiduciary hereunder, for purposes of construction, masculine pronouns may include a corporate fiduciary and neutral pronouns may include an individual fiduciary.

<u>ITEM XIV</u>

<u>Law Against Perpetuities</u>

Um: interesting

(a) Having in mind the rule against perpetuities, I direct that (notwithstanding anything contained to the contrary in this last will and testament) each trust created under this will (except such trusts as have heretofore vested in compliance with such rule or law) shall end, unless sooner terminated under other provisions of this will, twenty-one (21) years after the death of the last survivor of such of the beneficiaries hereunder as are living at the time of my death; and thereupon that the property held in trust shall be distributed free of all trust to the persons then entitled to receive the income and/or principal therefrom, in the proportion in which they are then entitled to receive such income. — attempted (poor) savings cl. re: RAP

(b) Notwithstanding anything else contained in this will to the contrary, I direct that if any distribution under this will becomes payable to a person for whom the Trustee is then administering a trust created hereunder for the benefit of such person, such distribution shall be made to such trust and not to the beneficiary outright, and the funds so passing to such trust shall become a part thereof as corpus and be administered and distributed to the same extent and purpose as if such funds had been a part of such trust at its inception.

ITEM XV

Payment of Estate and Inheritance Taxes

Notwithstanding the provisions of ITEM X herein, I authorize my Executor to use such sums received by my estate after my death and resulting from my personal services as identified in ITEM X as he deems necessary and advisable in order to pay the taxes referred to in ITEM I of my said will.

IN WITNESS WHEREOF, I, the said ELVIS A. PRESLEY, do hereunto set my hand and seal in the presence of two (2) competent witnesses, and in their presence do publish and declare this instrument to be my Last Will and Testament, this _3_day of March , ~~1976~~ 1977

s/ Elvis A. Presley
ELVIS A. PRESLEY

The foregoing instrument; consisting of this and eleven (11) preceding typewritten pages, was signed, sealed, published and declared by ELVIS A. PRESLEY, the Testator, to be his last Will and Testament in our presence, and we, at his request and in his presence and in the presence of each other, have hereunto subscribed our names as witnesses, this _3_day of March , ~~1976~~, 1977 at Memphis, Tennessee.

s/ *Ginger Alden* residing at (Omitted)

s/ *Charles F. Hodge* residing at (Omitted)

sl Ann Dewey Smith (Omitted)

STATE OF TENNESSEE)

)ss.

COUNTY OF SHELBY)

Ginger Alden, Charles F. Hodge and Ann Dewey Smith after being first duly sworn, make oath or affirm that the foregoing Last Will and Testament was signed by ELVIS A. PRESLEY and for and at that time acknowledged, published and declared by him to be his Last Will and Testament, in the sight and presence of us, the undersigned, who at his request and in his sight and presence, and in the sight and presence of each other, have subscribed our names as attesting witnesses on the 3rd day of March , ~~1976~~, 1977 and we further make oath or affirm that the Testator was of sound mind and disposing memory and not acting under fraud, menace or undue influence of any person, and was more than eighteen (18) years of age; and that each of the attesting witnesses is more than (18) years of age.

s/ *Ginger Alden*

s/ *Charles F. Hodge*

s/ *Ann Dewey Smith*

SWORN TO AND SUBSCRIBED before me this 3rd day of March, ~~1976~~ 1977

Drayton Beecher Smith II
Notary Public

My commission expires: Aug. 8, 1979

CPSIA information can be obtained
at www.ICGtesting.com
Printed in the USA
JSHW051608280722
28632JS00002B/6

9 781600 421945